# AXÉ BAHIA

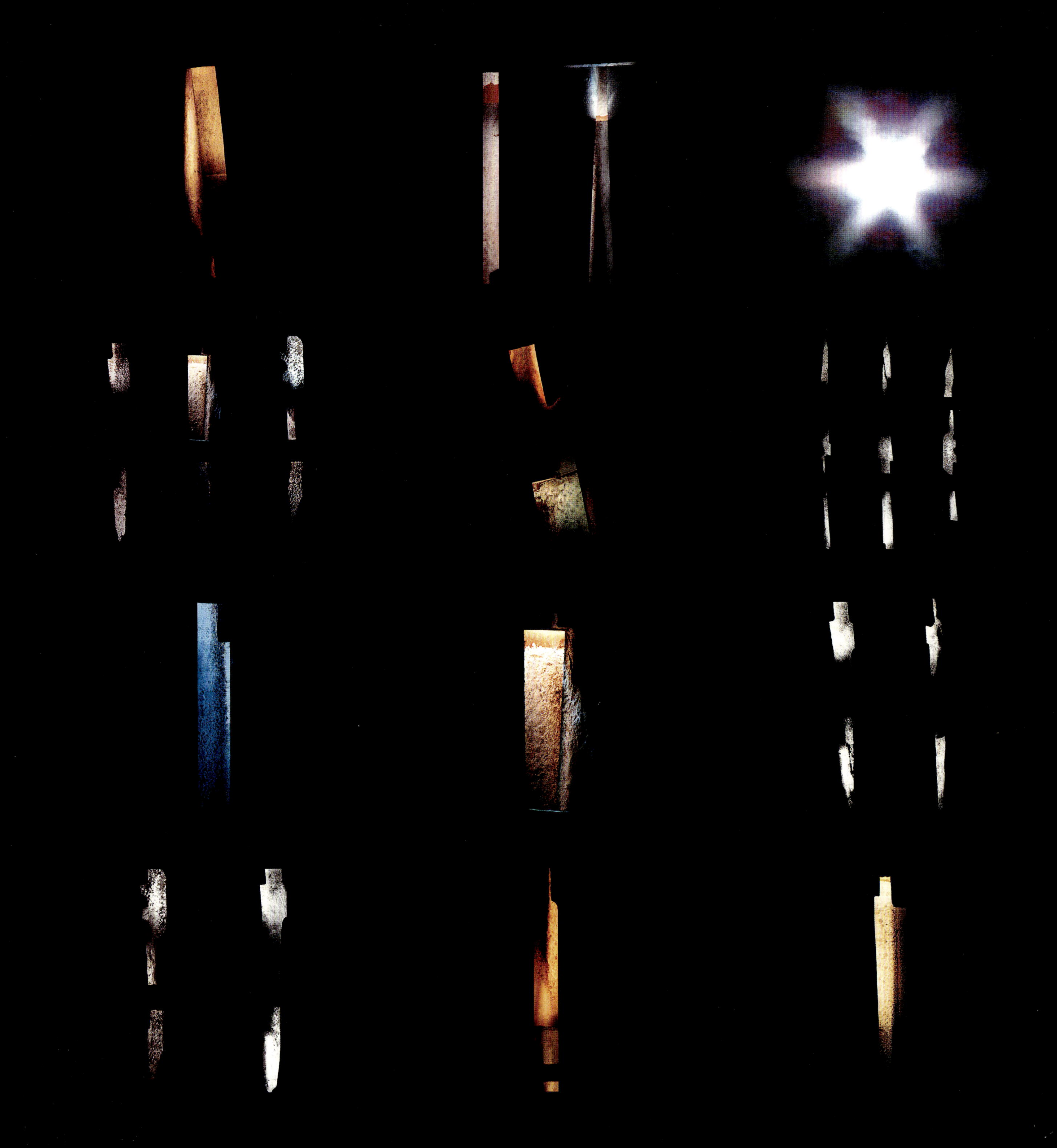

# AXÉ BAHIA

## The Power of Art in an Afro-Brazilian Metropolis

PATRICK A. POLK, ROBERTO CONDURU, SABRINA GLEDHILL, and RANDAL JOHNSON, *EDITORS*

*with essays by*

Scott Alves Barton
Sarah K. Chenault
Kimberly L. Cleveland
Roberto Conduru
Christopher Dunn
Cécile Fromont
Sabrina Gledhill
Ana Paula Höfling
Randal Johnson
Vanda Machado
Lucas Marques
J. Lorand Matory
Paulo Miguez
Patrick A. Polk
Anadelia Romo
Roger Sansi
Heather Shirey
Jeri Bernadette Williams

*Fowler Museum at UCLA*
*Los Angeles*

PUBLISHED WITH THE ASSISTANCE OF THE GETTY FOUNDATION

## *Lenders to the Exhibition*

Anonymous lenders
Bass Museum of Art
Maria Byington
Jose Antônio Cunha
Dallas Museum of Art
Caetano Dias
Estate of Mário Cravo Neto ©IMCN
Fundação Pierre Verger
Galeria Casa Triângulo
Galeria Luisa Strina
Galeria RV Cultura e Arte
Mark Steven Greenfield and Valerie Zavala
Helen Louise Allen Textile Collection, School of Human Ecology, University of Wisconsin-Madison
Pedro Buarque de Holanda and Adriana Varejão Fonseca
Goya Lopes
Museu Afro-Brasileiro (MAFRO)
Museu de Arte da Bahia (MAB)
Museu de Arte Moderna da Bahia (MAM-BA)
Paulo Darzé Galeria
Aroldo Oliveira de Peixoto
Pinacoteca do Estado de São Paulo
Research and Special Collections, University of New Mexico
Lucas Robatto and Yêda Robatto Stasi
Roberto Alban Galeria
Sam L. Slick Collection of Latin American and Iberian Posters, Center for Southwest
Slate Magazine

Pacific Standard Time: LA/LA is a farreaching and ambitious exploration of Latin American and Latino art in dialogue with Los Angeles. Supported by grants from the Getty Foundation, Pacific Standard Time: LA/LA takes place from September 2017 through January 2018 at more than 70 cultural institutions across Southern California, from Los Angeles to Palm Springs, and from San Diego to Santa Barbara. Pacific Standard Time is an initiative of the Getty. The presenting sponsor is Bank of America.

Pacific Standard Time: LA/LA
Latin American & Latino Art in LA

Presenting Sponsors
The Getty
Bank of America

Major support for this exhibition is provided through grants from the Getty Foundation.

The Getty Foundation

Additional support is provided by The Andy Warhol Foundation for the Visual Arts and the National Endowment for the Arts. Public programs and educational outreach activities are made possible in part by the Ralph M. Parsons Foundation. Travel support is provided in part by the Brazilian Ministry of Foreign Affairs through the Consulate General in Los Angeles.

The Andy Warhol Foundation for the Visual Arts

ART WORKS.
National Endowment for the Arts
arts.gov

# Contents

# Foreword

IN 2013 THE GETTY FOUNDATION ISSUED A CALL for proposals for their Pacific Standard Time: LA/LA initiative, a project seeking to explore Latin American and Latino art in dialogue with Los Angeles. At the Fowler Museum, Patrick A. Polk, Curator of Latin American and Caribbean Popular Arts, immediately registered a strong interest in spearheading a major exhibition and publication project centering on the history and current status of Afro-Brazilian arts in the northeastern state of Bahia. Initially titled *The Roads That Lead to Bahia: Visual Arts and the Emergence of Brazil's Black Rome*, his proposal aimed to expand the Fowler's engagement with the arts of the Black Atlantic. At the same time, Polk sought to deepen his long-standing research on the intersections of art and faith in the African diaspora and the roots of these junctures in indigenous African religious systems that had survived the violence of the Atlantic slave trade and European colonization of the Americas. This publication represents the culmination of the Fowler Museum's participation in PST: LA/LA: more than four years of intensive investigation and collaboration that has resulted in *Axé Bahia: The Power of Art in an Afro-Brazilian Metropolis*.

The Fowler has presented programming on the arts of the African diaspora since the 1980s. It organized the first major exhibition on *Afro-American Arts of the Suriname Rain Forest* in 1984, based on landmark field research undertaken in this South American country by anthropologists Richard and Sally Price. An exhibition on the *Afro-Bahian Arts of Candomblé and Carnaval* was presented in 1984, and accompanying it were two modest but significant publications: *From the Inside to the Outside: The Art and Ritual of Bahian Candomblé*, which drew on the dissertation research of UCLA doctoral scholar Mikelle Smith Omari, and *African Myth and Black Reality in Bahian Carnaval*, written by the late UC Davis Professor Emeritus and festival arts specialist Daniel J. Crowley. The Museum provided Omari with the funds to build a small collection of Candomblé-related dress and accoutrements during her time in Salvador, and items from it are included in the *Axé Bahia* exhibition and illustrated in this volume.

Perhaps better known is the Fowler's scholarly leadership in the dissemination of groundbreaking research on the *Sacred Arts of Haitian Vodou*. In 1995 this traveling exhibition and book of the same name became landmarks in Caribbean diaspora studies. The Fowler also has one of the foremost collections of Vodou-inspired arts. The legacy of this project has resonated over the intervening decades, inspiring other Fowler exhibitions on related topics and focusing attention on the work of Haitian contemporary artists who continue to address the triumphs and tragedies of this island nation's complex history. A solo exhibition on the Haitian-American artist Edouard Duval-Carrié, *Divine Revolution* (2004), was followed by *In Extremis: Death and Life in Twenty-First Century Haitian Art* (2012), a group show presenting the work of thirty-four artists, most living in Port-au-Prince. Haiti's social instability and the devastation caused by hurricanes and the horrendous earthquake of January 12, 2010, led to bold and original artists' responses. The powerful intervention of Haitian artists into ongoing reckonings with the past is mirrored in the work of artists living elsewhere in the diaspora, where slavery and colonialism are shared historical shadows.

Donald J. Cosentino, UCLA Professor Emeritus, and the late Marilyn Houlberg, Professor Emerita at the School of the Art Institute of Chicago—veteran scholars of Haitian Vodou arts—had closely tracked avant-garde developments in Haiti for decades. Patrick initially joined them in these efforts as a PhD student at UCLA and has continued this research to the present day as curator at the Fowler. He was co-curator with Cosentino of the *In Extremis* exhibition of 2012. Patrick's own curatorial trajectory has not strayed far from the Americas or from an intense engagement with artists whose work reflects complex relationships with the divine. His exhibition and accompanying publication *Sinful Saints and Saintly Sinners at the Margins of the Americas* (2014) looked at the work of contemporary artists from Mexico, Brazil, Guatemala, Argentina, and the United States as they grappled with the sacred figures "who walk the fine line between sinfulness and sanctity."

Drawing on his own considerable experience and insights into the conditions of diaspora, Polk has astutely led the curatorial team of *Axé Bahia* in its broad investigation of the artistic expressions of African heritage in the city of Salvador, a key hub of such practices in Latin America. His collaborators—Professor Roberto Conduru, Professor Randal Johnson, and Dr. Sabrina Gledhill, along with Curatorial Assistant Sarah K. Chenault—brought different disciplinary strengths and perspectives to the project, and we are deeply grateful to them for their major investment in and commitment to this ambitious effort. As the first exhibition to comprehensively treat the subject of Afro-Bahian arts, there was much to learn and to understand, and the team worked together beautifully to accomplish its goals.

This collection of essays and interleaves, edited by the curatorial team with Polk's oversight, gathers together their own research with that of many other international scholars. Our gratitude goes to all of them for their contributions (they are listed in the acknowledgments that follow). The many artists featured in the exhibition and publication are, however, the real stars of *Axé Bahia*. Some are well known, and others are only now receiving the attention they deserve as part of Brazil's diverse and multivalent art history.

The Fowler is indebted to the many private and institutional lenders who have shared key works of art for the exhibition and have provided crucial support. We would like to offer heartfelt gratitude to: Estate of Mário Cravo Neto ©IMCN (Christian Cravo); Fundação Pierre Verger (Angela Lühning and Alex Baradel); Instituto Carybé (Solange Bernabó and Gabriel Bernabó Duarte Guimarães); Museu Afro-Brasileiro (MAFRO; Graça Teixeira); Pinacoteca do Estado de São Paulo (Rafael Laterça, Fernanda D'Agostino, Valéria de Mendonça, Valéria Piccoli, and Manuel Ley Rodriguez); Museu de Arte da Bahia (MAB; Pedro Arcanjo); Museu de Arte Moderna da Bahia (MAM-BA; Zivé Giudice and Sandra Regina Jesus); Roberto Alban Galeria (Roberto and Cristina Alban); Galeria Luisa Strina (Luisa Strina, Flavia França, and Thamy Garcia); Galeria RV Cultura e Arte (Larissa Martina); Paulo Darzé Galeria (Paulo Darzé and Thaís Darzé); Galeria Casa Triângulo (Ricardo Trevis, Rodrigo Editore, and Julia Vaz); Bass Museum of Art (Silvia Karman Cubiñá and Sherry Zambrano); Dallas Museum of Art (Augustín Arteaga and Tricia Dixon); Helen Louise Allen Textile Collection, School of Human Ecology, University of Wisconsin-Madison (Sherry Harlacher and Natasha Thoreson); Sam L. Slick Collection of Latin American and Iberian Posters, Center for Southwest Research and Special Collections, University of New Mexico (Tomas Jaehn and Suzanne Schadl); and Slate Magazine (Andrew Kahn and Jamelle Bouie). Thanks also go to Maria Byington; Pedro Buarque de Holanda and Adriana Varejão Fonseca; Mark Steven Greenfield; Aroldo Oliveira de Peixoto; Lucas Robatto and Yêda Robatto Stasi.

The extremely handsome support provided by the Getty Foundation allowed the Fowler Museum to realize the sweeping aspirations of *Axé Bahia*. We received both PST: LA/LA planning and implementation grants, and have enjoyed the benefits of the Getty's comprehensive promotion of all the PST: LA/LA programs and events. I extend very special thanks to Deborah Marrow (Director of the Getty Foundation), Joan Weinstein (Deputy Director), Heather MacDonald (Program Officer), Gloria Gerace (Managing Director, Pacific Standard Time: LA/LA), and Selene Preciado (Program Assistant). Major funding for *Axé Bahia* also has come from The Andy Warhol Foundation for the Visual Arts and the National Endowment for the Arts. Public programs and educational outreach activities were made possible in part by the Ralph M. Parsons Foundation. Additional assistance and travel support was provided by the Brazilian Ministry of Foreign Affairs through the Consulate-General of Brazil in Los Angeles (Consul General Bruno Bath, Deputy Consul General Márcia Adorno) and Azul Brazilian Airlines (Beatriz T. M. Spira, Natasha C. Scaglione Ribeiro). We are grateful to all of these entities for their confidence in the project and in the Fowler's ability to produce and present all of its components with professionalism and excellence.

The entire Fowler staff is to be commended for its commitment to the stellar realization of *Axé Bahia*. The project required coordination and collaboration at every stage of development, and I am thankful for the outstanding work of every department and each of its members (please see the staff list at the end of this volume). I join the curators of *Axé Bahia* in singling out David Blair, Deputy Director, and Matthew Robb, Chief Curator, for their critical oversight of the project. As it developed over time, the *Axé Bahia* exhibition benefited from the contributions of the Fowler's curatorial team in helping to shape its themes and content. Later, the design team, under the inspired leadership of Director of Exhibitions Sebastian Clough, was instrumental in guiding the unfolding of its narrative and its beautiful presentation in the gallery. Collections staff under the supervision of Rachel Raynor, Director of Registration and Collections Management, dealt astutely with the complex details of bringing the art from Brazil to Los Angeles, and Bridget DuLong, Exhibitions Project Manager, carefully oversaw not only the workflow but also the schedules for participating artists and couriers. Director of Education and Interpretation Terri Geis and her staff creatively developed the many outreach programs and activities designed for all of our audiences. The departments of Development, Communications, Finance and Administration, and Security all performed the often-unsung behind-the-scenes work that allows the Fowler to shine.

This publication, like those before it, continues in the fine tradition of combining significant scholarship with high-quality reproductions, allowing readers to appreciate simultaneously the words of scholars and the work of the artists they discuss. This volume has been handsomely designed by Danny Brauer, Director of Publications, and skillfully and sensitively edited by Lynne Kostman in the final project of her twenty-year tenure as Managing Editor at the Fowler. Gassia Armenian, Curatorial and Research Associate, and Sarah K. Chenault, Curatorial Assistant, did their tenacious best in securing photographs and photo permissions.

Lastly, I return to Patrick A. Polk who has been the driving force of *Axé Bahia: The Power of Art in an Afro-Brazilian Metropolis*. He has infused it with his boundless energy, intelligence and insatiable curiosity, and his passionate devotion to the arts and artists of the African diaspora. He deserves our sincere thanks and congratulations.

Marla C. Berns
*Shirley and Ralph Shapiro Director*

# Acknowledgments

*EXÚ TIRIRI LONÃ, OXUMARÉ, IANSÃ, XANGÔ, Oxum, Iemanjá, Omolú, Ogum Ajá, Nanã*. These are titles of works included in *Axé Bahia: The Power of Art in an Afro-Brazilian Metropolis*. They are also the names of *orixás* (divinities) worshipped in Candomblé whose invocation and appearance in ceremonies is central to the practice of the African-derived religion. The impact of these divinities and their *axé* (vital force or energy) on the world is measured in great part through human action. Without their everyday presence—as embodied by adherents in Candomblé temples or as envisioned by artists—this volume and the exhibition that it accompanies simply would not exist. As objects of faith and study, the *orixás* have been very much at the heart of *Axé Bahia* project since its inception.

Beyond the deities who may be credited as key sources of inspiration, divine or otherwise, the success of this endeavor has depended—from start to finish—on the contributions of many individuals and organizations in Brazil, the United States, and elsewhere. As curators, we join Marla C. Berns, the Shirley and Ralph Shapiro Director of the Fowler Museum, in warmly thanking all of the lenders, funders, and others singled out in her foreword. We are extremely grateful to Marla herself for her unwavering support of this undertaking and her participation in planning and implementation activities in both Brazil and Los Angeles. As with other Fowler exhibitions, the value of her leadership cannot be overestimated. We are likewise indebted to David Blair, Deputy Director, for his superb management of countless project details and to Matthew H. Robb, the Fowler Museum's Chief Curator, whose let's-roll-up-our-sleeves-and-get-to-work attitude and insightful suggestions enabled us to accomplish the always-daunting job of translating an object list into a finished exhibition. Many thanks also go to our Curatorial Assistant Sarah K. Chenault who deftly handled an ever-expanding array of crucial tasks and helped to keep things running smoothly in the face of the occasional crisis. And we again echo Marla in commending the entire Fowler staff for enabling us to realize this complex collective effort.

In developing the ideas that would become *Axé Bahia*, the curatorial team received immensely productive input from a diverse body of formal and informal advisors that included Emanoel Araújo, Marcia Argolo, Jeferson Afonso Bacelar, Judith Bettelheim, James V. Burks, Dori Caymmi, Kimberly L. Cleveland, Paricia Cochée, Roberta Saraiva Coutinho, Marcelo Bernardo da Cunha, Henrique Dantas, Abigail Lapin Dardashti, Gustavo Falcón, Felipe Ferreira, Luiz Alberto Ribeiro Freire, Cécile Fromont, Sergio Guedes, Goli Guerreiro, Ayrson Heráclito, Erica P. Jones, Larry Lauerhass, Helena Leal, Maria Cecília Loschiavo dos Santos, Justino Marinho, J. Lorand Matory, Sergio Mielniczenko, Valéria Piccoli, Marcelo Rezende, Antonio Risério, Anadelia Romo, Sandra Salles, Roger Sansi, Juliana Bevilacqua Santos, Maria Eugênia Saturni, Heather M. Shirey, Elena Shtromberg, Barry Stinson, Edward J. Sullivan, Xavier Vatin, Jorge Vismara, Jeri Bernadette Williams, and Jerome Woods. Others whose help was invaluable are Barbara Cristiane Nunes Almeida, Alicio Charoth, Isis Maria Gledhill Barreto Damasceno, Hernani Hefner, Henrique Lima da Silva; Marta Luna, Christine Eida Madureira, Ailton Muniz, Gary Neeleman, Soraia Oliveira, and Linda Yudin.

Also providing immeasurable assistance to the development of *Axé Bahia* were Maria Stella de Azevedo Santos (Mãe Stella de Oxóssi, Odé Kayode) and Célia Silva of the Sociedade Cruz Santa do Ilê Axé Opô Afonjá; Márcia Adorno, Ana Christina Gonçalves de Oliveira, and Marcos Braga de Carvalho of the Consulate-General of Brazil in Los Angeles; Mitch Loch, Taylor Van Horne, and Augusto Albuquerque of the Instituto Sacatar; Ana Lúcia Lopes and Maria de Fátima Padua de Cruz of the Museu Afro Brasil; Bárbara Carvalho dos Santos and Simone Trindade of the Museu Carlos Costa Pinto; Antônio Carlos "Vovô" dos Santos and Ilê Aiyê; João Jorge Rodrigues and Olodum; Arany Santana and Jaime Oliveira do Nascimento of the Centro de Culturas Populares e Identitárias (CCPI); the Centro de Estudos Afro-Orientais da Universidade Federal da Bahia (CEAO); Amen Santo and Nayla Eva Santo of Brasil Brasil Cultural Center; Karen Mack of LA Commons; Ben Caldwell of KAOS Network; Patricia Leão and Heber Moreira of Brazilian Nites Productions.

Without artists there would be no curators. We begin with paying posthumous respect to Gil Abelha (Gildásio Feliciano Costa), Hansen Bahia (Karl Heinz Hansen), Carybé (Héctor Julio Páride Bernabó), Mário Cravo

Neto, Agnaldo Manoel dos Santos, Mestre Didi (Deoscóredes Maximiliano dos Santos), Detinha de Xangô (Valdete Ribeiro da Silva), Voltaire Fraga, Rubem Valentim, and Pierre Verger. Next we must thank the following for sharing their work and perspectives with us: Rosa Bunchaft, Tauan Carmo, Lita Almeida Cerqueira, Tracy Collins, José Luiz Natividade Costa, Akira Cravo, Christian Cravo, Mário Cravo Júnior, José Antônio Cunha, Marco Aurélio Damaceno, Caetano Dias, Aurelino dos Santos, Marcondes Dourado, Oscar Dourado, Adenor Gondim, Ayrson Heráclito, Àlex Ìgbó, Tacun Lecy, Goya Lopes, Pedro Marighella, Willyams Martins, Virginia de Medeiros, Eder Muniz, Thaís Muniz, Aislane Nobre, Oske (Hirosuke Kitamura), Junior Pakapym, Alberto Pitta, Bauer Sá, Helen Salomão, Eneida Sanches, Tiago Sant'Ana, Arthur Scovino, Denis Senna, Arlete Soares, Sérgio Soarez, Nadia Taquary, Gilmar Tavarez, Bárbara Tércia, Marisa Vianna, Rommulo Vieira Conceição, Vinicius S.A. (Vinicius Silva de Almeida), and Zé Diabo (José Adário dos Santos). While not all of the aforementioned were included in the exhibition, each played a role in shaping the foundation on which *Axé Bahia* was built. We would also like to offer our appreciation to Dr. Julio Casoy who donated to the Fowler Museum a remarkable personal collection comprised of paintings by the late Gil Abelha and *orixá* dolls by Detinha de Xangô. Generosity such as his enables institutions such as ours to thrive.

Given that this volume will be a long-lasting legacy of *Axé Bahia*, we are deeply indebted to the authors who shared their work with us: Scott Alves Barton, Sarah K. Chenault, Kimberly L. Cleveland, Christopher Dunn, Cécile Fromont, Ana Paula Höfling, Vanda Machado, Lucas Marques, J. Lorand Matory, Paulo Miguez, Anadelia Romo, Roger Sansi, Heather Shirey, and Jeri Bernadette Williams. We look forward to further conversations and collaborations with these colleagues. We likewise thank the photographers, arts professionals, and family members or representatives of artists among whom are: Shai Andrade, Edgar Azevedo, Sergio Benutti, Hugo Canuto, Pedro Chiodo, Juana Elbein dos Santos, Inaicyra Falcão dos Santos, Roberto Faria, Bruno Fraga, Genie Guerard, Darío Guimarães Neto, Christian Herrmann, João Lima, Sora Maia, Isabella Matheus, Marco Menezes, Wallace Nogueira and Tatiana de Lima, Edgard M. de Oliva Junior, Consuelo Pinho Medauar, Octavio Olvera, Nilton Souza, Silvestre Silva, the Thiré Family, Tiago Troccoli, Edison Vara, Antonello Veneri, Artur Viana, Alvaro Villela, Jorge Vismara, and Bob Wolfenson. Additionally, we owe a very special debt to Andrew Kemp and Edouard Fraipont who photographed many of the works in the exhibition prior to their shipment from Brazil to the United States.

We are also thankful for the number of organizations worldwide who granted image permissions: Biblioteca Nacional de Brasil, Bibiliothèque Nationale de France, Copyrights Consultoria Ltda, Editora Corrupio, Editora da Universidade Federal da Bahia, Fundação Instituto Feminino da Bahia, Fundação Jorge Amado, Fundação Pierre Verger, Gabinete de Estudos Arqueológicos da Engenharia Militar (Lisbon, Portugal), Museu Paulista da Universidade de São Paulo, Museu de Arte da Bahia, Museu Carlos Costa Pinto, Museu Castro Maya, National Library of Australia, Stanford University Special Collections, UCLA Special Collections, and the Württembergische Landesbibliothek, Stuttgart.

Lastly, as is the case with the innumerable gods and goddesses of Candomblé, there are far more people deserving of recognition than can be named at one time and place. For those not mentioned here, please know that your support was invaluable. *Axé*!

Patrick A. Polk
Roberto Conduru
Sabrina Gledhill
Randal Johnson

NOTE ON ORTHOGRAPHY: Much of the vocabulary of Candomblé derives from African languages, especially Yoruba. The spellings of names and terms associated with the religion as it developed in Brazil vary considerably as a result. Although we have attempted to standardize spellings to the extent possible, we have also acknowledged the strongly held preferences of scholars and practitioners in some instances.

# Introduction

## Have You Been to Bahia?

**Patrick A. Polk**

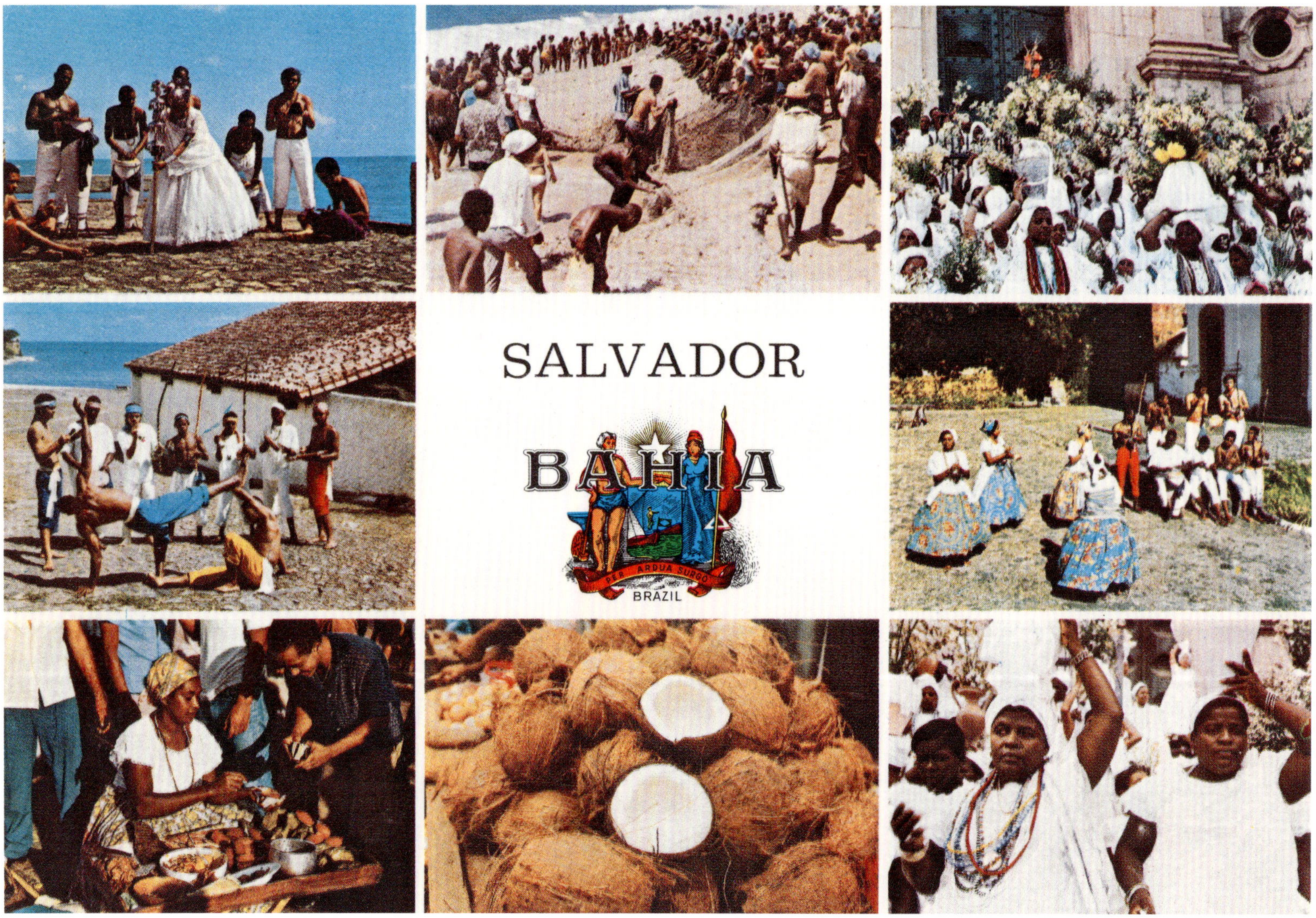

*Bahia... is a magical land—the city as well as the state. We are a mestizo people, of an intense culture, and every one of us is a magician.*

—Jorge Amado (1984, 19)

*Being black isn't about pigmentation*
*It's resistance that overcomes oppression; without pressure*
*Always fighting; equality and humility*
*I'm going to rise up with Ilê Aiyê*
*And change the whole city*

—Mario Pam and Sandro Teles[1]

FOR MORE THAN TWO DECADES several postcards from Brazil have been attached to the refrigerator door in my home. One of them, as the bold lettering announces, comes from Salvador in the Brazilian state of Bahia (fig. 1). Over the years it has ably done what travel-focused mementoes are supposed to do: entice visitors, shape their expectations, and encapsulate firsthand experiences of a particular place. Indeed, Salvador was in my kitchen long before I went to Bahia. In other words, the postcard served as an invitation to an unknown land and is now a reminder of a city whose streets I have traveled.

Nearly encircled by dark blue ocean, São Salvador da Bahia de Todos os Santos (Holy Savior of the Bay of All Saints) was the first capital of Portugal's Brazilian colony (fig. 2). Founded in 1549, it is one of the oldest cities in the Americas established by Europeans. Often referred to simply as "Bahia," it is the nation's third largest metropolis boasting a population of more than three million, the majority of whom have African ancestry. Widely regarded as the center of Afro-Brazilian culture, Salvador is frequently described as a *Cidade negra* (Black City) and has garnered the epithets *Roma negra* (Black Rome), *Capital negra do Brasil* (Black Capital of Brazil), and even *Coração do Brasil* (Heart of Brazil).[2]

This is the Bahia of my postcard. Produced in Curitiba in the Brazilian state of Paraná, it dates to the late 1970s or early 1980s. Still in circulation, it features eight small photographs, some clearly posed, emphasizing Bahian folk traditions. Positioned in the middle of these is the coat of arms (*brasão*) of the State of Bahia. Assuming a lack of local knowledge, the card gives a title for each vignette on the reverse.[3] Moving clockwise from the top left corner, the images represent:

A folkloric presentation of Afro-Brazilian religion featuring the Candomblé *orixá* (divinity) Oxalá holding his emblematic *opaxorô*, or staff surmounted by a dove (see Matory, this volume).

The massive handheld fishnets used to catch *xaréu* (*Caranx hippos*) along Brazil's northeastern coast.

Baianas, or Bahian women, at the annual Lavagem (washing of the steps) of the Igreja de Nosso Senhor do Bonfim (Church of Our Lord of the Good End; see interleaf C).

A festive *samba de roda* (circle samba) accompanied by drums in which dancers form a ring and take turns soloing in the middle.

Candomblé priestesses carrying water-filled clay jars to the Igreja de Nosso Senhor do Bonfim for the Lavagem.

Bahian coconuts, a dietary staple sold on beaches, streets, and in markets.

A Baiana with a table selling *acarajé*, deep-fried black-eyed pea fritters (see Shirey, this volume).

A capoeira bout (see Höfling, this volume).

This Salvador is a site of encounter with Afro-Brazilian culture; one routinely promoted by academics, artists, community activists, politicians, and a host of other interested parties (see Romo, this volume). As such, it appears an unequivocally black space.

These photographs essentially update long-standing tropes of local life and culture.[4] If the image of the Baiana vending *acarajé* had been taken in a studio rather than on the street, for instance, it could have been produced by Marc Ferrez (1843–1923), Guilherme Gaensly (1843–1928), or Rodolpho Lindemann (c. 1852–19?), all of whom created popular *cartes de visite* of Bahian market women in the late nineteenth century. Closer in style are some shots from the mid-twentieth century black-and-white postcard series by Foto Wessel entitled *Bahia typica* (Typical Bahia).[5] According to legend, one of these inspired Dorival Caymmi's ode to Afro-Bahian women entitled "O que é que a baiana tem? ("What Is It That the Baiana Has?") of 1938, a song that increased his national recognition and helped launch Carmen Miranda's international career (see Shirey, this volume, fig. 4.1).

**1**
Artist unknown
*Salvador, Bahia, Brazil*, late 1970s/early 1980s
Postcard
PARANÁ-CART, NO. 241, CURITIBA, PARANÁ, BRAZIL

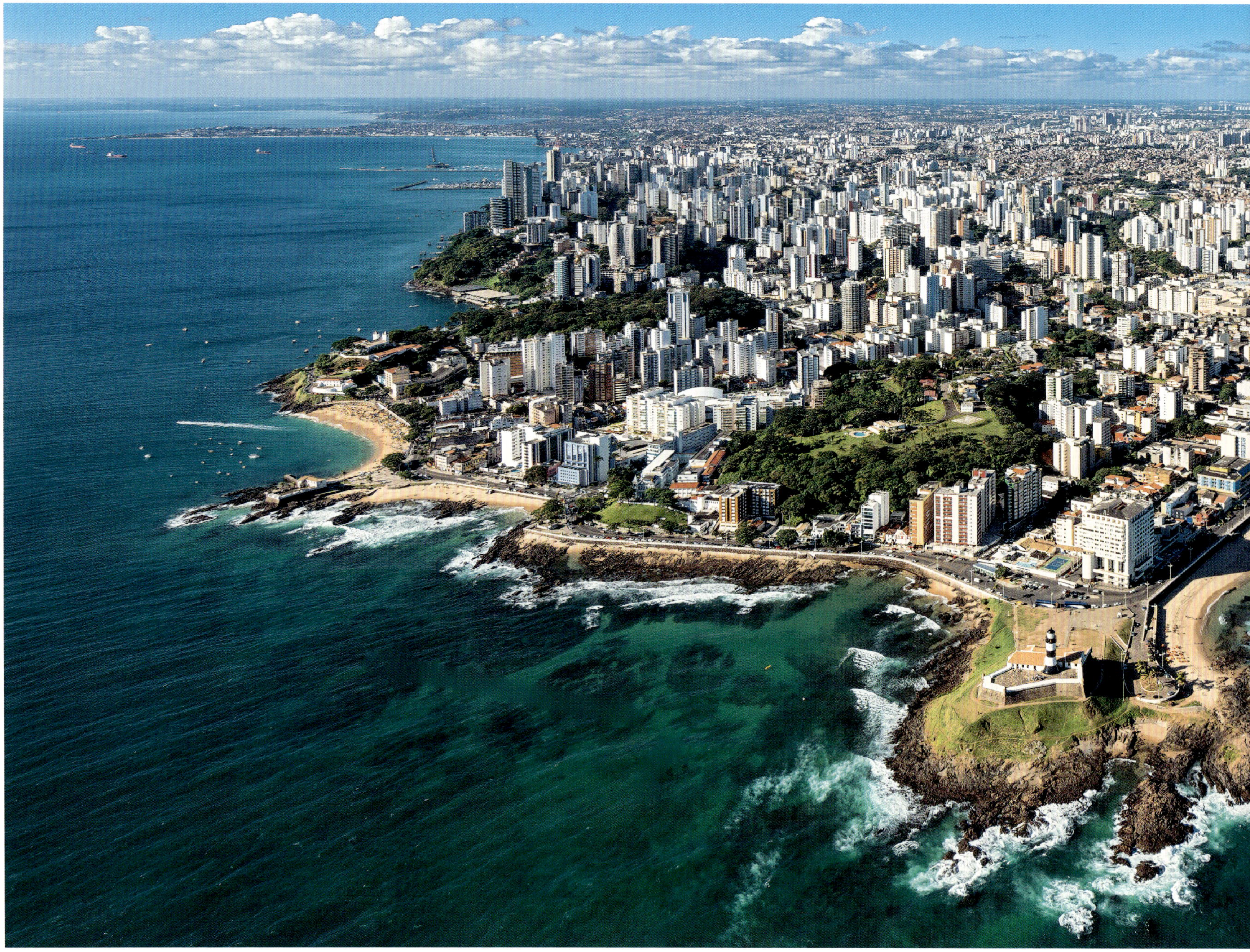

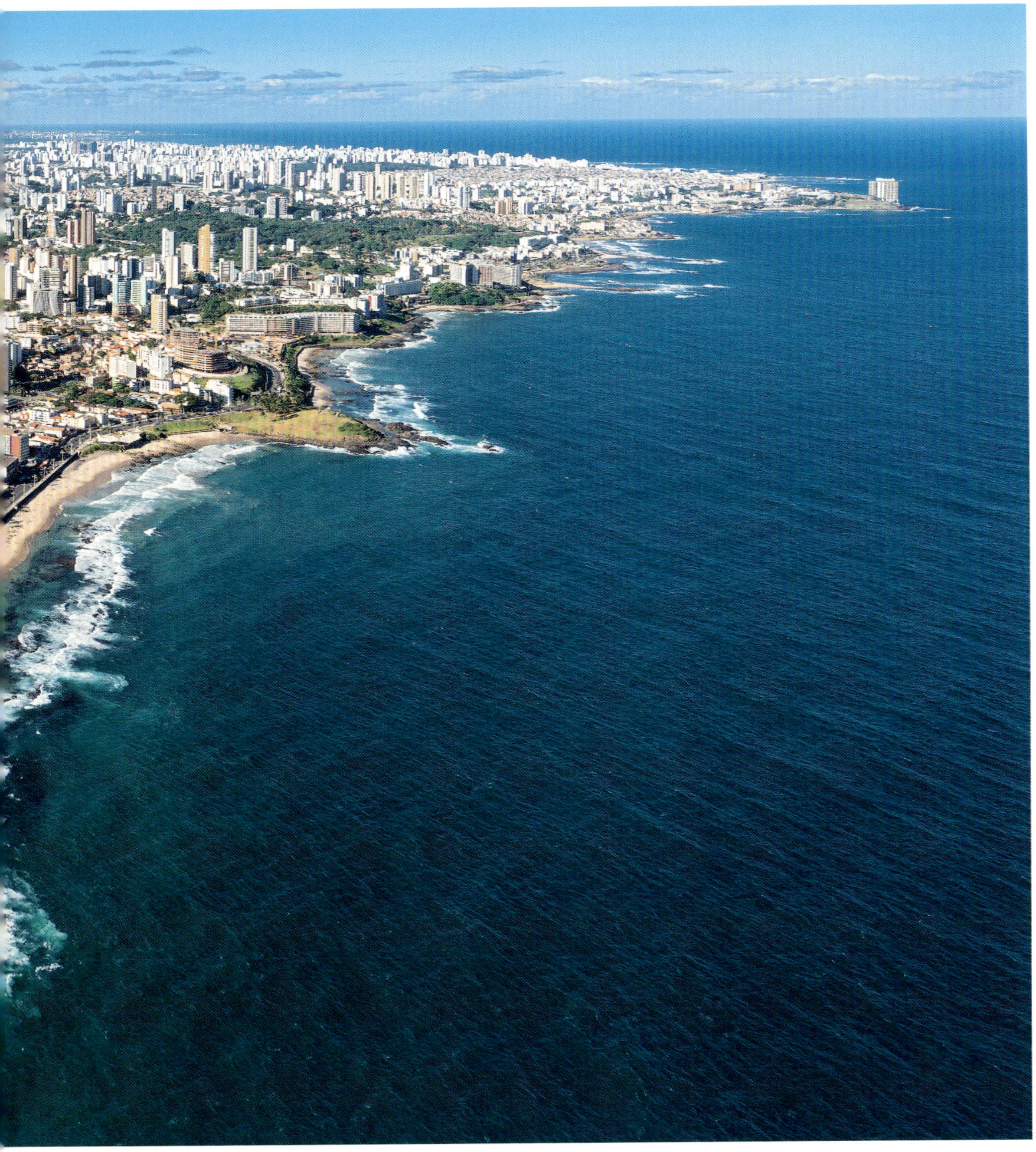

2
Nilton Souza (b. 1950, Varzedo, Bahia, Brazil)
*Vista aérea panorâmica da cidade de Salvador* (Panoramic Aerial View of the City of Salvador), August, 9, 2012
Photograph
COURTESY NILTON SOUZA

1re Div. Pl. 27.

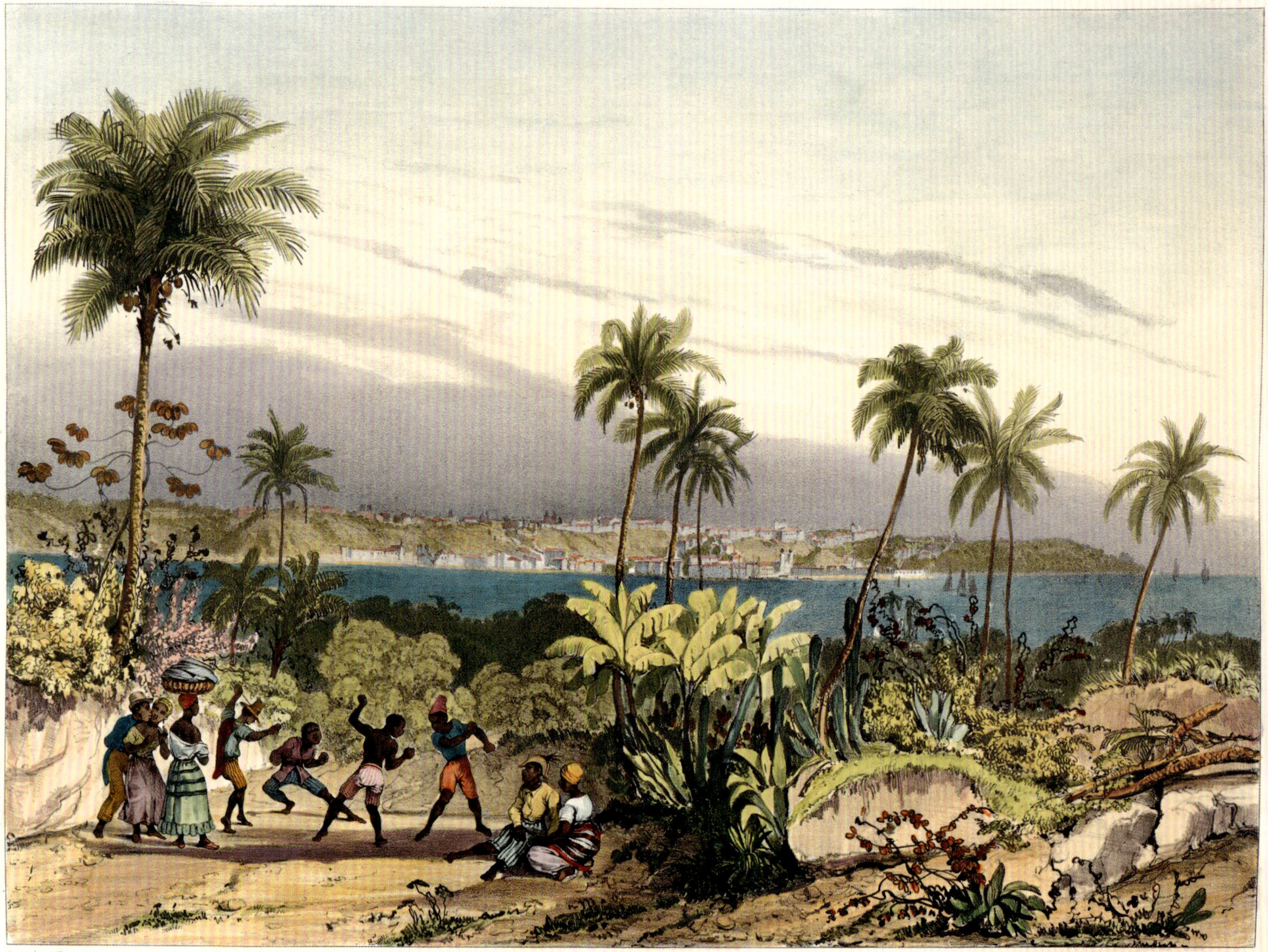

*Dessiné par Rugendas* *Lith de Thierry frères Succrs. de Engelmann à Paris.* *Lith. par Sabatier, Fig. par Wattier.*

SAN-SALVADOR.

Views of Bahia such as those displayed on my refrigerator have been crucial to popular notions of the region and its inhabitants since at least the late eighteenth century (see Fromont, this volume). The work of the German painter and illustrator Johann Moritz Rugendas (1802–1858) provides a good example (fig. 3). While many of his original drawings and watercolors illustrate flora and fauna or chart landscapes, a number of compositions are remarkable for their detailed, if often stereotypical and overly romantic, depictions of indigenous peoples and Afro-Brazilians. The color lithograph *San-Salvador* that appeared in his 1835 *Malerische Reise in Brasilien* (Picturesque Travels in Brazil) contains elements, or stock scenes, that are immediately familiar: a lush tropical seaport populated only by peoples of African descent; *jangadas* (single-sail fishing boats) plying the bay; coconut-laden palm trees; a bare-shouldered woman carrying a basket of goods on her head; four men playing capoeira as a seated couple look on; and another male and female caught in an amorous embrace. This is a once and forever Bahia.

Clearly, there is magic at work here, a glamour in the older than old sense of the word: the meeting point of grammar and incantation. Specifically, the Salvador conjured by Rugendas—and he was by no means the first—relies on a systematic visual language that makes of it an exotic land or magic kingdom. It is an enchantment that moves through time and space. More than one hundred years later Walt Disney and his animators realized their version of this *Bahia mágica* (Magical Bahia) with the classic *The Three Caballeros* (1944), which follows Donald Duck in a friendly wartime adventure through several Latin American countries. His dream-like visit to Bahia is saturated with rich pastels and set to the tune of Brazilian composer Ary Barroso's "Na Baixa Do Zapateiro" ("In the Shoemaker's Alley"), which was renamed "Baía [*sic*]" for the movie. Perfectly complemented by Ray Gilbert's English-language lyrics, the initial frames of the segment scan across a cityscape of antiquated buildings and notably empty streets:

> Oh Baía, when twilight is deep in the sky, Baía
> Someone that I long to see, keeps haunting my memory
> An' so the loneliness deep in my heart calls to you, calls to you!
> Oh Baía
> Oh Baía

An almost mournful song, it hinges on the proposal that Salvador is a land of romance whose spell is not easily broken. Look again at the flirtatious couple in the Rugendas print: a moment of passion frozen in time.

As Disney unfolds the allure of this eternal Bahia, two luminous orchids glisten with dew. Then a single *jangada* glides offshore. Next a lone white dove wings its way through dense vegetation. Alighting on one of the matching bell towers of a Baroque church, obviously patterned after Bonfim, it nestles with a second dove waiting there. After a tender greeting, they fly off together, soaring past twin palms before landing on an ancient wall beside a pond. A pair of spiraling wind-blown leaves briefly touch the water before flitting off-screen. Now the lonesome boat is joined by a second, and framed by the coconut trees, they sail into a ruby-colored sunset. Oh Bahia!

Artists working in many genres have found such charm in and around the Bay of All Saints. Magical realism infuses the writings of Jorge Amado, which have in turn fueled the imagination of countless others (see Johnson, this volume). Dorival Caymmi's famous samba "Você já foi à Bahia?" ("Have You Been to Bahia?") transports listeners to a bewitching terrain where the curves of dancing bodies merge seamlessly with the scrolled lines of colonial-era architecture (see Dunn, this volume). In addition to feasting on tantalizing cuisine, he assures visitors that they will count the rest of their days as fortunate ones if they go to Bonfim. "Everything," Caymmi exalts, "everything in Bahia makes us fall in love."

**3**
Johann Moritz Rugendas (b. 1802, Augsburg, Germany; d. 1858)
*San-Salvador* (São Salvador)
From *Malerische Reise in Brasilien* (Picturesque Travels in Brazil, Paris: Engelmann & Cie, 1835)
Lithograph
40 x 30 cm
WÜRTTEMBERGISCHE LANDESBIBLIOTHEK, STUTTGART

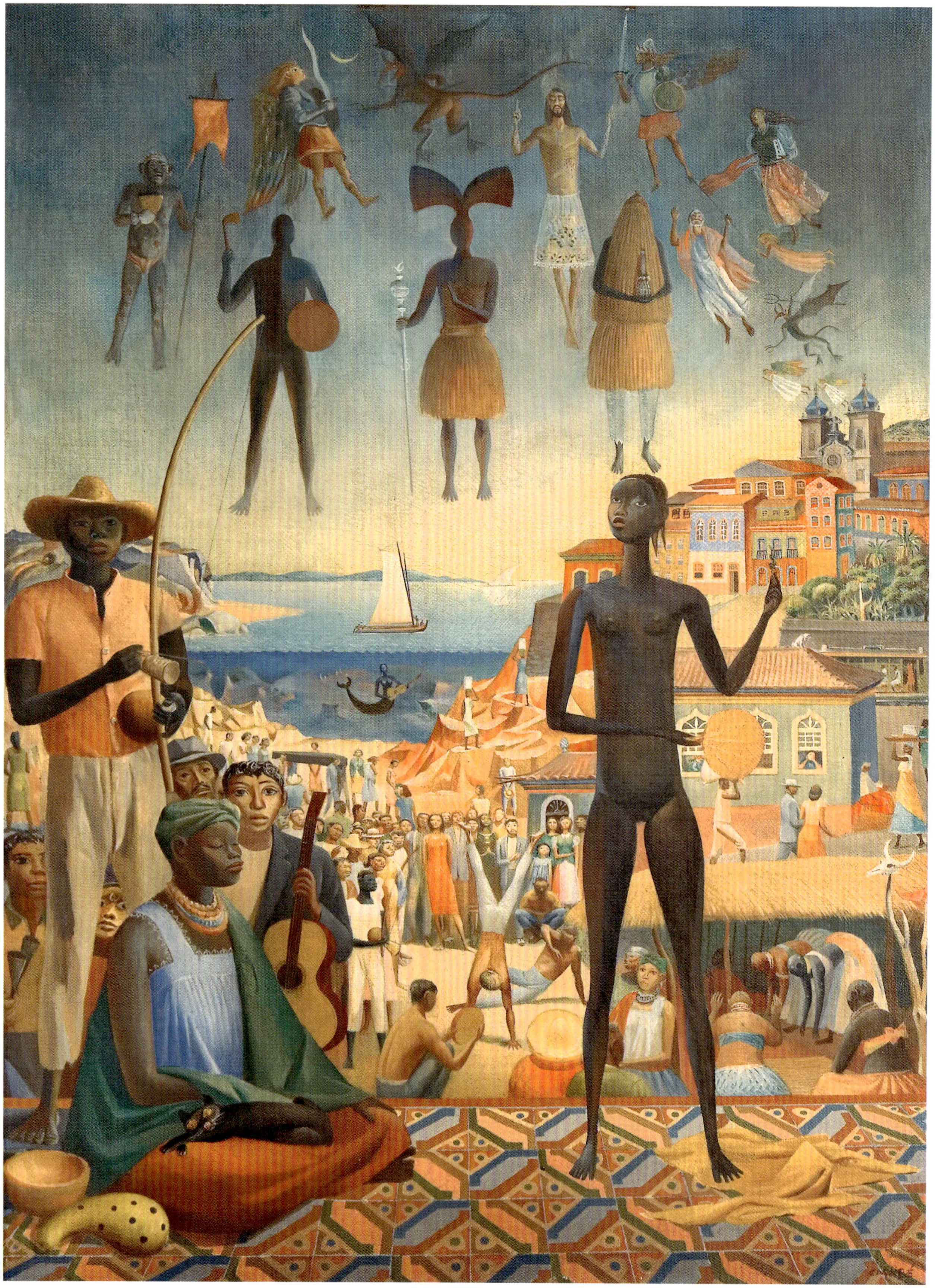

We can plainly see the paradigms of *Bahia típica* and *Bahia mágica* intersecting, as they generally do, in Carybé's painting of 1944 *Alexandrina e sua cidade* (Alexandrina and Her City; fig. 4). An Argentine-born immigrant, admittedly mesmerized by Amado and Caymmi, Carybé now ranks as one of Salvador's most renowned artists. Produced the same year Disney released *The Three Caballeros*, his Alexandrina presents a landscape pulsing with activity. We already know much of the realm. A *jangada* is anchored in the bay. The Church of Bonfim dominates the high ground to the right. Some residents watch a capoeira match while others go about their business carrying goods to and from market. Nearby a Candomblé initiation is underway. Musicians, one playing a *berimbau* and another holding a guitar, crowd up against a contemplative Baiana sitting cross-legged on an expanse of Portuguese tile. It is also a spirit-filled domain with the Afro-Brazilian *orixá* Iemanjá floating just beneath its waters in mermaid form while other *orixás* join with Jesus and Catholic saints to hold court and battle demons in the sky above.

Unencumbered but for a fan held in her right hand and a sprig of leaves in her left, Alexandrina stands naked before her birthright. Comparison to Caetano Dias's *O mundo de Janiele* (Janiele's World) of 2007 is compelling in that each centers on a young Baiana in the midst of a cityscape (see fig. 11.9). We are left to ponder not only their lives at that moment but also who they will become given the realities of where they reside. With regard to Alexandrina, though, Carybé has already told the end of her story in his *A morte de Alexandrina* (The Death of Alexandrina), 1939. Both paintings were inspired by a young Baiana with whom he was acquainted and who was murdered in the streets of the capital.[6] In terms of Carybé's professional trajectory, *Alexandrina e sua cidade* marks a defining moment in his career-long valorization of Afro-Brazilian culture and his ardent popularizing of Bahia as the premier *Cidade negra* of Brazil if not the Americas.

The French-born photographer Pierre Verger (1902–1996) is equally famous for his sensitive and beautifully framed portrayals of Brazilians of African descent (see Shirey, this volume). Like Carybé, Verger spent the majority of his life in Salvador, and his iconic black-and-white photographs, most dating from the late 1940s to the early 1960s, are indelible impressions of Bahia. Rolleiflex camera in hand, he haunted religious ceremonies, capoeira bouts, street festivals, markets, beaches, and harbors documenting the artistry of everyday life (figs. 5–8). As an anthropological researcher and social advocate, he was instrumental in the establishment of institutions dedicated to the study and preservation of Afro-Brazilian culture including the Museu Afro-Brasileiro (MAFRO) and the Fundação Pierre Verger. The influence of Verger's masterful command, or rebranding, of Bahian tropes on his contemporaries and subsequent generations is immeasurable, and his photographic practice remains an important point of comparison.[7]

Bahia continues to be introduced to audiences near and far following the well-rehearsed pattern. This is readily apparent in the recently released song "Muito prazer! Meu nome é Salvador" ("Pleased to Meet You! My Name Is Salvador") by Luiz Caldas, a Bahian who rose to fame in the 1980s as a leader in the *Axé* Music scene.[8] Presented as a gift in honor of the city's 468th anniversary (March 29, 2017), its first line proclaims: "Salvador is mystery." Caldas then details the ingredients of the *mistério*: the beach, the sounds of the *berimbau* and *atabaque* drums, the Church of Bonfim, capoeira, and *samba de roda*. Also mixed in are the sloped streets of the Pelourinho district (named a world cultural center by UNESCO in 1985), and the lighthouse at Itapuã. They make Salvador magical (*Faz da nossa Salvador, Um encanto*). The accompanying music video produced by the local government nicely accentuates both the African heritage of the contemporary city and its multiracial, multicultural diversity.

**4**
Carybé (Héctor Julio Páride Bernabó, b. 1911 Lanús, Buenos Aires Province, Argentina; d. 1997)
*Alexandrina e sua Cidade* (Alexandrina and Her City), 1944
Oil on canvas
110 X 80 cm
COLLECTION OF ADRIANA VAREJÃO, RIO DE JANEIRO, BRAZIL

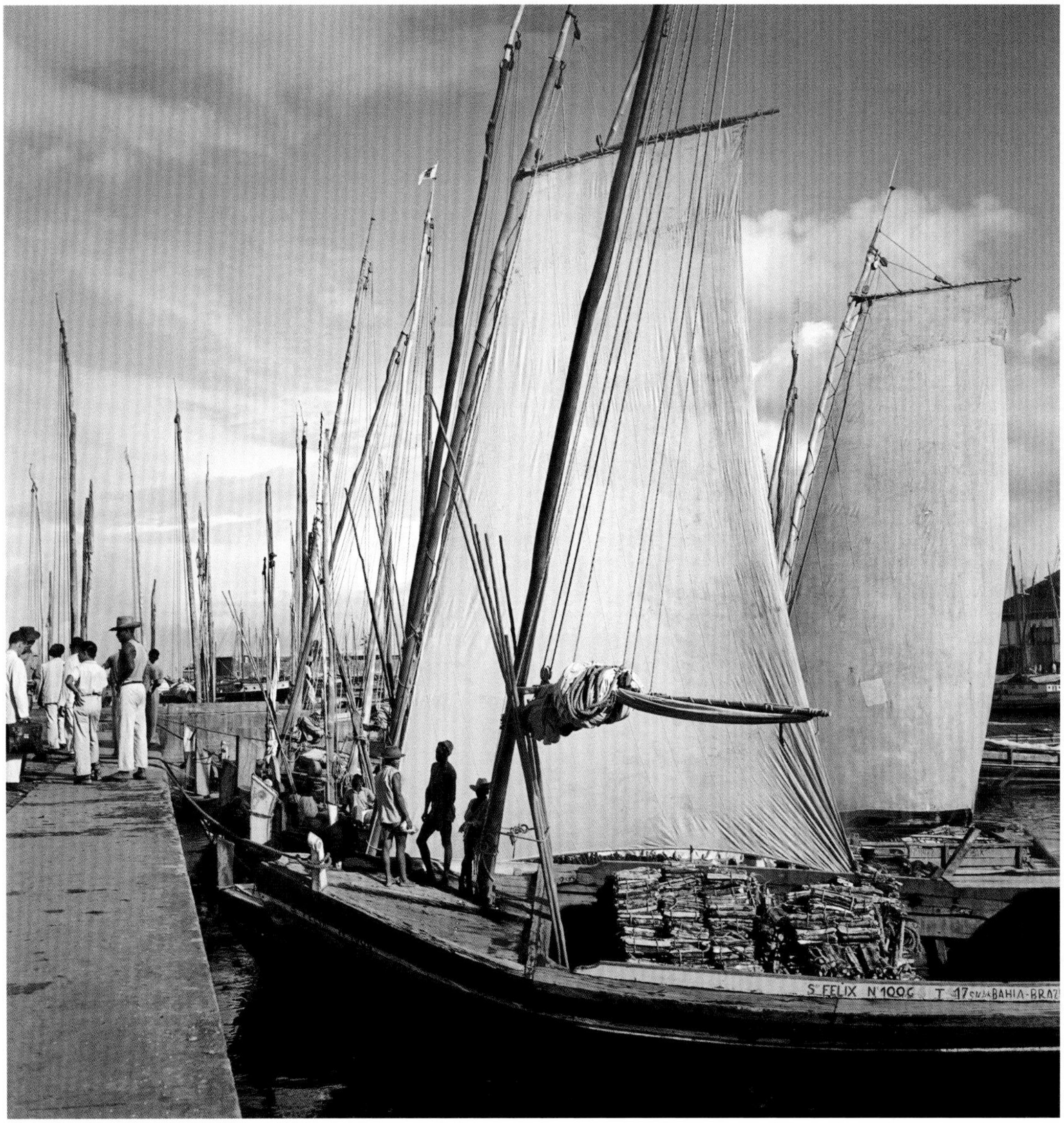

**5**
Pierre Verger (b. 1902, Paris, France; d. 1996)
*Porto dos Saveiros*, Salvador, Brazil, 1946–1948
Photograph
PHOTO PIERRE VERGER ©FUNDAÇÃO PIERRE VERGER

**6**
Pierre Verger (b. 1902, Paris, France; d. 1996)
*Capoeira*, Salvador, Brazil, 1946–1947
Photograph
PHOTO PIERRE VERGER ©FUNDAÇÃO PIERRE VERGER

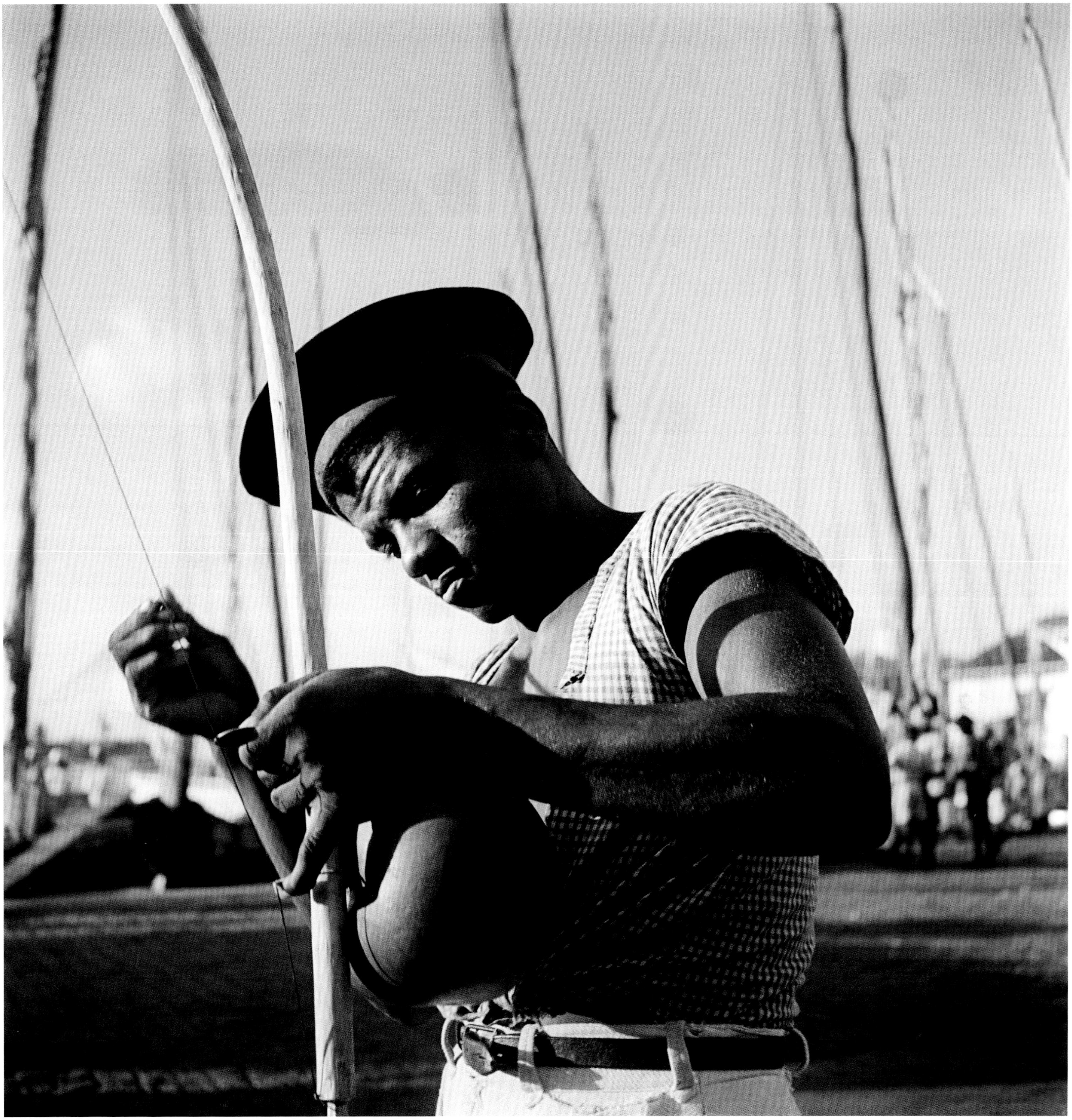

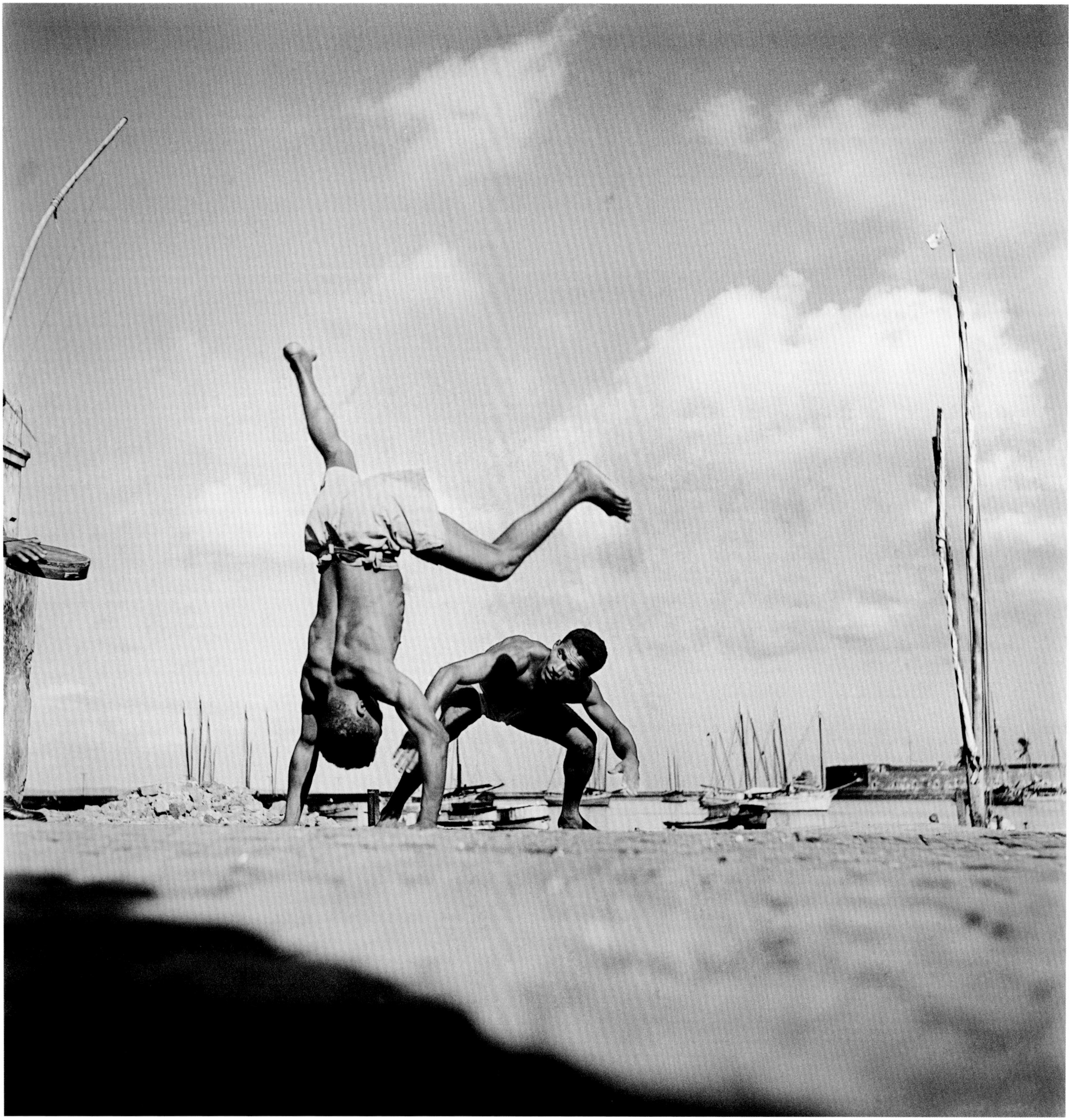

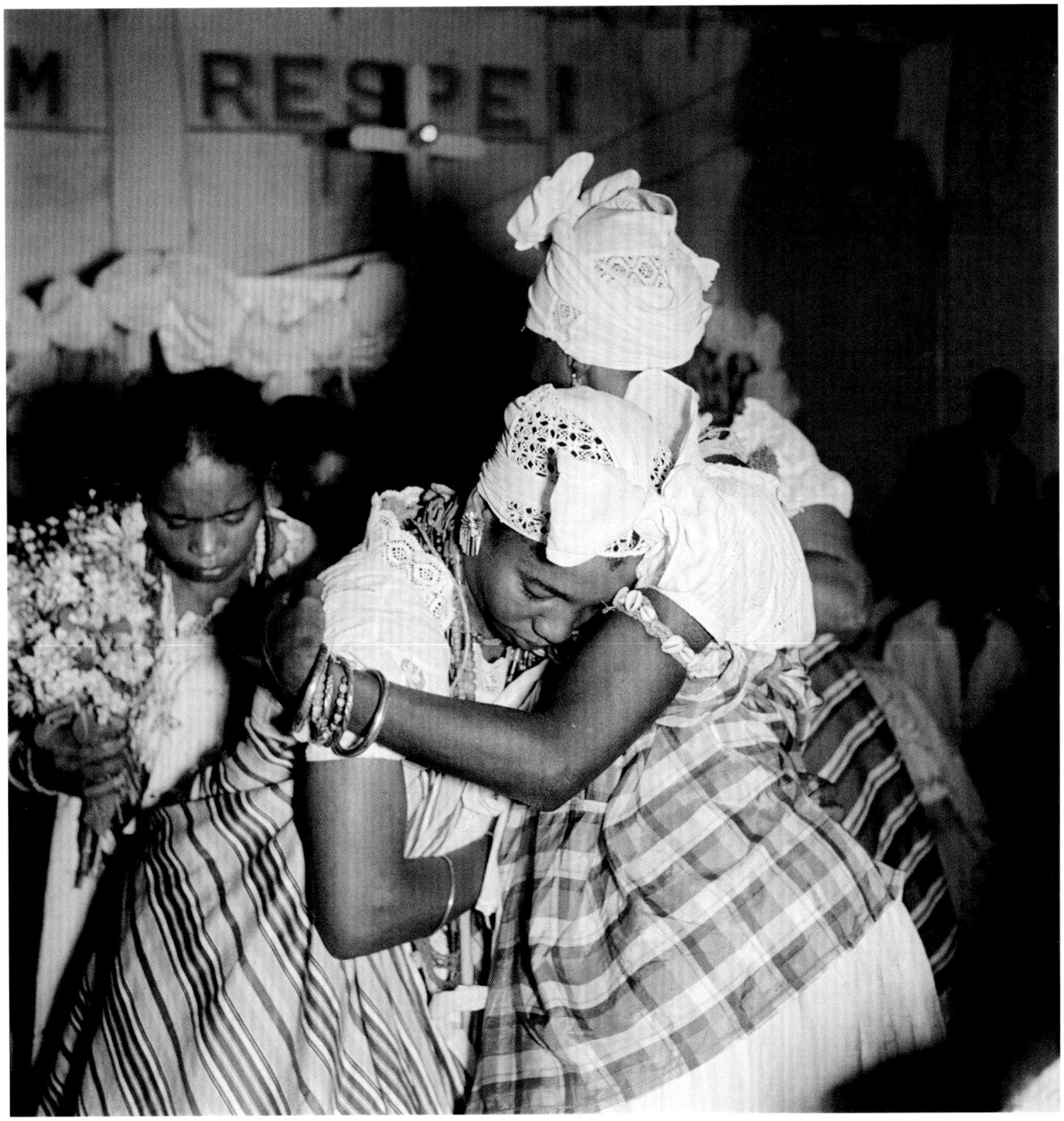

**7**
Pierre Verger (b. 1902, Paris, France; d. 1996)
*Capoeira*, Salvador, Brazil, 1946–1948
Photograph
PHOTO PIERRE VERGER ©FUNDAÇÃO PIERRE VERGER

**8**
Pierre Verger (b. 1902, Paris, France; d. 1996)
*Candomblé Miúda* (Candomble temple of Dona Miúda), Salvador, Brazil, 1946–1950
Photograph
PHOTO PIERRE VERGER ©FUNDAÇÃO PIERRE VERGER

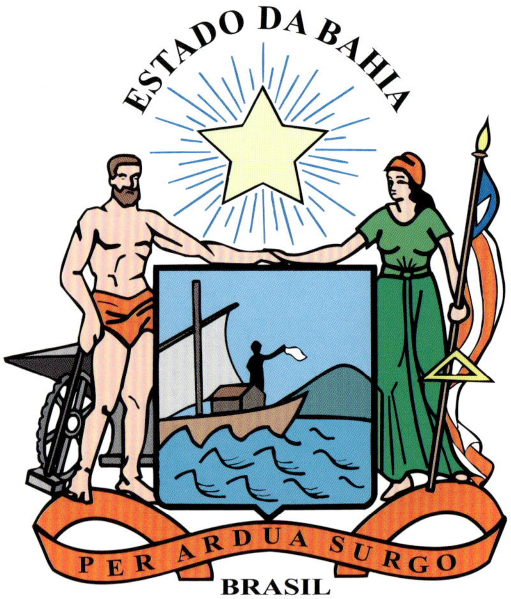


**9**
Artist Unknown
Coat of arms (*brasão*) of the State of Bahia, early twenty-first century

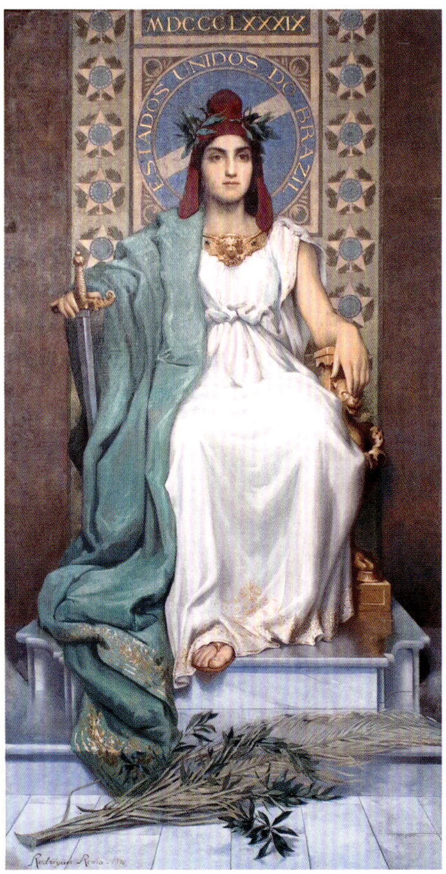


**10**
Manuel Lopes Rodrigues (b. 1860, Salvador, Bahia, Brazil; d. 1917)
*A República* (The Republic), 1896
Oil on canvas
228 x 118.5 cm
ACERVO DO MUSEU DE ARTE DA BAHIA

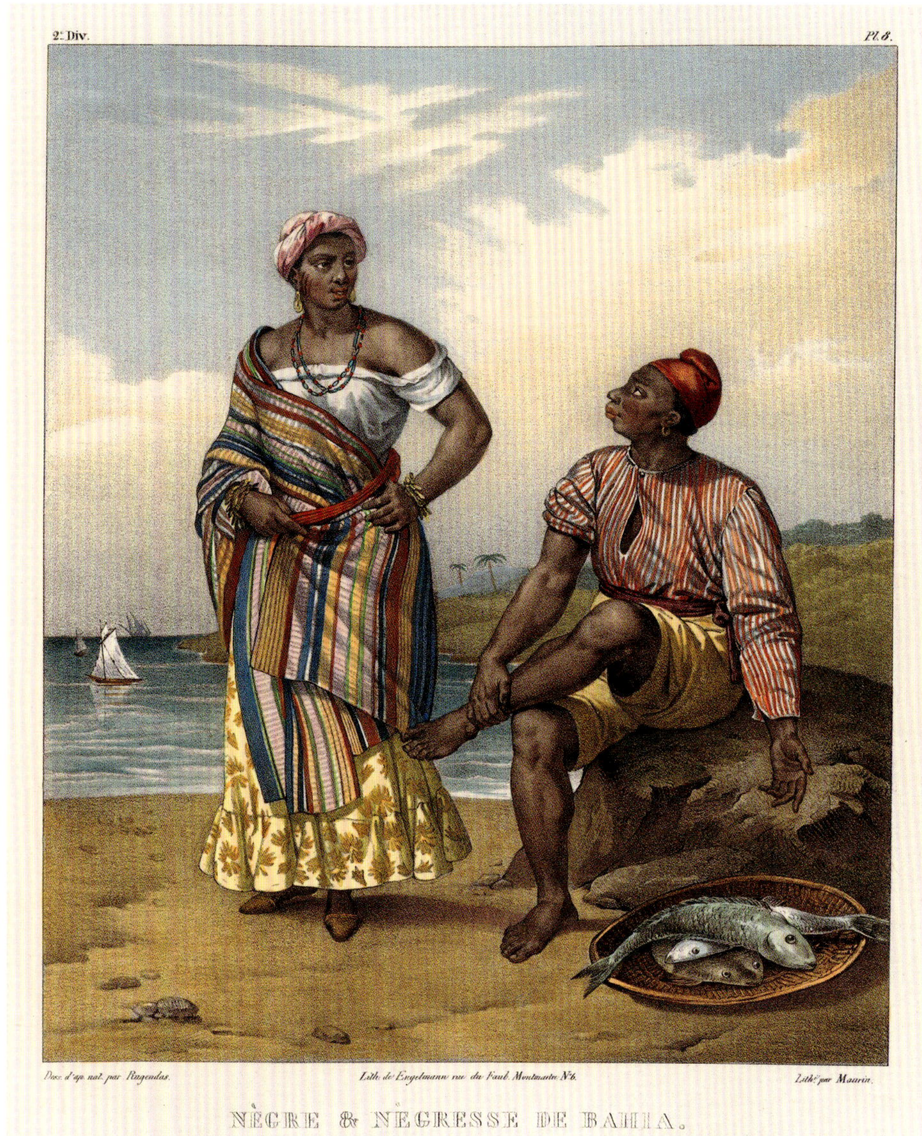


**11**
Johann Moritz Rugendas (b. 1802, Augsburg, Germany; d. 1858)
*Nègre & Nègresse de Bahia* (Black Man and Black Woman of Bahia), 1835
From *Malerische Reise in Brasilien* (Picturesque Travels in Brazil, Paris: Engelmann & Cie, 1835)
Lithograph
40 x 30 cm
WÜRTTEMBERGISCHE LANDESBIBLIOTHEK, STUTTGART

### *Per Ardua Surgo* (From Adversity I Rise)

*Out of the huts of history's shame I rise*
*Up from a past that's rooted in pain*
*I rise*
*I'm a black ocean, leaping and wide,*
*Welling and swelling I bear in the tide.*
*Leaving behind nights of terror and fear*
*I rise*
*Into a daybreak that's wondrously clear*
*I rise*
*Bringing the gifts that my ancestors gave,*
*I am the dream and the hope of the slave.*
*I rise*
*I rise*
*I rise.*

—Maya Angelou (1978)

Let's return to my postcard. There is no question that it celebrates Afro-Brazilianess. But take a closer look at the coat of arms (*brasão*) of the State of Bahia in the middle (see fig. 1). It is the only graphic element lacking a visual representation of a black Brazilian. Even the photograph of the coconuts contains a glimpse of the arm of a person of color. Instead, the *brasão* features almost cartoonish white personifications of Industry and Liberty (fig. 9). It is a notable break from the otherwise almost complete focus on peoples of African descent (Afrodescendentes). One initial way to read this might be to align it with a history in which Afro-Brazilians have been relegated to the periphery with regard to the construction of Brazilian national identity and institutional authority.

Adopted in 1891, just three years after the abolition of slavery in Brazil, the *brasão* is closely patterned after European models rooted in Greco-Roman mythology and iconography (see Romo, this volume). Thus Hephaestus/Vulcan, god of metallurgy, poses with hammer, forge, and flywheel, while Athena/Minerva, goddess of war and wisdom, firmly grasps the spear-tipped flag of Bahia. Known locally as "República," she stands for freedom and independence, as further evidenced by her Phrygian (Liberty) cap and the triangular device representing liberty, equality, and fraternity.[9] Situated between these fair-skinned embodiments of Industry and Liberty is the five-pointed star of the Federal Republic of Brazil. Also included is an illustration of Portuguese explorer Pedro Álvares Cabral's arrival near the present-day Bahian city of Porto Seguro in 1500. He waves a piece of white cloth as Monte Pascoal comes into view. A ribbon beneath, resembling the ubiquitous *fitas* associated with the Church of Bonfim, bears the Latin phrase *Per Ardua Surgo* (From Adversity I Rise).

It is an admirable motto to be sure; one that generations of Brazilians have lived up to. República, as painted in 1896 by the Bahia-born Manuel Lopes Rodrigues (1860–1917), appears serene and majestic (fig. 10). A revolutionary whose Phrygian cap and laurel wreath are well earned, *A República* (The Republic) is enthroned before the star of the nation. With flowing white gown, elegant swath of green fabric draped over her shoulder, and an elaborately worked necklace at her bosom, she is the epitome of feminine beauty. The sword on which she rests her right hand is a testament to sovereignty as is the bundle of palm branches and other leaves lying on the floor beneath her sandaled foot. There is no question that República cuts an impressive figure.

But one might ask: Why aren't these Bahian symbols of state and nation the Afro-descendants who constitute the majority of the populace and whose collective history surely better reflects the ideal expressed in the maxim "From Adversity I Rise"? Why must they be white? The answer, of course, is obvious. When all or nearly all of the other imagery in the postcard is either patently or obliquely coded as black, the juxtaposition reveals the crux of the issue. The likenesses are an expression of power. Even as peoples of African descent are seemingly being lauded, they can still be deliberately made to disappear through acts of identity definition that are shaped by dynamics of racism and institutionalized forms of privilege. Race matters. It did in 1890s, and it still does today.

What if we take a different road to Black Rome and envision some alternative Afro-Brazilian guises for Liberty and Industry? A well-known color print of 1835 based on drawings by Rugendas offers an excellent starting point (fig. 11). His *Nègre & Nègresse de Bahia* (Black Man and Black Woman of Bahia) could easily supplant the Greco-Roman god and goddess should viewers be willing to accept the couple as such. Doesn't the shoeless Baiano with rolled-up pant legs and a bare arm epitomize labor as he hawks fish freshly caught from the sea? And is the Baiana with her head and body enveloped in lavish cloth any less formidable a presence than República? There is certainly good reason to think that Rugendas and some abolition-minded nineteenth-century contemporaries saw the possibility even if others could not (figs. 12, 13).[10]

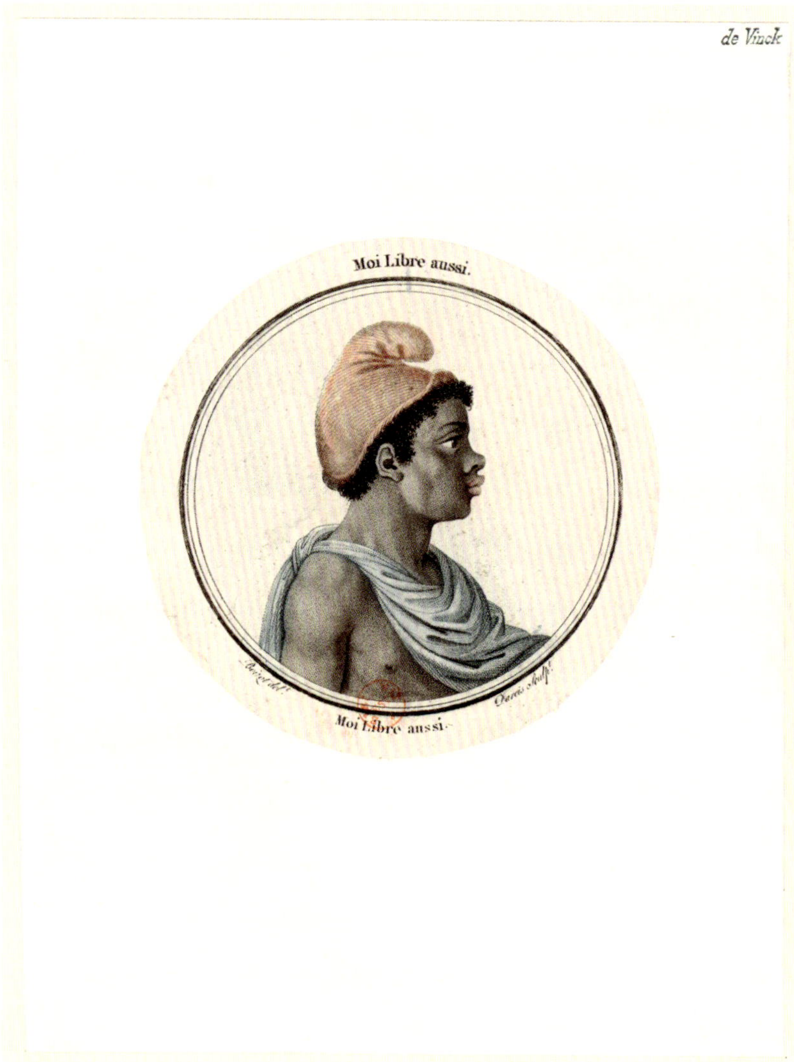


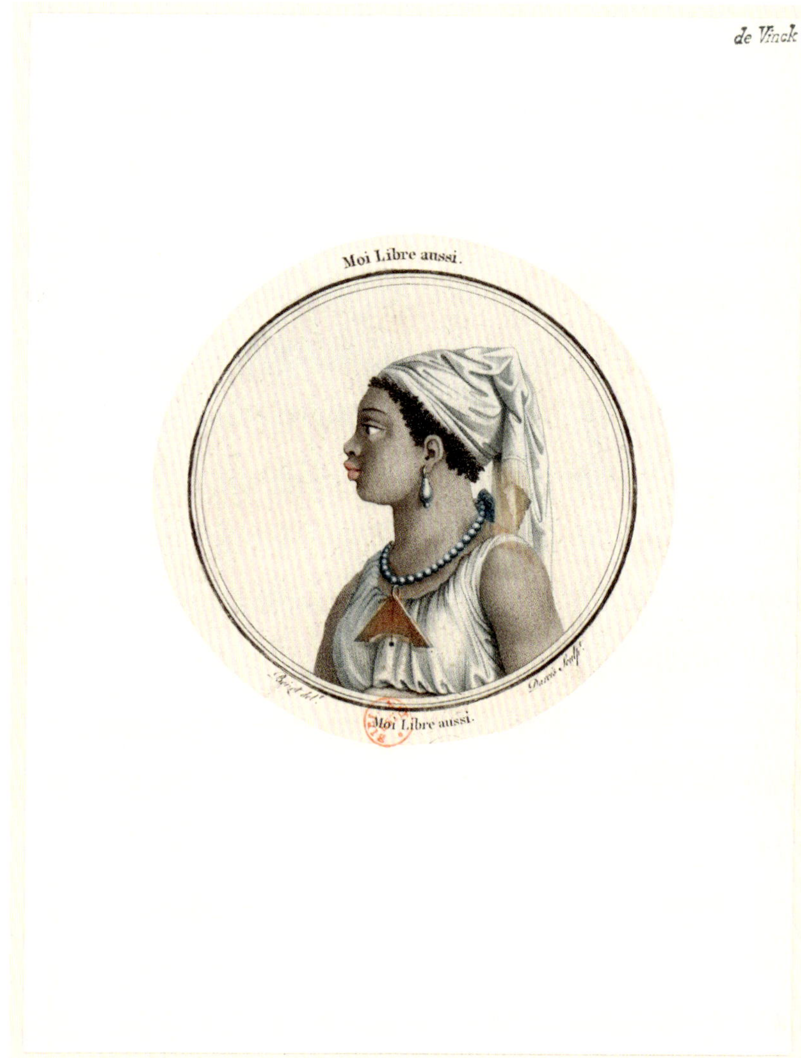


**12**
Louis-Simon Boizot (b. France, 1743; d. 1809), artist;
Louis Darcis (b. France, 17??; d. 1801), engraver
*Moi libre aussi* (I Too Am Free), 1794
Etching
Diam: 9 cm
BIBLIOTHÈQUE NATIONALE DE FRANCE, DE VINCK, 6036

This etching and its companion (fig. 14) were published on the occasion of the abolition of slavery in the French colonies, which was announced on February 4, 1794.

**13**
Louis-Simon Boizot (b. France, 1743; d. 1809), artist;
Louis Darcis (b. France, 17??; d. 1801), engraver
*Moi libre aussi* (I Too Am Free), 1794
Etching
Diam: 9 cm
BIBLIOTHÈQUE NATIONALE DE FRANCE, DE VINCK, 6037

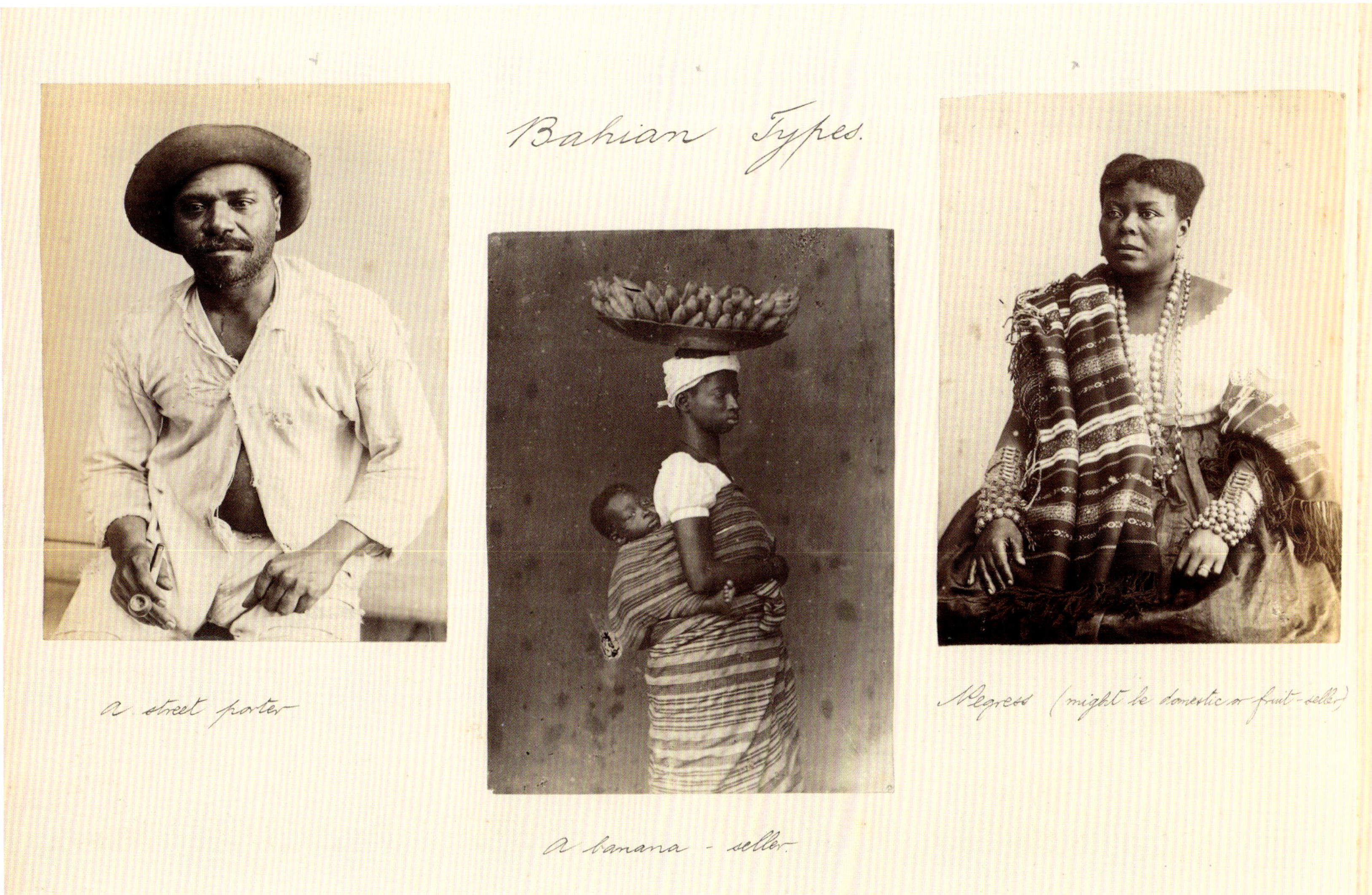


**14**
Left: Artist Unknown; Center: Marc Ferrez (b. 1843, Rio de Janeiro, Brazil; d. 1923), circa 1884; Right: Lindemann (b. 1852, Germany; d. ?), circa 1881
Photographs
Scrapbook compiled by an unidentified nineteenth-century visitor to Brazil.
SPECIAL COLLECTIONS, YOUNG RESEARCH LIBRARY, UNIVERSITY OF CALIFORNIA, LOS ANGELES

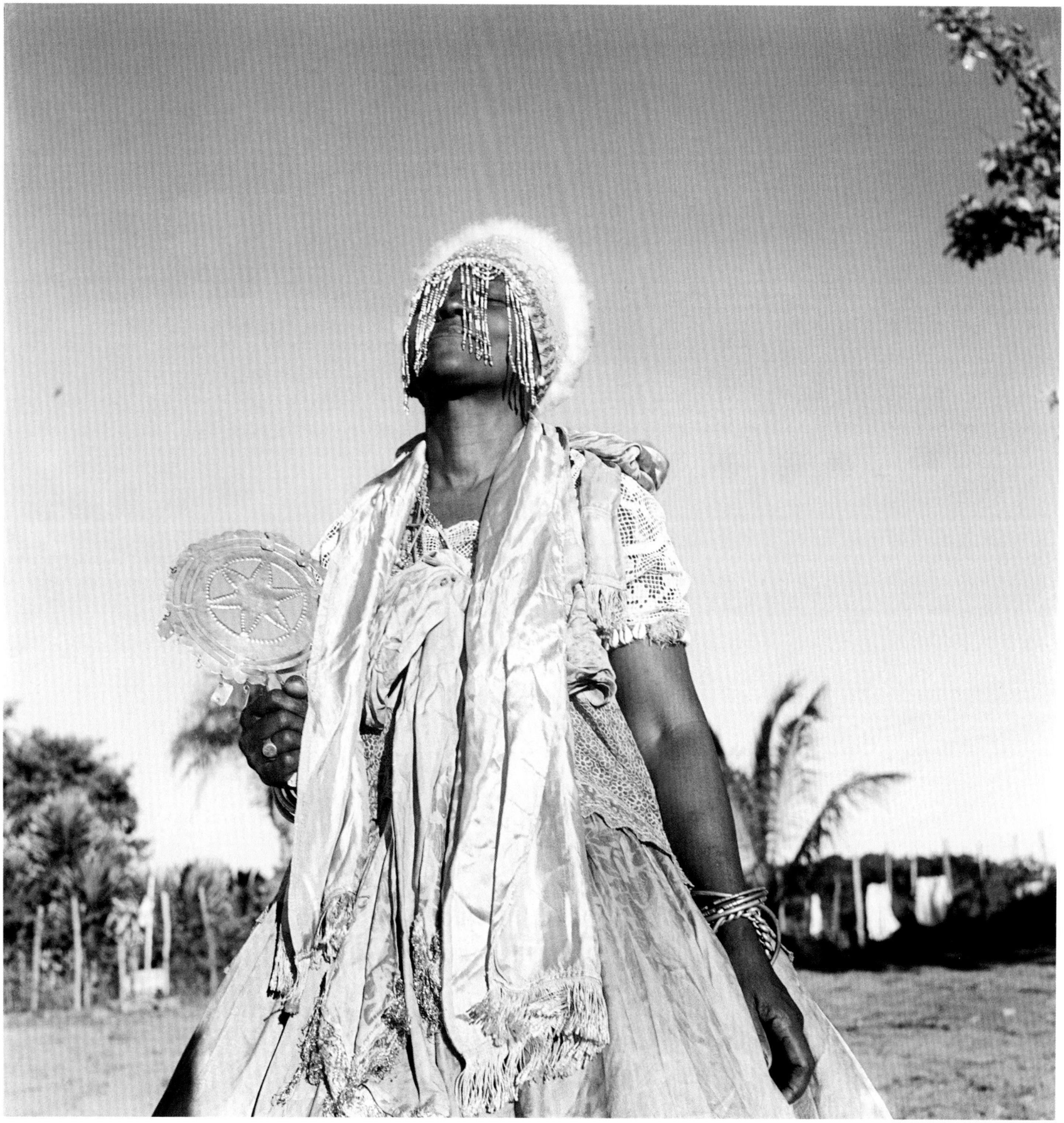

15
Pierre Verger (b. 1902, Paris, France; d. 1996)
*Candomblé Joãozinho da Goméia* (Candomblé Temple of Joãozinho da Goméia), 1946
Photograph
PHOTO PIERRE VERGER ©FUNDAÇÃO PIERRE VERGER

Another relic of a bygone but still critically relevant era is a late nineteenth-century scrapbook compiled by a visitor to Brazil that is filled with original works by Marc Ferrez, Rodolpho Lindemann, and other important early Brazilian photographers. One leaf of the album with three of these images is labeled "Bahian Types" in elegant cursive script (fig. 14). Here again is *Bahia típica*. Extra notes inked onto the page describe the man to the left as "a street porter," the woman carrying a child in the middle as "a banana-seller," and the female on the right as a "Negress (might be domestic or fruit-seller)." Postal cards imprinted with these portraits, especially those of the women, were mass-produced during the decades spanning the end of the nineteenth century and the beginning of the twentieth, and today they commonly illustrate histories of the Afro-Brazilian experience and more broadly those of the African diaspora. The individuality of the subjects has, however, been effectively erased. No personal names are given. No family lineage. Rather, they stand almost solely as tokens of a very specific identity: Afro-Bahian labor, free or enslaved, Industry personified.

Photographed by Rodolpho Lindemann in the late 1800s, the woman on the right exemplifies the elaborately dressed and ornately adorned black Baiana. Often described alternatively as a *crioula* (creole), her likeness has graced many publications, especially those dedicated to the art of Brazilian *joias de crioula* (creole jewelry) of the kind she wears in the portrait (see interleaf G, this volume). Although the sitter remains anonymous, her necklaces, bracelets, and other precious accessories suggest she was a person to be reckoned with. Her regal bearing would seem to make her as good a candidate as any to ascend Manuel Lopes Rodrigues's altar of Liberty. Maybe he did have her *pano da costa* (an African style of cloth often worn as a shawl) in mind when he draped luxurious fabric over República's right shoulder. Each wears it well. After all, they are both *crioulas*, are they not?

We also need to reflect on the potential of Afro-Brazilian religion to provide conceptual paradigms that embody collective ideals and infuse emblems with deep meanings. Historically, Brazil has made good use of European and indigenous mythological figures and culture heroes. Why not the *orixás* of Candomblé? Human-like in form and personality, they were given dominion over key aspects of the cosmos and human experience by the Supreme Creator Oludumaré (also known as Olorun). A robust body of sacred narratives augmented by arts and ritual performances makes of the *orixás* ready models of moral and ethical behavior (see Matory, this volume). To be fair, representations of Afro-Brazilian divinities are prominent in some contemporary Brazilian physical and virtual contexts, but these are often contested spaces (see Sansi, this volume). Every day, for example, thousands of Bahians pass by the *orixá* sculptures designed by Tati Moreno that tower over the waters of the Dique de Tororó in Salvador (see fig. B.2), while some evangelical Christians protest their presence there.[11] Similarly, the intersection of religious intolerance and racial tensions is central to Àlex Ìgbó's *Jexus* project (see chapters 3 and 11, this volume, and figs. 3.3, 3.4).

Candomblé emerged out of an Afro-Brazilian process of "world-building" and remains a generative mode of creating stability (cultural, familial, psychological, social, etc.) and a counter to the wide-ranging effects of inequality. Over the years much emphasis has been placed on how African deities were re-coded using elements from other iconographies of spirit and power, especially Catholic saints.[12] In theory, doing so diverted potential negative attention from authorities that discriminated against or outlawed African-derived practices. Thus, in Bahia the warrior *orixá* Ogum masqueraded as or merged with Santo Antônio de Pádua (Saint Anthony of Padua), the patron of Portugal and Brazil who was also closely linked to the colonial military. More expansive searches for analogy could extend the range of signification. Iemanjá, once a Yoruba river goddess, now surfaces from ocean waters as a European-style mermaid and Nossa Senhora da Conceição (Our Lady of the Immaculate Conception).[13] Some older personifications are transformed, other equally ancient guises persist, and new visions regularly arise. J. Cunha's monumental *Códice* argues this point forcefully: Afro-Brazilian religious iconography, like its theology, is a dynamically expansive system rather than a static one (see interleaf H, this volume).

With this in mind, I wonder now if I've been looking at the *brasão* of the State of Bahia emblazoned on my postcard in the wrong way. My initial interpretation of the white characters made them out to be Greco-Roman mythological figures (Athena/Minerva and Hephaestus/Vulcan) repurposed as the Brazilian República and her consort Industry. In so doing, however, I neglected the possibility of ongoing reinterpretation or revelation. Who says that they do not or cannot represent Afro-Brazilian *orixás*? Can't the muscular male figure be Ogum, the lord of iron and technology (see interleaf E, this volume)? Within Candomblé, divine presence isn't predicated on skin tone but rather embodiment through ritual enactments including choreographed movement and the use of sacred objects. Ogum responds to the salutation *Ogunhê*! Ogum dances in a certain way. He is African. He is Brazilian. He is Black. He is also the color of whatever hand holds his *ferramentas* (ritual implements) during a ceremony.

Likewise, it is possible to see Iemanjá in the body of República, especially as realized by Manuel Lopes Rodrigues. Or even a *mãe de santo* (Candomblé high priestess) seated on a throne-like chair in her *terreiro*, or temple (see fig. 10.5). As one of Pierre Verger's most renowned photographs reveals, not only do Iemanjá and República dress alike, they have been working with essentially the same *ferramentas* for a long time (fig. 15). Shot in 1946 at the *terreiro* of Joãozinho da Goméia (1914–1971), it shows an initiate embodying Iemanjá complete with her characteristic *adé* (crown) and *abebé* (star-shaped fan). Although the adherent is not holding an *espada* (sword), one normally completes her set of insignia (figs. 16–18). If we read further into the portrait, the fronds of the palm trees in the background have ritual significance as well. In that light, how might some interpret the leaves at República's feet? In Candomblé, each *orixá* has symbolic plants, many of which are cultivated on the grounds of *terreiros*, and these are used during initiations, for blessings and spiritual cleansings (*sacudimentos*), and a variety of other ceremonies (see interleaf K, this volume).

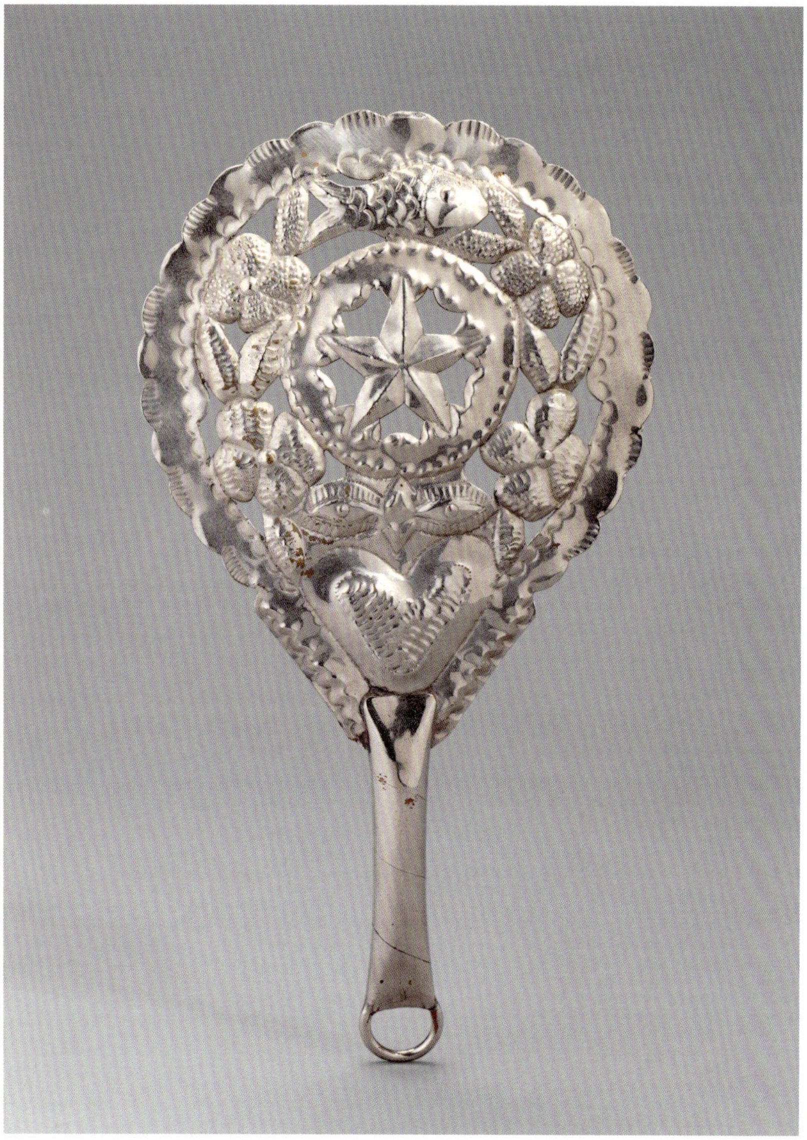

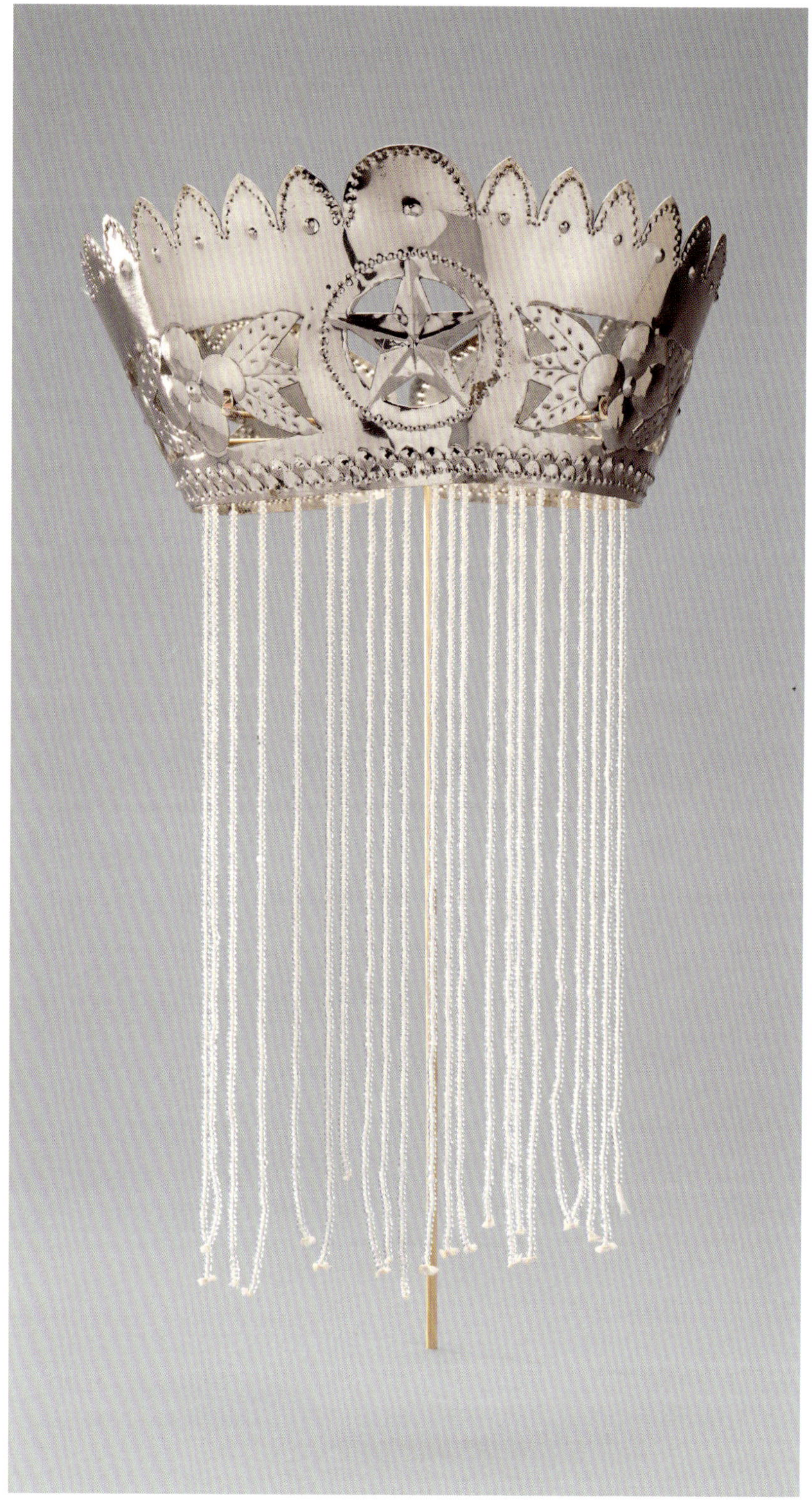

**16**
Artist Unknown
*Abebé* (fan) for Iemanjá, circa early 1980s
Tin
H: 28.9 cm
FOWLER MUSEUM AT UCLA X83.536B; ANONYMOUS GIFT

**17**
Artist Unknown
*Adé* (crown) for Iemanjá, circa early 1980s
Tin, glass beads
H: 37.8 cm
FOWLER MUSEUM AT UCLA X83.536A; MUSEUM PURCHASE

18
Artist Unknown
*Espada* (sword) for Iemanjá, circa early 1980s
Tin
H: 33.6 cm
FOWLER MUSEUM AT UCLA X83.524; ANONYMOUS GIFT

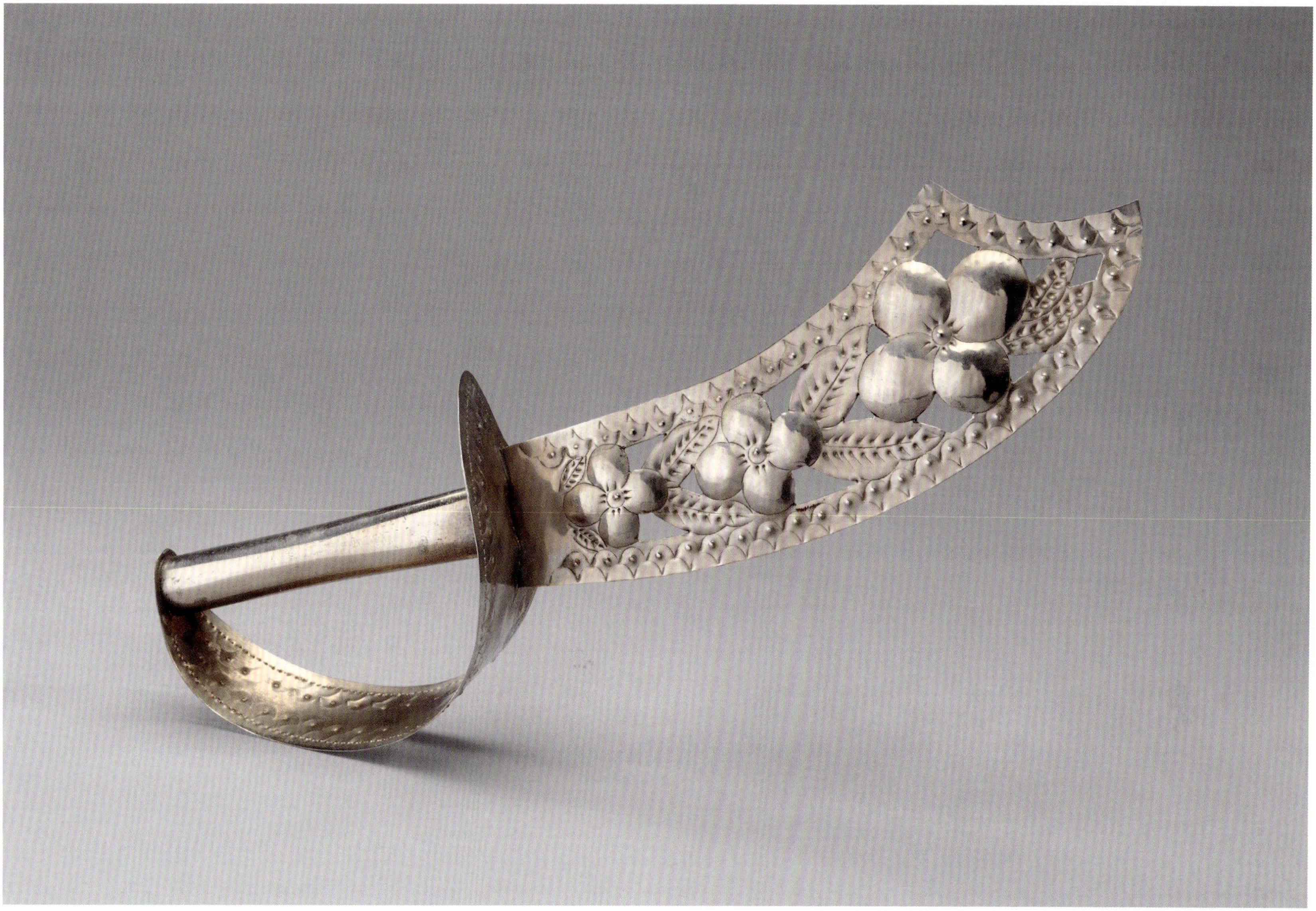

My point in making such comparisons is not to argue that Iemanjá and República are one and the same. Rather I'm suggesting that depictions of each—which may derive from very different cultural, historical, or religious perspectives—can overlap in profound ways. This enables multiple, and sometimes oppositional, interpretations. Thus, the iconographies of Euro-Brazilian nationalism and Afro-Brazilian religion can look very much alike even though some might hold them to be irreconcilable. Much of the ability of divinities and emblems of state to express notions of collective identity, to inspire action, and to summarize human experience lies in their symbolic elasticity (see Cleveland, this volume). Iemanjá and República are neither twins nor avatars of the same sacred essence, but they can help each other be present in the world and speak meaningfully to different audiences.

Here, it is critical to introduce the Afro-Brazilian concept of *axé* (pronounced "ah-sheh"). When vocalized, the term is a common way of saying "Blessings" or "Peace" and voicing approval. Understood within Candomblé theology as the intangible energy or vital force that infuses life, it carries the potential for positive change in the world when channeled appropriately. Although *axé* animates all things, it is most visible in ritual and art. Sacred symbols applied to the bodies of initiates, lavish ceremonial costumes, intricately designed icons, handcrafted portraits of *orixás*, and many other aesthetic practices all activate *axé*.

## Axé Bahia: From Orun to Aiyê and Back

*Then Caramuru, in the language and style*
*Of the natives, speaking to the new chief,*
*All standing in silence to hear him,*
*Shows the escutcheon of Bahia to the people:*
*Noah's dove, which, having found sanctuary,*
*Returns with an olive branch,*
*Signifying the peace the merciful king*
*Dispensed to the heathens through the faith.*

—José de Santa Rita Durão (1781)

*Up in the heavens a door opened*
*A white dove appeared*
*Let us all praise the divine Holy Spirit*
*Let us all praise the divine Holy Spirit*
*Hail mama Oxum–Ayeyeo*
*Hail my father Oxalá*
*Hail Nanã Buruque*
*Hail all the orixás*

—From *"Lá no céu abriu uma porta"*[14]

When Carybé composed *Alexandrina e sua cidade* with its heavenly host of *orixás*, he placed Oxalá's *opaxorô*, his metal staff, in the hands of Xangô, god of thunder and warfare whose signature *ferramenta* is the double-headed axe, or *oxê* (fig. 19). At first glance, this makes no sense. Divinity of wisdom, purity, and peace, Oxalá is generally envisioned as the progenitor of the other *orixás* and the creator of humankind. His bird-adorned insignia, often specifically representing a dove, exemplifies his *axé* and his bridging of the immaterial and material realms of existence: Orun (Sky or Heaven) where the orixás reside and Aiyê (Earth) where humans live (fig. 21). Yet, the hot, fiery Xangô is positioned in the middle of the panorama holding the primary implement of the cool, calming Oxalá. Carybé may well have been mistaken in his assignment of the *opaxorô*, or he might have been making reference to the sometimes problematic relationship between father and son. According to one myth, for example, Xangô held Oxalá prisoner for seven years, albeit unwittingly (see interleaf C). Or perhaps the artist had something else in mind. The question is likely irresolvable. Nonetheless, an easily overlooked detail of the *opaxorô* highlights an important fact: if ever there was a city where doves matter, it is Salvador.

Like the coat of arms of the State of Bahia, the *brasão* of the metropolis tells a remarkable tale. More accurately, it conflates several sacred narratives. Derived from classic European heraldry, its shield bears a white dove *volant* with wings spread (fig. 20). This device itself is held in place by fish-like supports and crowned by a castle with crenellated towers. Spelled out in large white letters on a curling blue banner is Salvador's Latin motto: *Sic Illa ad Arcam Reversa Est*. A direct reference to the biblical account of Noah, it may be translated: "And thus she [the dove] returned to the ark." Further accentuating the connection to the story of the Great Flood, the dove carries in its beak an olive branch. Based on an earlier design attributed to Portuguese explorer Tomé de Sousa (c. 1515–1573), who is credited as the founder of Salvador and was the first governor-general of the colony, the message of the present-day *brasão* is forthright. As the righteous and resolute Noah was guided to dry land by the hand of God following the Deluge, so too was de Sousa led to terra firma in Brazil by divine providence.

**19**
Bauer Sá (b. 1950, Salvador, Bahia, Brazil)
*Olhos de Xangô (Xangô's Eyes)*, 2007–2009
Photograph
COURTESY BAUER SÁ

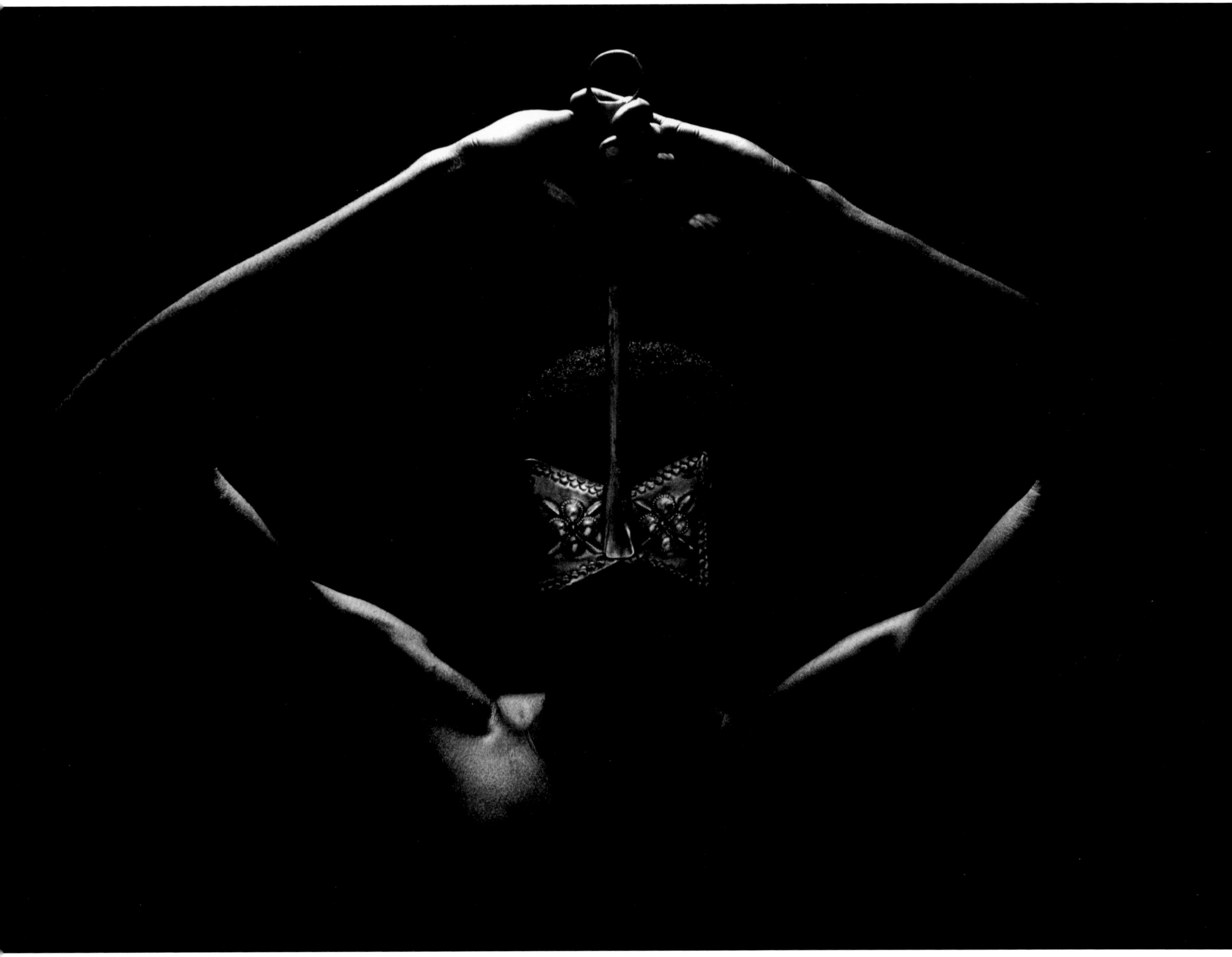

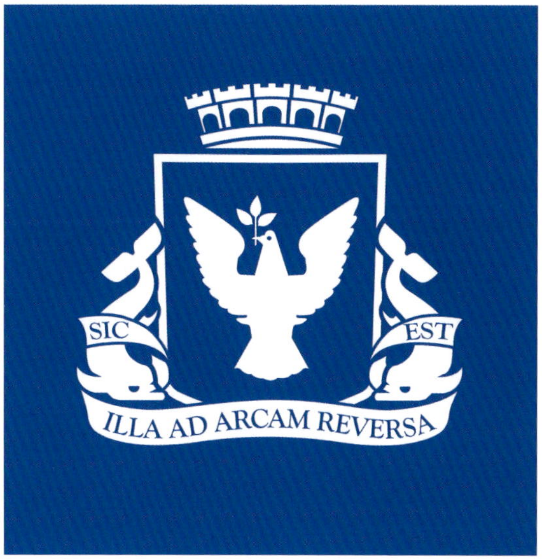


**20**
Artist Unknown
Coat of arms (*brasão*) of the City of Salvador, early twenty-first century

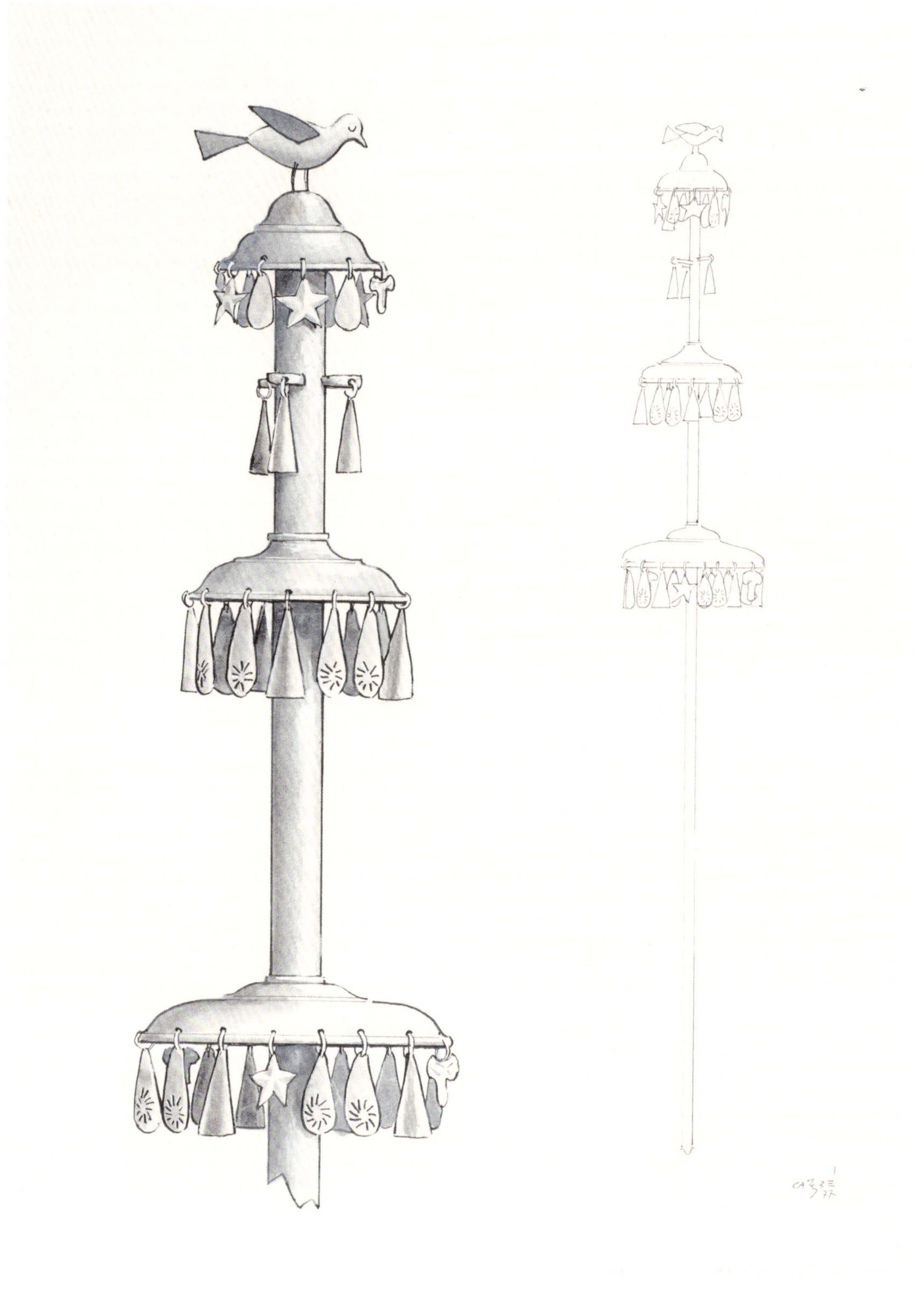

**21**
Carybé (Héctor Julio Páride Bernabó, b. 1911, Lanús, Buenos Aires Province, Argentina; d. 1997)
*Ferramentas de Oxalufã* (Ritual Implements of *Oxalufã* [or elderly Oxalá]), 1977
Ink and watercolor (gouache) on paper
83 x 63 cm

The castle on the coat of arms alludes to the fortification of the Bay of All Saints undertaken by Tomé de Sousa and his son Garcia de Sousa d'Avila (1528–1609), which solidified Portuguese control of the region. One of the initiators of plantation society in Bahia, d'Avila also constructed the infamous Casa da Torre (Tower Castle) at Mata de São João north of Salvador (see interleaf K, this volume). In their establishment of the colony, Tomé and Garcia were greatly aided by Diogo Álvares Correia (c.1475–1557), a Portuguese adventurer who had been shipwrecked on the coast years earlier. According to popular history, Correia, now known by the indigenous name Caramuru, married a Tupinambá woman who was christened as Catarina Álvares Paraguaçu (1495–1583). He, and presumably Catarina, served as valuable intermediaries between the native communities and the Sousa clan when they washed up on Salvador's shore. In later years, as the mythology of the colony evolved, Caramuru and his wife were deemed by some to be the veritable "Adam and Eve" of Brazil; Bahian parents of the first mestizo generation (see fig. 1.1).

That Tomé de Sousa, Garcia de Sousa d'Avila, and Caramuru rowed into Bahia on the wings of doves is no surprise. The bird is a Christian emblem of the first order. In the Old Testament, it has a variety of symbolic meanings including purity, fertility, and divine presence. The only avian appropriate for sacrificial atonement, it can represent suffering and salvation. All of this underscores why this creature and not the crow, which was chosen first but failed miserably, ultimately brought Noah the olive branch. In the New Testament, it is more firmly associated with the Holy Spirit (God's active force in the world) and is prominent in apostolic accounts of the baptism of Jesus in the River Jordan. Consequently, the Espírito Santo in the form of a *pomba* (dove) thoroughly marked the spiritual landscape of colonial Brazil and continues to do so today.

Perhaps the courting *pombas* that flew through the Salvador of Disney's *The Three Caballeros* can offer a useful metaphor for the meeting in Bahia of the Catholic Holy Spirit and the winged *axé* of Oxalá. In the traditional West African religions from which Candomblé Nações (nations or branches) such as Nagô or Jêje derive, the dove (or white pigeon) has a wide range of sacred implications including signaling divine benevolence, facilitating divination and communication with supernatural beings, and purification. The diverse, and frequently coinciding, meanings attached to these prime symbols in Africa and Europe surely provided unique opportunities to make sense of an inherently disordered and unruly Brazilian world-in-the-making. Many of the Portuguese colonists must have been confident that their bird would help make Christians, and hence good subjects, of non-Europeans ensnared in the imperial enterprise.

The very same avian can signify an alternative Afro-Brazilian worldview as well as express resilience in the face of hegemonic pressures. The *orixá* Oxum, to whom doves are also especially sacred, is widely viewed by Candomblé practitioners to be the protector of Salvador (Garcia 2009). And with Oxalá and his *opaxorô* in mind, Mário Cravo Neto's photograph *Pedro with Dove* offers a beguiling case study (fig. 22). Is this a visitation of the Holy Spirit? Or Oxalá? Does it depict pain or freedom from suffering? Is the tree branch a sign of divine intervention? Or are man and bird caged by it? Is one or the other a sacrifice? Or both? If so, for what purpose? For whose benefit? Isn't this stark contrast of black and white inherently the story of Salvador? Now compare the Cravo Neto work to the digital image *Afoxé, Filhos de Gandhy* (*Afoxé*, Sons of Gandhi)[15] of 2016 by his son Christian Cravo (fig. 23). Motivated by the activism of the Mahatma, the Sons of Gandhi are one of the oldest and most prominent Afro-Brazilian Carnaval associations in Bahia (see Miguez, this volume). Proudly Afrocentric, there is little ambiguity with regard to what the *pomba* on their banner represents: peace, calm, and serenity fostered by the enveloping celestial whiteness of Oxalá. Whether overtly stated or not, this is a Candomblé-inflected response to the legacies of the *brasão* of Tomé de Sousa and the standard planted in the soil of Bahia by Caramuru.

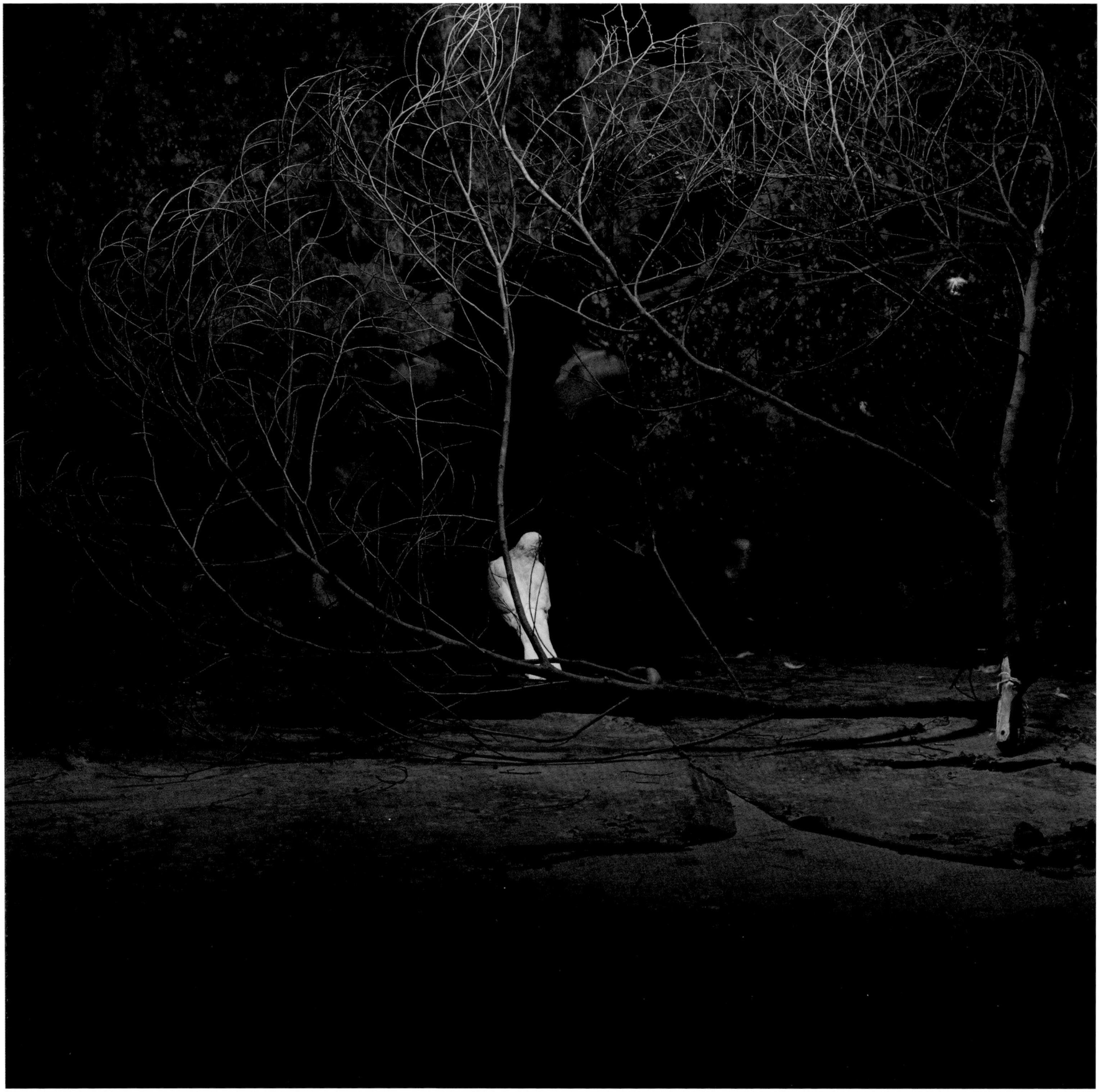

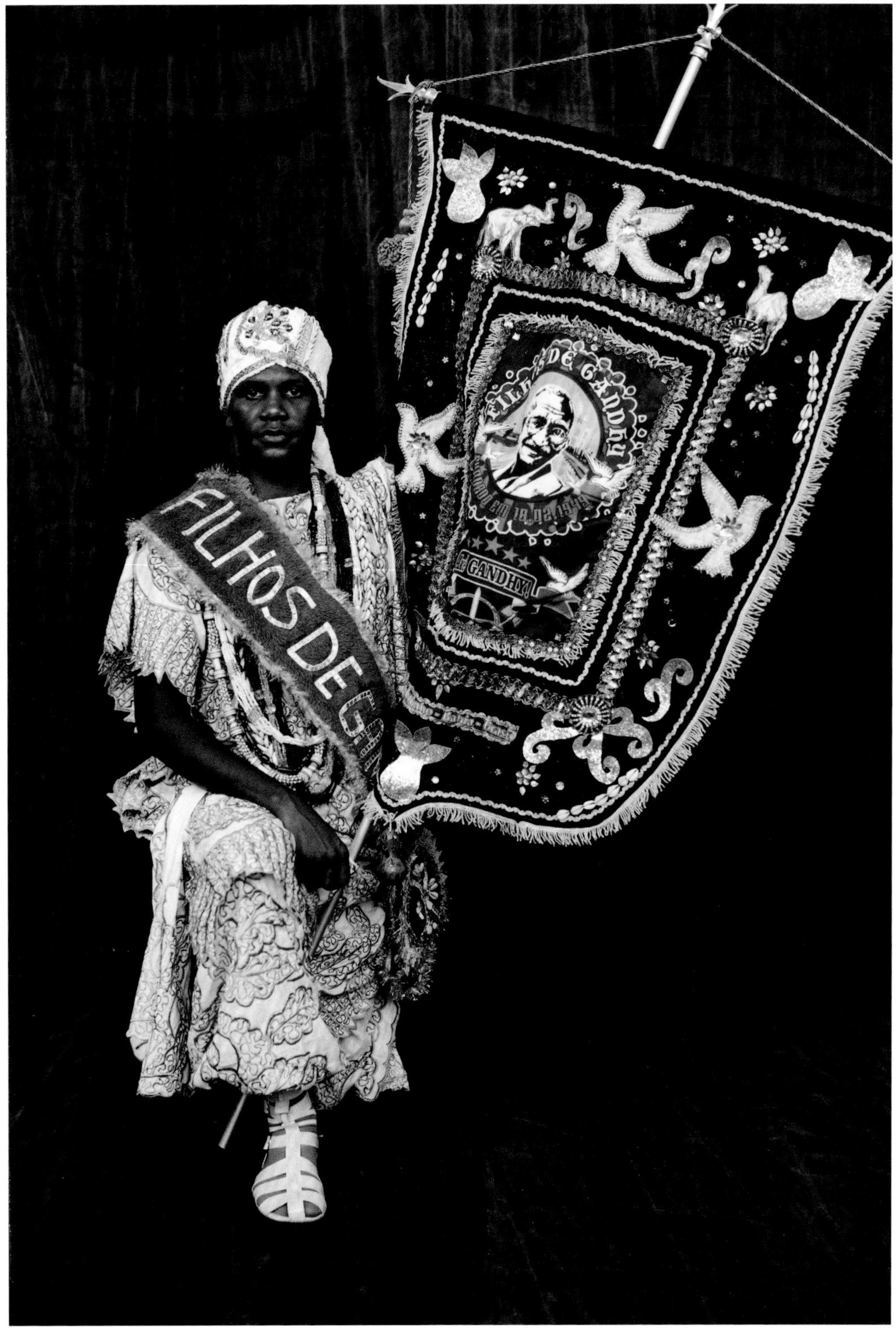


**22**
Mário Cravo Neto (b. 1947, Salvador, Bahia, Brazil; d. 2009)
Pedro with Dove, 1988
Photograph
COURTESY OF THE ESTATE OF MÁRIO CRAVO NETO ©IMCN

**23**
Christian Cravo (b. Salvador, Bahia, Brazil, 1974)
*Afoxé, Filhos de Gandhy* (Afoxé, Sons of Gandhi), 2016
Photograph
COURTESY CHRISTIAN CRAVO

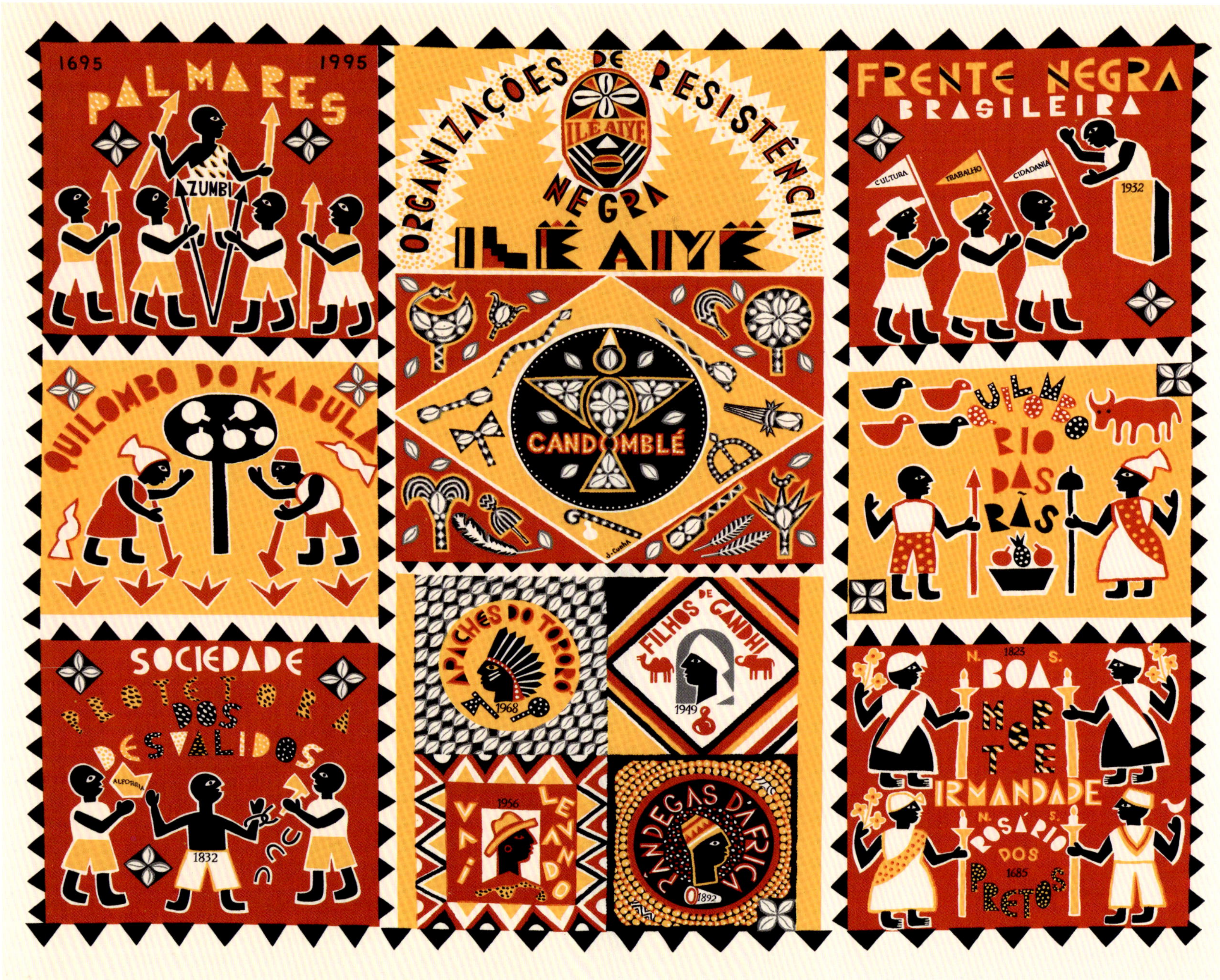


**24**
J. Cunha (José Antônio Cunha, b. 1948)
*Organizações de resistencia negra—Ilê Aiyê* (Black Resistance Organizaions—Ilê Aiyê), 1995
Block-printed cotton textile
120 x 147.3 cm
HELEN LOUISE ALLEN TEXTILE COLLECTION, UNIVERSITY OF WISCONSIN-MADISON

A vividly emblematic textile fashioned by J. Cunha for the Bahian Carnaval season of 1995 brings the *axé* of Afro-Brazilian art into sharp focus highlighting how it can summarize notions of self and counter stereotypes or misrepresentations by facilitating other discourses about Afro-descendant experiences in Bahia (fig. 24). The year it was produced marked the 300th anniversary of the death of Zumbi (1655–1695), a paramount icon of black resistance to the slave system. In light of that commemoration and the growing Black Consciousness movement in Brazil, the Carnaval *bloco afro* Ilê Aiyê chose to foreground Afro-Bahian history in their public performances. Moving clockwise from the top center, the panels represent:

> The head-like emblem of Ilê Aiyê as designed by Cunha and the overarching theme: *Organizações de resistência negra* (Black Resistance Organizations).
>
> Frente Negra Brasileira (The Black Brazilian Front), a national civil rights group that opened a chapter in Bahia in 1932.
>
> Quilombo Rio das Rãs, a maroon community (*quilombo*) located in the Bahian municipality of Bom Jesus da Lapa and dating back to the sixteenth century.
>
> Irmandade de Nossa Senhora da Boa Morte (Sisterhood of Our Lady of the Good Death) founded in Cachoeira, Bahia, in 1823 and Irmandade de Nossa Senhora do Rosário dos Homens Pretos (Confraternity of Our Lady of the Rosary of Black Men) established in 1685 (see interleaf D and timeline, this volume).
>
> Pândegas d'África (African Merrymakers, 1892), Filhos de Gandhi (Sons of Gandhi, 1949), Vai Levando (Keep Going, 1956), and Apaches do Tororó (Apaches of Tororó, 1968), all path-breaking Afro-Brazilian Carnaval associations in Bahia (see Miguez, this volume).
>
> Sociedade Protetora dos Desvalidos (Society for the Protection of the Underprivileged), an Afro-Brazilian social justice collective dedicated to the manumission of slaves instituted by the free African Manoel Victor Serra in 1832.
>
> Quilombo do Kabula, formerly a refuge during the era of slavery and now a neighborhood of present-day Salvador (see chapter 11, this volume, figs. 11.7a-c).
>
> Palmares, the capital of a federation of *quilombos* with thousands of residents, lasted roughly from 1605 until its destruction by Portuguese troops in 1694. Palmares and Zumbi, one of its last leaders, are often used to symbolize Afro-Brazilian empowerment.
>
> Candomblé, the center square contains a cowry-filled outline of Oxalá's dove and stylized renderings of the *ferramentas* of other *orixás* as well as more cowries, sacred leaves, and a feather.

A testament to a legacy of activism and autonomy, Cunha's block-printed cloth was primarily intended as fabric for the Carnaval outfits worn by members of Ilê Aiyê. Black Power on parade.

The resemblance of the *Organizações de resistência negra* textile to my refrigerator souvenir is unmistakable, and not necessarily coincidental. People in Bahia have lived with that nine-part touristic view of Salvador much longer and more intimately than I have. Thus, Cunha, in conjunction with Ilê Aiyê, co-opts a format commonly used to market *Bahia típica* and *Bahia mágica* to outsiders and instead presents an insider vision of *Bahia negra* (Black Bahia). While the postcard certainly honors traditions that, as we have seen, many Bahians proclaim to be core elements of their heritage, the perspective is significantly different.

To begin with, Cunha makes Candomblé the indisputable heart of the matter. In effect, he replaces the *brasão* of the State of Bahia with that of Oxalá, which is also a reconfiguration of Tomé de Sousa's dove-dominated coat of arms of the City of Salvador. The artist takes it a step further, however, as the *pomba* has now conquered the geometry of the national banner as well (fig. 25). Afro-Brazilian religion provides the *Ordem e Progresso* (Order and Progress) normally touted by the Brazilian flag and does so by reading Bahian cowries rather than Latin-named stars in the sky over Rio de Janeiro.[16]

Like the photographs on my keepsake, the panels of the Ilê Aiyê cloth emphasize black bodies in action but with a much greater emphasis on community building and social empowerment. *Ferramentas* in hand, these Afro-descendants re-order their world. Political activists from the Frente Negra Brasiliera carry banners dedicated to *cultura* (culture), *trabalho* (work), and *cidadania* (citizenship); residents of *quilombos* hold spears and hoes accentuating the fight for freedom and the significance of cultivating one's own land; members of the Sociedade Protetora dos Desvalidos use ensign and hatchet to achieve *alforria* (manumission); affiliates of the Irmandade de Nossa Senhora da Boa Morte and the Irmandade de Nossa Senhora do Rosário dos Homens Pretos clasp candles, flowers, and dove as acts of piety and public service; representatives of racially conscious Carnaval troops are surrounded by musical instruments and their respective emblems. And, as opposed to the touristic images, Cunha stresses dates. This effectively presents Afro-Bahian culture as a hard-fought and ongoing process of self-determination instead of a set of picturesque and relatively timeless activities. It narrates the story less often told.

As with any metropolis, the intense complexity of Salvador, past or present, is not easily illustrated. Today a densely populated urban center, its white-painted high-rises compete for space with dwellings situated nearer to the ground and closer in color to the red soil (fig. 26). Its streets are often congested with traffic and its plazas occasionally filled with revelers. Neighborhoods are wracked by violence and energized by religious fervor (fig. 27). Even as it is extolled as a location where Afro-Brazilian culture has flourished, this *Roma negra* is nonetheless a place to which many came via torturous paths and continue to do so. This legacy resonates with the lyrics of Bahia-born songwriter and political activist Gilberto Gil's song "Cidade do Salvador" ("City of Salvador"). While "Salvador" is "Savior," the last syllable of the word, "*dor*," means "pain" in Portuguese. "Pain and pain and pain" (*Dor e dor e dor*), Gil laments, "so much pain" (*tanta dor*).

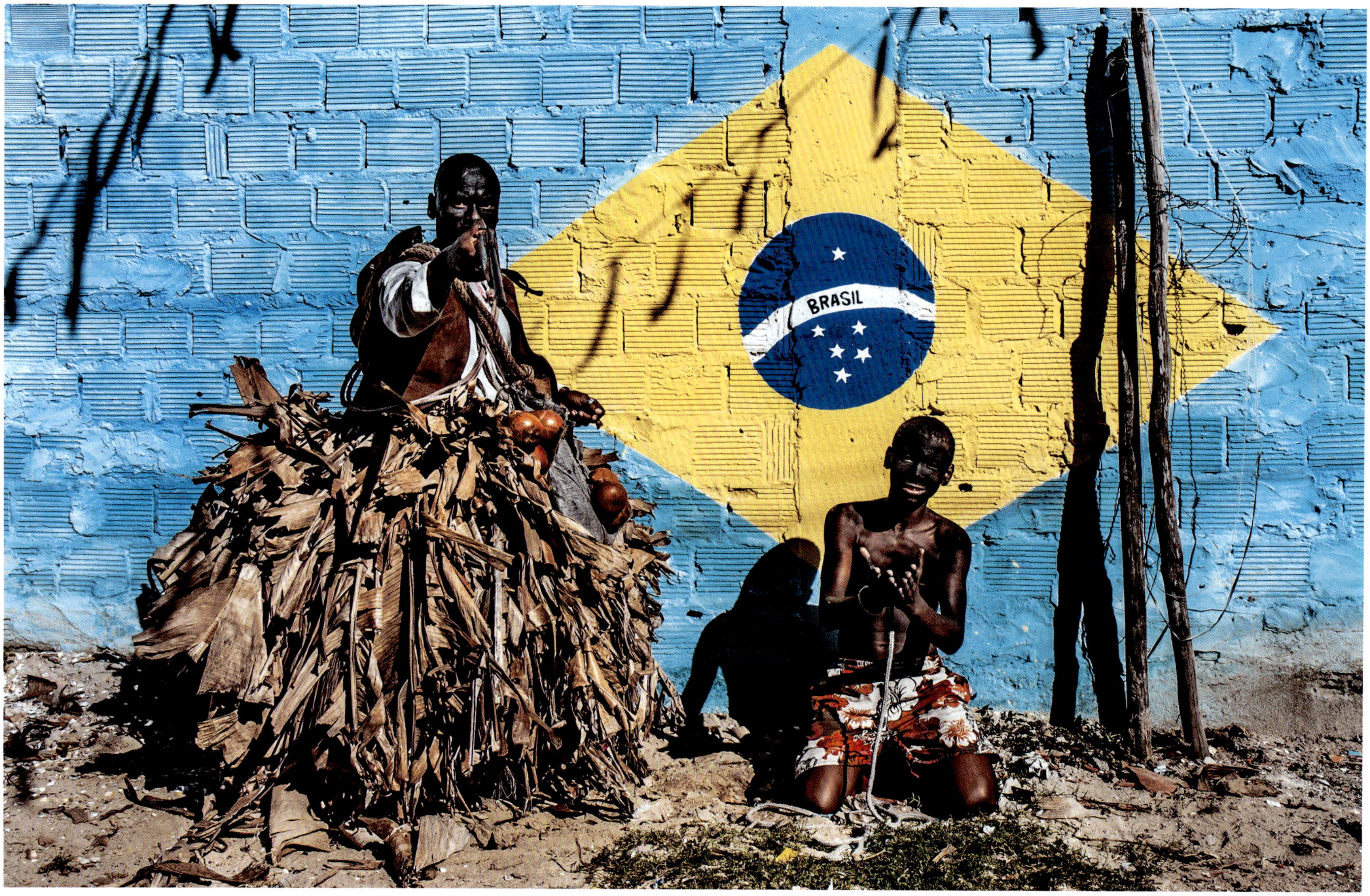


**25**
Adenor Gondim (b. 1950, Rui Barbosa, Bahia, Brazil)
*Nego fugido* (Runaway Slave), 2010
Photograph
COURTESY ADENOR GONDIM

Shown here are participants in the annual festival called *Nego fugido* (Runaway Slave) held in the town of Acupe, which was originally a *quilombo*, or settlement of escaped slaves. Masqueraders such as these adopt the guises of pursued and resistant Africans and Afro-Brazilians.

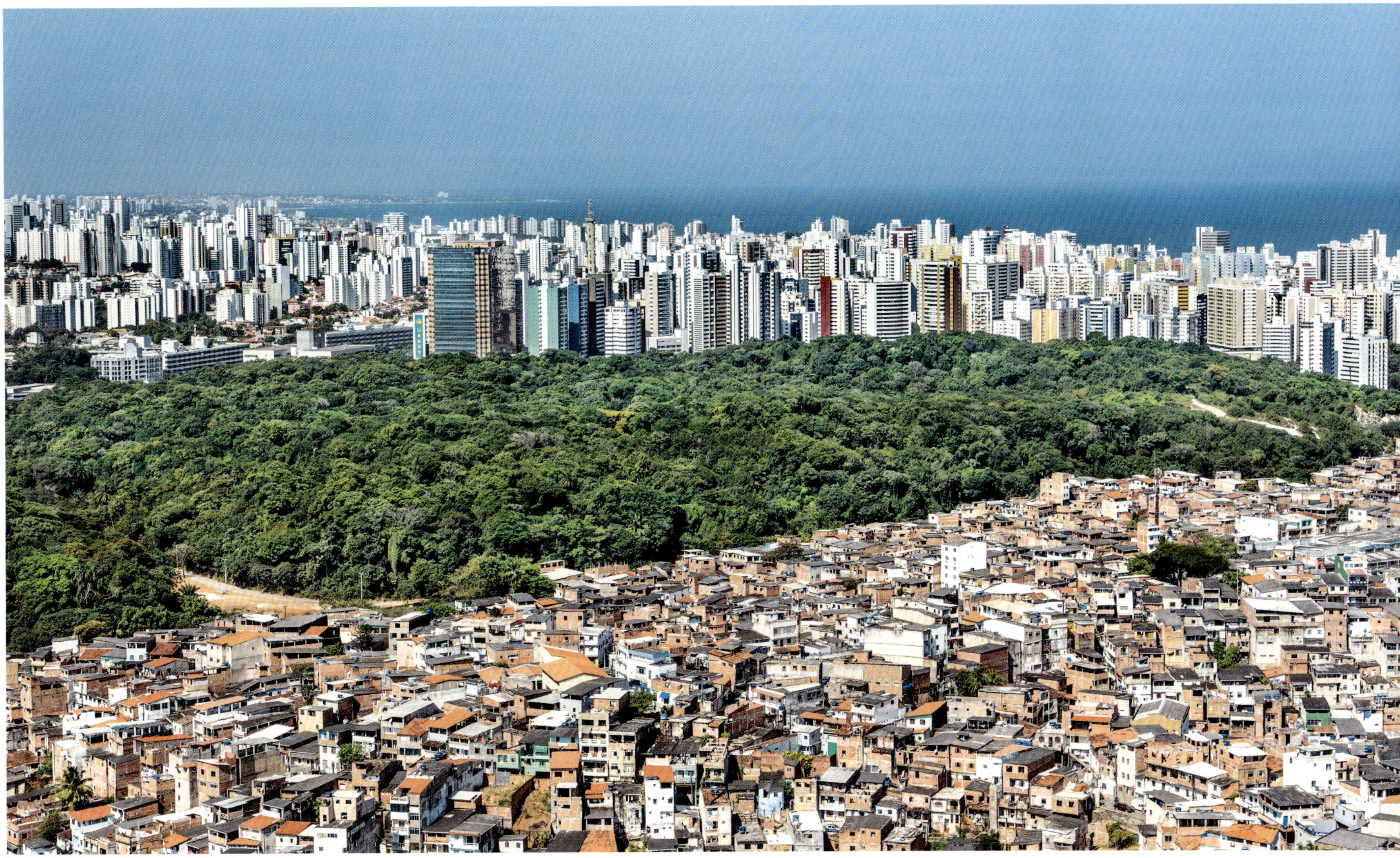

**26**
Nilton Souza (b. 1950, Varzedo, Bahia, Brazil)
*Cidade do Salvador e suas diferenças sociais* (City of Salvador and Its Social Differences), September 29, 2015.
Photograph
COURTESY NILTON SOUZA

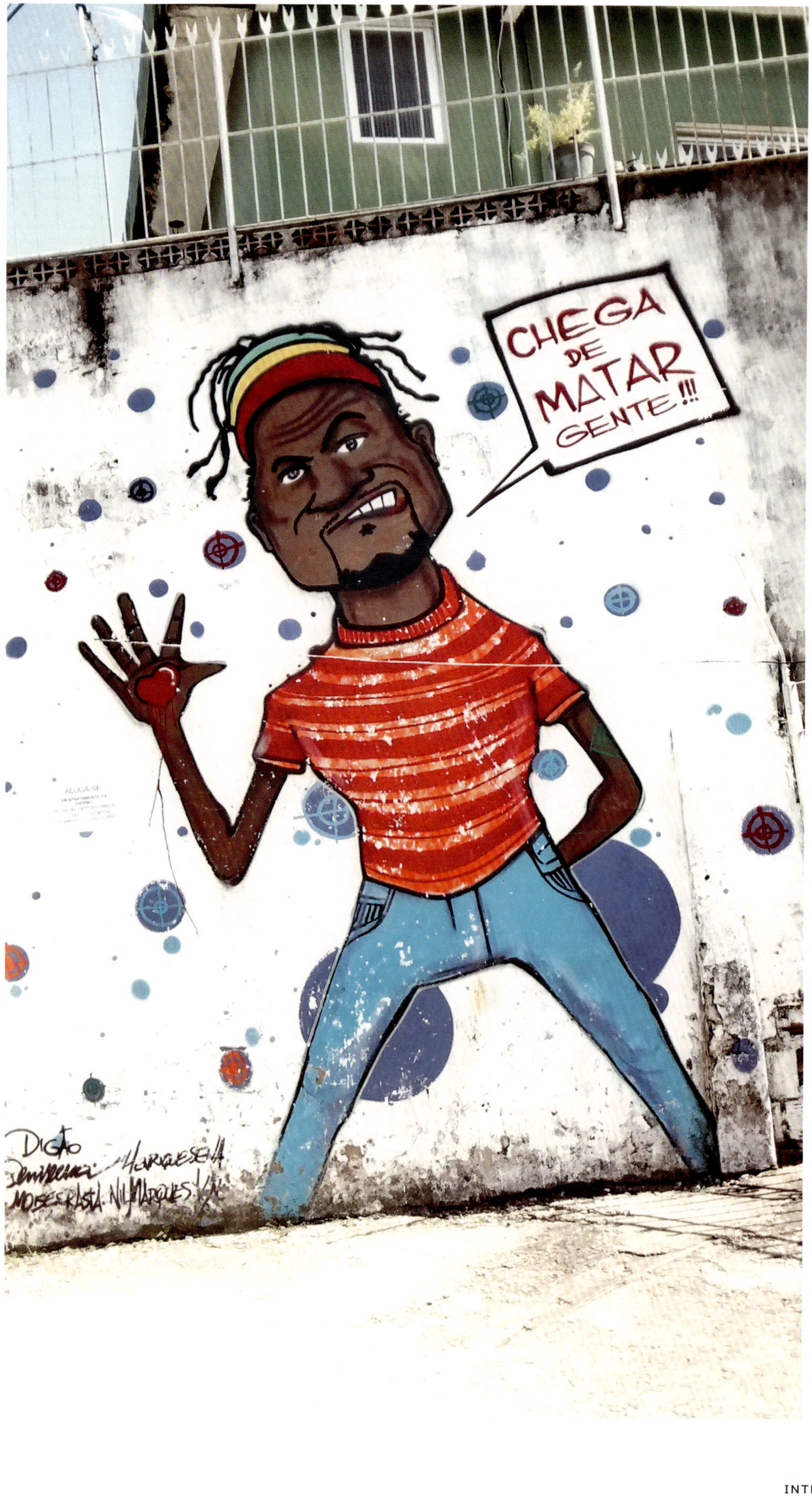


**27**
Denissena (Denis Senna, b. 1976, Salvador)
*Reaja* (React), April 2015
Mural
PHOTOGRAPH BY SABRINA GLEDHILL, SALVADOR, BAHIA, BRAZIL, 2015

This street mural in the Cabula neighborhood of Salvador protests the killing of twelve black youths known as the Cabula Massacre of February 6, 2015. The figure in the mural is saying "Chega de matar gente!!!" which may be translated as "Stop killing folks!!!"

The pensive, almost melancholic, atmosphere of Christian Cravo's photograph *Afternoon with Bonfim Church in the Background* (2003) seems to echo that sentiment (fig. 28). The ebullience of Rugendas's *San-Salvador* is missing as is the rhapsody of Disney's "Baía," and the Church of the Good End appears so much farther away than in Carybé's *Alexandrina e sua cidade*. This too is Bahia—the unfinished agenda of black resistance organizations such as those memorialized by J. Cunha and Ilê Aiyê who fight against what is often called *abolição falsa* (false abolition). In one way or another, all of the artists featured in this publication address the painful histories and troubling everyday realities faced by Afrodescendentes in Bahia (see especially chapter 11 and interleaves I, J, and K).

Yet, in "Cidade do Salvador," Gilberto Gil speaks also to the ability of religiosity and joy to alleviate if not overcome suffering. As with the wordplay involving *Salvador* (Savior) and *dor* (pain), he reminds us that *fé* (faith), *felicidade* (happiness), and *cidade* (city) are also deeply intertwined. In a similar way, *A força que habita em mim* (The Force That Resides within Me), a painting of 2017 by the Bahian street artist Eder Muniz, returns us to an Edenic Bahia where one's spiritual potential can be realized through Candomblé as referenced by an imaginative fish-like crown signifying Oxum, the female *orixá* of fresh waters (fig. 31). It is a paradisiacal world where the *axé* of plants, animals, sky, earth, and water enables transformative human experiences. A public mural of 2016 on the grounds of the Federal University of Bahia's Architectural School expands on Muniz's vision. Titled *O espírito maior* (The Greater Spirit) it is a tropical dreamland motivated by indigenous Yanomami mythology but also inspired by Afro-Brazilian religion (fig. 30). Teeming with life and spirit, this verdant rain-drenched heaven on earth is in some ways remarkably similar to the Bahia of *The Three Caballeros*, even though Disney colored Salvador from afar and Muniz generally spray paints *Bahia mágica* directly onto the walls of the city.

The bit of common ground found by a contemporary African-descendant Bahian muralist and North American animators laboring more than seventy years ago exemplifies the ambition of *Axé Bahia: The Power of Art in an Afro-Brazilian Metropolis*. This volume and the accompanying exhibition are intended as an exploration of how selected artistic practices express and shape notions of Salvador in general and Afro-Brazilian identity and experience in particular. Dating primarily from the mid-twentieth to the early twenty-first century and representing a variety of genres, the works collectively illustrate the ways that seminal artists (Brazilians and foreigners alike) have responded to the visual and cultural richness of Bahia and expanded upon it. More importantly, much of this art offers potent, and often provocative, counterpoints to racism and other forms of inequality. Some of the pieces included are invocations of the sacred; others are accusations. Some materialize trauma; others search for healing.

This focus on artistic intention, affect, and activism brings back to mind the intricate symbolism of doves and more specifically their ceremonial release into Orun, the sky, by participants in a variety of Bahian rituals and festive activities (fig. 29). Whether tossed into the air at a pivotal moment in the annual celebration of Nossa Senhora da Boa Morte, freed by members of Ilê Aiyê and the Sons and Daughters of Gandhy during Carnaval, or let loose by Candomblé adherents at *terreiros* and other sacred sites, they are messengers, cleansing agents, and harbingers of change. *Axé* incarnate. And just as the dove of Noah crossed nearly endless waters to find new land, the Espírito Santo will continue to widen its circles around the towers of Bonfim, and the *pomba* of Oxalá will spread its wings over Liberdade, Pelourinho, and ever more neighborhoods in Salvador and beyond. Art works this way too. *Axé Bahia!*

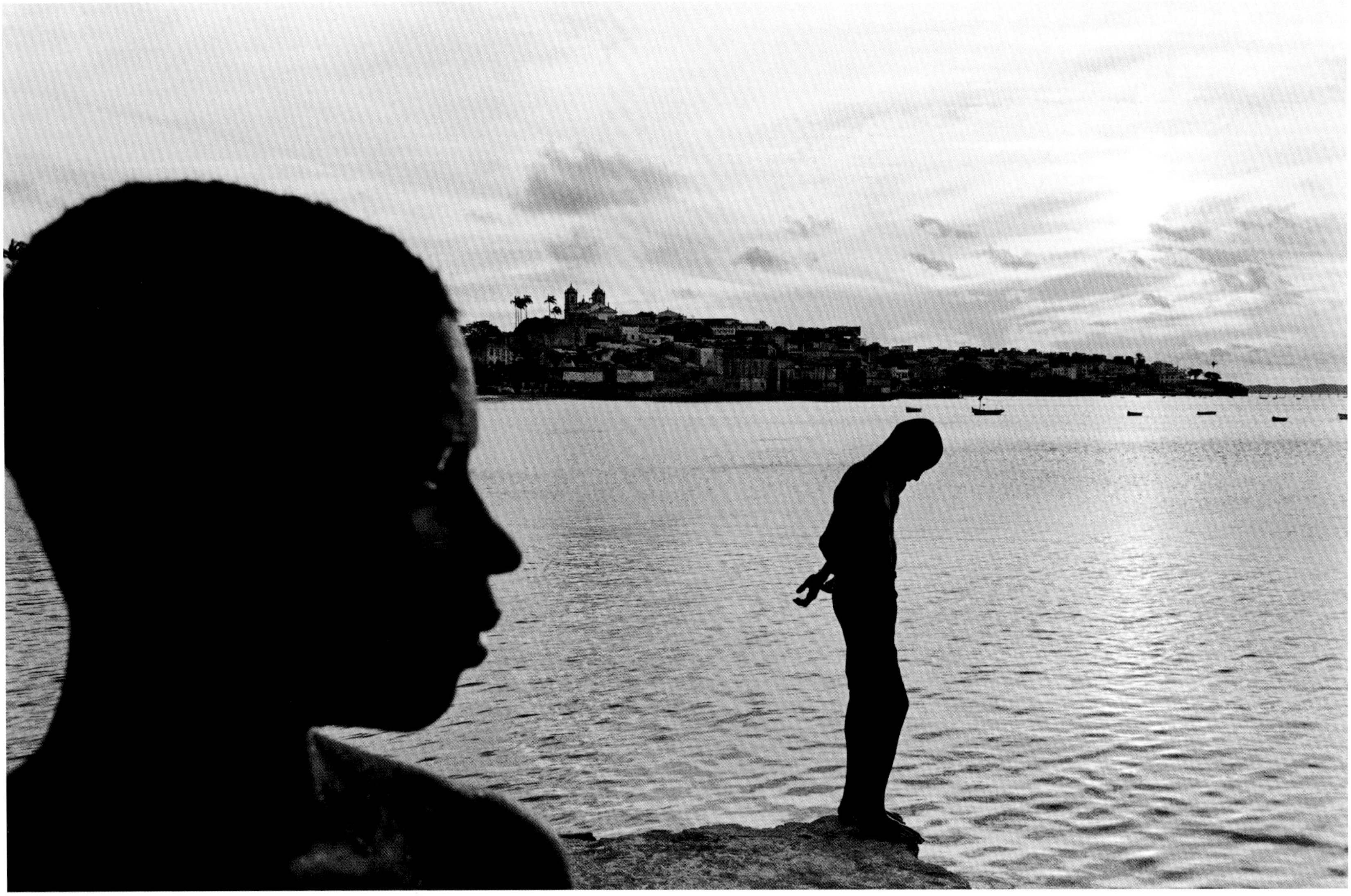

**28**
Christian Cravo (b. Salvador, Bahia, Brazil, 1974)
*Afternoon with Bonfim Church in the Background*, 2003
Photograph
COURTESY CHRISTIAN CRAVO

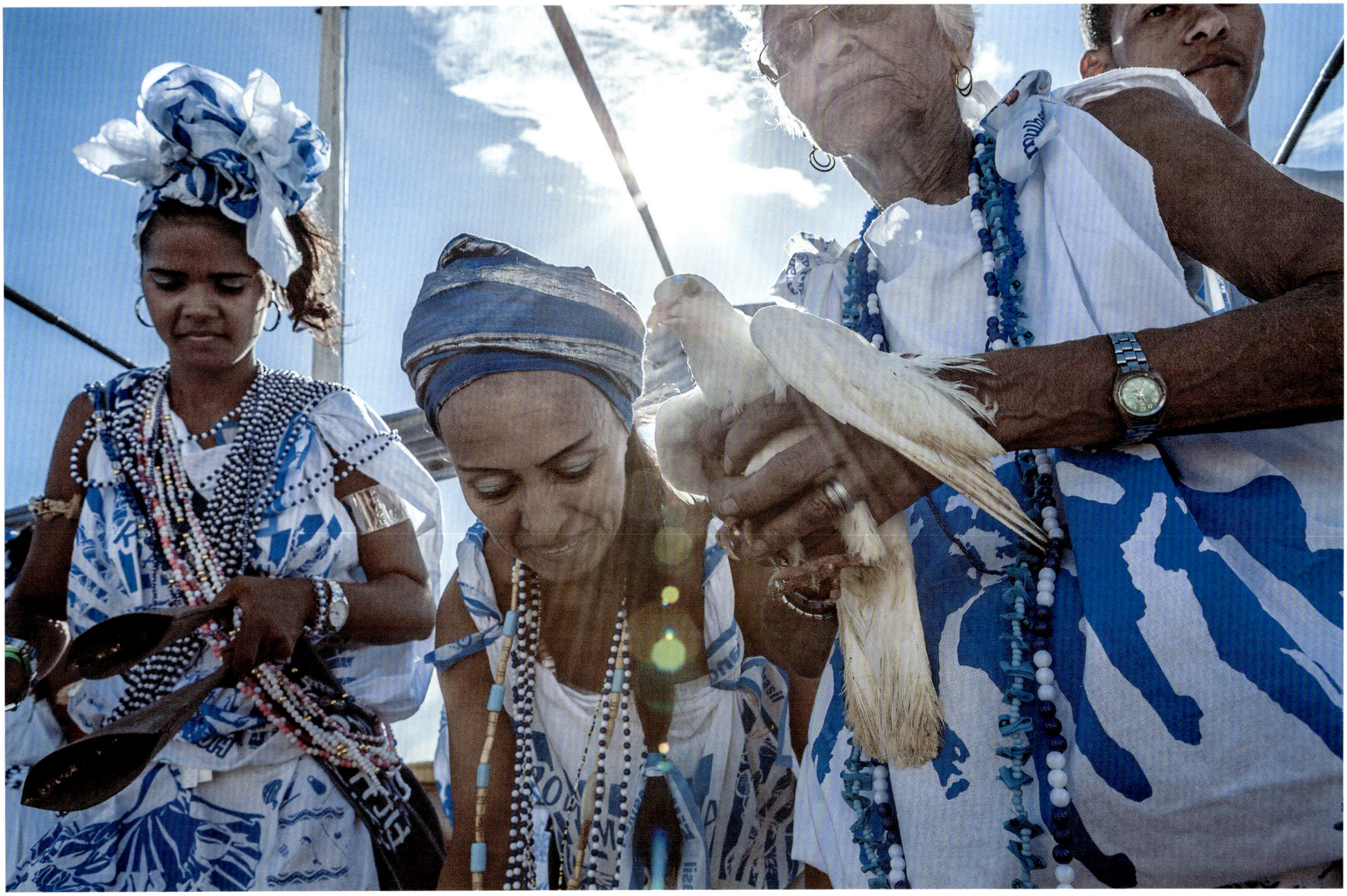

**29**
Antonello Veneri (b. 1973, Italy)
*Filhas de Gandhy* (Daughters of Gandhi), 2014
Photograph
COURTESY OF ANTONELLO VENERI

**30**
Eder Muniz (b. 1982, Salvador, Bahia Brazil)
*O espírito maior* (The Greater Spirit), 2016
Aerosol paint, varnish
5 x 16 m
COMMISSIONED BY THE FOWLER MUSEUM AT UCLA; COURTESY EDER MUNIZ; PHOTOGRAPH BY ANDREW KEMP

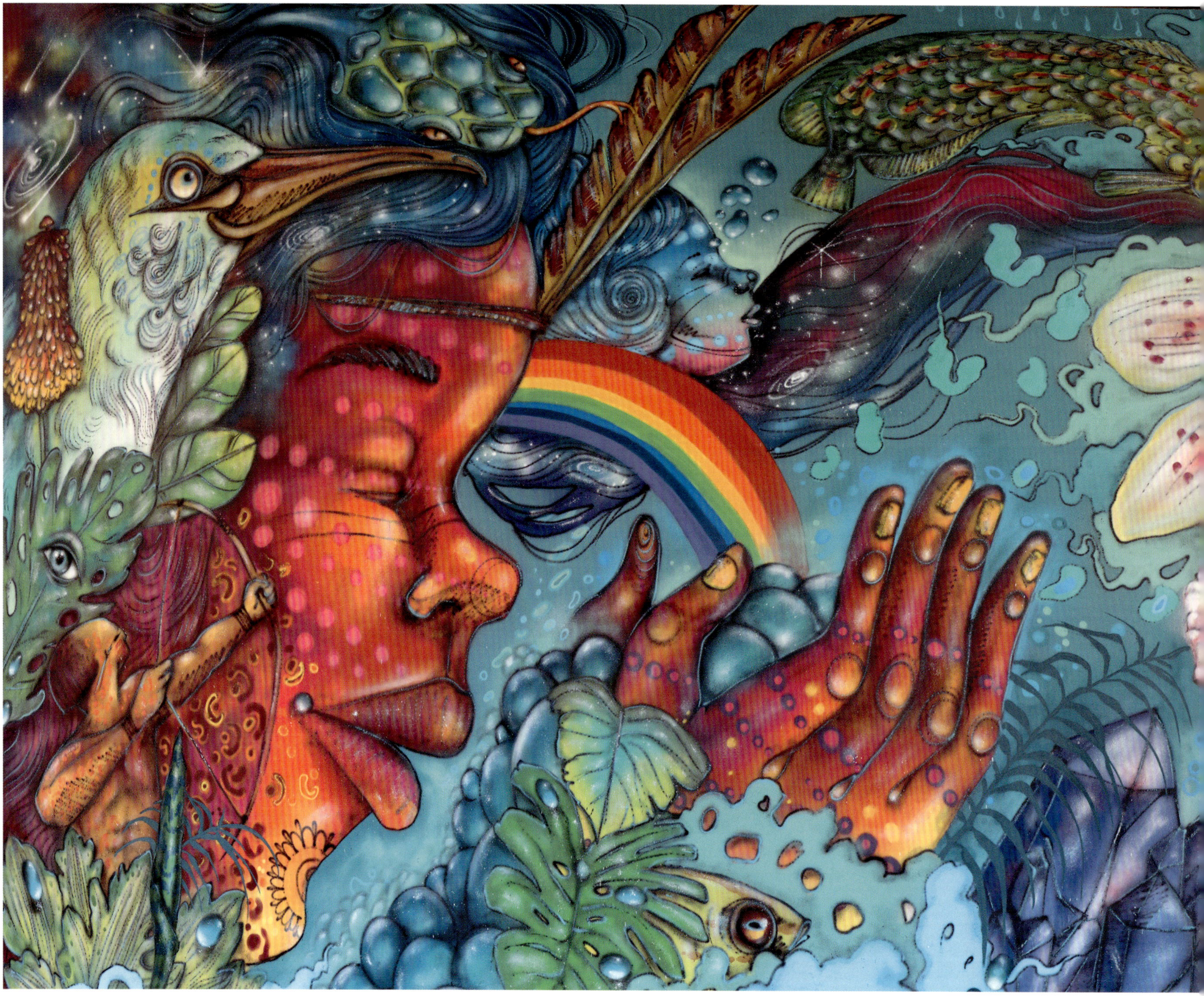

**31** (OVERLEAF)
Eder Muniz (b. 1982, Salvador, Bahia, Brazil)
*A força que habita em mim* (The Force That Resides within Me), 2017
Aerosol paint, varnish, wood
1.8 x 3.7 m
COMMISSIONED BY THE FOWLER MUSEUM AT UCLA; COURTESY EDER MUNIZ

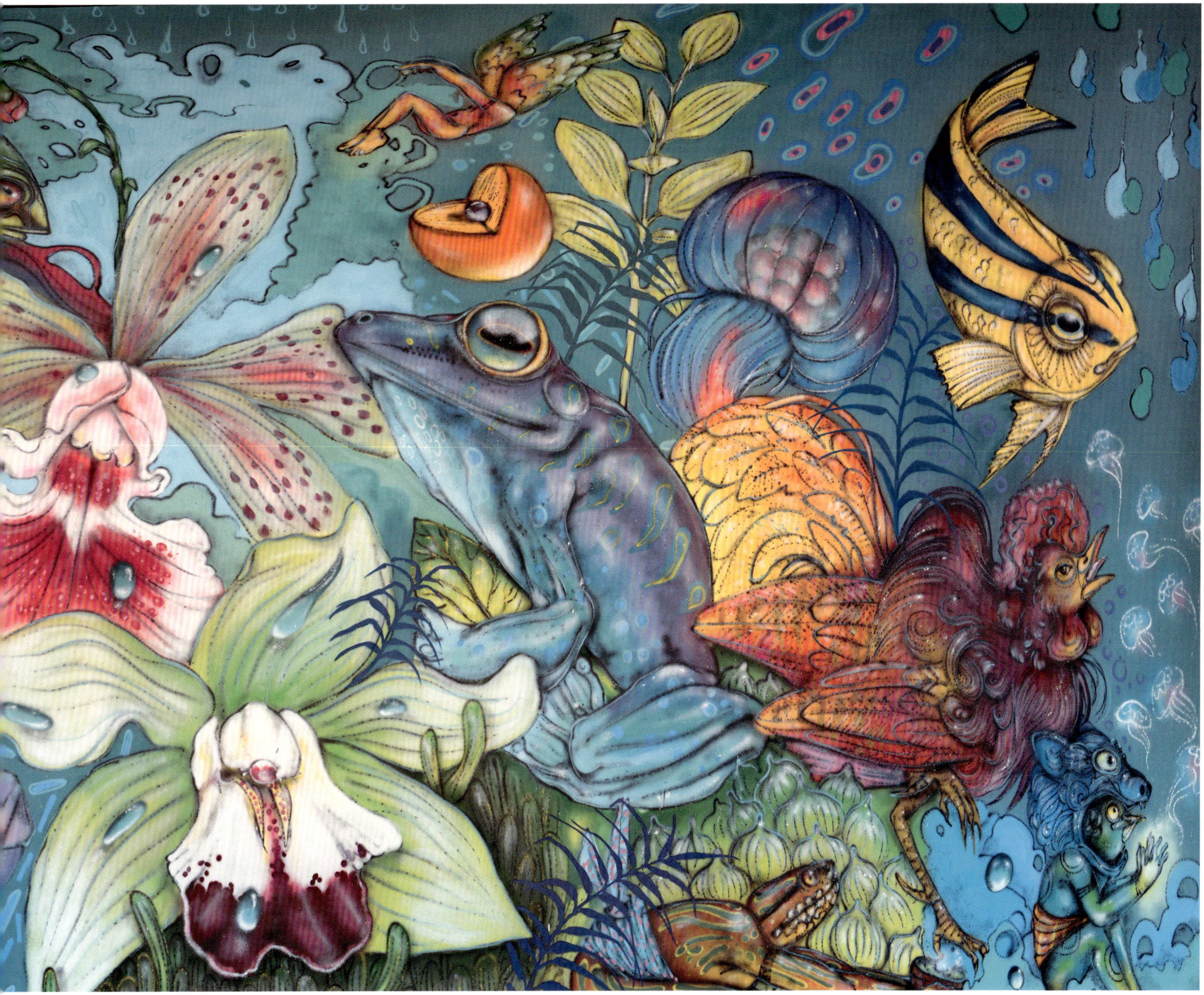

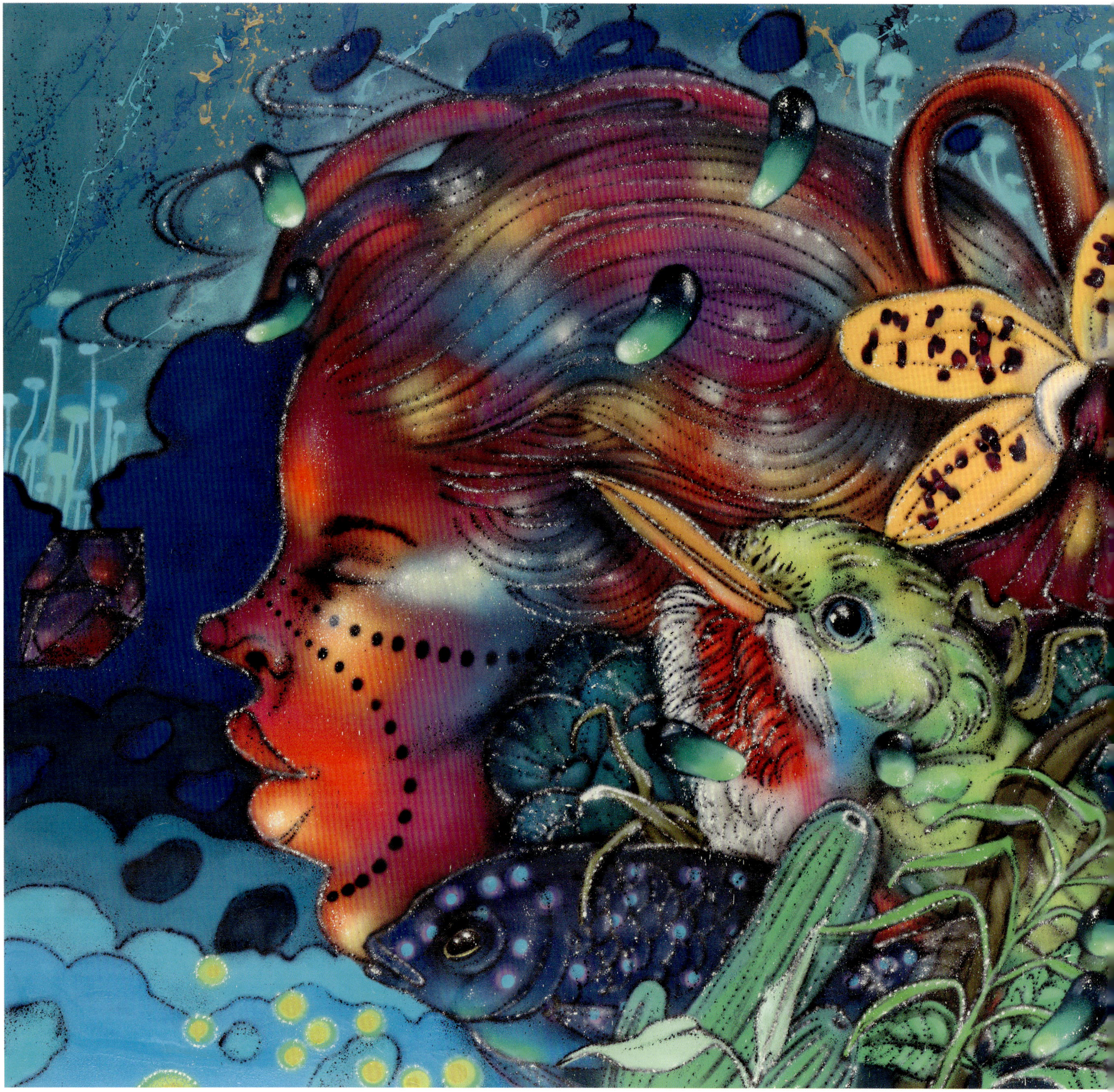

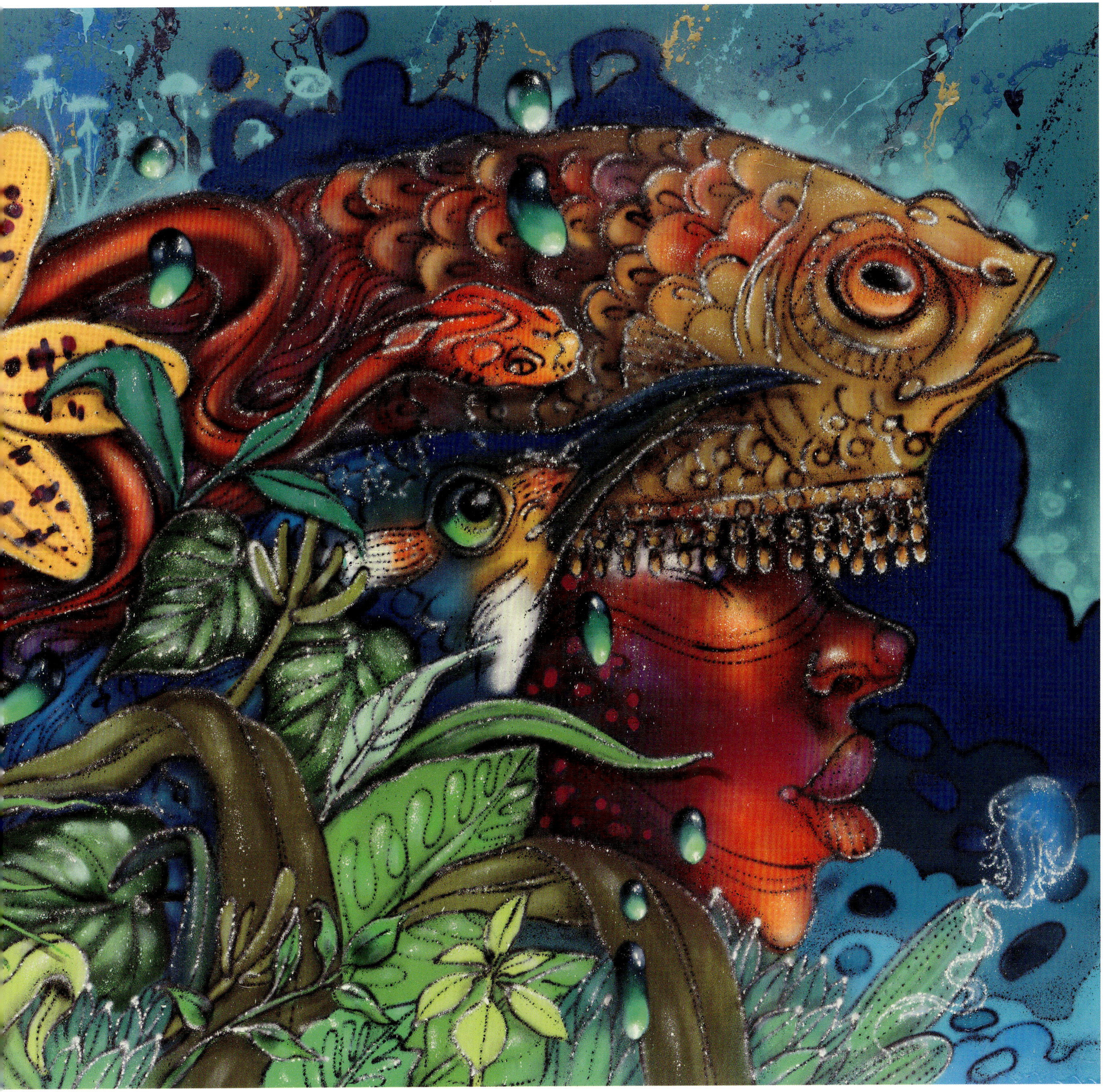

# Timeline

1500 Pedro Álvares Cabral arrives in the future town of Porto Seguro, Bahia, in what will eventually be called Brazil, and declares it a Portuguese colony.

1538–40 Portugal begins transporting enslaved Africans to Brazil.

1549 The city of São Salvador da Bahia de Todos os Santos is founded as the first capital of colonial Brazil.

1654 The black militia groups known as "Henriques" are formed.

1685 The Irmandade de Nossa Senhora do Rosário dos Homens Pretos (The Confraternity of Our Lady of the Rosary of Black Men) is founded in Salvador.

1691 A slave revolt occurs in Camamu, southern Bahia.

1694 Quilombo dos Palmares, Brazil's most famous maroon community, located in the present-day state of Alagoas, is destroyed.

1695 On November 20th (a date that will later be commemorated as Black Consciousness Day in Brazil), the leader of that maroon community, Zumbi dos Palmares, is reputedly killed.

1763 The colonial capital is transferred to Rio de Janeiro.

1817–18 The transatlantic slave trade is banned above the equator.

1820–30 Two of the oldest Candomblé houses in Bahia, Alaketu and Ilê Axé Iyá Nassô, are founded.

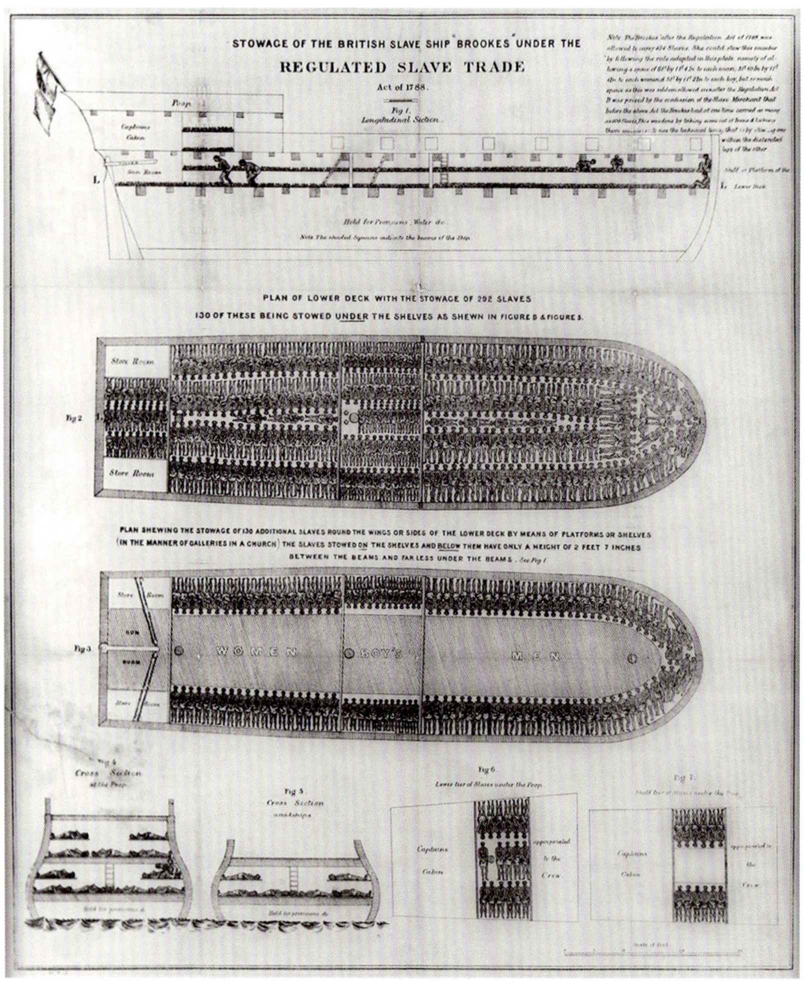


**T.1**
"Stowage of the British slave ship 'Brookes' under the regulated slave trade act of 1788," circa 1788
Original etching
LIBRARY OF CONGRESS RARE BOOK AND SPECIAL COLLECTIONS DIVISION WASHINGTON, D.C. PRINTED EPHEMERA COLLECTION. CALL NUMBER: BROADSIDE PORT. 282, NO. 43, LC-USZ62-44000

**T.2**
Johann Moritz Rugendas (b. 1802, Augsburg, Germany; d. 1858)
*Négres à fond de calle* (Blacks in the Ship's Hold)
From *Malerische Reise in Brasilien* (Paris: Engelmann & Cie, 1835)
Lithograph
WÜRTTEMBERGISCHE LANDESBIBLIOTHEK, STUTTGART

1822 Emperor Pedro I of Brazil declares his country's independence from the kingdom of his father, João VI of Portugal, on September 7th.

1823 Brazil wins its independence from Portugal in Bahia on July 2nd.

1831 Brazil officially abolishes the transatlantic slave trade under pressure from the British. Although the law passes, the Brazilian government soon ceases to enforce it.

1832 The Sociedade Protetora dos Desvalidos (Society for the Protection of the Underprivileged) is founded in Bahia.

1835 On January 24th and 25th, Yoruba-speaking Muslim slaves and free people allied with other African groups, stage the short-lived but pivotal Revolt of the Malês. This leads to a crackdown on Muslim slaves and the deportation of many freed Africans.

1845 Britain unilaterally enacts the Aberdeen Bill, authorizing the Royal Navy to pursue slave ships into Brazilian waters.

1850 The Queiroz Law definitively bans the already illegal transatlantic slave trade, although it persists to a small extent in the following years.

1865–70 The Paraguay War provides enslaved Afro-descendants an opportunity to obtain freedom if they survive their service in the armed forces (provided their masters allow them to enlist).

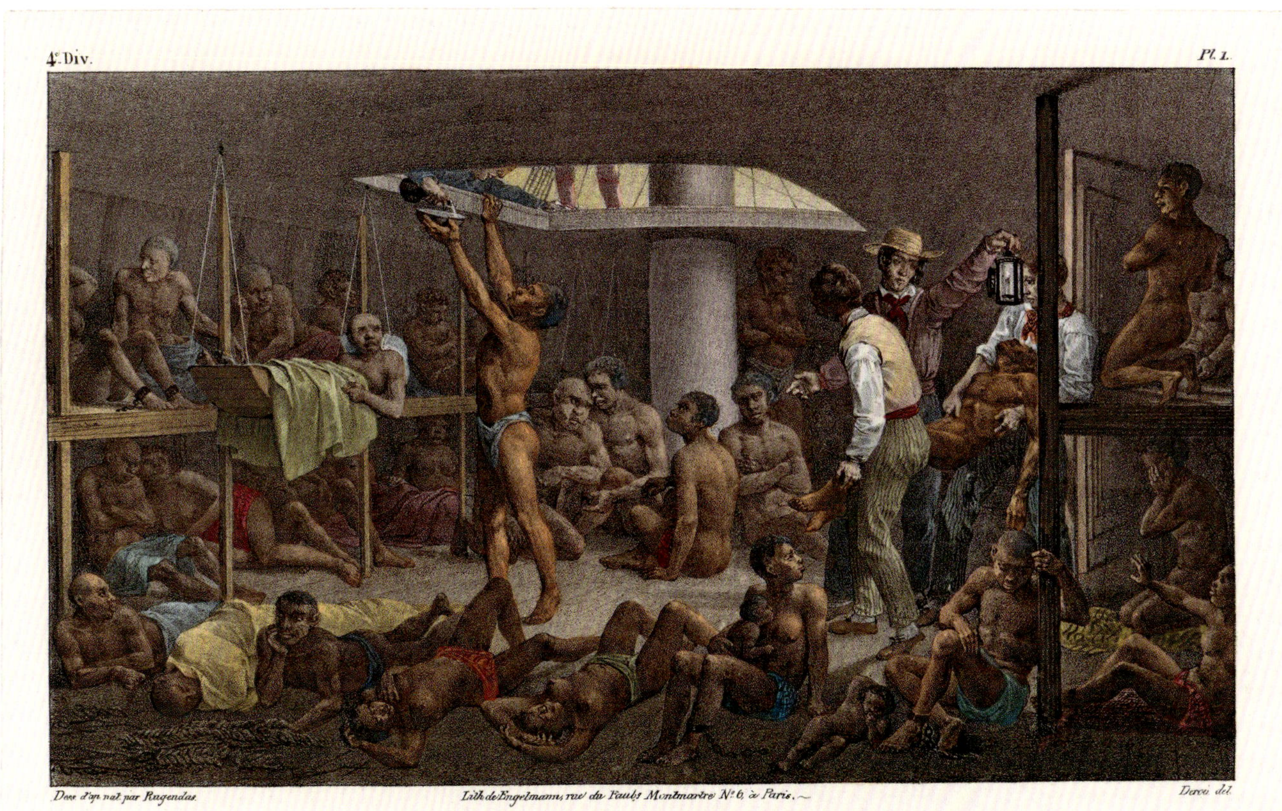


NÈGRES A FOND DE CALLE.

1871 On September 28th, the “Free Womb Law” emancipates the children of slaves born from that date forward, and slave owners are obliged to care for them until the age of eight. If the Brazilian State does not pay compensation, however, these so-called *ingênuos* are obliged to serve the slave owner until the age of twenty-one.

1885 The “Sexagenarian Law” frees slaves over the age of sixty. It is considered particularly cruel because these captives are emancipated without compensation or means of support.

1888 On May 13, Princess Isabel signs the “Golden Law” abolishing slavery in Brazil. It is the last country in the Americas to do so.

1892 The First Republic’s legal code criminalizes capoeira and Afro-Brazilian religions.

1910 The Revolta da Chibata (Revolt of the Lash) by black sailors against corporal punishment in the Navy takes place in Rio de Janeiro.

1931 The black movement Frente Negra Brasileira is founded.

1934 Afro-Brazilian studies are officially recognized following the First Afro-Brazilian Conference in Recife, organized by Gilberto Freyre.

1937 The Second Afro-Brazilian Conference, organized by Édison Carneiro, is held in Salvador.

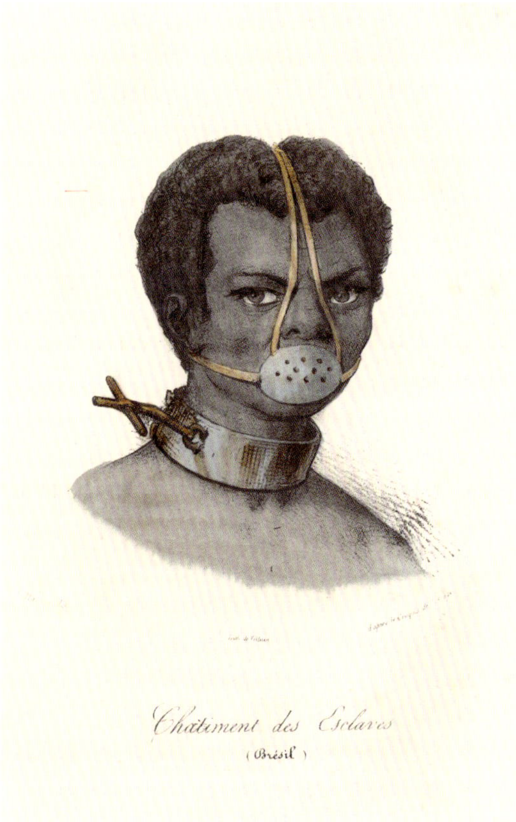


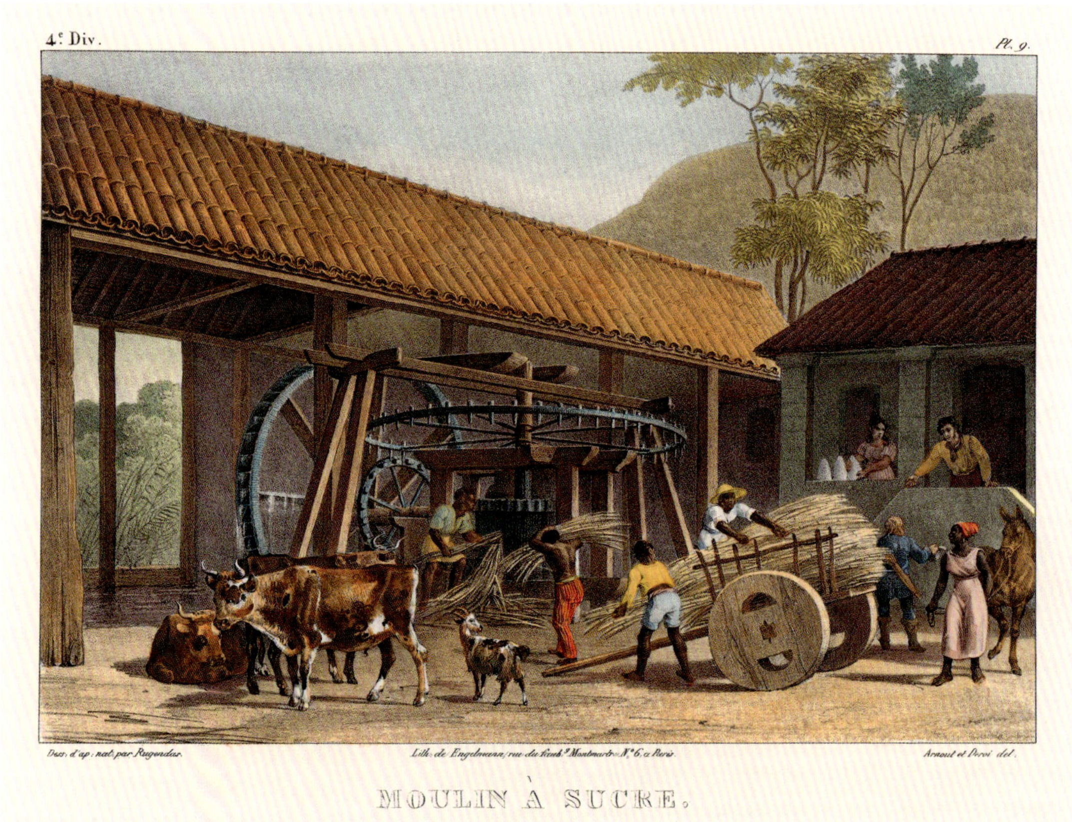

1945 Founded by Abdias do Nascimento, the Teatro Experimental do Negro (Black People's Experimental Theater) performs its first play in Rio de Janeiro.

1949 The Carnaval *afoxé* (group) Filhos de Gandhy is established in Salvador.

1951 The Afonso Arinos Law against racism, the first of its kind in Brazil, is enacted.

1974 The Carnaval group Ilê Aiyê is founded.

1979 The black movement Movimento Negro Unificado (MNU), or United Negro Movement, comes into being.

1988 The 100th anniversary of abolition is marked amid demonstrations and protests, and cries of "Cem anos sem abolição" (100 Years without Abolition) are raised.

1989 The Caó Law defining and punishing racism passes.

2003 Law no. 10.639/03 makes it obligatory for schools to introduce African and Afro-Brazilian history into the curriculum.

2012 Racially based affirmative action is introduced with Law no. 12711/12.

2016 Following the reform of secondary education (Provisional Measure 746) by the administration of Michel Temer (from 2016), it is no longer obligatory to teach African and Afro-Brazilian history in Brazilian schools.

**T.3**
Jacques Arago (b. 1790, Estagel, France; d. 1855)
*Châtiment des esclaves, Brésil* (Punishment of Slaves, Brazil)
From *Souvenirs d'un aveugle: Voyage autour du monde* (Paris: 1839–40), vol. 1
Lithograph
UNIVERSITY OF CALIFORNIA, SANTA CRUZ, SPECIAL COLLECTIONS

This image became associated with the popular saint known as Escrava Anastácia (Anastácia the Slave). Anastácia was known for her protective abilities and the equanimity with which she faced the cruelties visited upon her. See chapter 11 and fig. L.4b.

**T.4**
Johann Moritz Rugendas (b. 1802, Augsburg, Germany; d. 1858)
*Moulin à sucre* (Sugar Mill)
From *Malerische Reise in Brasilien* (Paris: Engelmann & Cie, 1835)
Lithograph
WÜRTTEMBERGISCHE LANDESBIBLIOTHEK, STUTTGART

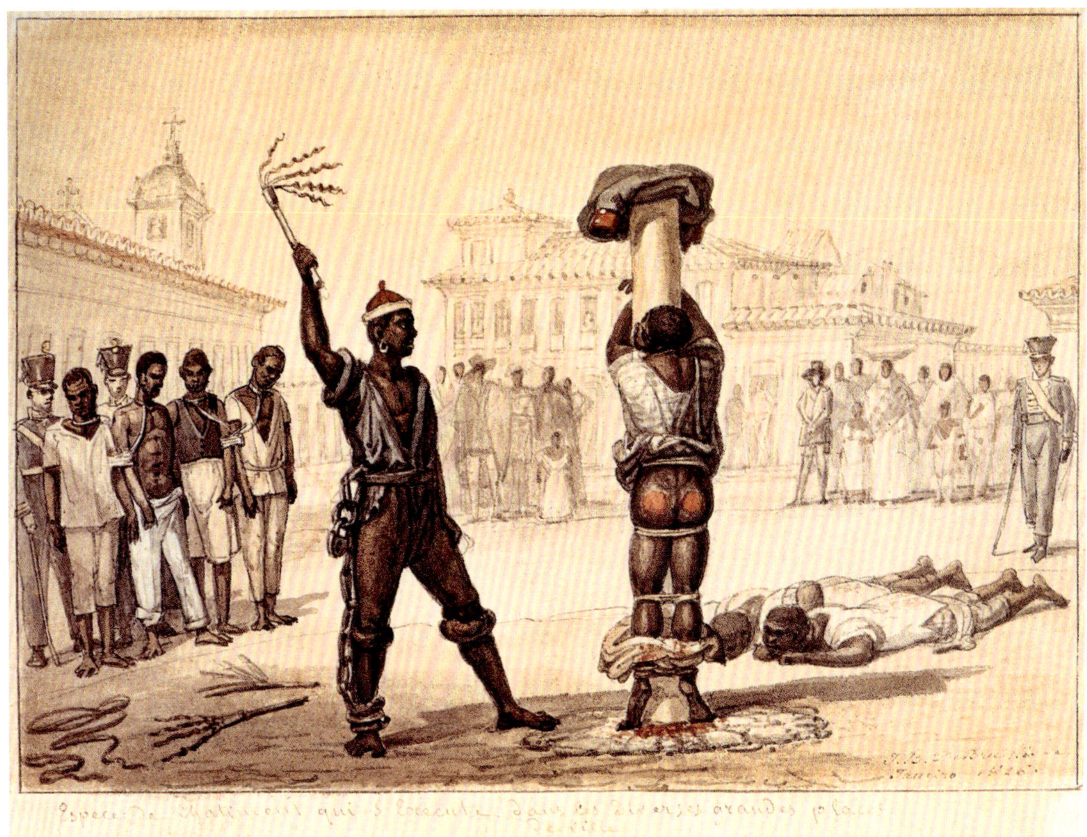

**T.5**
Jean-Baptiste Debret (b. 1768, Paris, France; d. 1848)
*Espèce de châtiment qui s'exécute dans les diverses grandes places de villes* (The Type of Punishment Carried out the Various Public Squares of the Cities)
From *Voyage pittoresque et historique au Bresil* (Paris: Firmin Didot Frères, 1834–1839), vol. 2., pl. 45
Lithograph
YOUNG RESEARCH LIBRARY, SPECIAL COLLECTIONS, UNIVERSITY OF CALIFORNIA, LOS ANGELES

# 1 Becoming the Black Rome

## Bahia, Africa, and the African Atlantic

**Cécile Fromont**

**1.1a**
Caetano Dias (b. 1959, Feira de Santana, Bahia, Brazil)
*Delírios de Catarina* (The Ravings of Catherine), 2017
Wood, metal, sugar, ox blood, resin
L: approx. 300 cm (variable)
COURTESY CAETANO DIAS
PHOTOGRAPH BY ANDREW KEMP

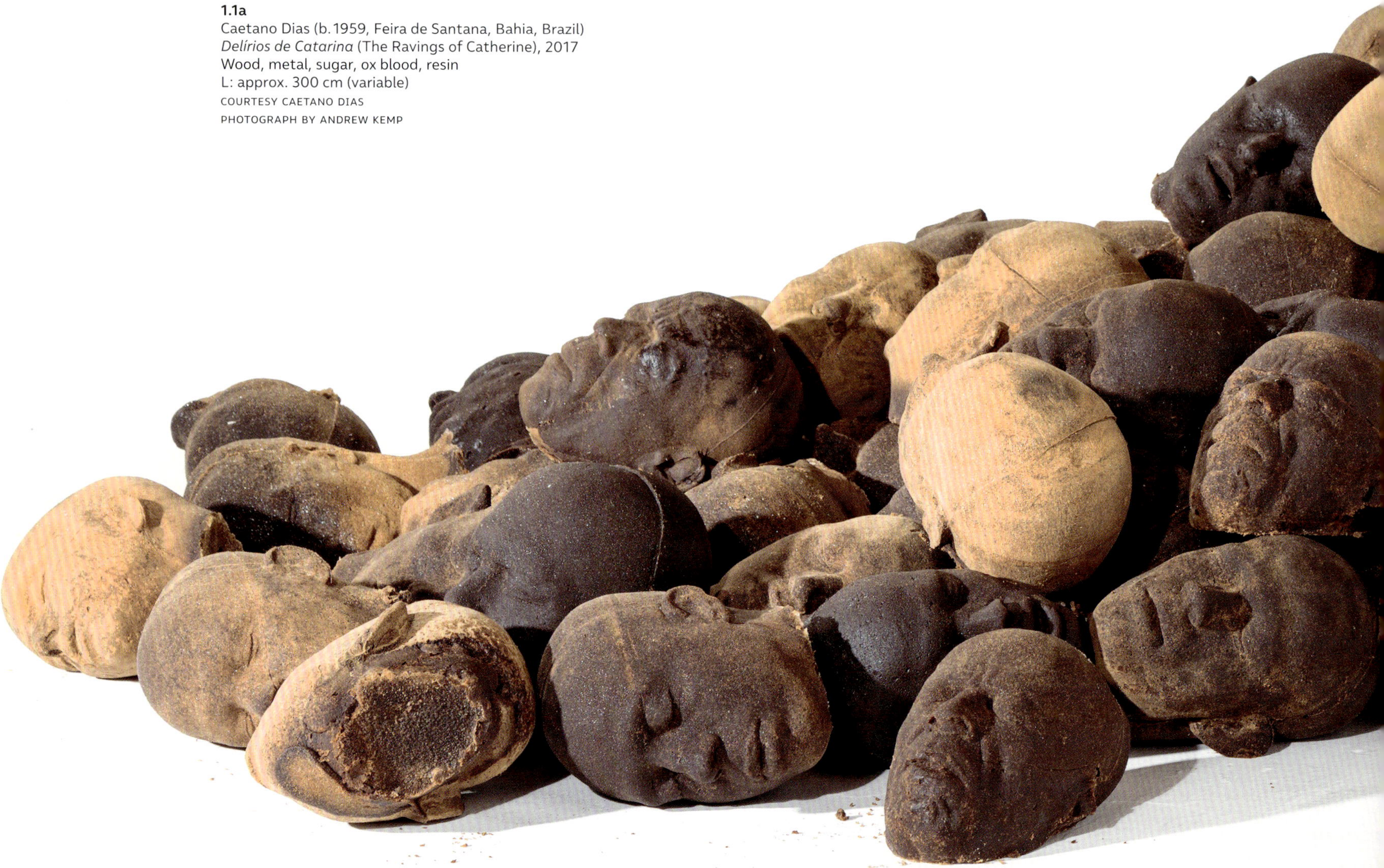

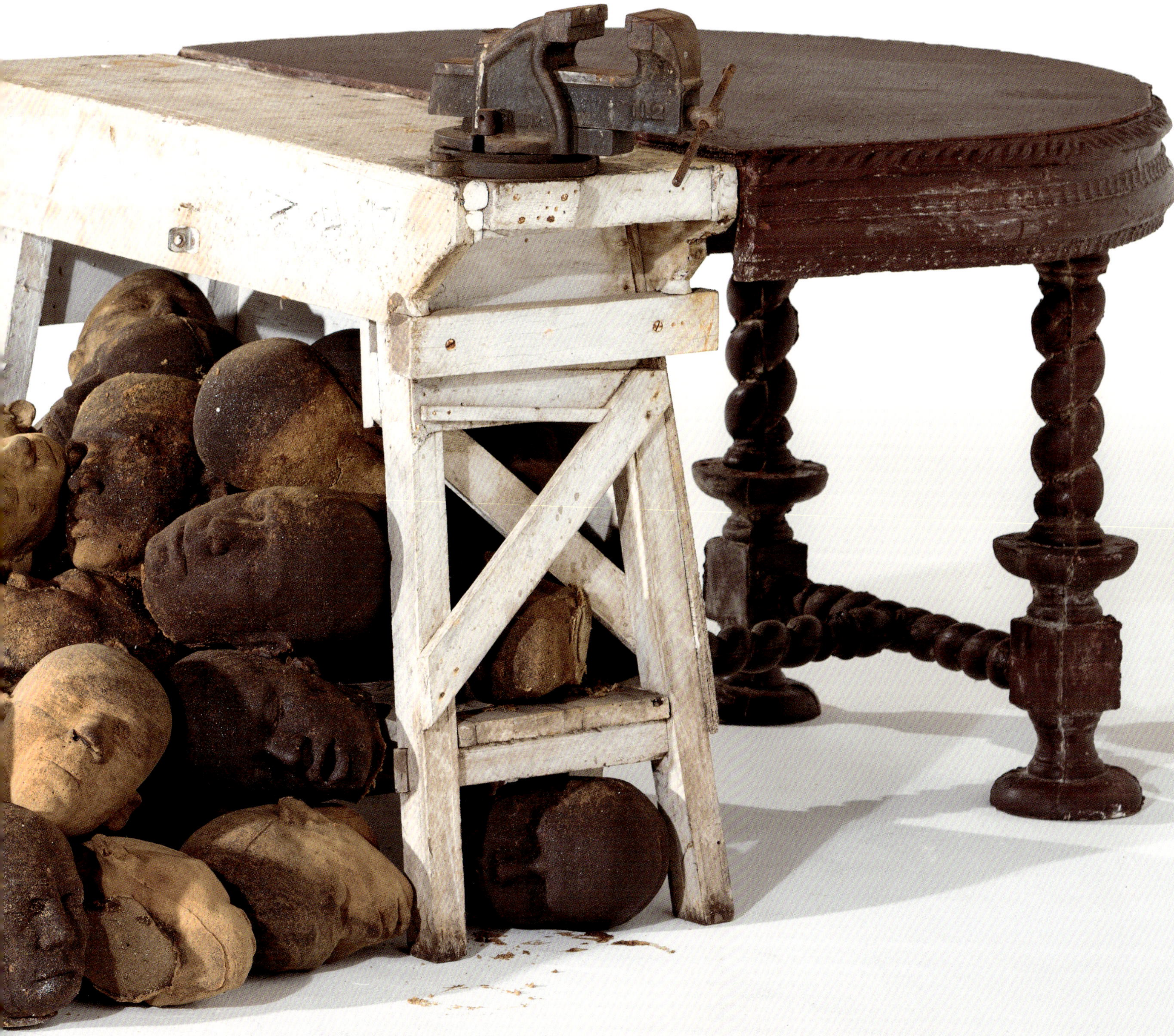

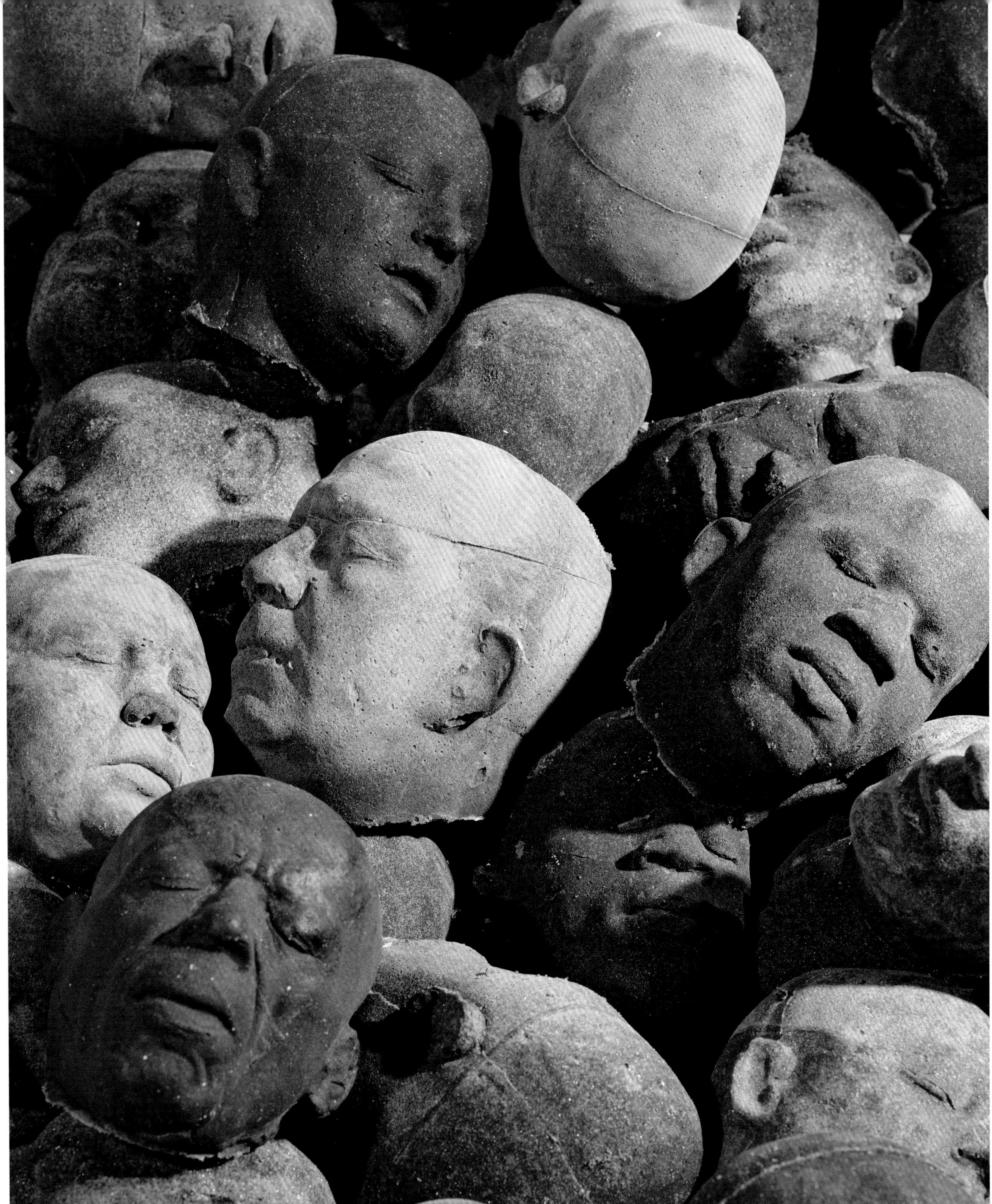

THE "VOYAGES" PLATFORM of the Trans-Atlantic Slave Trade Database details around 35,000 slaving expeditions, making accessible still incomplete, although rigorously compiled and organized, numerical information about the forced migration of an estimated 12.5 million individuals from the African continent to the Americas, and to a much lesser extent Europe, between 1514 and 1866.[1] The searchable database allows narrowing the information by region of embarkation or ports of landing, among many other variables, making it possible to inquire about and obtain a numerical scope of the trade for a given geography. A few clicks into the interface, anyone with access to the Internet can see these raw numbers gathered from the ledgers of slave traders. They can also sit through the vertiginous experience of visualizing within an animation the movement of each recorded ship for which Bahia was the "principal place of slave landing."[2] The minimalist animation tool is set on a map of the Atlantic Ocean and its surrounding continents. It soberly figures each of the voyages with a black dot appearing from its last port of call on the African coast, crossing the Atlantic in a schematic straight line, and ending on the east coast of Brazil, in and around the Bay of All Saints.

The online animation shows each voyage chronologically and on a timed scale. Watching dots appear and relentlessly cross the screen from right to left, seconds begin indeed to feel like decades, and minutes like centuries. Spurting slowly at first, then as fast as machine gun bullets from different points of the African coast, the black dots line up and move across the waters in orderly files. They then vanish into a single point recording Bahia on the left of the map. The once-sparse dots soon irrupt in a crescendo that turns dots into lines, and lines into a broad, fan-shaped surface. The discrete events of each slaving trip become before our eyes linear patterns of history, making apparent forced migration on a massive scale from one continent to the other. Filtered to show only the trips headed to Bahia, the lines of ships pictured in the animation assume a triangular shape, in which voyages originating from a large swath of the African Atlantic coast converge into a single point of arrival. This singular, flickering funnel-shape makes manifest several traits of the trade as prolegomena to the making of Bahia as an "African Metropolis." It shows the iterative and cumulative aspect of centuries-long migration produced by the trade. African men and women arrived in incessant waves of relatively small groups, streams from which the African and Afro-descendant population of Bahia grew over time, in spite of the appalling mortality rate of enslaved laborers. The funnel-shape trace that the diagrammed ships leave on the screen also makes explicit both the range of locales from which Africans came to Bahia and the predominance among them of two areas of provenance, west Central Africa, around Kongo and Angola, and the Bight of Benin. Finally, its focus on the Atlantic as a main stage inhabited, if fleetingly and over centuries, by millions, suggests the role of the ocean as a connecting space rather than a divide, where bonds of common fate tied Bahia with the places of the west coast of Africa involved in the trade.

Human experience is not an accounting matter, but the Atlantic slave trade was. The careful bookkeeping of profits and loss its entrepreneurs kept have left us with the data from which to reconstruct this double-ledger record of forced departures, deaths at sea, and hapless arrivals (figs. 1.1a,b). Where the database and animation end, however, is where Afro-Bahia begins. In spite of the unspeakable trauma of enslavement, the middle passage, and life at the wretched bottom of a slave society, the African men, women, and children who landed in the Bay and, after them, their descendants carved and affirmed a place for themselves that effloresced into a sophisticated, vibrant, and rightly celebrated culture of their own that would earn, in the twentieth century, decades after the end of the trade, the moniker of Black Rome. This essay, in an expansive take on Afro-Bahia, considers the *Cidade negra* in a broad Atlantic context, discussing its status, beyond the Bay of All Saints, as one of the cultural and spiritual centers that arose from and shaped the early modern and contemporary African Atlantic world.

**1.1b**
Detail of fig. 1.1a.

## African Roots

Capture, displacement, and enslavement are deeply transformative experiences that affected the fates of individuals and communities in all corners of the Atlantic world. Africans and Afro-descendants in Bahia lived in a wholly new ecological, social, and religious environment. Enslaved or free, they operated at the bottom of the hierarchies of power in slave societies. Over centuries, however, they made Salvador a center celebrated as a beating heart of African creativity and spirituality. The role that concrete or imagined connections with Africa played in the molding of Afro-Bahian identities, spirituality, and material practices in the past and present is the object of ongoing research and scholarly debate. Some scholars see a direct connection between the cultures of the two continents. Others focus on the novelty of African American cultures. Most, regardless, agree that the foundation on which the enslaved could and did build spaces of resistance to the "social death" of enslavement depended on some commonalities of language, experiences, and values honed in Africa (Patterson 1982).

The estimated 1.3 million Africans who reached Bahia through the trade came in great majority from ports of embarkation in the Bight of Benin (about 54 percent of the embarked who landed in the Bahia region) and west Central Africa (about 34 percent). The trade was a centuries-long phenomenon already in place in the Bay in the sixteen hundreds, but most active in the eighteenth and early nineteenth century. West Central Africans from regions in and around Kongo and Angola arrived in significant numbers all along, but individuals originating from the Gbe- or Yoruba-speaking areas of the Bight of Benin greatly dominated the number of arrivals throughout the period.

These statistical elements resonate deeply with historical and contemporary practices recorded in Salvador, the names and forms of which suggest identifiable links to these particular regions. The ritual vocabulary and pantheon of Candomblé, the religious phenomenon at the core of Afro-Bahia, point, for instance, to the enduring presence in the city's spiritual landscape of words and gods similar to those found in the places in Africa most involved in the slave trade. The name Candomblé refers to a range of Afro-Brazilian religious practices that emerged in the nineteenth century, and it is distinct from earlier ritual activities among enslaved and free Africans for its formal character and the extra-domestic location of its activities within a defined temple, the *terreiro* (see fig. 2.1). Candomblé heeds and draws from many sources, and each temple maintains distinct rituals and teachings. While there is no accepted typology of the religion's extremely complex and elaborate landscape, some of its appellations and ritual vocabulary highlight cross-Atlantic affinities with different areas of the continent. Variants of the religion include Candomblé Ketu wherein *iyalorixás*, or high priestesses, communicate with *orixás*, or deities, many of whom share names and character traits with those of the Yoruba pantheon. Other deities, in this case linked to Candomblé Jeje, resemble counterparts from Aja-Fon areas of Benin and Togo, themselves close to the Yoruba gods of the neighboring populations, as well as those of Haitian Vodou. Tata Inquice ritual leaders of Candomblé Angola, whose worshipers turn to *inquice* and other spirits, recall in name the spiritual vocabulary of west Central Africans, most notably the invisible forces they call *minkisi* (sing. *nkisi*).[3] These parallels also extend to the visual and material apparatus used in the religion's different groups. Godly attributes, power symbols, but also movement and music link expressions of spirituality from around the Atlantic. The double axe of the thunder god, the long hat of the trickster, empowered bundles, accumulative altars, or strings of beads masking the face of a powerful figure are examples of a shared vocabulary of form.

It is crucial to understand here, however, that the phenomena that connected Bahia to these regions of the west coast of Africa—first among which was the slave trade—formed a bond between Africa and the Americas that was in many regards reciprocal. A "Black Atlantic" emerged across and around the ocean that was, in the words of scholar Paul Gilroy, "continually crisscrossed by the movements of black people—not only as commodities but engaged in various struggles towards emancipation, autonomy, and citizenship."[4] This formative, two-way connection between the shores of the Atlantic arched back to long before the nineteenth century (fig. 1.2), the period Gilroy eloquently studied, and included, beyond the geography he analyzed—that is, North America and Europe—the Americas at large and, of course, the African continent itself. French-born Bahian ethnographer, historian, and *babalaô* (ritual specialist trained in the Ifá divination system) Pierre Verger described these centuries-old ties already in the 1960s as the "fluxes and refluxes" of the slave trade that linked specifically the Bight of Benin and Bahia, between the seventeenth and the nineteenth century (Verger 1968). In fact, alongside the infrastructure of the slave trade, an array of familial, political, commercial, and cultural relationships traversed and extended across the Atlantic. Far from a rigid divide, the ocean proved to be a space in which individual and collective histories unfolded. An "Atlantic community" (Law and Mann 1999) similar to the one that tied Bahia to the Bight of Benin also linked the material and immaterial fates, across the southern Atlantic, of the inhabitants of the Brazilian center with those of west Central Africa in and around the Portuguese *conquista* of Angola (Ferreira 2012).

**1.2**
Johannes van Keulen (b. 1654, Deventer, the Netherlands: d. 1715)
Claes Janszoon Vooght, engraver (d. 1696)
"Wassende-Grade-Kaart van de Aetiopische Ocean beslooten met de kusten van Guinea, Angola, de Caffers en Brasilia," printed in Amsterdam, 1753 (?)
51 x 59 cm
DR. OSCAR I. NORWICH COLLECTION OF MAPS OF AFRICA AND ITS ISLANDS, 1486–CIRCA 1865
SPECIAL COLLECTIONS, STANFORD UNIVERSITY

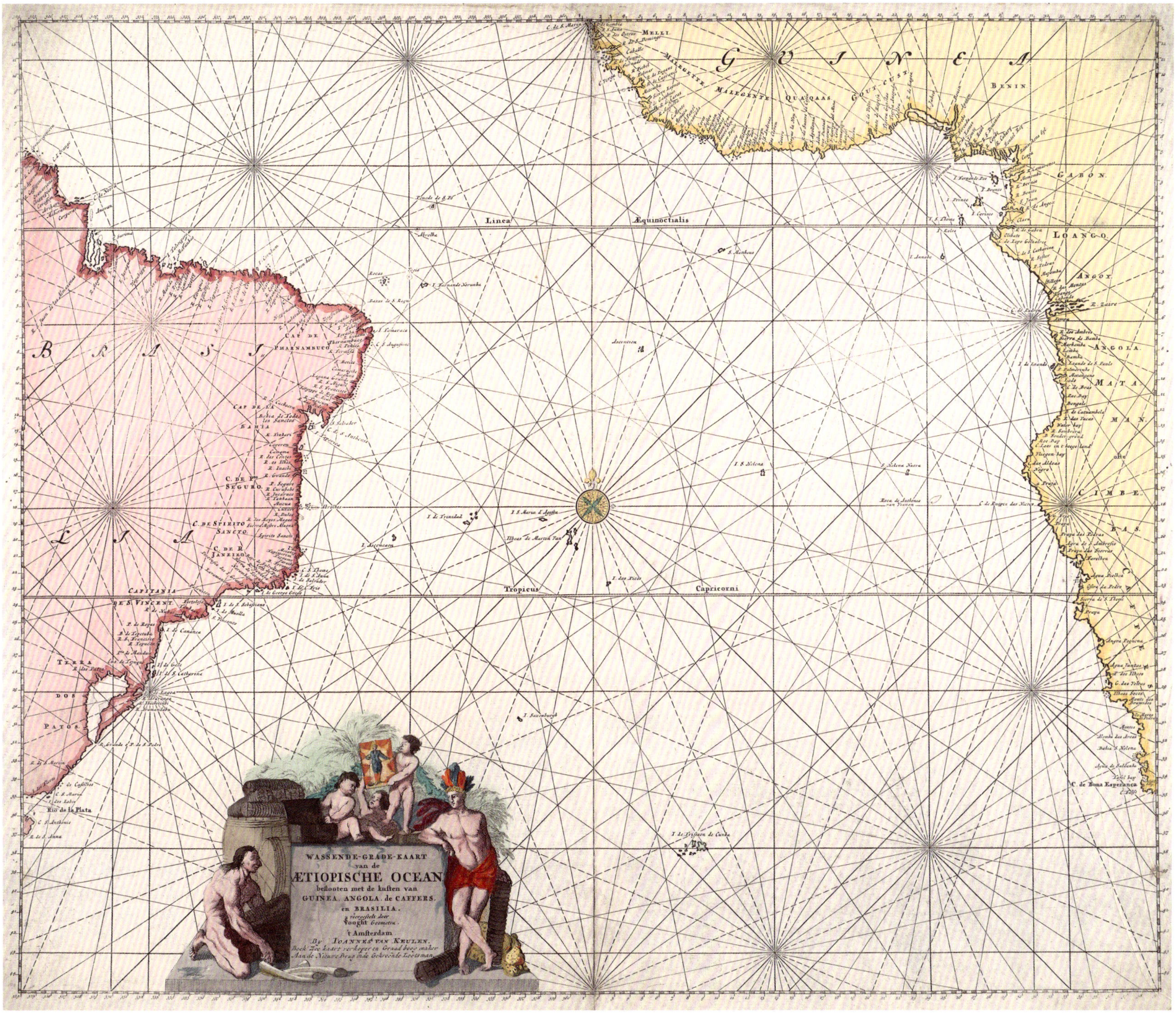

WASSENDE-GRADE-KAART
van de
ÆTIOPISCHE OCEAN
beslooten met de kusten van
GUINEA, ANGOLA, de CAFFERS,
en BRASILIA,
voorgestelt door
Vooght Geometra.
't Amsterdam
By IOANNES VAN KEULEN,
Boek Zee kaart verkoper en Graad boog maker
Aan de Nieuwe Brug inde Gekroonde Lootsman
G V I N E A
BENIN
GABON.
LOANGO.
ANGOLA
MATA
MAN.
CIMBE.
BAS.
B R A S I L I A
Linea
Æquinoctialis
Tropicus
Capricorni
CAP DE PHARNAMBUCO
C. DE SPIRITO SANCTO
CAPITANIA DE S. VINCENT
TERRA DOS PATOS
Rio de la Plata
C. de Bona Esperança

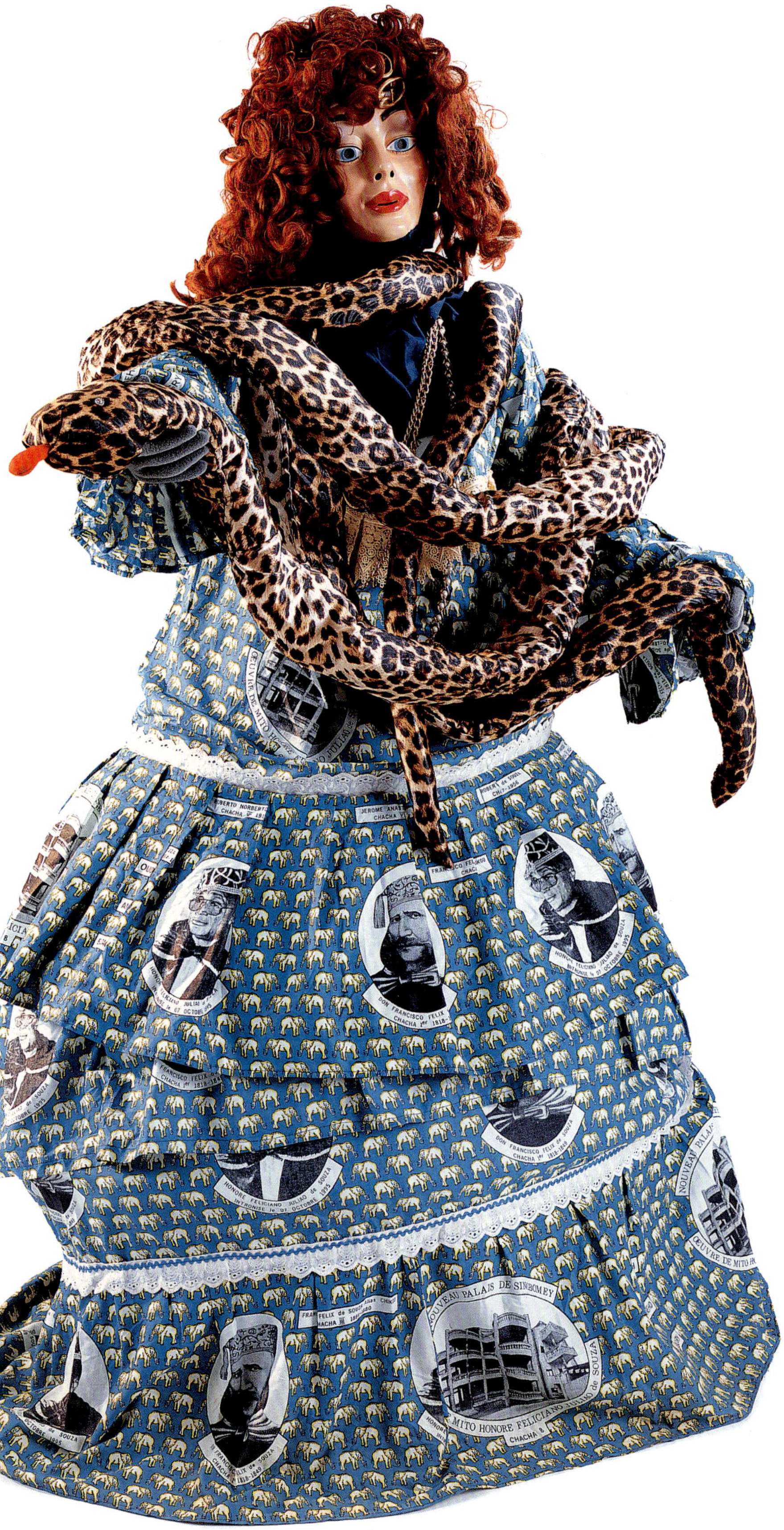

Keeping these complex material, cultural, and religious transoceanic connections in mind is key to understanding Afro-Bahia. They illustrate the city's status as one of several historic and contemporary centers that have contributed to and continue to partake in the construction of an African Atlantic (Verger 1968; Mann and Bay 2001). The Afro-Brazilian festival of *buriyan* (from the Portuguese *burinnho*, or little donkey) splendidly illustrates the multidirectional vortex of interconnections in which Afro-Bahia participates.[5] The performance has taken place in the coastal towns of present-day Benin and Togo since the nineteenth century and celebrates the feast of the Senhor do Bonfim, an immensely popular Bahian devotion feted with great pomp annually in Salvador da Bahia (Guran 1999, 154–55). Ostensibly a religious occasion, *buriyan* also celebrates the Agudás, Afro-Brazilian families descended from Portuguese and Brazilian merchants as well as from former slaves returned to the West African coast, who settled and thrived there since the eighteenth and nineteenth centuries, forming local lineages of their own. The dance appears for instance in Benin at the instauration of the head, or *chacha*, of the de Souza family, a merchant dynasty with fortunes rooted in the slave trade. Most recently the *buriyan* appeared during the festivities for the elevation of Mito Honoré Feliciano de Souza, as Chacha VIII, in 1995.[6]

Featuring masqueraders dancing samba dressed as the eponymous donkey, or as horse and riders inspired by northeastern Brazil's *bumba-meu-boi* dance, or as one of an heteroclite cast of global public figures (King Tut! Jacques Chirac! Mitterrand!), the festival is cosmopolitan Brazilian carnavalesque staged on the West African coast. The belle of this Agudá ball is Mami Wata, the charming and dangerous goddess come from "overseas" who lends her protection to devotees from all around the Afro-Atlantic (Drewal 2008). In her incarnation for the 2005 *buriyan*, now in the collection of the Fowler Museum, she displays her potentially deadly, snake-charming magnetism and cosmopolitan flare in a fancy ensemble (fig. 1.3). She wears a full-skirted and poufy-sleeved dress fit for the star of a Brazilian historic telenovela, an entertainment genre as popular in Benin as elsewhere in Africa. The sea-colored, blue fabric is printed with the emblematic elephant of the de Souza family, portraits of the *chachas* past and present, and images of their Singbomey palace. Her association with the commercial dynasty is not surprising as her powers emerged and grew in centuries past in synch with the trade relations between Africa and Europe. The prosperity and protection she promises devotees has made her and her diasporic counterparts beloved goddesses of the Afro-Atlantic pantheon. The blue-and-white lace outfit of a Bahian priestess devoted to Iemanjá, the Brazilian avatar of the water goddess (see interleaf B, this volume) for instance, celebrates her aquatic dimension and luxurious tastes on the western Atlantic shore.

Unselfconsciously mixing Yoruba- and Gbe-language chants and Portuguese devotional hymns, *buriyan* masqueraders also take part in Vodun festivals in spite of the Agudás' claims of Catholic or Muslim orthodoxy. In Brazil, too, devotees of the *orixás* have long recognized in Senhor do Bonfim, brought to the Bay by Portuguese sailors, a manifestation of one of their deities. As crowds converge each January in pilgrimage to the hilltop church dedicated to Bonfim in Salvador, devout worship and hearty devotion fill the city with a concert of spiritual energies arising from multiple religious horizons. Brazilian, Portuguese, African, Catholic, secular, and Vodun, the Feast of Bonfim in Bahia as in Benin challenges simple labels (see interleaf C, this volume). It also invites reflection on the term "Afro-Bahian" as implying a linear trajectory across the Atlantic from east to west, from roots to offspring, from original to memory. The festivals of Bonfim held on both shores bring to the fore a fuller, more accurate meaning of the phrase as an adjective labeling a complex and multidirectional history of physical and spiritual transatlantic contact, exchange, displacement, loss, and reinvention.

There is, in other words, no straight road that led to the Black Rome. Rather, the vibrant culture of *Cidade negra* emerged from bricolage, coincidences, detours, and back-and-forths. It became one of the centers where the fraught but generative interactions between Europeans, Africans, and also, often, others, produced the spiritual, social, and cultural realm of the Afro-Atlantic. The Benin/Bahia axis has a long history of scholarly interest, but other centers have emerged, strived, and sometimes waned in the last five centuries: Haiti and New Orleans, Peru and Paris, London and Luanda. Others are yet to come. What makes Salvador a Black Metropolis is not the success of its inhabitants in preserving an allegedly original African heritage against the threats of acculturation, but rather their past and present role in the making of an ever-changing Afro-Atlantic culture.

**1.3**
Members of the Souza family (Ouidah, Benin, Africa)
*Buriyan* ensemble for Mami Wata, 2005
Fabric, metal, jewelry, wig
H: 180 cm
FOWLER MUSEUM AT UCLA TR2007.6.1A–J

## Visualizing Afro-Bahia

Relatively few images have survived of Africans in Salvador before the nineteenth century. This makes a composition created in 1779 by Italian-born Portuguese officer Carlos Julião a particularly important document (fig. 1.4). A cartouche at the bottom center of the watercolor on paper describes its imagery and the circumstances of its making:

> Elevation with façade that shows a marine view of the city of Salvador of the Bay of All Saints in South America at 13 degrees of latitude and 345 degrees and 36 minutes of longitude, followed by the plans and views of all the fortifications that defend said city.
>
> This prospect was drawn by Carlos Julião Cap. M. of Miners at the Royal artillery regiment, on the occasion of his visit on the Ship Nossa Senhora Madre de Deus in May of 1779.[7]

The page portrays the city of Salvador in four different ways. A view of the coastline at the top shows its profile as seen from the sea, in a genre familiar for the representation of ports in the Portuguese world since at least the early modern period. Upper town and lower town emerge in the chorographic view, flanking the steep hill characteristic of Salvador and Portuguese port towns at large. Steeples and stately buildings at the top and galleries of doors and windows from commercial structures at the bottom speak of faith and commerce as the backbones of the town. Directly under the marine view, Julião puts to work his skills as draftsman of military engineering to give the plans and elevations of nine forts. The bottom register gives, in addition to the title in the middle, a numbered key of the buildings labeled in the top part. The largest section of the composition, the second register from the bottom, presents five vignettes in which Julião portrays Salvador not through its bricks and mortar, but through the diversity of men and women making up its society. The paintings, composed for a Portuguese audience in the upper political and military spheres back in Lisbon, each received a caption as a reading key. From left to right, Julião represented the "Way of Dressing of the Mulatto Women of the city of Bahia," a "Black who sells milk in Bahia," a "Carriage or Sedan Chair in which the Ladies of the city of Salvador Bahia de Todos os Santos Travel," a "Young woman dancing the Landú de bunda a cinta," and finally the "Clothing of the Mina Black Women Merchants of Bahia."[8] Significantly, most of these figures also appear in closely related versions in a series of watercolors attributed to Julião, now bound together in an album in the Biblioteca Nacional do Brasil in Rio de Janeiro, the *Riscos illuminados de figurinhos de brancos e negros dos uzos do Rio de Janeiro e Serro do Frio*.[9] Ostensibly about southeastern Brazil, according to the title and scenes from the mining district of Minas Gerais, the presence of some of its figures in the view of Salvador indicates that the full scope of the *Riscos* concerned Bahia as well as Minas Gerais and Rio de Janeiro, and probably relied on a typology of figures without strong regional ties.[10]

**1.4**
Carlos Julião (b. 1740, Turin, Italy; d. 1811)
Panoramic view of Bahia, 1779
Watercolor and india ink on paper
53 x 86 cm
COURTESY PORTUGAL/GABINETE DE ESTUDOS ARQUEOLÓGICOS DA ENGENHARIA MILITAR/DIREÇÃO DE INFRAESTRUTURAS DO EXÉRCITO – 4756-3-38-52

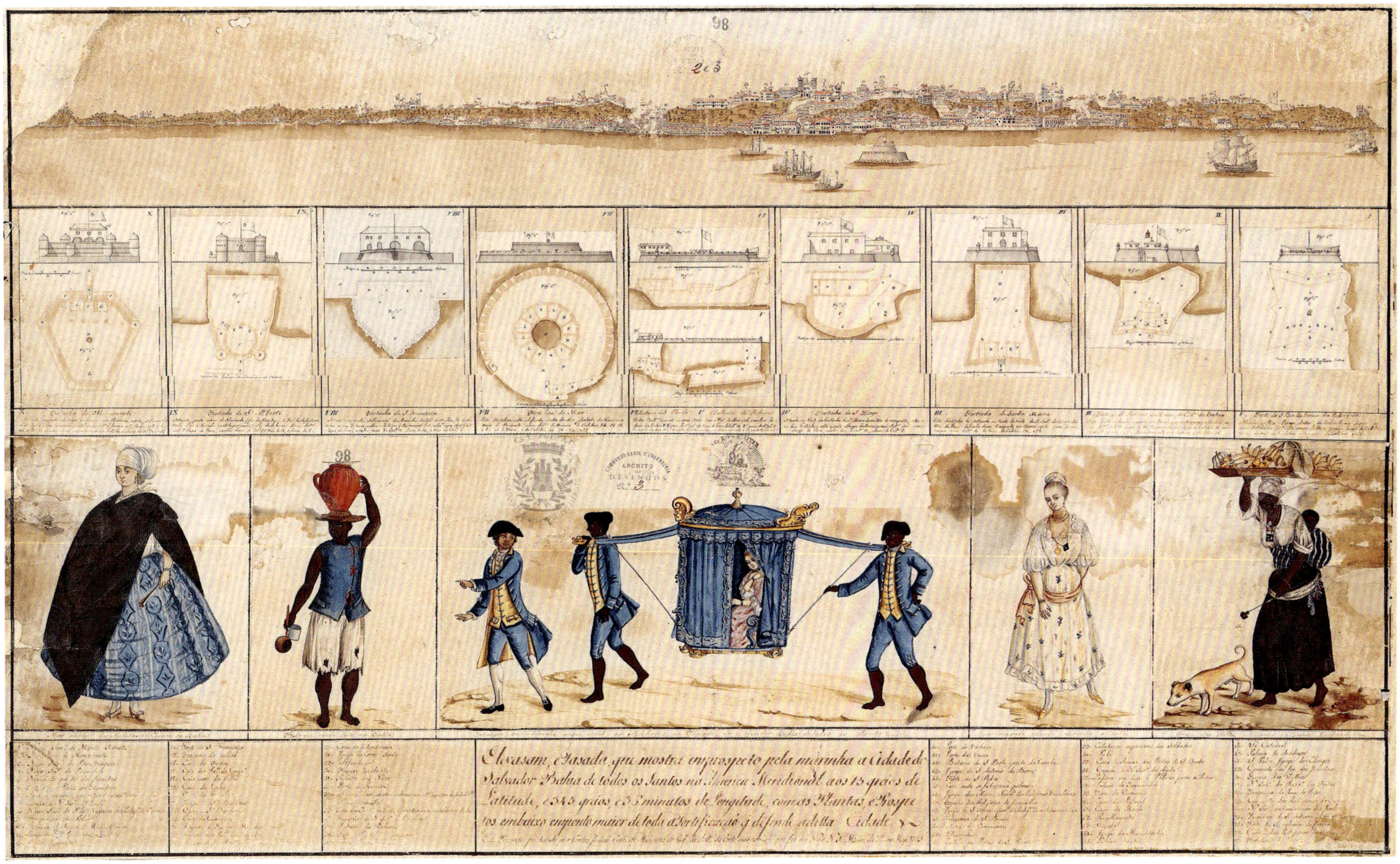

The European draftsman's representation of Bahia through human and social types in descriptive vignettes, akin to natural history illustrations, is in keeping with his scientific ambitions as a naturalist, which found fulfilment elsewhere in a botanical compendium.[11] He did not aim to be exhaustive in his panel, but in a somewhat accurate transposition of the demographics of the city, Julião included only one figure of exclusively European descent among the eight people he painted, a lady carried in a sedan chair. The richly dressed woman peeks through the curtain of her vehicle toward the intended viewers of her image, Portuguese men back in Lisbon. Symbolically placed at the center of the composition, she enjoys the luxuries that enslaved labor of the kind performed by the sedan-chair carriers affords her, in what forms a not so subtle allegory of Bahian society. A light-skinned, shod third man in a livery matching that of the barefoot carriers leads the traveling group. The woman to the right of the sedan chair vignette is of ambiguous racial background, but her clothing, dancing, and the label of "*mossa*" for "girl," rather than the word *senhora*, or "lady," used for the central figure, indicates her status as a *mulata* or, less likely, a European from a low social class. She also looks at the viewer, in this case flirtatiously, while stepping toward him, in a contrapposto aimed to suggest the provocative choreography of the Landú or Lundu dance, infamous for its overtly sexual tenor.[12] To the far left, another *mulata* stands, in contrast, poised and dignified, modestly covered with a black mantle that nonetheless reveals her thin white blouse and printed skirt and that threatens to fall at any sudden movement. The two last dark-skinned figures on the page are hard at work. Much like the chair carriers, each bears a load in service of the sustenance of Bahia: milk, fruits, vehicle, and even the next generation of laborers. One, a muscular black man in ragged clothing, carries a jar of milk to sell. He is likely as an *escravo de ganho*, a slave who would work independently and repay part of his gains to his owner. The other, a woman to the far right walking alongside a dog, holds a tray of fruits on her head to bring to market and carries a baby on her back tied in a *pano da costa*, the often-striped cloth identified in Bahian lore as from Africa.

While far from unfiltered representations of reality, Julião's images nonetheless carry some documentary value concerning the mores and customs, as well as the makeup, of late eighteenth-century Bahian society. We may turn to them, and in particular to the "preta Mina da Bahia" at the far right, to think about the emergence of Afro-Bahia within a broad Atlantic African sphere. The ethnonym "Mina," a term used broadly in the slave trade to refer to the coast of West Africa, could be construed as indicative of her recent arrival from the continent or point to an identity—self-defined or imposed—reaching back to that region of West Africa. Both the term itself and the manner in which Julião uses it in the phrase "Mina of Bahia" express the idea of a Mina *nação*, a social construct honed in Brazil itself. The woman's outfit accordingly prefigures what would become emblematic of the Baiana mode of dress. She wears a head scarf, a *pano da costa*, necklaces, bracelets, a bright white shirt, a dark skirt, and dangling pendants hung around her belt (see also Shirey, this volume).

The figure of the Baiana that already emerges from these early images comes into focus in the works of the traveling artists who crisscrossed Brazil in the nineteenth century creating wave after wave of genre scenes documenting their impressions of a country that seemed to them an endless source of local color and exoticism. French painter Jean-Baptiste Debret for instance sketched "Bahianas" on several occasions during the first decades of the nineteenth century (fig. 1.5). Dark skirt and light-colored lacy top falling off her left shoulder, jewels and head scarf, his "*Vie[i]lle Bahiana*" sits at a street corner selling produce, her *pano da costa* wrapped around her waist and hardly visible. Fellow traveling artist Johann Moritz Rugendas also sketched costume studies during his stay in Brazil between 1821 and 1826. His works, advertised as "from nature," served as sources for a set of prints that appeared in an editorial project titled in its simultaneous French and German editions *Voyage pittoresque au Brésil* or *Malerische Reise in Brasilien* (Rugendas 1835). The Bavarian artist pictures a strong, youthful Baiana, hand on the hip in a pose of great self-countenance and clad in a full skirt, head scarf, filmy white blouse, jewels, and an ostentatious *pano da costa*. At the other end of the century, Debret's Brazilian-born countryman Marc Ferrez also pictured Baianas in 1885, at the threshold of the abolition of slavery in 1888 (fig. 1.6). His photographs, marketed as postcards inviting sexualized comments, captured the women in similar but more lavish outfits, with extravagant amounts of lace and precious metals. They appear in the black-and-white prints richly adorned, their jewels, lace, and static poses making them apt counterparts to the portraits of Queen Victoria from the same period that may have inspired the photographer's compositions (see fig. 4.4).

**1.5**
Jean-Baptiste Debret (b. 1768, Paris, France; d. 1848)
*Vie[i]lle Bahiana* (Old Baiana), circa 1817–1829
Watercolor
8.1 x 13.9 cm
COURTESY CASTRO MAYA MUSEUM, RIO DE JANEIRO, BRAZIL

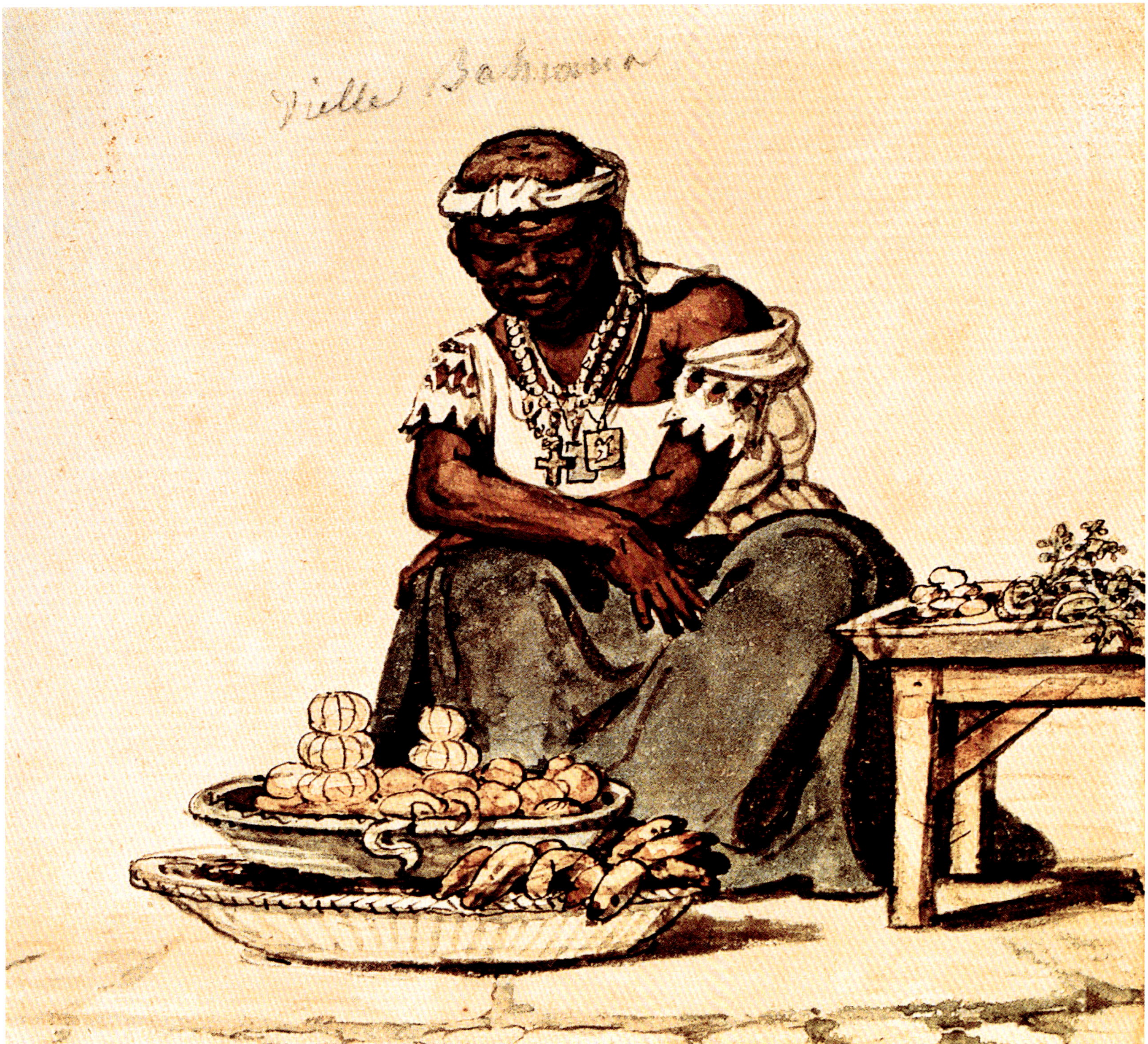
Vielle Bahiana

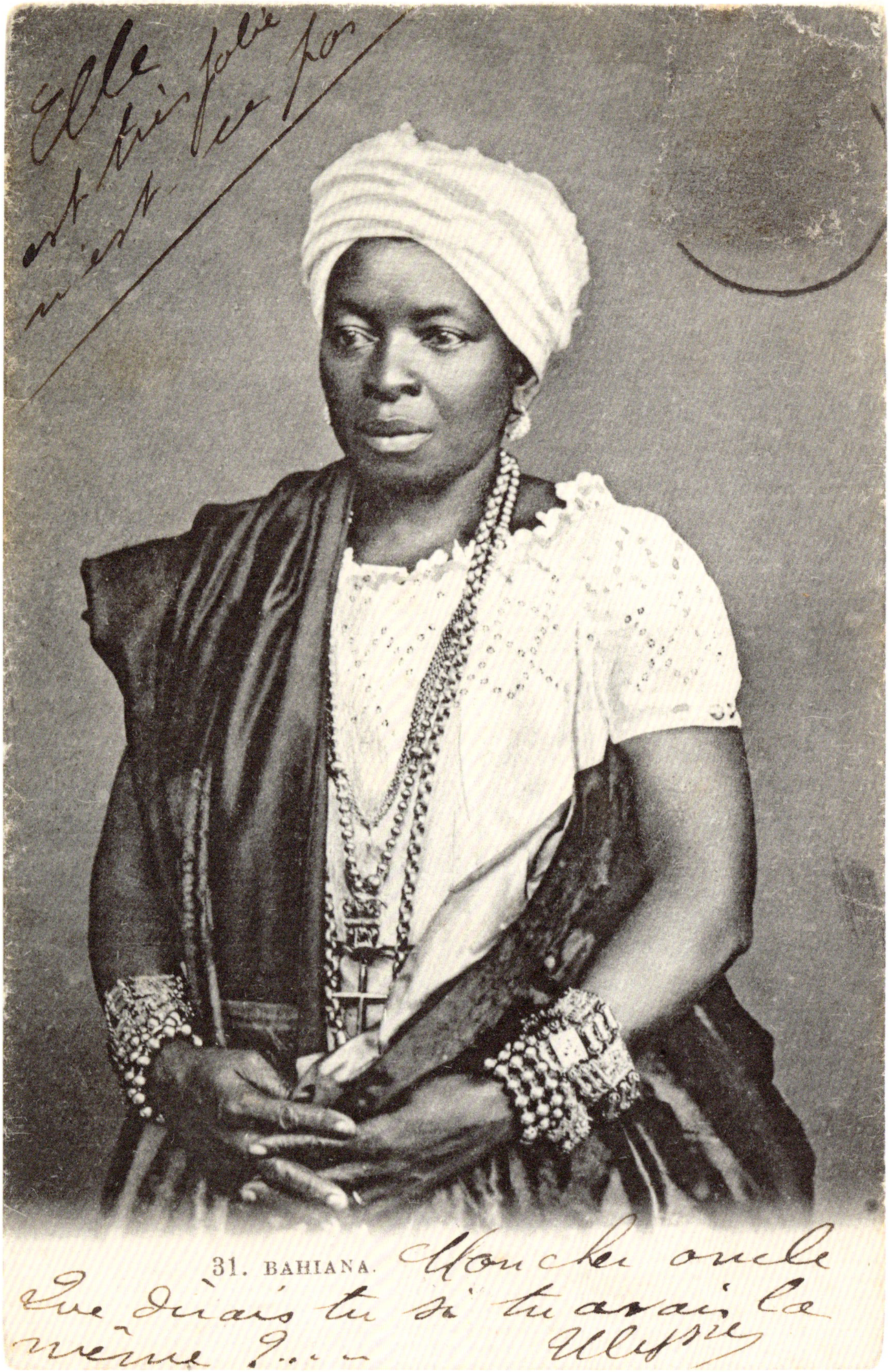
31. BAHIANA.

The unnamed figures captured by Julião and Ferrez usually wear a group of pendants at the waist (see fig. 4.4). In nineteenth-century images by Ferrez, these are *balangandãs*, a cluster of silver or gold charms (see interleaf G, this volume). In the older painting by Julião, the components are less defined, and the pendants mix metallic pieces with a type of amulet called *bolsas de mandinga*, or Mandingo bags. The *bolsas* were empowered packets that ritual specialists of African descent living in cosmopolitan nodes of the Portuguese Atlantic in the seventeenth and eighteenth century crafted and sold to clients seeking their mighty and trustworthy protection. Worn about the body, the small bundles drew their powers from a combination of relics of the Atlantic spiritual economy. They mixed empowered materials blessed or activated by Christian and non-Christian rituals from Europe and Africa with others indigenous to the Americas. The makers of the bags, called *mandingueiros*, trained through apprenticeship. They combined pieces of altar stones, consecrated hosts, sulfur, plants, and already-functioning amulets into spectacularly efficient shields against physical or social vulnerabilities.[13] Putting to work invisible forces from all horizons through a ritual and material apparatus borrowing from European, African, and native American esoteric practices, the *bolsas* were Atlantic objects par excellence used by a clientele of men and women of all origins, social classes, races, and religions.

The *bolsas* that we see at the waist and perhaps also on the neck of the *Preta Mina*, as well as likely on the chest of the *"mossa"* in Julião's panorama, illustrate the many ways in which the visual, material, and spiritual environment of Salvador was rooted in the vortex of cross-cultural exchange the Atlantic world system created. They also provide an apt metaphor for the making of Afro-Bahian culture at large. *Mandingueiros* created their packets by identifying, harvesting, and mixing empowered and empowering material from the four corners of the Atlantic world that, once brought together, changed in nature from heteroclite scraps to mighty objects recognized, respected, and celebrated by all. Crafted by Africans caught in the webs of the Atlantic trade, the *bolsas* became objects of broad social use, and their influence reached far beyond any racial or social confines. Over time, Africans and Afro-descendants in Bahia continued to turn to *bolsa*-like objects, but they eventually enshrined and galvanized the empowered ingredients and charms into durable, precious, yet still intimate objects of protection and ostentatious pride in the form of gold and silver *balangandãs*.

Afro-Bahia emerged from a similar form of alchemy in which African men and women under Portuguese colonial rule and suffering from the hardships of enslavement and disenfranchisement mixed and remixed cultural traits from around the ocean, morphing them into a new, broadly resonant, widely influential, and constantly evolving, galvanizing culture. Images such as those by Julião, Debret, Rugendas, and Ferrez allow us to visualize the historical depth of some of the emblematic figures, objects, and practices of Afro-Bahia and to bring to light the ways in which the inhabitants of the *Cidade negra* used and transformed them along the centuries and in response to their changing social, political, and cultural circumstances.

**1.6**
Marc Ferrez (b. 1843, Rio de Janeiro; d. 1923)
*Bahiana*, 1885
Postcard
Edição A. Moura Ouvidor, Rio de Janeiro
14 x 9 cm
PRIVATE COLLECTION

*Interleaf* **A**

# The Slave Ship

## *Castro Alves and Hansen Bahia*

**Sabrina Gledhill**

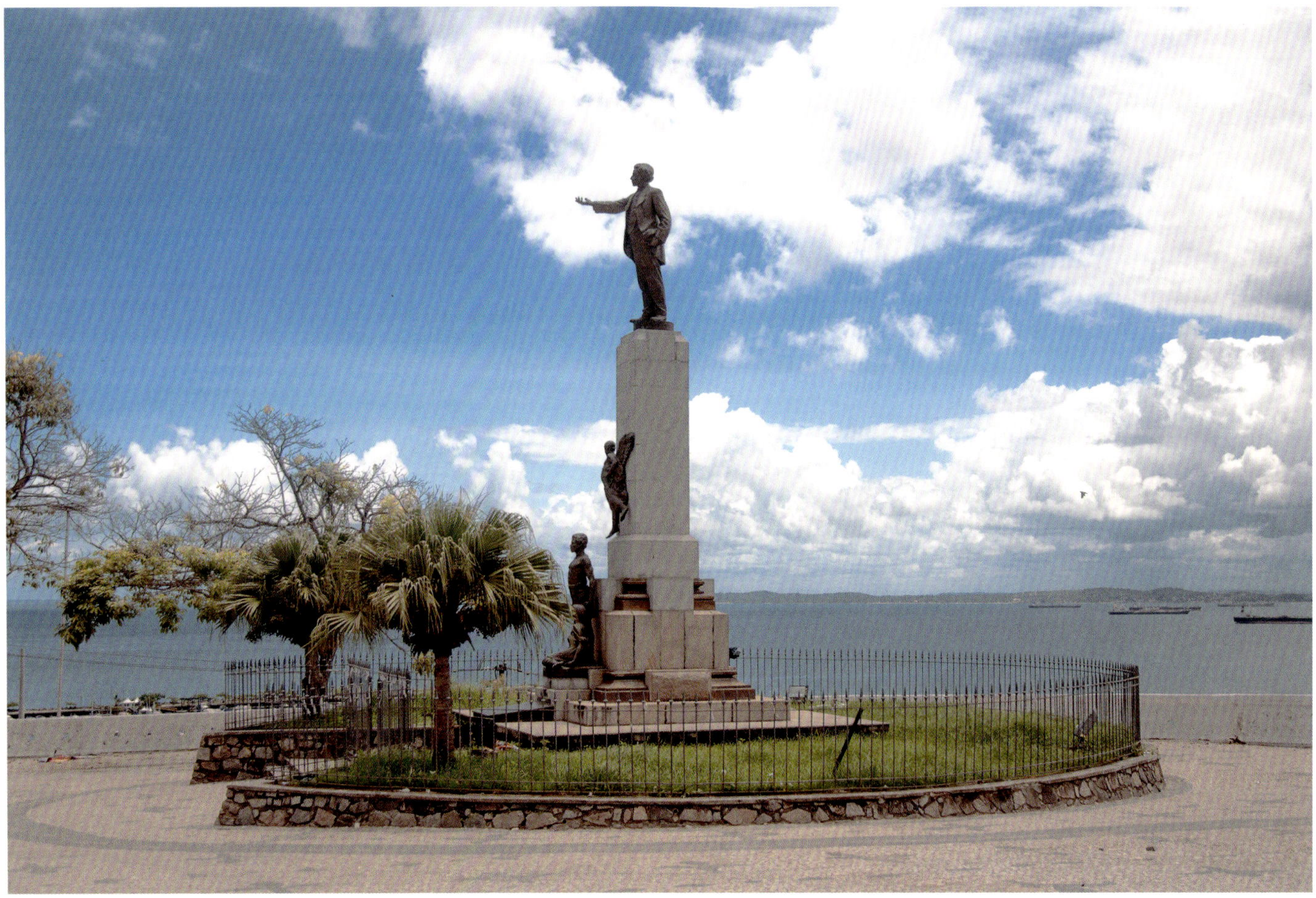

A.1
Adenor Gondim (b. 1950, Rui Barbosa, Bahia, Brazil)
Statue of Antônio Frederico de Castro Alves, 2014
Digital photograph
COURTESY ADENOR GONDIM

This sculptural tribute to Castro Alves stands in the square bearing the poet's name overlooking the Baía de Todos os Santos (Bay of All Saints).

"'STAMOS EM PLENO MAR." So begins the epic poem *O navio negreiro—Tragédia no mar* (The Slave Ship: Tragedy at Sea) by Antônio Frederico de Castro Alves (1847–1871). "We are out on the high seas." The moonlight is a "gilded butterfly cavorting in space" and "stars leap down from the heavens like golden foam." Then a "Dantean dream" defiles this natural beauty and pollutes the sea: a blood-soaked deck, clanking chains, cracking whips; African captives forced to dance to the point of madness, while chained together on the deck of a slave ship crossing the Atlantic; babies draining the life from their mothers' breasts; terrified maidens dragged out to be raped; a whip falling on an old man's back (fig. A.2).

> Yesterday full liberty
> Desire for power...
> Today...the height of perversity
> They are not even free to die...
> The same chain binds them
> —Iron, ghastly snake—
> In the coils of slavery.
> And so mocking death,
> The ghastly cohort dances
> To the sound of the lash...Derision!...[1]
>
> (Castro Alves, stanza V)

In concluding, the poet invokes a sense of shame in Brazilian patriots by revealing the colors flying from the slave ship's mast to be none other than the green and yellow of Brazil's national flag, a symbol of independence.

Known as the "Bard of the Slaves," Castro Alves is strongly identified with the Afro-Brazilian metropolis of Salvador, and today his statue stands—in a square that bears his name overlooking the Baía de Todos os Santos (Bay of All Saints)—with one arm outstretched as if reciting his work (figs. A.1, A.3). He may have adopted abolitionism as a theme of his poetry because of his racial background (he could be considered black according to the one-drop rule),[2] but it is more likely that he was attracted to the movement during his days as a law student in Recife. He wrote *O navio negreiro* on April 18, 1868, eighteen years after the second and final ban of the transatlantic slave trade in 1850, and two decades before the official abolition of slavery in Brazil in 1888.

The transatlantic slave trade had been officially abolished in Brazil in 1831, but it only ceased following the enactment of the Eusebio de Queiroz Law, which definitively criminalized it in 1850. The slave ship and Middle Passage nonetheless continued to be enduring symbols, and Castro Alves's abolitionist poetry inspired a generation of Brazilian poets and novelists to concentrate their creative efforts on abolitionism and other social issues, such as poverty. Given his brief and brilliant career—he died of tuberculosis at the age of twenty-four—the abolitionist movement, which gained strength after his death, under the leadership of Rui Barbosa, Joaquim Nabuco, and José do Patrocinio, among others, adopted Castro Alves as a tragic, heroic, even a Christ-like figure, and made him a focus of their campaign to abolish slavery (Haberly 1983).

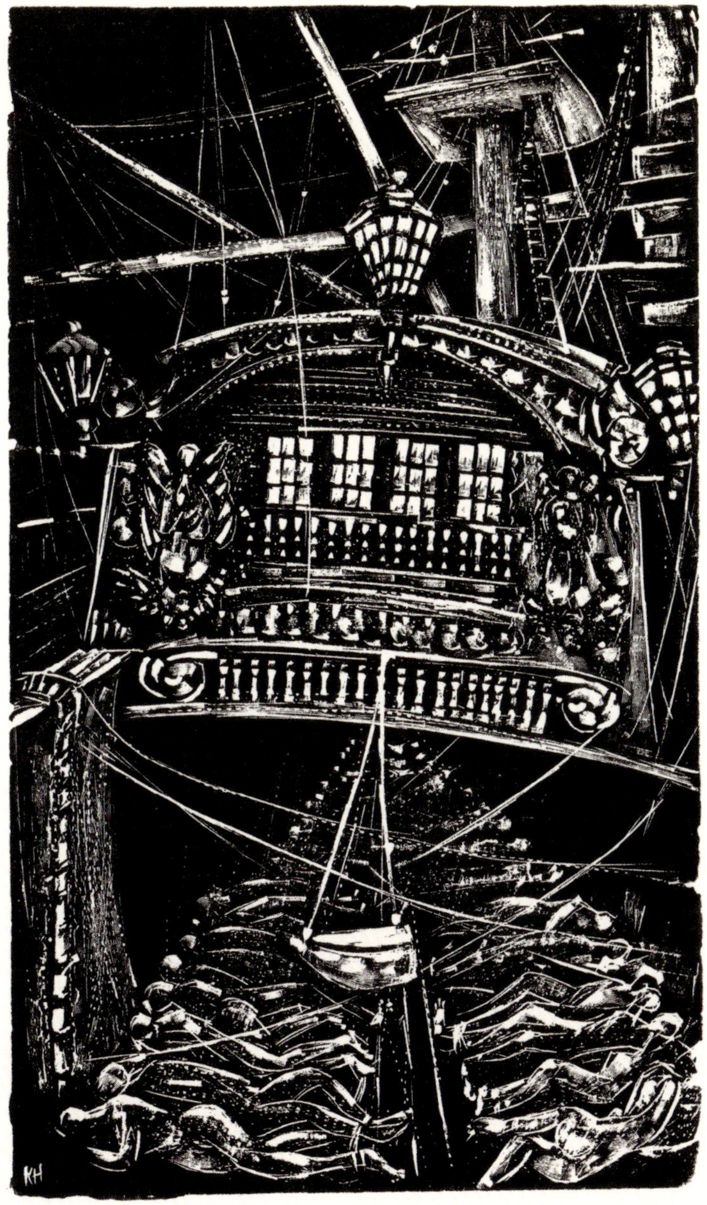


**A.2**
Hansen Bahia (Karl Heinz Hansen, b. 1915, Hamburg, Germany; d. 1978)
*Caminho de lágrimas* (Trail of Tears), 1958
Woodcut print on paper
H: 42 cm
PRIVATE COLLECTION

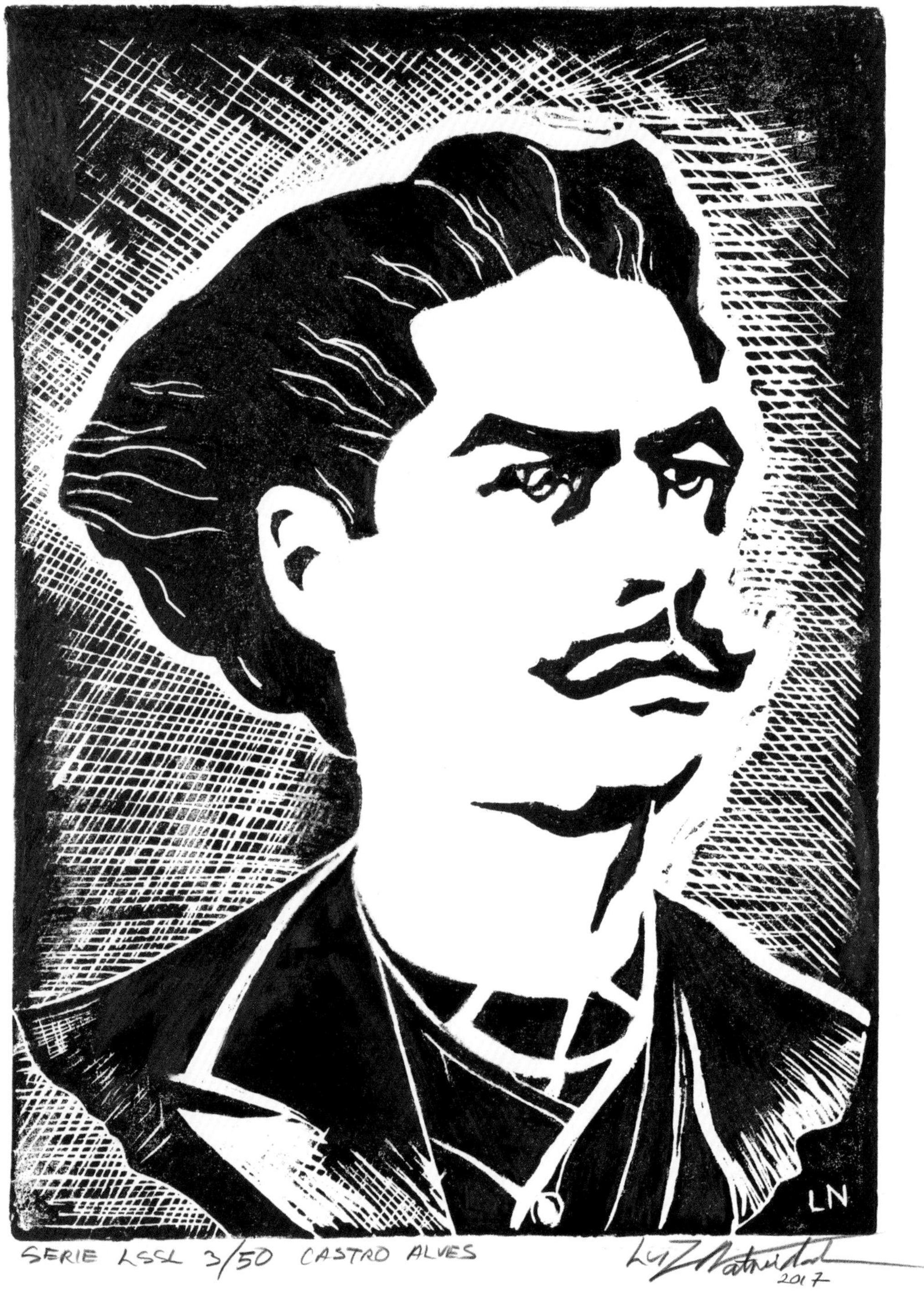


**A.3**
José Luiz Natividade Costa (b. 1961, Junqueiro, Alagoas, Brazil)
*Antônio Frederico de Castro Alves*, 2017
Woodcut print on paper
70 x 50 cm
PRIVATE COLLECTION

In 1957 Brazilian publisher Manoel Pinto de Aguiar commissioned the German-born Brazilian artist Hansen Bahia to produce woodcuts to illustrate an edition of Castro Alves's poem that would portray the suffering aboard a slave ship. The book was published in 1958 with a preface by the Afro-Brazilian anthropologist Édison Carneiro, a leading figure in establishing Afro-Brazilian studies as a respectable academic pursuit (fig. A.4). The xylographs, or woodcuts, Hansen Bahia created for *O navio negreiro* reflect a combination of German Expressionism, African art, and Brazilian *cordel* traditions. (While in Brazil he was also influenced by the spontaneity of the naive woodcuts that illustrate chapbooks of folk poetry known as *literatura de cordel*.) Already recognized for works that intensely portrayed his tragic view of life, the artist compared them to scenes of Calvary, calling this series the Caminho de lágrimas (Trail of Tears). Although most of his illustrations do not specifically portray scenes from Castro Alves's epic poem—in fact, the artist created his own *Navio negreiro*—Hansen Bahia uses writhing Expressionist lines, the bold contrast of black and white found in *cordel* woodcuts, and even the flaws inherent in the woodblocks to heighten the sense of human suffering, particularly mothers and children (fig. A.6), enchained bodies, and even hanged captives—suicides or "examples" set to quell rebellion (fig. A.5).

Best known for his xylographic works, Hansen Bahia was born Karl Heinz Hansen in Hamburg, Germany, in 1915, and worked there as a xylographer and illustrator, producing religious scenes inspired by Albrecht Dürer. His service in the German Army in World War II confronted him directly with what the Scottish poet Robert Burns called "man's inhumanity to man." In 1950 he emigrated to Brazil, where he lived in São Paulo and held several exhibitions of his works, which were already markedly Expressionist, before moving to Salvador, Bahia, in 1955. The Brazilian Modernist movement was in full swing in that city, where he befriended Carybé and Jorge Amado (see Johnson, this volume).

Between 1959 and 1966, he lived and worked in Germany and Ethopia, where he co-founded and taught graphic arts at the School of Fine Art in Addis Ababa, before acquiring Brazilian citizenship and returning to Brazil. While in Germany, he had added "Bahia" to his surname. He moved to the riverside village of São Félix in the Bahia Recôncavo region in 1970, and before his death in 1978, he bequeathed his works to Cachoeira, São Félix's sister town across the River Paraguaçu. The Hansen Bahia Foundation was established there to house his collection of prints, woodblocks, tools, and books. Today, the name Hansen Bahia is indelibly linked to the towns of Cachoeira and São Félix.

The works of Castro Alves and Hansen Bahia serve as a reminder that the myth of "racial democracy" is founded on another misconception: that slavery was kinder and gentler in Brazil. The end of the slave trade marked the beginning of the end of slavery in that country, which depended on a regular influx of young African captives to replace those who were worked to death on the plantations. Castro Alves helped bring slavery down years after his death. Hansen Bahia's works keep alive the memory of the unspeakable suffering of the Middle Passage and its aftermath—a life spent in chains—with images that evoke the tragic side of human existence.

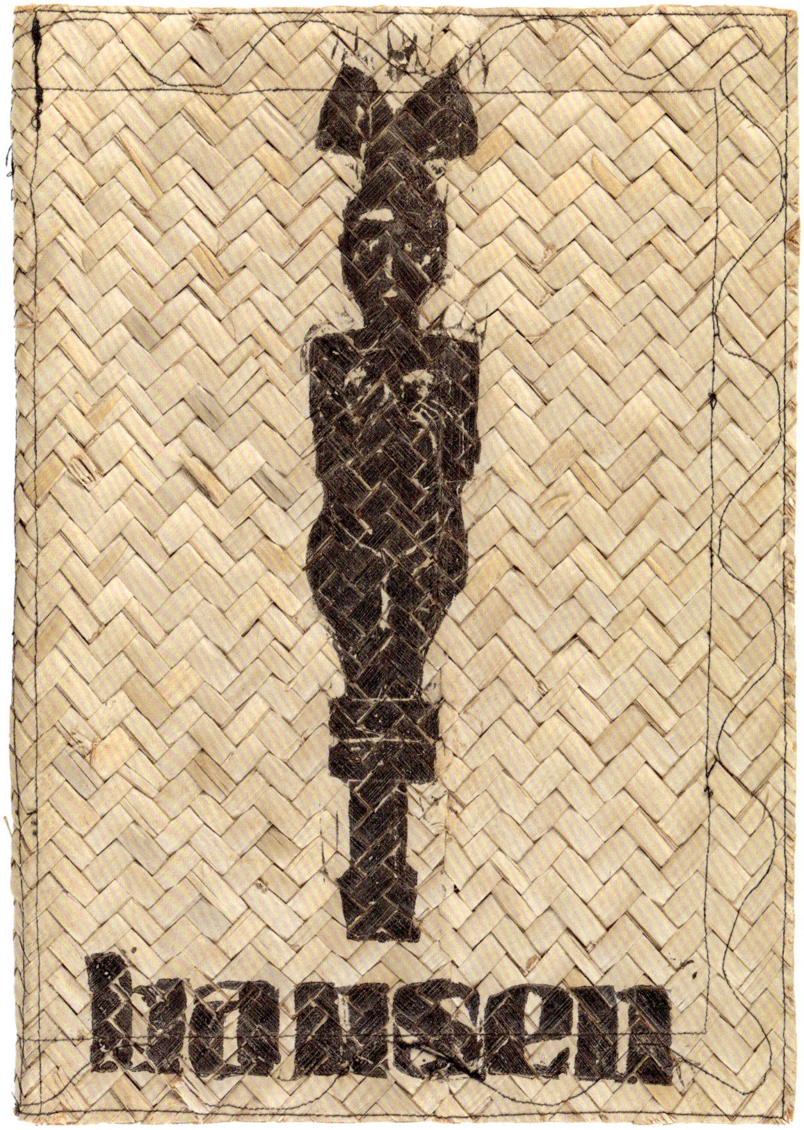


**A.4**
Hansen Bahia (Karl Heinz Hansen, b. 1915, Hamburg, Germany; d. 1978)
Cover for a special printing of *Caminho de lágrimas* (Trail of Tears), 1958
Ink stamp on woven plant fiber
H: 44.5 cm
PRIVATE COLLECTION

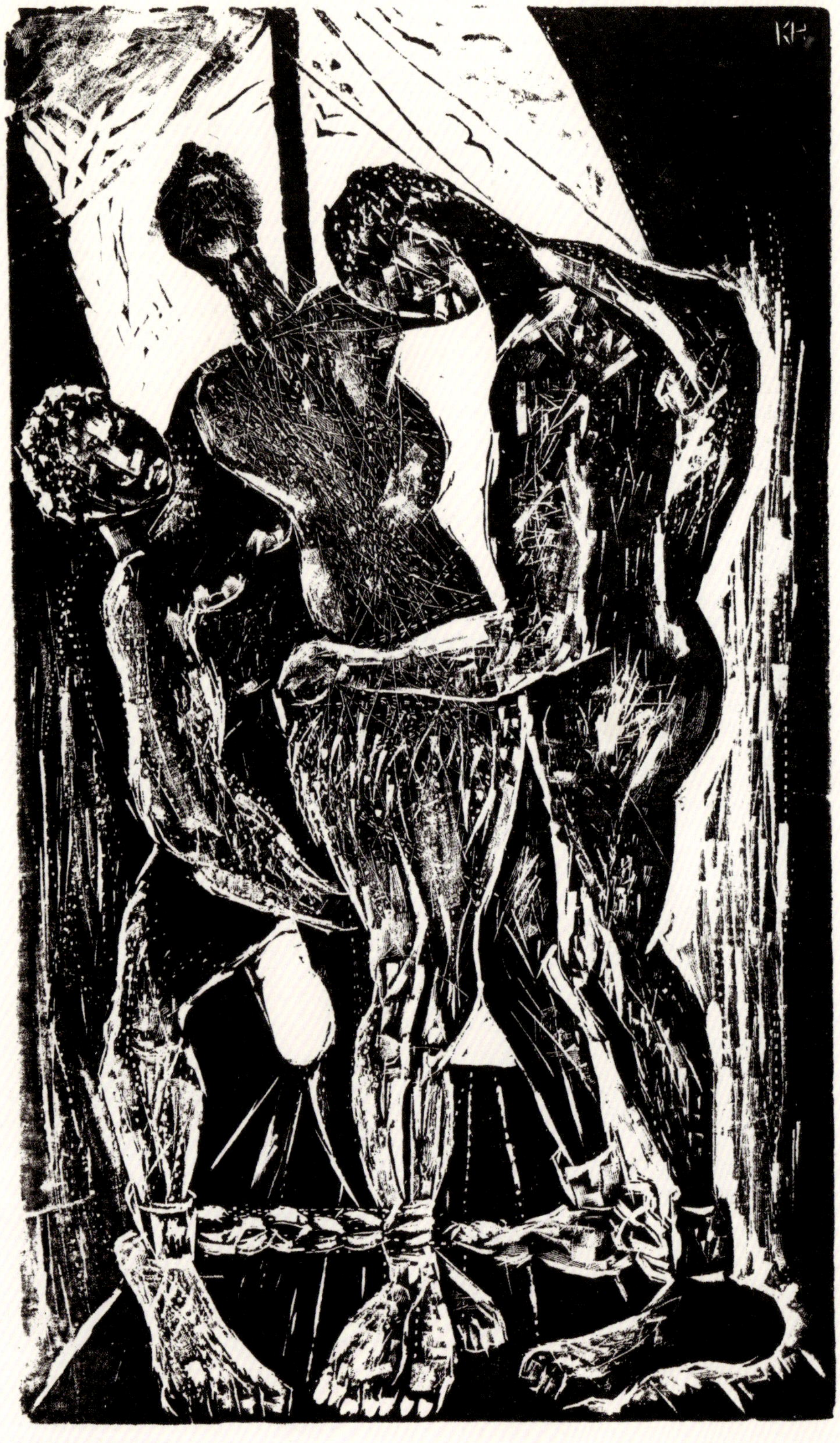

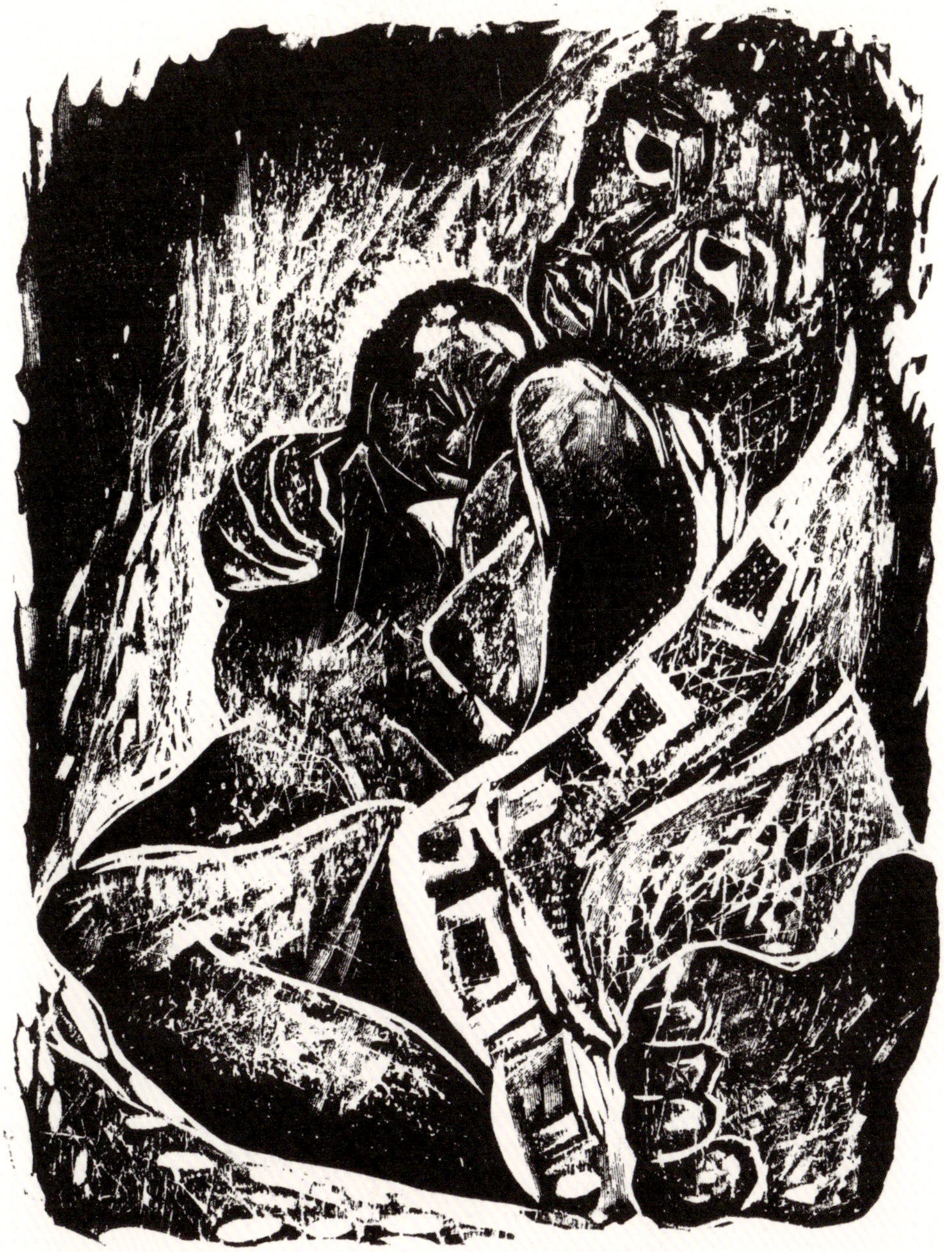

**A.5**
Hansen Bahia (Karl Heinz Hansen, b. 1915, Hamburg, Germany; d. 1978)
*Caminho de lágrimas* (Trail of Tears), 1958
Woodcut print on paper
H: 42 cm
PRIVATE COLLECTION

**A.6**
Hansen Bahia (Karl Heinz Hansen, b. 1915, Hamburg, Germany; d. 1978)
*Caminho de lágrimas* (Trail of Tears), 1958
Woodcut print on paper
H: 42 cm
PRIVATE COLLECTION

Interleaf **B**

# *The Iemanjá* Festival

**Sabrina Gledhill**

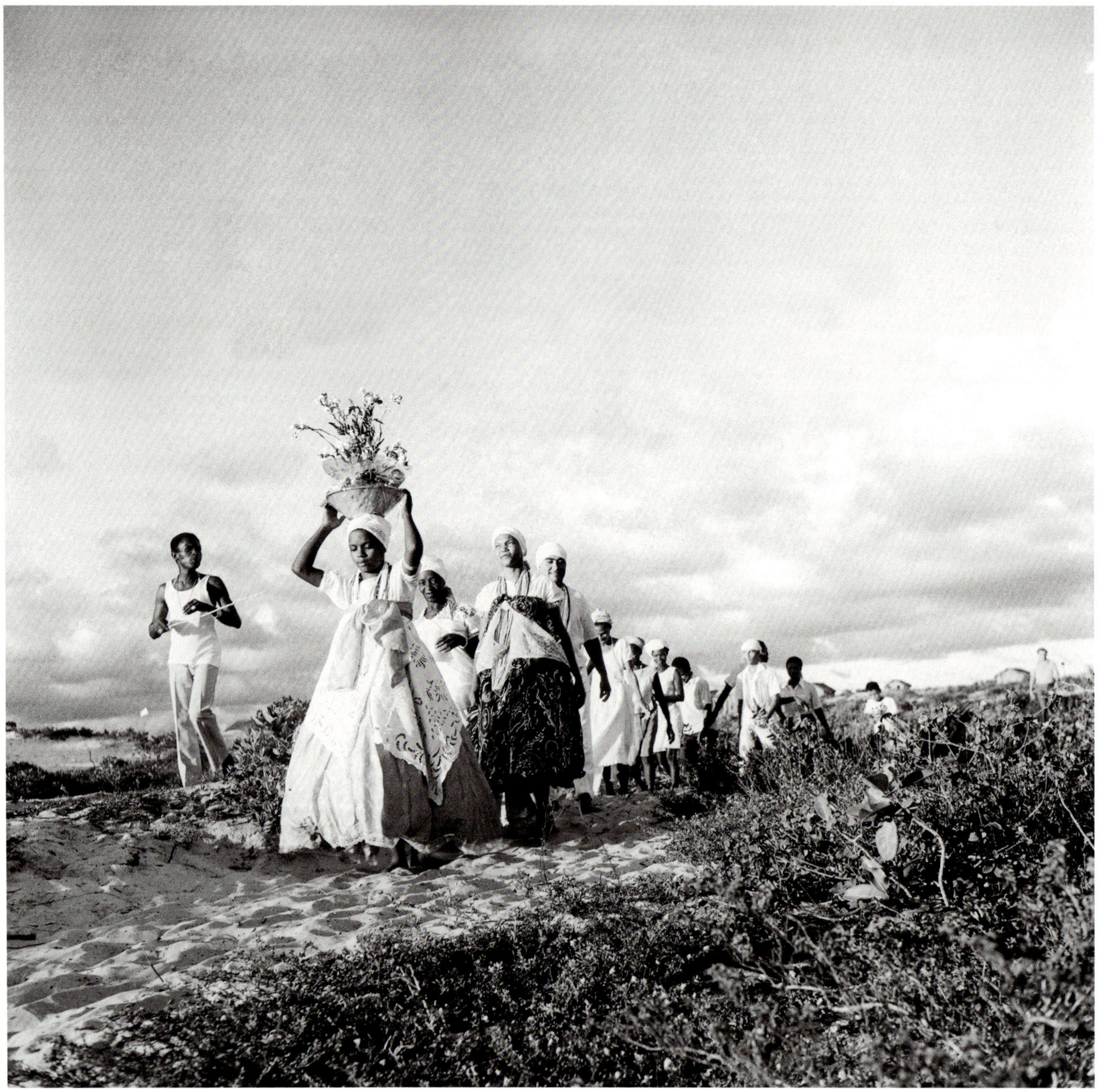

**B.2**
Jorge Vismara (b. 1945, Salvador, Bahia, Brazil)
*Dique do Tororó*, 2015
Photograph
COURTESY JORGE VISMARA

Tati Moreno's sculptures of the *orixás* rise from the Dique (Dike).

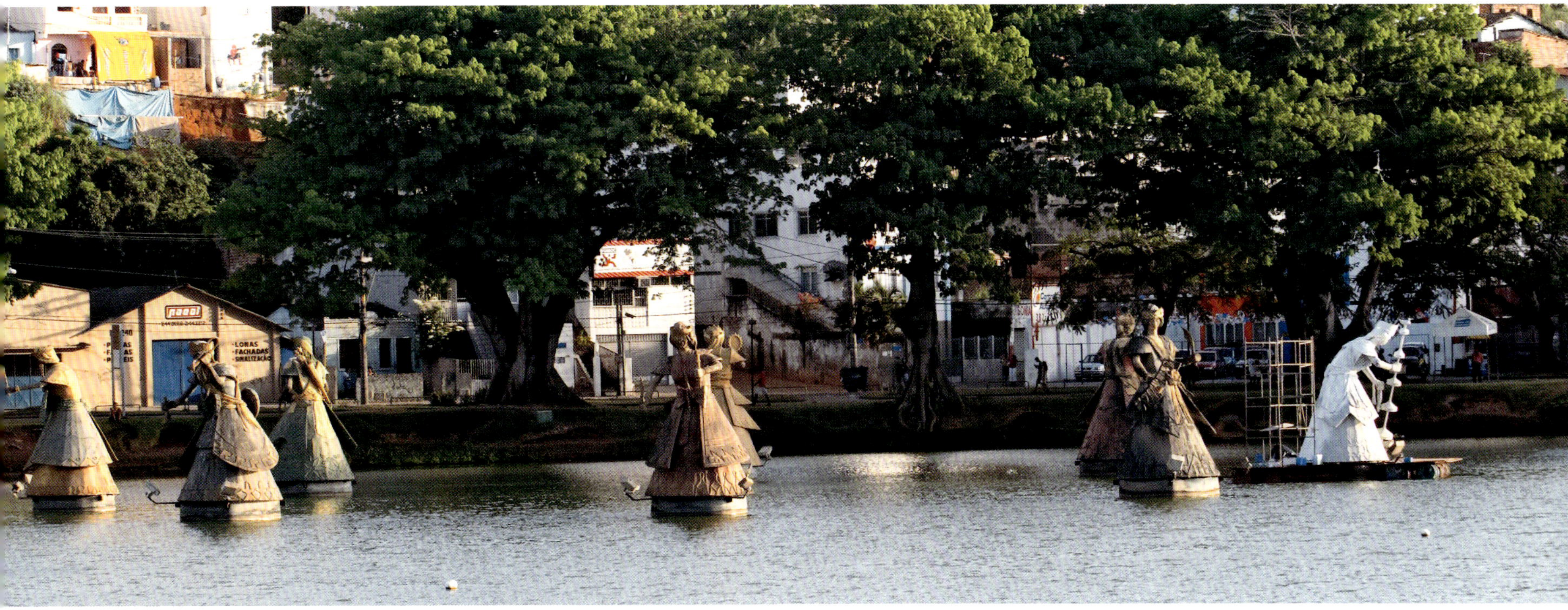

*ODÔ IYÁ!* is the salutation used to greet Iemanjá, the Afro-Brazilian divinity of the sea, mother of many *orixás* (fig. B.1). While she is worshiped as a river deity in West Africa, Iemanjá is thought to rule the ocean in Brazil. There, she is honored by millions of adherents of Candomblé, Umbanda, and Spiritism, with fishermen as her most devoted followers. Folklorist and Black vindicationist Manuel Querino (1851–1923) noted that prior to the abolition of slavery, the festival of the *mãe d'água* (mother of the waters) was held on the third Sunday of December, in front of Fort São Bartolomeu[1] in Itapagipe (a peninsula just northwest of the commercial district of Salvador), and was attended by thousands of Africans and Afro-descendants, including the *pais de santo* of several *terreiros*. It lasted for two weeks, and the offerings made included "combs, bottles of hair oil, flasks of scent, and cubits of cloth" that were placed in a large clay jar or pot and then tossed into the sea halfway across the bay, "a spot well known to sailors, especially when strong winds reign" (Querino 1955b, 127).

Today, public festivities for Iemanjá usually take place in February. They are still primarily organized by fishing communities throughout Bahia (from Itapuã on the northeast coast, near the dunes of Abaeté Lagoon and Salvador's airport, to the island of Itaparica). The most popular celebration is held in Rio Vermelho, once a remote fishing community and now a middle-class district of Salvador. Long before dawn, Candomblé followers gather at the Dique do Tororó to give offerings to Oxum on the second of February (fig. B.2). This is the feast day of Our Lady of the Lamp, the avatar of the Virgin Mary associated with the *orixá* Oxum, who is believed to have ceded her own celebration to Iemanjá. The faithful then head for the beach beside the fish-weighing station, near a statue of a mermaid. A shed full of baskets has been set up especially for the occasion. By the afternoon, those containers and many more will be brimming with flowers, bottles of lavender water, dolls, jewelry, china—anything the attendees think a lovely young goddess might desire (fig. B.3). Encouraged by spiritual leaders like Mãe Stella de Oxóssi (Maria Stella de Azevedo Santos), the preferred gifts today are biodegradable to protect the environment. Most devotees wait in line for hours to add their contributions. A flotilla of yachts and schooners sets off around 3:30 p.m. from the Marina and casts anchor offshore, setting these offerings afloat to the delight of those who watch from the shore (fig. B.4). Some people prefer to pay a boatman to row them out to sea so they can deposit their baskets themselves. This is the climax of the spiritual side of the festivity.

**B.1**
Pierre Verger (b. 1902, Paris, France; d. 1996)
*Presente á Mãe d'Água* (Present to the Mother of Waters), 1940s/1950s
Photograph
PHOTO PIERRE VERGER ©FUNDAÇÃO PIERRE VERGER

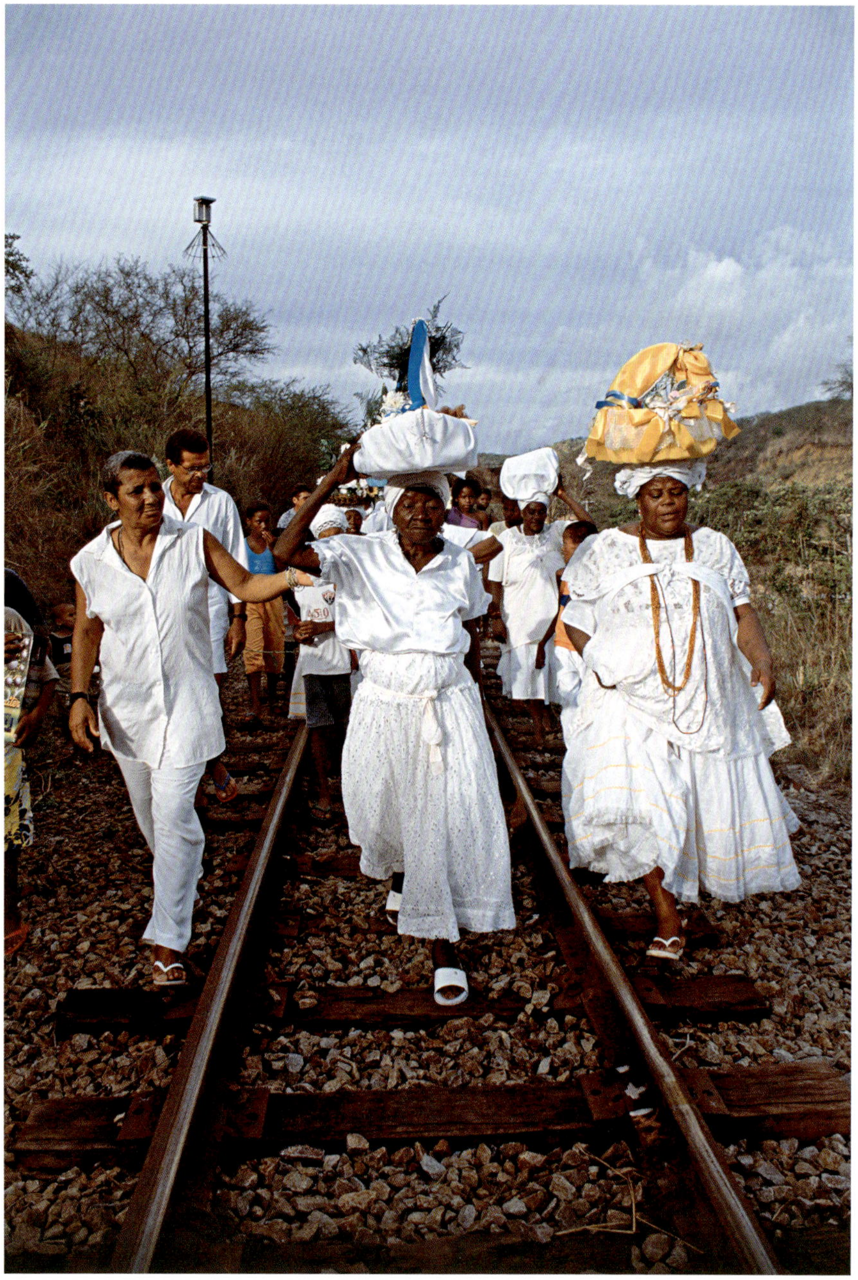

**B.3**
Adenor Gondim (b. 1950, Rui Barbosa, Bahia, Brazil)
*Presente para Iemanjá* (Present for Iemanjá), February 2, 2005
Photograph
COURTESY ADENOR GONDIM

**B.4**
Tacun Lecy (b. 1977, Salvador, Bahia, Brazil)
*Festa de Yemonjá* (Festival for Iemajá), February 2, 2014
Photograph
COURTESY TACUN LECY

**B.5**
Adenor Gondim (b. 1950, Rui Barbosa, Bahia, Brazil)
*Terreiro de Mãe Filhinha* (Temple of the High Priestess Filhinha [Narcisa Cândida Conceição]), February 2, 1990
Photograph
COURTESY ADENOR GONDIM

Over the past few years, the city government has set up stalls on the beach where visitors can be spiritually cleansed by being brushed down with leaves or showers of popcorn in stalls specially set up for use by Candomblé practitioners. Members of the *bloco afro* Filhos de Gandhy have been known to appear, as well as popular musician Carlinhos Brown and his Zárabe band, who play trumpets and wear Islamic-inspired headgear. The gathering in the street soon turns into a mini-Carnaval that continues into the night, fueled by pop-up bars and food stands.

The gift of the fishermen's association of Rio Vermelho (Colônia de Pescadores Z-01 do Rio Vermelho), which is loaded on a boat and placed in the water in the late afternoon, is always the pièce de résistance—usually a gigantic statue of their queen or associated symbols, such as a ship or fish. In 2017 their offering to Iemanjá was a huge statue of a white woman in a long blue dress, in accord with her portrayal within Spiritism and Umbanda and some Candomblé communities.[2] Although now commonly found in works by artists like Camasi Guimarães and Gil Abelha, portrayals of Iemanjá as a black woman have previously angered fishermen and sparked controversy. This is because, for many, the divinity—who was originally a river goddess in Africa—is not only thought to have expanded her purview to the ocean but to have become white, syncretized with Our Lady of the Conception, the patron saint of Brazil (fig. B.5), and with Our Lady Star of the Sea (Stella Maris). In 1997, the fishing community of Rio Vermelho rejected artist Floriano Teixeira's portrayal of a black mermaid. Teixeira died in 2010, three years before the fishermen decided to accept his gift.[3]

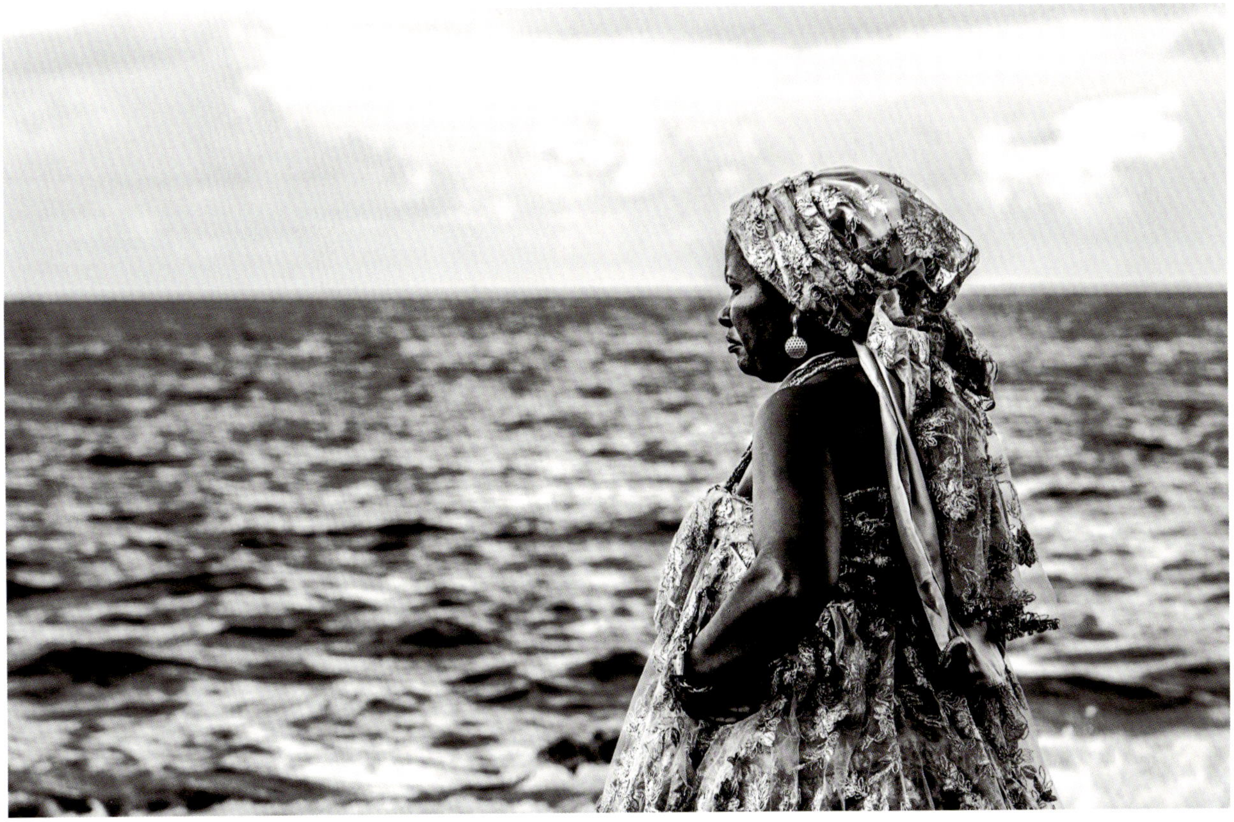

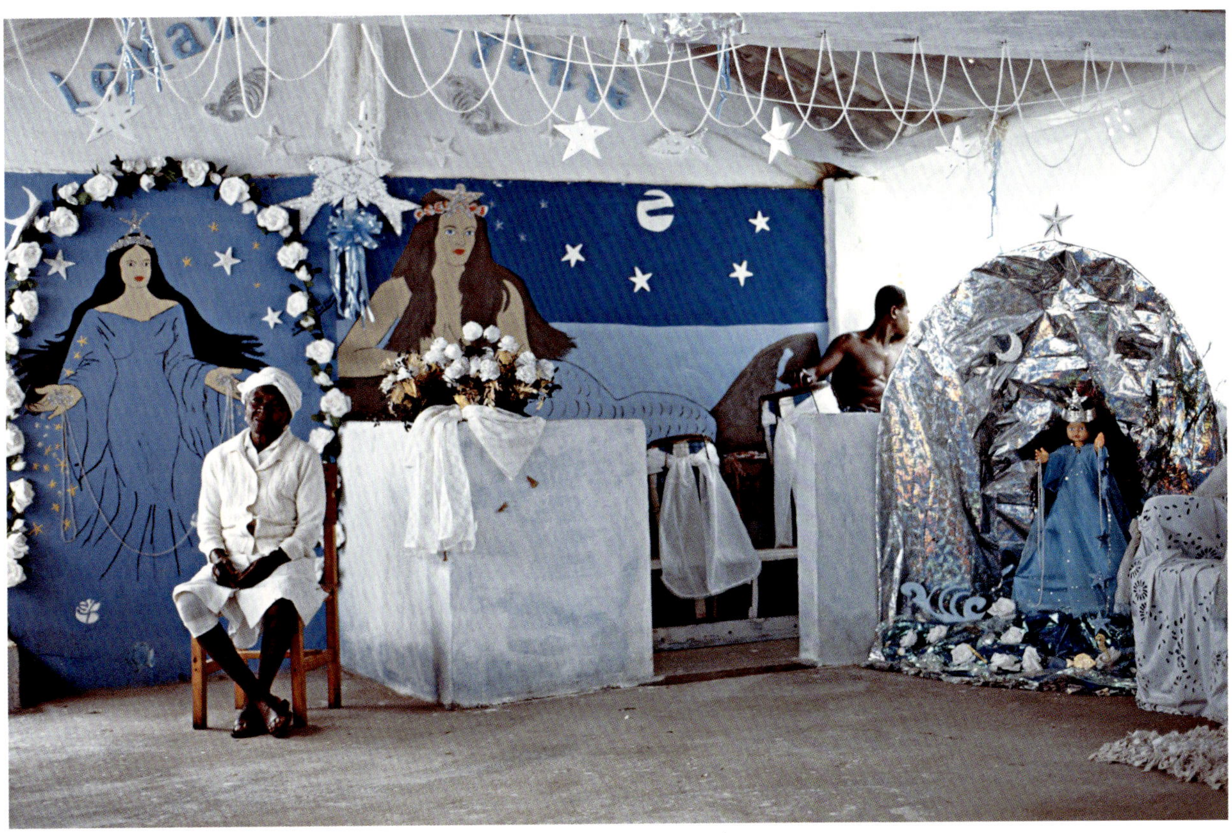

# 2 Candomblé Making the Saint, Making History, and Making Spirited Things

J. Lorand Matory

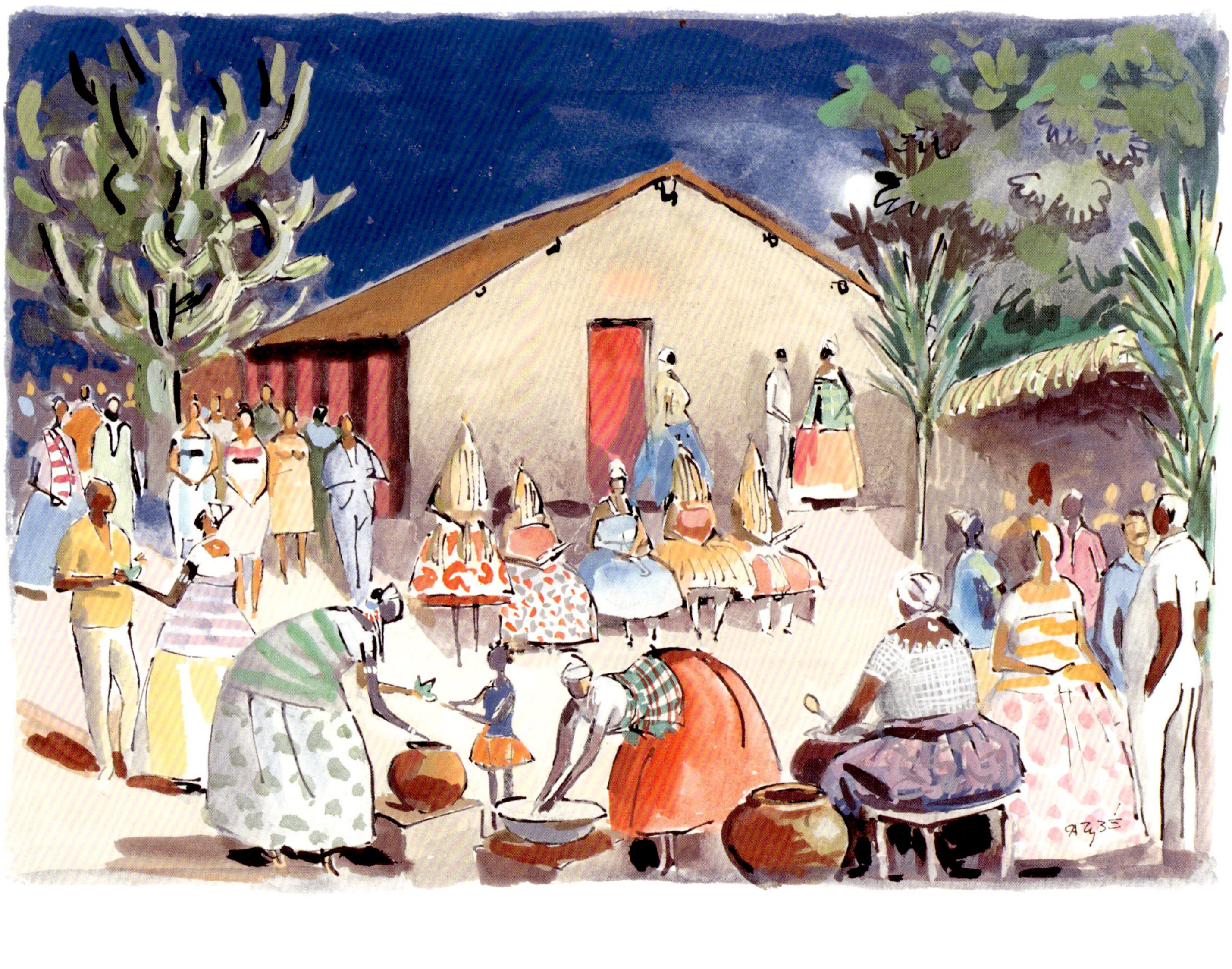

CANDOMBLÉ IS AN AFRO-BRAZILIAN RELIGION of divination, sacrifice, healing, music, dance, and spirit possession. Although it is headquartered in the coastal Brazilian state of Bahia, it has counterparts and offshoots all over urban Brazil, including religions known as Umbanda, Xangô, and Batuque. Believers attribute miraculous powers and exemplary flaws to gods known as *orixás*, *voduns*, *inquices*, and *caboclos*, depending on the Candomblé denomination. The adventures, personalities, and kinship relations of these deities are described in an extensive mythology and a body of oracular wisdom, which also serve to explain the personalities and fates of their human worshipers, as well as the worldly relations among those adherents. Through prayer, blood sacrifice, music, and lavish ceremonies of spirit possession, the gods are persuaded to intervene beneficently in the lives of worshipers and to keep their foes at bay.

The Candomblé *terreiro* (temple or house) also serves the social and economic needs of its largely urban membership, which is diverse in terms of both class and race (fig. 2.1). It is usually the primary residence of the chief priest, some of his or her lieutenants, and their wards, as well as a temporary shelter for fugitives from police persecution, domestic crises, and poverty. The temple is also often a conduit of bourgeois largesse, a source of job contacts, an employer in its own right, and a major port of call for politicians. The priests and practitioners, however—no less than the social scientists and politicians who seek to speak for them—tend to emphasize the ancientness and fixity of Candomblé and of the ritual "tradition" that both constitutes its ultimate purpose and shapes the deepest part of community life (Matory 2005).

### The African "Nations" of Candomblé

Similarities between Candomblé, on the one hand, and the spirit possession religions of the West African Yoruba, Ewe, Gen, Aja, and Fon peoples, on the other, give evidence of the long-running historical relationship between the Gulf of Guinea coast and Bahia. From the early sixteenth century until the mid-nineteenth, kidnapped Africans were transported from the Guinea coast to dig the precious minerals, till the fields, process the crops, build the cities, and manage the homes of Bahia.

The conditions of slavery in Brazil were brutal. Long after the enslaved population of the United States became self-reproducing in the early nineteenth century, the ongoing large-scale overseas slave trade to Brazil made it more profitable to work the enslaved to death than to encourage their reproduction. Consequently, from the time of their arrival in Brazil, they lived an average of seven to eight years. In urban Brazil, however, large numbers of the enslaved were *negros de ganho* (wage-earning blacks), who lived and moved about independently and simply owed their masters a fixed weekly or monthly sum. With their portion of the wages, many of the enslaved were able to purchase their own freedom and that of their families. Their relative independence allowed them to organize with fellow Africans and to build institutions that embodied African-inspired but also adaptively Brazilian methods of worship, technologies of healing, and strategies of mutual assistance.

**2.1**
Carybé (Héctor Julio Páride Bernabó, b. 1911 Lanús, Buenos Aires Province, Argentina; d. 1997)
*Olubajé de Omolú: Opô Afonjá* (Annual Festival for Omolú: Opô Afonjá Temple), undated
Ink and watercolor (gouache) on paper
83 x 63 cm (unframed)
COURTESY INSTITUTO CARYBÉ / COPYRIGHTS CONSULTORIA LTDA.

**2.2**
Johann Moritz Rugendas (b. 1802, Augsburg, Germany; d. 1858)
Illustration of African "nations"
From *Malerische Reise in Brasilien* (Paris: Engelmann & Cie, 1835)
Lithograph
49 x 39 cm
WÜRTTEMBERGISCHE LANDESBIBLIOTHEK, STUTTGART

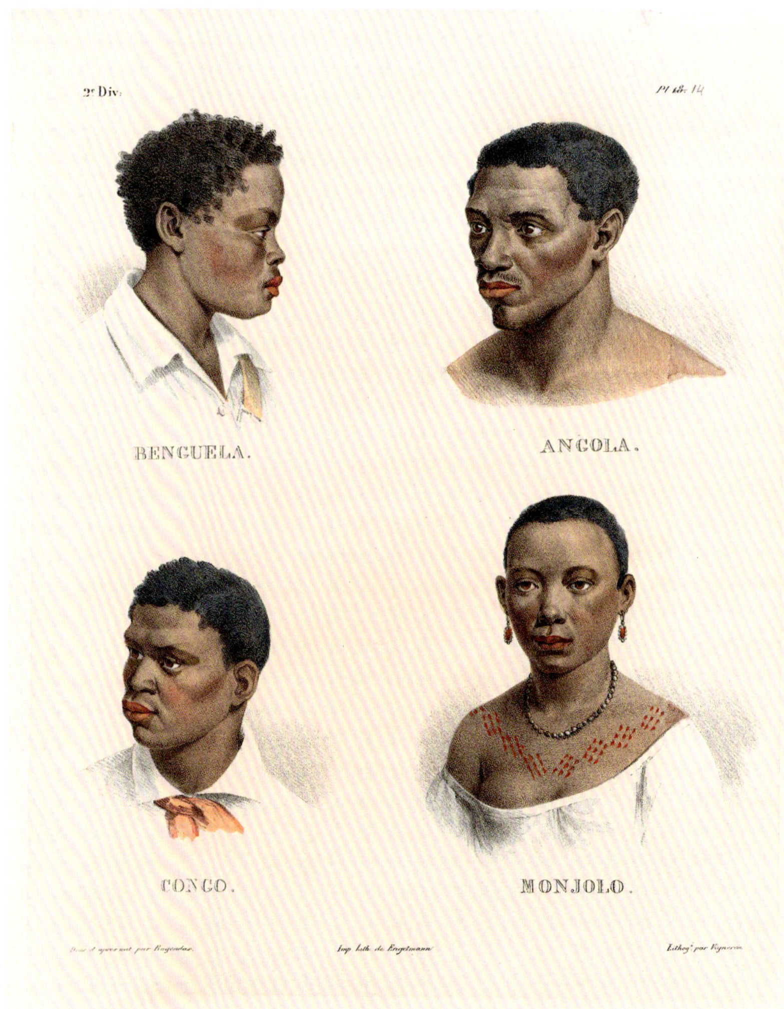

The Africans frequently organized themselves around African-inspired ethnic identities—called "nations"—that were considerably broader than the continental African identities that they encompassed. For example, in Brazil, people from linguistically related polities as diverse as Ọyọ, Ileṣa, and Ketu came to be collectively called "Nagô," corresponding to the designation given to all of them by the European slave-traders, or "Ketu" (in Portuguese "Quêto"). The speakers of the Ewe, Gen, Aja, and Fon languages came to be known collectively as "Jejes," an ethnonym apparently invented in Brazil (Matory 2005, 299–300). Various populations of west Central African origins—in what are now Congo-Brazzaville, Congo-Kinshasa, and Angola—came to be called "Congo" and "Angola" (fig. 2.2).

Indeed, Brazilian state and church authorities consciously encouraged the adoption and embrace of these identities, assuming that an ethnically divided African population would be less inclined to rebel or coordinate resistance. The Africans of Bahia and their descendants formed work crews, Roman Catholic brotherhoods and sisterhoods (see interleaf D, this volume), and Candomblé temples organized around African-inspired and European-endorsed rubrics, producing some of the most enduring, popular, and celebrated institutions in Bahian history. These temples continue to pledge allegiance to their "nations" of origin, which today constitute multiple religious denominations, the most populous of which are the Congo/Angola, the Quêto/Nagô, and the Jeje nations (Matory 2005).

#### The Live Dialogue between Brazil and the Guinea Coast

Amid the extensive exchange of practices and ideas among these nations, the Quêto/Nagô nation has been the most influential, followed by the Jeje nation, at least partly because of the frequency with which the free members of these nations traveled back and forth between Bahia and the Guinea coast—for the purposes of commerce, education, and pilgrimage—up until World War I. Indeed, from the 1830s until the early twentieth century, thousands of African- or Brazilian-born Nagôs and Jejes moved to the cities of the Guinea coast—such as Lagos, Porto-Novo, Ouidah, Agoué, Lomé, and Accra. Along with the itinerant Saro (Gulf of Guinea captives rescued from the slave trade by the British Royal Navy and educated in Freetown by English, German, and African American missionaries), "returnees" from Brazil and their counterparts from Cuba formed the early bourgeoisie of these cities and turned British colonial Lagos into the capital of the "Yoruba" identity, an amalgamation of the West African Ọyọ, Ẹgba, Ẹgbado, Ijẹbu, Ketu, and Ekiti peoples with the returnees from Freetown, Brazil, and Cuba.

In the 1890s the Lagosian Cultural Renaissance[1] not only canonized a new Yoruba identity but, in its struggle against white British racism, also actively borrowed the black nationalist ideas of black American political leaders like W. E. B. Du Bois and Booker T. Washington and Danish Virgin Islander Edward Wilmot Blyden, whose writings were serialized in the Lagosian press. The transatlantic circular migration of Afro-Brazilian priests like Otampê Ojarô, Marcos Pimentel, Marcelina of Ilê Axé Iyá Nassô Oká temple, Bamgboxê, Felisberto Sowzer, and Martiniano do Bonfim brought to Bahia sacred knowledge, religious artifacts, and ritually important commodities (such as handwoven cloth, red palm oil, and kola nuts) also establishing the superiority of African goods and West African bloodlines. Influenced by the Lagosian Cultural Renaissance, these travelers also introduced black cultural nationalism and black-nationalist political strategies into the heart of Bahian Candomblé. Martiniano's early twentieth-century collaboration with the founder of Bahia's august Ilê Axé Opô Afonjá temple, Mãe Aninha (Eugênia Anna Santos), established the explicit principle of black racial dignity that remains at the heart of Candomblé. Moreover, equipped with the cultural nationalist publications of the Lagosian Cultural Renaissance, as well as their personal literacy and their fluency in English, such transatlantic Afro-Brazilian travelers were living proof of the exceptional dignity of the Yoruba-affiliated Quêto/Nagô nation in particular. They made that dignity evident to the founder of Afro-Brazilian studies, Raimundo Nina Rodrigues, and, through his research, to the founder of Afro-Cuban studies, as well—Fernando Ortiz.

#### The *Orixás*

Despite the richness of the Jeje and Congo/Angola contributions to Candomblé and to African-diaspora civilization in general, the Yoruba-affiliated nations, such as the Quêto/Nagôs of Brazil and the Lucumís of Cuba, enjoyed the greatest prestige and exemption from police persecution. In Brazil, their Yoruba-inspired pantheon has become, as culture critic Antônio Risério put it, the lingua franca of all the nations of Candomblé. In order to make itself understood by outsiders, each nation must explain its gods as its own version of a Quêto/Nagô *orixá*, who is assumed to be familiar to most Bahians (Matory 2005).

There are more than twenty widely known *orixás*, each with up to twenty-one different avatars (see also Omari 1984; Verger 1981). I will identify here some of those most frequently encountered and their iconography, with the caveat that their color and numerical symbolism varies somewhat from nation to nation and that the Roman Catholic saints with which they are correlated, or "syncretized," may vary from one Brazilian region and or devotee to another.

Exu (also Exú) is the lord of phallic virility, commander of the crossroads, and the gatekeeper of all communications between humans and gods (fig. 2.3a). His sacred number is seven, and he is most often invoked with the color combination of red and black. In any ceremony, he must be propitiated first. Worshipers honor him with the salutation "Laroiê!" Most Candomblé devotees dispute the association between him and the Christian devil.

Oxalá is the lord of wisdom, age, purity, peace, and procreation (fig. 2.3b). He is widely regarded as the father of all of the other gods. The older of his two main avatars is Oxalufã, an arthritic elder whose sacred color is pure white and whose sacred numbers are ten and sixteen. His emblematic symbol is the *paxorô*, or *opaxorô*, a tall metal cane with up to eight vertically arrayed and pendant-adorned umbrellas. Doubled over as he rounds the festival space, he shakes the *opaxorô*, driving away malign forces and filling the air with the light tinkling of its pendants. The image of one of Oxalá's emblematic animals, the white dove, sits at the top. The younger of these two main avatars is Oxaguiã, a warrior whose sacred number is eight and whose sacred color combination is light blue and white. When he possesses his devotee, he wears a cuirass and carries a sword, a pestle, and a shield, all of silver-colored metal.

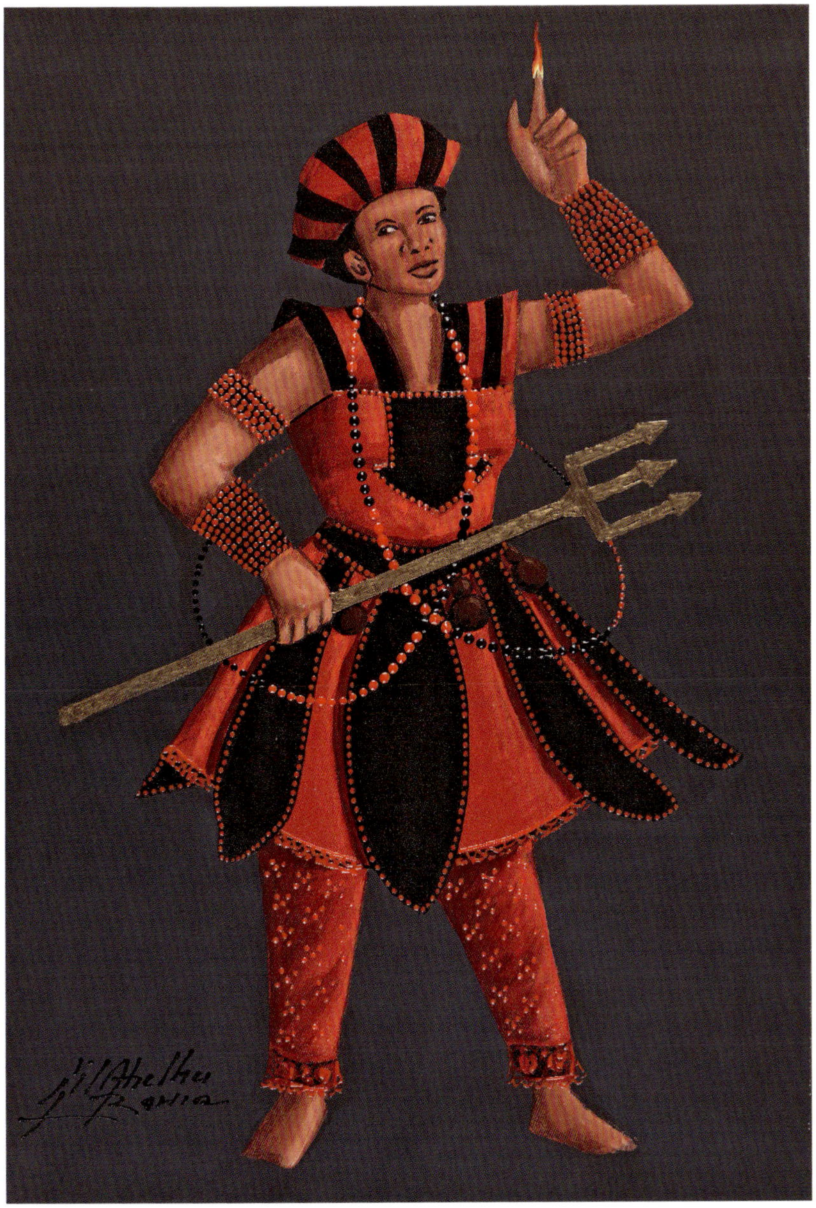

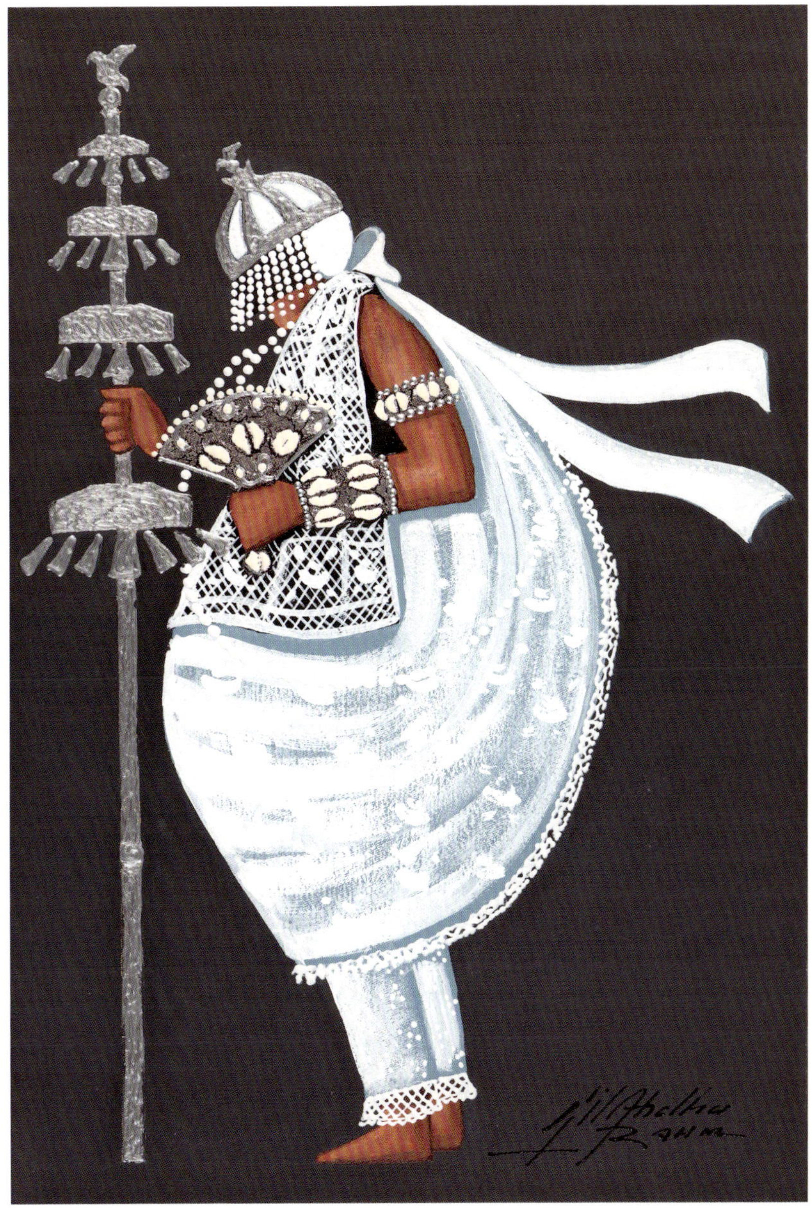

**2.3a-l**
Gil Abelha (Gildásio Feliciano Costa, b. 1955, Salvador, Bahia, Brazil; d. 2006)
*Orixá* Series
Acrylic on wood
60 x 40 cm
FOWLER MUSEUM AT UCLA; GIFT OF DR. JULIO CASOY

A. Exú, X2015.4.109
B. Oxalá in his avatar as Oxalufã, X2015.4.89

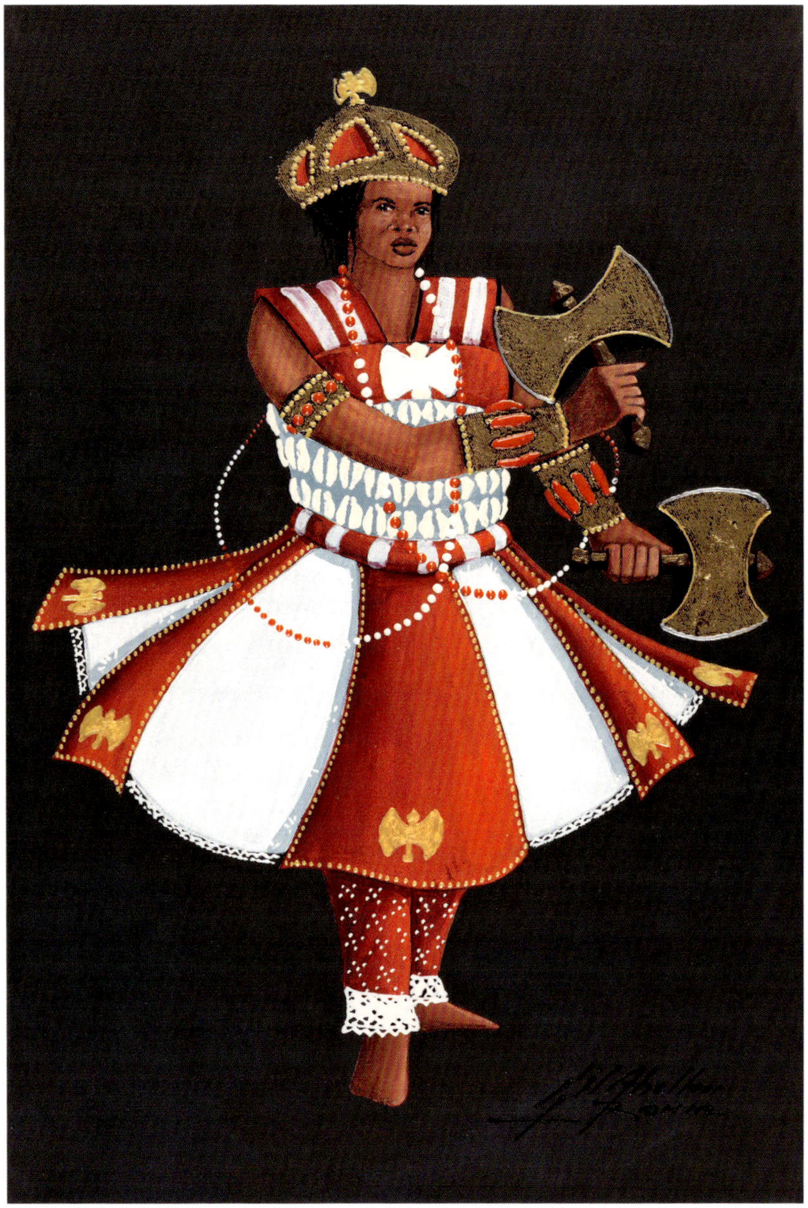

C. Xangô, X2015.4.105

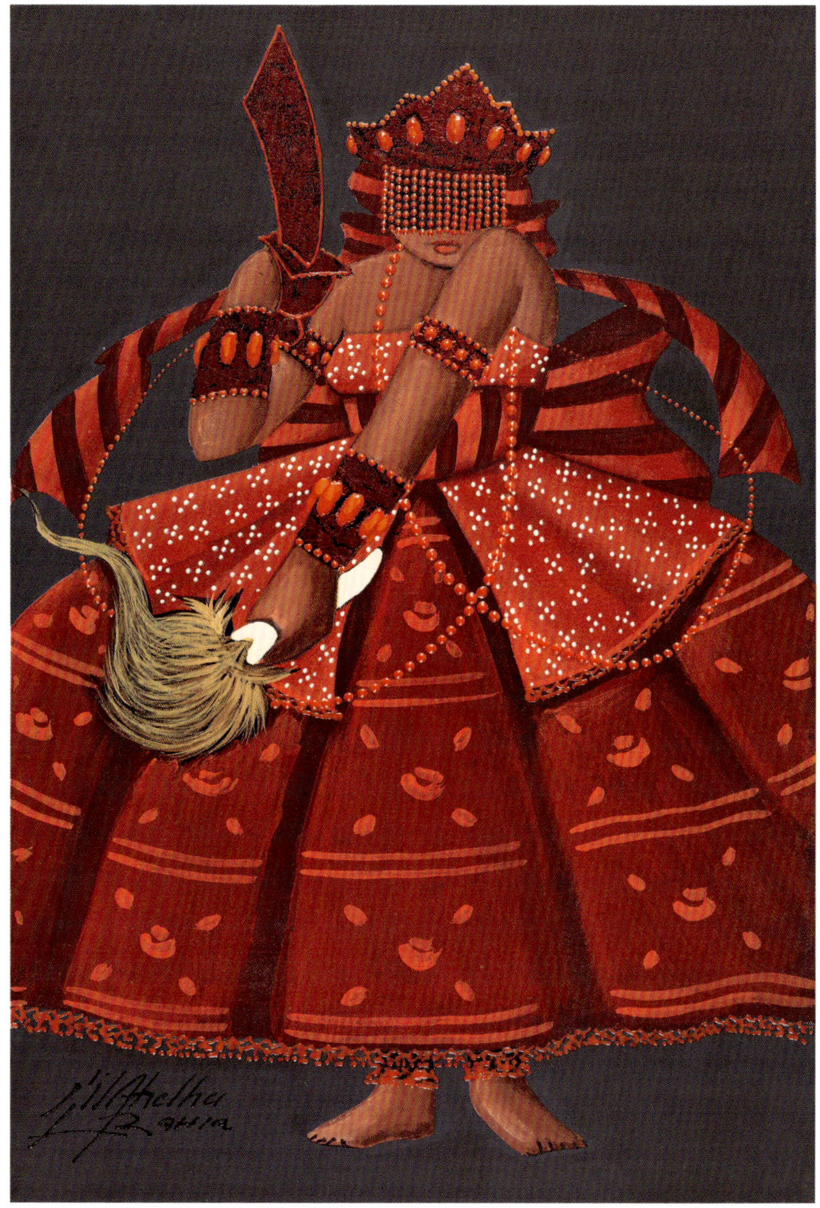

D. Iansã, X2015.4.98

Candomblé devotees debate the precise relationship between the *orixás* and the saints of the Roman Catholic Church. Some devotees regard these gods and the saints as versions of the same reality, while others believe that the saints were merely temporary camouflage for the gods, displayed in order to evade prohibitions against African-inspired religion. Some people say both, depending on the moment. By all of these logics, Oxalá is closely associated with Jesus Christ and particularly with Our Lord of the Good Death, whose church is the site of one of Candomblé's largest annual events, the Lavagem do Bonfim (Washing of the Church of Our Lord of the Good Death; see interleaf C, this volume). In many cases, however, the saint-*orixá* correlations are varied: different worshipers and people in different regions draw different correlations. Oxalá's salutation is "Epa Babá!"

Xangô is the lord of fire and lightning, as well as justice (fig. 2.3c). He is a born ruler and epicurean. His sacred number is twelve. His emblematic color combination is red, ochre, and white. His defining implement is the double axe, or *oxê*. He is closely identified with the ram and is syncretized with Saint Peter, Saint Jerome, and John the Baptist. His salutation is "Kaô Kabiesilé!" Xangô is regarded as the husband of three wives: Iansã (the goddess of wind and storm, whose numbers are four and nine and whose foremost sacred color is red ochre; fig. 2.3d); Oxum (the goddess of fresh water, whose sacred numbers are five, eight, and sixteen and whose sacred colors are yellow and gold; fig. 2.3e); and Obá (another freshwater goddess, whose color is red ochre and whose numbers are four and nine; fig. 2.3f). When they dance in the body of a possession priestess or priest, Iansã carries a sword and a fly whisk, Oxum carries a sword and a fan/mirror, and Obá carries a sword and a small shield. In addition, Obá normally dances with her hand covering her ear, in commemoration of a self-inflicted injury. As the third and newest wife of Xangô, she asked her co-wife Oxum about their husband's preferred foods. Manipulatively, Oxum told her that his favorite food is human-ear soup. Unable to find any human ears for sale in the market and overly anxious to please her husband, she severed her own ear and served it to him in a soup. Seeing the disgusted look on his face when she served it, she realized she had been tricked. So she covered her ear and ran away. Iansá is greeted with "Repa Rei Oiá!"; Oxum with "Ora Ieiê ô!"; and Obá with "Obá Xirê!"

Ogum is the god of war and iron (fig. 2.3g). His sacred number is three, and his sacred color in the Quêto/Nagô nation, green. In the Angola nation, it is blue. He is hard working and joyless. His salutation is "Ogunhê!" He is associated with Saint Anthony. His brother Oxóssi is the charming and adventurous hunter god (fig. 2.3h). In the Quêto/Nagô nation, his emblematic color is turquoise, while, in the Angola nation, it is green. Five is his a sacred number. When manifest in his possession priestess or priest, he carries a hunter's pouch, a fly whisk, and a combined bow and arrow. To honor him, worshipers shout, "Ôquê Arô!"

Iemanjá is the brooding, motherly goddess of the sea (fig. 2.3i). Her sacred number is nine, and her colors are crystal clear, transparent light blue and transparent green. She, too, carries a fan. Her salutation is "Odô Iá!" She is syncretized with the apparition of the Virgin Mary known as Our Lady of the Conception of the Beach.

Omolu (Omolú) is the somber lord of skin diseases and other forms of pestilence, which he can vengefully spread or lovingly heal (fig. 2.3j). His color combination is black and white or red, black, and white. His possession priest or priestess carries a stylized and decorated African-style broom made from the ribs of the leaves of the oil palm. It is called a *xaxará*. To shield his scarred body from the gaze of others, he wears a suit of shredded raffia-palm leaves. "Atotô!" is his honorific salutation. He is associated with Saint Roch and Saint Lazarus.

As the son of Oxóssi and Oxum, the god Logunedé wears a combination of turquoise for his father with clear yellow and/or gold for his mother, and he carries both the combined bow and arrow of his father and the fan of his mother (fig. 2.3k). His emblematic number is five. In character, he is delicate, refined, and discerning. Over the course of the year, he also vacillates between male and female. His salutation is "Logum!" He is associated with Saint Michael.

Ossaim is the one-legged lord of herbs, whose color is leaf green with touches of red ochre and whose sacred number is four (fig. 2.3l). Ossaim is indispensable to Candomblé because virtually every ritual operation requires the use of leaves. Each god owns specific species of leaves, which embody that god's powers, or *axé*, such that leaf infusions can cleanse objects and people of malign influences or transfer these powers to the objects and people who are bathed in them.

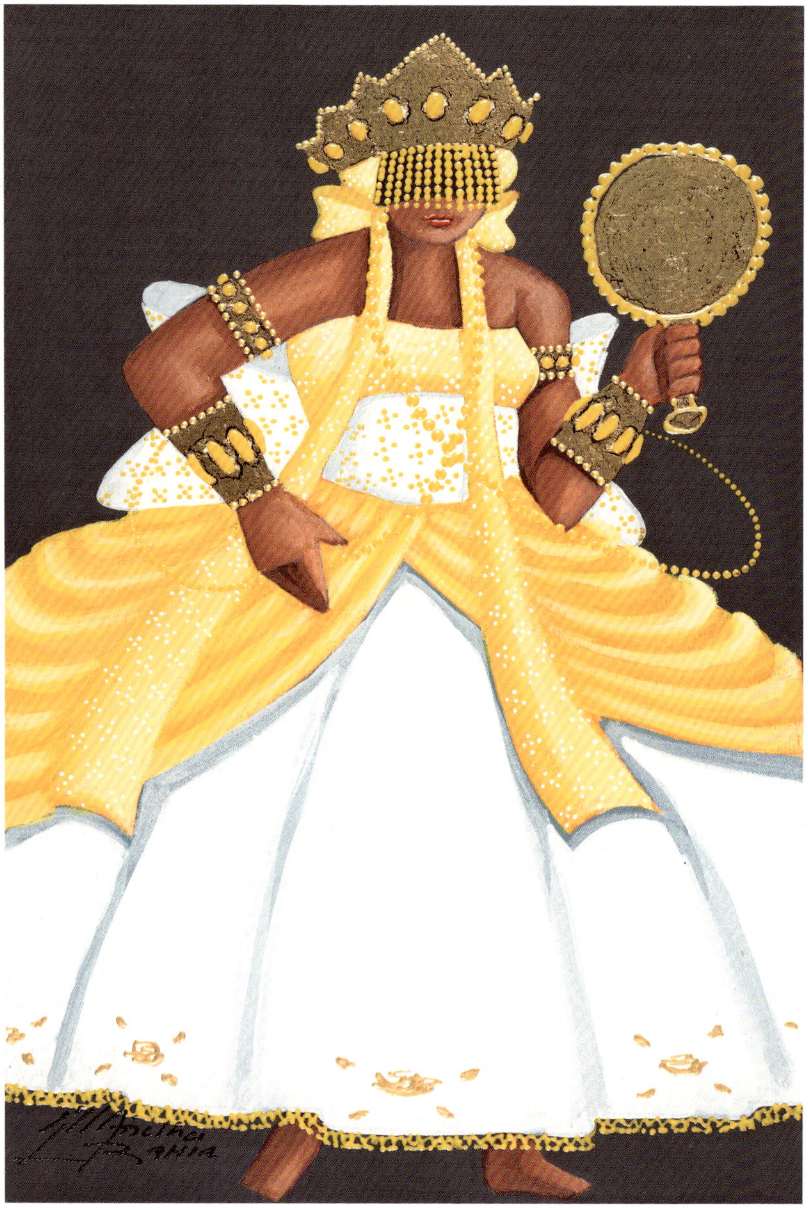

E. Oxum, X2015.4.90

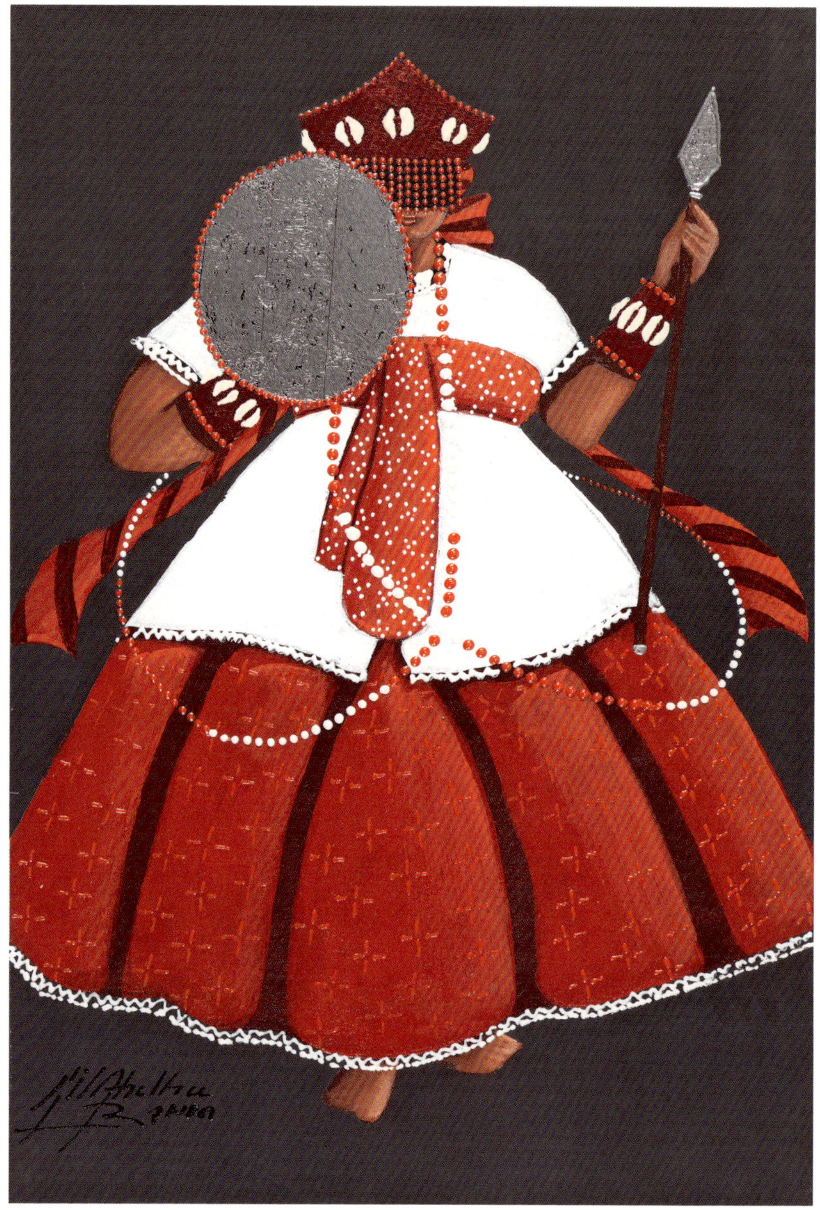

F. Obá, X2015.4.110

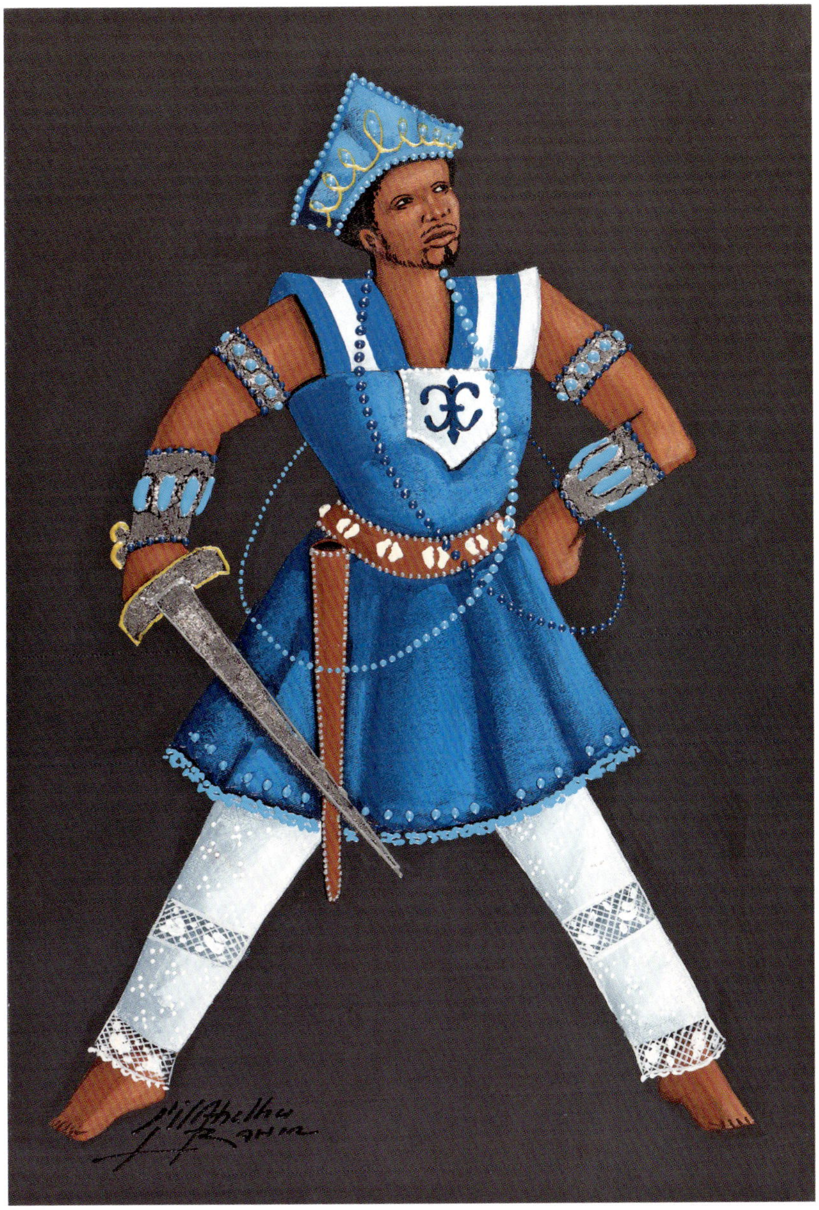

G. Ogum, X2015.4.107

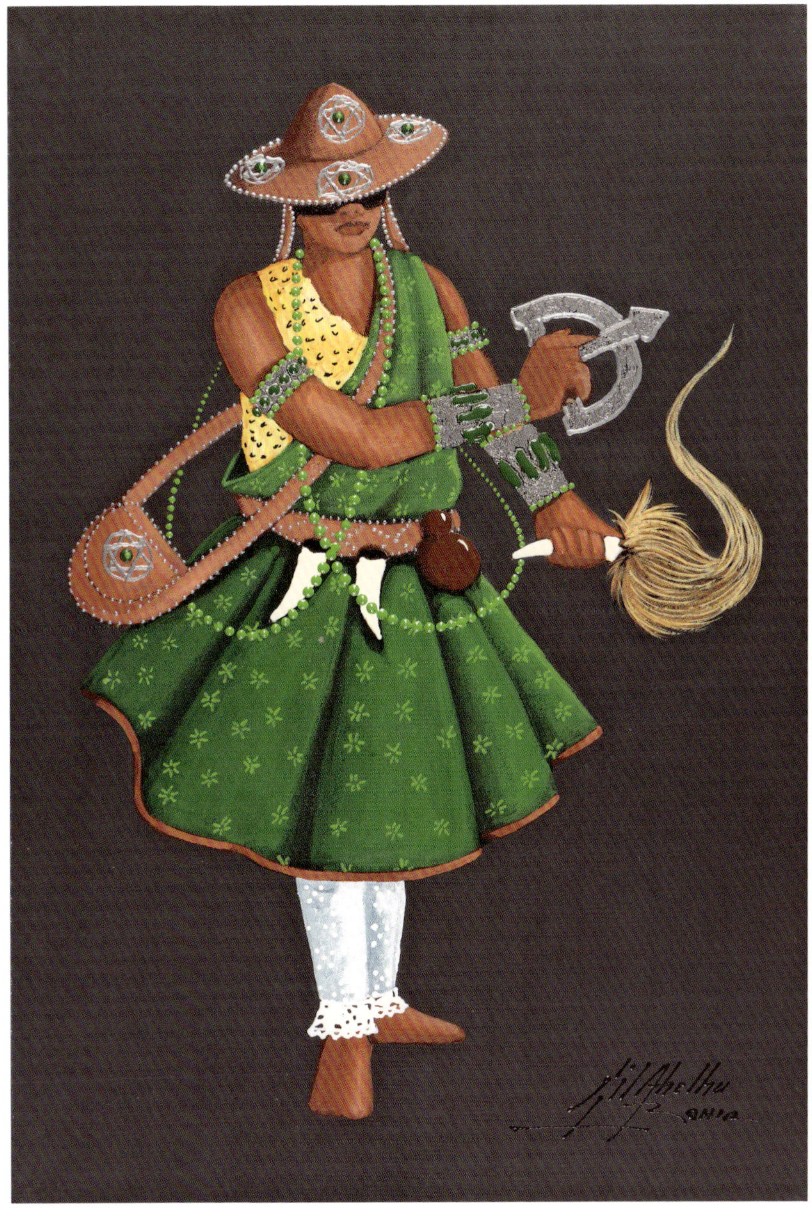

H. Oxóssi, X2015.4.91

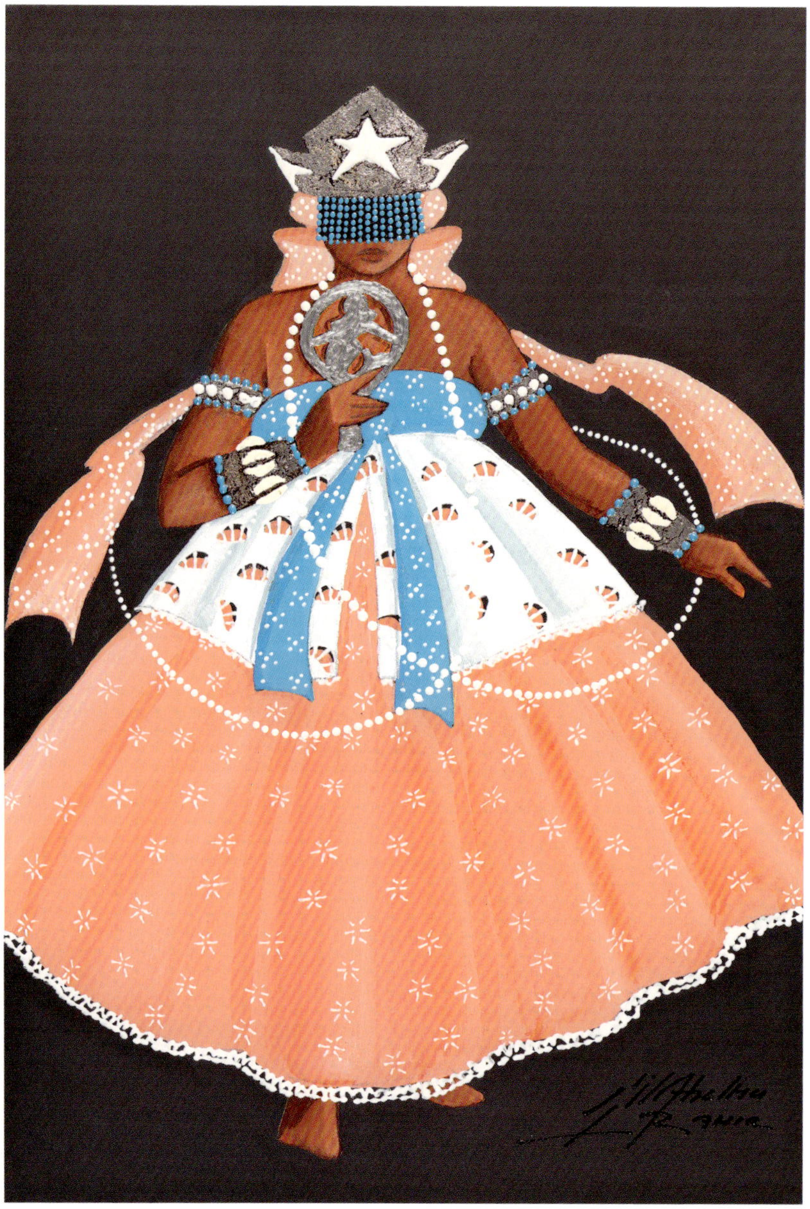

I. Iemanjá, X2015.4.103

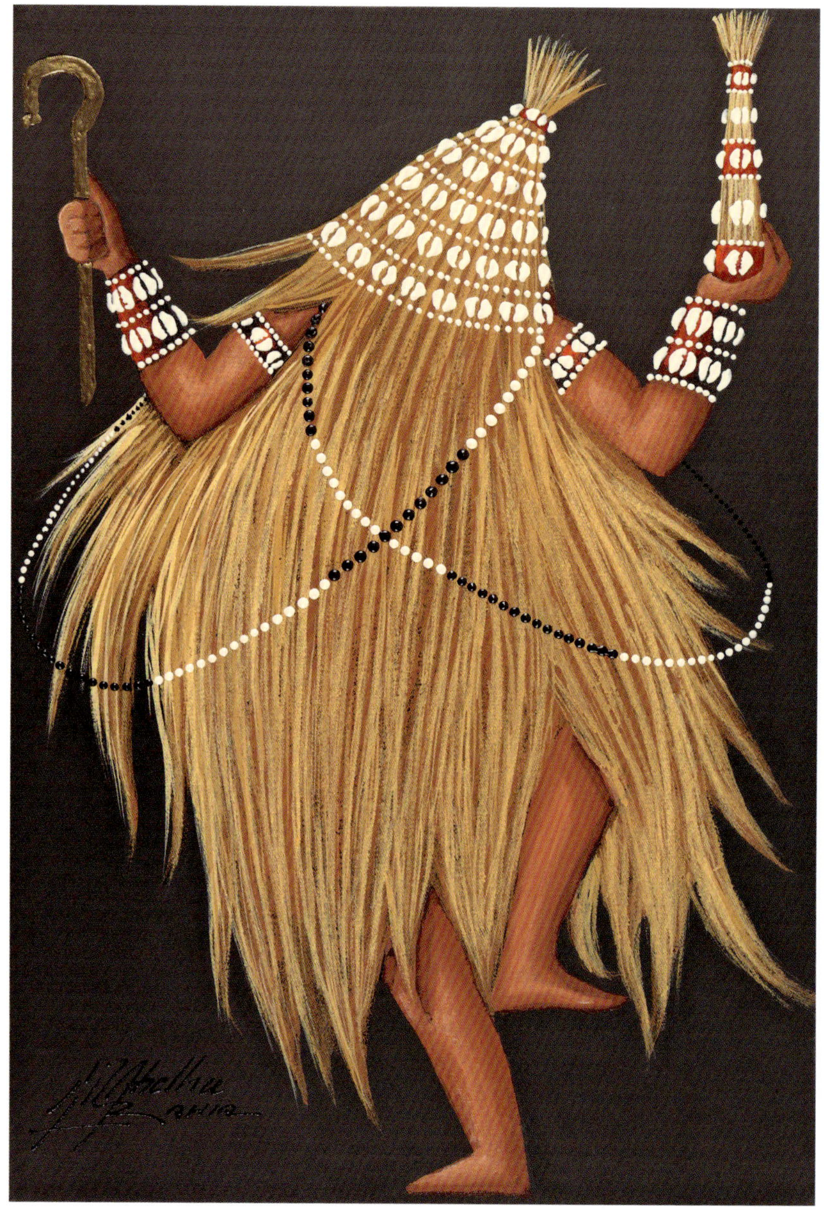

J. Omolú, X2015.4.101

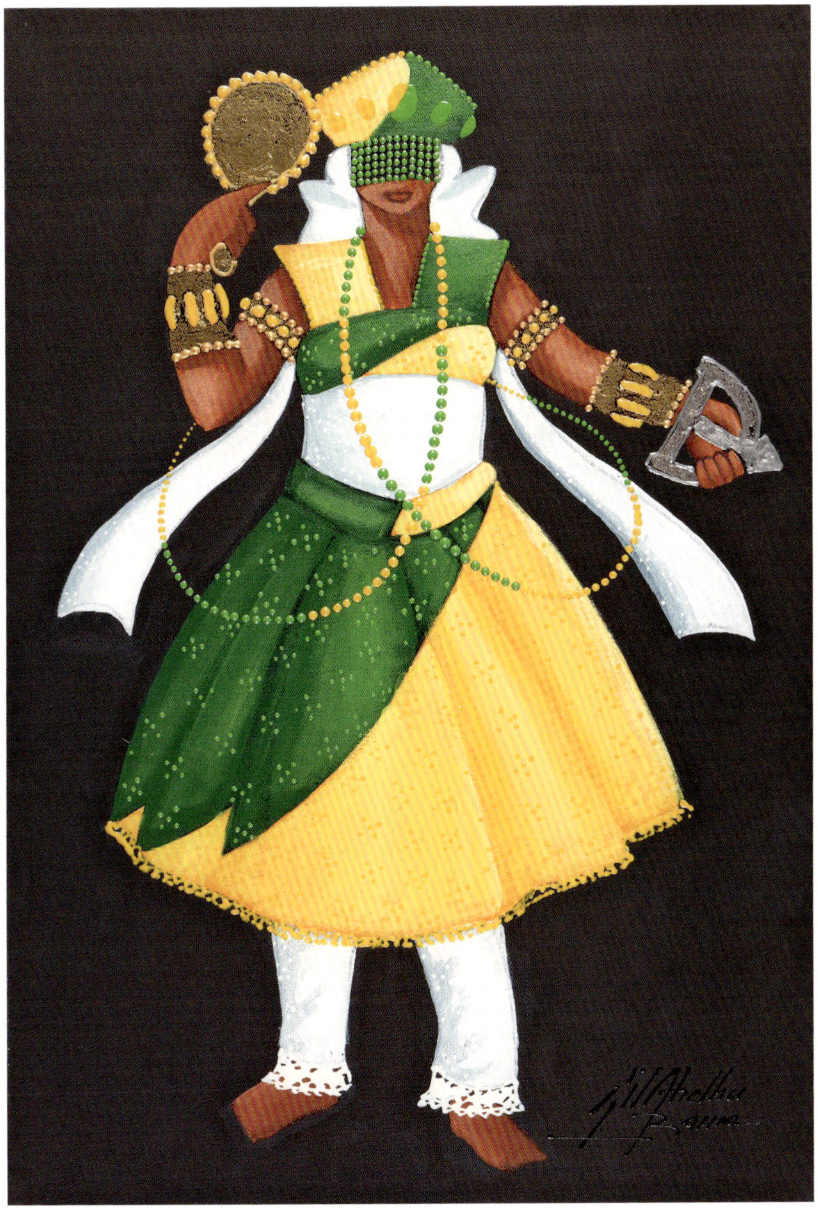

K. Logunedé, X2015.4.108

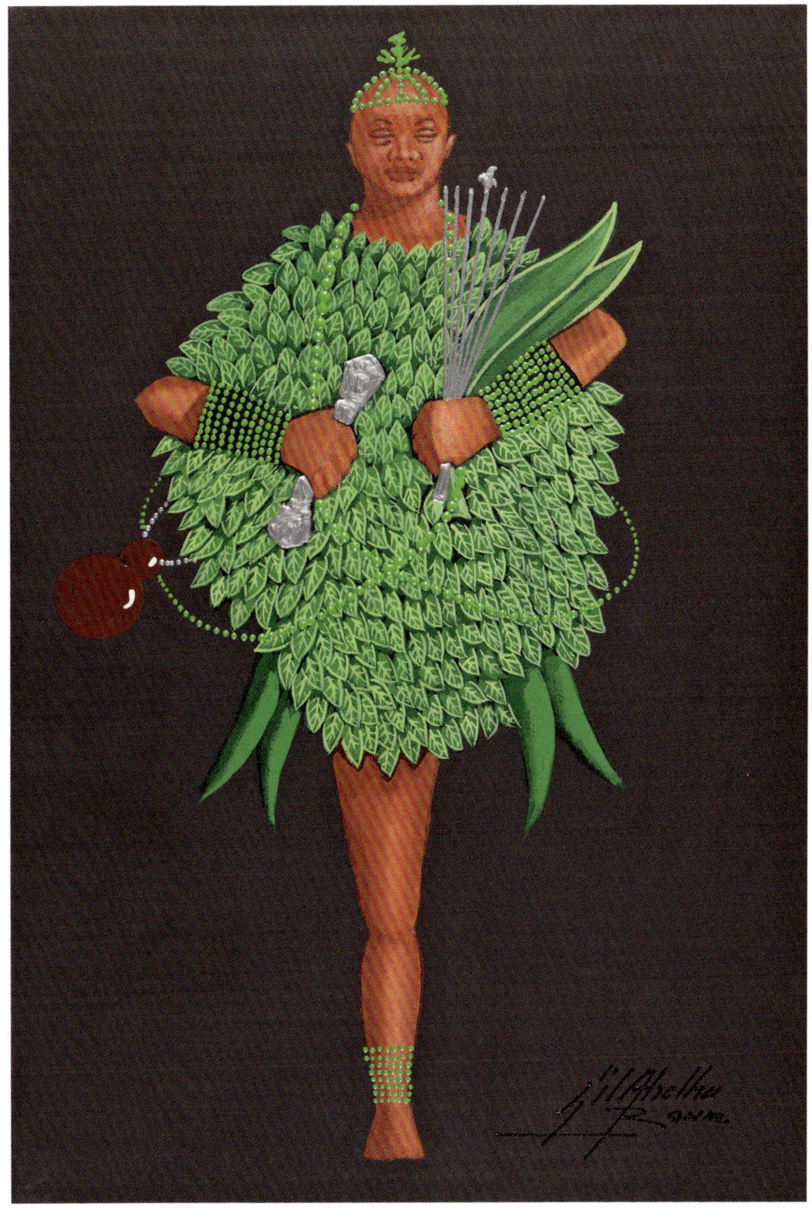

L. Ossaim, X2015.4.102

### Candomblé as a Ritual Technology of Self-Making

Like astrology, Candomblé entails a widely discussed personality theory. Most Bahians believe that each person is born under the protection and preeminent influence of one or another *orixá* and that one's appearance and personality reflect those of the god. Expert priests are nonetheless aware that this reflection is often oblique. The archetypal character of one's governing *orixá* may be evident in one's personality, or it may correspond to an aspect of one's personal character that one is struggling against or an aspect with which one must develop a better working relationship.

Indeed, Candomblé is not so much a set of lessons about good and evil as a technology for the management of the multiple personified social and natural forces that constitute the self. Candomblé priests regard any given human body as not only a biological entity subject to natural health and illness but also the vessel of multiple invisible beings and forces that spiritually affect the person's health, well-being, and good fortune. Each of those beings links one's experience to a network of animals, plants, geographical and meteorological phenomena, colors, numbers, possession priests, and altars that make up the god.

If a devotee has the gift of receptivity, the god will periodically displace her or his consciousness and fully "mount," "ride," or "manifest" in the person's body. Such a devotee will become a possession priest—that is, a "horse" or *adôxu*—of the god. Most, but not all, of the people with this gift are women or homosexual men. Heterosexual men very seldom possess this gift, but there are exceptions. In these cases, however, the men must also master the skills of cooking, cleaning, couture, decoration, nurturance, and graceful self-display, as these are all indispensable to the success of a temple and its leader. As in West African Yoruba religion, however, women are considered the paradigmatic vessels of the gods.

Male priests—including possession priests—have long been common in Candomblé, as they have been in Yorubaland and in the related religions of Haitian Vodou and Cuban Santería/Ocha. In Bahia, men formed the majority of chief priests before the 1930s. Something changed in Bahia during the 1940s, however, soon after an anthropologist from the United States, Ruth Landes, published an article (1940) and a widely read book (1947) intent on constructing Candomblé as proof that some cultures are matriarchal and that, as a result, there is nothing uniquely natural or inevitable about patriarchy in the United States. Candomblé has always included highly respected chief priestesses, as well as a class of high-ranking non-possession priestesses known as *ekédis*. As I have argued in a number of venues, however, the overwhelming predominance and prestige of chief priestesses in present-day Candomblé is not an inheritance from Africa; nor does it date from the nineteenth-century Brazilian roots of Candomblé. It is instead an artifact of the selectiveness of state and bourgeois sponsorship since the 1940s. In response to Brazilian embarrassment about Landes's derogatory and pathologizing account of the male "homosexual" presence in Candomblé, the patterns of financial and political patronage shifted radically in favor of the priestesses (see Matory 2005; [1994] 2005; 2003; 1988). Today, the structures of opportunity for men and women in Candomblé have diverged sharply. The greatest state largesse has been reserved for the temples headed by females, such as Casa Branca, Gantois, and Ilê Axé Opô Afonjá. Entrepreneurialism has nonetheless brought great wealth and/or reputation to a number of male-led temples, such as Pai Aizinho's Pilão de Prata, Pai Amilton's Terreiro Vodunzô, Pai Balbino's Ilê Axé Opô Aganjú, and Ilê Axipá, the temple to the ancestral spirits made famous by the late priest Didi dos Santos (Deoscórides Maximiliano dos Santos).

Despite the omnipresence of women's cookware in the mimetic insertion and the removal of spiritual forces, Candomblé altars, altar rooms, and sacred festival halls, temples are also filled with vertical metal staffs honoring the male gods—such as Exu, Ogum, and Oxóssi—and made with aesthetic finesse by heterosexual men, who, in their downtown ateliers, also make most of the crowns and the fan/mirrors for the goddesses. Within the Candomblé temple grounds, typically heterosexual non-possession priests, known as *ogãs*, are also responsible for most of the animal sacrifices and for the care of the spirits of the dead.

Candomblé is historically neither a matriarchy nor a patriarchy but a world in which there is a role assignment for each person in a heterogeneous array of classes, races, and gender types—including not only roles normatively assumed by homosexual men and heterosexual men but also the divergent rights and responsibilities assigned to: (1) men governed by goddesses, (2) women governed by goddesses, (3) men governed by male gods, and (4) women governed by male gods. This complex division of labor has, perhaps, been one of the keys to Candomblé's success and longevity.

Most people attend public Candomblé festivals for fun. They are beautiful and entertaining performances of drumming, singing, dancing, and mysterious ritual. Many attend in the hope that a prayer to the gods who "descend" and dance during the festival will enhance their fortunes. When the faithful need general guidance or are troubled by misfortunes that resist natural and material solutions, they seek a consultation with a priestess or a priest, who tosses sixteen consecrated cowry shells (*merindilogum*) in order to discern the cause of the problem (fig. 2.4). The number of cowry shells that fall with the natural mouth up corresponds to the god governing the supplicant's concern and also suggests the nature of the solution. If the issue is deemed natural, the supplicant may be sent to a physician or mental health worker, or she may be given practical advice about possible solutions. If the problem is deemed spiritual, the priestess or priest will likely perform a ritual intent on correcting it. Some spiritual difficulties result from the malevolence of enemies, especially jealous people who have bribed an Exu to cause harm. Some harm comes from the malign spiritual "influences," "heat," and stray spiritual beings that one has accidentally picked up on the street. Other harm comes from the misguided efforts of dead loved ones to intervene in one's life: relative to ours, their world is upside-down, so their efforts to help us actually do harm. In addition, sometimes, as a way of calling us to serve them, the gods themselves cause us harm or open the path for other beings to do so.

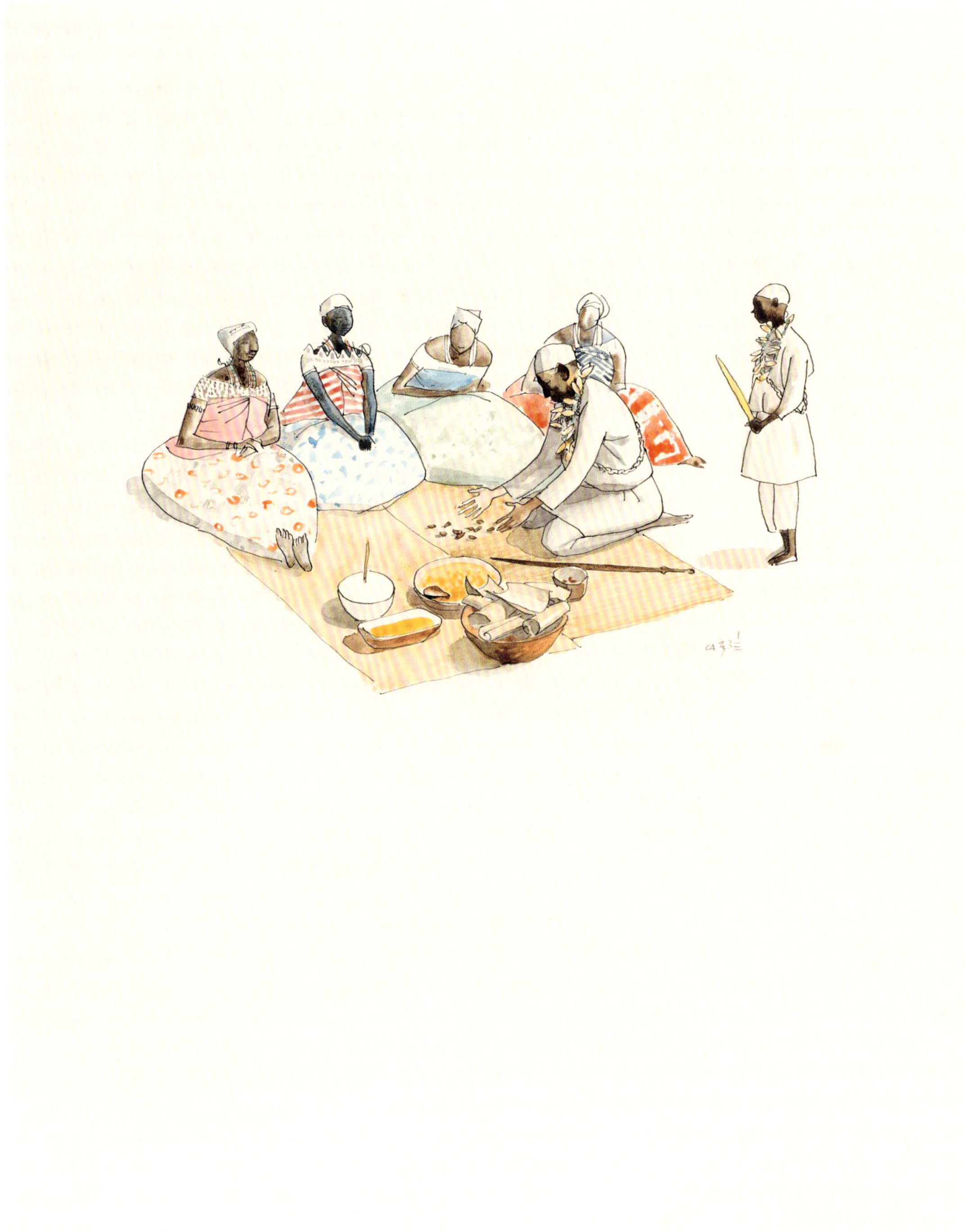

**2.4**
Carybé (Héctor Julio Páride Bernabó, b. 1911 Lanús, *Buenos Aires Province, Argentina; d. 1997)*
*Festa de Ifá: Olga do Alaketu* (Festival of Ifá: Olga do Alaketu), undated
Ink and watercolor (gouache) on paper
83 x 63 cm

The priest's first course of ritual action is usually baths or expiatory rituals (*ebós*) intent on cooling a person down and removing malign influences and beings from the supplicant's body or environment. During an *ebó*, various food substances, objects, and an animal are wiped over the supplicant's body to absorb those malign influences and beings. These absorbent substances and objects are destroyed and the animal killed. The priest then deposits the remains in a vessel, which is rushed out of the temple and deposited in a space far away from the supplicant, who must avoid that space for a time, lest the malign influences and beings that have been removed re-enter or re-attach themselves to his or her body. If the supplicant's problems are actually a calling from a god, other sorts of *ebós* can be performed as temporary stopgaps in order to relieve the symptoms. If such a supplicant wants permanent relief, however, she or he will ultimately have to undergo initiation and serve the god for the rest of her or his life.

During the initiation, herbal baths, the application of chewed kola nuts and bitter kola to the body, and animal sacrifices cleanse the body of the initiand, or *iaô*—a term cognate with the Yoruba term for "bride" (*iyàwó*) but which Candomblé devotees translate as either "bride" or "child." These operations also strengthen the *iaô's* body and turn her or him into a "blood" relative of the sacred family that is the temple community. The filling of several vessels with consecrated stones, cowry shells, and other objects specifically emblematic of each god governing the person's life mime the creation and the deposition of that god in the head or body of the initiand. A unique version of the god governing the initiand's head is created and "seated" in his or her body, alongside two or more other gods who serve as the tutelary god's auxiliaries. The series of initiation rituals—which is called the "making of the saint, or the god" (*fazer o santo*)—is much like a marriage, binding the initiate in a reciprocal relationship of mutual empowerment with a set of gods who thus become part of the initiate's very essence.

Outside the ritual context, the vessels used in initiation and in the tandem making of the gods are reserved for use chiefly by women in the preparation or serving of food. The most common of these are soup tureens for the goddesses and earthenware bowls called *alguidares* for the gods. Even the jugs of water favored by the gods reflect their gender. The goddesses prefer jugs with handles that resemble the arms of a woman standing akimbo, while the gods prefer jugs without handles. One priest told me that the lack of handles makes these jugs evocative of the male erection.

A whole range of other commercial products is necessary for initiation in and for the practice of Candomblé—including red palm oil (*epo pupa*), cowry shells (*búzios*), kola nuts (*obi*), bitter kola (*orobô*), river lime (*efum*), indigo (*waji*), raffia (*palha da costa*), African black soap (*ossé dudu*), African wild buffalo horns, water pots, handwoven African cloth (*pano da costa*), lace (*richelieu*), farm animals, razors and knives, decorative metalwork, and beads from Africa, Europe, and China. Many of these products are necessarily or ideally imported, with the result that in the nineteenth and early twentieth centuries, several Afro-Bahian men, some of them priests, made their fortunes through transatlantic commerce in these goods, and a number of Bahian priestesses found success through the retail sale of these items.

Candomblé initiation rituals, and the years of ritual devotion that follow, bind the person to an extensive and, in some cases, circum-Atlantic liturgical community structured around mutual assistance, physical healing, and spiritual succor. Yet, like all cosmologies and communities, Candomblé also structures ambitions, rivalries, hierarchies, and anxieties.

**Candomblé as an Art and a Technology of Community Building**

If there is one key term that encapsulates the logic of self and community in Candomblé, it is *axé*, which refers to the power and authority embodied in human agents, animals, and inanimate objects. It can also, however, mean "amen" or "let it be so." In general, it denotes the "life force" that is inherent in all things and creatures. *Axé* is concentrated and transferable in the form of leaf infusions and, most intensely, animal blood.

This blood is generated through a sacred process quite different from the carnage and cruelty practiced in slaughterhouses in the United States. In Candomblé, the priests bathe and consecrate the chicken, duck, guinea fowl, tortoise, goat, or ram with collective song and prayer before it is exsanguinated over the altar with further songs and prayer. No unhealthy animal is pushed or dragged by bulldozers. Nor is the fact that an animal has given its life for the benefit of a human community hidden by distant feedlots and industrial abattoirs. Their blood is offered with much gratitude in order to fortify a community and to amplify the "life force" and power of Candomblé altars, including the possession priests themselves, who, at pivotal moments, embody the gods through possession trance.

*Orixá* priests share the related view that initiatic families (as opposed to birth families) can be constructed through the applications of sacrificial blood that link the initiand to the initiating priest and, in turn, to the priest who initiated the initiator. People, communities, and their residences are like vessels, which are rendered functional, orderly, and effective by their regulated containment of the proper *axé*, as well as their continual expiation of malign or misdirected influences. *Axé* reifies the solidarity and power of geographically dispersed groups, initiatic lineages, and whole sacred "nations," or denominations, that cut across nation-states.

Hence, *axé* is also the membership of a temple (or family of temples), united by the same continuous ritual transmission of *axé* from the founding priest or priestess to the "children-in-saint" (*filhos de santo*) whom he or she has initiated and so forth. Thus, one may ask a worshiper which *axé* he or she belongs to. In reply, he or she might identify the lineage by the name of its founder, its temple of origin, or its currently ranking temple. An *axé* (that is, a temple community or family of temples) is held together by shared *axé* (or a ritually constituted life force) and, ideally, by a shared set of ritual conventions that are supposed to have remained unchanged since the founding of that *axé* (or family of temples).

In truth, innovations do take place, and the prestige of some temples or *axés*, such as Ilê Axé Opô Afonjá, is closely tied to the spread of the innovations that they introduced. Such innovations are, however, usually justified by the assertion that they are actually restorations of an original, West African ritual standard that preceded the founding of that family of Brazilian temples. The most influential of these reforms—such as the valorization of "African purity" and the early twentieth-century appointment of a set of secular officeholders and sponsors known as the "Twelve Mamgbas (or Obás) of Xangô" in the Ilê Axé Opô Afonjá temple—emerged from the transatlantic circuit of commerce and pilgrimage that united Bahia with colonial Lagos and other cities on the Guinea coast long after the mid-nineteenth-century termination of the slave trade (Matory 2005).

Members of the same *axé* are more likely to trust each other than to trust outsiders to have contact with their young and vulnerable novices, to witness and participate in their important and secret rites, and to manage a possessed member of that *axé*, because the ritual techniques from one *axé* might interfere with or harm the gods, altars, and lives of people from another *axé*. The purity of an *axé*'s rituals is an important idiom of social boundedness and distinction. Through rituals and the blessings of elders, *axé* can be accumulated; people can lose it, gain more of it, and possess more or less of it than others do. Thus, it corresponds quantitatively with rank within a community. Within any given temple, an initiate's authority and degree of respectability depend in large part on his or her initiatic age—that is, how long he or she has been initiated. Increased *axé* and rank can nonetheless be achieved through apprenticeship, special rituals, travel to sacred places, and the special blessings of gods and higher-ranking priests.

Each initiate's authority, degree of respectability, and very legitimacy depend greatly on the legitimacy of his or her lineage of temples and on the clarity of the initiate's links to that lineage. This legitimacy relies, in turn, on the time depth of its traceably uninterrupted priestly genealogy and (in theory) its inherited, unadulterated liturgical practice. The age of a temple is frequently used as a metonym of its respectability and authority. Thus, various *axé*-founding temples in Brazil—such as Casa Branca (Ilê Axé Iyá Nassô Oká) and Alaquêto (Ilê Maroialaje)—are described by their affiliates, with some symbolic truth, as three or four hundred years old. According to these indexes, some *axés* clearly rank higher than others.

There is no single priest with authority over the entire Candomblé religious community. Some *axés*, however, have institutional power and some priests, such as Mãe Stella of Ilê Axé Opô Afonjá, achieve degrees of projection in the media that give their public pronouncements and ritual protocols overwhelming authority, inspiring widespread deference, quotation, and imitation. The temples of such *axés* and of such priests are called the "great houses" (*grandes casas*), and the "greatest" of these are linked to the *axé* of Iyá Nassô, the founder of Casa Branca.

The clothing and jewelry of priests and gods elaborately dramatize two further preoccupations in the social order of Candomblé. Priestly attire encodes the compound gender and rank of the wearer, reminding everyone of the proper order of social relations among gods and people. As a festival for the gods begins, most of the priests dress in white—men in trousers and long shirts, and women in elaborate ensembles of blouse, skirts, multiple slips, shawl, and head tie, recalling the nineteenth-century attire of prosperous white women and the mulatta mistresses of northeastern planters (Omari 1984). Priestesses serving male tutelary gods wear their head ties in the form of a turban, while the head ties of priestesses of serving goddesses are tied in the *borboleta*, or "butterfly," fashion, so called because of the wings at the top. In some denominations of Candomblé, such as the Marrim subgroup of the Jeje nation, only a woman with a male tutelary god can rule the temple as chief priestess. In many denominations, there are also elaborate rules about who—among the four priestly genders—must cook, clean, serve, and rule. For example, the position of chef in the kitchen where the foods of the gods are prepared is, in the great houses, typically reserved for a priestess under the protection of a goddess. The devotees of gods who can be playfully tricked into performing servile duties for the devotees of a goddess can be fined (Santos 2010).

In most denominations, the possession priestesses who dance in ensemble for the audience wear as many starched slips as possible, in order to give their skirts buoyancy and flair. These relatively low-ranking women wear pantaloons in order to keep men from looking up their skirts as they prostrate themselves on the floor before more senior initiates and higher-ranking priests (fig. 2.5). They also wear a shawl-like "cloth from the [African] coast" (*pano da costa*) under their arms and around their torsos. By contrast, for their comfort while they are sitting down, high-ranking priestesses wear fewer skirts, and they wear the "cloth from the coast" over one shoulder. Because they are not expected to prostrate themselves often, they also typically eschew the pantaloons.

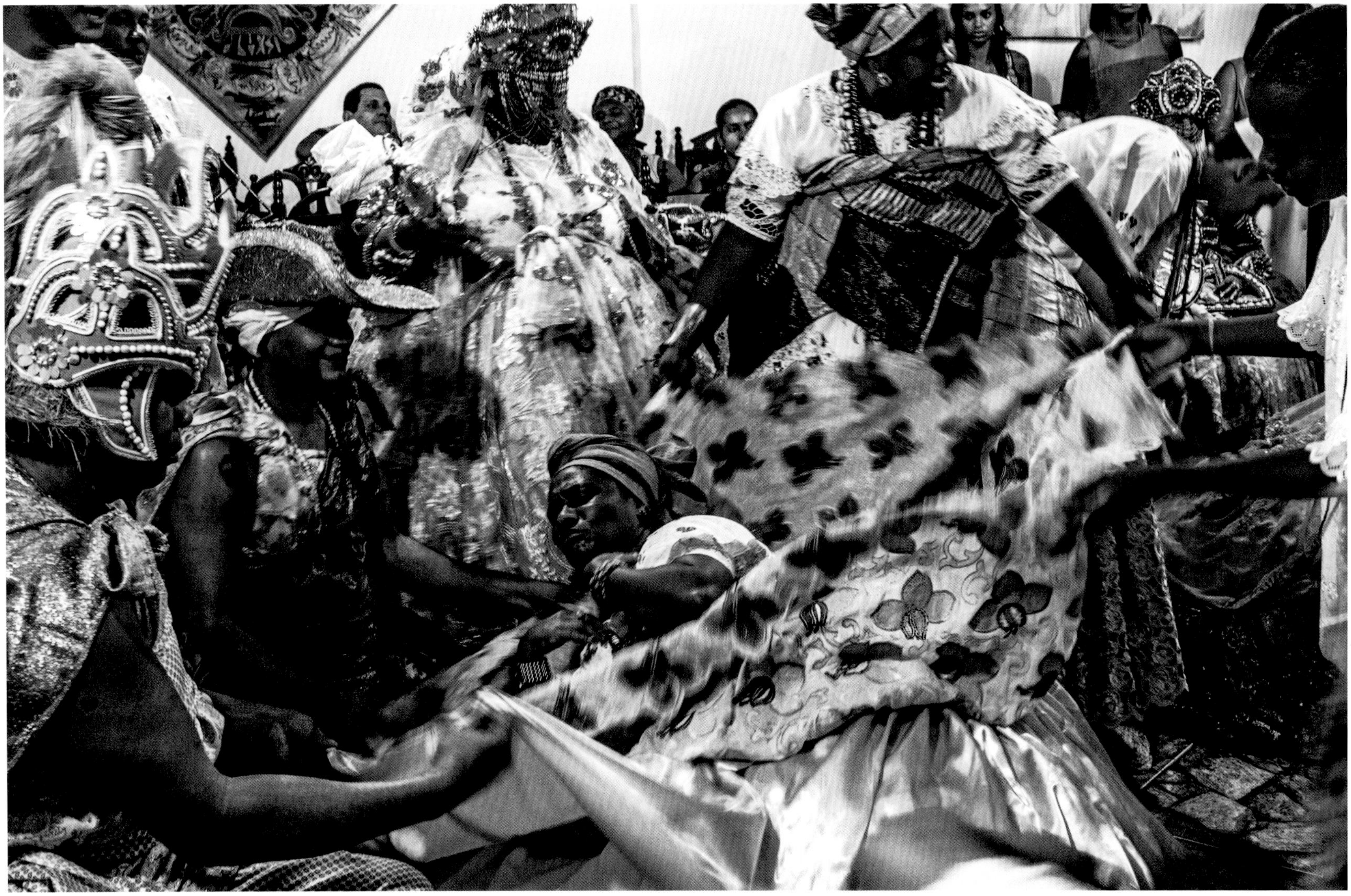

**2.5**
Tacun Lecy (b. 1977, Salvador, Bahia, Brazil)
*Candomblés Nagô: Ilê Axé Ogunjá* (Nagô Candomblés: Axé Ogunjá Temple), May, 17, 2015
Photograph
COURTESY TACUN LECY

The cloth worn by priestesses and manifest gods during sacred ceremonies is often lacy or full of openwork, suggesting the wind-like character of the gods who are invited to penetrate the bodies of the priests. Once manifest in a priest or priestess, the god dons clothing in the emblematic colors of that deity. His or her accessories and handheld objects refer allegorically to the manifest god's character and powers. Elaborate number- and color-coded bead necklaces also identify the gods who protect the unpossessed human wearers, as well as the manifest gods themselves.

This is the cosmological, social, and aesthetic context in which a Candomblé priest is made and the life of the priestly community is lived. Each person is born under the protection of one *orixá* or another, as well as that god's corresponding Roman Catholic saint. Certain special people, however, are called into the service of the god, and a unique version of that tutelary god is created and "seated" in such a person's body, alongside two or more other gods who serve as the tutelary god's auxiliaries (see also Sansi, this volume). The most special of these initiates are the *adôxu*s, or "possession priests," who, on ritual occasions, cede their consciousness to that of the lavishly dressed gods, giving visible reality to the gods and to the hierarchical lineage communities they substantiate.

While most members of these initiatic lineages and nations are black or mulatto Brazilians, Candomblé priests and devotees come in all colors and many nationalities. The elaborate ritual, aesthetics, and personality theory of this religion permeates the entire society. Candomblé argot is now omnipresent in Brazilian gay culture, youth culture, and mass-market advertising. For example, the term *axé* is also shouted by young people and sung by hip musicians as an exclamation meaning "Right on!" or "Wow!" or "Cool!" The rituals, art, and celebrity priestesses of Candomblé inspire the deference and devotion of a national array of politicians and businesspeople, as well as an international array of artists, musicians, philosophers, activists, and social scientists.

Candomblé is and, since its founding in the nineteenth century, has always been enmeshed in a multireligious, politically stratified, and transnational world. Its rituals and liturgical art do not simply express a primordial, otherworldly belief system. Instead they turn the products of twenty-first-century production and commerce into gods who, in an African-inspired idiom, embody and act upon the conditions of a world that you and I share with the Bahian devotees of the *orixás*, the *voduns*, the *inquices*, and the *caboclos*.

*Interleaf* **C**

# *Lavagem do Bonfim*

**Sabrina Gledhill**

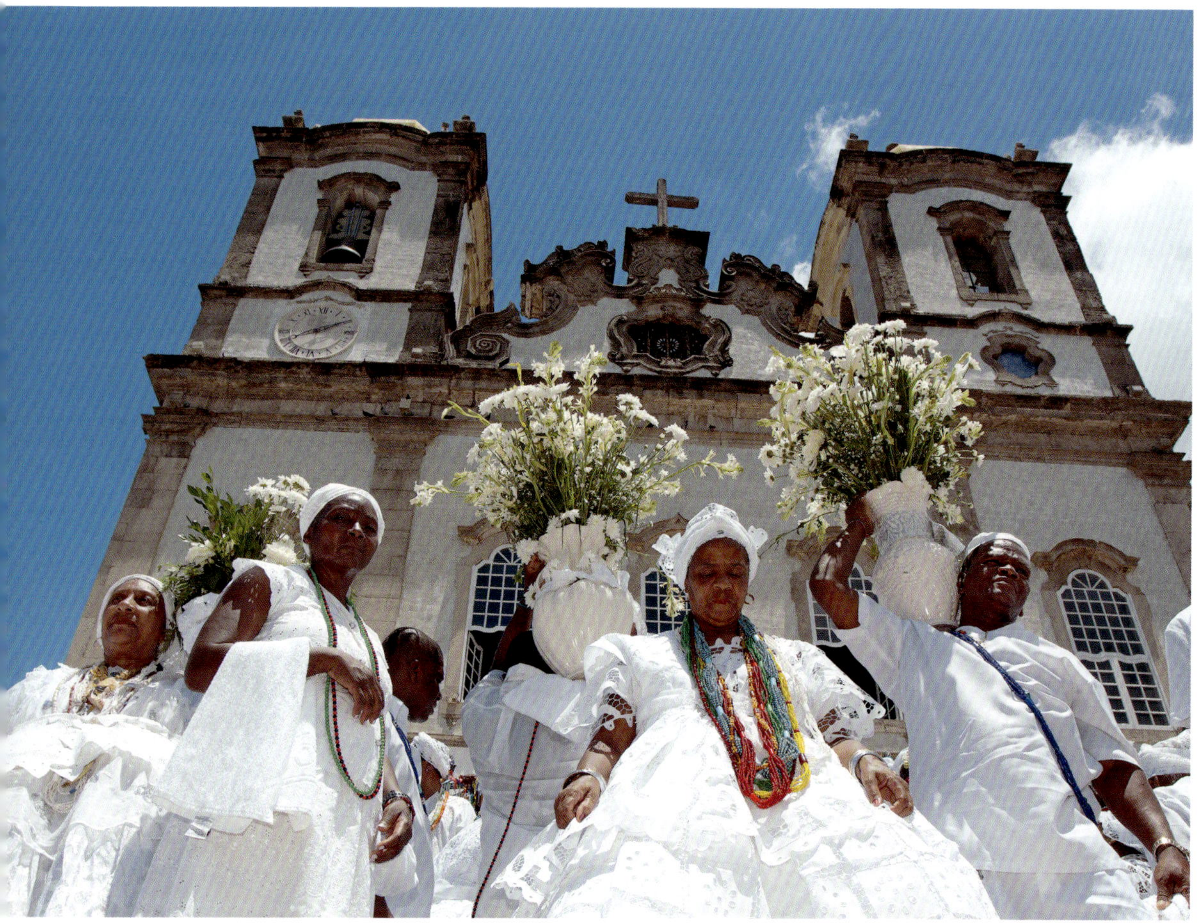

C.1
Roberto Faria (b. 1968, Salvador, Bahia, Brazil)
Pilgrims gather in front of the Igreja do Nosso Senhor do Bonfim (Church of Our Lord of the Good End) on Salvador's Itapagipe Peninsula, 2009.
Photograph
COURTESY ROBERTO FARIA

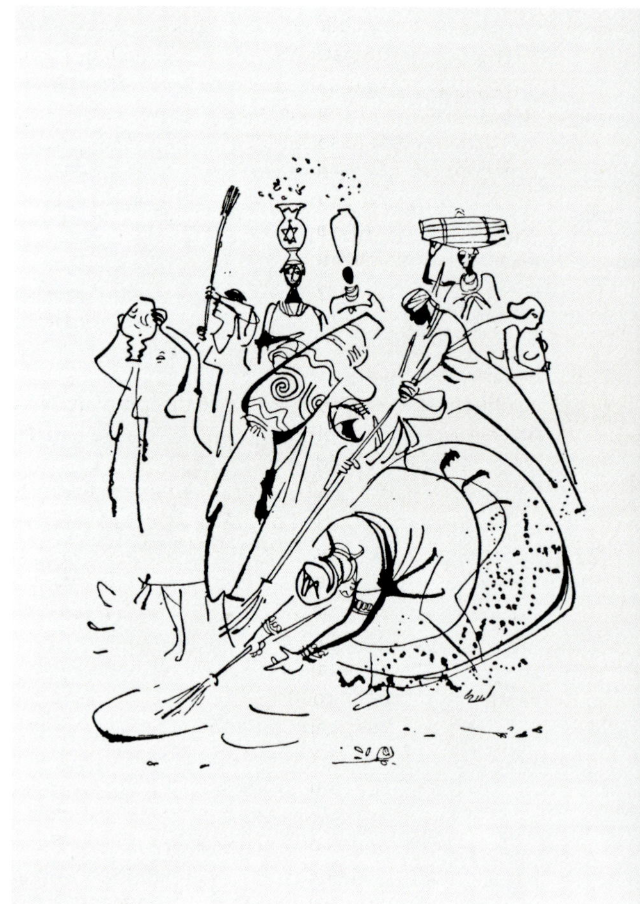

C.2
Carybé (Héctor Julio Páride Bernabó, b. 1911, Lanús, Buenos Aires Province, Argentina; d. 1997)
*Lavagem do Bonfim* (Washing of Bonfim), date unknown
Ink on paper
Dimensions unknown
COURTESY INSTITUTO CARYBÉ / COPYRIGHTS CONSULTORIA LTDA.

EVERY YEAR, ON THE SECOND THURSDAY of January, following Epiphany, which celebrates the visit of the three magi bearing gifts for the infant Jesus, a procession sets off from Conceição da Praia Church, next to the Lacerda Elevator, which links the entrance to the Historic District in the Upper City with the port area in the Lower City. From there, it follows a nearly five-mile route to the Igreja do Nosso Senhor do Bonfim (Church of Our Lord of the Good End) situated atop the Sagrada Colina (Holy Mount) on Salvador's Itapagipe Peninsula (fig. C.1). Some of the pilgrims carry brooms and flowers. Others bring clay jars filled with scented water that will be used to cleanse not only the church steps and yard but also many of those taking part in the trek: Candomblé practitioners, Catholic devotees of Christ Crucified (patron of the church), local residents, and tourists. Most of the participants wear white, chief among them the Baianas, women, usually African or Afro-descendants (fig. C.2), attired in long, full skirts, lacy smocks, beads, and head ties (see Shirey, this volume).

Although the association of Candomblé and Catholicism has always been uneasy at best, adherents of Afro-Brazilian religions have long been intimately involved in the ceremony known as the Lavagem do Bonfim (Cleansing of the Church of Bonfim). Baianas used to clean the interior of the church until 1890, when they were banned from doing so by Catholic authorities, allegedly due to the "ruckus" they were making near the high altar. Today, they sweep the exterior stairs. The procession remains a high point of the festival calendar in Bahia, second only to Carnaval, as it climaxes in a festival with drumming, dancing, food, drink, and capoeira bouts. Because of this, leaders of the Catholic Church still tend to view it with disapproval. They particularly frown on the "syncretism" of Catholic saints and Afro-Brazilian divinities—a feeling shared by some Candomblé leaders.

The involvement of the Afro-Brazilian religious community in this ceremony is due to the association of Christ Crucified with the *orixá* Oxalá. The color of this deity is white, and Candomblé *terreiros* hold a similar ceremony known as Águas de Oxalá (Waters of Oxalá). At the Ilê Axé Opô Afonjá temple, this takes place in late September and is restricted to members and friends of the religious community. White-clad participants wearing head ties retire on straw mats at the *terreiro*, awaken after midnight, and silently form a line according to rank. They then make the rounds of the temple three times (circumambulation is also a Catholic practice), carrying clay jars filled with water on their heads and pouring them onto the shrine of Oxalá. The ceremony ends with drumming at dawn.

Pierre Verger recounts the legend behind the rite, which tells of the journey of Oxalufã (the elderly avatar of Oxalá) to visit his friend Xangô, the king of Oyó, despite the warnings of an Ifá priest. After the deity Exú tricks him into getting covered in palm oil or charcoal three times, obliging him to change clothes and wash himself in a stream, Oxalufã comes across a stray horse in Xangô's kingdom and recognizes it as one he had given his friend some time before. Just then, Xangô's men come upon him, mistake him for a horse thief, beat him, and throw him in jail. For seven years, the kingdom of Xangô is plagued by disease, dead livestock, and bad harvests until another Ifá priest reveals that these disasters are due to the unjust imprisonment of an old man. When Oxalufã is brought before him, Xangô immediately recognizes his old friend, even though he is covered in filth and grime, and the king orders everyone in his palace and realm to wear white and do penance by carrying jars of water on their heads to cleanse Oxalufã. Verger explains that this legend is commemorated by both Águas de Oxalá and the Lavagem do Bonfim (Verger and Carybé 1997, 65–68).

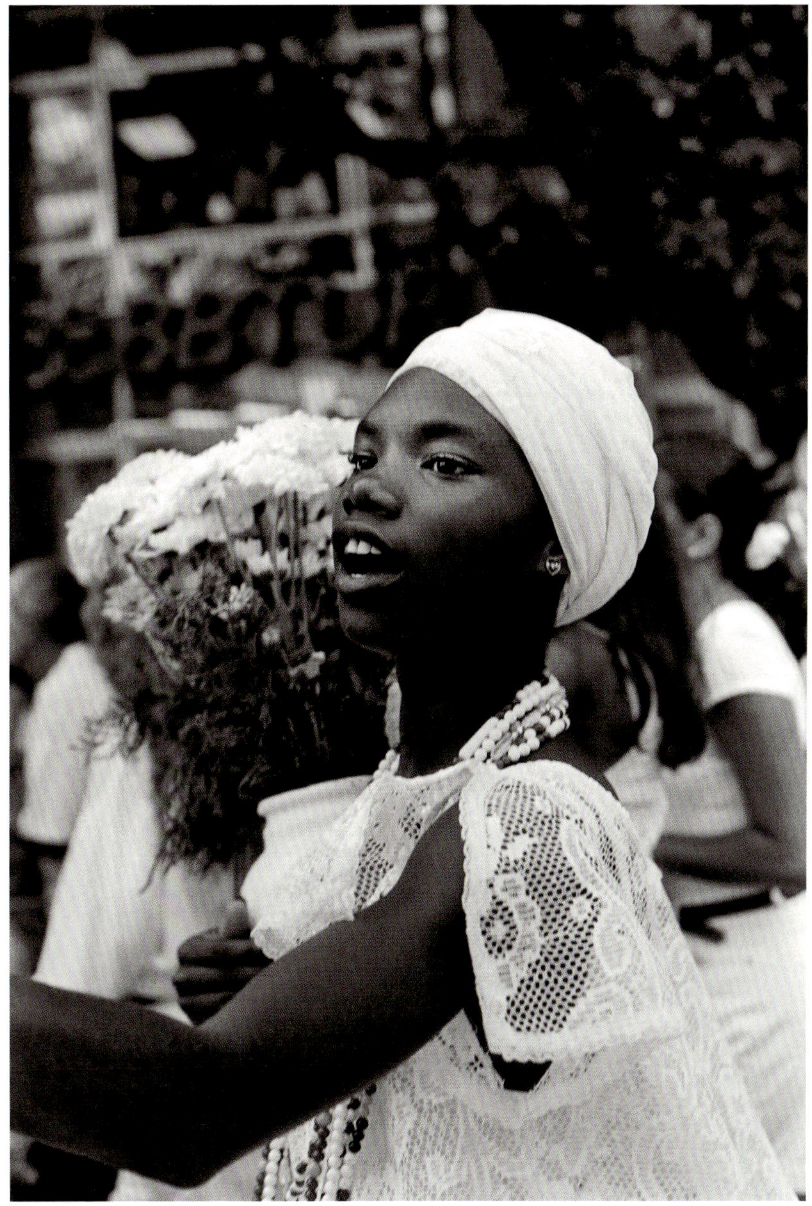

**C.3**
Lita Almeida Cerqueira (b. 1952, Salvador, Bahia, Brazil)
*Menina na Lavagem do Bonfim* (Young Woman at the Lavagem do Bonfim), 1994
Photograph
COURTESY LITA ALMEIDA CERQUEIRA

*Interleaf* **D**

# Adenor Gondim and the Irmandade de Nossa Senhora da Boa Morte

**Scott Alves Barton**

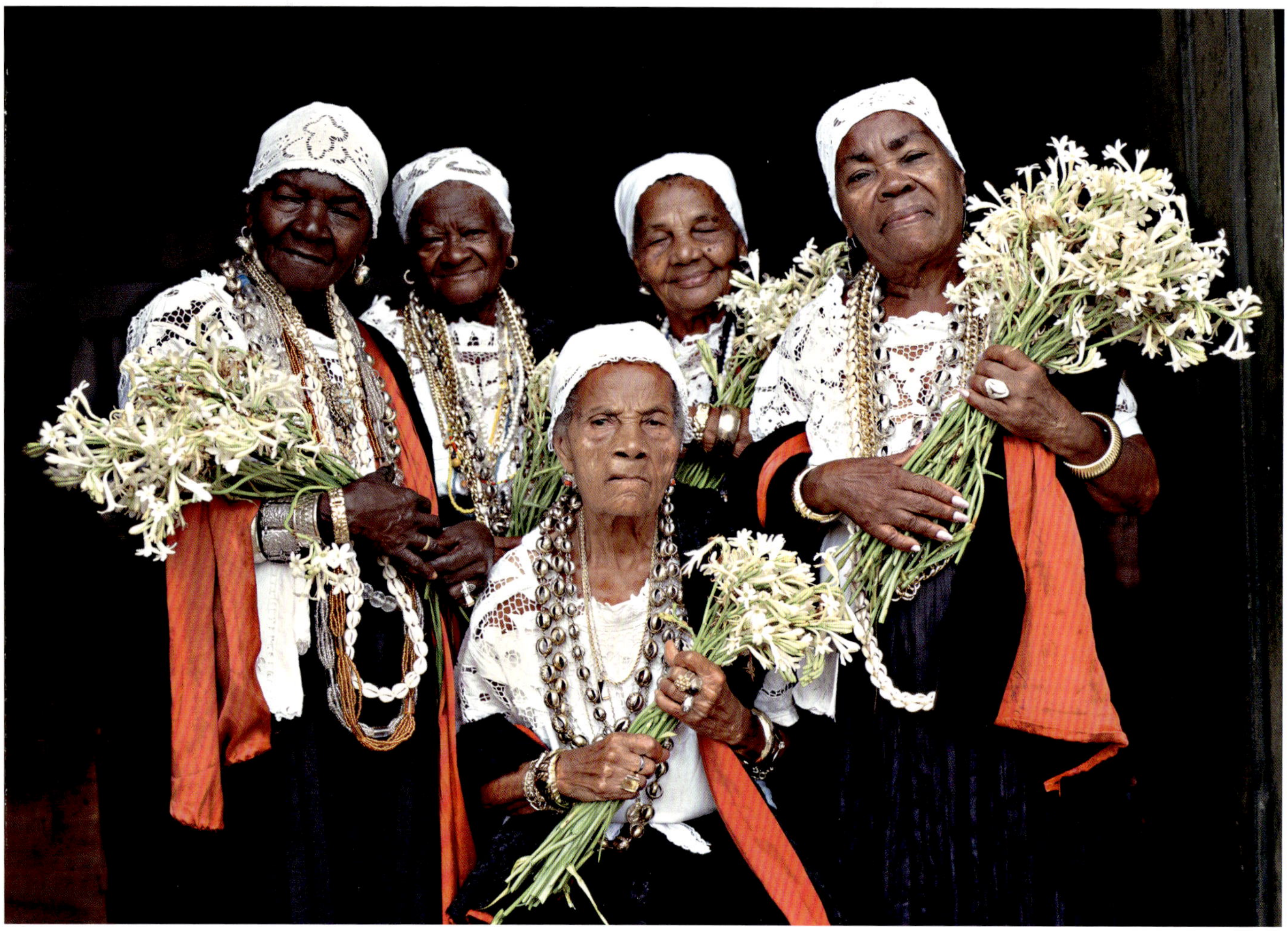

**D.1**
Adenor Gondim (b. 1950, Rui Barbosa, Bahia, Brazil)
*Velma guarda da Irmandade de Nossa Senhora da Boa Morte*
(Old Guard of the Sisterhood of Our Lady of the Good Death), June 8, 1994
Photograph
COURTESY ADENOR GONDIM

SINCE THE EARLY NINETEENTH CENTURY the Festa da Boa Morte (Festival of the Good Death), which is held in Cachoeira, seventy-five miles west of Salvador, has existed to honor and ameliorate the suffering and torment of enslaved ancestors. Through the festival, as well as through prayer and charitable works maintained in perpetuity by the Irmandade da Boa Morte (Sisterhood of the Good Death), it is believed that the misery, heartache, and corporeal torment suffered during enslavement can end in *alforria* (liberation). The majority of the sisters in the Irmandade are concurrently Catholic devotees and *mães de santo* (priestesses) or initiates in the Afro-Brazilian Candomblé religion. Boa Morte is one of the key regional festivals to foster appreciation of these syncretic roots (fig. D.2).

In the Catholic calendar, the Virgin Mary's ascension into heaven is celebrated as the Feast of the Assumption on August 15th. In the Barroquinha district of Salvador, between 1820 and 1835, the Assumption was observed as part of the Festa da Boa Morte and viewed as a means for the souls of deceased slaves to achieve redemption. The Irmandade da Boa Morte, which persists to the present, also came into being at this time. It is made up of middle-aged and elderly women, many of them widows, who are descendants of Bahia's enslaved. The sisters pay homage and maintain fealty to the interventions of Nossa Senhora, the Virgin Mary, their blessed change agent, and to their creed of ancestral worship (Castro 2006, 40–48, 75–78, 110).

After its beginnings in Salvador, the Festa da Boa Morte quickly moved inland to the former colonial state capital of Cachoeira. Oral histories recount that once there the festival initially took place in a neighborhood renowned for its West African cultural and Jeje[1] religious traditions. This site was near the original location of Brazil's foundational Candomblé temple, Ilê Axé Iyá Nassô Oká, popularly known as the Terreiro da Casa Branca (White House). In the early twentieth century, two hundred members of the Sisterhood participated in the *festa*; today there are less than twenty-five members (fig. D.1).

Scholars and local elders often define the sisters as exponents of Gẹlẹ dẹ worship, the female analogue to traditions of male Egungun ancestral worship in Bahia. Egungun traditions venerate deceased mortals whose spirits have returned to earth and provide communion and communication between the living, the dead, and the deities (fig. D.3). Gẹlẹdẹ is a secret women's religious group within traditional Yoruba society. Through collective worship of ancestral dead associated with land or water deities, its members represent fertility and feminine power and serve as guardians of the earth and community. Iemanjá, Oxum, and Nanã Buruku are three key *orixá* who are honored during the Festa da Boa Morte. Iemanjá in particular is a foundational figure within Gẹlẹdẹ societies.[2] The identities of all these deities are related to water: oceans, rivers, waterfalls, and swamps. Oxum is linked to fertility. Nanã, a primordial *orixá*, is older than creation itself. Within Yoruba spiritual tradition, the Gẹlẹdẹ cosmology sees Iemanjá as the mother of all *orixás* and all living things. The Virgin Mary, Iemanjá, and various *orixás* are concurrently honored during the *festa*. Whereas the festival is public, attended by local residents, Brazilian travelers, and international tourists, there are ancillary rites and aspects of the ceremonies that are shared only among the women initiated into the Irmandade.

As with most Catholic religious orders, members of the Sisterhood should be mature women dedicated to their communities (fig. D.4). Personal recommendations must accompany applications for admission to the group, and in a few cases mothers and daughters both serve. Historically their charity work would raise funds for funerals and to support the families of the deceased. Although the Sisterhood had the blessing of the Catholic Church, it arose at a moment when enslaved West Africans and free people of color were not seen to be as worthy of salvation as whites and the indigenous population. One of the fundamental ways that the deceased and the living were nourished through their grief was with an offering of food, simulacra of the sacred banquet for the *orixás*, prescribed in the Candomblé liturgy. Either foodstuffs or monies can thus be offered to support the local community and the sisters' mission.

Early in the Festa da Boa Morte, members of the Irmandade enact a funeral ceremony for their patron saint. They wear black, knee-length, A-line skirts that are pleated; simple white lace smock blouses; and vibrantly colored necklaces and bracelets that are linked to each sister's particular *orixá*. Some of these ornaments have late nineteenth- or early twentieth-century pedigrees.[3] The sisters also wear reversible stoles; one side is red satin, but it is the black velvet side, which signifies mourning, that is displayed at this moment. Moorish-style white cotton eyelet-lace veils cover their faces. During candlelit or moonlit processions, these veils impart an ethereal glow to their faces. Every aspect of their dress has its own significance within Catholic, Muslim, or Candomblé traditions.

The ten-day festival cycle begins with an *esmola* (a call for alms and foodstuffs to fund the festival), followed by a private luncheon for the sisters. Iconic foods are prepared by the Sisterhood and distributed among the community every other day of the festival. These meals recall both biblical and West African culinary and ceremonial protocols. The festival's apex occurs on the Feast of the Assumption with a Catholic High Mass. This is followed with a *feijoada* (a stew of various meats and beans that is ascribed to the ingenuity of the enslaved); a *valsa portuguesa*, or colonial-style formal waltz by the sisters; and the regional *samba de roda*. The *festa* ends two days later with the celebratory *caruru* (a rich gumbo-like soup of okra, palm oil, and smoked, dried shrimp), a community feast symbolizing good luck. Fried plantains, boiled black-eyed peas, *vatapá*, and white rice are served with the *caruru*. This final meal mirrors the West African-inspired dishes enjoyed at Bahia's secular and sacred (Candomblé) tables. It is accompanied by nearly endless samba. The festival also heralds the beginning of the Candomblé ritual season for several sects of this Afro-Brazilian religion.

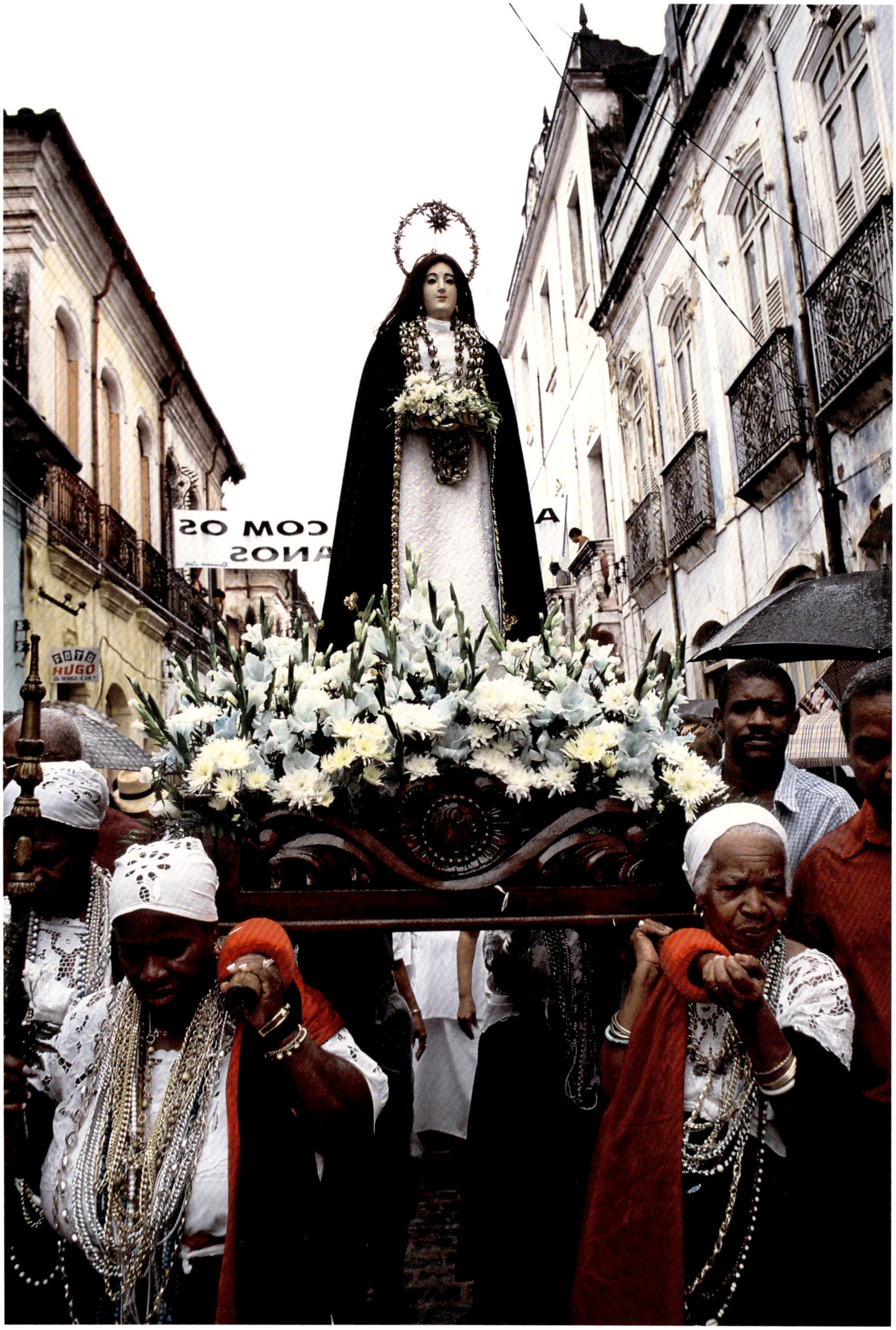
FOTO
HUGO

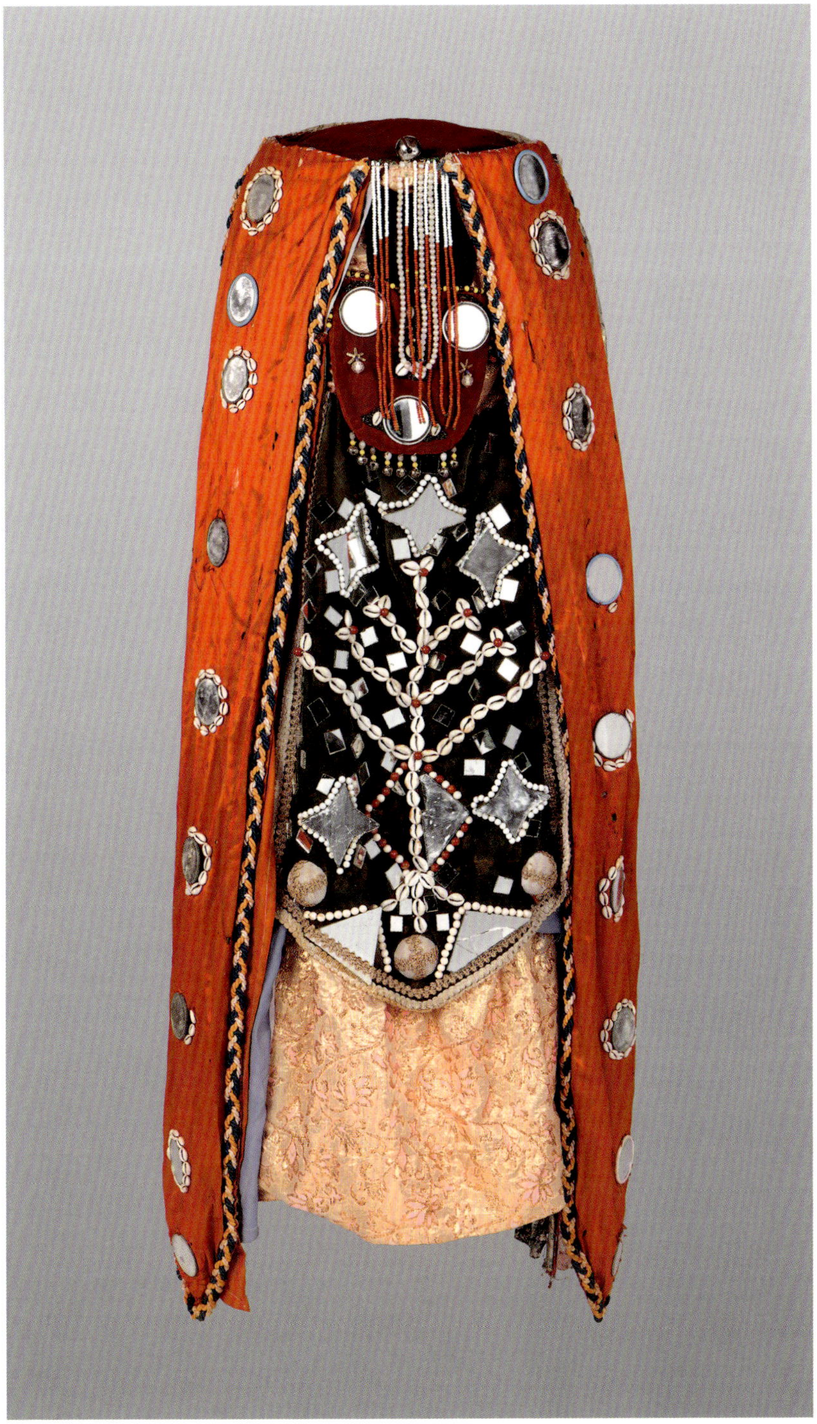

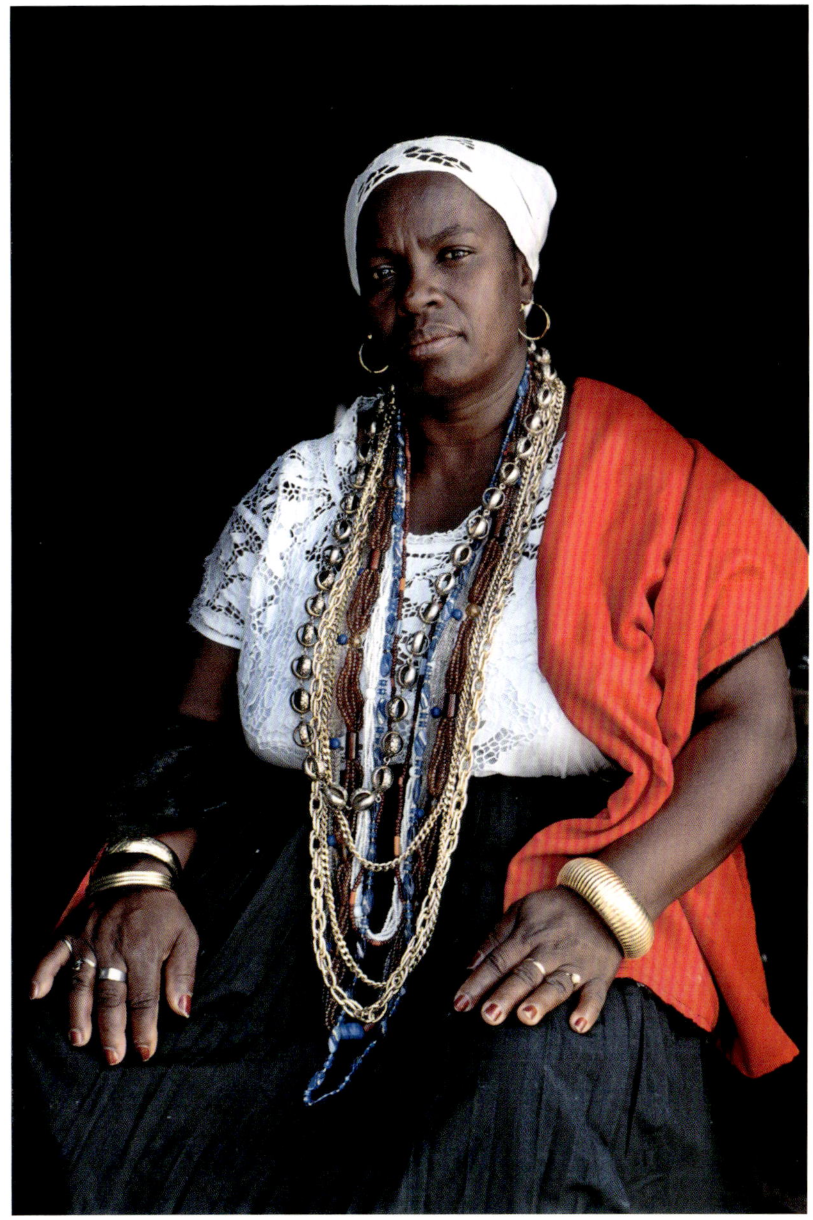

**D.2**
Adenor Gondim (b. 1950, Rui Barbosa, Bahia, Brazil)
*Procissão—Nossa Senhora da Gloria* (Procession—Our Lady of Glory), 2006
Photograph
COURTESY ADENOR GONDIM

**D.3**
Artist Unknown
Egungun masquerade ensemble representing an Egun (ancestral spirit) called Babá Xangô
Itaparica, Bahia, Brazil, early 20th century
Cloth, beads, cowry shells, mirrors
L: 1.5 m
GIFT OF MRS. THOMAS DAVIS, X82.1359; FOWLER MUSEUM AT UCLA

**D.4**
Adenor Gondim (b. 1950, Rui Barbosa, Bahia, Brazil)
*Irmã Deleci—Irmandade de Nossa Senhora da Boa Morte* (Sister Deleci—Sisterhood of Our Lady of the Good Death), 1997
Photograph
COURTESY ADENOR GONDIM

### The West African Umbilical Cord

The images of the Festa da Boa Morte presented here are by Adenor Gondim. They represent only a fraction of the photographs of the Irmandade and the *festa* that he has taken over two decades. Gondim is one of the most influential and virtuosic documenters of regional Bahian life, and he has been acknowledged as such for over forty years. The son of a portrait photographer from the small town of Rui Barbosa in the interior of the state of Bahia, he has focused on Afro-Brazilian and Brazilian cultural traditions of the northeastern region.

Born in 1950, during Brazil's Second Republic, Gondim's youth was marked by a brief democratic period bookended by political turmoil. He lived through the dissolution of agrarian oligarchies that ushered in rapid growth of industrial capitalism and its attendant industrial bourgeoisie intent on nation building. These petty elites initiated social reforms meant to contain and sublimate the nascent urban working class. Creatively, this period was marked by monumental modernist architectural projects, among them Oscar Niemeyer's futurist Brasilia. It was also during this era that Italian architect Lina Bo Bardi developed MAM (Museu de Arte Moderna) in Bahia, highlighting both high and popular art movements. These political, social, and cultural changes affected Gondim's life and philosophy.

As a teen, he began working as his father's photo studio assistant. Both men were influenced by the images and entrepreneurship of the itinerant photographers who traveled throughout Bahia's *sertões* (backlands), particularly Ernesto Frick who was accompanied by Gondim's uncle Maninho. In the mid-1960s, Gondim's father expanded the family business, Foto Gondim, moving it closer to the coastal city of Itabuna. As Adenor relates,

> My work moved beyond the mechanical snapping images here and there, to creating portraits, including the documentation of *candango*, rural migrant workers who flooded cities for work during the construction boom. Much to the consternation of my father, I started to walk the periphery of Itabuna, or take my bike and go out photographing everything I found sad and cheerful, ugly and beautiful, in the universe of poverty and nature. My father saw my images as being unnecessary and a waste of film stock.[4]

Not content to simply record portraits and social events, Gondim struggled with the nature of the relationship between the photographer and the subject. In the 1970s he trained as a biologist at Bahia's Federal University and briefly ceased taking photographs. Following an exhibition at MAM in 1980, however, Gondim fell in love with the imaginary of an "enchanted universe" of popular Catholic culture in the Romaria district of Bom Jesus da Lapa deep in central Bahia (fig. D.5).

> Then in 1990, I became impassioned by the Irmandade de Nossa Senhora da Boa Morte in Cachoeira. I offered my services to voluntarily photograph the festival and the sisterhood. I fell in love. I didn't just dive in I swooned. It is a story without end, a blind alley with no exit.[5]

Gondim's photos have since been featured in many exhibitions, acquired for public and private collections, and reproduced in numerous books. He has photographed the Festa da Boa Morte and the Sisterhood nearly every subsequent year. Following his initial agreement, he has been asked to photograph the festival

> as a means of articulating cultural practices that are a foundational aspect of Bahian identity. Documenting the festival as an exemplar of self-determination and creolized culture held the potential to portend cultural reform by circulating images of heritage practices that upon my arrival [at the festival] were in shambles.[6]

In 1998 Baiano artist and curator Emanoel Araújo, then director of the Pinacoteca de São Paulo (São Paulo Modern Art Museum), invited Gondim to present a photo essay on the Irmandade da Boa Morte in the exhibition *Arte e Religiosidade no Brasil—Heranças Africanas* (West African Heritage in Brazilian Religiosity and Art). This was followed in 2000 by his inclusion in the exhibition *500 anos do descobrimento do Brasil nos módulos negro de corpo e alma* (500-Year Anniversary of the Discovery of Brazil through the Mode of Black Body and Soul). In 2002 he participated in the exhibition *Acts of Faith—Brazilian Contemporary Photography* at the Pitt Museum, Oxford University.

Adenor characterizes his maturity as a photographer through his selection of subjects,

> I have passionately photographed the prayers, processions, walks, masses, shrines, and offerings for Iemanjá, Caboclo ceremonies, fairs, and food from Bahia. I am not a photographer of nature, nor violence, human misery or pain.... I am a photographer of the dignity of a people who scorn hunger and abandonment by reveling in the joy of the party.... There are times when the emotion makes me leave aside the act of photographing to live them. I like to shoot essentially in black and white, but I recognize the importance of color...I'm interethnic. In my veins, Indian, black, Portuguese blood and its derivatives run. I'm ecumenical, having limboed between the Baptists, Spiritists, Catholics, and Candomblé. I have learned and incorporated some of the goodness of each one. Realizing that through everything, both good or evil are in Man. I am against religious intolerance. I am against cultural globalization. I am against any kind of prejudice. I am Bahian, Brazilian, and South American. I am a citizen of the World. My world is Bahia. Bahia is enough for me.
>
> In conclusion, I believe at times it is better to stop taking pictures and live in the moment happening in front of my eyes. I have been given permission as the designated photographer, allowing me to be there in that moment. Yet I would rather delay my process, stop everything, and experience the moment until I am no longer overcome with emotion.[7]

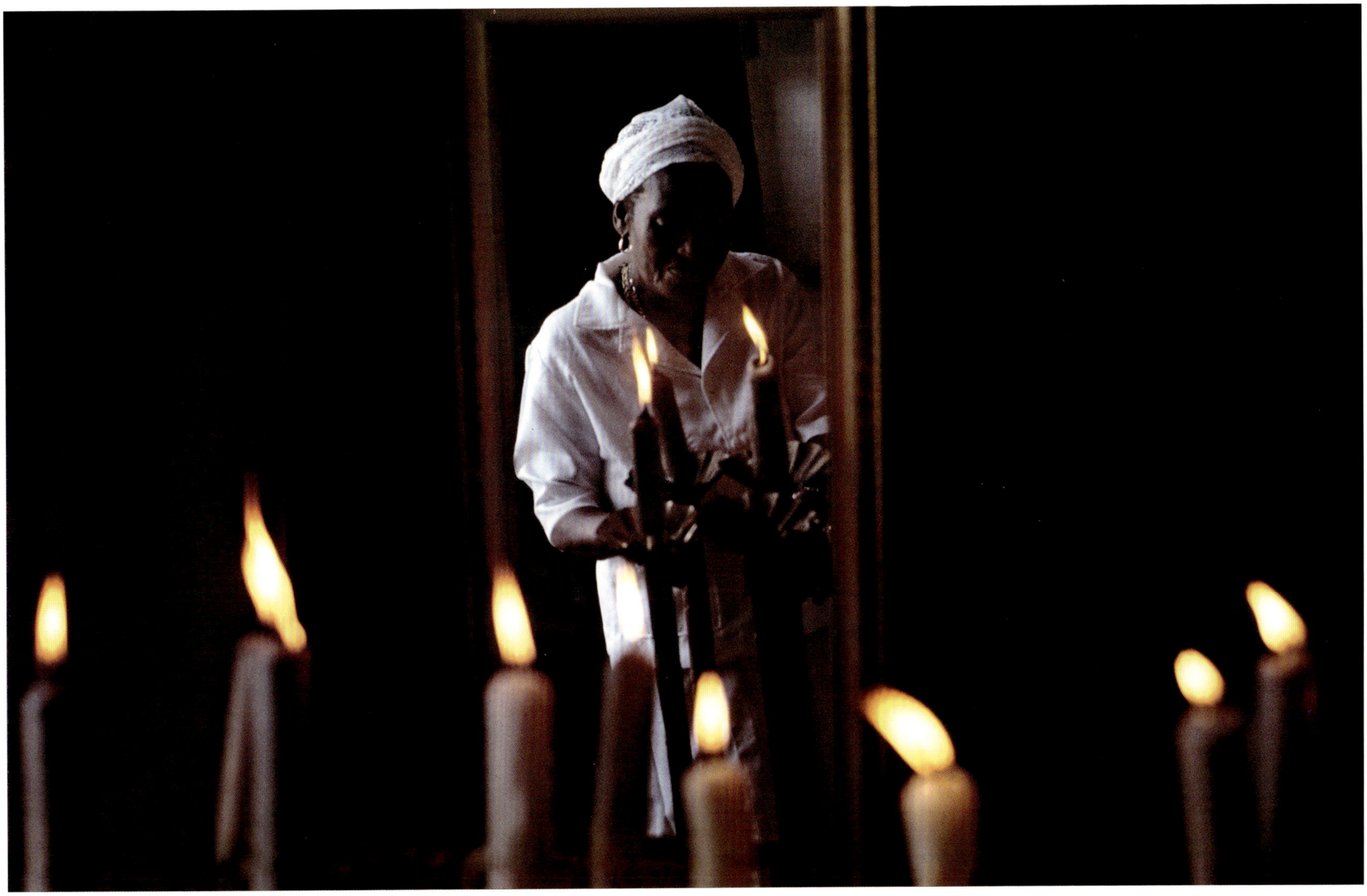

**D.5**
Adenor Gondim (b. 1950, Rui Barbosa, Bahia, Brazil)
*Prece* (Prayer), 1999
Photograph
COURTESY ADENOR GONDIM

# 3 To Have *Axé* — To Be *Axé*

Roger Sansi

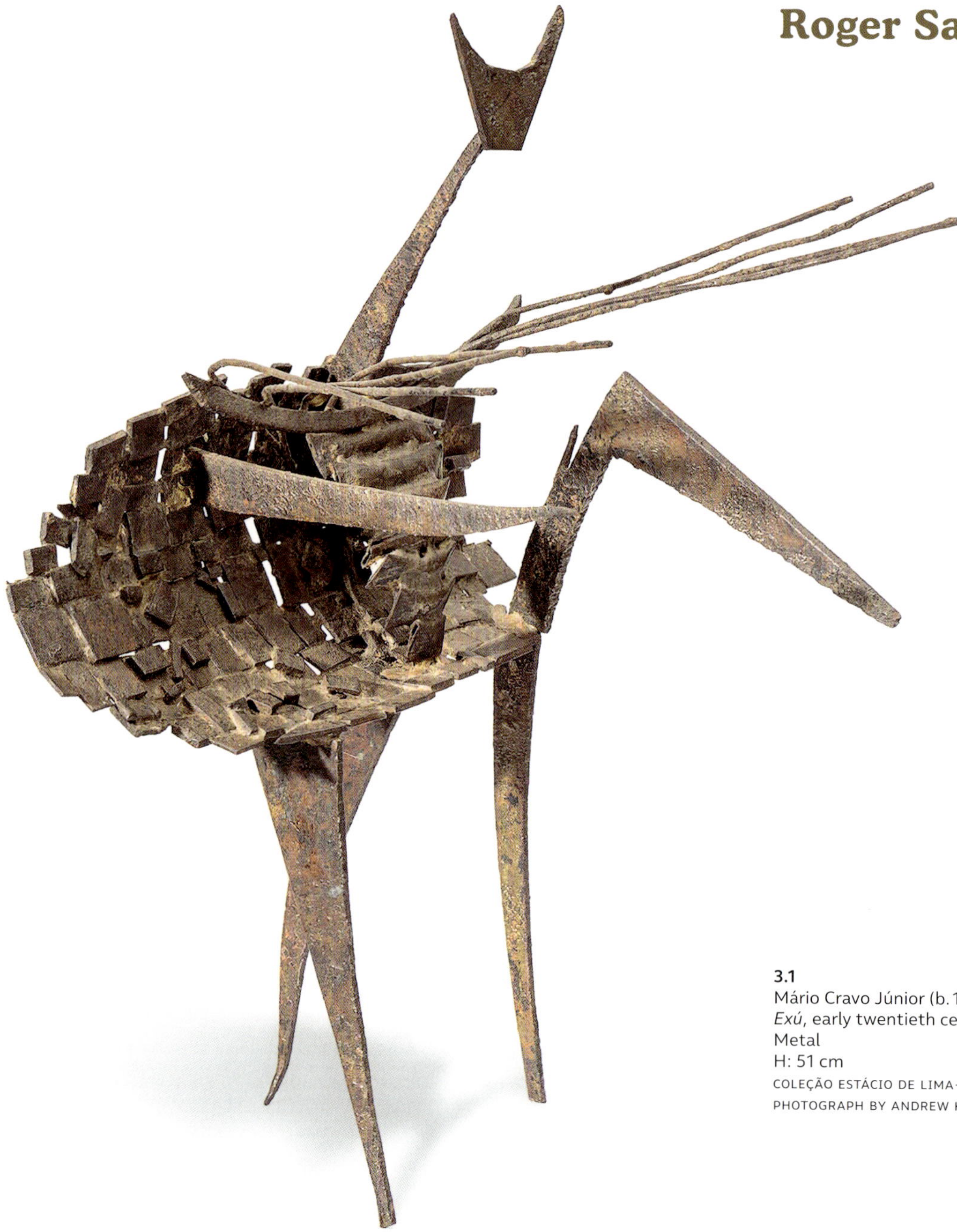

**3.1**
Mário Cravo Júnior (b. 1923, Salvador, Bahia, Brazil)
*Exú*, early twentieth century
Metal
H: 51 cm
COLEÇÃO ESTÁCIO DE LIMA—MUSEU AFRO-BRASILEIRO DA UFBA
PHOTOGRAPH BY ANDREW KEMP, 2017

DURING THE FIRST DECADES of the twentieth century, news accounts of police breaking into Candomblé houses were frequent in Bahia. Such articles described the scenes of spirit possession encountered during raids in a tone vacillating between derision and contempt. They also detailed how officers removed concealed "weapons of sorcery" (Maggie 1992; Lühning 1995–1996; Sansi 2005). Some of the objects confiscated, among them chairs and stones, were not on the surface particularly exotic or strange, but they did have a particular value in Candomblé (fig. 3.2). We can assume, therefore, that some members of the police were actually quite familiar with the practice of Candomblé and that it was not for them an exotic religion. If it had been, they wouldn't have removed these ostensibly mundane objects.

All of these materials ended up in police collections and were displayed for decades in the Museu de Medicina Legal Estácia de Lima (Museum of Forensic Medicine of Bahia), together with weapons, drugs, and other objects of forensic interest—including deformed fetuses and embalmed corpses. Only in recent decades have the changed public perception of Candomblé and the rising consciousness of Brazil's colonial past aroused ire over the shameful treatment of these objects as curiosities in a freak show (Rafael and Maggie 2013).

The Museum of Forensic Medicine is currently closed. Nearly a century following these scurrilous journalistic accounts, however, the practice of Candomblé remains under threat. This time the attack comes primarily from Neo-Pentecostals who identify Candomblé with idolatry and devil worship (Silva 2007). These iconoclastic attacks are also directed at Catholicism, but Afro-Brazilian religions are the main victims of religious intolerance, according to recent statistics (Puff 2016). Candomblé houses continue to be violated and their objects of worship destroyed. In the Federal District of Brasilia in 2015, for example, arsonists reportedly burned thirteen Candomblé houses (Puff 2016). The battle to restore dignity to Afro-Brazilian religions and assure their public recognition is far from over. In spite of the efforts on the part of black cultural movements and state institutions in the last decades, Afro-Brazilian religions are yet to be seen as equal to their European counterparts in Brazil. In fact their status as religions has been challenged by federal courts as recently as 2014.[1]

If we are to understand the material and visual culture of Candomblé, however, we have to consider it in wider terms than cultural politics. The attacks on Candomblé houses are not solely the result of colonialism and racism. The enemies of Candomblé are often very familiar with the religion; it is, in fact, part of their background, and in spite of all their contempt, they take it very seriously. They might believe in the power (*axé*) of Candomblé, even if they view it as an evil—as the power of the devil (Selka 2014; Giumbelli 2007). The desire for public recognition of Afro-Brazilian culture should not overlook the fact that the "art" of Candomblé is something much more than that of selected objects displayed in a museum. It is part of a religion, of a culture where the relationships between people, things, and spirits take a particular shape—one that may be very different from what we conventionally call art, aesthetics, representation, or even religion, following European perspectives.

In the following pages I will describe in very general terms the material and visual culture of Candomblé. I will initially look at the body as a central site of its practice. I will then address the life of shrines and their relation to bodies; and finally, I will focus on a variety of images. I will broadly examine the religious imaginary of Candomblé: its capacity to recognize the holy in the multiple things of everyday life and its ability to invent and reinvent itself.

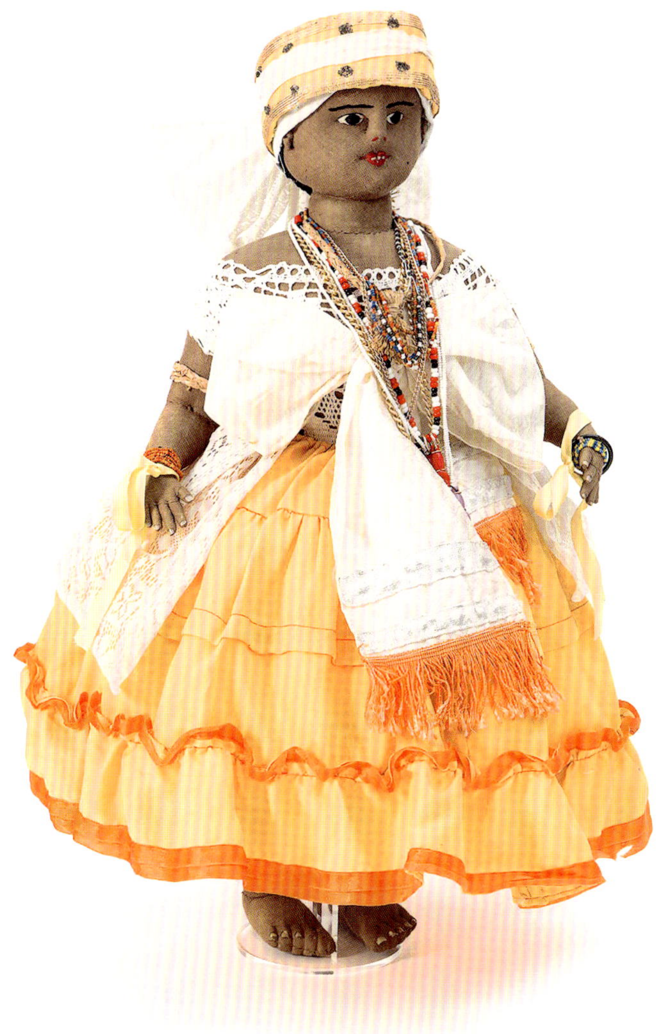

**3.2**
Artist Unknown
Doll, early twentieth century
Cloth, beads, metal
H: 45 cm
COLEÇÃO ESTÁCIO DE LIMA–MUSEU AFRO-BRASILEIRO DA UFBA
PHOTOGRAPH BY ANDREW KEMP, 2017

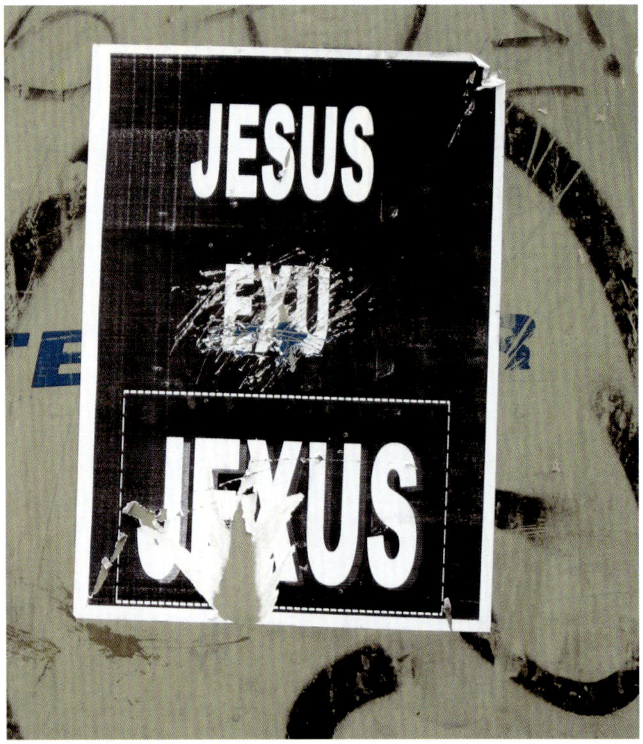


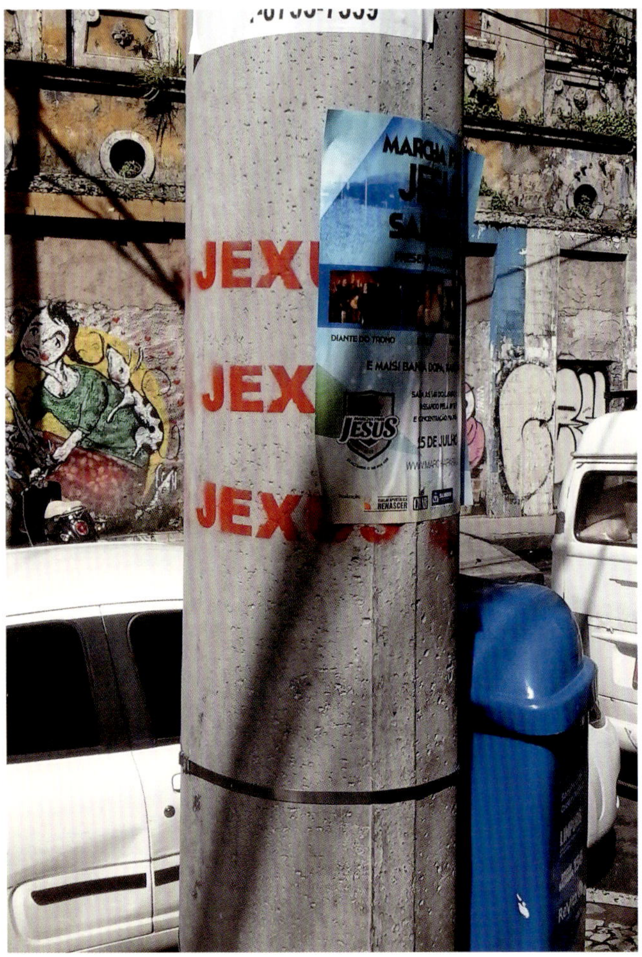

### Spirits

Candomblé is based on the worship of the *orixás* or *voduns*. A term most commonly used in speaking of them in Candomblé today is *santo*, or "saint" in Portuguese, which should not be understood as a generic holy person—a "saint" in the Catholic tradition or a "god" in a polytheistic system. Instead, the *santo* refers to the particular incarnation that the generic spirit, the *orixá*, has for a particular person. Thus there are as many "*santos*" as there are people initiated into Candomblé—despite the fact that the generic entities, as some of the more purist theologians maintain, are limited to sixteen (Xangô, Iemanjá, Oxum, Ogum, Oxóssi, et al.). These generic *orixás* are those of the African tradition, but every Candomblé adherent has a particular version of them—his or her own *santo*.

Traditionally, people are initiated into Candomblé through the call of the *orixá*. They do not "convert" through personal conviction, they are drawn to it because the *orixá* calls them. Historically, from the point of view of Candomblé, it was not unacceptable to practice other religions, such as Catholicism, as well (figs. 3.3, 3.4). What described the practice was the expression of duty to one's *santo*, in Portuguese, "*obrigação*." In recent decades, however, there has been a growing "anti-syncretist" movement that has rejected the historical submission of Afro-Brazilian religions to Catholicism and has fought for the public recognition of Candomblé as a religion on its own terms. In tandem with growing acceptance of its practices, it has attracted adherents of higher social status and background. Perhaps paradoxically, the result is that many have started to relate to Afro-Brazilian religions in "modern" terms: through sincerity, personal faith, belief, and spirituality (Johnson 2002; Sansi 2007; Duccini 2016). These new forms of worship are, however, outside the scope of this essay.

In Candomblé, everyone, everything, belongs with an *orixá*—one of the generic spirits that define the world (figs. 3.5–3.9). Oxum, for example, is the spirit of fresh water, of young female beauty and seduction, of sorcery, of wealth. Her color is gold, and there are particular objects that she accepts as presents, like perfumes and beauty products, and foods like eggs. Some people belong with her, but they may never know this if they fail to ask. This may be done through the oracle of the cowry shells (*búzios*) or, more spectacularly, the body may be possessed by the *orixá* without notice.

**3.3**
Àlex Ìgbó (b. 1986, Salvador, Bahia, Brazil)
*Jexus*, Bairro Garibaldi, Salvador, 2014
Ink on paper
COURTESY ÀLEX ÌGBÓ

**3.4**
Àlex Ìgbó (b. 1986, Salvador, Bahia, Brazil)
*Jexus*, Centro Histórico-Praça da Sá, Salvador, 2015
Stencil, paint
COURTESY ÀLEX ÌGBÓ

Afro-Brazilian religions have long been attacked by the intolerant. In the Jexus series however, Àlex Ìgbó considers the possibility of a symbolic connection between Jesus and Exú, one that moves beyond misunderstanding and conflict.

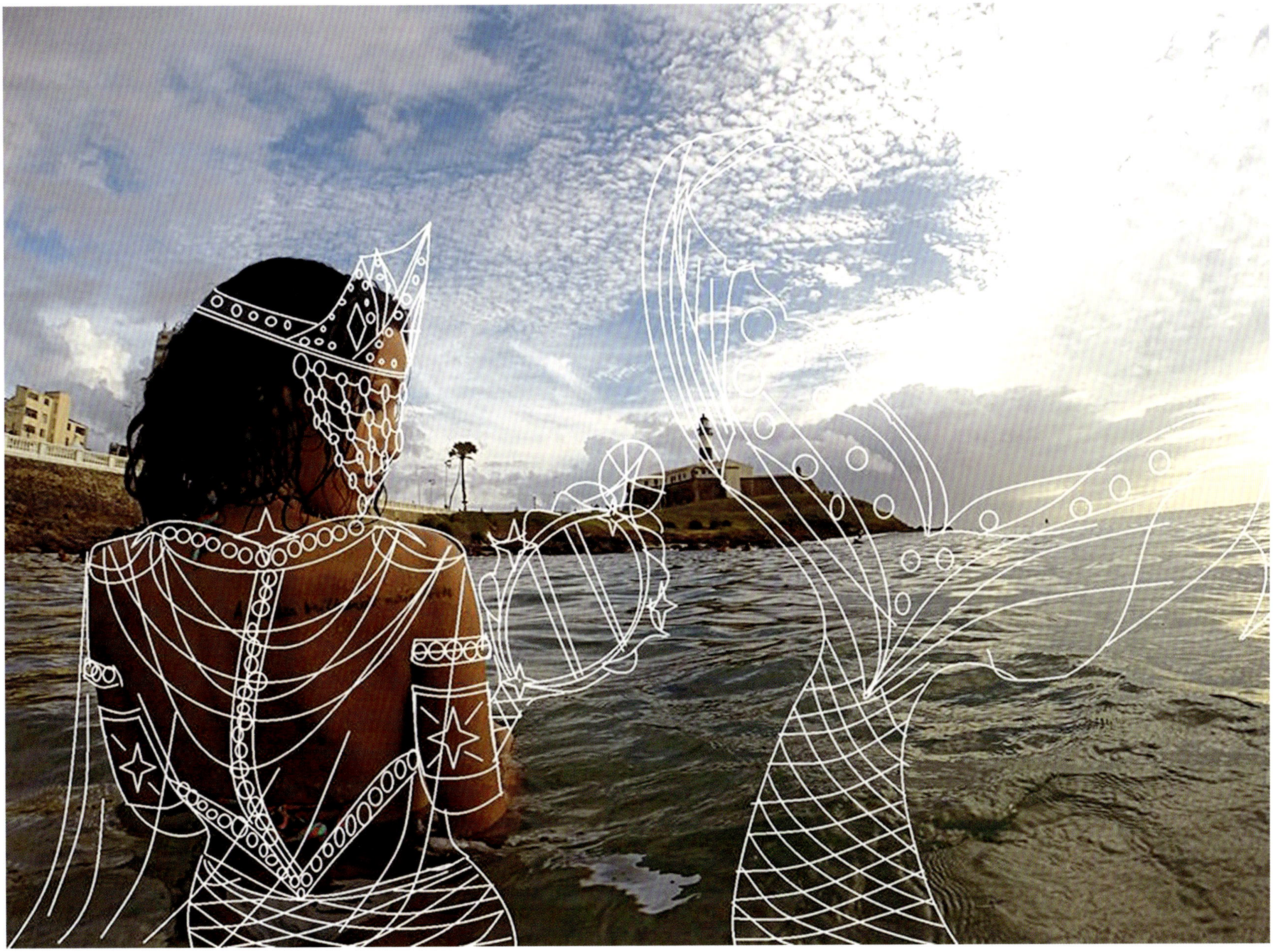

**3.5**
Tauan Carmo (b. 1993, Salvador, Bahia, Brazil)
Drawing by Tauan Carmo, photograph by Tiago Troccoli
*Oxum—A Rainha das águas doces* (Oxum—The Queen of the Fresh Waters), 2016
Digital photograph enhanced with Microsoft Paint
COURTESY OF TAUAN CARMO

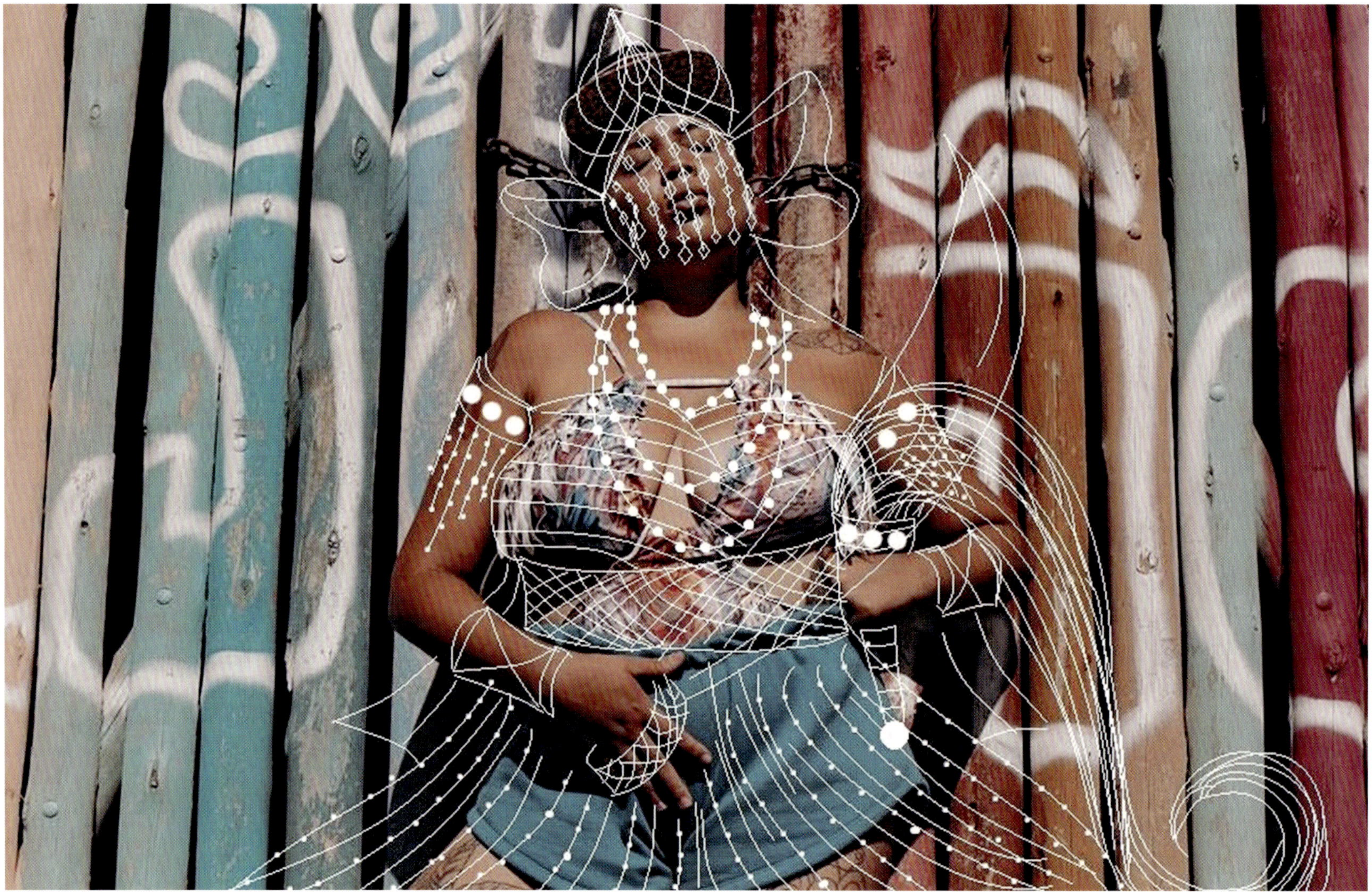

**3.6**
Tauan Carmo (b. 1993, Salvador, Bahia, Brazil)
Drawing by Tauan Carmo, photograph by Edgar Azevedo *Iansã—A rainha dos raios* (Iansã—The Queen of Lightning), 2016
Digital photograph enhanced with Microsoft Paint
COURTESY OF TAUAN CARMO

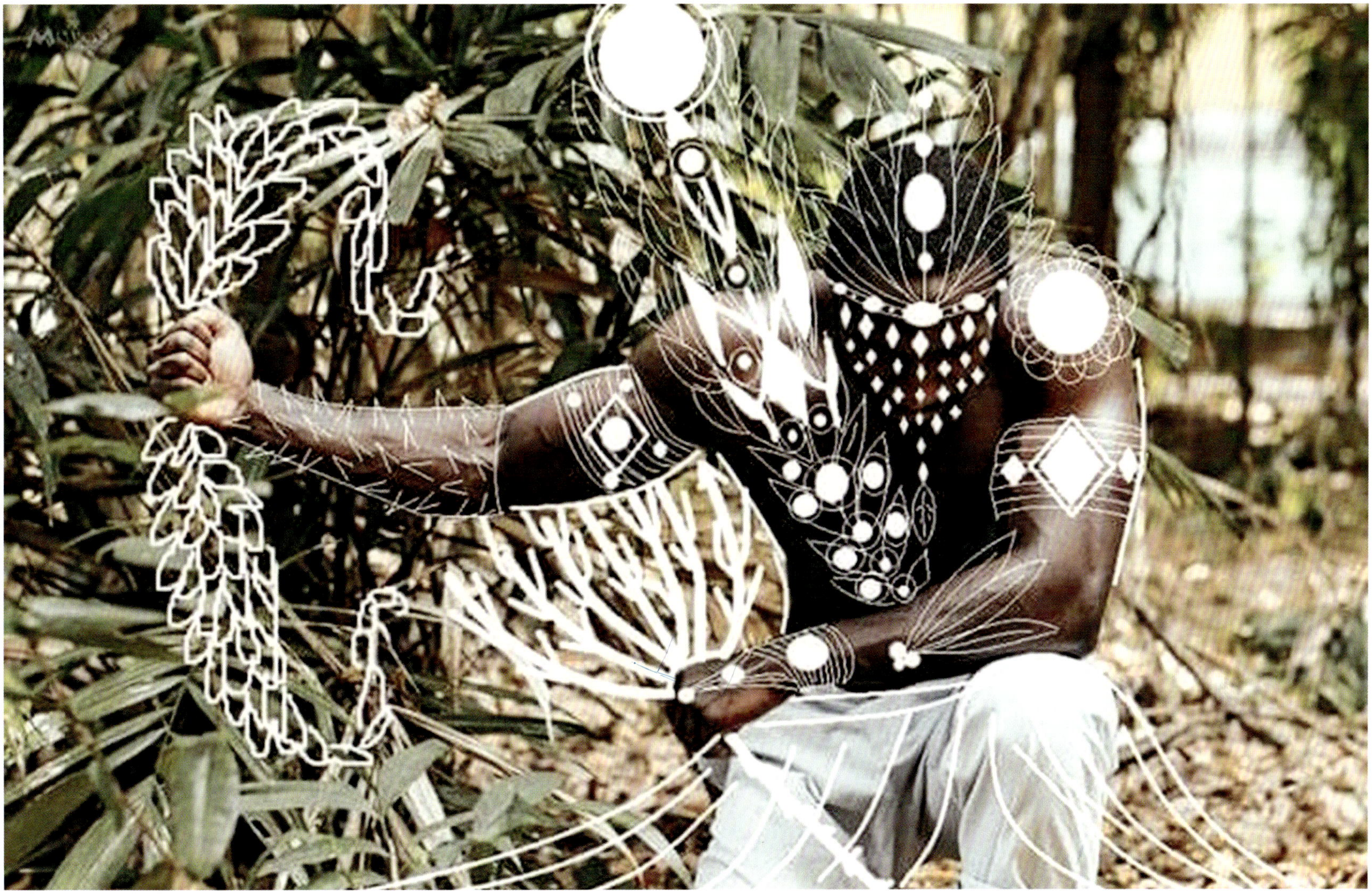

**3.7**
Tauan Carmo (b. 1993, Salvador, Bahia, Brazil)
Drawing by Tauan Carmo, photograph by Marco Menezes
*Ossain—O senhor das folhas* (Ossaim—The Lord of the Leaves), 2016
Digital photograph enhanced with Microsoft Paint
COURTESY OF TAUAN CARMO

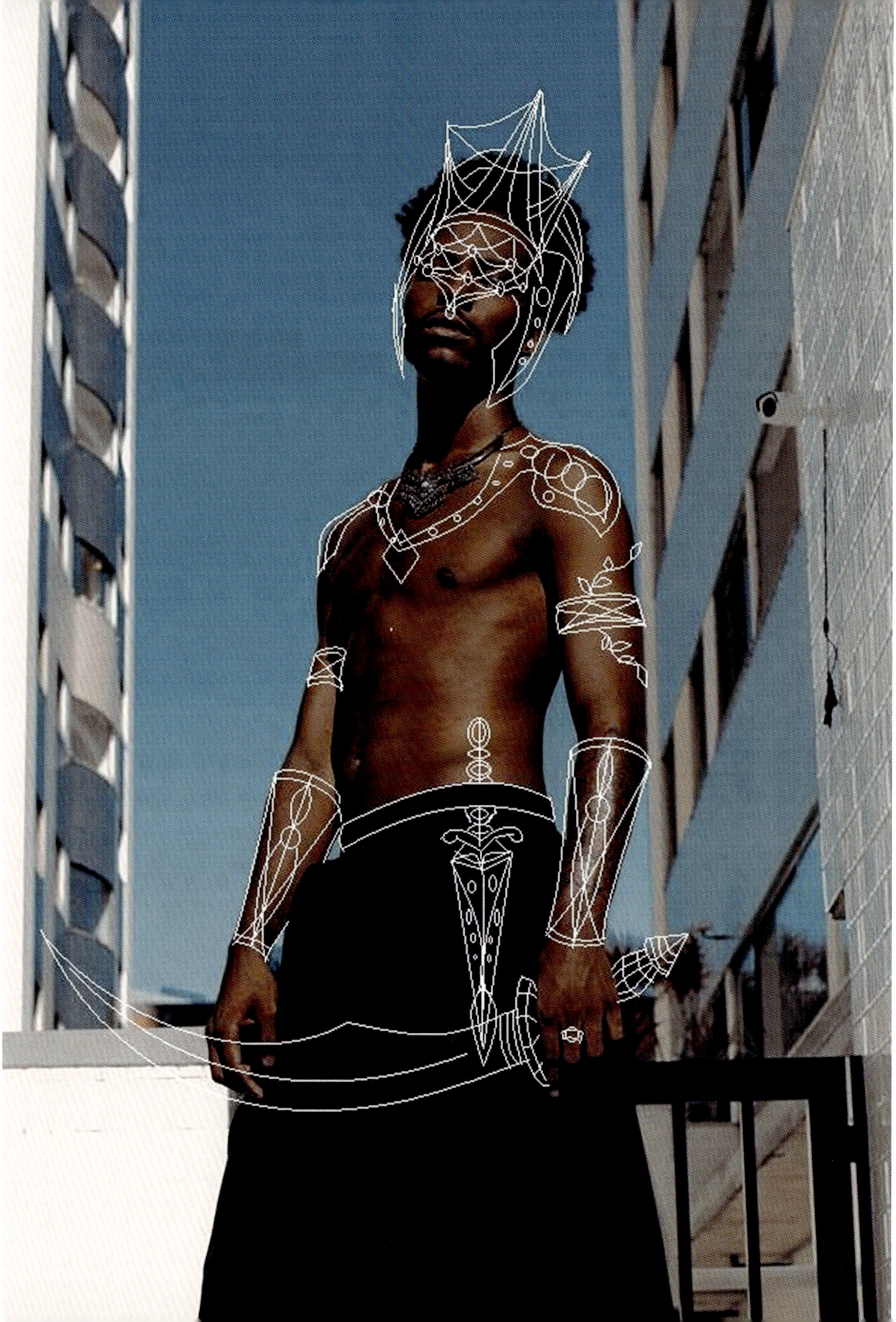

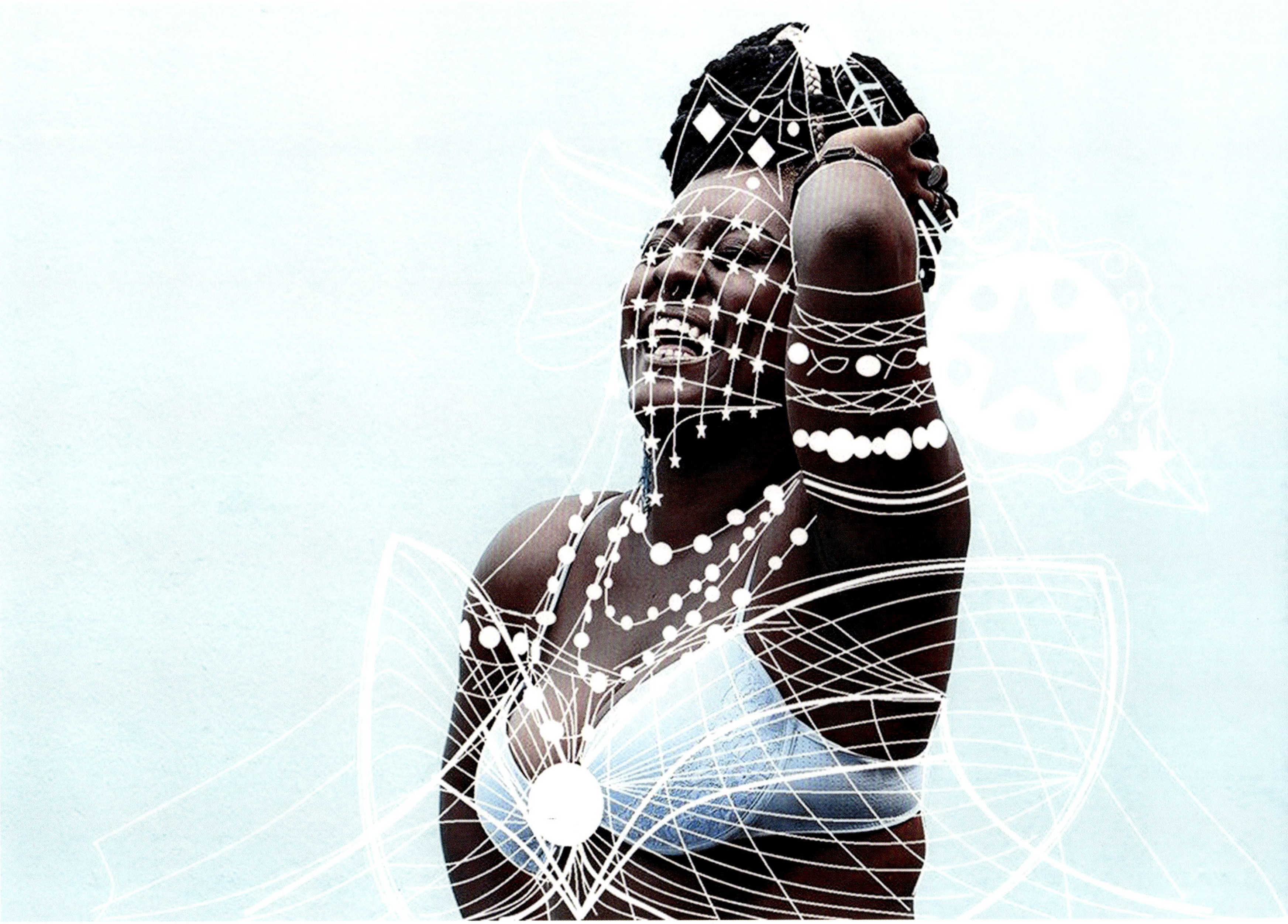

**3.8**
Tauan Carmo (b. 1993, Salvador, Bahia, Brazil)
Drawing by Tauan Carmo, photograph by João Lima
*Ogum—O senhor do ferro* (Ogum—The Lord of Iron), 2016
Digital photograph enhanced with Microsoft Paint
COURTESY OF TAUAN CARMO

**3.9**
Tauan Carmo (b. 1993, Salvador, Bahia, Brazil)
Drawing by Tauan Carmo, photograph by Helen Salamão
*Iemanjá—A rainha do mar* (Iemanjá—The Queen of the Sea), 2016
Digital photograph enhanced with Microsoft Paint
COURTESY OF TAUAN CARMO

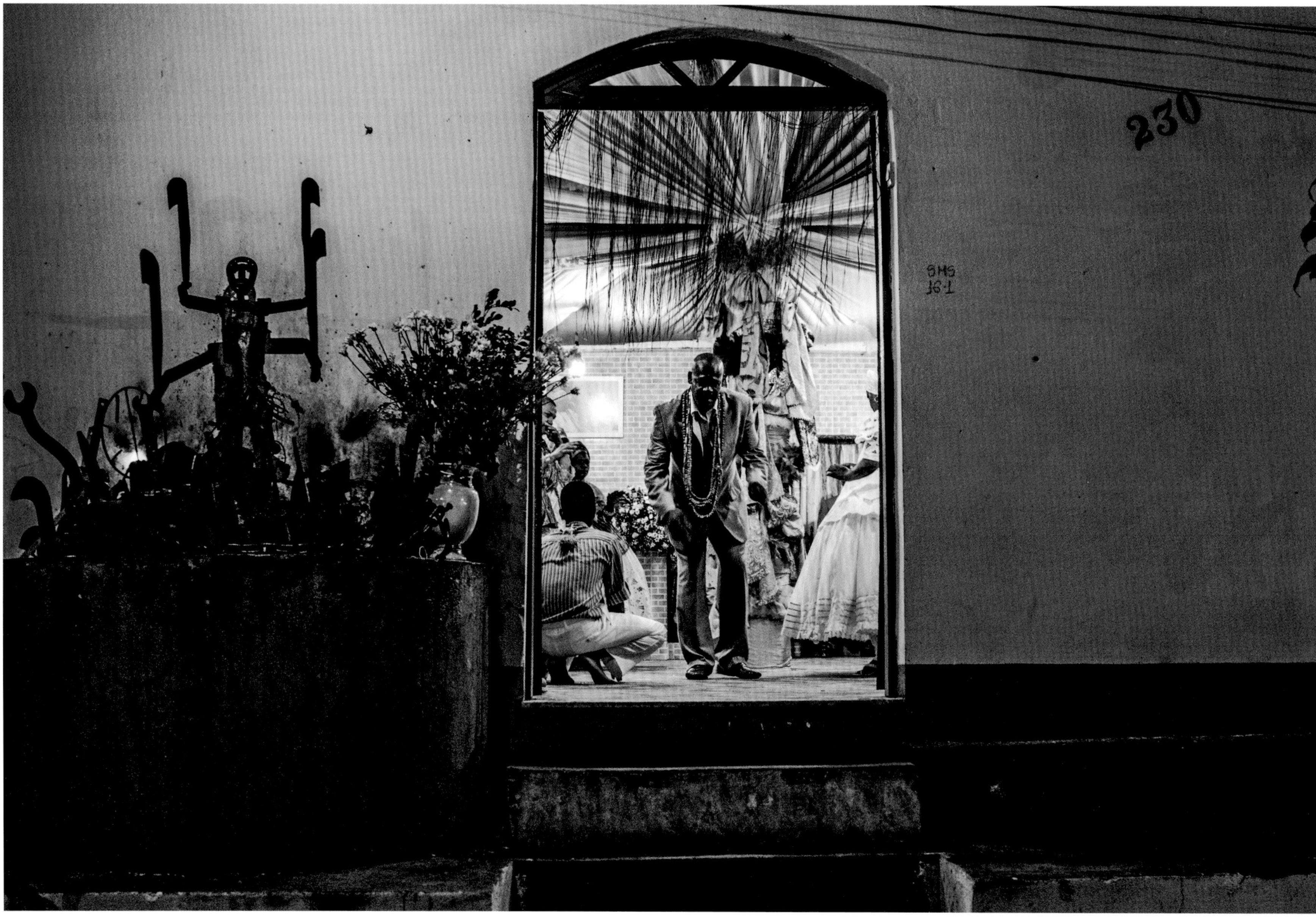


**3.10**
Tacun Lecy (b. 1997, Salvador, Bahia, Brazil)
*Candomblés Nagô: Ilê Axé Ogunjá* (Nagô Candomblés: Ilê Axé Ogunjá Temple), January 18, 2014
PHOTOGRAPH
COURTESY TACUN LECY

## The Body

People may spend a whole lifetime without knowing that they belong to an *orixá* (see Matory, this volume). In some circumstances, however, the *orixá* asks for worship: we could say, people who belong *with* are asked to belong *to*. The *orixá* can cause physical, mental, and social afflictions if those they choose do not fulfill their duty (*obrigação*) to them. Candomblé houses are organized to make people understand what these duties are and to allow them to perform them correctly (fig. 3.10). Of course not everything is about obligation, these are communities built upon conviviality, but there is a very strong discourse relating to hierarchy and order, described in the language of the family and the "house." There, a *mãe de santo* (a high priestess, or "mother of the saint") or *pai de santo* (a high priest, or "father of the saint") will identify the *orixá* and what it requires. This could be a simple offering, but it could also be much more than that: the *orixá* may want to seize the body of a person through spirit possession. In that case, the person will need to go through initiation, or *fazer o santo* (making the saint). This involves a very long and complex process during which the initiate will be confined in the Candomblé house of the priest, and his or her *santo* will be "made" (*feitura de santo*), meaning that the relationship between the initiate and the *orixá* will be ritually fixed. Just as the initiator is known as the *mãe de santo* or *pai de santo*, the initiate will be called *filha/filho de santo* "daughter/son of saint." The relationship between them is strictly hierarchical, as the kin terminology would indicate. The outcome of the initiation process is twofold. First, the person will learn to deal with the phenomenon of spirit possession with the *santo* who will periodically possess her or his body in the rituals of the Candomblé house. Second, the *santo* will be present in a shrine, as each initiate adds a personal shrine to the general shrine of each *orixá* (the generic spirit) in the Candomblé house. The *santo* is formed through this process. It is the outcome of the particular relation between the *orixá* and the individual.

To understand this process in more detail, we should explain the ritual of the *bori*, or "giving food to the head." The head (*ori*) is the receptacle of *axé*, and by "feeding the head," one makes it strong and protects it from spells. *Bori* is also the signature of an alliance with the *orixá*, because the head is the place where *orixás* seize power over their acolytes. In the ceremony of the *bori*, the *mãe de santo* or *pai de santo* makes offerings to the head of the person and to the *orixá* who owns this head. Several kinds of foods are passed around the head of the participant, as well as deposited on it and spit on it (figs. 3.11a-l), and part of the food will be given to the *assento* (seat) of the person's *orixá* in the temple. At that point an animal is sacrificed, and its blood is placed or daubed on the body of the participant and the shrine of the *orixá*. After that, the participant must sleep in the Candomblé house, perhaps even spend some days there, so that his or her *ori* has time to eat.

The *bori* creates a link between the Candomblé house and the participant, the *mãe de santo* has "put her hand on the head" of the new initiate and fed it. After this, the initiate belongs to the *axé* and the house, which also means that he or she is now "obliged" to the *orixá* and to the house. The initiate is at the base of a hierarchical structure, led by the *mãe de santo* and must now periodically attend the ritual washing (*ossé*) of the *assento* with water and sacred leaves (*amassi*).

A Candomblé shrine is typically composed of a central, or house, *assento*, surrounded by the pots of the initiates—their particular *assentos*, which extend and reproduce the main *assento*, the *axé* of the house. Thus, the *assento* reproduces materially the hierarchy of people in the Candomblé house. In the rituals of possession the *santo* is first called in the *assentos* with sacrifices and offerings. These offerings, followed by drumming, enable the transference of spiritual power from *assento* to the *ori*, from the object to the person possessed.

**3.11a-l** (OVERLEAF)
Ayrson Heráclito (Ayrson Heráclito Novato Ferreira, b. 1968, Macaúbas, Bahia, Brazil)
*Bori* (Feeding the Head), 2008–2011
Photographs
COURTESY AYRSON HERÁCLITO

Heráclito's work is a contemporary art performance inspired by the Candomblé ritual of *bori*.

A. Ogum
B. Oxóssi
C. Omolú
D. Xangô
E. Ossaim
F. Oxumaré
G. Tempo
H. Oxum
I. Iansã
J. Iemanjá
K. Nanã
L. Oxalá

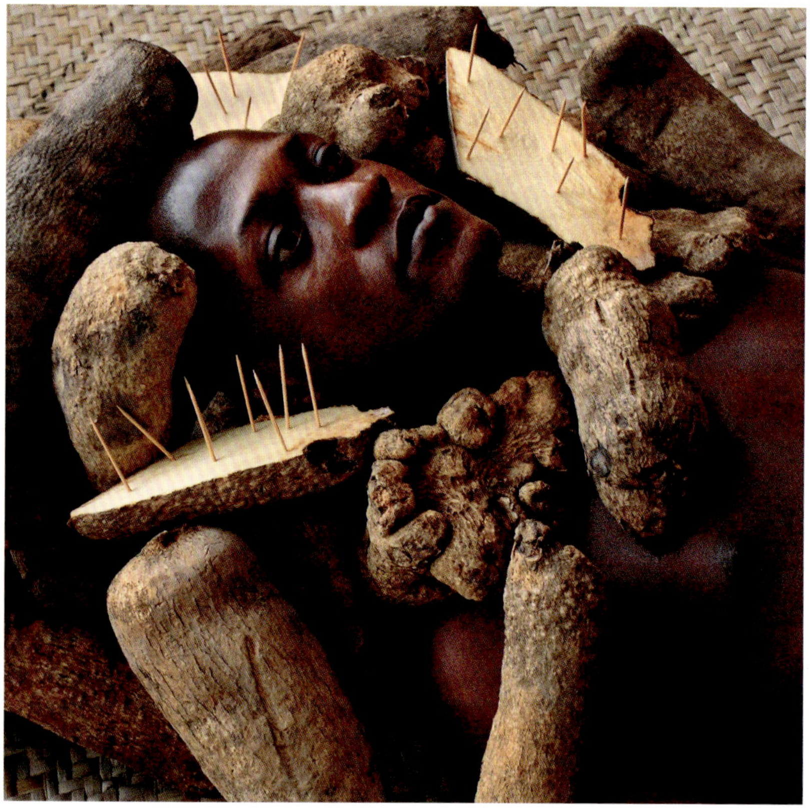

A.Ogum

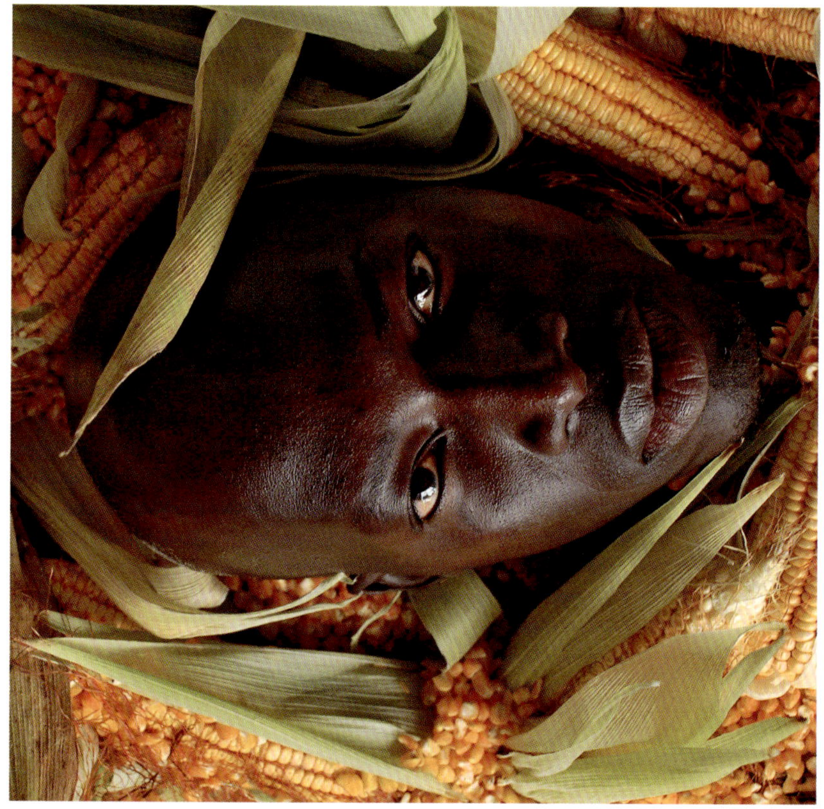

B.Oxóssi

B.Omolú

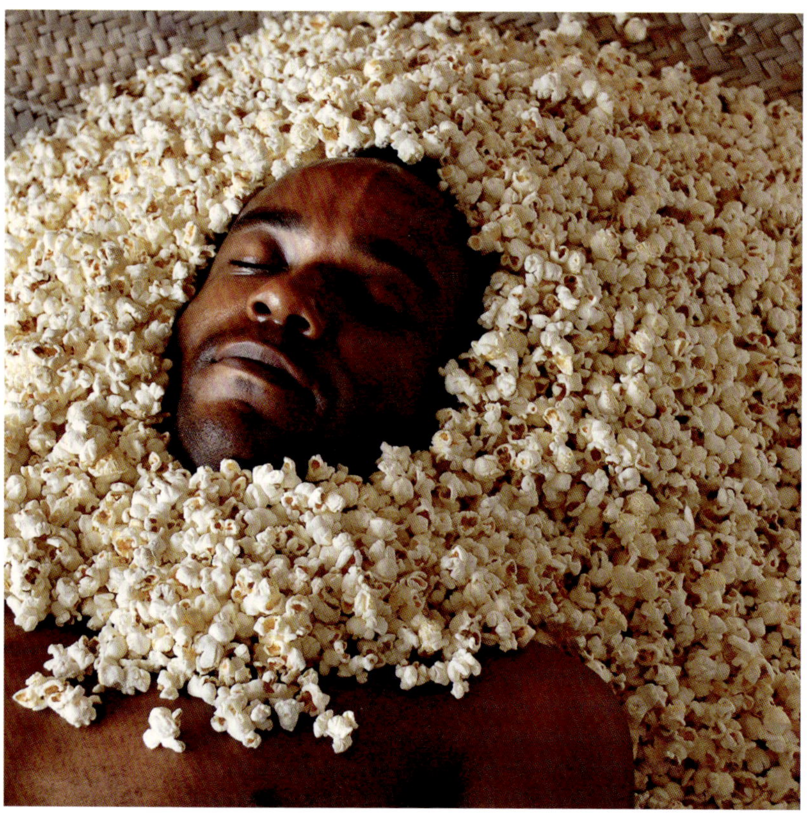

D.Xangô

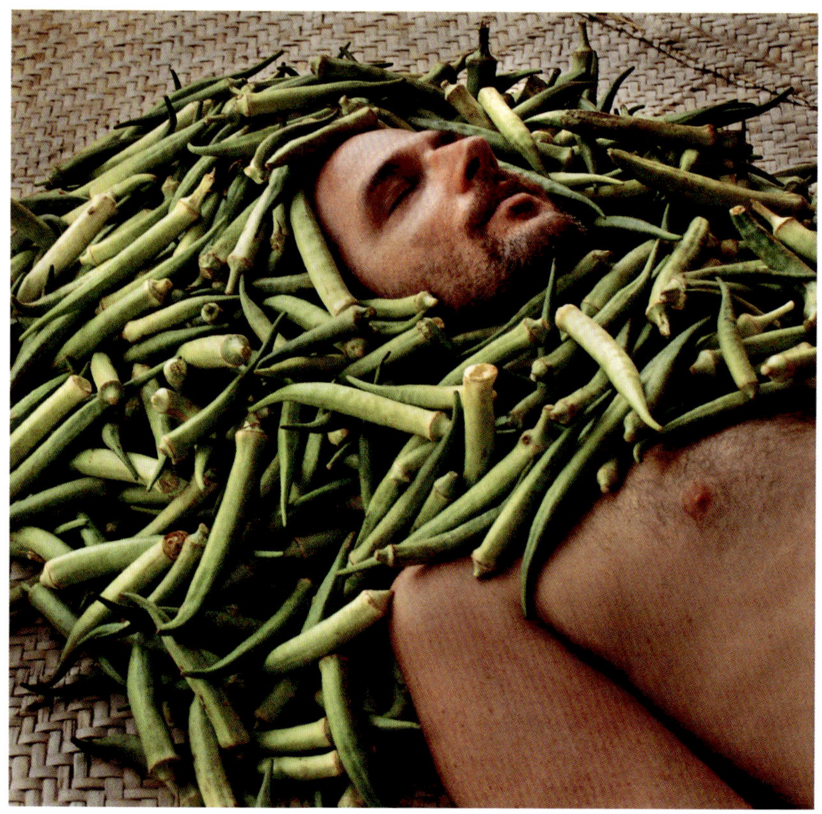

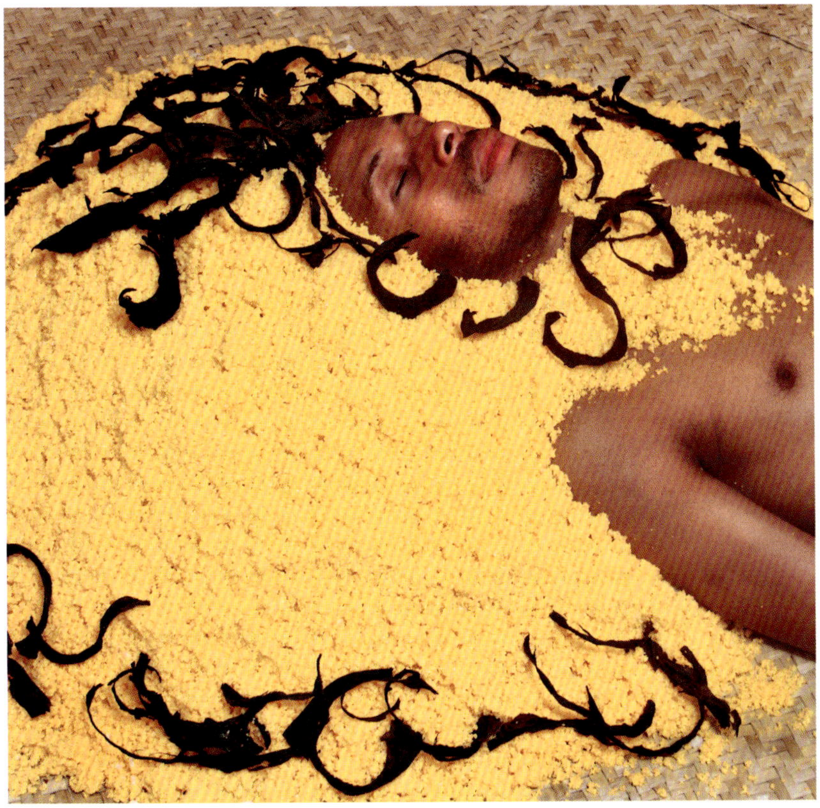

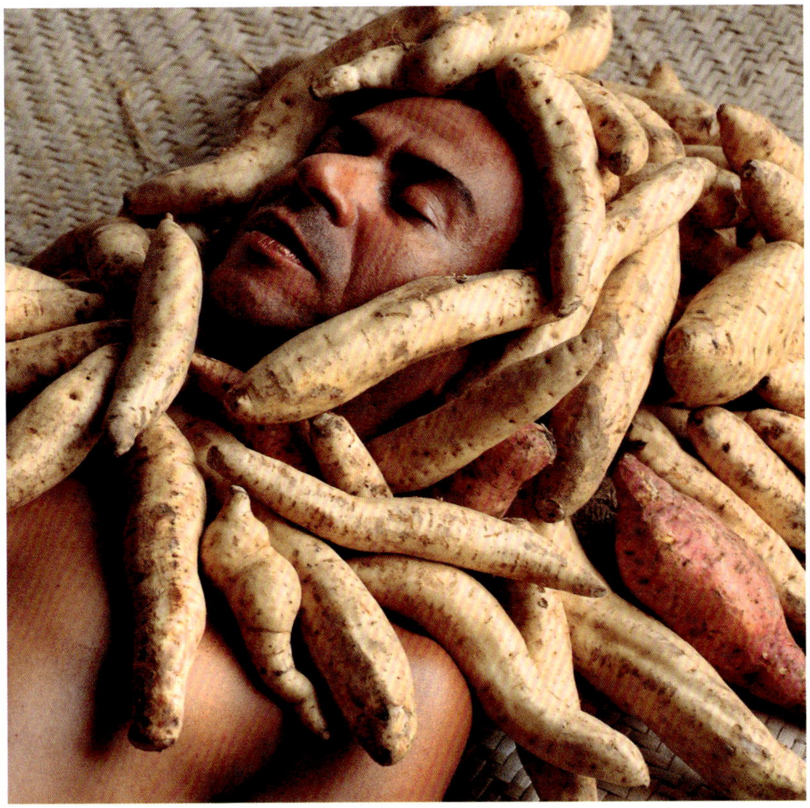

E. Ossaim

F. Oxumaré

G. Tempo

H. Oxum

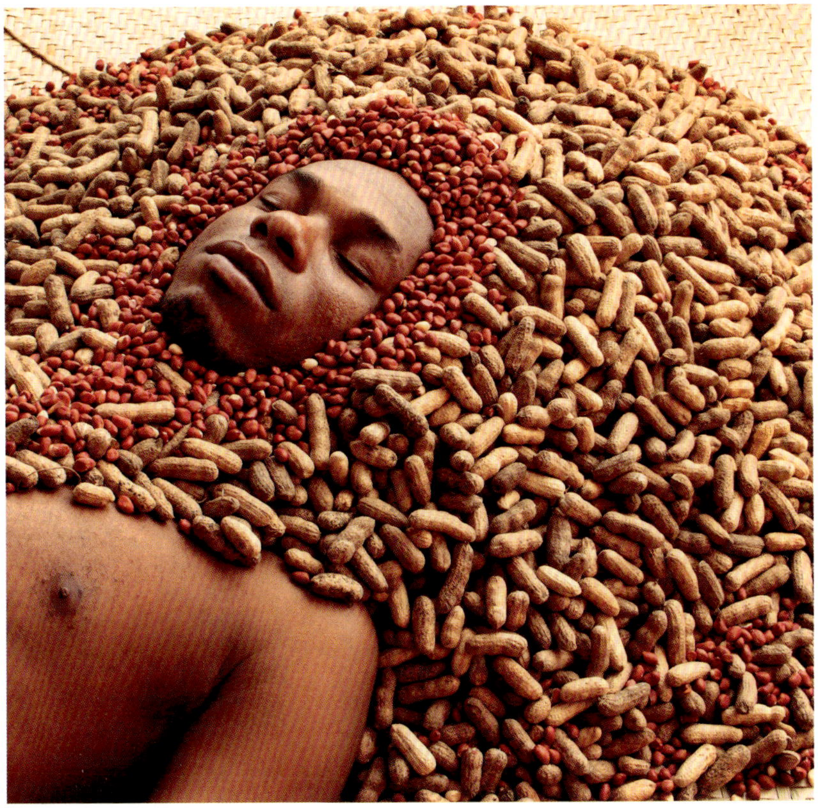

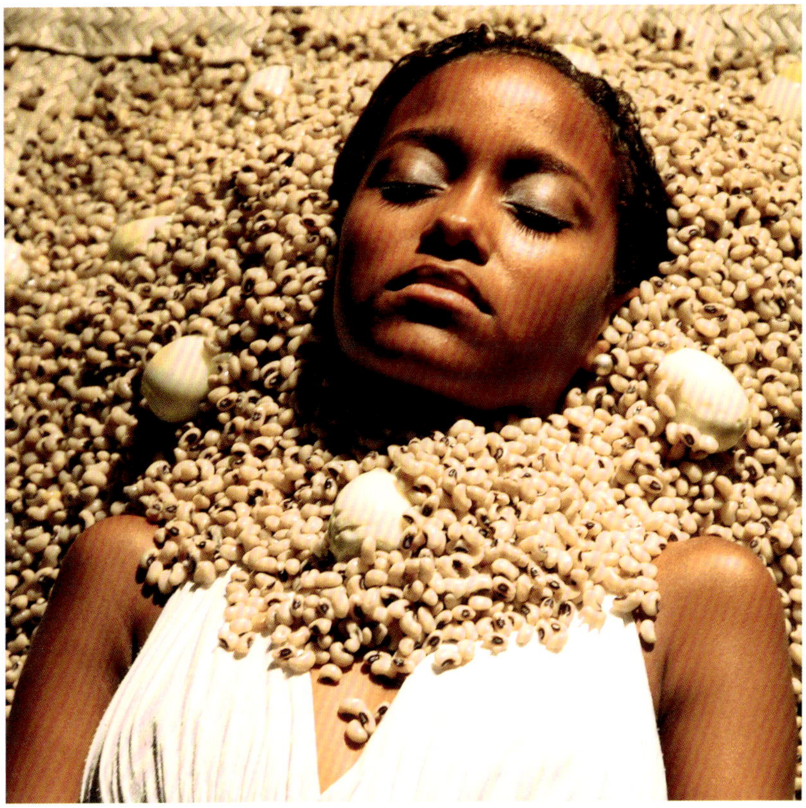

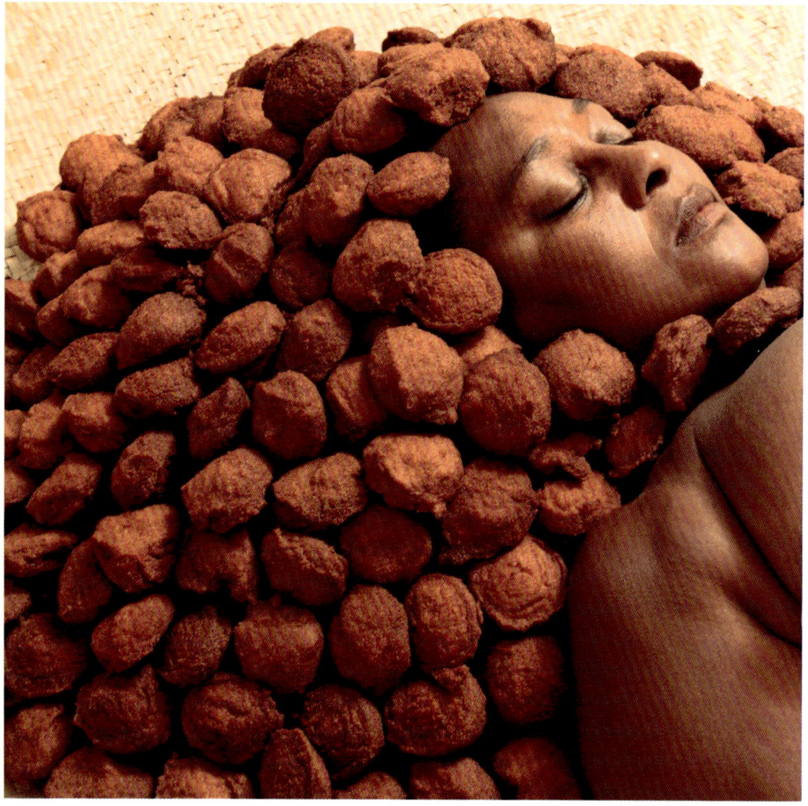

I. Iansã

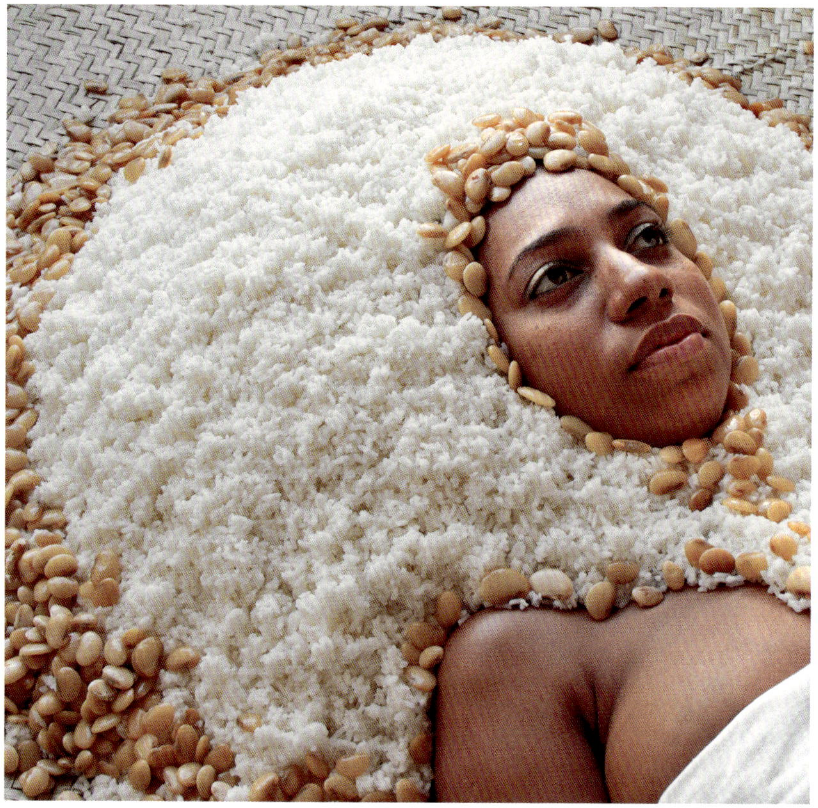

J. Iemanjá

K. Nanã

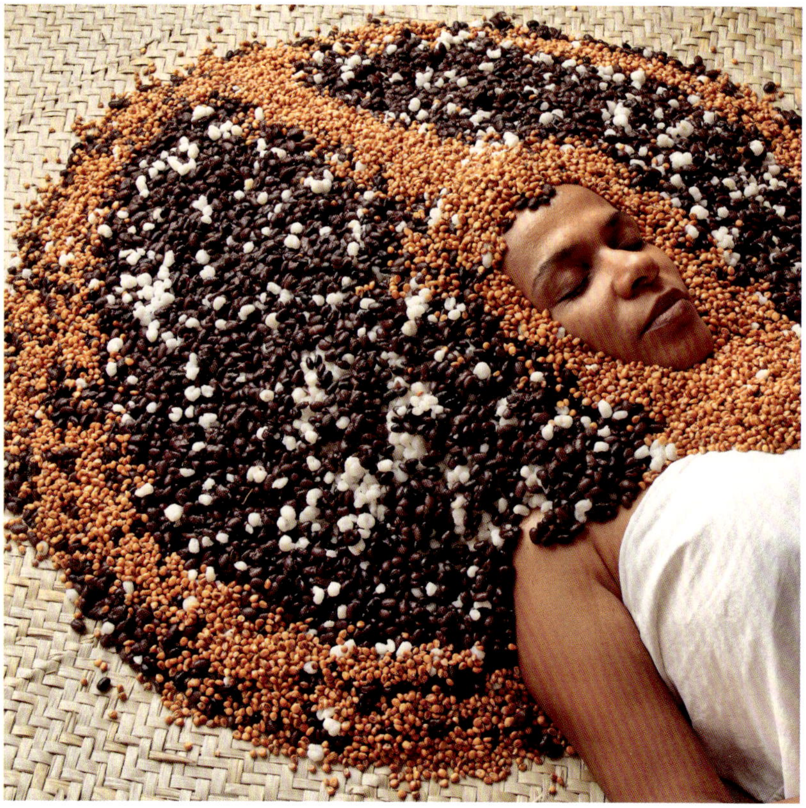

L. Oxalá

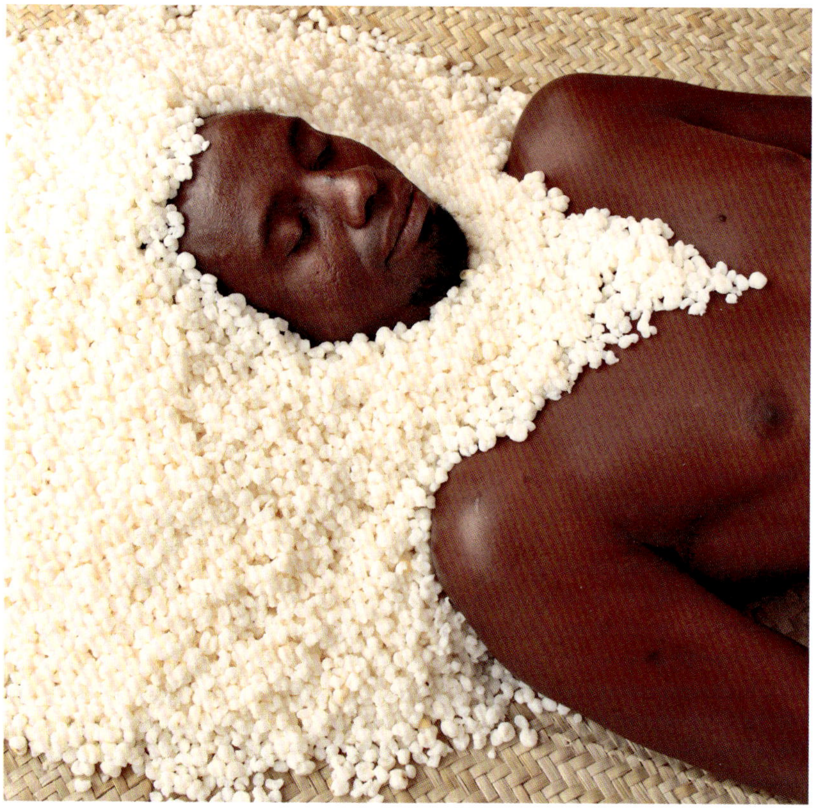

After this process, the initiate can "make the saint," that is to say incorporate the *orixá*, in the event that the *orixá* wants this. After a long seclusion and intimacy with the *assentos*—spent in the *quarto do santo* (the room of the *assentos*) and learning the secrets— the initiate's head is shaved (*raspada*) by the *mãe de santo*, and a little cut is made in the top of the head, where the blood of sacrifices and other elements of *axé* are shed. Then the head is painted with the motifs of the *orixá* (fig. 3.12), and the initiate comes out in a public ritual known as *saída de santo* (coming out of the saint). The initiate is possessed and the *santo* cries out loud his or her initiation name.

The *filhas/filhos de santo* take part in the *roda de santo*, or *xirê*, the "round" dance in which the *orixás* are incorporated. These elaborate ceremonies are the more public and stereotypical face of Candomblé, where everyone—even outsiders and tourists—is invited to eat foodstuffs related to the *orixá* being celebrated, partake of drinks like *aluá* (a fermented beverage incorporating ginger, brown sugar, and white corn), and witness the beauty of the spirits. The *filhas/filhos de santo* dance for a long time until they start to shake and lose their balance. Sometimes, it appears almost as if they have been struck by lightning. They throw away shoes, glasses, anything that bothers them. Their bodies become stiff with their arms stuck to their sides, and they make only slight movements leaning their shoulders forward, as if somebody were "riding" on their backs and clenching the reins. Their faces become hieratic, their eyes close, and their mouths make strange grimaces. The attendants (*ikede*) help them take off their clothes, and they wrap a cloth called *ojá* around the waists of the *filhas/filhos de santo* in a particular way depending on the *orixá* (if it is male or female, essentially). Then, barefoot and wearing the *ojá*, the saints start dancing, hesitantly at first. After some songs, however, they will retire to the room or house where the implements of the *orixás are kept*. They come back fully attired, impersonating the *orixás* Ogum, Iansã, Oxum, and so forth, in all their splendor. They dance freely and make distinctive cries or sounds that identify them. Their faces, however, remain mask-like: they never open their eyes. Their regal attire demonstrates that they were once queens and kings in Africa. It combines African-inpired fabrics and styles with elements reminiscent of Catholic saints (for example, the Roman helmets associated with Saint George, and also with Xangô or Ogum). The *orixás* can also carry other implements in their hands, like the fan (*abebé*) of Oxum or the sword of Ogum.

After seven years of "making the saint," the *filha/filho de santo* can be become a *mãe de santo*, following the *deca*, a ritual that gives a person the power to open her or his own house of Candomblé. It is also referred to as *dar a navalha* (to give the razor) because it bestows the capacity *raspar cabeça* (to shave the head), that is, the power to initiate people, *assentar* and to seat and to make the saints, *fazer o santo*.

The *orixás* are present, therefore, in people and things: in the body of initiates and in shrines (Sansi 2005). Their presence is described in terms of force, or *axé*. *Axé* is particularly expressed in and through sacrifice, although it is not only through sacrifice that it comes into being. This force is present in varying degrees in different people, places, and things. Powerful *mães de santo* and shrines that have witnessed many initiations and sacrifices are said to have a lot of *axé*, which is given, not bought or sold. The *orixás* give *axé*, and powerful *mães de santo* in turn give *axé* to their *filhas/filhos*. This is a gift-giving relationship that creates community; but this community is clearly hierarchical, there are people with more and people with less *axé*. It should be made clear, nonetheless, that *axé* is not exactly an objectified power. It is not something that people have as property, but is something that they *are*—it is not detachable from them as persons, it is inalienable.

The house of Candomblé can also be called the *axé*, since the house is the assemblage of all the instances of this *axé* in people and things. Thus, an initiate who becomes a *mãe de santo* and opens a new house of Candomblé, must take her or his shrine to the new location. The new house will, however, have the *axé* of the original house because they are, in fact, the same.

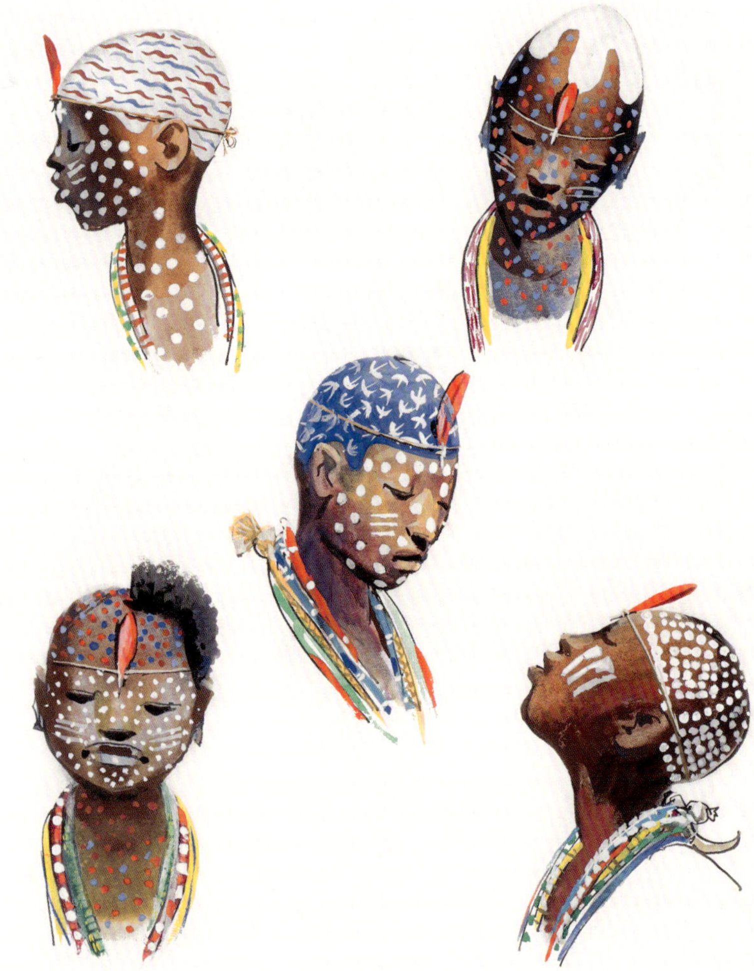

**3.12**
Carybé (Héctor Julio Páride Bernabó, b. 1911, Lanús, Buenos Aires Province, Argentina; d. 1997)
*Iaôs de Oxumaré, Ogum, Oxossi, Oxum* (Initiates of Oxumaré, Ogum, Oxóssi, and Oxum), undated
Ink and watercolor (gouache) on paper
66 x 48 cm


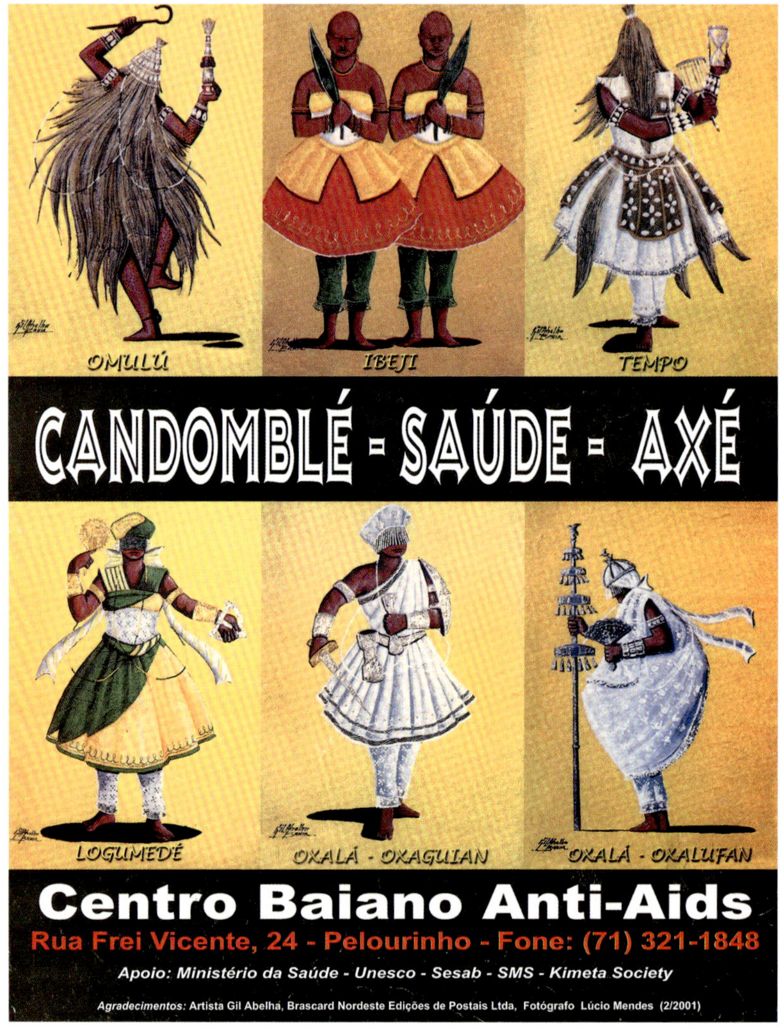


**3.13**
Lûcio Mendes, photographer
Centro Baiano Anti-AIDS (Bahian Anti-AIDS Center)
*Candomblé-Saúde-Axé* (Candomblé-Health-Life Force), circa 1980s
Ink on paper
38 x 28 cm


This AIDS prevention poster uses popular images of the *orixás* by Bahian artist Gil Abelha (Gildásio Feliciano Costa; see figs. 2.3a-l).

### Shrines

Popular art based in Candomblé, like that of the painter Gil Abelha (fig. 3.13, and see figs. 2.3a–l), often portrays scenes of spirit possession, the best-known feature of the religion. Candomblé, however, remains a religion of the secret (Johnson 2002; Van de Port 2011). Some things can be seen by all, but others are forbidden even to devotees. The lifelong process of initiation is one of partial revelation, wherein the initiate gains access not only to discursive or practical knowledge but also to the right to *see*, eventually becoming the guardian (*zelador*) who will allow or restrict the view of others.

The distinction between what should and should not be seen is, however, fundamentally ambiguous. Despite these separations, as Van de Port has shown (2011), nothing is totally concealed or invisible, just as what appears to be public or visible is never totally accessible. Concealment and revelation are dynamically related; they are interdependent. The rituals of possession are ephemeral and take place in a building or room set aside for ceremonial purposes (*sala* or *barracão*). Candomblé shrines, however, are for the most part kept in closed rooms or buildings with restricted access.

Altars are accumulations of objects related to the *orixás* on a dais or other supports, together with pots and other containers, generally covered with cloths and hidden from public view. Inside of these there are other objects, generally stones (*otá*) that embody the *axé* of the *orixás*. On the pots we often find *ferramentas*, or tools made of iron, with emblems of the *orixás*, like those made by José Adário dos Santos (Zé Diabo; see interleaf E, this volume). Shrines are not supposed to be seen, and thus the devotee is not supposed to look at them directly. The Candomblé shrine, the *assento*, is thus very different from Catholic altars where images of the saints are supposed to be seen. Candomblé shrines are composed of active elements that do not simply represent, but make present the saints. That is no obstacle, however, to the inclusion of Catholic images in Candomblé shrines as we will see below.

The *assento* is not the image, but the house of the *santo*. Shrine offerings open the circulation of *axé* that will culminate in spirit possession. The living image of the *santo* is the body of the *filha/filho de santo* possessed, dancing, and dressed in the clothing of the *santo*. This image changes through time as the relationship between *santo* and initiate changes. The initiate progressively grows and deepens in knowledge, and the body becomes better adapted to the ritual of possession, which becomes less violent. At the same time the person's shrine becomes bigger, richer, filled with presents that serve as an objectification of this intense interaction. The *filhas/filhos de santo* talk, pray, and sing to their shrines, and ask for help from their *santos*; offerings and gifts are added continuously; periodically, the pots are washed and their contents changed. The "life" of shrines is always renewed through interaction with the initiates. The constant ritual feeding establishes a highly determined and determinant relationship between shrine and initiate; the shrine becomes an extension of the practitioner.

The objects accumulated in the shrines are part of the *santo*. Ogum, *orixá* of war and iron, whose color is blue, receives iron tools and blue robes. Iansã, *orixá* of storms, whose color is red, receives copper, jewelry, red fruits, red robes, and *acarajé* (a bean pastry fried in palm oil). Despite the fact that we often find similar objects in different shrines, there is virtually no limit to what can be added. The association with the *santo* can be extended to many kinds of objects that the *filha/filho de santo* finds suitable. Presents are difficult to locate, and those that are felt to be most appropriate are often found through coincidence or an element of chance. These fortuitous encounters are described as necessary: moments of revelation that had to happen. The found object is an index of the saint, who left it there to be seized upon by the initiate. That means that anything can become part of a shrine, if the saint wants it. An Ogum shrine can accumulate pots, tools, car parts, or typewriters, if he wants it to. It is important to understand the apparently random and disordered character of the objects in shrines. They do not stand for specific qualities intended to form a logical ensemble, on the contrary, they are accumulations of things that people have found and feel to fit naturally with the spirit that lives in the shrine.

### Images

Figurative images are among the objects found in shrines. Some scholars maintain that the *orixás* of Candomblé are not "represented" in sculptures, pointing out that in Africa the wood carvings found in shrines represented the initiates in a state of possession, rather than the *orixás* themselves (Santos 1967). The fact is, however, that like other shrine objects, images are often found objects and have been recognized by initiates as their saints. In this way, they are not seen so much as representations of Catholic religion, but as indexes of this personal encounter. If Catholic images were once dominant in Candomblé shrines, it was not only due to an implicit project of "syncretism" between religions but also because Catholicism was overwhelmingly hegemonic in the production of public images. Through time, however, Afro-Brazilian religions like Umbanda, have borrowed imagery from many other sources of popular culture (figs. 3.14, 3.15). For example, Oxum or Iemanjá may be represented as mermaids—Oxum strawberry blonde and Iemanjá, brunette.

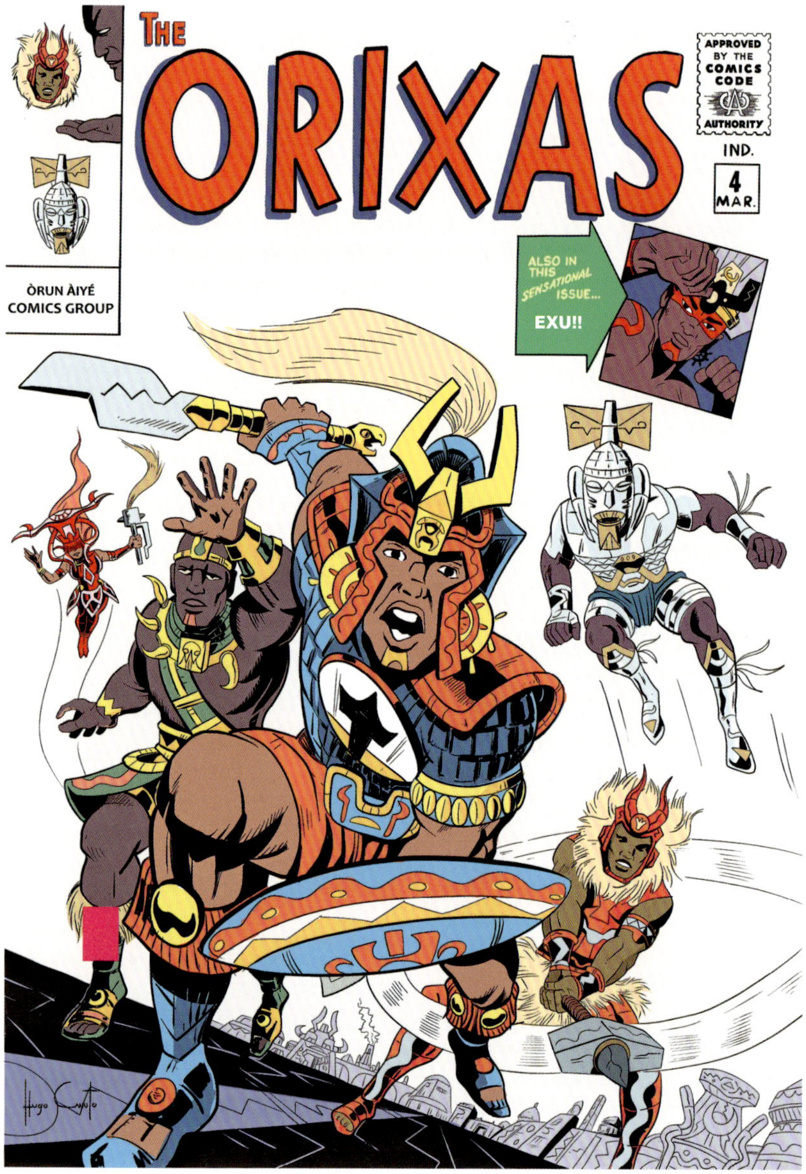


**3.14**
Hugo Canuto (b. 1986, Salvador, Bahia, Brazil)
*The Orixás*, 2016
Pencil and digital art
59.4 x 42 cm
COURTESY HUGO CANUTO

Canuto created this work, patterned after Marvel's *The Avengers*, as a tribute to the celebrated American comic book artist Jack Kirby on his birthday. This is a case of popular culture borrowing from Afro-Brazilian religion.

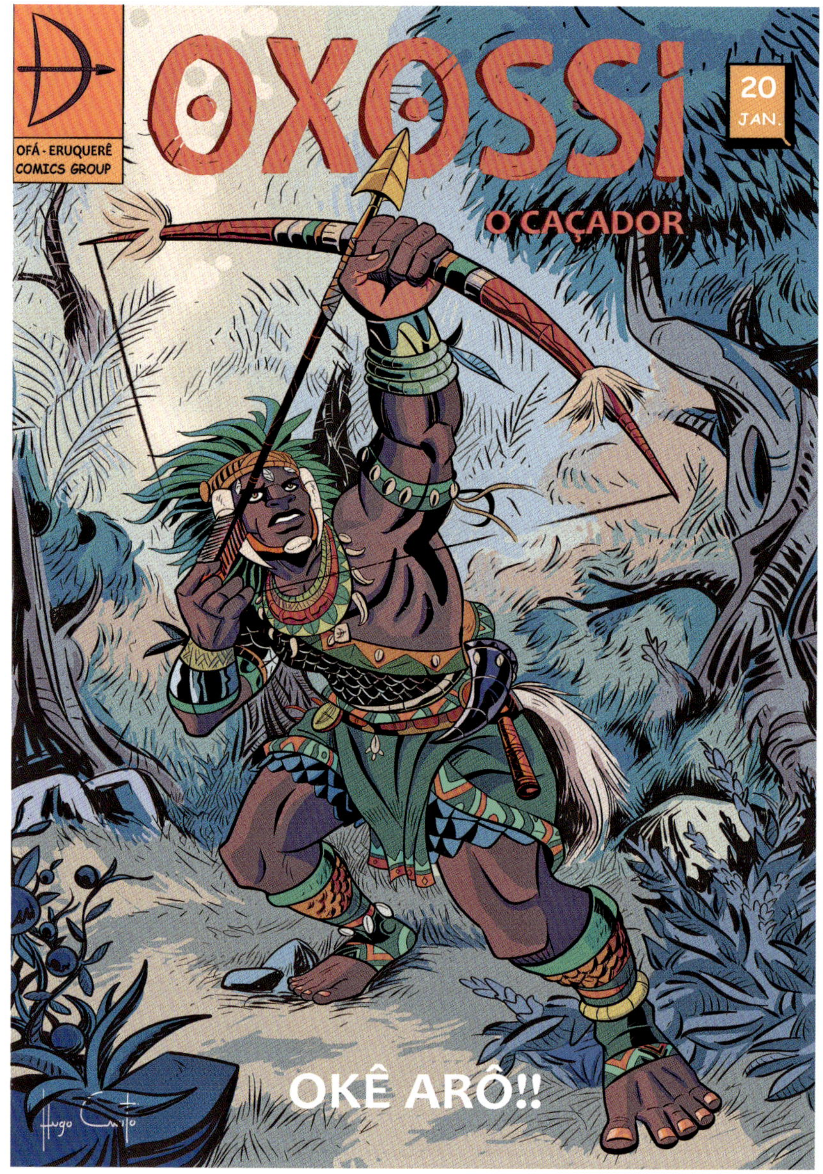


**3.15**
Hugo Canuto (b. 1986, Salvador, Bahia, Brazil)
*Oxóssi—O Caçador* (Oxóssi—The Hunter), 2016
Pencil and digital art
59.4 x 42 cm
COURTESY HUGO CANUTO

### Moving Images

Visitors to Candomblé houses are often told that taking pictures or videos is not allowed. This is explained in different ways. It could be said that you can't represent the *orixás* in pictures: they are dynamic entities, pure force, and their images are the moving bodies of the initiates incorporating their saints. Although the ritual of possession is structured and routinized, the dance always includes unexpected turns, swirls, and improvisations, happening at a pace that is difficult to follow for those who are not acquainted with the *orixás*. They have to be seen live. According to anthropologist Patricia de Aquino, the *orixás* can't be "freeze-framed"(2002), they are dynamic entities that can't be reproduced in static images.

Today, given the normalization of digital media, pictures and videos of the rituals are regularly taken and used privately, as family photo albums and home videos by Candomblé communities. It is true that visitors, outsiders, or tourists taking pictures of rituals will not always be welcome. Perhaps the issue with photography is not so much the technique as the control of its outcomes (Castillo 2008), that is, who takes the pictures and for what purpose. The censorship of the visual reproduction has to do not just with the aesthetics of Candomblé, but with its notion of the person. Photographs are, obviously, indexes. Our image is a part of ourselves, we don't feel comfortable giving it away to outsiders. That is true for a Candomblé ritual as it would be for any ritual in private life—a wedding, baptism, and so forth. "Freeze framing" the gods, the control over the mechanical reproduction of images in Candomblé is first and foremost an issue of privacy and intimacy. Furthermore, particularly in relation to sorcery (*feitiço*), objects that emanate from the body, including photographs, can be used to cast spells against the people they index. Intimacy and sorcery are in many ways coextensive: the question is who will use the image, for what purpose, and to what extent these images can be considered a part of the person.

If the reproduction and distribution of images is controlled by the Candomblé house, the "danger" of these reproductions seems to be less urgent. They are used, as "personal memory banks" (Van de Port 2011). What is important is that these images keep a record of the past. The question becomes what past, which events are being recorded, and to what extent these records manage to encapsulate the miraculous. More important than the ways in which Candomblé is represented is the presence of the sacred. Through photographs and videos, the adherants can see an image of their own *santos* that they had not seen before as manifested in their own bodies.

### Art and Spirits

I will close this chapter with a story. In 1996 a group of intellectuals, artists, and Candomblé houses, constituted as Societies for the Protection and Defence of Afro-Brazilian Cults, filed a legal complaint against the Museum of Forensic Medicine of Bahia for threatening public decency (Sansi 2005). During the trial, the plaintiffs argued that beautiful creations of sacred black art should not be displayed in an exhibition with a racist and perverse ideological discourse wherein these works of art were exhibited as objects of criminological and pathologic interest. What the representatives of the Candomblé houses were asking was precisely that the material culture of Candomblé be made equal to Western art.

Most of the items comprising the collection of confiscated objects are now held by other, more community-focused museums, such as the Museu Afro-Brasiliero (Afro-Brazilian Museum), which now holds 199 of them in its Estácio de Lima Collection. Others have not been displayed, including, for example, the *otás*, the sacred stones of Candomblé. These cannot be displayed in public and are not displayed publicly in Candomblé houses. As opposed to the other objects, they are not works of art or artifacts. Their immanent power must be respected and hidden.

Although one might expect that they would be returned to the Candomblé temple they came from, this has not happened. The archives of the museum were not exhaustive, and apparently they were destroyed in a fire some decades ago (Sansi 2005). From the point of view of Candomblé, however, there may be other sources of information about their origin: through the oracle of the cowry shells, one could try to identify the *orixás* of these *otás* if they were still there (they could have departed). They could be taken to a Candomblé house, if somebody would assume the responsibility for caring for them. When an *orixá* doesn't want to leave her or his shrine, after the *mãe de santo* has died, some other *mãe de santo* can take responsibility for it. So in the end, the stones were left in the old museum. Recently, originators of an art project for the 3rd Bahia Biennial (2014), conducting research for an exhibition on *Archive and Fiction*, discovered a stone in the deposits of the museum and decided to include it in the Biennial (Pato 2015), together with other objects from the museum, in order to display the recent colonial past of the city. After the Biennial, the stone went back to the storage area of the museum, perhaps making the case that in spite of good intentions, there are things in Candomblé that should not be made public.

Interleaf **E**

# Visiting the Forge of Ogum

## The Iron Work of José Adário dos Santos

**Lucas Marques**

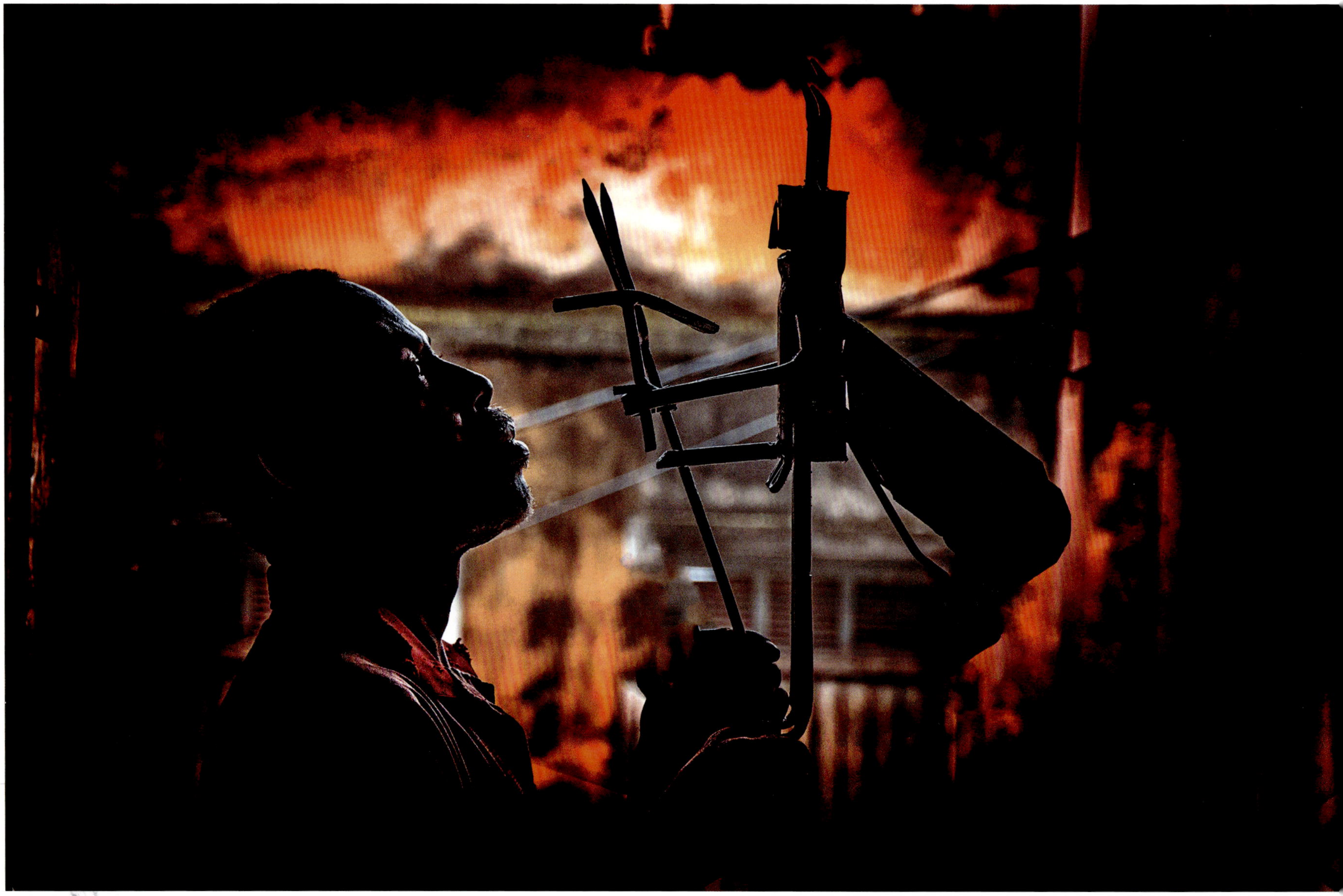

**E.1**
Adenor Gondim (b. 1950, Rui Barbosa, Bahia, Brazil)
Zé Diabo, 2010
Photograph
COURTESY ADENOR GONDIM

**E.2**
Zé Diabo, aka Zé Bahia (José Adário dos Santos, b. 1947, Salvador, Bahia, Brazil)
*Ogum Ajá*, 2015
Metal
H: 68 cm
FOWLER MUSEUM AT UCLA X2015.17.1; MUSEUM PURCHASE

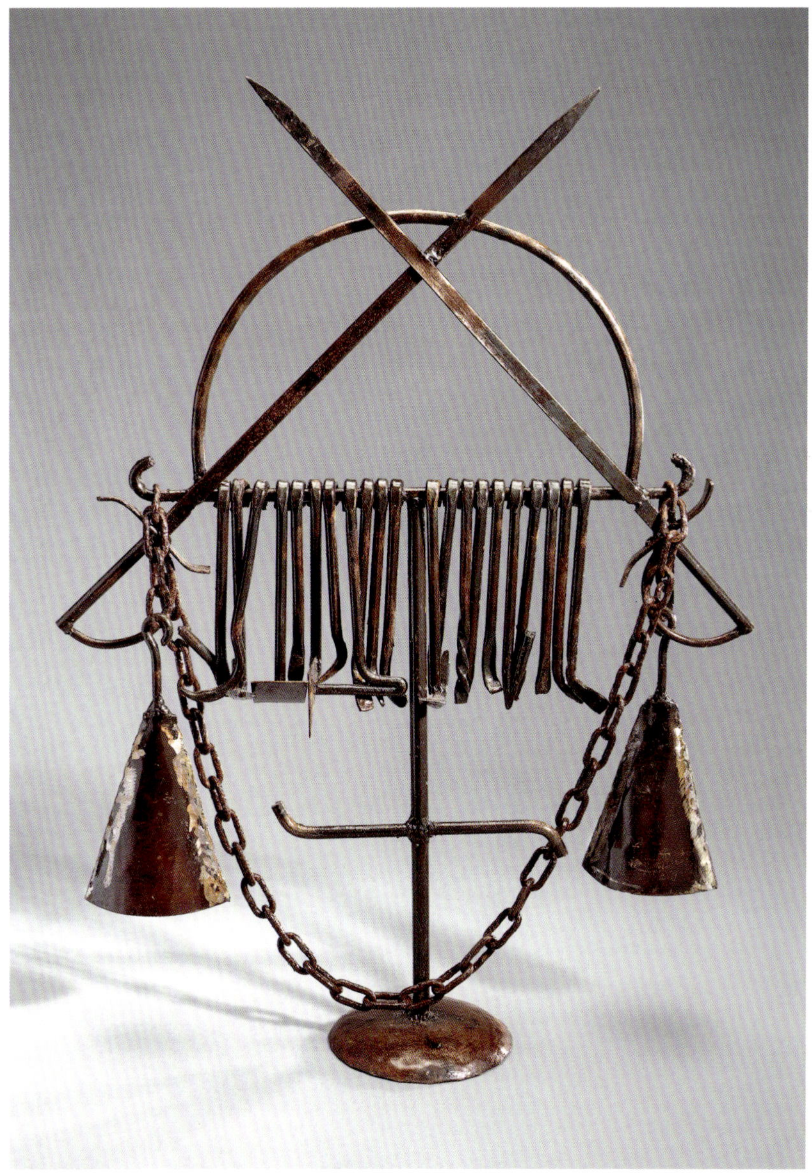

WHEN AFRICAN PEOPLES CAME TO THE AMERICAS, crossing the Atlantic in a forced migration, they brought with them their customs and practices, ways of life and subjectivities. Once they disembarked on the "new continent," those traits were brutally violated: their homelands became accursed, their customs, barbarous; their practices were reduced to "superstition," their personhood massacred. Nevertheless, as Roger Bastide once said, the slave ships carried not only men, women, and children, but also their gods (Bastide 1971), and it was through them that those peoples imaginatively re-created their subjectivities in what was certainly the greatest process of reterritorialization in human history. This gave rise to the broadest and most varied range of religions of African origin in the Americas—among them, Afro-Brazilian Candomblé.

Of all the divinities that arrived in Brazil, Ogum is certainly one of the most popular. He is the *orixá* of war and the deity of iron, farming, and technology, particularly the forge (figs. E.2, E.3). In some places, like Rio de Janeiro, Ogum is associated with Saint George, the warrior saint, while in Bahia he is linked to Saint Anthony, mainly because of his military characteristics and his ability to "open up pathways." Very close to his brother Exú, Ogum is the one who removes obstacles from our way and who rules over production and labor—the blacksmith, warrior, artisan *orixá*.

It is Ogum who commands the work of José Adário dos Santos, or "Zé Diabo," one of the best-known *orixá* blacksmiths in Bahia. This traditional form of labor consists in the creation of *ferramentas de orixás* (*orixá* "ritual implements" or "tools"), artifacts that become—or are consecrated for—entities that belong to Afro-Brazilian religions: *orixás*, *exús*, *voduns*, *inquices*, *caboclos*, etc. Even though the *orixás* of Zé Diabo are Oxalufã (an incarnation of Oxalá) and Omolú, Ogum rules his whole path. Ogum is his *compadre* (partner), the one who shows him the way so he can work with iron: "Because everything in my path is iron, is the *jabá* of Ogum, so I follow the path of Ogum. Oxalá was never a blacksmith, neither was Omolú, so no; so I follow the path of Ogum. He's the one who gives me the strength to beat the iron, to follow my path," says Zé. His connection with the *orixá* is so close that he only produces implements for entities using iron. Working with other materials, as he says himself, would require him to deal with other forces and skills, to follow different paths: "What I was really born to do is to work with raw iron. I was raised that way. It was Ogum that made me that way."

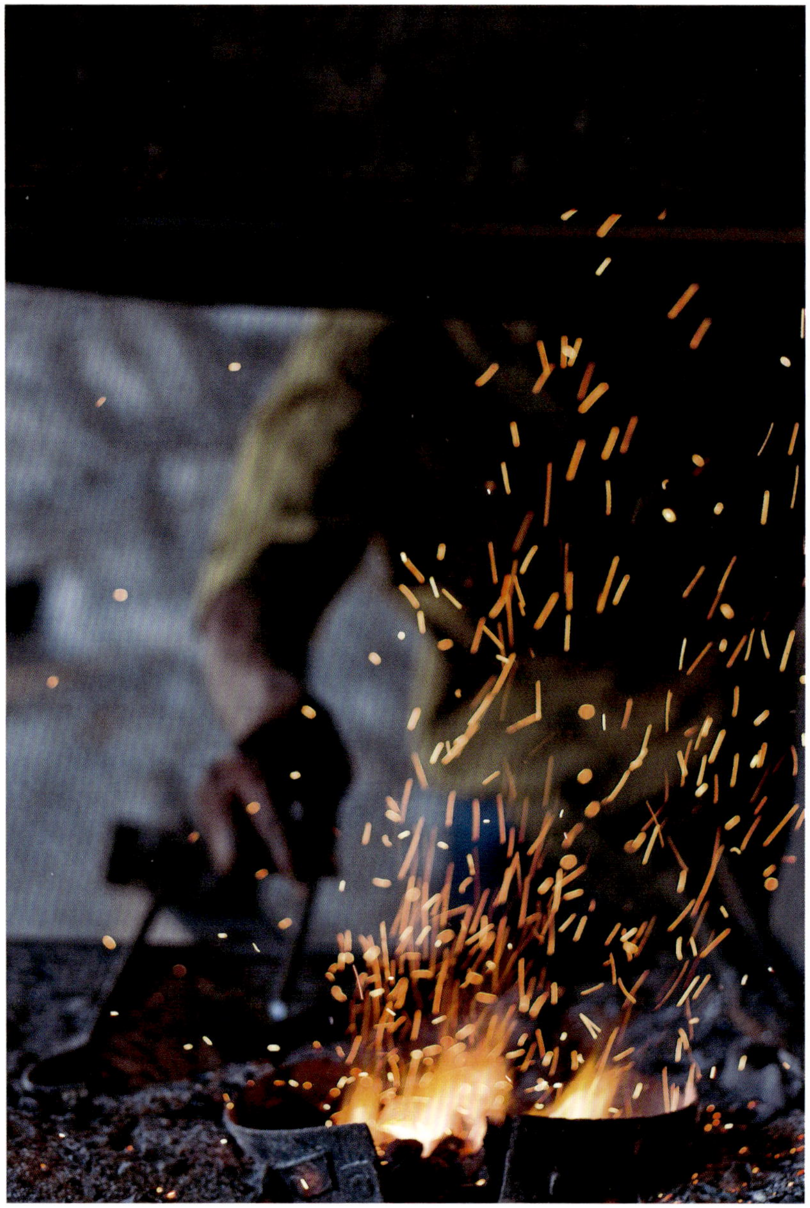

**E.3**
The forge of José Adario dos Santos (Zé Diabo)
PHOTOGRAPH BY LUCAS MARQUES, 2013

My first impression when I met Zé Diabo was that he was Ogum in the flesh, standing right in front of me (fig. E.1). His deep gaze, his black body protected by a string of blue beads hanging from his neck, his calloused hands, and the dog who accompanied him at the time—an animal traditionally associated with this *orixá*—all created the right atmosphere to foster that impression. When I saw him working, this link became even clearer. As he connected a bare wire to a precarious power source, Zé began to show me an entirely unknown world: the forge of the *orixás*. Once the motor for the bellows was switched on, the fire began to come to life, heating the iron bars brought into contact with it (fig. E.4). Meanwhile, Zé waited in silence, leisurely enjoying a cigar, creating an ambiance of smoke and mystery. It took no more than few minutes for him to grab the iron bars and, with just a few strokes of the hammer—a veritable extension of his arm—bend them as if they were slender wires, creating all kinds of shapes under the rhythm of the blows: spears, arrowheads, knives, birds, and so on. As I witnessed that scene—Zé Diabo working with iron bars in the heat of the fire, like the conductor of an orchestra arranging with different rhythms, gestures, and actions—I had the feeling that all this work took place in an atmosphere that was more than human. Sacred.

Endowed with profound practical knowledge, Zé learned the art of smithing in the same street where he works today, the historic Ladeira da Conceição da Praia in Salvador. It was there, in 1958 at eleven years of age, that José began learning the *orixá* blacksmith's craft. A few years later, after the passing of his teacher and mentor, Martiniano Prates, he opened his own workshop, Nação José (José Nation), specializing in the making of *ferramentas de orixás* and *agogô* bells. His technical apprenticeship in forging metal paralleled his learning process with Candomblé itself. Initiated into that religion by his maternal grandmother, Barbara do Sacramento, when he was eight, Zé Diabo is also considered a great *babalorixá*, or Candomblé high priest.

The nickname, Zé Diabo, is related to one of the most important deities in Candomblé: Exú. Exú is the *orixá* who comes first in the pantheon of Afro-Brazilian gods (figs. E.5, E.6). Nothing can be done without honoring him first. He is the messenger between the *orixás* and humans in the spiritual and material worlds, respectively the Orun and Aiyê. His realm is the streets and crossroads, the passages. Something of a trickster figure, Exú is also the *orixá* of cunning and sexuality, endowed with an enormous phallus (*ogó*) and a propensity for turning the tables and playing games. Because of this, one of the multiple versions of Exú—the one with horns and tail—was associated with the "Devil" of popular Catholicism, and it was because of this *ferramenta* of Exú that Zé got the nickname "Diabo" ("devil" in Portuguese), which he has borne all his life. He carried so many statuettes of Exú around the Mercado Modelo (a Bahian arts and crafts marketplace) that when people saw him they just had to say: "Look, there's the devil," or "Here devil, devil." As a result, as he tells it, the nickname caught on and was adopted and respected: José Adário dos Santos, or "Zé Diabo."

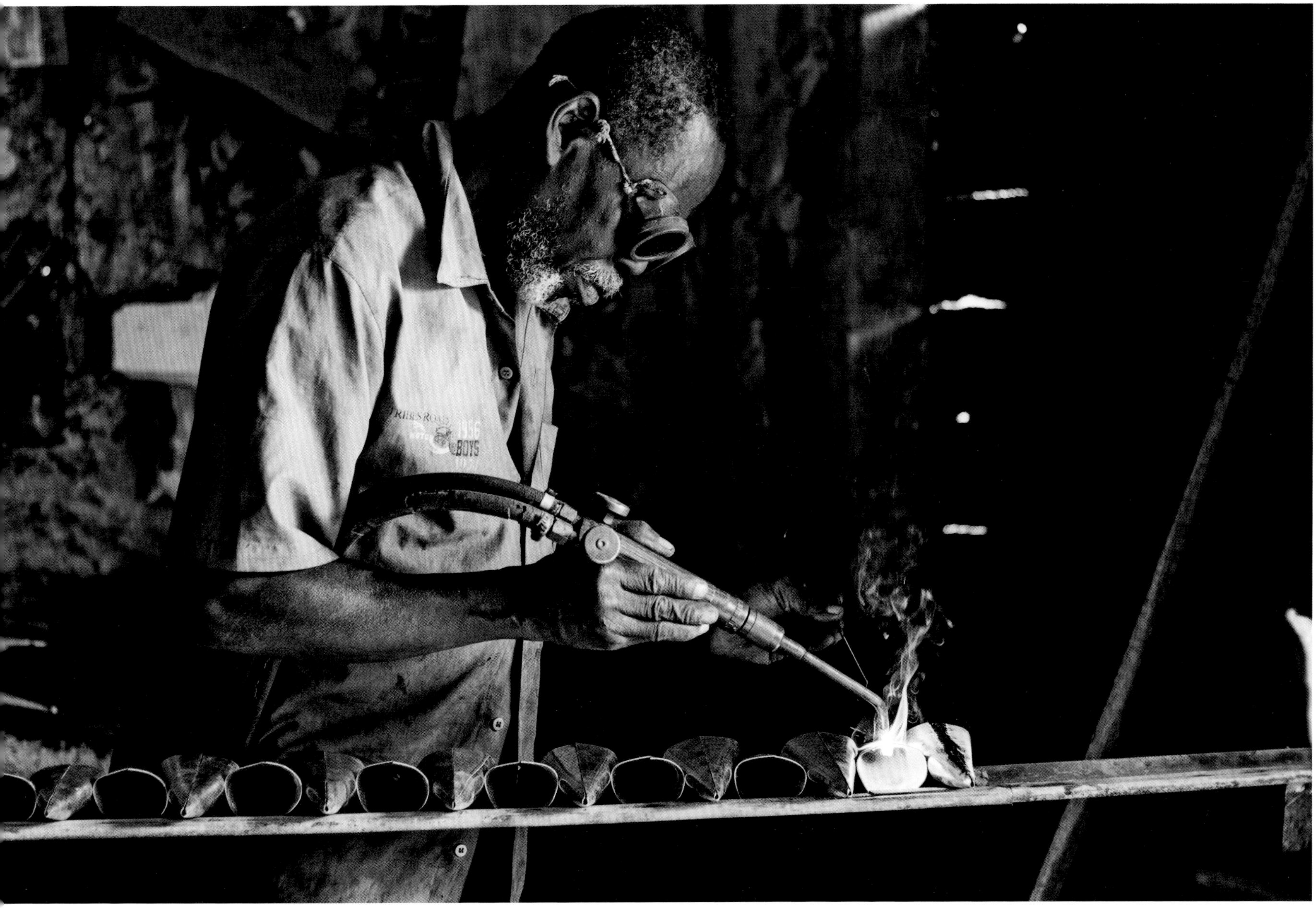

**E.4**
Zé Diabo welds *agogô* bells at his forge.
PHOTOGRAPH BY LUCAS MARQUES, 2013.

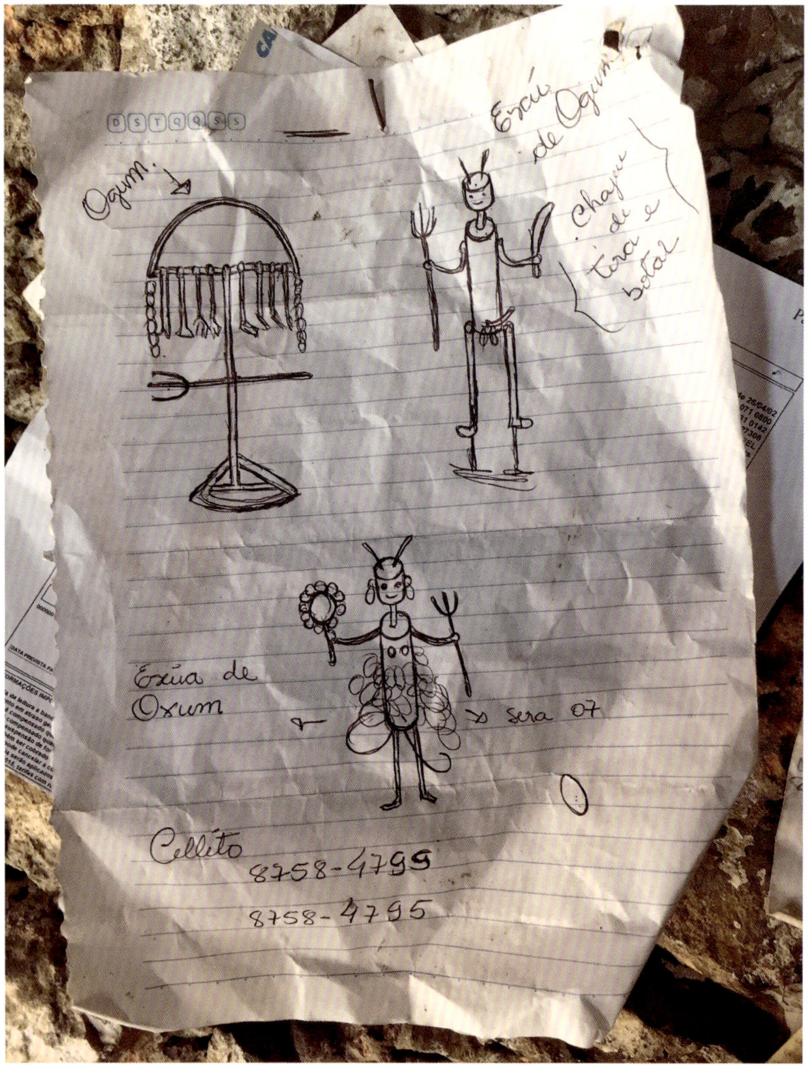


Combining technical and religious knowledge, the work done in Zé Diabo's workshop is imbued with rituals and mysteries. Zé always starts by invoking and making Exú, the first *orixá*, and then goes on to Ogum, Oxóssi, Ossaim, and so forth, respecting the order of the Candomblé pantheon. Not only that, but the preparatory prayers, lit candles, characteristic silence, tobacco smoke, rhythmic gestures—everything seems to converge into a true dialogue between gods, materials, and the blacksmith.

Each of Zé Diabo's sculptures is unique, made exclusively as an intermediary in the special relationship between the individual and his *orixá*. That is why he now only works on commission, refusing to produce standardized items like those found in the main markets of religious objects. Singular in character, each implement undergoes a specific process of creation: from the start, the blacksmith must intuit the shape and details characteristic of each *orixá*, creatively exploring the possibilities the iron affords and the traditional shapes of each entity. Here, invention and tradition go hand-in-hand in the creative process. Each detail will express the intensive power of the *orixá*, inscribing in the artifact the characteristic mysteries of the religion.

Once made, these sculptures do not just become representations of the gods but the *orixás* themselves, embodied in them (see fig. E.2). When the *ferramenta* leaves the workshop it goes to a Candomblé *terreiro*, where it will experience other rites. There, the *ferramenta-orixá* will grow with the offerings that feed it and will become the main expression of the power of the *orixá*. From the outset, however, this power is present in the strength of the iron, and it is that power, also called *axé*, which must be channeled, transformed, and sculpted by the blacksmith, charging the *ferramenta* with the *jabá* of Ogum, Zé Diabo's expression for the *axé* of that *orixá*. Transforming the iron is then to create the very gods of Candomblé, materializing them in the world.

After spending a few years with Zé Diabo, I have come to realize that my first impression was not off the mark. By following the path of Ogum, Zé Diabo has in fact become something of the *orixá* himself. This "becoming," however, is not just a representation of the *orixá*, nor is it a complete resemblance, but something close to the concept developed by Deleuze and Guattari (1980): an assemblage that connects his work to the force of the *orixá*—the *jabá* of Ogum. It is as if each blow of the hammer on the hard iron brings with it the power of his ancestors, conducting a mythical return voyage to an ancestral Africa.

**E.5**
At the upper right is the sketch that Zé Diabo made preparatory to creating *Exú* (see fig. E.6); at the upper left is a sketch that resembles the *ferramenta* in figure E.2.
PHOTOGRAPH BY PATRICK A. POLK, 2015

**E.6**
Zé Diabo, aka Zé Bahia (José Adario dos Santos, b. 1947, Salvador, Bahia, Brazil)
*Exú Tiriri Lonã*, 2015
Metal
H: 60 cm
PRIVATE COLLECTION

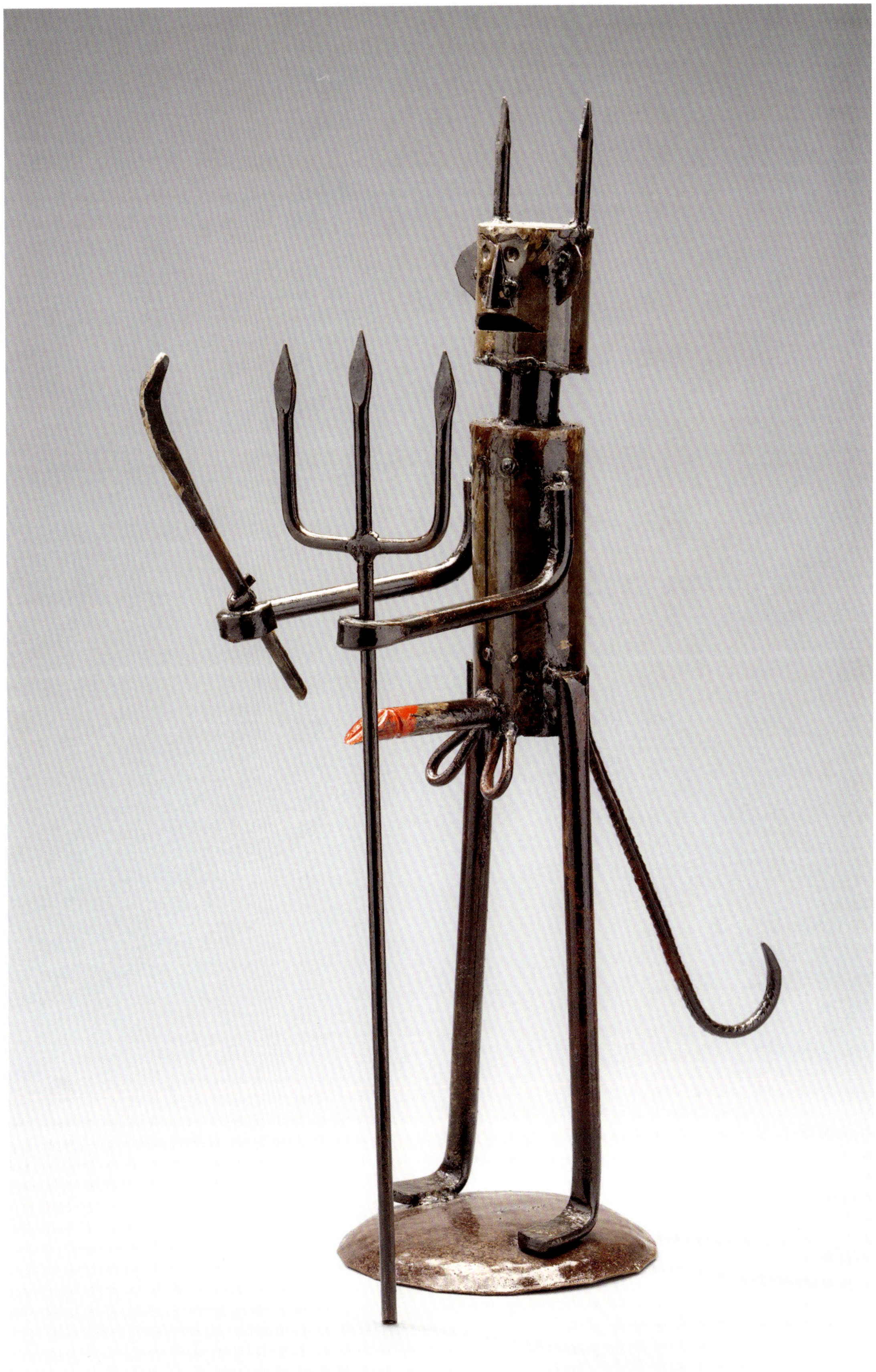

Interleaf **F**

# Art, Tradition, and Ancestry

## The Wisdom of Tia Detinha

**Vanda Machado**

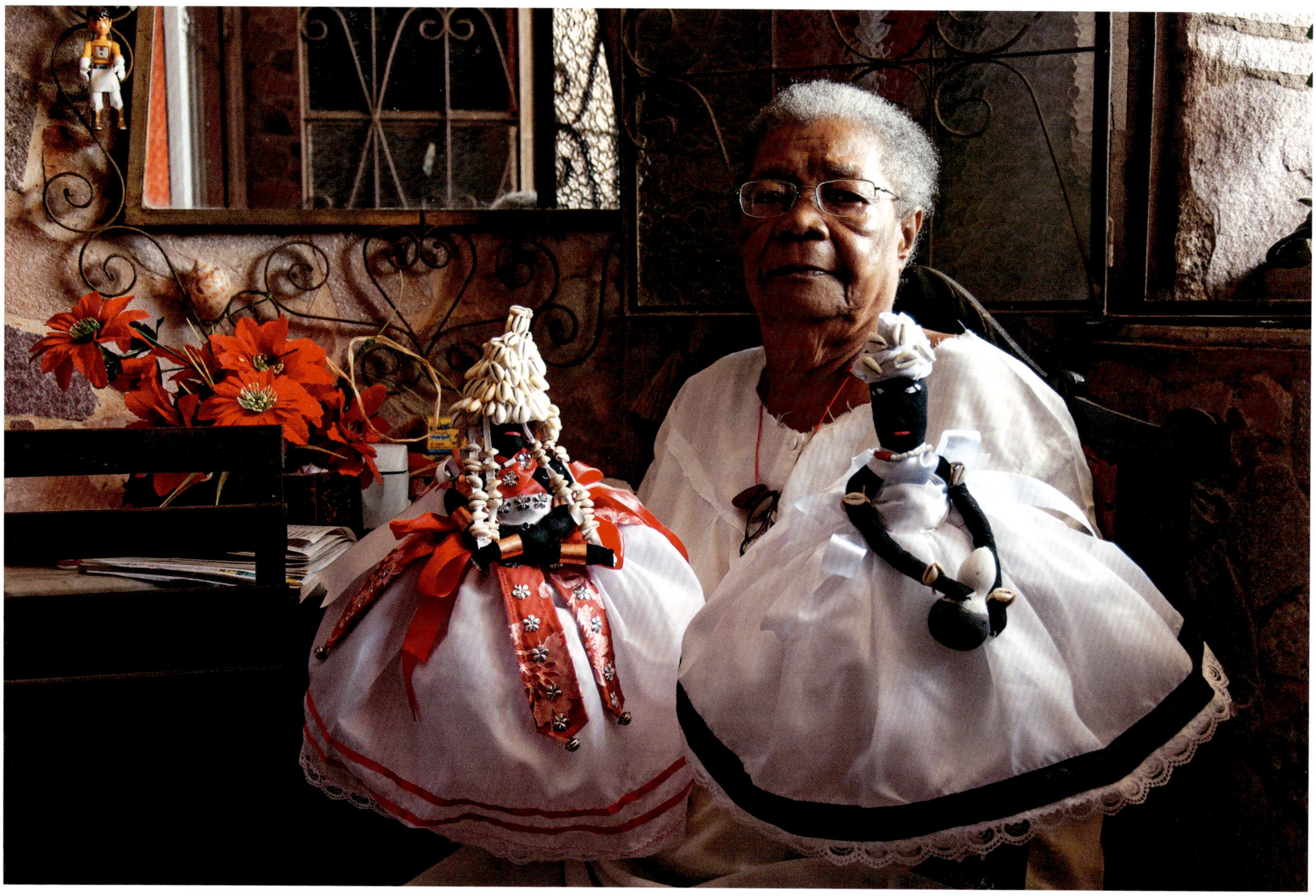

**F.1**
Adenor Gondim (b. 1950, Rui Barbosa, Bahia, Brazil)
*Detinha de Xangô* (Portrait of Tia Detinha [Valdete Ribeiro da Silva]), 2010
Photograph
COURTESY ADENOR GONDIM

I REMEMBER THE FIRST TIME I visited the Ilê Axé Opô Afonjá *terreiro* (temple) as pure enchantment. I entered the gate with bated breath but immediately felt welcomed by every tree that waved its branches and leaves. I was filled with joy at the invitation to enter the house with white walls and red doors, the house of Xangô. A few people were sitting on the wide red sofas, waiting for Mãe Stella, the mother and manager of the community, to consult the cowries. I didn't go in right away.

From the porch, I could see scraps of colored fabric, gold braid, glue, scissors, needles, buttons, gold and silver material, thread, wire, beads, elastic, ribbons, lace, pliers, and unfinished black dolls on the dining table. At the end of the table, a stuffed, cloth-covered figure stood ready to be dressed. I wondered who was working at that table, making dolls?

Just then, a genial black woman with very short, nearly white hair and very thick glasses, walked in from the porch (fig. F.1). She was wearing a full dress printed with red flowers that made her look like a returning ancestor, brimming with intuition and steeped in poetry and philosophical narratives. That day, Tia Detinha de Xangô (Valdete Ribeiro da Silva) entered Mãe Stella's room, asked her blessing, and sat down at the table, ritualistically resuming her task.

Young initiates into our religion approached Tia Detinha in silence. She started to dress a figure, recounting a legend of the *orixás*. Her quiet words were like a discourse on archetypes that could have been inspired by Jungian thinking, had she been familiar with it. But the fact is, they were the words of a person who gave herself the authority to speak truth steeped in wisdom, the heritage of the fifth generation of the Afonjá family. The elders taught ways of being and interacting to their children by recounting legends and stories of the tangible world, penetrating a reality that did not necessarily include religion. They were just ways of preparing people for life (see box, p. 129).

Tia Detinha asked a younger initiate to come closer. "You're a daughter of Oxum, aren't you?" The young woman said she was. Dona Detinha continued, "It's good for you to know who your *orixá* is, the owner of your head and your life [figs. F.2–F.5]. Part of your life carries the energy of Oxum, who is elegant, refined, and hates scenes and gossip. She is the mistress of fresh water. Her dance is as light as a breeze ruffling the peaceful waters of the river." Then Tia Detinha dressed the black doll in a yellow skirt made of golden fabric. She put on necklaces, rings, earrings, and lace trimmings. Oxum is an *ayabá*, a female *orixá*, the mother of all of us. She likes jewelry and beautiful things. Tia Detinha related that

> Oxum takes care of children from their conception until they learn to talk. That is the moment when the *orixá* who will watch over that child all their life appears. Oxum is the protector of families and pregnant women. Oxum is enchanted motherhood. Do you know why Oxum carries the mirror called an *abebé*? The mirror isn't to sit around admiring her own beauty. The mirror serves as an instrument of enlightenment so Oxum can see everything around her and protect her children's lives in any situation.

**F.2**
Tia Detinha, aka Detinha de Xangô (Valdete Ribeiro da Silva, b. 1928, Salvador, Bahia, Brazil; d. 2014)
*Oxum*, circa 1990s
Cloth, metal, beads
H: 48 cm
FOWLER MUSEUM AT UCLA X2015.4.3; GIFT OF DR. JULIO CASOY

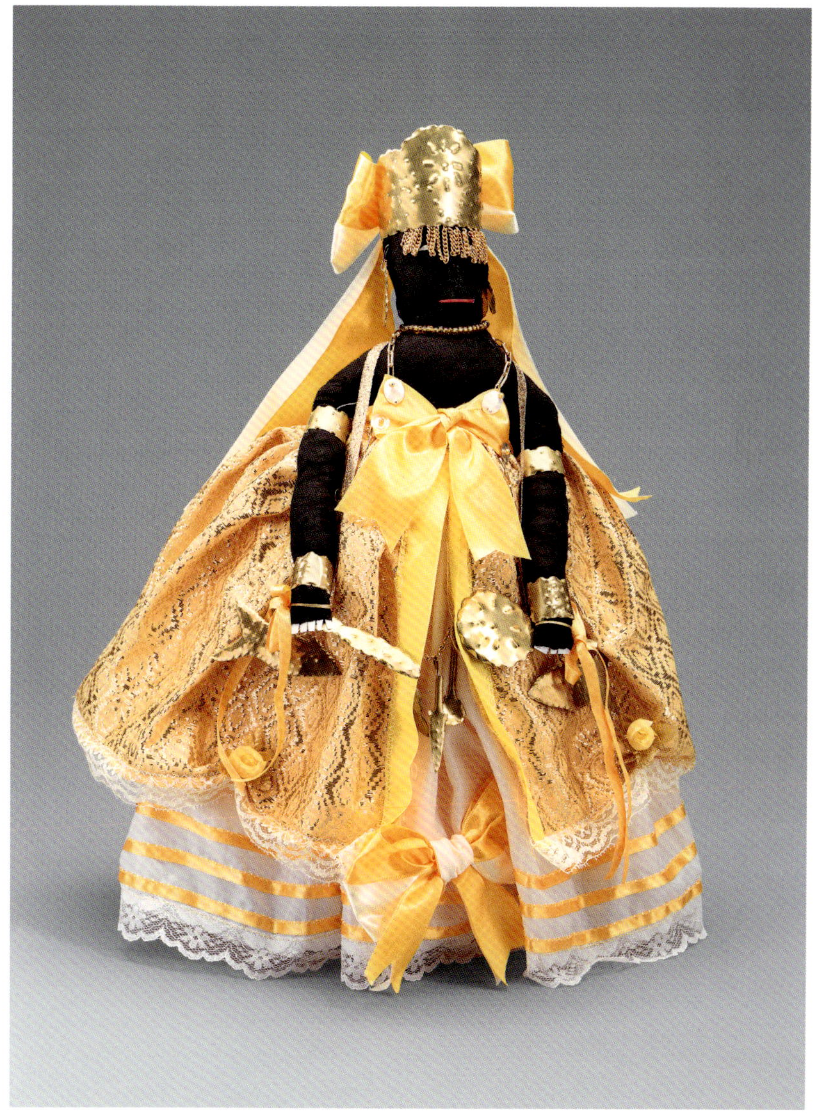

**F.3**
Tia Detinha, aka Detinha de Xangô (Valdete Ribeiro da Silva, b. 1928, Salvador, Bahia, Brazil; d. 2014)
*Xangô*, circa 1990s
Cloth, metal, beads
H: 48 cm
FOWLER MUSEUM AT UCLA X2015.4.7; GIFT OF DR. JULIO CASOY

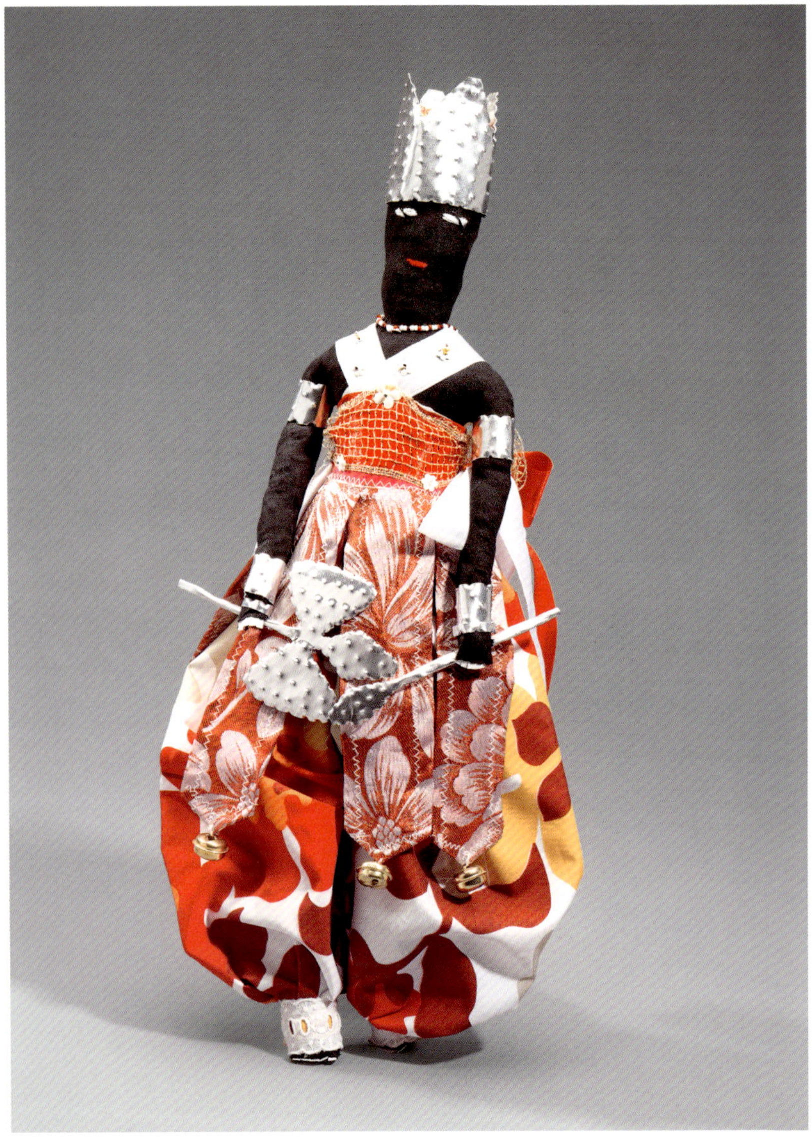

**F.4**
Tia Detinha, aka Detinha de Xangô (Valdete Ribeiro da Silva, b. 1928, Salvador, Bahia, Brazil; d. 2014)
*Exú*, circa 1990s
Cloth, metal, beads
H: 46 cm
FOWLER MUSEUM AT UCLA X2015.4.16; GIFT OF DR. JULIO CASOY

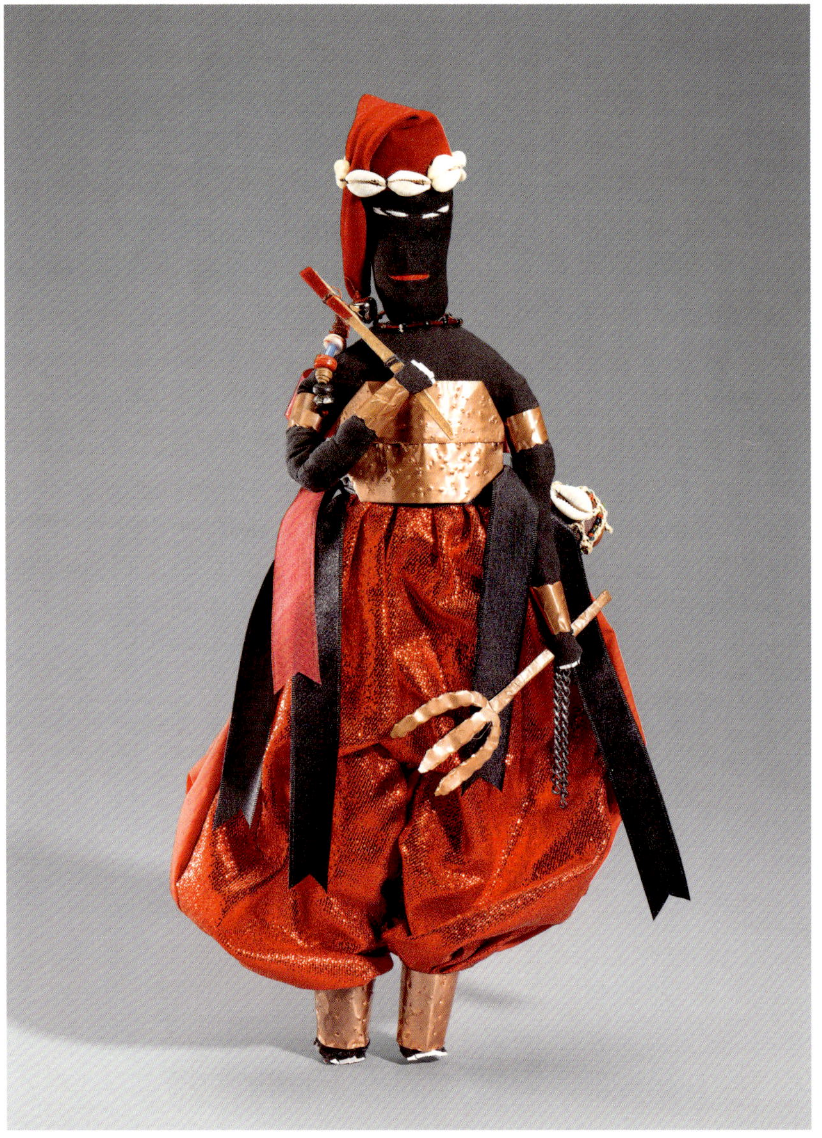

It is said that seeing that her people were in trouble, Oxum once went to the king to ask him to do something. She started to complain, asking the king if it was fair for him to enjoy such opulence while his people were living so poorly? She carried on until the day the king ordered, "Give this woman everything she asks. After all, she just wants to help her people." As a result, she became the lady who distributes wealth.

Tia Detinha never faltered in her teaching mission, deriving from her art the feelings that affect our identities, as well as lessons on community life and rituals. This apparently spontaneous encounter was part of the rite of initiation, essential lessons for understanding and community living that will last a lifetime. We know that logic is efficient and rational, but it cannot produce the experience of becoming religious and fully human individuals. Mythology, in contrast, is an art form that permeates our being, spreading emotions like droplets of ancestral wisdom. Or as Leopold Senghor would say, "I feel the other, therefore I am" (Nussbaum 2003, 22).

Dona Detinha's dolls tell stories that are spun with the joy that sustains a religion that is not only humanizing but interdependent, in which caring, being cared for, giving and taking are the rule. For me, every word Tia Detinha spoke became like precious beads, strung together to form a sacred necklace for Oxum that I carry close to my heart, because that is what gives identity, comprises my way of being in my community and the world.

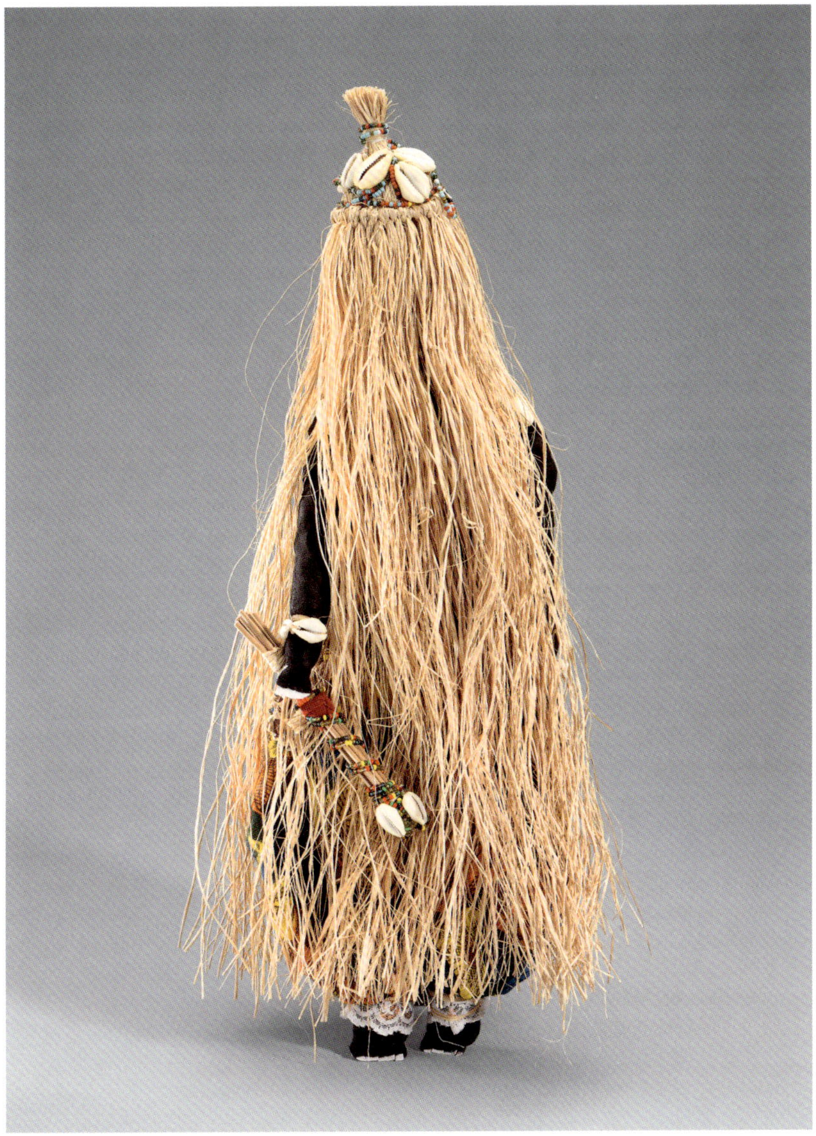

**F.5**
Tia Detinha, aka Detinha de Xangô (Valdete Ribeiro da Silva, b. 1928, Salvador, Bahia, Brazil; d. 2014)
*Omolú*, circa 1990s
Cloth, metal, beads
H: 47 cm
FOWLER MUSEUM AT UCLA X2015.4.20; GIFT OF DR. JULIO CASOY

### "I Am Exú"—A Story Told by Tia Detinha

There was once a strange leafy tree with an iron symbol in the shape of a giant fork. Black men went there to deposit offerings and they spoke in their own language. Not far away there was a chapel dedicated to Saint Cajetan, and its caretaker used to sweep it and dump all the detritus among the roots of the tree, without any respect or scruples. Withered old flowers, candle wax, in short, trash. He'd say, "Take that, Devil!," and he would pick up all the old shoes tossed on the scrap heap and dump them there, always saying, "Take that, Devil!"

One day, a large number of valuables were stolen from the chapel's sanctuary. The caretaker was arrested and charged, tried and sentenced to hang. On the day of the hanging, right at noon on the dot, an expectant crowd filled the square. As he was mounting the scaffold with the noose around his neck, waiting for the king to give orders to his overseer, suddenly a loud voice was heard to say, "Hold it!"

Everyone was amazed at the horseman's arrogance and boldness in stopping something ordered by the king himself, who was so fearsome and unyielding. The king was also frozen in his tracks by that imposing man riding a horse with all its tack, whose harness was blinding bright. And the rider went on in his powerful voice, "This man is innocent. Release him!" And then he grabbed a man who shouted, "Hang him. Hang the thief!"

The horseman cried, "This is the real thief! The belongings that were stolen are buried six feet underground in back of his house." And the valuables were brought forth. The king ordered, "Hang the thief!"

Then the rider made his way through the crowd, carrying the caretaker behind him, and took him to the tree. Dismounting from his horse, he asked, "Do you know me?" The caretaker replied, "No sir, I've never seen you before." The rider then gave him a sack and ordered him to open it. Inside it were all those old shoes. And the rider introduced himself:

"I am Exú, my name isn't the Devil! The man who was applauding your hanging, the thief himself, is worse than the Devil! That tree with the trident, those who know me and respect me place their offerings to me among its roots. As for you, your lack of respect and scruples knows no bounds! I will give you a word of advice—never meddle with what you don't know! The shoes you gave me out of contempt and derision, you gave to the Devil, and I am Exú! Put the sack on your back and go and give it to him or ask your Saint Cajetan for help! And when you've managed to deliver the shoes to the Devil, return to the chapel and ask forgiveness, because your journey is long and the weight of the sack is due to your imprudence. You will only be free of it when Iku [Death] takes you."

And Exú mounted his horse and disappeared, followed by a whirlwind. LA RÔE EXÚ!

[This story was adapted from a mythical narrative of 2006 and originally published in Portuguese in *Cartilha de Contos de Detinha de Sàngó* (Salvador, Bahia: Sociedade Cruz Santa do Opô Afonjá, 2010).]

—Translation by Sabrina Gledhill

# 4 What Does the Baiana Really Have? The Baiana and Afro-Brazilian Identity

Heather Shirey

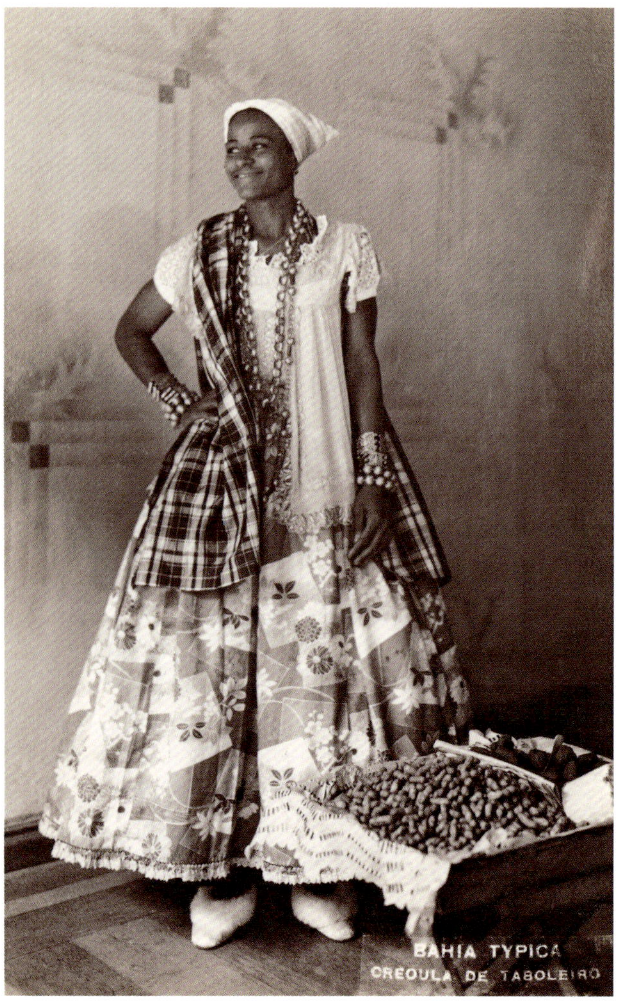


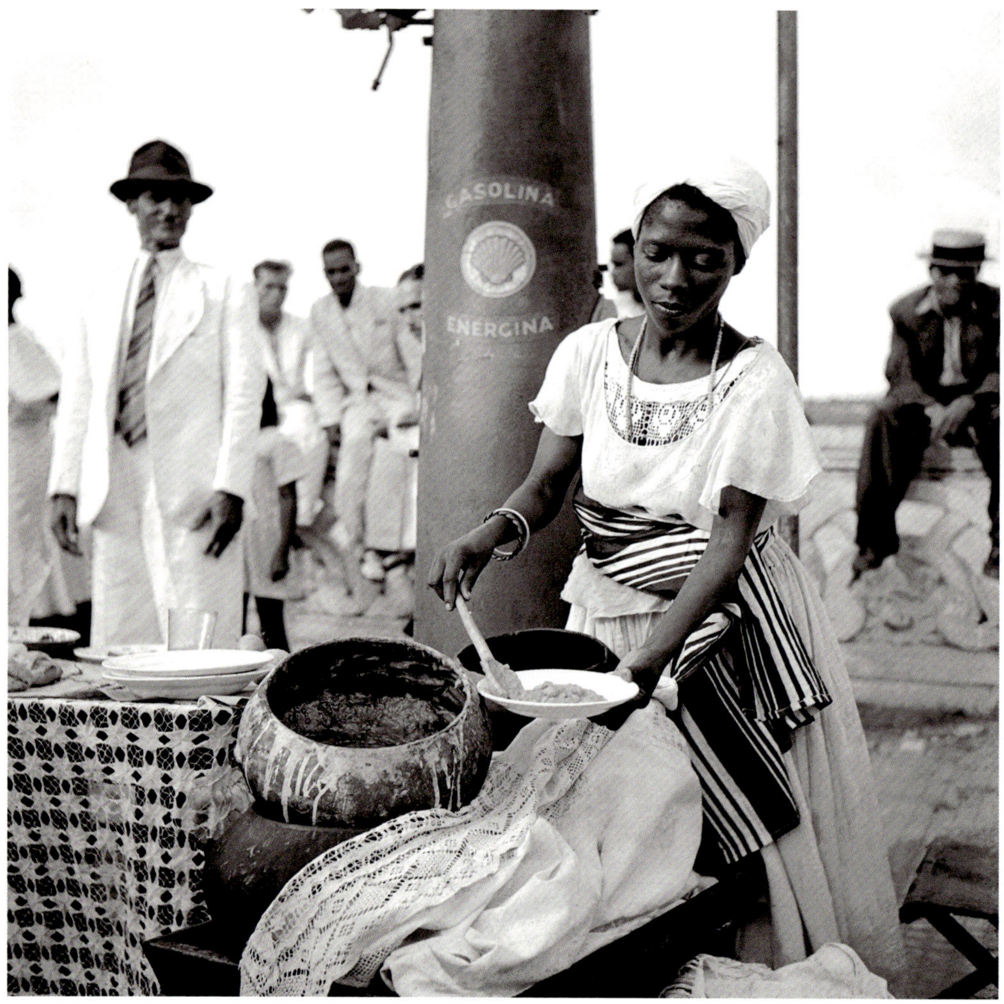

TODAY, THE CONSTRUCTED IDEA of an eternal and unchanging Baiana (literally, "a woman from Bahia") often uncritically evokes a past defined by racial oppression and gender inequity and problematically seizes upon this as a key component of Bahia's contemporary identity. As a concept that has long been appropriated by the dominant class, the Baiana is an essentialized vision of Bahian femininity that is frequently exoticized, "othered," frozen in time, and commercialized (fig. 4.1). An examination of visual representations over time, however, reveals that the Baiana is a complex image of black, Bahian femininity that also has the potential to speak to the strength and resistance of powerful women of African descent, dominant figures in the commercial world, and leaders of spiritual communities.

As cultural theorist Stuart Hall suggests, the construction of the image of the Baiana, as with any representation of identity is "never complete, always in process, and always constituted within, not outside, representation" (Hall 1990, 222). Ultimately, the Baiana exists in a complicated position in relation to notions of beauty and "authenticity" in the dominant culture. Early studio photographs of Bahian "types," images by Pierre Verger, and the constructed Baiana persona of Carmen Miranda shed light on the continuously evolving image of the Baiana, both inside and outside of Bahia. The tensions between an "exotic," "eternal" image of the Baiana and contemporary notions of black female power and beauty can be seen in a *Vogue Brasil* "Black Issue" of January 2011, as well as in the work of photographer Helemozão (Helen Salomão da Silva e Silva) and performances by Thaís Muniz, contemporary artists who contend with notions of black female beauty, power, and Bahian identity.[1]

## Baianas, Markets, and Adornment

In nineteenth-century Salvador da Bahia as well as in other urban centers, particularly Rio de Janeiro, Baianas were identified as women of African descent who sold regional Afro-Brazilian culinary specialties and goods including soap, beads, and cloth—sometimes imported from West Africa[2]—in the city's public spaces. As such, Baianas constituted a powerful subculture on which the dominant class was dependent. Brazilian anthropologist Raul Lody notes that other terms, such as *baianas de rua* (Baianas of the street) and *baianas de tabuleiro* ("Baianas of the tray," referring to the table or tray used for displaying food), were used to refer to these women as well (Lody 2015, 23). Some Afro-Brazilian women vendors achieved a high level of success and were renowned for their beautiful clothing and the use of elaborate bracelets, necklaces, rings, and other adornments made of gold, silver, coral, and African beads.[3] A *penca de balangandã*, a collection of charms joined together and often worn as a pendant at the waist, was a particularly potent emblem of the Baiana (see interleaf G, this volume).[4]

The role that Baianas played in urban markets allowed women vendors a degree of autonomy that was otherwise denied in the context of slavery and the continued racial and gendered oppression that defined social space after its abolition.[5] In some situations, earnings allowed women to support their families, assist others in need, and participate in the culture of conspicuous consumption, using attractive and valuable jewelry to make a statement about their social status (Soares 1996, 57–72).

In addition to jewelry, particular articles of clothing became identified as the attire of the Baiana (fig. 4.2). These included a loose, full skirt (*saia*) and blouse (*camizu* or *camisa*), both of which generally allowed for great freedom of movement. These were typically made of white cotton fabric, embroidered and decorated with lace, and highly starched. *Richelieu*, the term used to describe a hybrid production method using embroidery and lace, elevated the clothing beyond what was practical for everyday use and served as an indicator of sufficient wealth to purchase cloth for its beauty rather than simply for its utility.[6] The full skirts and use of lace also reflected European influence. At the same time, the addition of multiple *panos da costa*, rectangular pieces of cloth that can be folded and worn in any number of ways, such as over the shoulder or as a head wrap, could be read as a signifier of African influence. Of these accoutrements, the head wrap was an especially powerful mode of representing African identity, as it marked a strong deviation from European-inspired head coverings.

Jewelry served as a portable bank of sorts (Lody 2015, 28–29), but these ornaments played a spiritual role as well, as many of them featured empowered elements used for protection or devotion (see interleaf G, this volume).[7] Similarly, several items of the Baiana's clothing were associated with Candomblé and were worn within the sacred spaces of the Afro-Brazilian religious community as well as at urban public festivals. For that reason, many women who were identified as Baianas might be *baianas de acarajé* (vendors of *acarajé* specifically) or *baianas do Bonfim* (women performing the annual purification of the Igreja do Nosso Senhor do Bonfim, or Church of Our Lord of the Good End; see interleaf C, this volume), as well as *mulheres de fé* (women of faith), practitioners of Candomblé (see Matory, this volume). The core elements of clothing were quite similar, and there was much overlap among these populations.[8]

**4.1**
Artist Unknown
*Bahia Typica Creoula de taboleiro* (Typical Bahia: Creole Woman with a Tray), 1925
Postcard
14 x 9 cm
PRIVATE COLLECTION

Luiza Franquelina da Rocha (1909–2005) was the model for the photograph used on this postcard.

**4.2**
Voltaire Fraga (b. 1911, Salvador, Bahia, Brazil; d. 2006)
*Baiana de acarajé, vatapá na Barra*
(Seller of *Acarajé*, Vatapá, in Barra), 1940
Photograph
IMAGE COURTESY OF AROLDO DE OLIVEIRA PEIXOTO

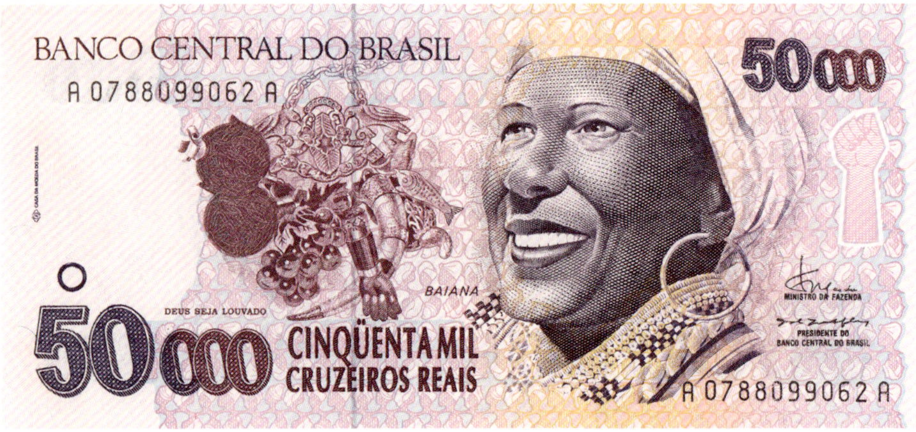


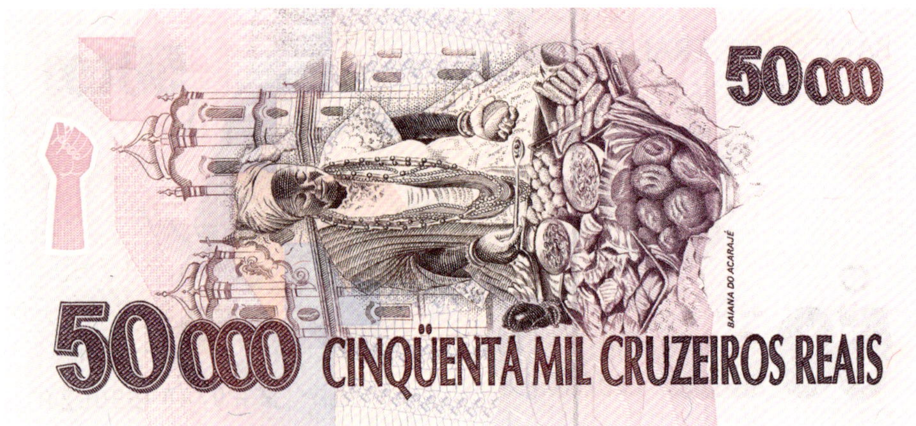


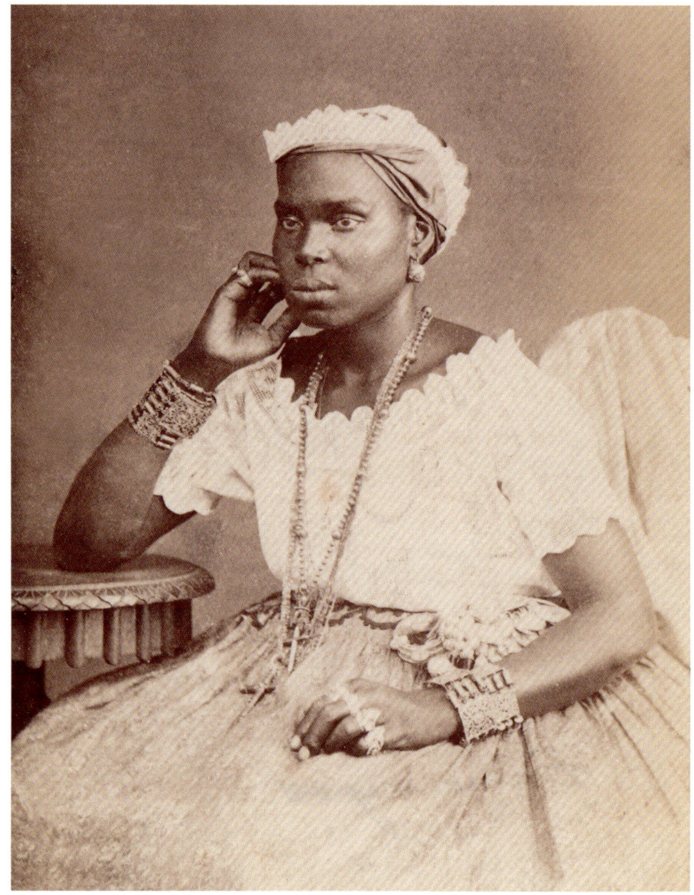

**4.3a**
Brazilian, 1994 CR$50,000 banknote, obverse

**4.3b**
Brazilian, 1994 CR$50,000 banknote, reverse

**4.4**
Marc Ferrez (b. 1843, Rio de Janeiro, Brazil; d. 1923)
*Negra da Bahia* (Black Woman from Bahia), 1885
Photograph
SPECIAL COLLECTIONS, YOUNG RESEARCH LIBRARY, UNIVERSITY OF CALIFORNIA, LOS ANGELES

Not surprisingly, the representation of the Baiana on the CR$50,000 Brazilian banknote of 1994 features the traditional attire, including the *penca de balangandã*.[9] The note shows a *baiana de acarajé* on the obverse coupled with a *balangandã*, enlarged to emphasize its details (fig. 4.3a). The reverse of the banknote shows the *baiana de acarajé* and a traditional food stand (fig. 4.3b). On both sides, the illustrations place emphasis on African identity as well as on the blending of cultures. The Baiana wears a head wrap, large hoop earrings, and multiple strands of beads and cowry shells that presumably indicate an affiliation with Candomblé. The enlarged *balangandã* includes a pomegranate and grapes (references to fertility), a wooden *figa* (fist) and animal tooth (signifying protection), a cashew (sign of abundance), fish (referencing Christianity as well as the *orixá* Iemanjá), and the dove or Espírito Santo.[10] On the reverse of the banknote, the Baiana is situated in the yard in front of the Igreja do Nosso Senhor do Bonfim (Church of Our Lord of the Good End), the site of an important annual festival (Lavagem do Bonfim) that has great significance in both Candomblé and Catholic spheres. This banknote series sought to move beyond the celebration of the political accomplishments of individual men by referencing landscapes (Iguaçu Falls), popular traditions (Bumba-meu-boi) and cultural "types" (in addition to the Baiana, the gaucho was featured on the CR$5,000 note).

**Studio Photography and the Baiana as a "Type"**

Foreign and Brazilian photographers working from the late nineteenth century to the early twentieth century often used Afro-Bahian women (or women perceived to be Afro-Bahian) to represent the Baiana and the role of this urban "type." Photographs were frequently produced in studios and these were sold as portrait images or *cartes-de-visite* and served to reinforce the racial and socioeconomic hierarchy by constructing a visual image of otherness that contrasted with representations of feminine beauty and modes of dress and adornment in the dominant culture.

Importantly, the Baiana as a "type" had relevance not just in Bahia, but also underwent a significant process of crystallization in Rio de Janeiro. While best known for his large body of work focusing on landscapes and urban scenes, Marc Ferrez (1843–1923), a photographer who originated from and spent most of his professional career in Rio de Janeiro, created many studio images representing racial and social "types," including Baianas. *Negra da Bahia* (1885) is one such photograph of a woman in Baiana clothing (fig. 4.4). While Ferrez had traveled to Bahia previously and produced cityscapes and images of individuals and groups of people in the street, this image, created just before the abolition of slavery, appears to be posed in a photographer's studio.[11] Within Ferrez's oeuvre, it is reasonable to imagine that he conceived of this portrait as one representing not a specific individual, but rather a regional "type."[12]

The subject of the photograph is seated in a high-backed chair with her elbow positioned on the table to her right. She rests her face against her hand, a pose likely intended to allow for stability during the long exposure time while also imparting a casual air to the otherwise stiff posture. Her photograph and her clothing, which represent the typical attire of a Baiana, are perfectly arranged. In a context in which enslaved men and women were often photographed in order to support racist ideologies (Wood 2013, 197), Ferrez's photograph captures the subject in a manner that seems nonintrusive and dignified, if perhaps a bit awkward and stiff. She is presented to the viewer as a picturesque and exotic example of a "type" unique to Brazil, and particularly representative of the northeast, making this sort of image, often reproduced in *carte-de-visite* format, of interest to collectors and tourists (Wood 2013, 198).

Ferrez's *Negra da Bahia* is dressed in the clothing most commonly associated with the Baiana in the late nineteenth century and echoed in many present-day representations. Although her full skirt is not white, it is typical of the voluminous style with embroidered details. She wears the lace *camizu* covering her shoulders and upper arms. Her head wrap is starched to perfection and meticulously arranged, and she is laden with jewelry, including rings on each visible finger, multiple heavy bracelets on her wrists, dangling earrings, long strands of beads and jeweled chains around her neck, and a large *balangandã* at her hip. A woven *pano da costa* is draped across the back of her chair. It is evident that the nineteenth-century viewer was interested in the clothing and adornment associated with the Baiana, and we learn little of the specific identity or life of the woman depicted. This clothing, markedly different and "exotic" in style when compared to that worn by women of the dominant class, served as a signifier of race. At the same time, the immense quantity of jewelry and the attention given to the clothing served to indicate wealth and elevated social status. In the case of this photograph, produced prior to the abolition of slavery, however, there is a distinct possibility that such indications would be read as a reflection of a slaveholder who may have provided the model or the photographer with clothing and jewelry in order to create a statement about his or her own position in society (Godoy 2006).

Because the photograph provides us with frustratingly little information about the sitter, it is difficult to determine if it was commissioned as a portrait and to what degree she had agency in determining her presentation within the image. In any case, it is worth noting that she appears in a contemplative pose in a studio setting. In this photograph, Ferrez did not re-create a street scene or set up a mock stand displaying her wares, as some of his contemporaries did, nor did he actually choose to photograph his subject as a vendor in the city's streets, as he had done previously.[13] This photograph serves to emphasize to its late nineteenth-century audience the "otherness" of black Bahian women not only through physical characteristics but also clothing and accessories. The fact that these images were not simply intended as private portraits for the sitter, but were also reproduced and sold to represent "types" allows us to understand the emergence of not only the black female body but also the clothing and jewelry as exotic tropes representing blackness as related to a Bahian identity.

Raul Lody argues that the Baiana has become as meaningful a signifier of Bahia as dance, music, and food (Lody 2015, 20–21), and certainly that process began with photographs such as this, whether produced in Bahia or Rio de Janeiro. Baianas asserted a powerful counter-cultural role in urban commercial spaces, and we may read their clothing and jewelry as emblems that represent this autonomy and empowerment (Harding 2000, 127–30). At the same time, photographs like those by Ferrez, when reproduced and distributed in order to reinforce existing hierarchies in society, involved the erasure of individual black Bahian identities and the multitude of experiences that become invisible when people are reduced to "types."

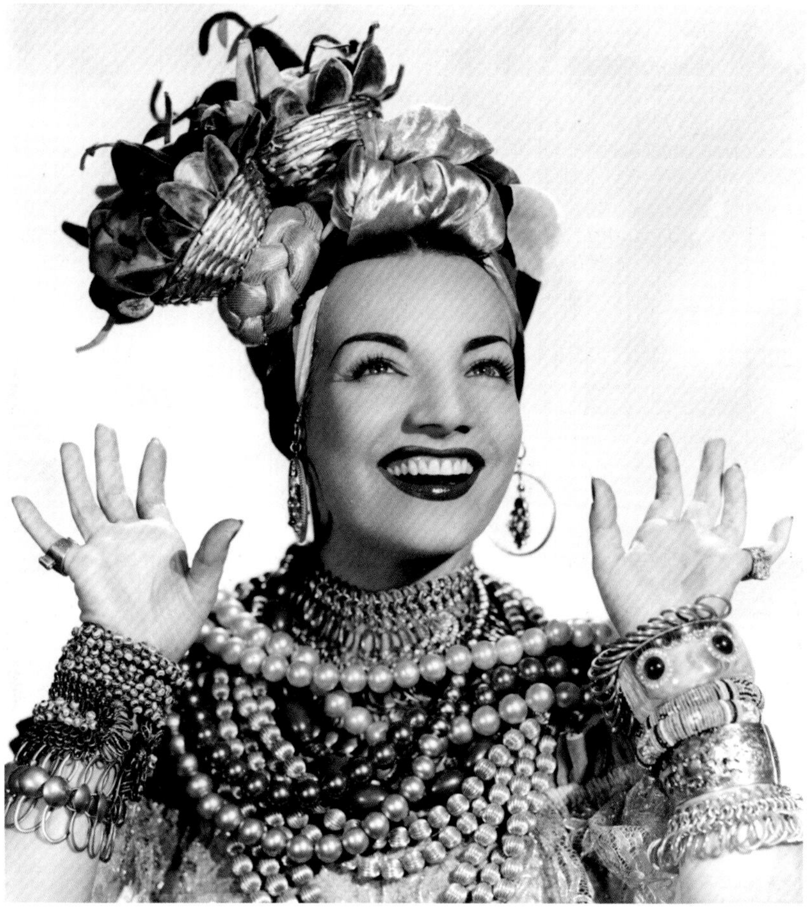

**4.5**
This promotional photograph of Carmen Miranda was taken circa 1945. IMAGE COURTESY MPTVIMAGES.COM.

Both inside and outside Bahia, images such these were consumed by a dominant-class audience that exoticized and marginalized women of African descent. By the turn of the century, a sizable Bahian population resided in Rio de Janeiro, struggling to maintain a position in society and shaping the cultural landscape of the city. Stereotypes of *tias baianas* (Bahian aunts) emerged in popular visual culture and performance, emphasizing a mode of dress and comportment that deviated from that of the ruling class (Moura 1983; Veloso 1990, 207–28; Gomes 2003, 175–88). Simultaneous with the popularization of photographs that exoticized Bahian women of African descent, the Baiana was performed in theaters and samba schools, both in Salvador and in Rio de Janeiro (Ickes 2013a, 118–19). The Baiana, for example, was performed at the Teatro de Revista in Rio de Janeiro as early as 1889, including performances by white actors in blackface (Yunes 2011). Additionally, the Baiana as a visible "type" in Rio de Janeiro, already evident in postcards and *cartes-de-visite*, became further engrained in the city's visual culture by way of popular samba schools associated with Carnaval, especially in the 1920s and later (Araújo and Ferreira 2012, 301–15).

In the media and public discourse of the time, Baianas were frequently accused of being dirty and uncivilized, as historian Scott Ickes has noted. The popular press about Baianas from the early twentieth century focused on their perceived "backwardness" and the need to impose "civilizing" efforts (Ickes 2013a, 117). Ferrez's photograph countered negative stereotypes that envisioned marginalized Bahians as unclean and impoverished by showing a carefully composed and meticulously dressed image of the Baiana, but at the same time his representation of a "type" served to "other" the experience of blackness and remained deficient in terms of its representation of individual experience, thus contributing to the perpetuation of stereotypes.

### Nationalization of the Image of the Baiana

In the 1930s and later, the Baiana became increasingly present in Rio de Janeiro's Carnaval culture; the existence of Baianas in celebrations was perceived to be a sign of a Carnaval tradition "of the people" and one that was, therefore, more "authentic" (Araújo and Ferreira 2012, 304). The poet Cecília Meireles exhibited a series of drawings in 1933 that included images of the Carnavalesque Baiana. Meireles's drawings and sketches, like those that Carybé would produce in the decades to come, were largely stripped of references to individual identity, further cementing the focus on clothing and accessories as the primary mode of identification of an authentic Bahian tradition (Meireles 2003).

Between the late 1930s and the 1950s, the image of the Baiana became increasingly widespread both nationally and internationally. Scholars such as Scott Ickes, Anadelia Romo, and Patricia de Santana Pinho have investigated the process by which the Baiana was transformed into a national symbol in the midst of the changing political climate of the Estado Novo (1937–1945).[14] Ickes notes that a new focus on popular traditions played a central role in the creation of an expansive notion of regional identity that co-opted rather than erased the presence of Afro-Brazilians (Ickes 2013a, 119). During this period, articles in the popular press, like those by Brazilian ethnologist Édison Carneiro in *Estado da Bahia*, for example, produced broader coverage of Afro-Brazilian culture, associating it positively and in relation to a developing national identity (Ickes 2013a, 112).

**The Internationalization of the Baiana Persona**

By the mid-twentieth century the image had also taken hold in the United States, where Carmen Miranda's Baiana persona came to represent not only the entirety of Brazil but also all of Latin America. The international popularity of Carmen Miranda's appropriated version of the Baiana, which "whitened" the image and stripped away racial politics that challenged the status quo, also had an impact on the positive representation of the Baiana in the popular press during the period of the Estado Novo (Ickes 2013a, 118).

Born in Portugal in 1909 and reared in Rio de Janeiro, Carmen Miranda was instrumental in developing a version of the Baiana that proved highly palatable in Brazil and in the United States. She expanded that persona on Broadway and in Hollywood films such as *That Night in Rio* (1941), which made the Baiana an international icon and crystalized her image. Her costume, a glamorized version of the typical Baiana clothing, became truly iconic, sexualizing, whitening, and therefore redefining Baiana identity as one associated with Brazilian and even Latin American women more generally (Yunes 2011; Pullen 2014). From Walt Disney's Donald Duck in *The Three Caballeros* (1944), which featured Miranda's sister, Aurora, to present-day Halloween costumes, popular culture has continued to emphasize the Baiana's sensuality and sexual availability.[15] Miranda's Baiana performed for audiences in the United States also shed overt references to Afro-Brazilian spiritual traditions that were an important part of the identity in Brazil, thus secularizing it.

In film, Miranda first performed Dorival Caymmi's samba "O que é que a baiana tem?" ("What Is It That the Baiana Has?") in the Brazilian musical comedy *Banana da Terra* (1939). Notably, the lyrics to Caymmi's song place an emphasis on the material culture of the Baiana and erase references to her racial identity (see Dunn, this volume). Miranda in effect sings a list of Baiana accessories in response to the question posed by the samba's title: The Baiana has a silk head wrap, golden earrings, a gold chain, cloth from the coast, a lace blouse, a gold bracelet, a starched skirt, adorned sandals, a gold rosary, and *balangandãs*.

The lyrics serve as an inventory of required objects for the "authentic" Baiana, some of which might simply be associated with wealth and good taste. Others, however, are specific to the Baiana, to Afro-Brazilian culture, to vendors of *acarajé*, and to Candomblé: the *pano da costa*, the lace blouse and starched skirt, the *balangandãs*, and the head wrap. The lyrics also reference a visit to Bonfim as the ultimate test of authenticity: "Só vai no Bonfim quem tem" ("Only those who have it go to Bonfim"). Bonfim here refers to the famous Igreja do Nosso Senhor do Bonfim (Church of Our Lord of the Good End, the patron church of Salvador), the steps of which have been and continue to be traditionally cleaned by Baianas. The festival surrounding this act is marked by a tremendous procession of Baianas—many, but certainly not all, with spiritual connections to Candomblé. Historically, the black women of Bahia were not allowed inside the church to wash its floors, and from this restriction the ritual of washing the steps emerged. The washing of the steps of Bonfim is racialized at its core, but this legacy of institutionalized racism is absent from the Baiana fantasy Miranda developed, just as her Baiana persona is stripped of references to Afro-Brazilian spirituality.[16]

Caymmi's lyrics focused on the material presence of the Baiana rather than her racial identity, and Miranda's whiteness reinforced the separation of race from this particular type of "exotic" identity. As has been noted previously, Miranda's performance of the Baiana in "O que é que a baiana tem?" was certainly not the first, and the Baiana was, by this time, a central element of Carnaval celebrations. It was, however, Miranda's particular representation of exotic beauty, now perceived to be white rather than Afro-Brazilian, that took hold in mainstream culture and internationally. In the promotional image of Carmen Miranda as a Baiana, we see the great attention given to her head wrap, often transformed into a large display of exotic fruits (read as produce for sale at market), as a primary signifier of identity (fig. 4.5). Also important are her multitude of bracelets, necklaces, and earrings. The white cotton and lace associated with the traditional Baiana as well as with Candomblé, however, are now rendered in a midriff-baring top and long skirt, made of flashy colorful fabrics. Notably, Miranda's light skin and petite frame conformed to standard ideals of beauty in Brazil and in the United States.

Once she skyrocketed to success in Hollywood, Miranda was criticized in Brazil for what was perceived as an appropriation of Bahian culture, especially since this very local identity came to stand for a much larger Latin American identity when it was exported (Pullen 2014; Coelho 1998). Even so, Miranda's popularization of Baiana clothing and accessories certainly had an impact on the development of regional identity in Bahia.[17] The translation of the Baiana persona that Miranda popularized certainly complemented the representation of regional identity in the displays created by curator José Valladares in the Museo do Estado in Salvador. By 1940 Valladares had made the then-unprecedented decision to display the clothing and accessories of a Baiana as part of an exhibition defining regional identity in Bahia (Romo 2010, 98; Ickes 2013a, 116).

## Pierre Verger, the Baiana, and Ethnographic Photography

On August 5, 1946, the French photographer Pierre Verger arrived in Bahia, where he ultimately established residence until his death in 1996. By the time of his arrival in Bahia, Verger had already established a reputation as a photojournalist with a penetrating eye, working for magazines such as *Paris-soir*. He had spent the preceding fifteen years traveling through much of Europe, Asia, Oceania, as well as North, East, and West Africa and the Americas. He saw himself as an ethnographic photographer, who, as a perpetual outsider using the supposedly "neutral" lens of his camera, captured the lives of others. It is with the gaze of an outsider that Verger produced his images of Baianas.

Verger dedicated himself to documenting city life in the streets and in places of worship. In no small part due to his status as an ex-patriate, his photographs most often captured public life, and he rarely photographed in private spaces. While Verger would later become known for his historical research and his use of photographs as key pieces of evidence in an intellectual debate about Afro-Brazilian culture and its connection to West African traditions, during the 1940s and 1950s most of his work was published in glossy magazines produced in Brazil's cosmopolitan south (Verger and Lühning 2003).

"Baianas de saias rodadas" ("Baianas with full skirts") featured photographs by Pierre Verger, accompanying text by José Leal, and was published in the February 5, 1949, issue of *O Cruzeiro*. A popular illustrated magazine published in Rio de Janeiro, *O Cruzeiro* featured articles and editorials about famous people, politics, movies, sports, and other topics of popular interest to Brazil's growing educated middle class (fig. 4.6). Verger made frequent photojournalistic contributions to the magazine, particularly in the form of stories that explored regional identity in Brazil (Barbosa 2007, 29–42). In the feature about Baianas, Verger published fifteen black-and-white documentary photographs that, while showing the "typical" attire of a Baiana, capture the individuality of the women and the wide variety of choices made in how clothing and accessories are used. Some of the photographs were taken within the sacred space of a *terreiro*, while others show women participating in a popular public festival. Some, such as an image of two women embracing and smiling at the camera, seem posed, while others have a more spontaneous feel (fig. 4.7).

When compared to Ferrez's nineteenth-century studio photographs, as well as to the popularized image of Carmen Miranda, Verger's images are remarkable for their sensitive and nuanced approach to the treatment of the Baiana. Rather than being portrayed as a one-dimensional "type," a trope focused largely on clothing and accessories, here multiple ways of dressing like and of being a Baiana are demonstrated. A *pano da costa* may be worn over the shoulder, but it may also be wrapped around the torso. Head coverings are essential, and they come in many forms, as do accessories such as necklaces and bracelets. The Baianas in Verger's photographs exist within both secular and religious spaces. They interact with one another and with the space in which they live. We see a variety of ages, body types, and skin tones, all within a range that viewers would have identified as belonging to African descendants. In sum, this variation allows Verger to present Baianas as individuals rather than as a "type."

That said, Verger only produced the photographs and had little control over how they were presented in the magazine. Of particular note, the article on Baianas, which seems to capture the lives of individual women of African descent—many of whom are working or involved in ritual practice—appeared in the same issue as, and in fact adjacent to, an article on white bathing beauties in Rio. The net effect of which was the contrasting of whiteness and blackness, a situating of white within the dominant framework of beautiful, and a further "othering" and exoticizing of blackness.[18] The contrast of these two articles also associates black women with labor and the upholding of traditional cultural and ritual practices, shown in the majority of the photographs, while white women are depicted enjoying leisurely activities on the beach.

Another photograph by Verger seeks to show the Baiana as an individual who has the autonomy to create her own pose and expression. This photograph was shot in Cachoeira, a city in the interior of Bahia and a place especially associated with the power of women and Afro-Brazilian religious practices.[19] As in Ferrez's image, the subject is dressed in the clothing and accessories most clearly associated with a Baiana—the *richelieu* top, the abundant jewelry, and head wrap (fig. 4.8). In contrast to Ferrez's studio image, however, Verger's photo, although no doubt carefully posed and composed, conveys a sense of informality. Whereas the attire of Ferrez's subject was presented in an overly flawless manner, here the subject's lace collar is slightly turned down, and her head wrap is positioned much more casually and naturally with a few stray pieces of hair escaping just above her ear. She gazes off in the distance as if unaware of the presence of the photographer and seems to touch her earring almost unconsciously. Verger effectively used the bright exterior light to draw attention to the network of deep wrinkles on the subject's face as well as the much more subtle evidence of aging on her forearm. Here we are invited to reflect on her thoughts and experiences and how they shape her as an individual. Compositionally, Verger forces the viewer to focus on the woman's face rather than simply on the objects she wears. For that reason, this image and others by Verger, though perhaps romanticized by the European gaze, counter the appropriation that is so evident in Carmen Miranda's use of the Baiana costume and identity, as well as the anonymity and reduction to a "type" evident in late nineteenth- and early twentieth-century photographs.

## The Baiana in *Vogue*

For *Vogue Brasil*'s "Black Issue" of January 2011, fashion photographer Bob Wolfenson worked with Afro-Brazilian supermodel Gracie Carvalho to evoke Verger's images of the Baiana. The title of the spread, "O que a baiana tem?" ("What does the Baiana have?") refers to Dorival Caymmi's samba, and as with Verger's images, the Baiana serves as a symbol of Bahia. Carvalho is situated in various urban locations associated with Salvador, including streets of Pelourinho, the Igreja de São Francisco (Church of Saint Francis), the lighthouse, and the beach in Barra, an upscale neighborhood. In one photograph, she appears surrounded by a group of men whose head wraps and drums reference the popular mutual aid society and Carnaval group Filhos do Gandhy (fig. 4.9a). In another, she claps as she watches two men play capoeira, a recognizable symbol of Bahia. Carvalho's ensembles vary and include a short, empire-waist, embroidered and lace tunic; a long, fitted maxi-dress; a fitted jacket; a light, breezy sundress; and shorts and a sophisticated but casual top. In all cases, it is the contrast of pure white clothing with dark skin and the use of chunky bracelets that evoke the image of the Baiana, who in this sense, is reduced to these essential elements.

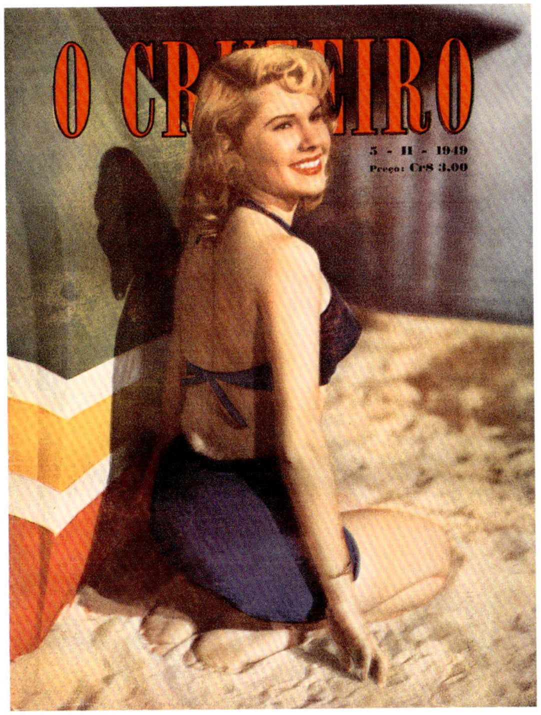



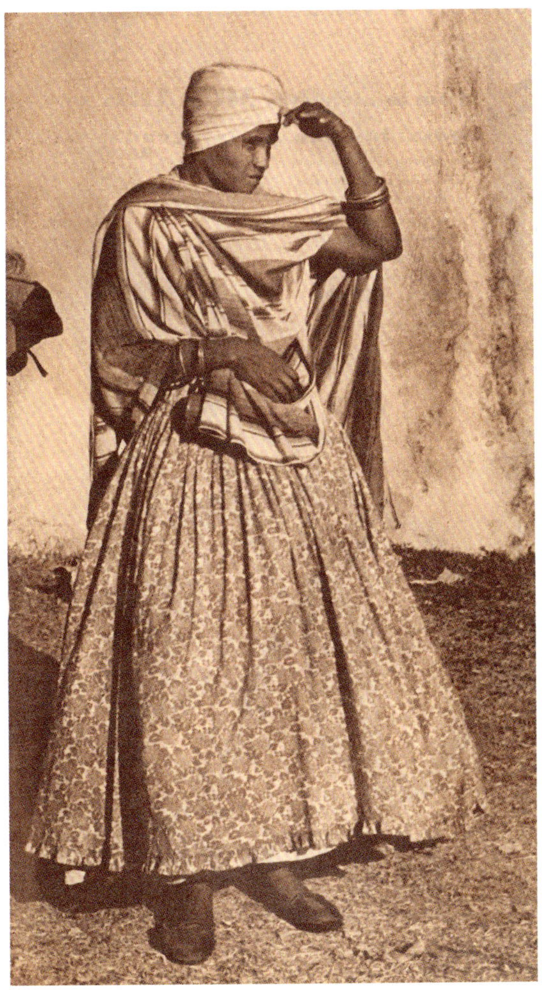

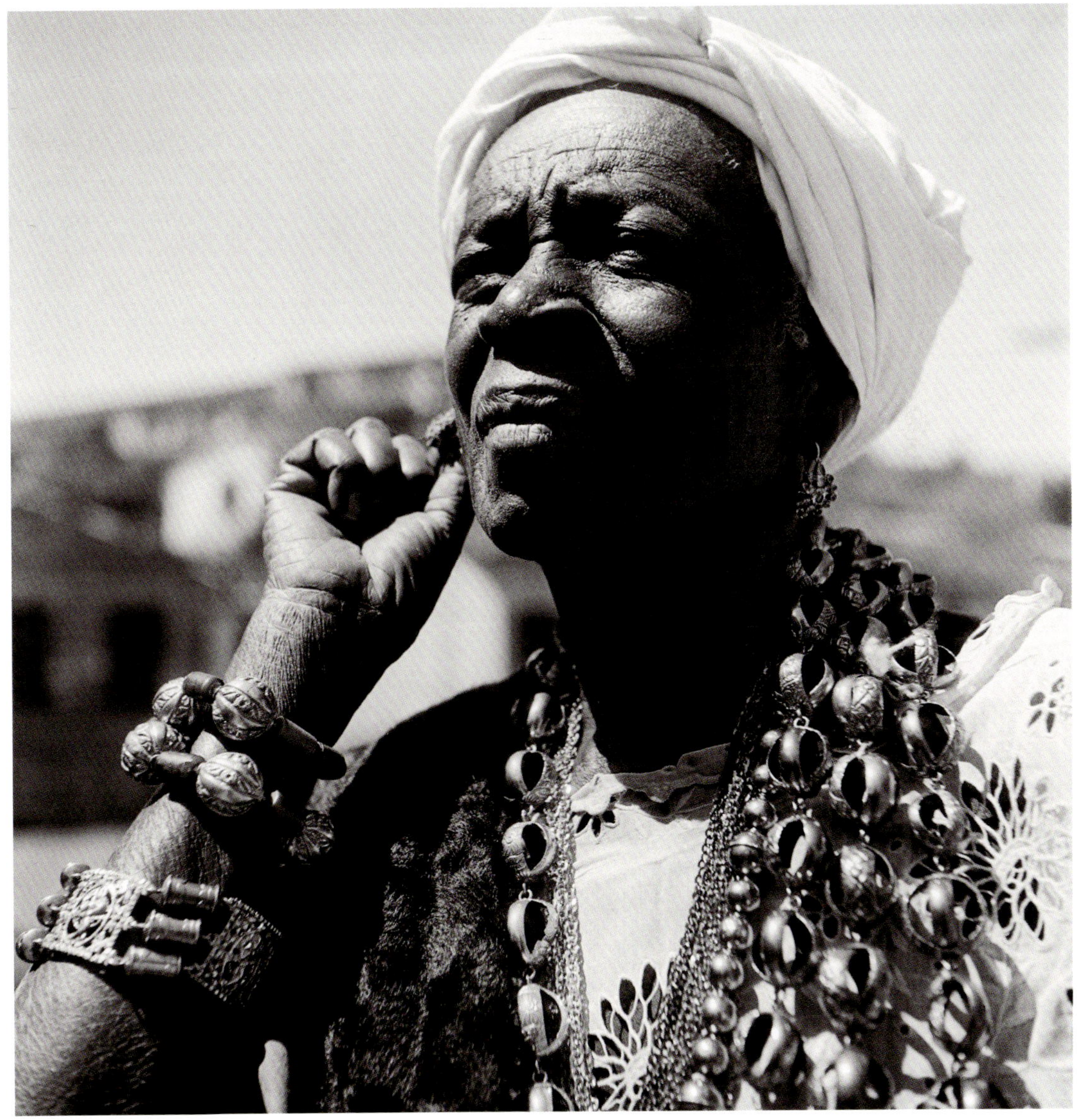

**4.6**
The cover of the magazine *O Cruzeiro* (February 5, 1949, issue) in which Pierre Verger's photo essay on the Baiana (see fig. 4.7) appeared. PRIVATE COLLECTION.

**4.7**
Pierre Verger (b. Paris, France, 1902; d. 1996)
"Baianas das saias rodadas" (Baianas with Full Skirts), 1949
Opening page of the photo essay by Verger with text by José Leal in *O Cruzeiro*'s February 5, 1949, issue
PRIVATE COLLECTION

**4.8**
Pierre Verger (b. Paris, France, 1902; d. 1996)
*Festa da Irmandade de Nossa Senhora da Boa Morte* (Feast of the Sisterhood of Our Lady of the Good Death), 1950s
Photograph
PHOTO PIERRE VERGER ©FUNDAÇÃO PIERRE VERGER

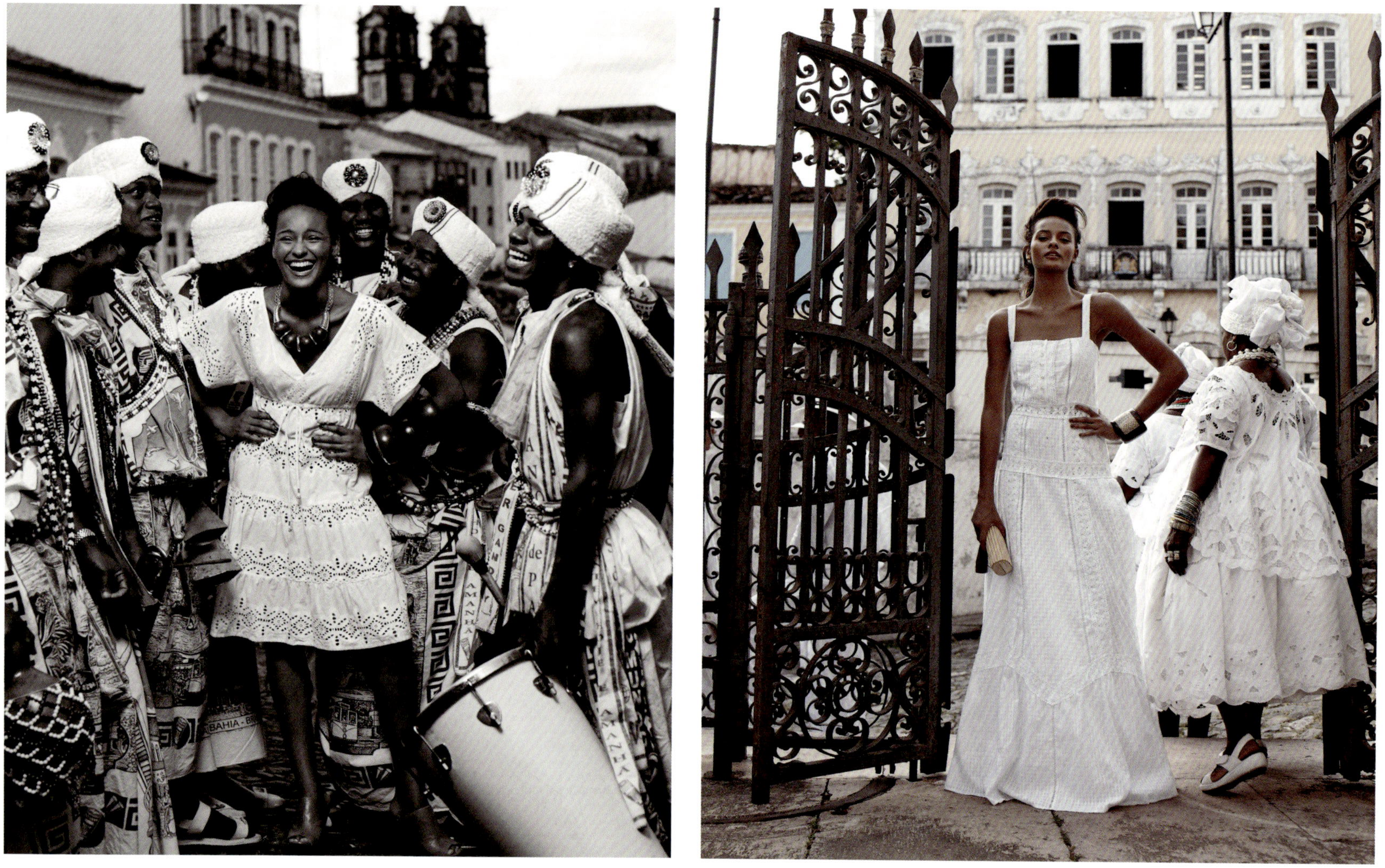

**4.9a,b**
Bob Wolfenson (b. 1954, São Paulo, Brazil)
Model Gracie Carvalho poses in Salvador for *Vogue Brasil*, January 2011
Photographs
FASHION EDITOR GIOVANNI FRASSON
COURTESY BOB WOLFENSON

Among the images Wolfenson produced for this shoot, two stand out for the striking contrast they present between the traditional representation of "authentic" Bahian culture in the form of the Baiana and the figure of a fashion model—juxtaposing representations of feminine beauty. In one photo Carvalho's long, lean form is emphasized by a floor-length dress, fitted through the torso with a slight flare at the bottom (fig. 4.9b). She stands in a gateway, gazing confidently at the viewer. On the right side of the composition, we see two women, the "real Baianas" (identified by traditional clothing) exiting. Photographed from behind, these two women conform to expected representations of the Baiana. In comparison to Carvalho, they are shorter and stockier; their mid-calf flounced skirts, shoulder-covering lace tops, and head wraps contrast with the model's high-fashion attire and her straightened hair, styled in an updo. In the second photo, Carvalho stands in the threshold of an open portal dressed in a sophisticated, fitted outfit of cropped pants and a stylish jacket. While Carvalho is in the background of the photograph, she is illuminated. In the foreground, concealed by dark shadows, we see two "traditional" Baianas in conversation.

The use of the Baiana in the context of a contemporary fashion magazine illustrates the centrality this iconic figure in representing Bahia. It also demonstrates that the Baiana, while celebrated as a core figure in the visual representation of Bahian identity and black femininity in Brazil's northeast, continues to exist outside of the boundaries of what is considered conventional, contemporary, mainstream beauty. The "authentic" Baiana, who appears as a background prop in a photograph that features Carvalho and contemporary fashion in the foreground, has darker skin, a larger body, and a posture of inaction that contrasts with Carvalho's thin frame, uncovered head, light skin, angular features, and, significantly, her active body language. The inclusion of "authentic" black Bahian culture in juxtaposition with the figure of Carvalho also makes the model appear more European, less "black," an interesting tactic in Vogue's annual issue dedicated to celebrating women of color. The Baiana in the *Vogue* spread may be read as a figure from the past, a frozen image of "authenticity," whose mode of representation through clothing has remained fixed over the course of time; her timelessness is further punctuated by comparison with Carvalho's of-the-moment fashion.

The pairing of Carvalho with the image of the "authentic" Baiana also reveals the continued reinforcement of standards of beauty that emerge from the dominant class. The Baiana serves in this context as a foil, standing in sharp contrast to mainstream ideals of beauty, even in an issue of *Vogue* that seeks to promote diversity. While the Baiana has been viewed positively, the specific construction of beauty used to represent black, Bahian, feminine identity has served to set her apart from white constructs of beauty, thus emphasizing exoticism.

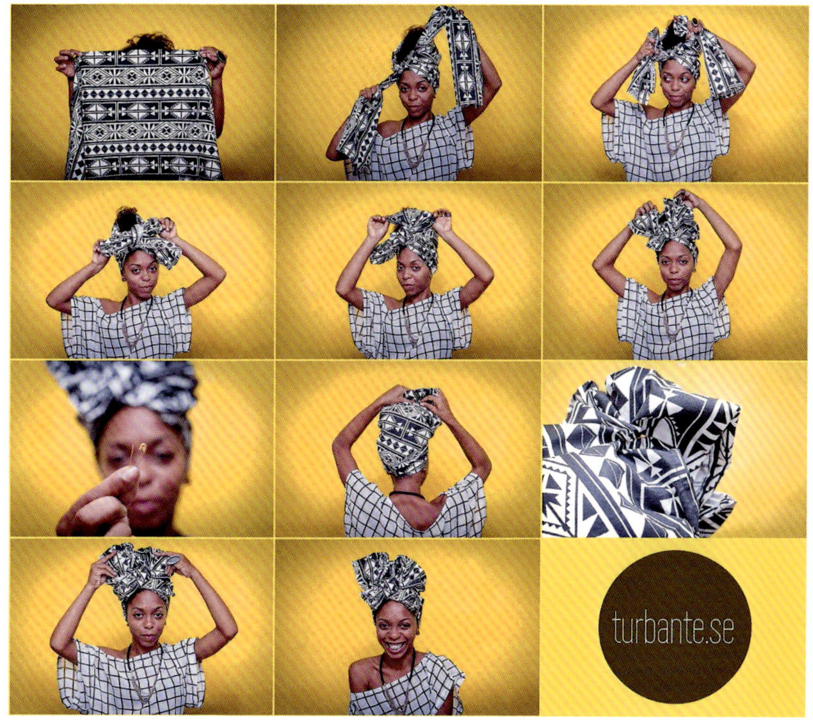


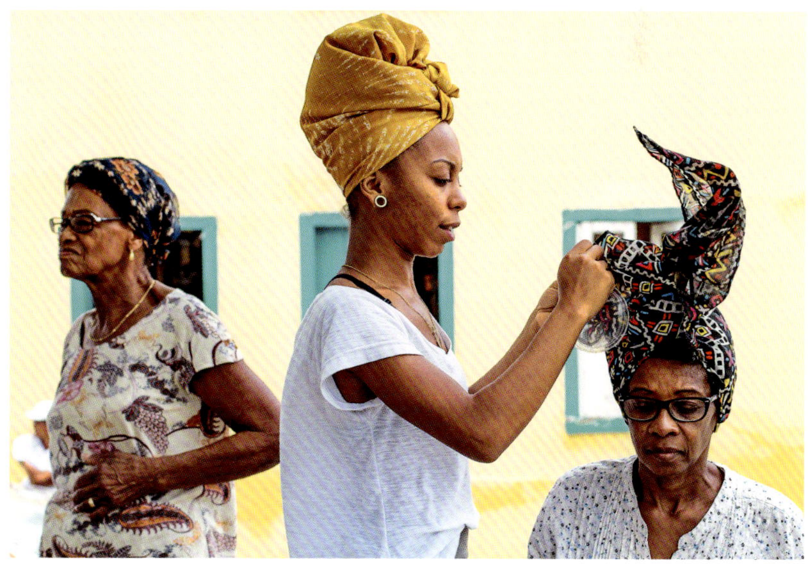

**4.10a,b**
Thaís Muniz (b. 1987, Feira de Santana, Bahia, Brazil)
a. *Turbante-se* (Turban Yourself), 2012–2016
b. *On Her Ori—Crowning Ceremony*, Rio de Contas, Bahia, Brazil
Performative workshop
PHOTOGRAPHS BY SHAI ANDRADE (B. 1992, SALVADOR, BAHIA, BRAZIL)
COURTESY THAÍS MUNIZ

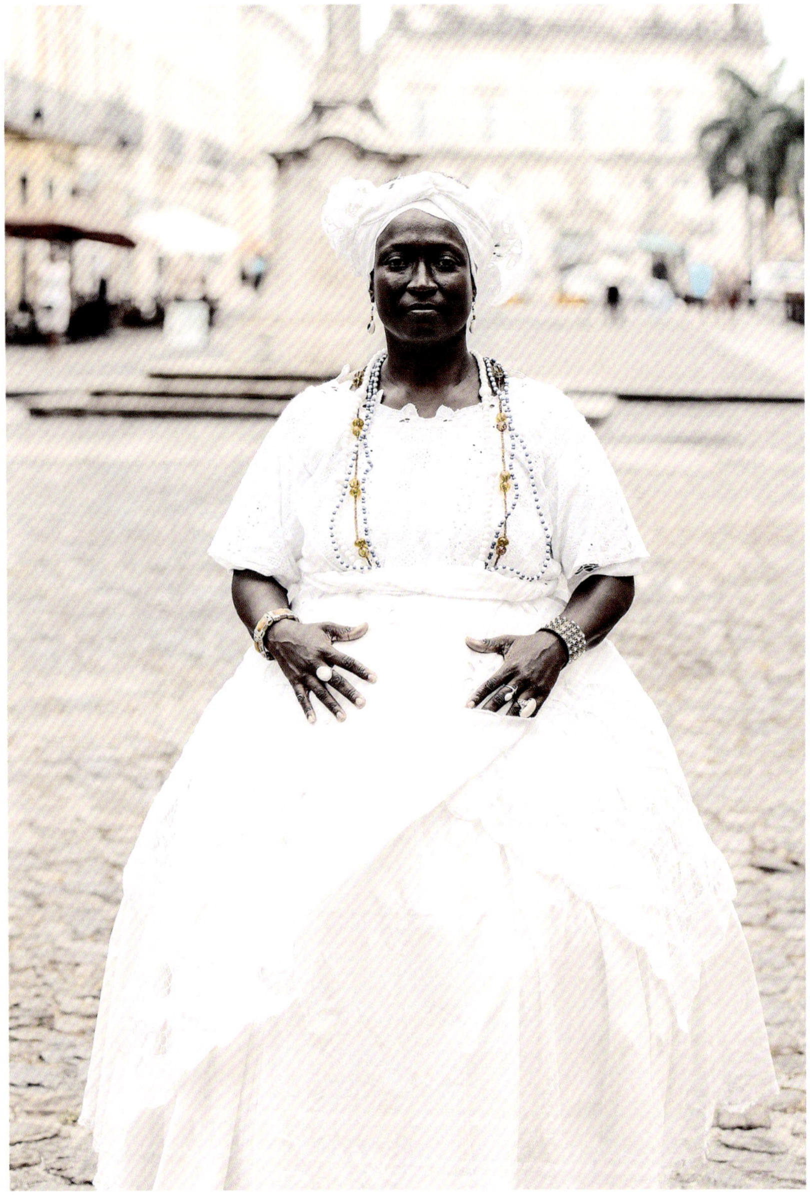

**4.11**
Helen Salomão, (b.1994, Salvador, Bahia, Brazil)
*Igbagbo (Fé)* (Faith), 2015
Photograph
COURTESY HELEN SALOMÃO

Posing for the photograph is Anita Costa.

**What the Baiana Really Has**

From the time of Verger and up to the present moment, black women, and especially Bahian women, have served as a central theme in the work of some of Brazil's most recognized photographers, among them Adenor Gondim, Voltaire Fraga, and Mário Cravo Neto. But what of images produced *by* Bahian women artists of African descent not merely *of* black women of Bahia? For contemporary women artists from Bahia, engaging with the representation of the Baiana can be an act of affirmation, a radical and empowering reclamation, as seen is the art and social practice of Thaís Muniz. Muniz lives and works in Dublin, but Bahia remains central to the creation of her interactive, performative workshops called *Turbante-se* (Turban Yourself). In *Turbante-se*, Muniz presents the history of head wraps throughout the world, emphasizing their significance as a symbol of identity and resistance in Africa and the African diaspora while also exploring the history of their appropriation (figs. 4.10a,b). Participants in the workshop are taught to wrap a turban in exchange for a photograph, which becomes a record of the interaction.

*Turbante-se* is interactive and collaborative, intended as an ephemeral experience that results in knowledge and a sense of belonging and empowerment rather than in a consumable product. The head wrap, a core element of the Baiana's attire and a potent symbol of blackness, is at the center of the work *Turbante-se* and the title—"Turban Yourself"—evokes the artist's active stance and her dedication to teaching and through participation, challenging the notion that knowledge of cultural practices is an innate skill. The step-by-step photographs emphasize that culture is learned, whether it be passed down through generations or presented by way of artistic interventions in daily life. Muniz presents the preparation of a head wrap in a didactic manner, stepping away from the "exoticism" that served to "other" in early representations of the Baiana.

Similarly, Helen Salomão gives women of color the agency to represent the complexity of feminine Bahian identity (fig. 4.11). She explodes the conventional depiction of beauty that dominates *Vogue*, where lighter skin, straightened hair, and ultra-thin bodies rule the day. The series Gorda Flor (Full Bloom) was shot in the streets of the Santo Antônio neighborhood of Salvador.[20] Here the women of Bahia engage with the viewer through confident poses and expressions. Hairstyles and clothing are used to express individuality, challenging the tendency to reduce the women of Bahia to a "type" defined by a style of dress.

In one image shot in the streets of Salvador, three women pose in front of a colonial-style facade covered with graffiti. They strike a pose, raise a fist, and gaze directly at the viewer (fig. 4.12). Gone are the traditional lace outfits. These Baianas wear brightly colored prints and stripes, the head wraps replaced by a Hashtag-logoed cap, eye-catching braids, and a gold headpiece evoking the Candomblé *orixá* Oxum. Skin tone, hair (from natural to long braids), and clothing all come together to challenge the tendency to reduce women to a single "type" and expand the mainstream standards of beauty seen in the pages of *Vogue*. It is in this work that the photograph's subjects show us what today's Baianas *really* have: power, strength, individuality, confidence, beauty, and pride.

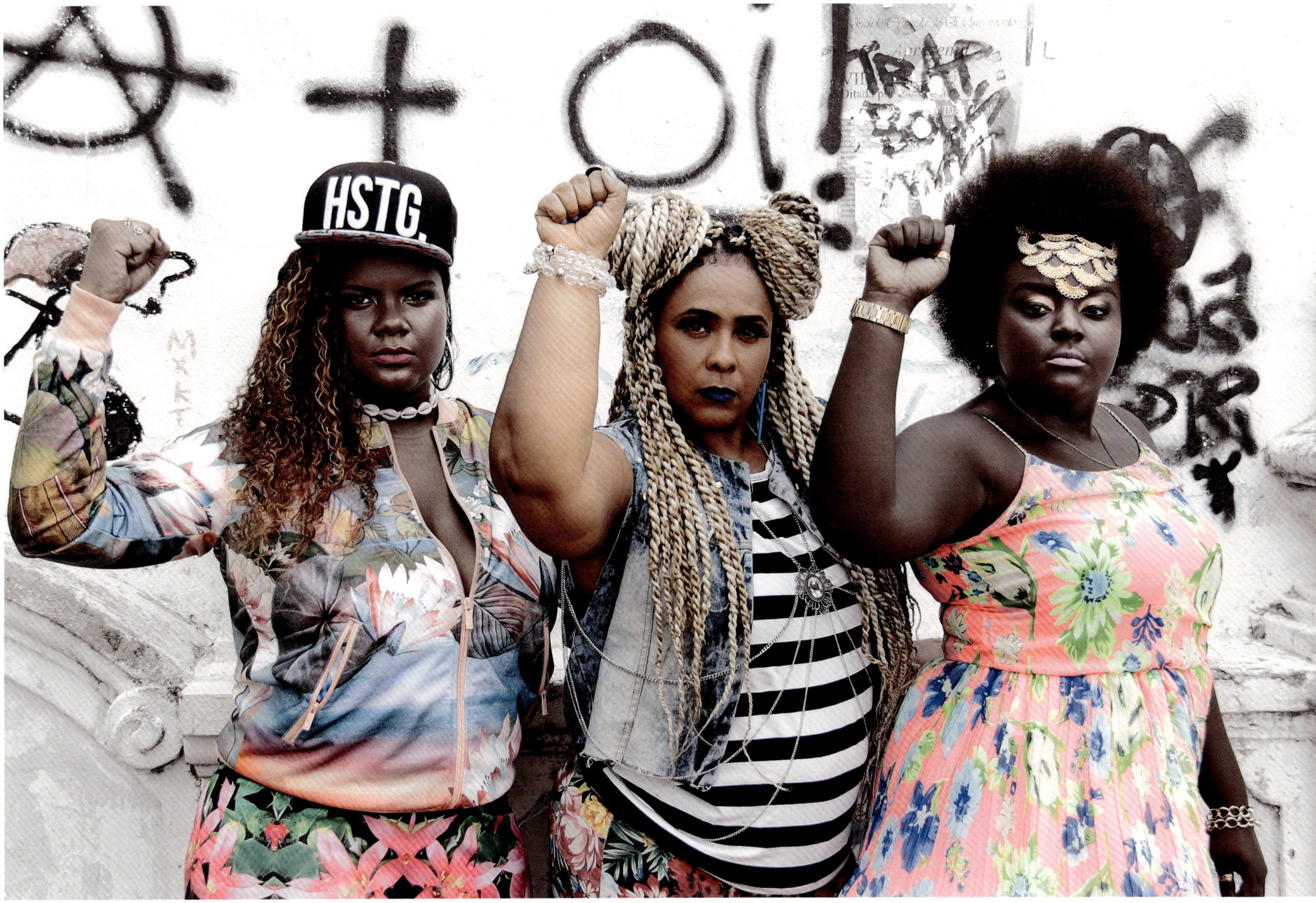


**4.12**
Helen Salomão (b. 1994, Salvador, Bahia, Brazil)
*Gorda Flor* (Full Bloom), 2016
Photograph
COURTESY HELEN SALOMÃO

Models: Lailane Dórea, Tania Neres, and Dandana França.

*Interleaf* **G**

# Bound in Beauty

## *Creole Jewelry in Bahia*

**Sarah K. Chenault**

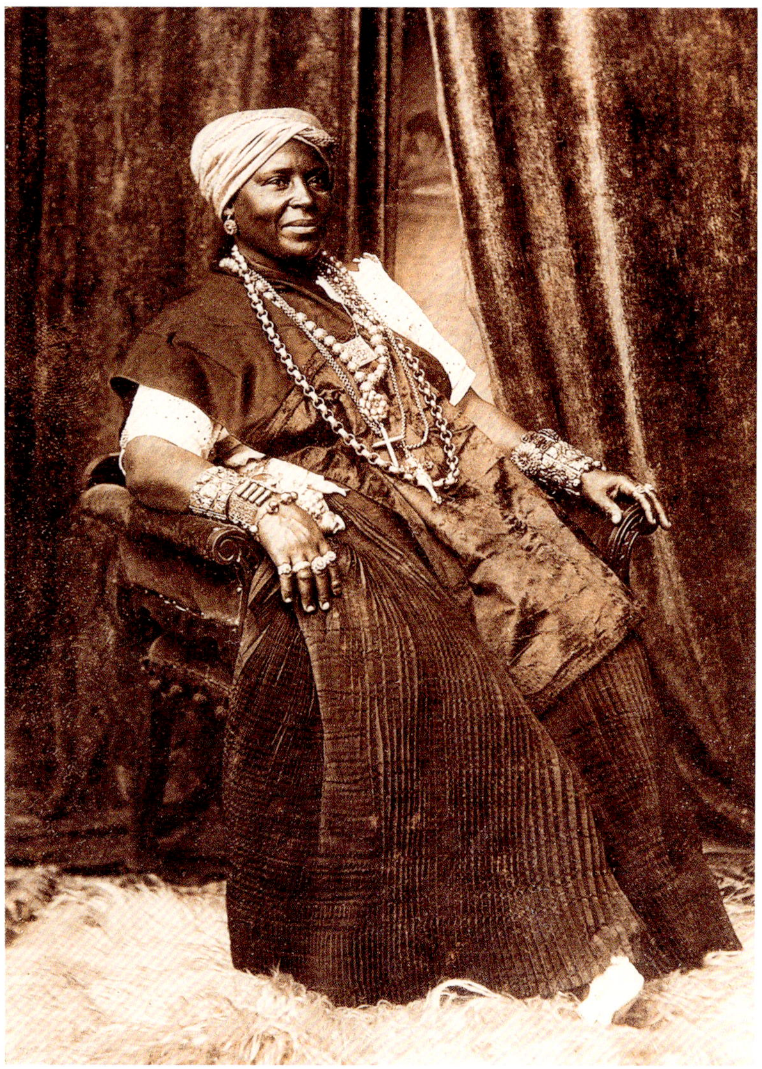

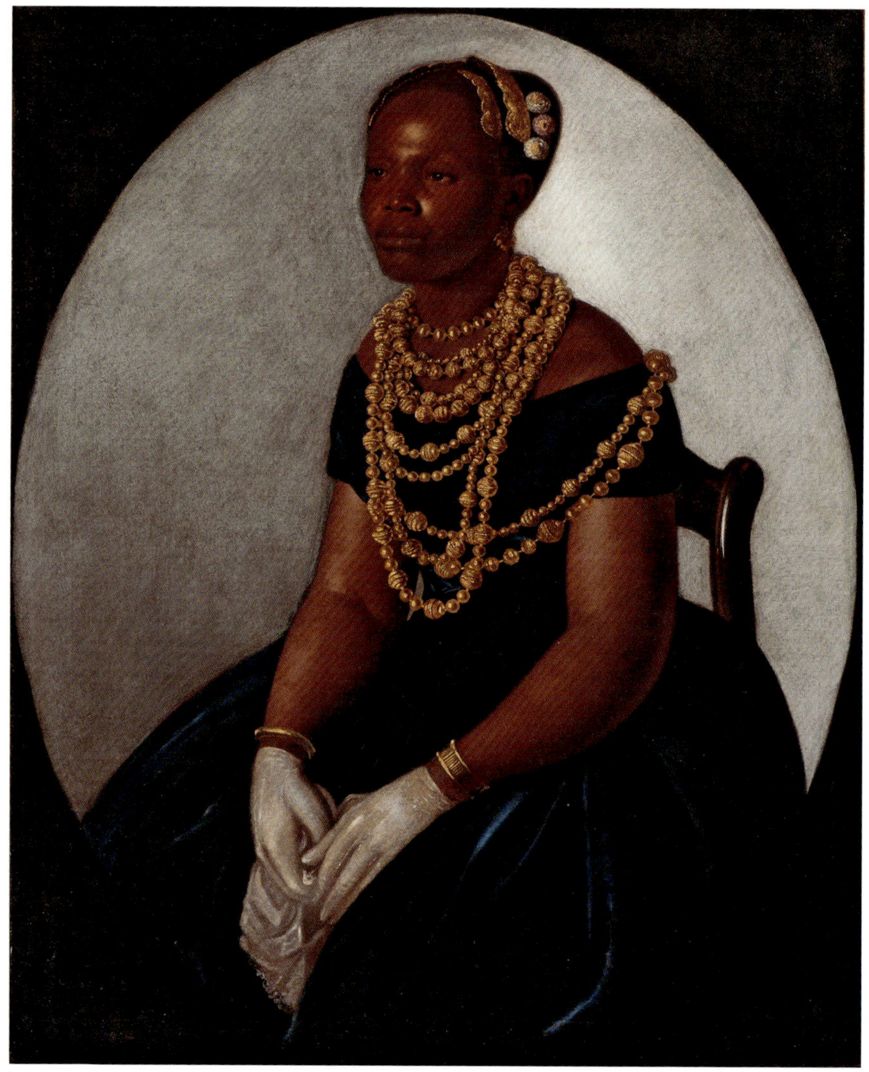

**G.1**
Photographer Unknown
Florinda Ana do Nascimento (b. unkown, Salvador, Bahia, Brazil; d. May 11, 1931), late nineteenth century?
Photograph
COLLECTION OF THE INSTITUTO FEMININO DA BAHIA, MUSEU DO TRAJE E DO TÊXTIL

Florinda Ana do Nascimento grew up on a farm outside of Salvador and eventually worked in at least two bourgeois homes, one of a doctor and the other of a colonel (Monteiro and Ferreira 2005).

**G.2**
Artist Unknown
Baiana, circa 1850
Oil on canvas
Unframed: 96 x 77.5 cm
COLLECTION OF THE MUSEU PAULISTA DA UNIVERSIDADE DE SÃO PAULO
PHOTOGRAPH BY HÉLIO NOBRE

**G.3a-d**
Arrangement of four necklaces

**a.** (INTERIOR ROW)
Necklace, eighteenth century
Coral and silver; L: 57 cm

**b.** (SECOND ROW)
Necklace, date unknown
Gold alloy; L: 76 cm

**c.** (THIRD ROW)
Necklace, eighteenth century
Gold plated silver; L: 32 cm

**d.** (FOURTH ROW)
Necklace, eighteenth century
Gold plated silver; L: 29 cm;
PRIVATE COLLECTION

Multiple necklaces were typically worn at once, as suggested by this photograph.

A LATE NINETEENTH-CENTURY PHOTOGRAPH of Florinda Ana do Nascimento shows her seated in front of a draped backdrop. She appears both regal and self-assured (fig. G.1). Her dress is that of the stereotypical Baiana, consisting of a head wrap or turban, a lace blouse, a long pleated skirt, and a *pano da costa* (a type of cloth worn as a shawl and associated with Africa). Her jewelry—all most likely of gold and silver—includes several long chains, earrings, rings, and multiple bracelets worn on both wrists. In an mid-nineteenth–century painting from the Museu Paulista da Universidade de São Paulo (G.2), another Baiana is also posed elegantly dressed and seated in a chair. This younger woman wears a deep blue dress, white gloves, and a stunning collection of gold hair combs, long necklaces, earrings, and bracelets. While her style of dress may derive from a European aesthetic, the layered and heavy gold pieces, known as *joias de crioulas* (creole jewelry), which appear almost to weigh her down, do not. Euro-Brazilian women and their descendants in Bahia in the eighteenth and nineteenth century typically also wore a tremendous amount of jewelry, but it was imported from Europe (Cunha 2011, 46) and was very different from the large and opulent style made in Brazil that was particularly associated with Bahia (Godoy 2006, 13).

Many eighteenth- and nineteenth-century Baianas, both freed women and slaves, wore the uniquely Brazilian *joias de crioulas* (figs. G.3–G.6). While some of these women could earn a wage and save to purchase such lavish adornments themselves, they and their enslaved counterparts may also have received them as gifts. Slave owners gave such jewelry to enslaved women or allowed them to wear it, possibly as a form of acknowledgment or reward but certainly also because the recipient, who often accompanied the lady of the house to church, to market, and elsewhere in the public sphere, became a living testament to the wealth of the family. This form of "conspicuous consumption" was not unique to Bahia, but has become closely associated with the Baiana in Brazilian collective memory and popular culture (Veblen 1947, 257, and see Shirey and Dunn, this volume). One traveler to Brazil commented that the total monetary value of such accoutrements was worth more than the living being they adorned (Lara 2000, 184). Tellingly the bracelets, hair combs, and chains—sometimes called "shackle" necklaces (Godoy 2006, 72), presumably because they bound the wearer to her owner—could, however, also be sold by the recipient to purchase the freedom of friends and family members (Lody 2001, 50).

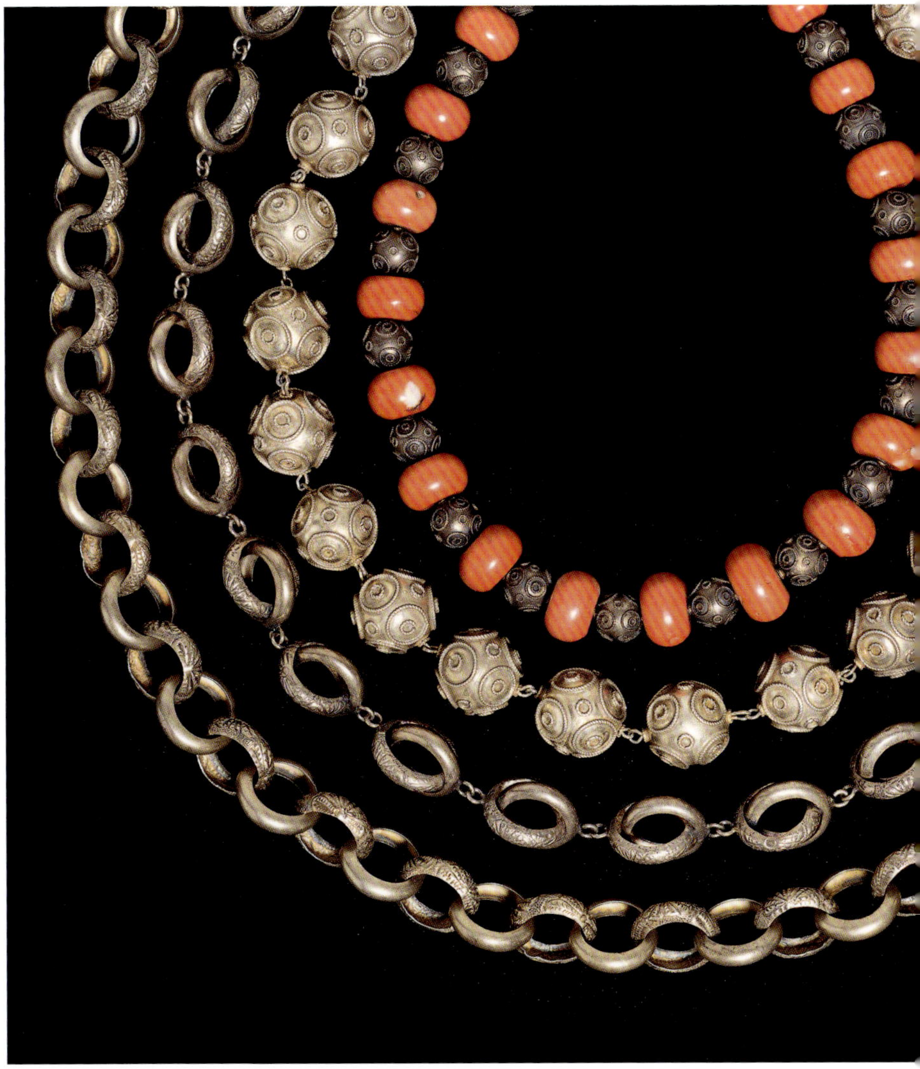

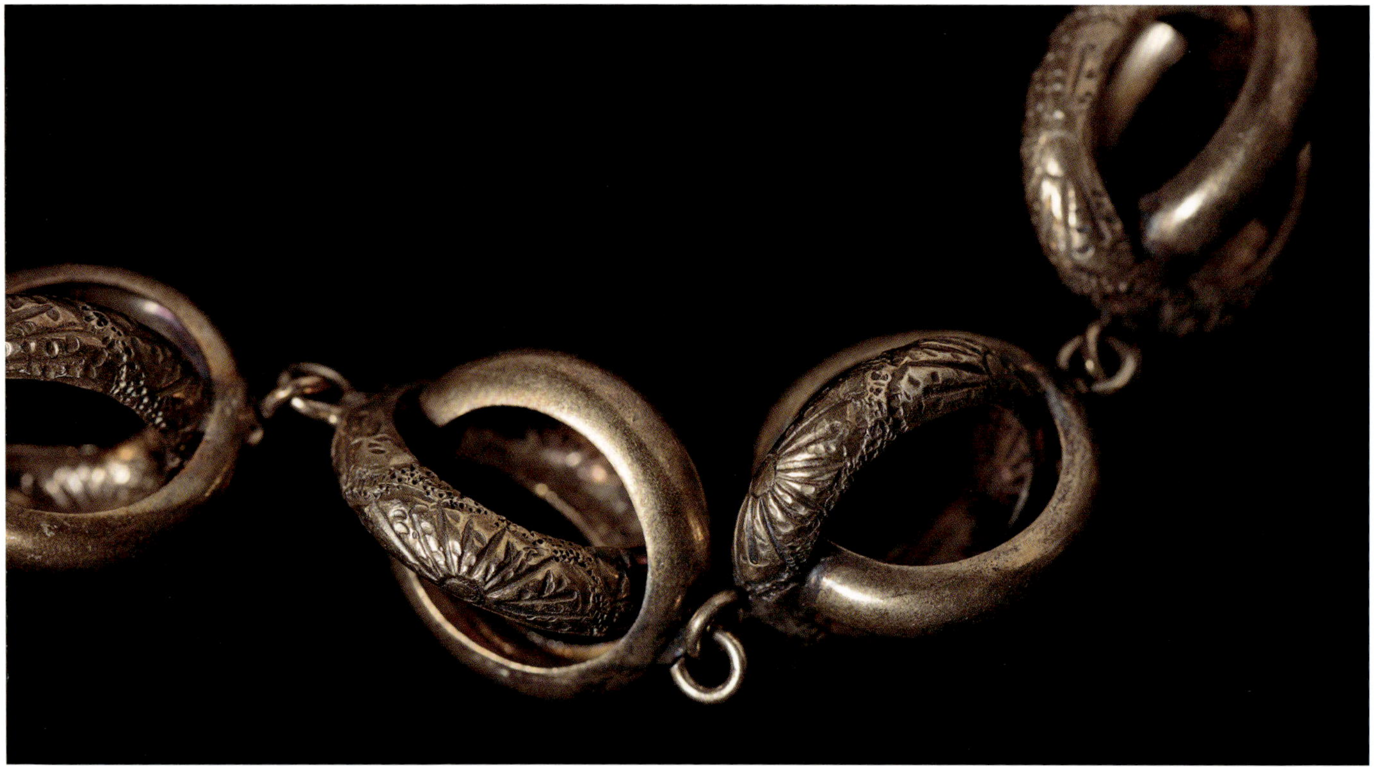

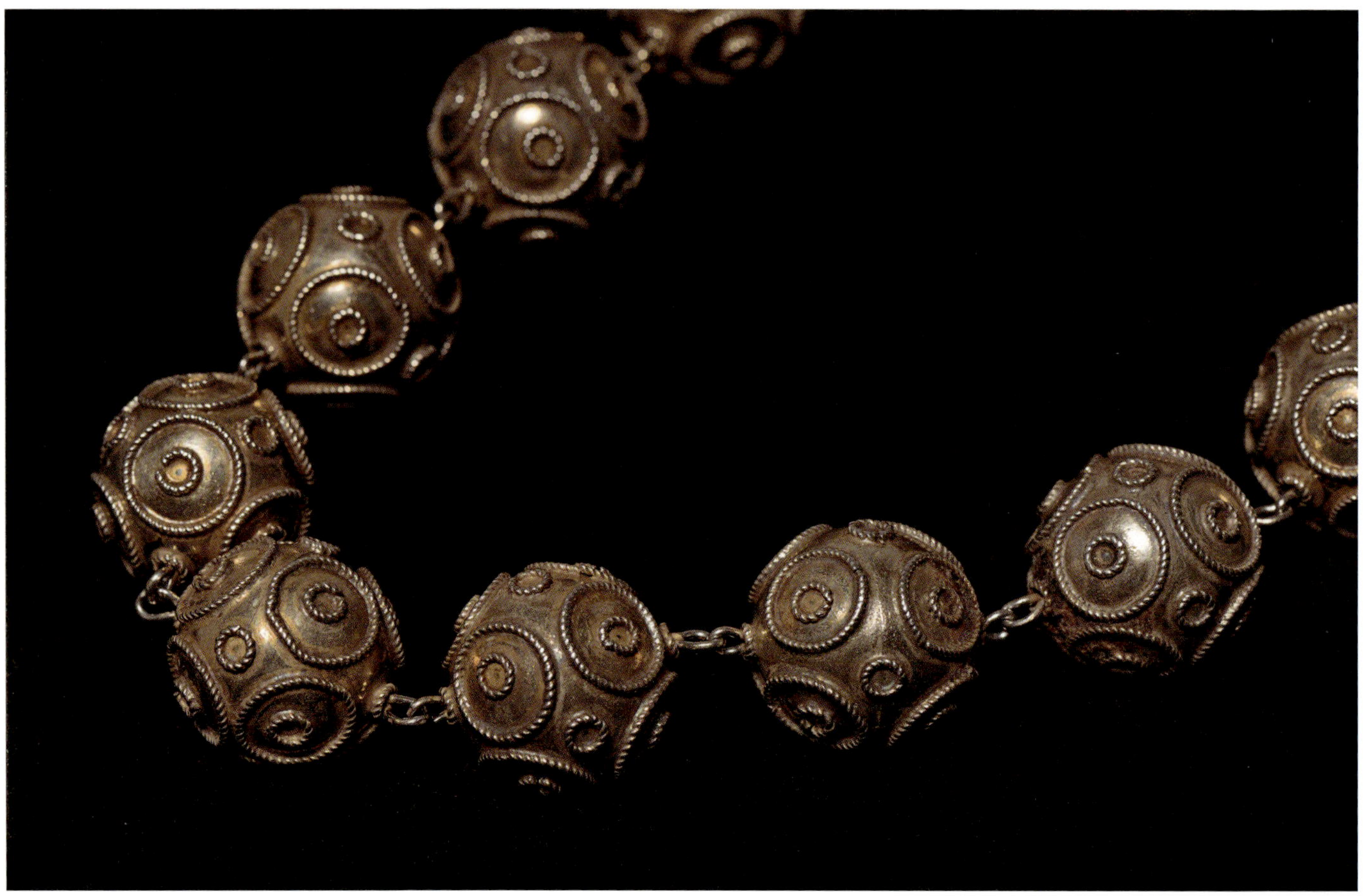

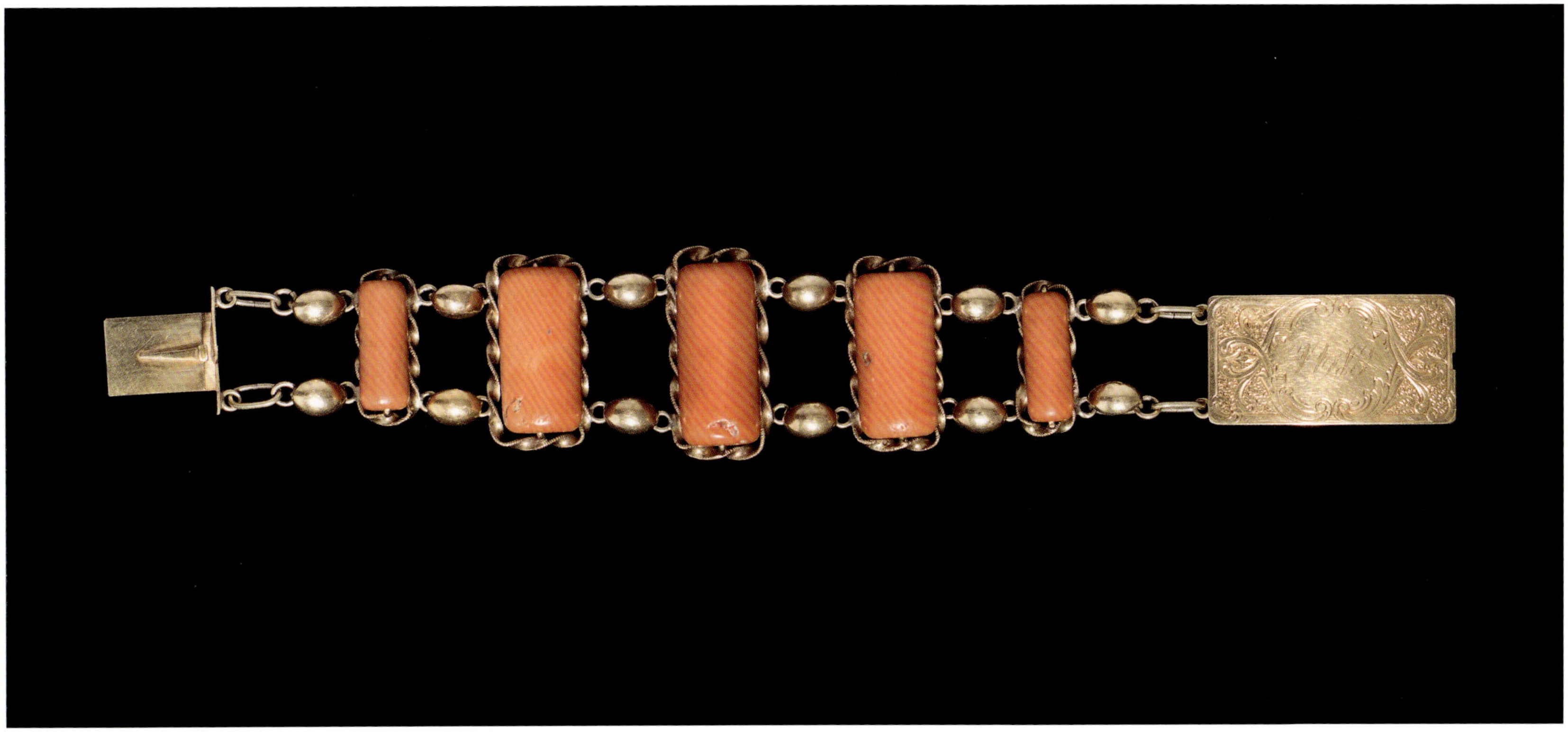

Creole jewelry is celebrated in the song "O que é que a baiana tem?" ("What Is It That the Baiana Has?") by Dorival Caymmi, one of Bahia's most well-known composers. The verses ask what makes up the archetypal appearance of the Baiana? A long list of responses follows, itemizing her gold jewelry and fine clothing (see Dunn, this volume). The lines that appear at the end of the song are noteworthy: Um rosário de ouro, uma bolota assim/Ai, quem não tem balangandãs/não vai no Bonfim (A rosary of gold, a pendant like this/They who have no *balangandãs*/Do not go to Bonfim). Alluded to as well is the *penca de balangandãs*, a collection of amulets characteristic of the Baiana.

Peeking from beneath her *pano da costa* at the left of the photograph of Florinda Ana do Nascimento (see fig. G.1) is a *penca de balangandãs* (figs. G.7, G.8). This group of charms was typically worn at the waist, and each was unique to the woman who selected it (Lody 2001, 21). The *penca de balangandãs* could at once include objects associated with Catholicism, such as a cross, and others associated with Candomblé, for example, a tiny metal tool to represent Ogum, the *orixá* associated with ironwork and warfare and linked by many to the fight for freedom from slavery (Lody 2001, 21).

One charm more likely present than not was the *figa*, a closed hand with the thumb placed between the index and middle finger (fig. G.10). Historically a symbol of fecundity rooted in ancient Mediterranean customs (Farelli 1981, 15), the *figa* is said to offer protection and to ward off the *mau olhado* (evil eye). It was often the first piece acquired by a Baiana (Ewbanks 1856, 246) and has become emblematic of Afro-Brazilian ritual if not identity. One can clearly see its contemporary resonance in the work of Nadia Taquary. She has expanded upon the creole jewelry tradition and focused upon the iconic role of the *figa* (fig. G.9). Her large-scale pieces are no longer intended to be worn, however, but are meant for display on walls and tables. Taquary sources her materials from scavengers who find old hardwoods, such as jacaranda, which were once used in building the foundations of colonial houses (Taquary, personal communication, 2015). Through her sculptures, these fragmentary sources of support gain a new life as a form of spiritual protection.

**G.4**
Detail of figure G.3c.

**G.5**
Detail of figure G.3b

**G.6**
Bracelet, eighteenth century
Coral, gold
L: 20 cm
PRIVATE COLLECTION

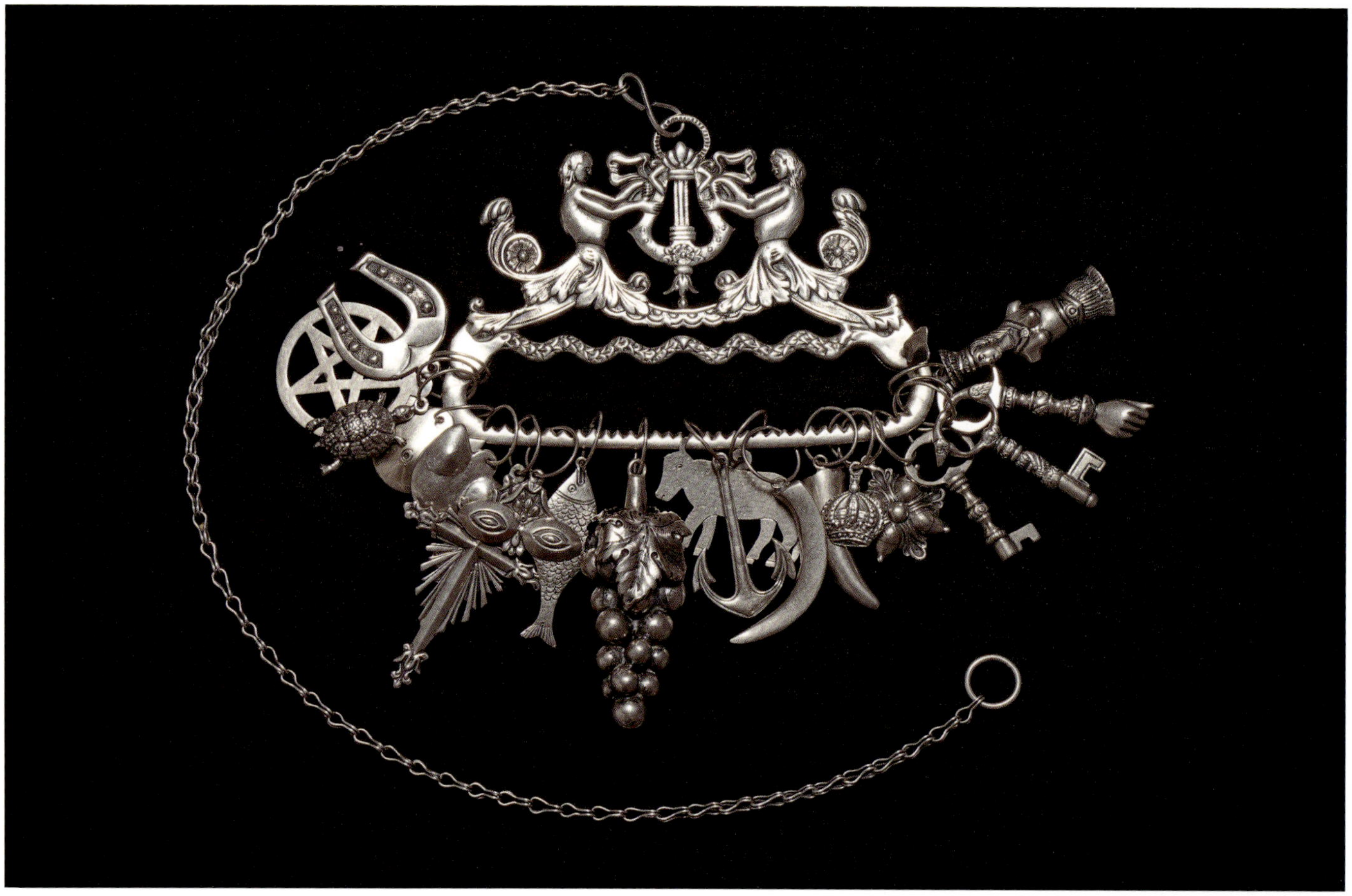

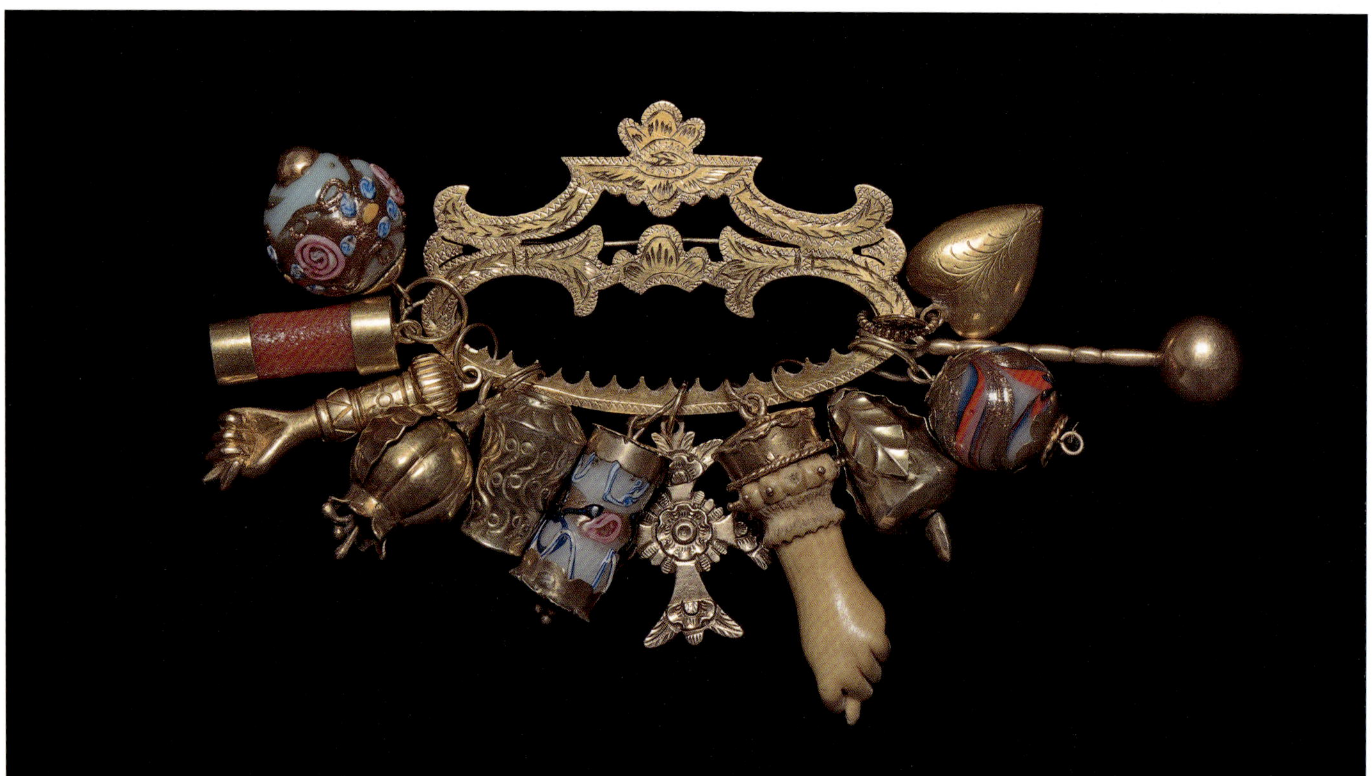

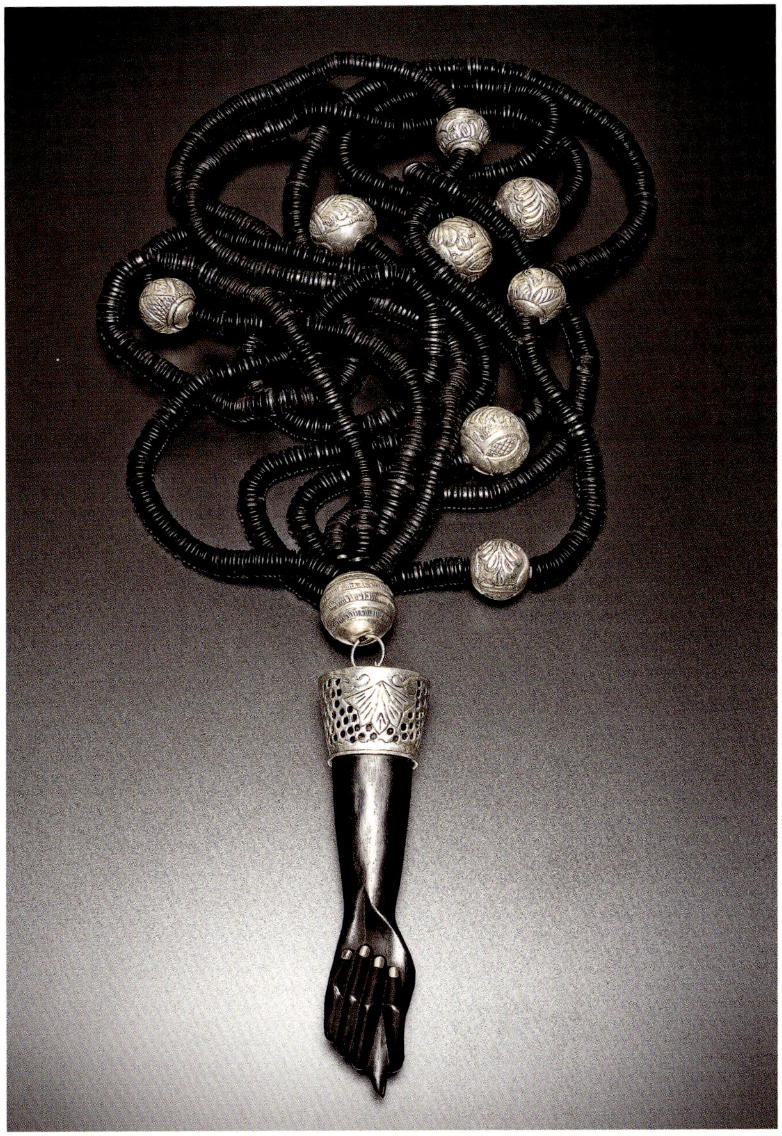

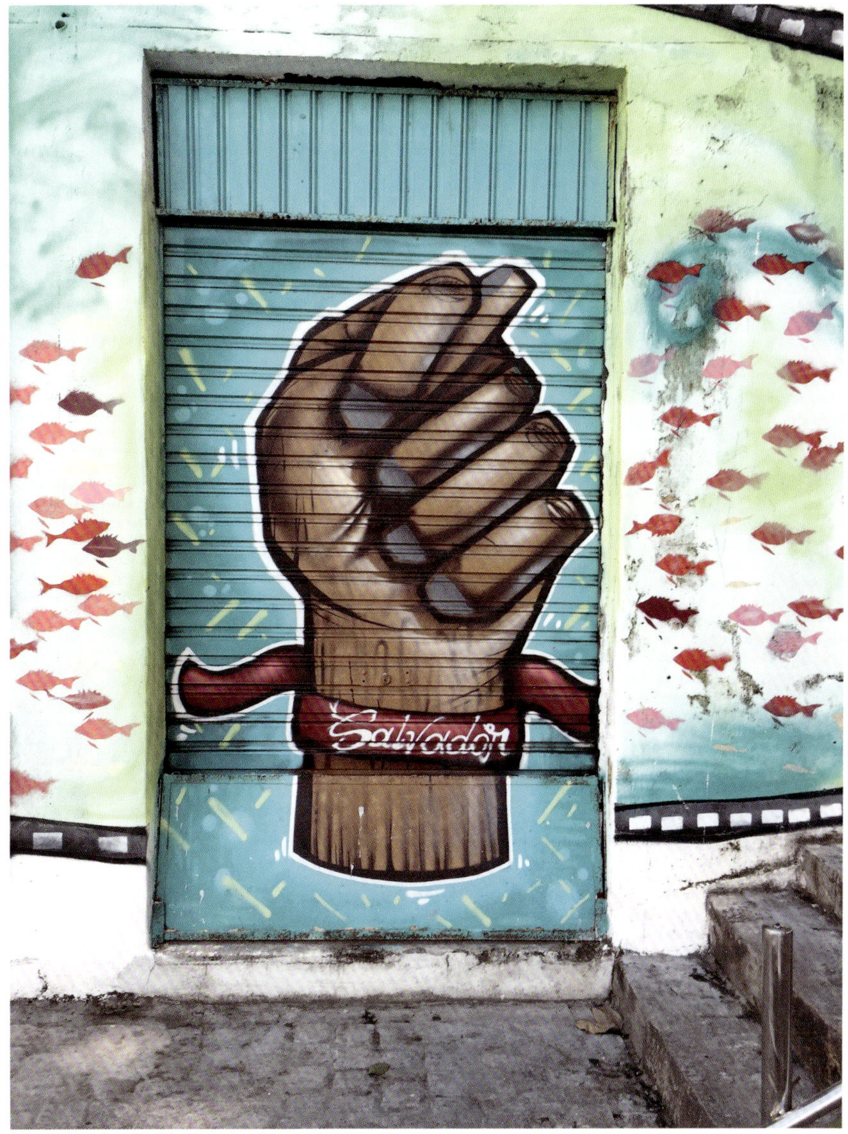


**G.7**
*Penca de balangandãs*, nineteenth century
Silver
L: 18 cm
PRIVATE COLLECTION

**G.8**
*Penca de balangandãs*, nineteenth century
Gold, unindentified metal
L: 8 cm
PRIVATE COLLECTION

**G.9**
Nadia Taquary (b. 1967, Salvador, Bahia, Brazil)
*Béerè—A filha primeira* (The First Daughter)
Coconut, brass, silver, wood
L: 50 cm
COURTESY NADIA TAQUARY
PHOTOGRAPH BY SERGIO BENUTTI

**G.10**
The *figa*, a hand with the thumb tucked between the index and middle fingers, appears as the subject of a street mural in Salvador. PHOTOGRAPH BY PATRICK A. POLK, 2016.

# 5 Capoeiras of Bahia

Ana Paula Höfling

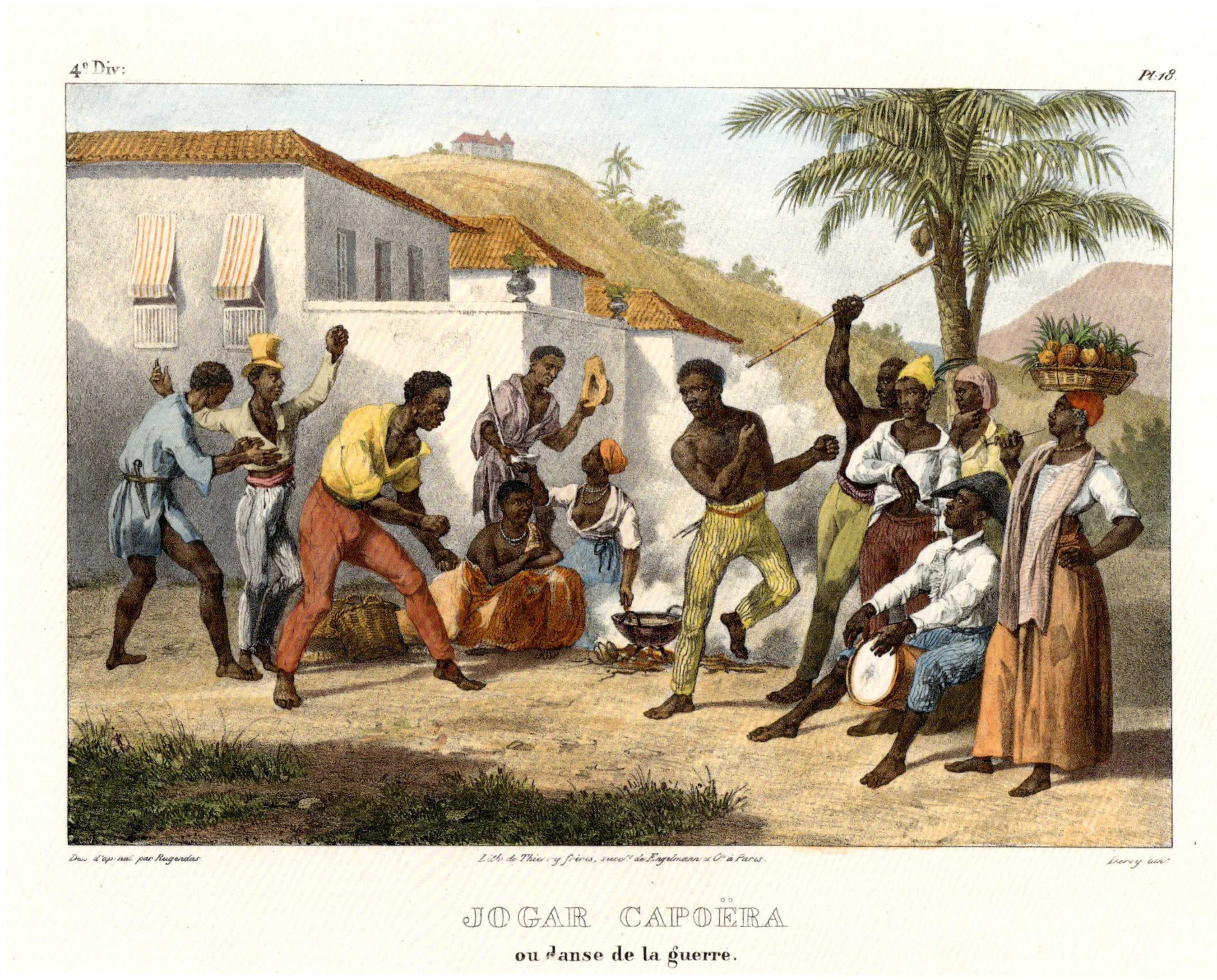

JOHANN MORITZ RUGENDAS, a German painter who first traveled to Brazil in 1821, provides us with one of the earliest descriptions of capoeira in his book *Malerische Reise in Brasilien* (Picturesque Travels in Brazil), published in 1835:

> [T]wo champions advance against each other, trying to hit with their heads the chest of the adversary they want to knock down. Attacks are avoided with jumps to the side and parrying equally as dexterous; but, throwing themselves against each other like rams, they hit head against head, not infrequently causing the game to degenerate into a fight and knives are brought in making it bloody.[1]

Rugendas describes capoeira as a violent and bloody combat game, marked by headbutts and dexterous evasive maneuvers (fig. 5.1). Charles Ribeyrolles, an exiled French journalist who moved to Brazil in 1858, briefly describes capoeira in *Brasil pittoresco: História, descripções, viagens, instituições, colonisação* (Picturesque Brazil: History, Descriptions, Travels, Institutions, Colonization), a bilingual French/Portuguese book divided in several tomes and published in 1859. Ribeyrolles classifies capoeira as a type of dance in a section titled "Games and Dances of Negroes": on weekends and holy days, he notes, "blacks are allowed one or two hours for dancing[....] Here, [we find] capoeira, a kind of pyrrhic dance, of daring and combative maneuvers, to the sound of the drum from the Congo" (Ribeyrolles [1859] 1980, 51).

These two nineteenth-century travelers' descriptions exemplify capoeira's duality: its graceful and dance-like quality—evasive moves seamlessly and effortlessly merging into circular kicks and hand balances—and the violent potential inherent in these graceful movements. Nineteenth- and early twentieth-century capoeira was often violent (it was common for practitioners to wield weapons such as straight razors), and the practice was criminalized as an act of "public disorder" in the Brazilian penal code of 1890 (fig. 5.2).

Capoeira today is no longer considered an illicit activity: it has become a respected aspect of Afro-Brazilian culture, and it is taught at schools, clubs, community centers, and private studios. Some capoeira teaching methods have been highly codified, and several schools of capoeira indicate a practitioner's levels through belts (*cordões*) of various colors. Capoeira practice involves learning its movements (strikes and evasive maneuvers) and its music; often students are taught to play capoeira's iconic musical bow, the *berimbau* (as well as other accompanying instruments) and sing capoeira songs (see figs. 5.4, 5.5). The *roda* (circle), an event often held on evenings and weekends, separate from regular instruction, provides capoeira students with an opportunity to put into practice the skills learned in class as they enter the circle, two at a time, in friendly matches or games (*jogos*) of capoeira, overseen by a *mestre* (master teacher) and always accompanied by live music (fig. 5.3).

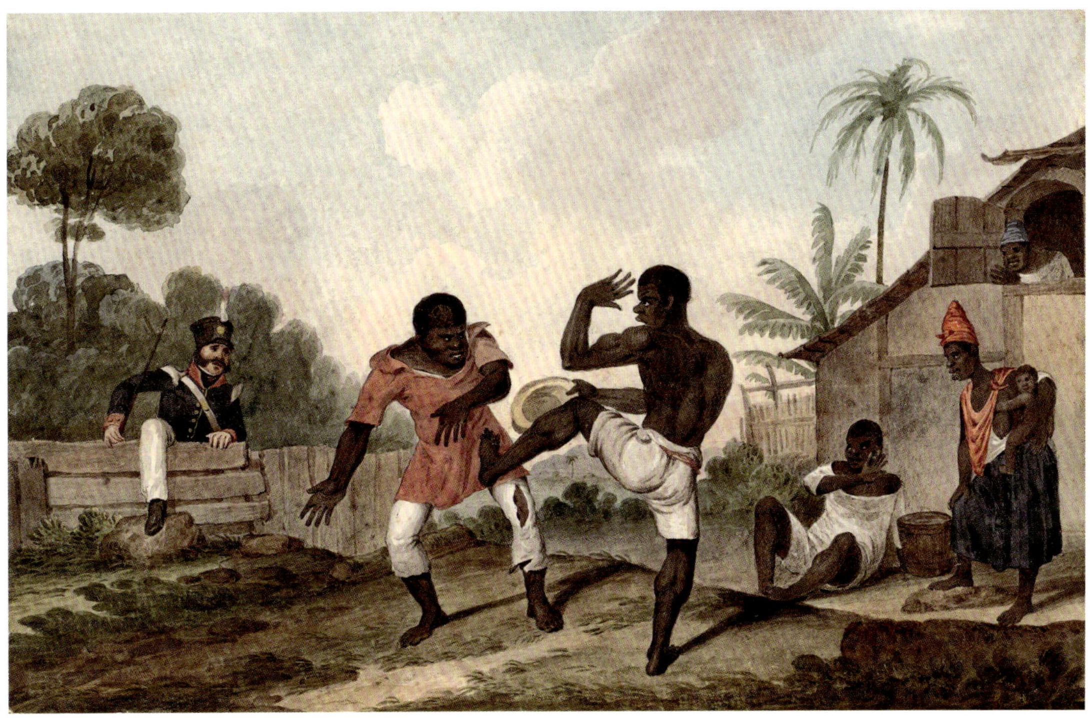

**5.1**
Johann Moritz Rugendas (b. 1802, Augusburg, Germany; d. 1858)
*Jogar capoëra; ou, Danse de la guerre* (Playing Capoeira; or, Dance of War)
From *Malerische Reise in Brasilien* (Picturesque Travels in Brazil, Paris: Engelmann & Cie, 1835)
Lithograph
39 x 49 cm
WÜRTTEMBERGISCHE LANDESBIBLIOTHEK, STUTTGART

**5.2**
Augustus Earle (b. 1793, London, England; d. 1838)
Capoeira, circa 1822
Watercolor on paper
16.5 x 25.1 cm
NATIONAL LIBRARY OF AUSTRALIA; REX NAN KIVELL COLLECTION, NK12/103

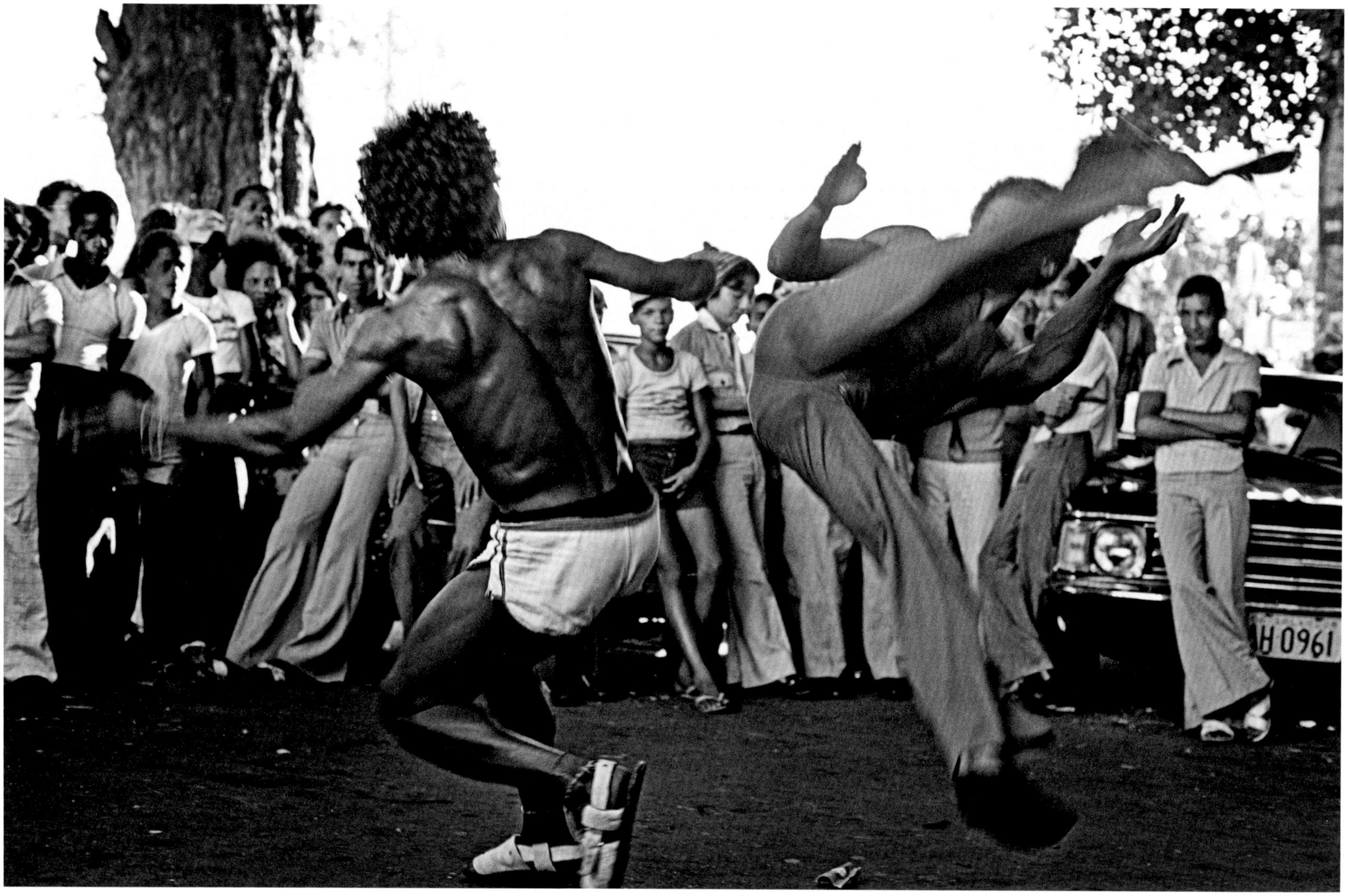

**5.3**
Lita Almeida Cerqueira (b. 1952, Salvador, Bahia, Brazil)
*Dança da capoeira II* (The Dance of Capoeira II), 1976
Photograph
COURTESY LITA ALMEIDA CERQUEIRA

The respect and popularity capoeira enjoys today can be traced back to the development of the practice as symbolic of the State of Bahia in the mid-twentieth century. Until the 1930s, the practice was known as *capoeiragem* or *vadiação*,[2] and *capoeira* referred to the practitioner. While today a *capoeirista* practices capoeira, up until the 1930s a *capoeira* practiced *capoeiragem*. Throughout the 1930s, *capoeiragem* was gradually transformed into what we know today—its violent aspects downplayed and its new identity as Afro-Bahian folklore established. In a collaborative effort involving both capoeira practitioners and Bahian intellectuals interested in ending police persecution of Afro-Bahian practices, capoeira was reimagined as both a regional sport and a folkloric practice. *Capoeiragem* gave way to two styles of capoeira: *capoeira regional* and *capoeira angola* (initially called *capoeira de Angola*, or capoeira from Angola). Although created in opposition to each other, both focused on codifying, organizing, and ultimately legitimizing the game of capoeira.

Mestre Bimba (Manuel dos Reis Machado, 1900–1974), in collaboration with his students (many of whom were white, college-educated young men), developed a codified training method divided into set sequences, which he later published in a manual titled *Curso de capoeira regional* (Capoeira Regional Course), where readers could learn capoeira in fourteen lessons, accompanied by music recorded on an LP. By calling his innovative style of capoeira "regional," Mestre Bimba emphasized its affiliation with the region of Bahia, which, paradoxically, was being reimagined as the repository of Afro-Brazilian tradition (see figs. 5.5a,b).

Mestre Bimba's *capoeira regional*, an Afro-diasporic practice that flaunted its own modernity, was met with skepticism by Bahia's intellectual elite. In Jorge Amado's *Bahia de Todos os Santos*: *Guia das ruas e dos mistérios da cidade do Salvador* (*Bahia de Todos os Santos: Guide to the Streets and Mysteries of the City of Salvador*, 1945), he addresses the "problem" of *capoeira regional*:

> A great debate is taking place nowadays in the *capoeira* community in Bahia. It happens that mestre Bimba went to Rio de Janeiro to show residents of the Lapa [neighborhood] how *capoeira* is played. And there he learned moves from *catch-as-catch-can*, jiu-jitsu, and boxing. He mixed all this with *capoeira de Angola*, the one born out of a dance of Negroes, and returned to his city speaking of a new capoeira, "*capoeira regional*." Ten of the most respected *capoeiristas* told me, in an open and democratic debate we had about mestre Bimba's new school, that the "*regional*" is not to be trusted and it's a disfigurement of the old *capoeira* "*angola*," the only true [capoeira]. (Amado 1945, 183)

Here, Amado distances Mestre Bimba's innovations from Bahia, relocating them to Rio de Janeiro, where the *mestre* was allegedly introduced to foreign fighting techniques. The capital of Brazil at the time, Rio de Janeiro came to symbolize modernity, while Bahia was refashioned as its counterpart: the cradle of Brazilian tradition.

Mestre Bimba unapologetically portrayed himself as an innovator while at the same time connecting his own capoeira lineage to Africa, often reminding interviewers that he first learned capoeira from an African named Bentinho. Although Mestre Bimba was an Afro-descendant Bahian man whose capoeira practice was, in fact, not that different from *capoeiragem*, his innovations were criticized as a "loss" of tradition by Bahian intellectuals who viewed culture from the prism of loss or retention. Capoeira scholar Letícia Vidor de Sousa Reis, in *O mundo de pernas pro ar: A capoeira no Brasil*, proposes that Mestre Bimba's innovations were not, in fact, a "whitening" of capoeira, as they were often understood until the end of the twentieth century. Instead, Reis frames Mestre Bimba's innovations as Afro-diasporic appropriations of hegemonic symbols and rituals deployed to legitimize capoeira (Reis 2000, 107–8). In her essay "Capoeiras e intelectuais: A construção coletiva da capoeira 'autêntica,'" anthropologist Simone Pondé Vassallo (2003) notes that Bahian intellectuals such as Édison Carneiro and Jorge Amado championed the preservation of cultural forms deemed pure and saw *capoeira regional* as a threat to capoeira's integrity (the word *descaracterização*, or "loss of character" was often used to refer to this process). Instead, they lauded the style they believed best represented capoeira's tradition: *capoeira de Angola*.

Mestre Pastinha (Vicente Ferreira Pastinha, 1889–1981) has been memorialized as the guardian of capoeira's African traditions, and his name has become synonymous with the *angola* style of capoeira today (fig. 5.4). Bahia's intellectual and artistic elite continually praised Pastinha for preserving capoeira's traditions "from Angola." Vassallo proposes that the term *capoeira de Angola* was initially disseminated by Édison Carneiro in his book *Negros bantus* (1937) and adopted by Mestre Pastinha in the process of establishing his own style of capoeira, constructed as authentic in opposition to Mestre Bimba's modernized *capoeira regional* (Vassallo 2003, 117). Capoeira historian Matthias Röhrig Assunção, in his essay "Angola in Brazil: The Formation of *Angoleiro* Identity in Bahia," notes that even though Angola identity was considered "impure" in Candomblé, it was associated with a capoeira style believed to have retained the "purity" of its African traditions (Assunção 2015, 135–36).

Mestre Pastinha, like Mestre Bimba, drew a direct link to Africa through claims of first studying capoeira with an "old African" from Angola. Mestre Pastinha often recounted the story of his introduction to capoeira as a frail and skinny ten-year-old who was often bullied by a larger, stronger boy in his neighborhood. They often got into fights, but Pastinha always lost. One day, an old African named Benedito watched the fight and invited Pastinha to come to his home to learn capoeira. After some practice, Pastinha was able to defeat the bully "with one blow."[3] The fact that both Mestre Pastinha and Mestre Bimba report having learned directly from Africans is important in that it decidedly dissociates the capoeira techniques of both these innovators from the marginal and criminal status of nineteenth-century, straight-razor-wielding tough guys (*valentões*).

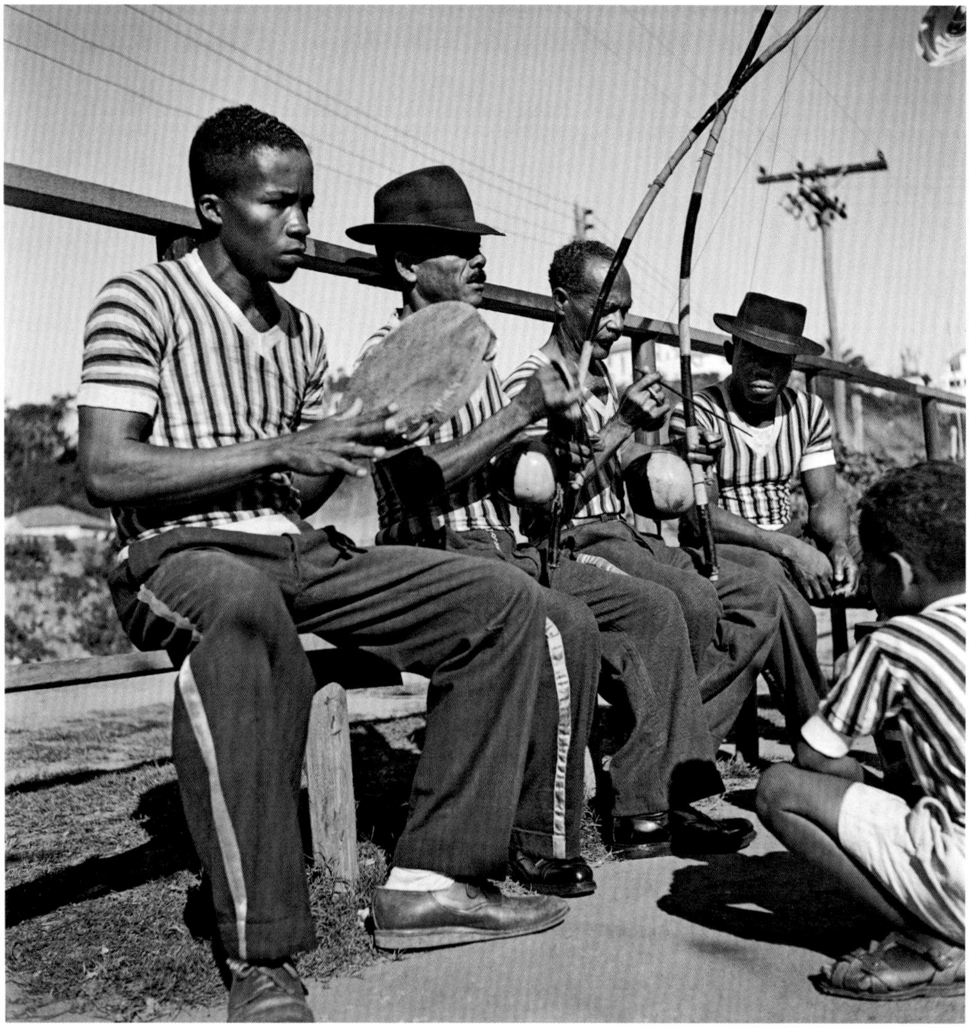

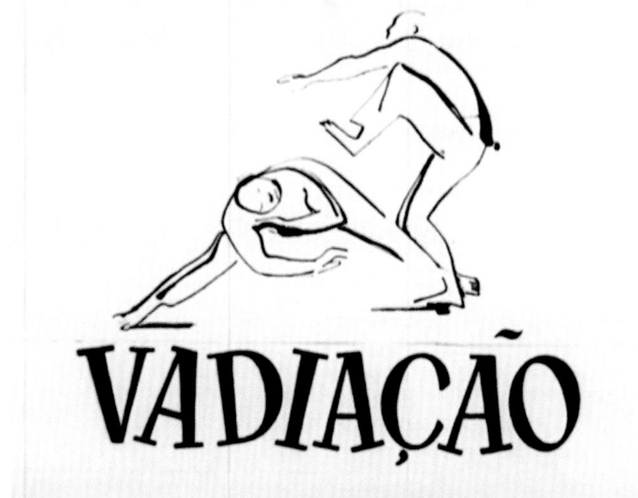


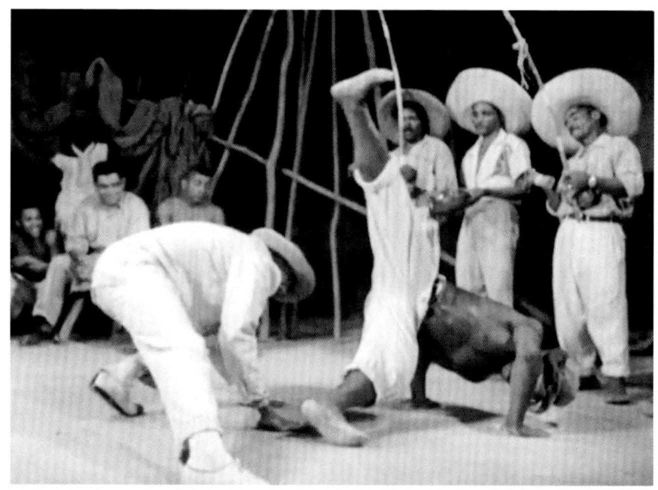

**5.4**
Pierre Verger (b. 1902, Paris, France; d. 1996)
*Capoeira,* Salvador, Brazil, 1946–1948
Photograph
PHOTO PIERRE VERGER ©FUNDAÇÃO PIERRE VERGER

Mestre Pastinha, third from the left, plays the *berimbau*.

**5.5a,b**
Alexandre Robatto Filho (b. 1908, Salvador, Bahia, Brazil, b. 1981)
Stills from *Vadiação* (Vagrancy), 1954
Film
COURTESY YÊDA ROBATTO STASI

Robatto's film featured Mestre Bimba and his students as musicians and Mestre Waldemar and his students as *capoeiristas*. The drawing on the title frame and the set design are by Carybé.

Mestre Pastinha further dissociated himself from violent street capoeira by stating that he stopped practicing for nearly three decades (1912–1941) and returned only when he was invited to "take care" of capoeira's tradition. Mestre Pastinha recounts this story in his unpublished manuscripts: on February 23, 1941, at the urging of Aberrê (Raymundo Argolo, 1895–1942), his former student, he went to watch a capoeira *roda* led by Mestre Amorzinho, who shook his hand and said: "I have been waiting for a long time to hand over this capoeira to you; so you can teach it." Reluctantly, and only with the support of the other *mestres*, Mestre Pastinha accepted the charge of guardian of *capoeira angola*. In the same year, he founded the Centro Esportivo de Capoeira Angola (Capoeira Angola Sports Center; Pastinha circa 1952–1957, 5, 24).

Mestre Noronha (Daniel Coutinho, 1909–1977), a contemporary of Mestre Pastinha, offers a different account of how Pastinha came to be the director the Centro Esportivo de Capoeira Angola. Mestre Noronha claims that he and a collective of twenty other capoeira players founded the first center of *capoeira angola*, and it was only after the death of its director, Mestre Amorzinho, that the group handed over the leadership to Mestre Pastinha (Coutinho 1993, 17). Mestre Noronha's writings portray Mestre Pastinha not as a trailblazer, single-handedly defending tradition, but rather as one capoeira player among many, chosen to assume a position of leadership in a thriving *capoeira angola* collective.

Mestre Pastinha insisted that his students be model citizens, always appearing in public wearing the school's uniform. His Capoeira Angola Sports Center was ruled by a statute and hierarchically organized, with a president, vice-president, three secretaries, two treasurers, and one librarian (Silva 1952, 9). His advanced disciples were assigned specific functions: field master, song master, percussion master, training master, archivist, supervising master, and *contra-mestre*, a term borrowed from the navy used to refer to the disciples who were just below the *mestre* in rank. In his unpublished manuscripts, written throughout the 1950s and early 1960s, he stated proudly, "we are registered, we have a building [for our school], we have identification, legal documents signed by the country's parliamentary leaders[.]"[4] Although Mestre Pastinha did not codify capoeira to the same extent that Mestre Bimba did, he certainly institutionalized the practice and successfully redeemed the reputation of its practitioners. The institutionalization of capoeira in formal schools (*centros* or *academias*) in the 1940s was an important step in the process of legitimization of the practice.

Throughout the 1930s and 1940s, folklorist Édison Carneiro advocated for the valorization and legitimization of both capoeira and Candomblé. In 1937 he organized the Second Afro-Brazilian Congress, which, in addition to presentations by scholars, included demonstrations by capoeira and Candomblé practitioners—an innovative move that differentiated this second congress from the first, organized by Gilberto Freyre in 1934.[5] For the capoeira demonstration, Carneiro invited Samuel Querido de Deus (Samuel de Souza, 1880–1955?),[6] whom he considered "the greatest *capoeirista* of Bahia" (Romo 2010, 74). In her ethnography *The City of Women*, US anthropologist Ruth Landes, whose local mentor was Carneiro himself, describes a capoeira game she observed during her fieldwork in the late 1930s featuring Samuel Querido de Deus (Landes 1947, 102–7). Carneiro's preference for Querido de Deus signals both his disapproval of Mestre Bimba's *capoeira regional* and the fact that Mestre Pastinha was still unknown at this time.

By the early 1950s, Mestre Pastinha had replaced Samuel Querido de Deus as the representative of "traditional" capoeira, and ethnographic filmmakers began focusing on Mestre Pastinha and his students. At this time, folklorist Alceu Maynard Araújo made a short film titled *Veja o Brasil* (See Brazil) that featured scenes of Brazilian folklore from various regions. Not surprisingly, Maynard chose capoeira to represent Bahia, and Mestre Pastinha and his students to represent capoeira.

Curiously, Mestre Pastinha is absent from Alexandre Robatto's film *Vadiação* (Vagrancy), released in 1954 (fig. 5.5a,b). The film features Mestre Bimba and his students in charge of the music, and Mestre Waldemar (Waldemar Rodrigues da Paixão, 1916–1990) and his group as the featured *capoeiristas*. The film is neither strictly ethnographic nor a work of fiction; instead, it seems to be a staged re-creation of capoeira as it would be found "in loco," on the docks of Salvador. Robatto introduces his capoeira footage with a brief text he superimposes on the opening image of three capoeira musicians playing two *berimbaus* (capoeira's iconic musical bow) and one *pandeiro* (tambourine). The text associates capoeira with the state of Bahia and echoes the theory of capoeira as a "fight disguised as dance," which permeated the discourse on capoeira at the time: "[...] Capoeira, widely disseminated especially in Bahia, was constituted as a secret weapon among the tough guys and the hustlers [*bambas e capadócios*] in the times of the monarchy. The violence of the strikes and four centuries of police repression caused it to evolve into a strange dance[,] disguising the fight into *vadiação*."[7] Robatto's choice of the word *vadiação* as his title, rather than, say, *capoeira de angola*, points to the fact that he aimed for a broader portrait of capoeira, as well as to his refusal to choose camps in the already-heated debate surrounding the opposing styles of *capoeira angola* and *capoeira regional*.

As it gained legitimacy, reconfigured as regional sport and Afro-Bahian folklore, the practice of capoeira increasingly attracted the attention of scholars, filmmakers, visual artists, and tourists (figs. 5.6–5.8). Bureaucrats charged with the development of the tourism industry in the state of Bahia saw capoeira as an asset and began sponsoring capoeira demonstrations, which later developed into full-fledged folkloric shows for tourists. Mestre Canjiquinha (Washington Bruno da Silva, 1925–1994) studied capoeira with Mestre Aberrê, a respected capoeira fighter and *mestre* whose practice largely predated the *regional/angola* split of the early 1940s. Like his teacher, Mestre Canjiquinha never aligned himself with either style. In fact, he openly and vehemently denied the existence of separate styles, and insisted that "*capoeira é uma só*" (there is only one capoeira), exposing both styles as marketing strategies. Unlike Mestre Bimba and Mestre Pastinha, who attained fame by founding a particular style or school of capoeira, Mestre Canjiquinha made a name for himself as a performer—both through his folkloric shows and his participation in numerous films.

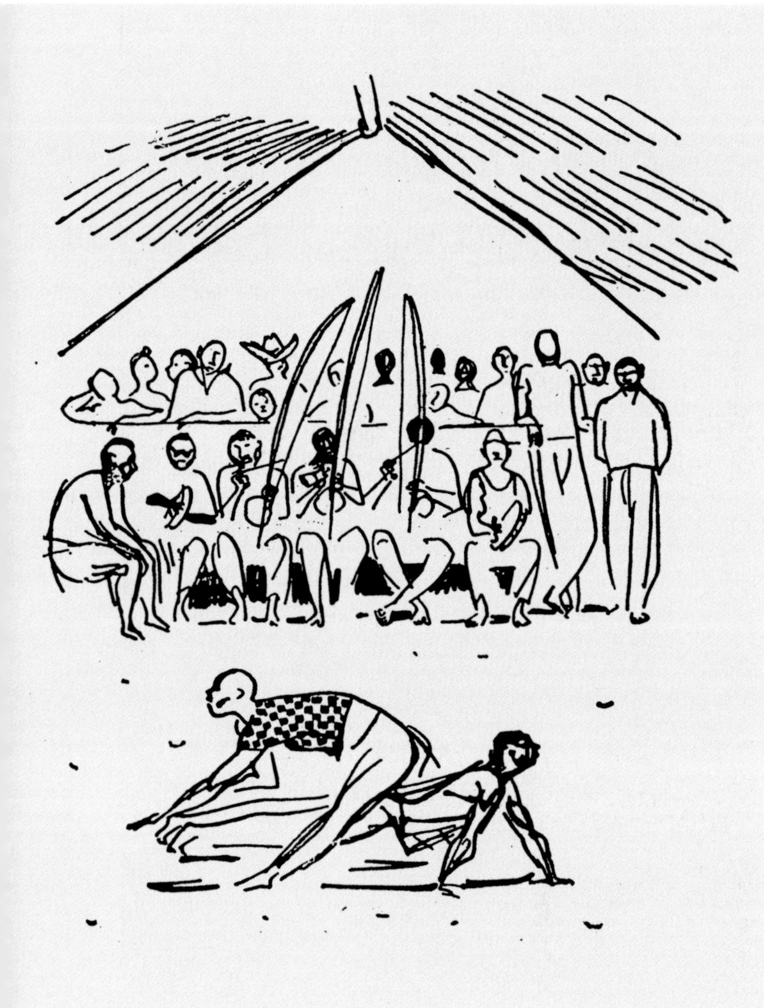

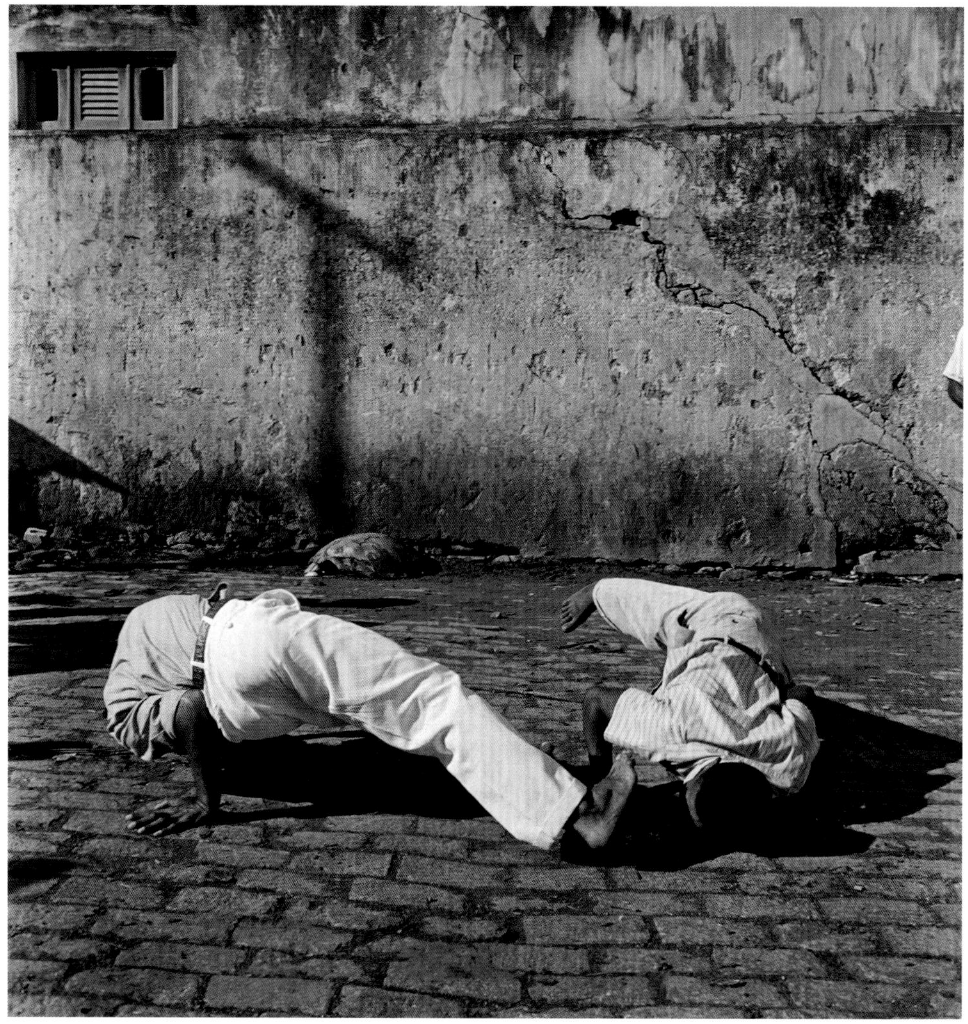

**5.6**
Carybé (Héctor Julio Páride Bernabó, b. 1911 Lanús, Buenos Aires Province, Argentina; d. 1997)
Illustration for the booklet "Jogo da capoeira" ("Capoeira Game"),
Recôncavo Collection, 1951
China ink on paper
29.7 x 21 cm


**5.7**
Pierre Verger (b. 1902, Paris, France; d. 1996)
*Capoeira*, Salvador, Brazil, 1946–1947
Photograph

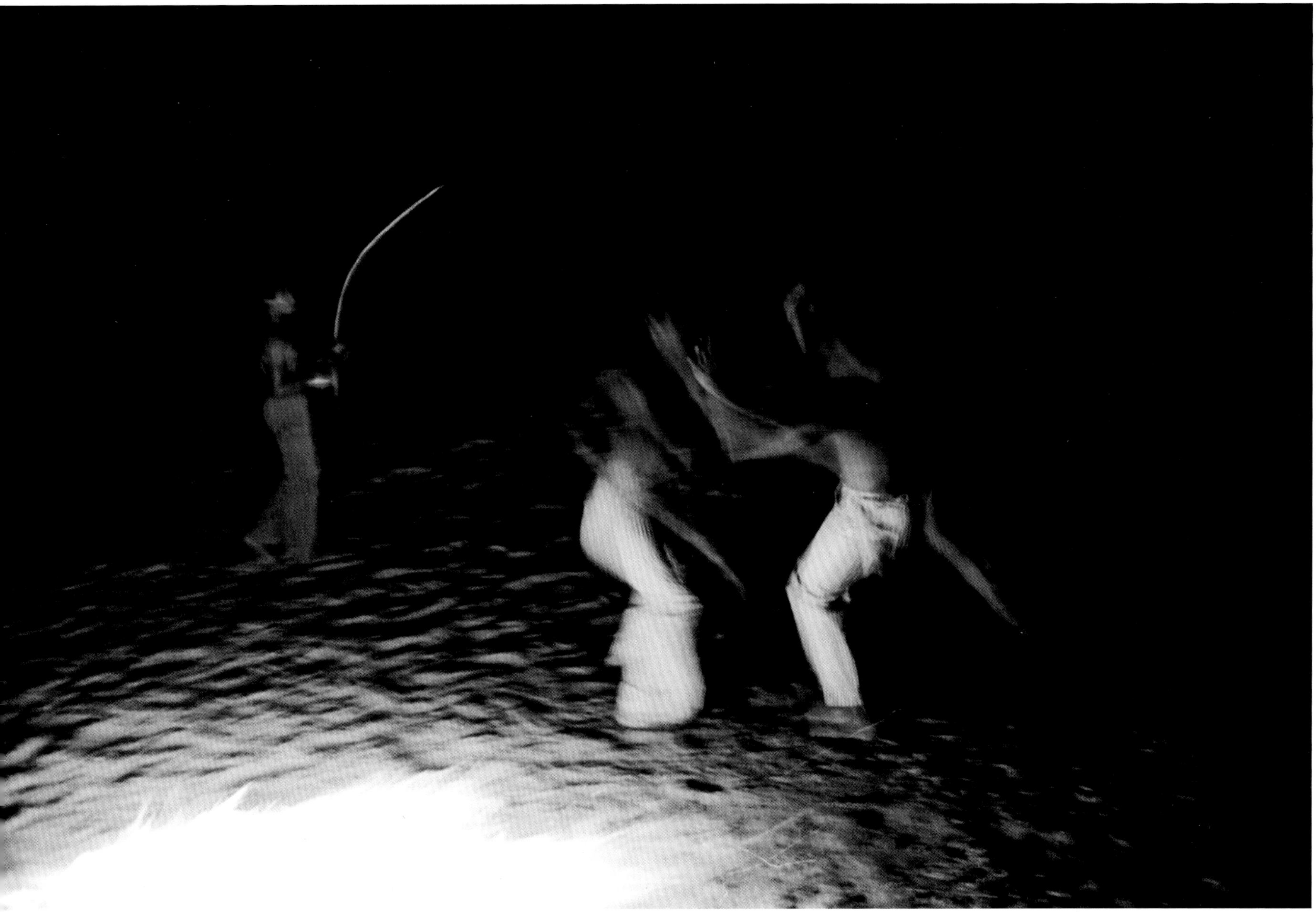

**5.8**
Arlete Soares (b. 1940, Valença, Bahia, Brazil)
*Capoeira*, 1973
Photograph
COURTESY ARLETE SOARES

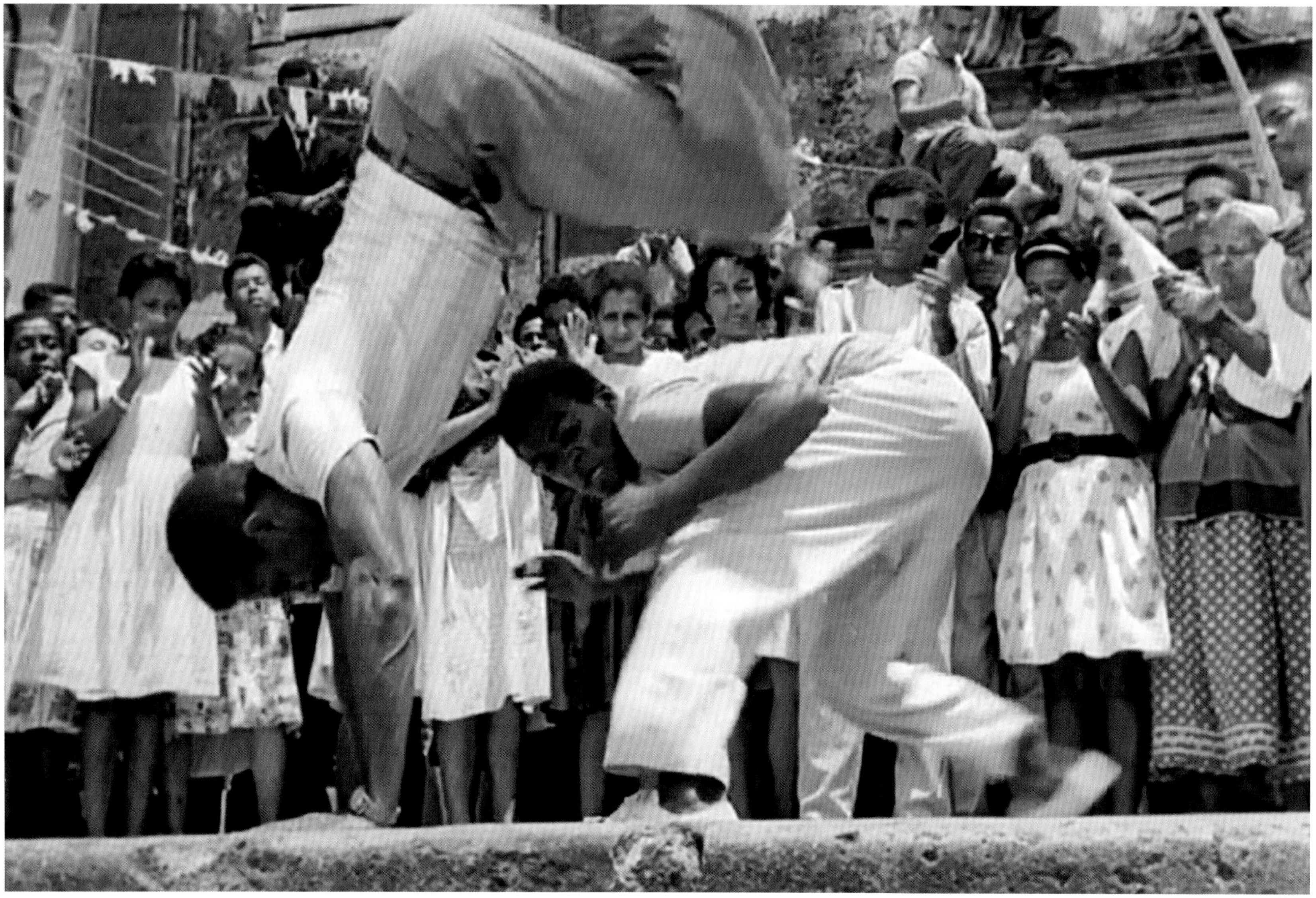

**5.9**
Anselmo Duarte (b. 1920, São Paulo, Brazil; d. 2009)
Still from *O pagador de promessas* (Keeper of Promises), 1962
Film

Mestre Canjiquinha appears at the left of the image, standing on his hands. The other *capoeirista* is the actor Antônio L. Sampaio (known today as Antônio Pitanga).

In the early 1960s, Mestre Canjiquinha participated as an actor and capoeira "consultant" in several movies, including two that went on to receive international recognition: *Barravento* (The Turning Wind) and *O pagador de promessas* (Keeper of Promises), both released in 1962 (fig. 5.9). Throughout the 1960s, he was placed in charge of the shows held nightly at the tourism department at the Belvedere da Sé in Salvador, directing an ensemble of *capoeiristas* that would later perform at other venues as Conjunto Aberrê, named after Canjiquinha's *mestre*. Although these presentations began as capoeira demonstrations, they gradually included other "folkloric" practices, such as *samba* dancing and *maculelê* (a stick-fighting dance), as well as capoeira variants that Canjiquinha created for the stage: *muzenza*, *samango*, and *samba de angola*.[8]

Mestre Canjiquinha was also the main informant for the most oft-cited book on capoeira, Waldeloir Rego's *Capoeira angola: Ensaio sócio-etnográfico* (Capoeira Angola: A Socio-Ethnographic Essay; 1968), although his contributions to the book are downplayed by its author. Rego, a tourism administrator and self-taught ethnographer, acknowledges Mestre Canjiquinha as the source for many of the songs transcribed in the book, but it is probable that the *mestre* contributed much more than song lyrics. Likely based on information obtained from Mestre Canjiquinha, Rego proposes a plausible alternative to Mestre Pastinha's capoeira lineage: rather than having learned from an African from Angola, he speculates that Aberrê might have been Mestre Pastinha's teacher rather than his student (Rego 1968, 270–71). Given the unqualified support that Mestre Pastinha received from other Bahian intellectuals, it is interesting that Rego not only questioned Mestre Pastinha's unbroken "African" lineage but also showed appreciation and respect for Mestre Bimba's *capoeira regional*. Rego disagrees with Carneiro's assertion that Mestre Bimba's capoeira had nothing to do with the "legacy of Angola." He notes that this conclusion shows that Carneiro had "never watched or studied Mestre Bimba's capoeira. Even stylized capoeira, performed on theatrical stages, on television and danced in the samba groups of Bahia and [Rio de Janeiro], still has a lot of this legacy of Angola that Édison Carneiro speaks of, and even more so with Mestre Bimba's capoeira, which, as I have said before is the very same as *Capoeira Angola*" (Rego 1968, 269). Rego went on to direct the new Centro Folclórico administered by the municipal tourism department of Salvador (inaugurated in 1968), where several capoeira groups performed for tourists.

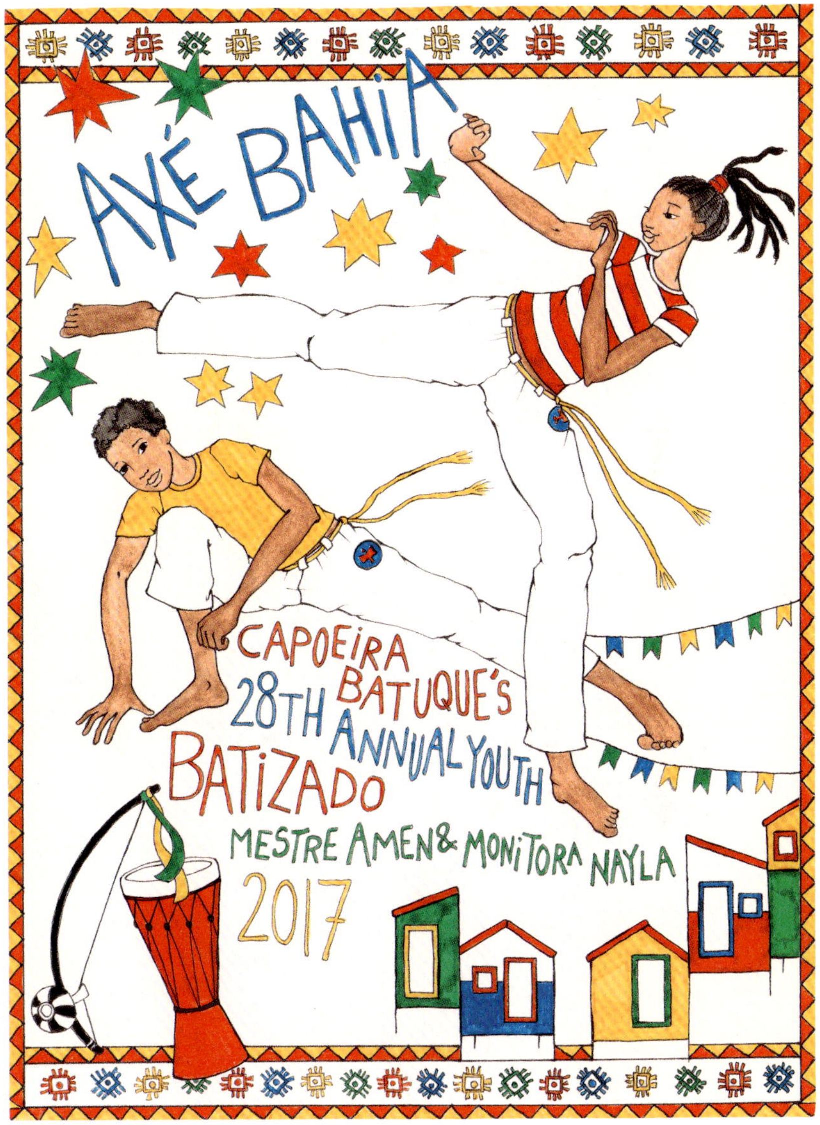


**5.10**
Artwork by Brown Crayons
Original artwork for the announcement of the Brasil Brasil Cultural Center & Capoeira Batuque's Twenty-Eighth Annual Youth Batizado, 2017
Ink on paper
38.5 x 28 cm
COURTESY OF BRASIL BRASIL CULTURAL CENTER & CAPOEIRA BATUQUE, CULVER CITY

Brasil Brasil Cultural Center & Capoeira Batuque in Culver City, California, commissioned this design to use in e-mail notifications and to be printed on T-shirts to announce its Twenty-Eighth Annual Youth Capoeira Batuque Batizado. The event is a celebration of Brazilian culture and includes capoeira demonstrations. The Center is run by Mestre Amen (Joselito Santo) and Nayla Eva Santo.

Throughout the 1960s, performances of capoeira and Afro-Bahian folklore could be found everywhere in the city of Salvador: from capoeira schools (including those of Mestre Bimba and Mestre Pastinha) and official folkloric stages to nightclubs and hotels. A few ensembles, such as the Grupo Folclórico da Bahia and the Conjunto Folclórico Viva Bahia secured short engagements at "high-brow" venues such as Salvador's Teatro Castro Alves and later toured nationally and internationally, introducing the world to capoeira. In 1964, a group of Bimba's disciples—Acordeon (Ubirajara Guimarães Almeida), Itapoan (Raimundo César Alves de Almeida), Camisa Roxa (Edvaldo Carneiro e Silva), and Beijoca (Francisco Benjamin Muniz)—created the Grupo Folclórico da Bahia. By 1969 the group had reorganized as Olodum, under the direction of Camisa Roxa and Beijoca, and by the late 1970s it was renamed Brasil Tropical, under the direction of Camisa Roxa.

Around the same time, Emília Biancardi Ferreira's Conjunto Folclórico Viva Bahia began attracting media attention and invitations to perform outside of Bahia. Biancardi, a music teacher trained in *canto orfeônico*,[9] organized a "folkoric" group, initially composed only of her students, and began inviting *mestres* to teach them various folk practices. Biancardi was the only non-*capoeirista* and the only woman to direct a folkloric ensemble. She sought capoeira expertise from Mestre Pastinha, who taught capoeira to Viva Bahia's performers and later recommended one of his top students, João Grande (João Oliveira dos Santos, the founder of the Capoeira Angola Center in Manhattan, the "mecca" of *capoeira angola* outside of Brazil) to tour with the ensemble. Several other capoeira performers who toured with Biancardi's Viva Bahia went on to become internationally renowned capoeira *mestres*, such as Lua Rasta (Gilson Fernandes), Amen (Joselito Santo; see fig. 5.10), Jelon Vieira (Jelon Gomes Vieira Filho), and Loremil Machado (Josevaldo de Souza Machado), among others. Although *maculelê* was initially the featured dance (often the finale) in Viva Bahia's shows, capoeira became its main attraction during its international tours in the mid-1970s.

In the mid-1970s, Viva Bahia split into two companies for two simultaneous tours: one headed to Europe and Iran, Capoeiras da Bahia, and another scheduled to tour Canada and the United States, Festa Brazil. As I have discussed elsewhere, Festa Brazil, featuring emerging vocalist Simone Bittencourt de Oliveira (today known only as Simone), presented an image of Brazil as a sultry and exotic destination, while Capoeiras da Bahia drew on primitivist fantasies of Brazil. Despite playing into stereotypes, these shows provided an outlet for *capoeiristas* to approach their practice creatively, thus disrupting the notion of capoeira as static "folk" knowledge tied to purportedly ancient traditions that should be preserved.[10]

Since the codification and "academicization" of capoeira in the mid-twentieth century, capoeira practice has been organized around lineages: who one's *mestre* is and one's group affiliation have become questions of primary importance. These concerns are, however, fairly recent in the history of capoeira and are directly related to projects of legitimization led by Mestre Bimba and Mestre Pastinha respectively. Through a convergence of discourses (anxieties about cultural loss, calls for preservation and legitimization) articulated by intellectuals, artists, culture policymakers, and "folk" cultural producers, *capoeiragem* or *vadiação* was reconfigured as capoeira, or rather, as various types or "schools" of capoeira. On stage and on screen, however, there was only one capoeira.

In his book *Negros bantus*, Édison Carneiro lamented the inevitable demise of capoeira, despite its current vitality (Carneiro 1937, 159–60). He predicted that capoeira, along with other elements of black folklore, would recede to small coastal villages and eventually disappear. Carneiro could not have imagined that capoeira would become a vibrant and increasingly globalized form in the late twentieth and early twenty-first centuries (figs. 5.10, 5.11a,b). Through performances on screen and on stage in the 1960s and 1970s, capoeira was disseminated around the globe, and today it is possible to find classes and *rodas* in practically every major city in the world. Despite (or because of) its global reach, capoeira remains iconic of Brazil and strongly connected to the state of Bahia, both symbolically and geographically. A visitor to Salvador today will find multiple references to capoeira around Pelourinho, the historic district of the city, from images of *capoeiristas* on T-shirts to shops selling *berimbaus* to live capoeira practiced daily on the Terreiro de Jesus square. Several hotels and *pousadas* in Pelourinho provide their guests with a list of places where they can find capoeira classes or watch capoeira *rodas*. Since the early 2000s, *capoeira mestres* of international renown have purchased land in southern Bahia near pristine beaches, waterfalls, and hiking trails, and built cultural and ecological sustainability centers where they host annual or semi-annual capoeira retreats, such as Mestre Suassuna's (Reinaldo Ramos Suassuna) *Capoeirando* near Ilhéus, Mestre Cabello (Éldio Rolim) and Mestre Tisza's (Helena Coelho) *Dancebatukeira* near the village of Serra Grande, and Mestre Cobra Mansa's (Cinésio Feliciano Peçanha) *Permangola* near Valença. These retreats attract *capoeiristas* and capoeira enthusiasts from around the world and offer, in addition to daily capoeira practice, experiences in other Afro-Brazilian movement and music practices, such as *maculelê*, samba, and dances from Candomblé. As malleable as the movement of two *capoeiristas* in a *roda*, the practice of capoeira itself has shown a remarkable ability to adapt and make itself relevant to the present, while firmly anchored in the past.

**5.11a,b**
Marco Aurélio Damaceno (b. 1965, Aracajú, Sergipe, Brazil)
Stills from *Encruzilhada: Troca de passagem* (Crossroads: The Passage), 2017
Video
COURTESY MARCO AURÉLIO DAMACENO

Filmed in Rio de Janeiro (fig. 5.11a) and Salvador (fig. 5.11b), Encruzilhada reflects on capoeira as a meeting point of Africa and Brazil by conflating the ring in which it is performed with the spherical Kongo cosmogram and a sidewalk sewer cover. The circle, like water, is an enchanted realm of encounter and a means of passage, at least symbolically, to other places.

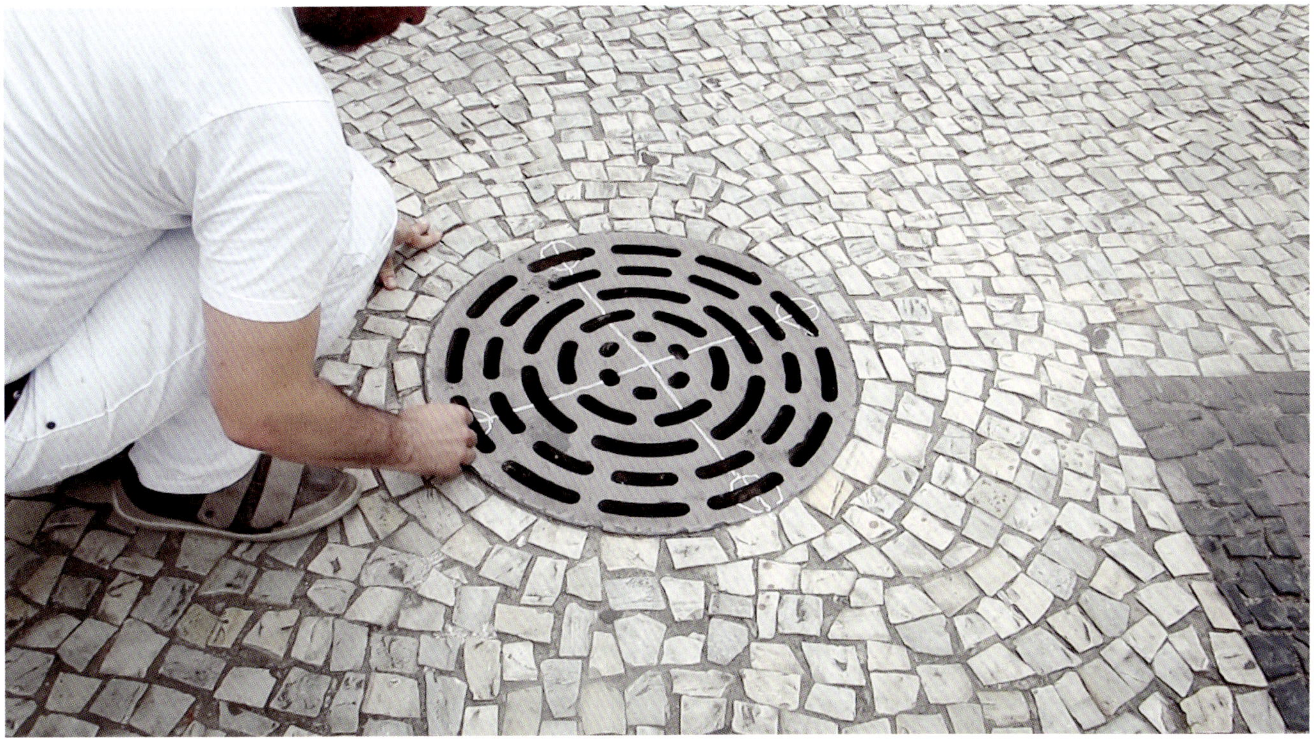

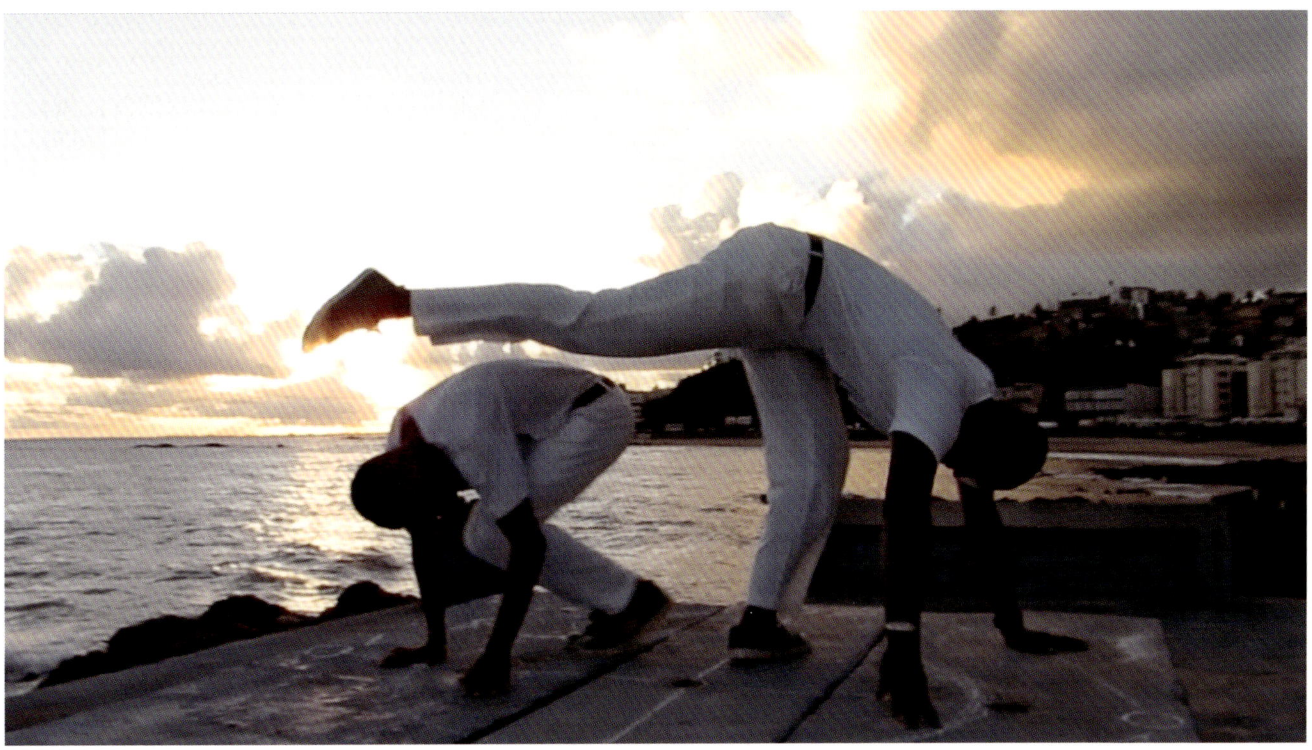

# 6 Reinventing Roots
## From Athens to Africa in the Making of Salvador's Identity

**Anadelia Romo**

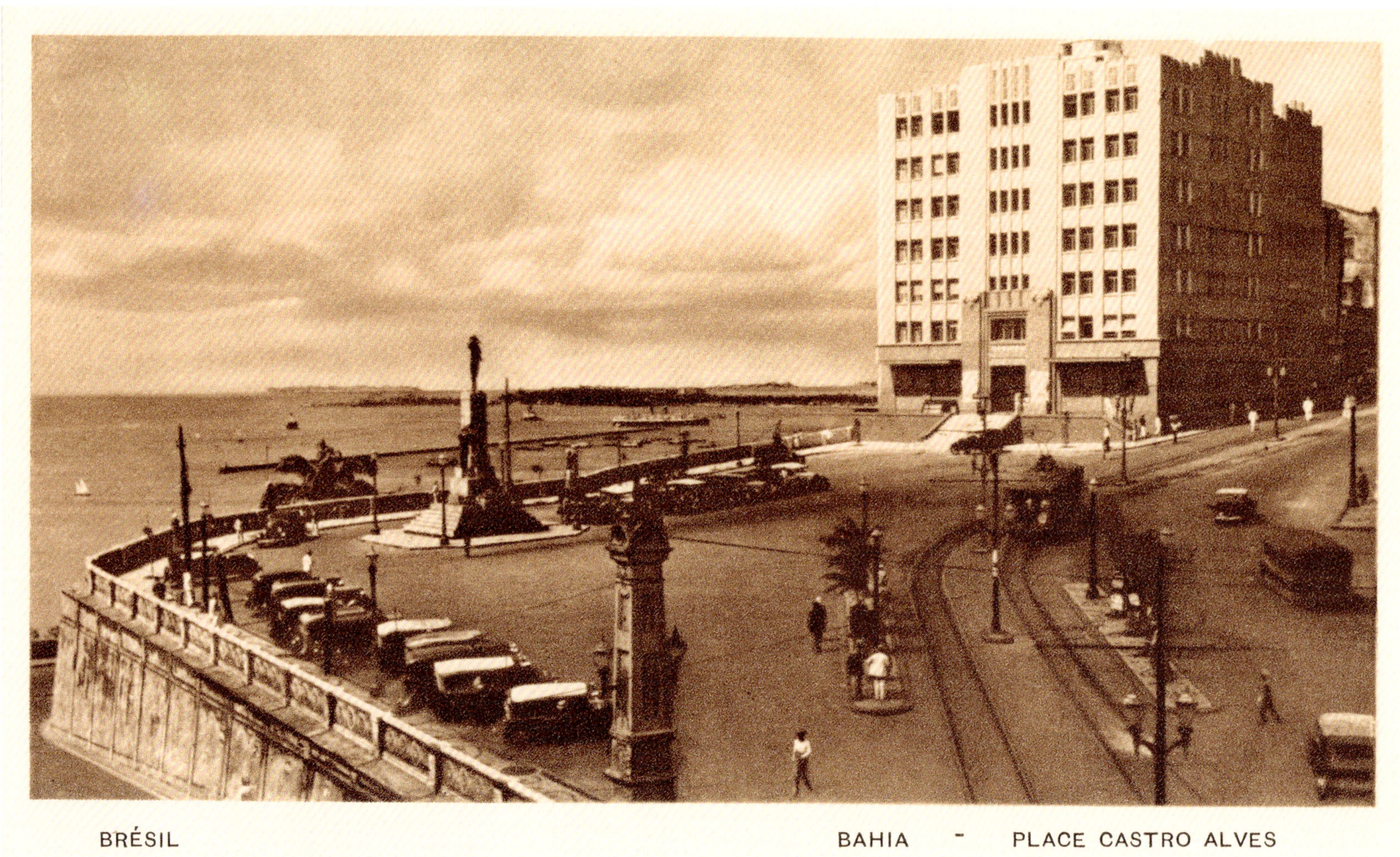

6.1
Artist Unknown
View of Bahia, 1930s
Postcard
Ink on paper
9 x 14 cm
PRIVATE COLLECTION

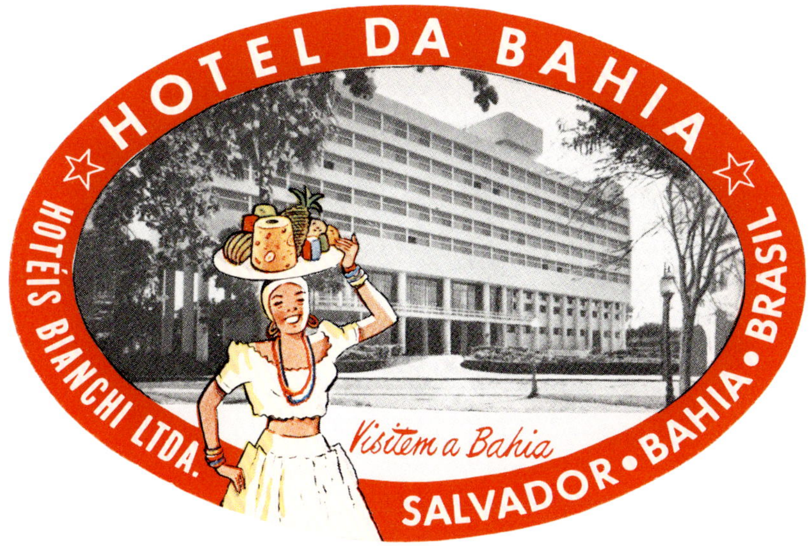


6.2
Artist Unknown
Luggage tag from the Hotel da Bahia, 1950s
Ink on paper
9 x 13 cm
PRIVATE COLLECTION

THE SOCIAL AND POLITICAL ELITE of Salvador, Bahia, ushered in the twentieth century claiming allegiance to the culture of ancient Greece rather than their native Brazil. Finessing their oratory and naming their children after Greek philosophers, these men and women found in Athens a symbol that expressed their ideal of whiteness and their connections to a broader European heritage (fig. 6.1). Their admiration for Athens did not, however, extend to democratic political ideals. Instead, in crafting an identity aimed at garnering national status and prestige, the wealthy of Bahia ignored the profound and undemocratic inequalities of their region, which had only recently seen slavery abolished. Such inequalities remained especially evident in a city like Salvador, which had a small, white political elite and a large, disenfranchised black majority. Accustomed to comforts accumulated through centuries of slave owning, the powerful closed their eyes to racial barriers that kept the black majority far from hopes of literacy, let alone Greek philosophy.

By the close of the twentieth century, however, the power brokers of Bahia, still predominantly white, had done a complete about-face. Now, stressing their connections to Afro-Bahian religion, music, and dance, they claimed Africa rather than Europe as the origin of many of their most cherished cultural ideals. Remarkably, these new beliefs had come to be shared by a wide swath of the Bahian population, regardless of racial background. Within a relatively short time span, Bahian identity, or "Baianidade," was reframed to make Salvador the center of a uniquely harmonious culture focused on African-based rhythms and ways of life.[1] Though it may be tempting to see this version of Bahia as a "truth," long understood by Salvador's Afro-Brazilian population and gradually accepted by a reluctant white elite, this new narrative was just as much an invention as its Athenian predecessor. This chapter turns attention to the constructed and shifting nature of Bahian identity over the first half of the twentieth century. Tracing this complicated story in broad strokes provides a sense of the cultural transformations that took place in Salvador and the host of dynamic actors who shaped them. It should be stressed, however, that many of the racial inequalities that existed at the beginning of the twentieth century have yet to be resolved, despite the theme of inclusion that became a central feature of Baianidade. The vision of the city may have been completely reversed, but the racism and poverty that characterize its population tragically still remain.

To understand Salvador, one has to grasp the fundamental role that the enslavement of Africans played in shaping the city and its history. Enslaved Africans had become the backbone of the new colony by the late 1500s, and Bahia was one of the earliest and most important slave centers within Brazil. Over the course of almost four centuries, Brazil enslaved over five million Africans, more than any other single country in the Americas. Despite horrifying rates of mortality, Africans and their descendants became the majority of the population, whereas those considered white remained a minority, comprising 44 percent of the population by the time of abolition in 1888.[2] This percentage varied greatly, however, depending on the state. Indeed, for the city of Salvador and the state of Bahia, it was lower, precisely because of the region's slave economy and the production of sugar.

The slaves within this economy fashioned vibrant cultures in rural plantations as well as the urban sphere. The rich soil surrounding Salvador and other regions in the northeast proved ideal for growing sugar cane, creating a plantation culture whose heart lay far beyond the edges of the city. At the same time, and as a result of the sugar economy, Salvador gained importance for its port, the protected Bahia de Todos os Santos, or Bay of All Saints. The entry of thousands of slave ships and the departure of massive amounts of sugar and other exports created an urban slave culture, based around trade, transport, and commerce. Indeed, by the early nineteenth century a large number of slaves in Salvador were owned by merchants, and many more belonged to those who rented them out as general labor for hire (Reis 1993, 13). Though plantation slavery and urban slavery each created their own particular dynamic, together they resulted in a dense concentration of Africans and their descendants in and around Salvador. Candomblé, an African-based religion with origins in Salvador and its surroundings (Parés 2013), emerged as a result of this, as did numerous other cultural practices. Indeed, it was precisely this historical setting that allowed slaves to carve out social networks and new religious and cultural communities, even as repression remained a mainstay of the slave regime.

As the slave regime marched slowly to its end, the impact of African descendants in Bahia remained powerful. Bahia's white population, for example, was lower than the national average, and reported by the census of 1872 to be 24 percent. Only two states showed a lower number of whites in their population.[3] Correspondingly, a large segment of the population of Bahia had some degree of African heritage. Color categories used at the time indicated that the state was 46 percent black (*preto*) and 27 percent brown (*pardo*), the latter a result of intermixing between Africans and Portuguese, whether consensual or forced.[4]

In the late nineteenth century, as the profitability of sugar declined and the prospect of abolition loomed, the enslaved population, once viewed as an economic benefit, came to be seen as a social liability by the white ruling minority. Though abolition brought new legal rights, freedom remained restricted due to widespread poverty as well as new social hierarchies that worked to maintain a white power structure. Brazilians now embraced a new reverence for "progress" and "modernity," defined inevitably in terms of European, primarily French, culture and explicitly framed in racial terms. Meanwhile, scientific racism gaining credence across the West posited not only the superiority of whiteness but also the undesirability of racial mixing. This proved an obvious dilemma for Brazil, which had a very large number of people with mixed heritage and a very small number of people deemed white.

Brazil pursued two solutions to the problem of scientific racism, neither of which challenged its essential assumptions. The south of Brazil, with new wealth from coffee and budding industrialization, aimed to solve the problem with a large-scale importation of Europeans. São Paulo aggressively began a state-sponsored program of immigration. Planters and industrialists viewed former slaves in explicitly racist terms as not sufficiently modern, or lazy, or generally unsuitable for the agriculture that they had long dominated as well as skilled factory labor (Andrews 1991; Weinstein 2015).

The second solution took aim not at the demographic reality of the country, but its interpretation. Brazilian intellectuals began to challenge European and American racial theorists by revising racial doctrine in important ways. Most critically, they reframed the "problem" of racial mixing, or as they termed it, "miscegenation." In their view it was a source of strength, rather than a cause of degeneration and decline. In this reframing, it became a positive force that made for a stronger population and ultimately, and most critically, a whiter population. This theory of "*branqueamento*," or whitening, meant a redeemed future for those with both African and European heritage, but it also ultimately endorsed whiteness as Brazil's ideal.

To what extent the *branqueamento* ideal found acceptance in Bahia still remains unclear. What is clear, however, is that one of Brazil's most pessimistic racial theorists Raimundo Nina Rodrigues (1862–1906), a medical doctor, was a Bahian resident. At the turn-of-the century he issued dire warnings about the limited potential of Africans, the instability of racial mixture, and, most remarkably, the possibility that Brazil could "turn black." At the same time, however, as an amateur ethnologist, he collected many detailed observations about African cultural connections in Bahia and its Candomblé community. As I have argued elsewhere, Nina Rodrigues actually gave credence to as large a role for environmental factors as he did for race, and was not nearly as deterministic as he has often been portrayed.[5] He was nonetheless undeniably racist, and his disastrous predictions arose from the particular context of Salvador and Bahia. For wealthy and powerful whites hoping to portray themselves as an enclave of genteel philosophers, Nina Rodrigues was surely an embarrassment, an obstacle, and an uncomfortable proponent of the view that Salvador was predominantly black with a culture that drew as much or more from Africa than from Athens.

Nina Rodrigues undoubtedly pulled his ideas of Africa's centrality from many sources. Perhaps most important, however, was Bahia's black population itself. In his role as ethnologist, Nina Rodrigues spent some time with informants, particularly within the religious communities of Candomblé, who stressed their African connections. It is likely that during this fieldwork, he was impressed with the centrality of African roots and their importance in Salvador. It was within this context that he became one of the first to treat the material culture of Candomblé as art. Significantly, he did so at a dynamic moment when African linkages were being established in important ways among Salvador's black community. As J. Lorand Matory has documented, British colonial officials in Africa and a Yoruba elite helped establish ideas of a grand African past in West Africa and helped consolidate the notion of Yoruba primacy among other ethnicities. At the same time, Africans in Bahia traveled back and forth to the region for trade and immersed themselves in these ideas, circulating them within Salvador as well.[6]

These ideals may have been powerful within the Candomblé communities, but they were far from mainstream in the early twentieth century. Candomblé occupied tenuous legal territory, and though technically it should have been guaranteed religious freedom under the constitution, it was regarded as witchcraft, deemed illegal, and often heavily repressed into the 1930s (Lühning 1995–1996). Indeed, not even academics took up the banner of religious liberty until the late 1930s in an attempt to guarantee some minimal protections from rampant police raids. Their campaign, however, faced an uphill battle. At the turn of the century, Nina Rodrigues had documented in his work numerous journalistic accounts that revealed middle-class and elite

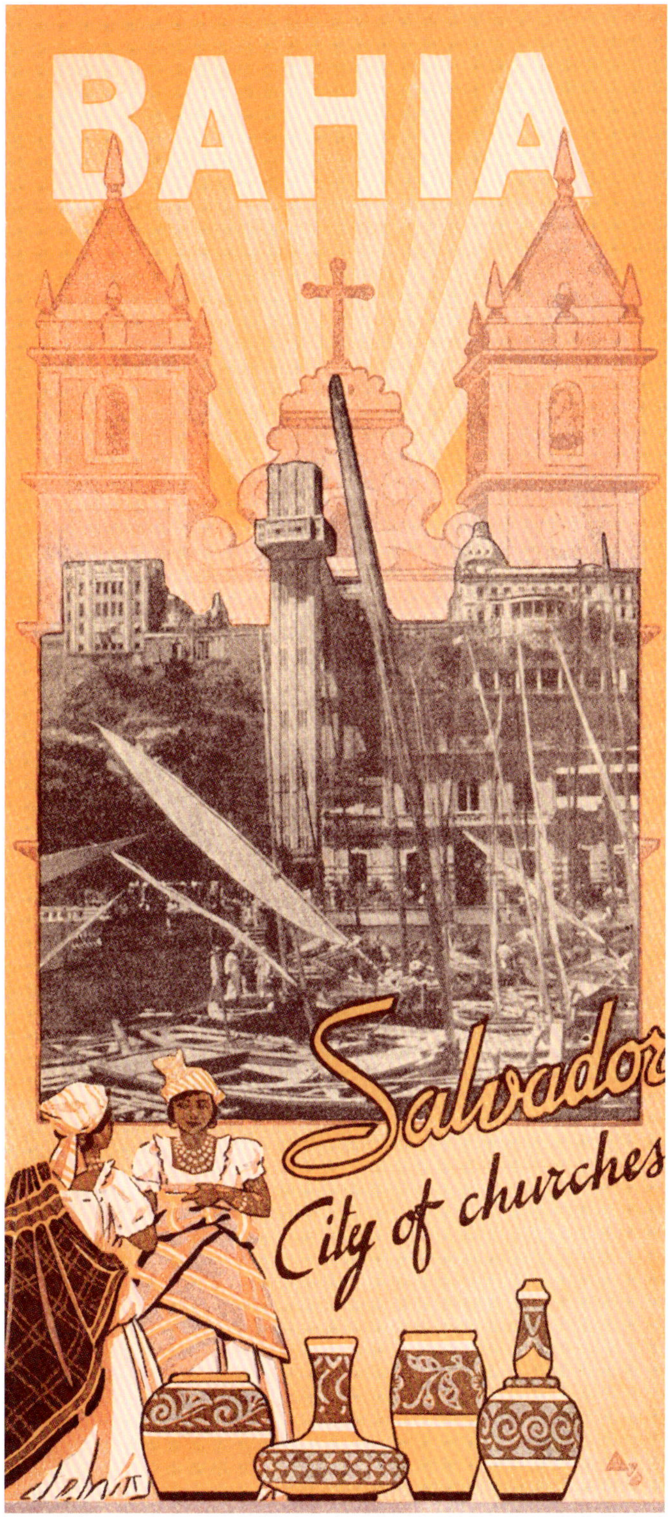


characterizations of the religion as barbaric, dangerous, and savage. Although the national climate had changed by the 1930s, inclusion remained tenuous and African identity still controversial.

The shift in Brazil's political and cultural climate can be traced to the impact of President Getúlio Vargas. Vargas came to power through a coup in 1930, and his policies had a deep impact in part because he was able to remain in power until 1945. His fascist-inspired dictatorship, declared in 1937, allowed him even greater control. In the realm of culture Vargas was exceptionally interested in forging a strong sense of nationalism and therefore dedicated his cultural policies to enhancing these goals. His regime encouraged practices deemed to be particularly Brazilian, and it aimed to displace any European ideal that portrayed Brazilians as inferior. Authenticity became a watchword for the time, and cultural ministers took a new interest in uncovering what was unique to Brazil. Within this context, Afro-Brazilian practices such as capoeira, a martial art and dance form, gained government endorsement for the first time (see Höfling, this volume). And samba, originally viewed as an exclusively black dance and music, came to dominate elite ballrooms and government radio waves (McCann 2004; Hertzman 2013).

Rio and Bahia both laid claim to capoeira and samba. Regardless of the reality, however, it was Bahia that gained steady acknowledgement as the site of inspiration and the most authentic practice of Afro-Brazilian culture.[7] Samba in particular drew on Bahian motifs to indicate its authenticity, and sambas of the 1930s created a host of songs about Salvador. The Bahian musician Dorival Caymmi (1914–2008) became critical in this movement, but so was the Rio-based composer Ary Barroso (1903–1964), who wrote early rhapsodies about Bahia although he didn't actually visit until late in his career (see Dunn, this volume). Such songs and many others celebrated Afro-Bahian culture and referred often to the charms of the Baiana (famously reinterpreted by Carmen Miranda for American audiences; see Shirey, this volume). Whether in capoeira or in samba, Salvador was portrayed as the wellspring of authentic practice.

This broader acceptance and celebration of Afro-Brazilian traditions fit into a larger national pattern but in distinctive ways. Historian Daryle Williams has analyzed how the Vargas era promoted a national agenda of arts that privileged both modernity and tradition (figs. 6.2, 6.3). Bahian state officials occasionally tried to promote both of these axes, but increasingly chose to reinforce an image of Bahia as the most authentic preserve of Brazilian traditions and the birthplace of Brazil. National authorities endorsed this vision as well. When he arrived for a visit in 1933, President Vargas, for example, insisted that he felt in Bahia "the excitement of drawing close, for the first time, to the birthplace of our nationality" (Vargas 1938–1941, 2: 114).

**6.3**
Artist Unknown
"Bahia: Salvador City of Churches," 1939
Cover of a tourist guide from the New York World's Fair of 1939
Ink on paper
10 x 23 cm
PRIVATE COLLECTION

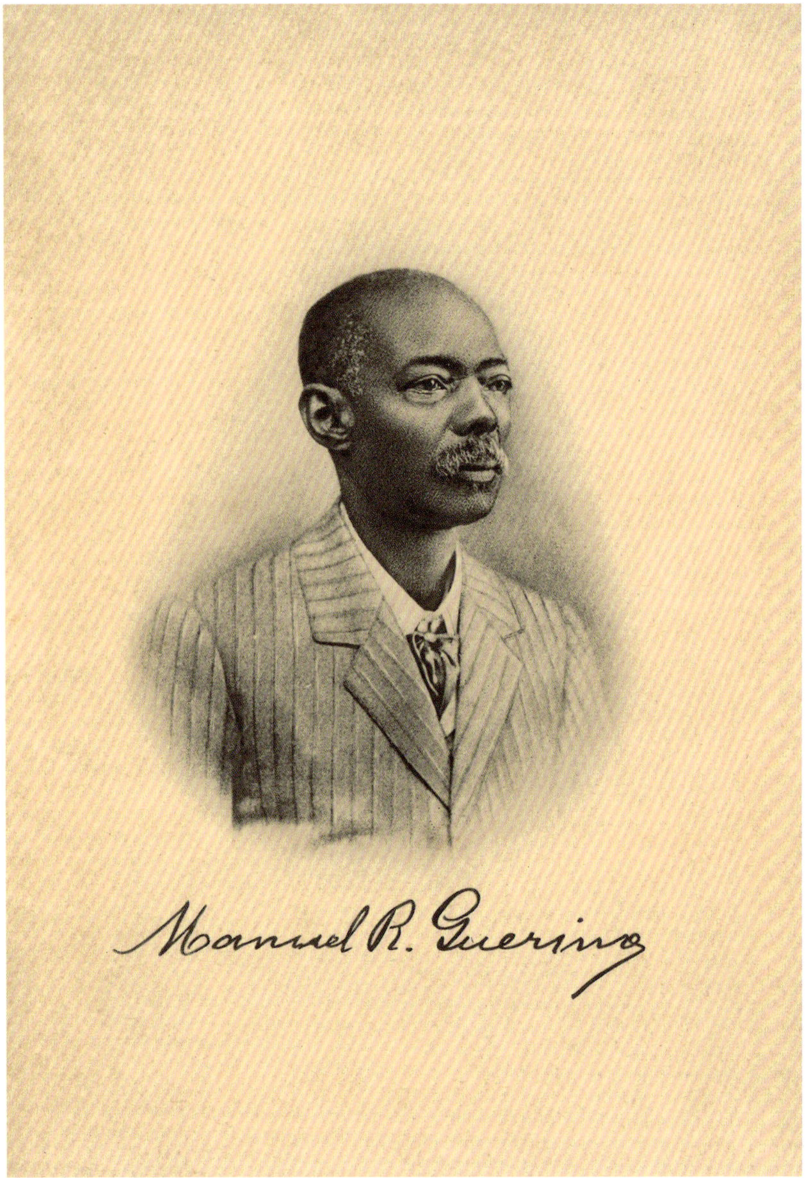


**6.4**
Artist Unknown
Portrait of Manuel R. Querino (b. 1851, São Paulo, Brazil; d. 1923)
Engraving after a photograph
REPRODUCED FROM *ARTISTAS BAHIANOS*, 2ND ED.
(BAHIA: OFFICINAS DA EMPREZA, 1911)
PRIVATE COLLECTION

While many of Salvador's political elite embraced the celebration of the city's colonial glory, others began to herald the city for its role in preserving the most authentic Afro-Brazilian culture in the nation. The first interpretation was certainly the most solidly consolidated and gained official endorsement during the 1930s. As historian Paulo Santos Silva has brilliantly documented, local intellectuals of the time rewrote Bahia's history to construct a glorious representation of the sugar elites' culture of the past, while also claiming the existence of a more mild form of slavery within the region (Silva 2000). The second interpretation, however, gained power through some remarkable alliances among local intellectuals and local black leadership.

This second view saw Salvador as central not for its colonial contribution to Brazil but for its black and African culture. It gained significant traction during the thirties through a confluence of events. Some of the most important of these were the Afro-Brazilian Congresses of 1934 and 1937. The first was held in Recife, under the direction of scholar Gilberto Freyre; the second was held in Salvador, organized by journalist and scholar Édison Carneiro and colleagues. Overall the scholarly presentations at the first congress revealed an ambiguous regard for Africa, in many cases preferring instead to highlight Brazilian culture as the most formative for Afro-Brazilians (Romo 2007, 31–54; 2010). The Bahian congress, however, set important new precedents as participants turned more clearly to celebrating African roots and connections. Its organizers insisted that Bahia was the true epicenter of Afro-Brazilian culture and aggressively campaigned for this view through the press. In the process Édison Carneiro and fellow scholars gave official endorsement to the legitimacy of Candomblé. Furthermore, leaders of the religion such as Mãe Aninha (Eugênia Anna Santos) of the Ilê Axé Opô Afonjá temple and her colleague Martiniano do Bonfim hosted several religious ceremonies and participated more broadly in the congress. The end result was the creation of a union of Candomblé leaders who sought official protection for their religious freedoms. Furthermore, in many ways the congress can be seen as a successful public relations campaign for Afro-Bahian culture. Gaining press coverage as well as new scholarly focus, the event marked important victories for Afro-Bahian culture and for the vision of Salvador as dominated by that culture.

All of this was controversial to Gilberto Freyre, the organizer of the first congress, who was uncomfortable with the more politically minded Bahian conference and who would have liked instead to prioritize his own hometown of Recife as the heartland of Afro-Brazilian studies. Although he ultimately rose to dominate much of Brazil's thinking about race, he lost this particular regional turf war (Dantas 1988; Romo 2010). His work was nonethless important for the movement in Salvador, particularly his *Casa grande e senzala* (*The Masters and the Slaves*, 1933). In this book Freyre celebrated the contributions Africans had made to colonial Brazil and insisted that the country was unique in its harmonious combination of indigenous, Portuguese, and African cultures and peoples. In fact, an Afro-Bahian named Manuel R. Querino (fig. 6.4) had published scholarship two decades earlier that emphasized the importance of Africans in the making of Brazil and gave serious treatment to African culture more generally (Leal 2009; Gledhill 2014). Freyre's work, however, emerged at a more receptive moment in the middle of the Vargas era and allowed him a remarkable impact on national thinking.

Jorge Amado, a young novelist steeped in socialism who would become Brazil's most famous and most translated author, attended the 1937 congress and played a critical role in promoting Afro-Brazilian culture as the heart of Salvador (see Johnson, this volume). His first novels, published in the early 1930s, took the city as their setting and focused on black culture and life. Perhaps most celebrated was his novel *Jubiabá* (1935), which placed Candomblé at the center of the story. In this book—in ways that would prove a precursor to his travel guide for the city—Amado portrayed Salvador as remarkable for its poverty, rather than its Athenian oratory. More importantly, he heralded it as a "black city," relegating more traditional portrayals of it as a Catholic center of Brazil's colonial administration or as a preserve of European-inspired sugar elites to the margins.

The framing of Salvador as a center of popular and Afro-Bahian culture was further reinforced in the 1940s through the work of Walt Disney. As is now well-known, Disney was commissioned by the US government to produce films to help fight fascism during World War II. Part of this agenda included encouraging closer relations between the United States and Latin America, an effort known as the Good Neighbor policy. As a part of this initiative, Disney produced two feature films: *Saludos Amigos* in 1942 (which premiered in Rio) and *The Three Caballeros* in 1944 (which premiered in Mexico City).[8] The premise of these films centered on a curious but ignorant Donald Duck who visited sites across Latin America to learn about their "folk" cultures and national traditions from compatriot animated birds. The films introduced the figure of José Carioca, or Zé Carioca, a dapper animated parrot from Rio who shepherded Donald through Brazilian life. Indeed, Brazil featured prominently in both films, and in the *Three Caballeros*, Salvador took a starring role.

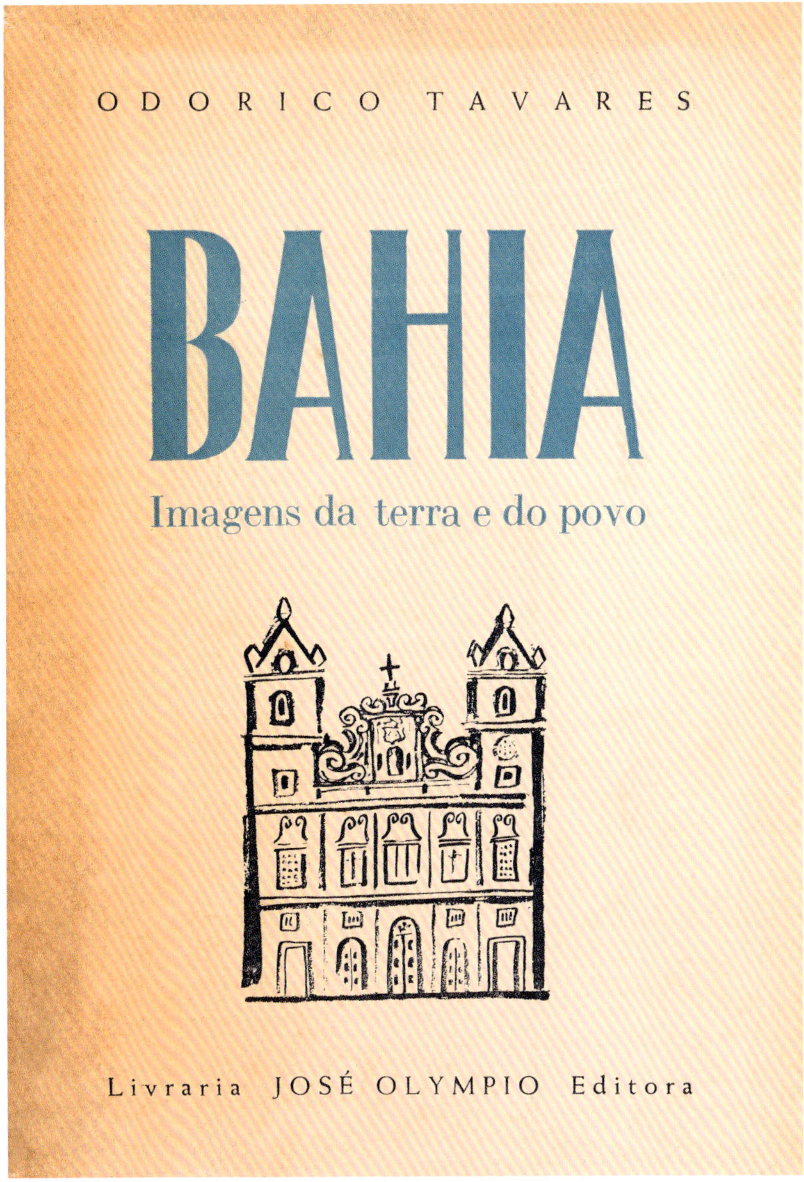


**6.5**
Odorico Tavares (b. 1912, Timbauba, Pernambuco, Brazil; d. 1980), author; Carybé (Héctor Julio Páride Bernabó, b. 1911, Lanús, Buenos Aires Province, Argentina; d. 1997), illustrator
Cover of *Imagens da terro e do povo* (Images of the Land and People; São Paulo: Livraria José Olympio Editora, 1951)
Ink on paper
24 x 17 cm
PRIVATE COLLECTION

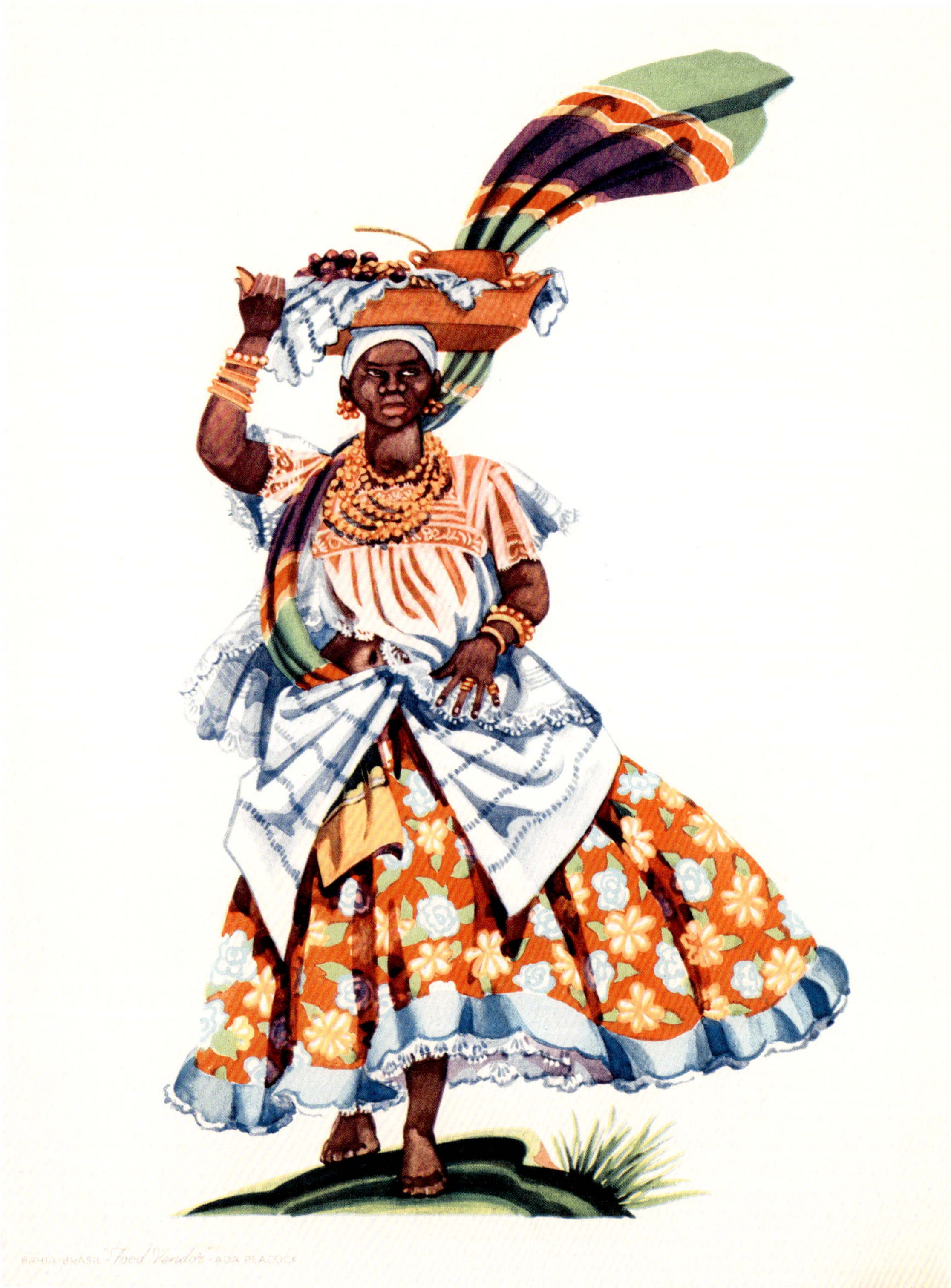


**6.6**
Ada Peacock (b. United States; dates unknown)
*Food Vendor*, early 1940s
Cover art for a menu for the SS *Argentina*, Moore and McCormack Lines, Barbados to Bahia, Tuesday, July 7, 1953
Ink on paper
23 x 30.5 cm
PRIVATE COLLECTION

The Good Neighbor Policy promoted tourism to Bahia in terms that often emphasized its exotic nature.

The *Three Caballeros* played upon several sambas already in circulation within Brazil that celebrated the charms of Bahia and urged the listener to go to visit. Zé invites Donald to Salvador in a scene that played with a twist on the song made popular in 1941 by Dorival Caymmi, "Você ja foi à Bahia?" ("Have You Been to Bahia?"). While Zé announces to the befuddled Donald Duck that he will show him Brazil, "the land of samba," the extended musical number set in the streets of Salvador made clear that the heart of samba was Bahia itself. Indeed, the song, and the vision of an Afro-Brazilian Bahia, was so central to the film that Disney studios chose to use it for the film's title in Brazil.

Within the film, the musical number that received the most attention was a samba performed by Aurora Miranda (sister of Carmen) among brightly colored drawings of Salvador's Pelourinho, or colonial center. In the scene, Salvador, deemed the "city of romance," enchants Donald so deeply that he loses his mind. He also becomes enamored with Miranda, who appears dressed as a Baiana street vendor.[9] The tropes followed closely the lyrics for the dance number "Os quindins de yayá," written by Ary Barroso. In the song, the city is represented by the captivating and mysterious Baiana, the Afro-Bahian sweets sold by Miranda, and samba itself. This was a vision of Salvador with music in the streets and colorful animated colonial buildings that literally vibrated and danced to its beat.

The trope of Salvador as the land of street festivals and Afro-Bahian influence gained prominence through Walt Disney, but it had a life of its own within the city as well. Autonomous forces within Salvador worked through the 1930s and 1940s to push acceptance of Afro-Bahian celebrations into the mainstream. As historian Scott Ickes argues, some of the most important players in this effort were members of the Afro-Bahian working class, who insisted on celebrating public festivals with distinct Candomblé connections. As his insightful analysis reveals, festivals were sites of contestation, and the determination of Afro-Bahian actors to celebrate their culture in public spaces helped forge a new Bahian identity that became more accepting of their vision (Ickes 2013a).

Tourism also influenced the development of a Bahian ideal (fig. 6.6). While scholars have often acknowledged the way in which Bahian tourism became tied to the region's black and African roots, they have generally viewed these developments as relatively recent. I argue instead that the roots of Bahian tourism began in the 1930s, were put on hold during the war, and then reemerged with new vigor in 1945. This is based on my research into sources that scholars of Bahia have not formally considered as a genre: the tourist guide. Yet the corpus of Bahian guidebooks that emerged in the mid-twentieth century demonstrate a richness and a dynamism unequaled across Latin America. The 1950s in particular witnessed a small boom in the publications written by native Bahians, or residents of Salvador, that were intended to entice domestic visitors from across Brazil. Written in Portuguese, they appealed to Brazilians to visit a land paradoxically described as unique within the country and central to it. While a limited number of visitor guides in Portuguese were produced in the 1920s and 1930s, their nature changed by the end of the war, and a completely new type appeared in the 1950s. They provide a window into the shifting ways that elites and intellectuals viewed the city and its identity. Such authors invested an immense amount of work in reshaping and reenvisioning Salvador, but in their vision, the stakes were important.[10] Hoping to bring increased status for the native city, and perhaps for themselves, they set out to put Salvador at the center of Brazil's cultural map.

Anthropologist Osmundo Araujo Pinho has noted the importance of such books within an expanding sector of works he terms guides to Bahianness. In his view, novels by Amado, local histories, and select guidebooks ultimately served to teach readers about the ideal Bahian identity, one which may not have actually existed but was in the midst of formation (Pinho 1998, 109–20). This highlights the constructed nature of Bahian identity, which is critical to understanding these texts: they were prescriptive and imagined more than a faithful reflection of reality. I argue, however, that the guidebooks in particular, which Araujo Pinho mentions only in passing, deserve much more attention and played a critical role that has thus far been unappreciated.

What is stunning about many of these guidebooks is their intersection with and embrace of the nascent modern art movement in Bahia. Indeed, one of the events that best highlights this important connection is generally acknowledged as the first modern art exhibition in Salvador. Held in 1944 at Bahia's State Library, it was organized by Amado, newspaper editor Odorico Tavares, and artist Manoel Martins from São Paulo, the illustrator of Amado's newly completed tourist guide.[11] What is less commonly remembered, however, is that the exhibition came about as a result of Amado's guide, which had brought Martins to Salvador to begin with, along with select modern artworks on loan.

Amado's very curious and idiosyncratic guide established a new view of the city and featured some tropes that would be adopted by almost all of the intellectuals who produced their own versions in the 1950s. It, also nonetheless, presented a view of the city unique to Amado, one in which poverty played a starring role. Amado was perhaps the only writer of this genre who romanticized the city while drawing attention to its serious social problems. These issues would virtually disappear from the treatments of the 1950s, and so it is worth highlighting that Amado not only forged a new path that would be enthusiastically followed but also established a social realism that would be put aside.

By the 1930s, as noted above, Amado was already foregrounding Afro-Bahians and the city of Salvador in his novels. His guidebook, however, went further, defining Salvador as a "black city par excellence"[12] and highlighting the influence of Candomblé. The book in fact opens with Candomblé drumming and includes a remarkably detailed listing of temples. Amado further insisted that the city was dark and mysterious, hinting at magic and enchantment and even possession that might overcome one during a visit. These themes would be revived over and over again by successive authors and indeed, had already been explored by the samba industry and Disney.

In the final analysis, Amado's guidebook failed to provide a consistent tone or framing for Salvador. His very inconsistency demonstrates, however, that in the 1940s no single view of the city had consolidated. This would only occur—and at a heightened pace—during the 1950s when the tour guides played a primary role in shaping the definition of the city as black, dominated by Candomblé, and driven by popular festivals that created a celebrative mood and rhythm year round.

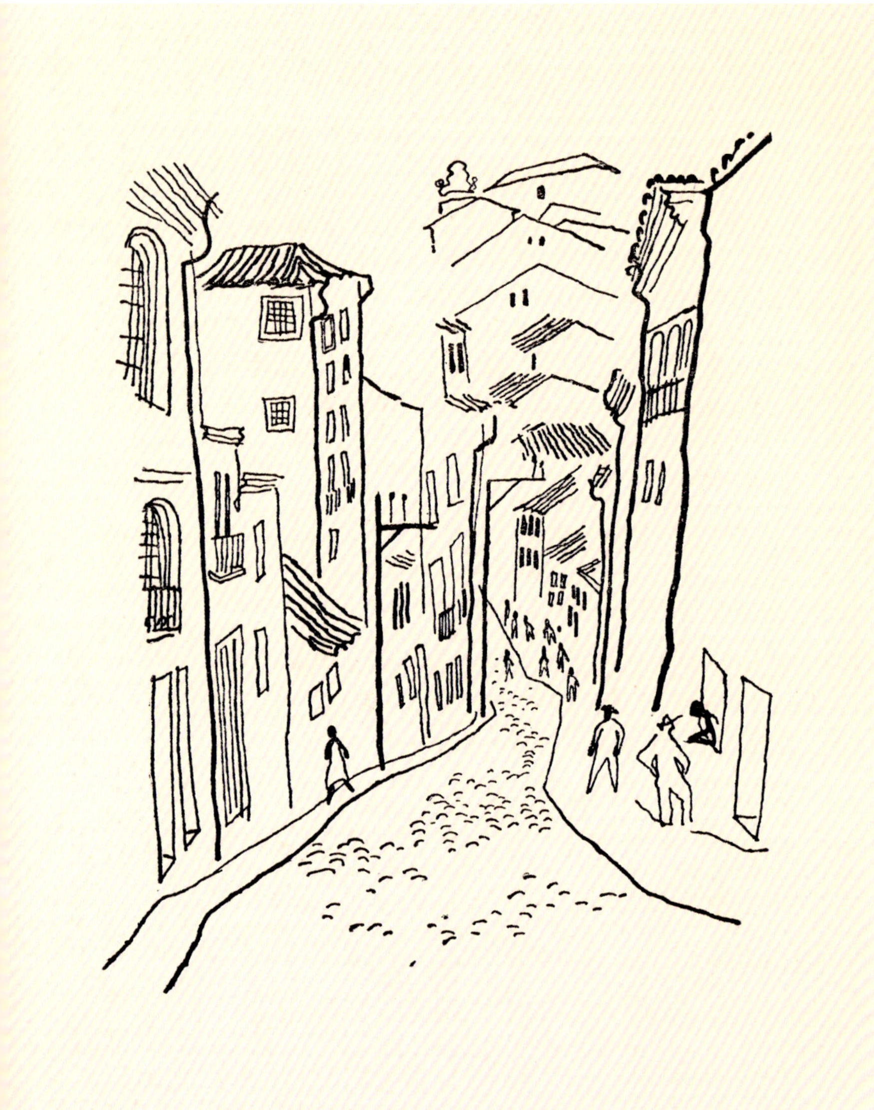

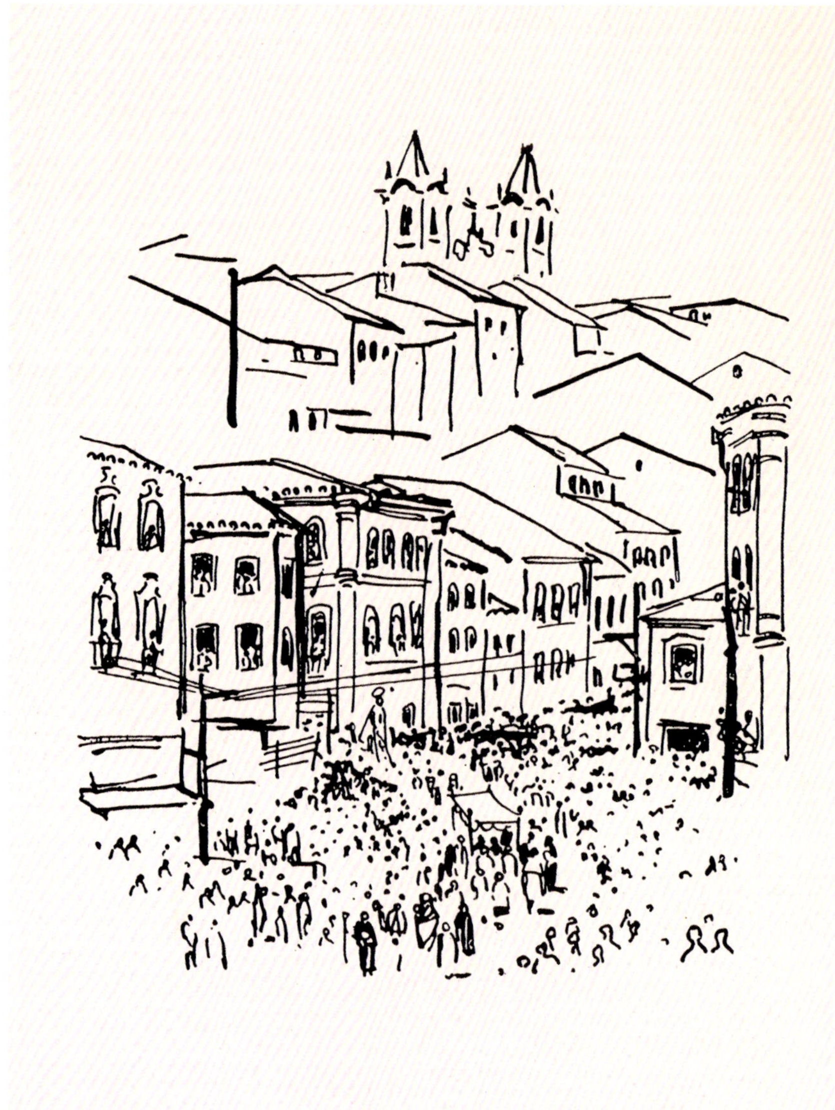

**6.7**
Carlos Thiré (b. 1917, Rio de Janeiro, Brazil; d. 1963)
Illustration from José Valladares, *Bêabá da Bahia: Guia turístico* (Salvador: Livraria Turista, 1951)
Ink on paper
Original dimensions unknown


**6.8**
Carybé (Héctor Julio Páride Bernabó, b. 1911, Lanús, Buenos Aires Province, Argentina; d. 1997)
From *O Pelourinho* (Recôncavo Collection), 1951
China ink on paper
29.7 x 21 cm

One of the most important figures to craft this ethos was Tavares, the editor of two of Bahia's most highly circulated newspapers. Tavares lent authority to this newly solidifying vision of Bahia through the columns that he and others wrote in his newspapers, and he penned his own guide to the city in 1951 (Tavares 1951). While his importance has long been overlooked, Tavares and his tourist guide played a critical role in publicizing a view of Salvador as a black and festive city (fig. 6.5), as Ickes demonstrates (Ickes 2013b, 437–66). His chatty, idiosyncratic guide accompanied with illustrations by Carybé, was organized around festival themes. The previous year, moreover, Tavares had worked with Pierre Verger to publish a series of articles on Afro-Bahian culture in Salvador in *O Cruzeiro*, the most important illustrated magazine of the time. As is now well known, Verger also contributed to establishing a particular visual language for Salvador, one dominated by many of the same preoccupations.

Some embraced this new vision more than others. Bahian art critic José Valladares, for example, also wrote an illustrated guide in 1951, but his was perhaps more split between the dual visions of Salvador as a preserve of colonial tradition and as a center for authentic Afro-Brazilian culture (Valladares [1951] 2012). Valladares served as director for Bahia's State Museum and played an important role in encouraging modern art. As I explore elsewhere, he also experimented with the inclusion of popular and African-based culture in the museum and his publications (Romo 2010; 2009). More so than many others of his time, however, he hesitated to embrace the city as exclusively black or as dominated by its festive life, to which he dedicated less attention. His guide was illustrated by the artist Carlos Thiré of Rio, who echoed Valladares's stance in his images (fig. 6.7).

The artist who dominated and shaped the vision of Salvador in the guides of the 1950s was Carybé, although Carlos Bastos also played a prominent role. Indeed, the work of Carybé served as a visual tour guide for the city in a thematic series of line drawings he published with government sponsorship in the early 1950s (fig. 6.8). Prominent intellectuals and scholars introduced each of these works, framing both the art and its reflection in the city itself. The texts and the drawings worked to define a new Salvador, one that had been in the making through the 1930s and 1940s. This Salvador highlighted Afro-Bahian culture and developed an idea of an authentic popular "folk" culture that dominated the city's festivities and daily life.[13] Not content to let his drawings speak for themselves, however, Carbyé would eventually write his own guide to the city some years later in 1962 (see fig. 7.2). Here he described Salvador as a city of confusion, of mixture, and of mystery, with the deities of Candomblé integral to everyday life.[14]

Though these depictions now seem natural, even expected for the city, at the time they were still the source of some debate. Guides of the early 1950s produced exclusively by municipal authorities, for instance, emphasized a much more conservative vision of the city, one dominated by its colonial culture and defined by its Roman Catholic churches (fig. 6.3). Popular culture and Afro-Bahian culture entered these guides briefly, if at all, during the early 1950s. Indeed, the municipal tourism board devoted much of its energy to sponsoring an extended series of guides on the city's colonial churches, none of which mentioned popular faith, practice, or even popular church celebrations.

By the early 1960s, all of this had changed. Official city tourism efforts shepherded visitors to sponsored capoeira exhibitions, and a stop at a Candomblé temple was obligatory. These efforts would be further solidified during the 1960s and 1970s, particularly with the reforms of the colonial district of the Pelourinho and the establishment of the historic center of Salvador as a UNESCO heritage site (Santos 2005; Riggs 2008). As anthropologist John Collins has noted, the commodification of the city in the 1990s created policies that aimed to preserve its colonial architecture but ultimately perceived the Afro-Bahian inhabitants of the crumbling historic buildings as both hindrances to a true representation of the city and as a commodity themselves (Collins 2015). The origins of these policies can be found in Salvador's budding tourism industry of the 1940s and 1950s and the tourist guides of the era. In creating a romanticized and idyllic portrait of the city, these efforts failed to address the poverty of the population, viewing the Afro-Bahian majority as a tourist "attraction" in ways that frequently neglected its general social welfare.

Although Amado has often been criticized for his romanticism, which undeniably deepened over the years, it is worth remembering that his guide was also a plea for help. Denouncing the high rates of infant mortality, poverty, and inequality, he called for visitors to do something. What precisely he meant by this is unclear. His portrayal of Salvador nonetheless remains equal parts celebration and denouncement. It is worth remembering that in the midst of all of the celebration of Salvador, much of it justified, it is also incumbent upon observers and locals to recognize the poverty and suffering that created the city and that shaped Afro-Brazilian reality. Racial inequality, though often written out of Salvador's narrative, has been as much a part of the city as its celebrated Afro-Bahian culture.

# 7 Jorge Amado and Friends

Randal Johnson

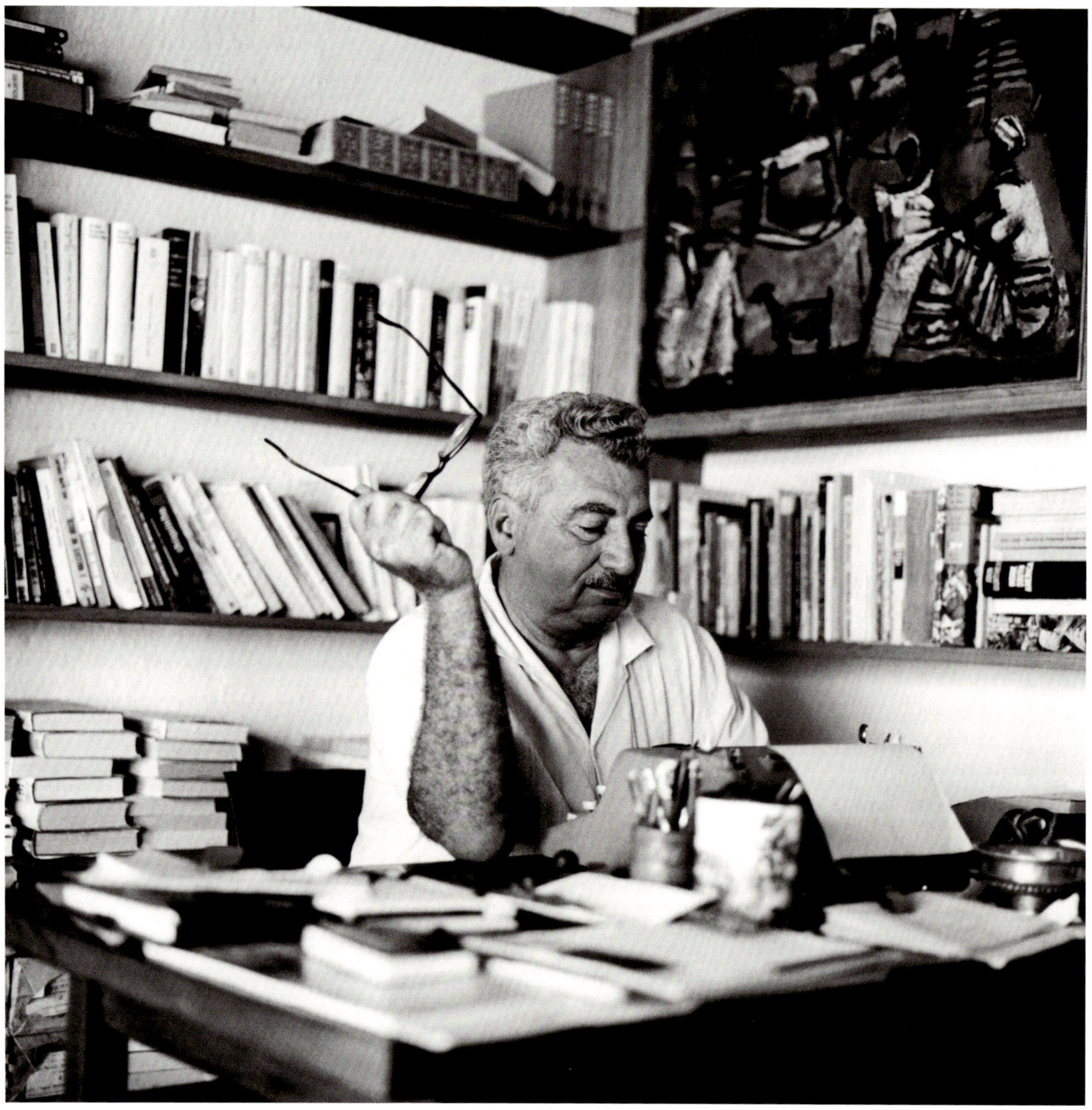

I am a man who throughout his life has struggled to defend the rights of blacks, poor people, and Candomblé communities. My lifetime struggle against racism is a struggle that directly supports black religion.

—Jorge Amado (Raillard 1990, 82)

THE BRAZILIAN MODERNIST MOVEMENT of the 1920s involved, in addition to aesthetic renewal, a concern with the nation's cultural identity, culminating in 1928 with Mário de Andrade's novel *Macunaíma*, which reflects on the possibility of an original Brazilian civilization, and Oswald de Andrade's "Anthropophagic Manifesto," which offered a radical proposal for the interaction of Brazilian and foreign cultures. At the same time, the idea that Brazilian society was constituted through the convergence of three races was commonplace as writers began to reflect, perhaps timidly, on the legacy of slavery and the African contribution to Brazilian culture.

The process of self-exploration intensified in the 1930s with the publication of numerous books and essays in which intellectuals of different political persuasions attempted to understand, reinterpret, or reconceptualize Brazil's social and cultural formation. In *Casa grande e senzala* (*The Masters and the Slaves*, 1933), Gilberto Freyre undertook a broad analysis of the historical development of Brazilian society by casting racial mixing in a positive light (in stark contrast to nineteenth-century conceptions of it as a form of mongrelization), while at the same time discussing the positive contributions of European, indigenous, and African cultures to Brazil's cultural formation. Various other studies from the period also examined the contribution of black culture to Brazilian society, in what literary scholar Antônio Dimas has referred to as a "veritable collective desire for a national self-inquisition": *O negro brasileiro* (Artur Ramos, 1934), *Religiões negras* (Édison Carneiro, 1936), *Negros bantus* (Édison Carneiro, 1937), and *Senzala e macumba* (Jacy Rego Barros, 1938), among others (Dimas 2008, 339–40).

Such studies obviously held significance for Bahia and its capital, Salvador, long considered the most African city in Brazil (fig. 7.2). Numerous scholars, including several contributors to this volume, have written of the transformation, in the first half of the twentieth century, of Bahia's identity as the nation's cultural bedrock, particularly because of the positive valuation of racial mixing and the recognition of the importance of Afro-descendants in the state, and particularly in Salvador and the area surrounding the Bahia de Todos os Santos (Bay of All Saints), known as the Recôncavo. This transformation eventually led to the elaboration of a distinctive and hegemonic Afro-Bahian cultural identity, although it did not lead to significant changes in the economic or political structure.[1] As Edward Telles has noted, Salvador is a city "where blacks are granted nearly free run of the cultural realm, and where the culture of Africa is celebrated, apparently in exchange for relinquishing claims to economic and political power so that it can continue to be monopolized by a small white elite" (Telles 2004, 213; cited in Dunn 2007, 851).

**7.1**
Jorge Amado works at his desk. A painting by Carybé hangs above him, at his left. PHOTOGRAPH BY FRANCO RUBARTELLI, 1968. COURTESY CONDÉ NAST VIA GETTY IMAGES.

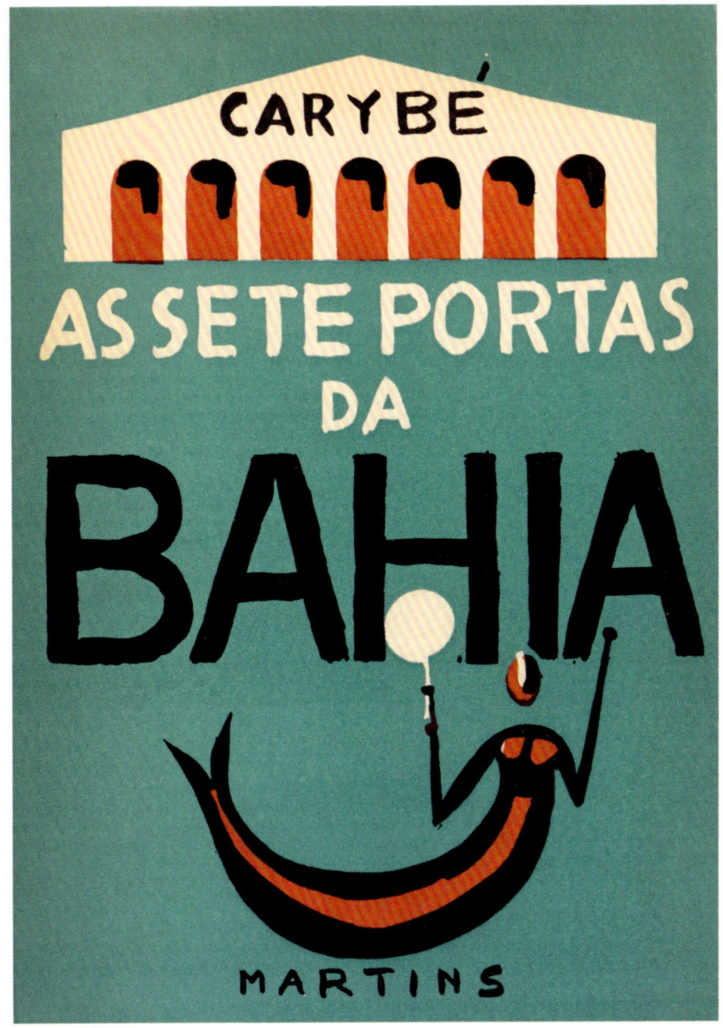


**7.2**
Carybé (Héctor Julio Páride Bernabó, b. 1911, Lanús, Buenos Aires Province, Argentina; d. 1997)
*As sete portas da Bahia* (The Seven Gates of Bahia; São Paulo: Livraria Martins Editora, 1962)
Ink on paper
23.5 x 16 cm
PRIVATE COLLECTION

This author-inscribed copy of Carybé's illustrated guidebook to Salvador with additional texts by Jorge Amado and Pierre Verger was presented to the musician, actor, and civil rights activist Harry Belafonte and his wife, Julie Robinson Belafonte.

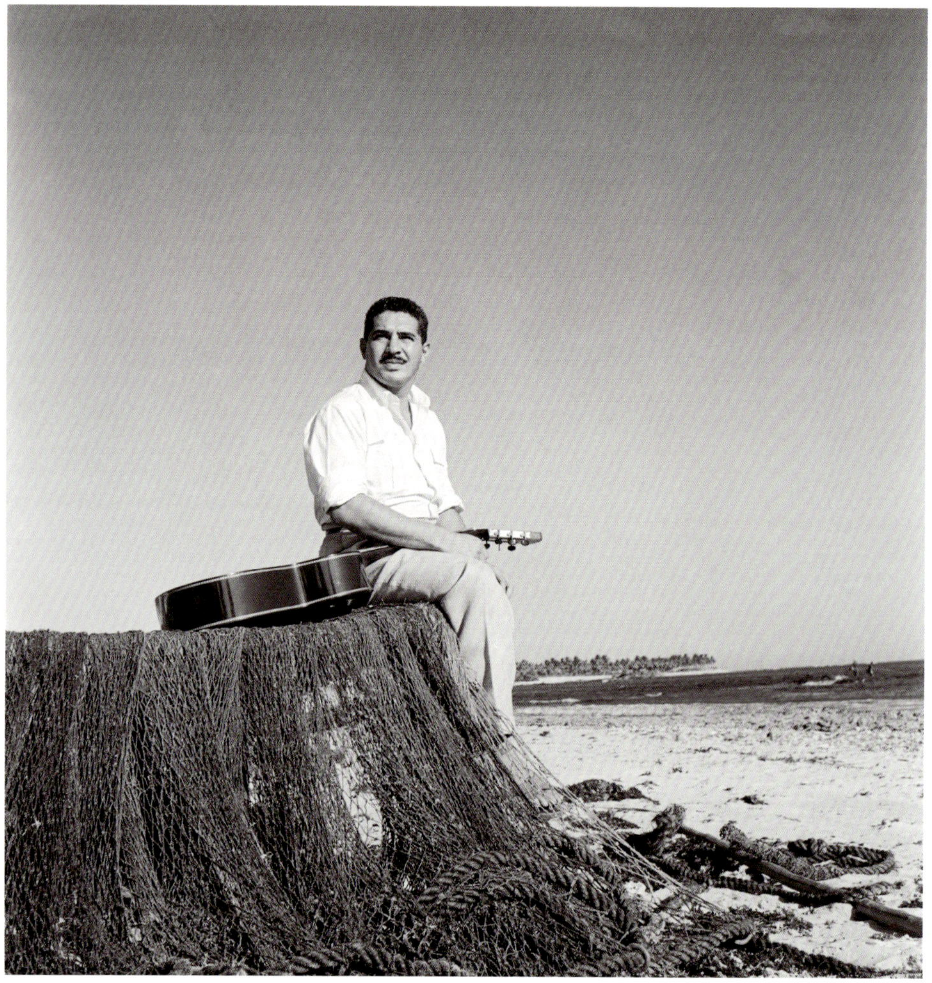

7.3
Pierre Verger (b. Paris, France 1902; d. 1996)
*Dorival Caymmi*, Salvador, Brazil, 1946
Photograph


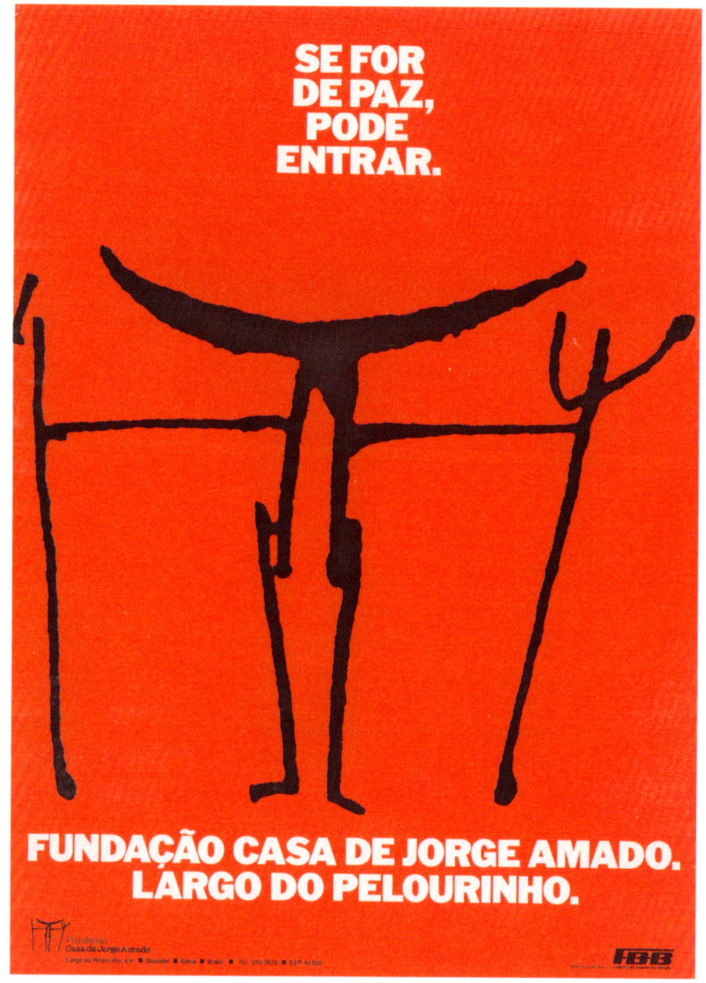


7.4
Artist Unknown
*Se for de paz, pode entrar* (You Can Enter If You Come in Peace), circa late 1980s
Poster
Ink on paper
59.5 x 39.5 cm
PRIVATE COLLECTION
COURTESY FUNDAÇÃO CASA DE JORGE AMADO

The symbol on this poster, which represents the *orixá* Exú, was designed for Amado by Carybé.

Despite—or perhaps because of—such social contradictions, Bahia's image has often tended to be idealized or romanticized. This is evident in such characterizations of the city as a "Black Rome," an expression apparently coined by Candomblé priestess Mãe Aninha[2] in the mid-1930s (Carneiro and Ferraz 1940, 7 n.1; Ickes 2013a, 2; Romo 2010, 119); in official tourism promotion campaigns (e.g., "Sorria, Está na Bahia," or "Smile, You're in Bahia"); and in many popular songs, works of art and literature, films, and television programs. One might think, in this regard, of a number of songs composed by non-Bahian Ary Barroso starting in the early 1930s, all of which offer a very romantic view of the city, its culture, and its people: "Bahia" (1931), "Nega baiana" (1931), "Terra de iaiá" (1931), "No tabuleiro da baiana" (1936), "Quando penso na Bahia" (1937), "Na Baixa do Sapateiro" (1938), and "Os quindins de iaiá" (1941). These last two songs were used to represent Bahia musically in Disney's animated film *The Three Caballeros* (1944).[3]

Many people and institutions—ranging from the Candomblé community and Carnaval organizations to the tourism industry, from political leaders to local and non-local artists and intellectuals, and from certain sectors of both the white elite and the black working class—contributed to this process of identity formation.[4] Four artists stand out above all others (figs. 7.1, 7.3, and see figs. 7.5, 7.7), however, for having expressed and solidified what may well be seen as the dominant image that many people have of Bahia today: novelist Jorge Amado (1912–2001), singer/song-writer Dorival Caymmi (1914–2008), fine artist Carybé (Héctor Julio Páride Bernabó, 1911–1997), and anthropologist/photographer Pierre Verger (1902–1996). As Roger Sansi has written of Carybé and Verger, to which we can clearly add Amado and Caymmi, "[Their] influence...on the image of Bahia is incommensurable. Their portraits of popular life in Bahia's streets and of Candomblé almost became a trademark of the city" (Sansi 2007, 131).

This situation is filled with paradoxes. One of the paradoxes is that although the identity in question is clearly *Afro*-Bahian, only one of the four—Caymmi—was arguably black (official records list him as "*pardo*," or "brown"), and two others—Carybé and Verger—were not even Brazilian by birth, much less Bahian. The former was born in Argentina, the latter in France. Carybé established residence in Salvador in 1950; Verger in 1946. Both lived much of their adult lives in the city, and Carybé became a naturalized Brazilian citizen in 1957. Regarding this paradox, it might be helpful to keep in mind a distinction that art historian Roberto Conduru makes in his book, *Pérolas negras* (Black Pearls), when he writes that the term "Afro-Brazilian art" has not always been characterized as that produced exclusively by Afro-descendants. Conduru gives as examples precisely Carybé and Verger, along with German-born Karl Heinz Hansen (1915–1978), who is known as Hansen Bahia, all of whom explored Afro-Brazilian themes in their artistic production (Conduru 2013a, 16), as did Amado and Caymmi.

The importance of these artists—and close friends—is evident in their official recognition as icons of a dominant view of Bahian identity. For example, in 1953 the municipal government of Salvador named a plaza in the neighborhood of Itapuã in honor of Dorival Caymmi (fig. 7.3). The homage was no doubt made in Itapuã rather than another area of the city because in 1948 he had written a song that has since become a classic of Brazilian popular music, "Saudades de Itapuã" (roughly, "Missing Itapuã"), but it was rendered because of his contributions toward the creation and dissemination of a positive image of Bahia in the rest of the country (Caymmi 2001, 295–99).

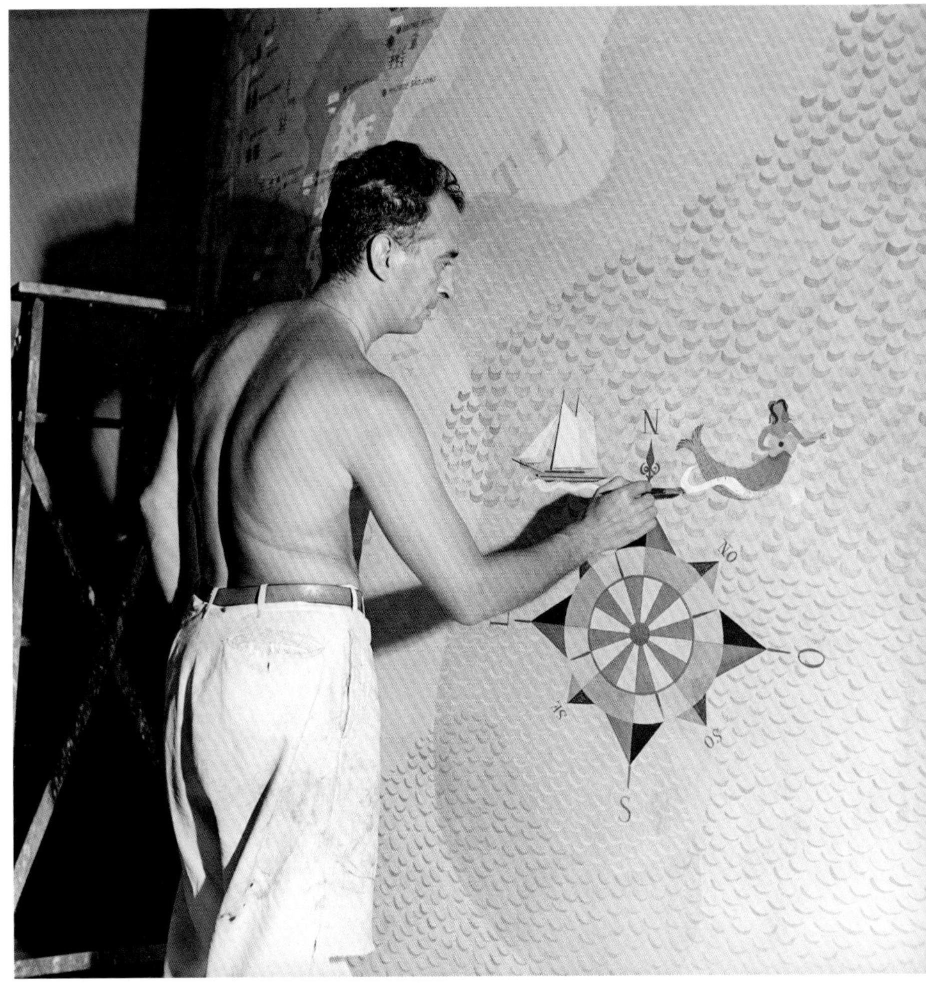

**7.5**
Pierre Verger (b. Paris, France, 1902; d. 1996)
*Carybé*, Salvador, Brazil, 1948–1951
Photograph
PHOTO PIERRE VERGER ©FUNDAÇÃO PIERRE VERGER

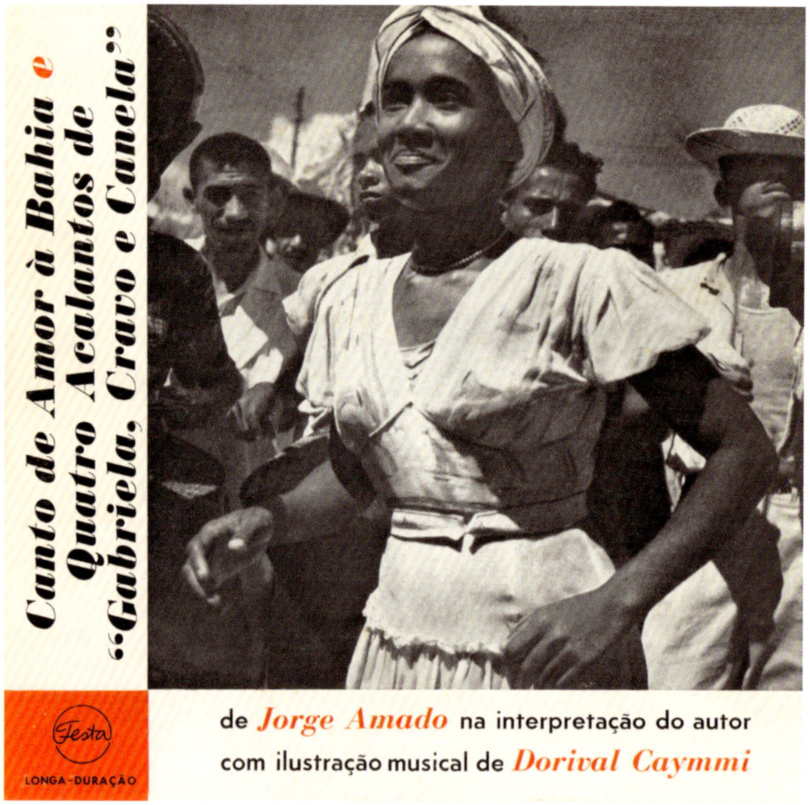


**7.6**
Pierre Verger (b. 1902, Paris, France, d. 1996)
Cover of an LP with lyrics by Jorge Amado and music by Dorival Caymmi
*Canto de amor à Bahia e quarto acalantos de Gabriela, Cravo e Canela* (Love Song for Bahia and Four Lullabies from "Gabriela, Clove and Cinnamon"), 1958
Ink on paper
26.5 x 26.5 cm
Private Collection
PHOTO PIERRE VERGER ©FUNDAÇÃO PIERRE VERGER

**7.7**
Carybé (Héctor Julio Páride Bernabó, b. 1911, Lanús, Buenos Aires Province, Argentina; d. 1997)
*Obrigação do Ojá Obalá: Opô Afonjá* (Ritual for Ojá Obalá: Opô Afonjá), undated
Ink and watercolor (gouache) on paper
83 x 63 cm
COURTESY INSTITUTO CARYBÉ / COPYRIGHTS CONSULTORIA LTDA.

Represented in the center of the foreground is Pierre Verger wearing glasses.

One might also think of Salvador's historic center, Pelourinho, which is the setting of numerous novels by Jorge Amado and the subject of many paintings by Carybé and photographs by Verger. Since its inauguration in 1987, the Fundaçâo Casa de Jorge Amado (Jorge Amado Foundation) has been housed at the top of the Largo do Pelourinho in an iconic eighteenth-century Baroque building (*casarão*), which had been designated part of the state's historical patrimony (fig. 7.4). The Foundation's opening was attended by Brazil's president at the time, José Sarney, and other state and national dignitaries and celebrities (Coelho 2012). In addition to the privileged position of the Foundation, two of Pelourinho's main internal plazas are named for characters in Amado's novels: Pedro Arcanjo, from *Tenda dos milagres* (*Tent of Miracles*, 1968) and Tereza Batista, from *Tereza Batista, cansada de guerra* (*Tereza Batista, Home from the Wars*, 1972). In 2014, Amado's Rio Vermelho residence, where he had lived since the early 1960s with his long-time spouse, writer Zélia Gattai (1916–2008), became a museum with the support of the municipal government of Salvador and the federal Ministry of Culture, among other public and private institutions.[5] Furthermore, in 2016 the municipal government of Salvador and Brazil's army collaborated to open, in historical forts (São Diogo and Santa Maria) on either side of famed Porto da Barra Beach, cultural centers in honor of Carybé and Pierre Verger. At night, images of their work are projected on the sides of the respective forts ("Salvador ganha" 2016).

These four artists came together at different moments in time based on their enthusiasm for and defense of Afro-Brazilian culture and Bahia's popular classes. Amado was a pioneer, starting in the 1930s with the publication of a series of novels about Bahia's black population, notably *Jubiabá* (1935), *Mar morto* (*Sea of Death*, 1936), and *Capitães de areia* (*Captains of the Sands*, 1937). By the time he published the novels, however, he was living in Rio de Janeiro, the country's center of artistic legitimation, and he did not publish another literary work set in Salvador until the late 1950s. He only again established residence in the city in the early 1960s.

Dorival Caymmi also began his career in the mid-1930s, but it only took off after he too established residence in Rio de Janeiro and began to perform on Radio Tupi (Caymmi 2001, 121–22). His first recorded songs date from 1939, when he released, with Carmen Miranda, "O que é que a baiana tem?" (see Dunn and Shirey, this volume) and, on Side B, "A preta do acarajé," both of which allude to Candomblé, even though they do not directly mention the religion.

Pierre Verger and Carybé arrived in Salvador later, both with a solid body of work behind them. Verger had traveled extensively between 1932 and 1946, supporting himself through his photography. Even after establishing residence in Salvador, he did not cease traveling, particularly to Africa, where he explored cultural, social, and religious connections between Africa and Brazil.[6] Carybé, in turn, had studied in Rio de Janeiro's Escola Nacional de Belas Artes in the late 1920s and had worked as a graphic designer and illustrator for numerous publications in Argentina and Brazil, while at the same time pursuing his own artistic career. He had first visited Salvador in 1938, and in 1950, Bahia's secretary of education, Anísio Teixeira, invited him to produce murals for the Centro Educacional Carneiro Ribeiro in Salvador, where he established permanent residence that would last until his death.

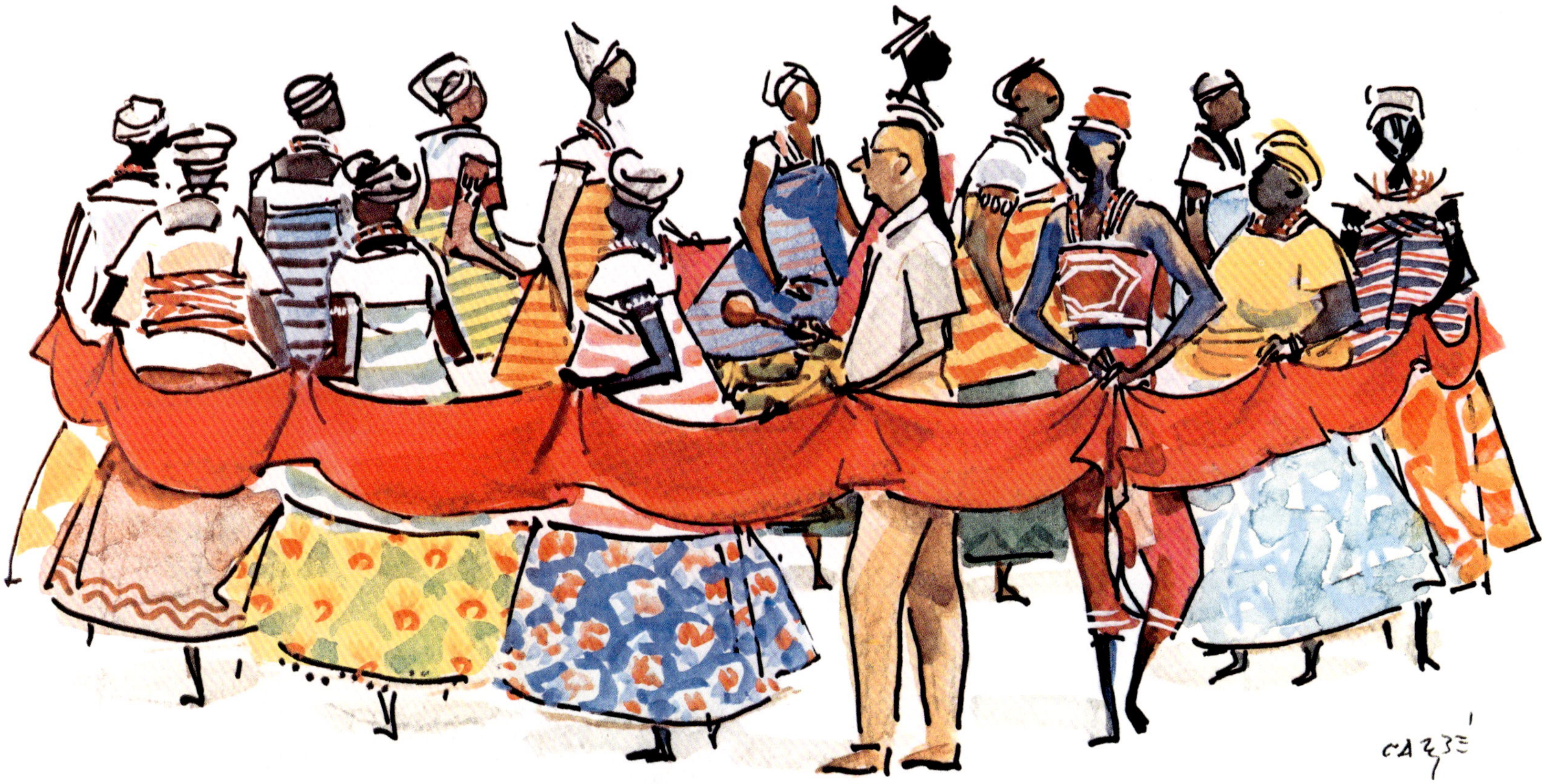

Amado, Caymmi, Carybé, and Verger all documented Bahia's people and culture in their own way and respective artistic mediums. Taken together, they left a remarkable body of work which, as Roberto Conduru suggests in chapter 11 of this volume, has at its core an exaltation of Bahia. They did not, however, celebrate Bahia's white elite; rather, they championed the common people, popular culture, and Afro-Brazilian religion.

Although each is an important artist in his own right, Jorge Amado would seem to be the central figure of the group. Three novels he published in the mid-1930s—*Jubiabá* (see fig. 7.8), *Mar morto*, and *Capitães da areia*—already contain many of the elements that would later come to constitute the Bahian identity the artists represented and defended. His tourist guide, *Bahia de Todos os Santos* (1945)—written during a brief period of residence in Salvador, when his literary writing tended to focus on struggles for power in the cacao region of southern Bahia and his political militancy was intense—offers a view of the city that is both romanticized and political, talking about the magic as well as the hardship of this black city: "In its lyrical mystery and its tragic poverty, truth and legend become one" (Amado 1945, 16; see Romo, this volume, for a brief discussion of this work).

In some cases, however, Amado's influence is more direct than the elaboration of certain themes. Some of Caymmi's early "canções praieiras" (songs of the sea) were inspired by Amado's 1936 novel, *Mar morto*, and the novelist is credited with contributing to the lyrics of "É doce morrer no mar" (1941), whose title is taken directly from the novel, as well as a number of other Caymmi songs and artistic projects. One is the LP *Canto de amor à Bahia e quatro acalantos de Gabriela, Cravo e Canela* (1958), with lyrics by Amado, music by Caymmi, and a photograph by Pierre Verger on the cover (fig. 7.6; Caymmi 2001, 368–69).

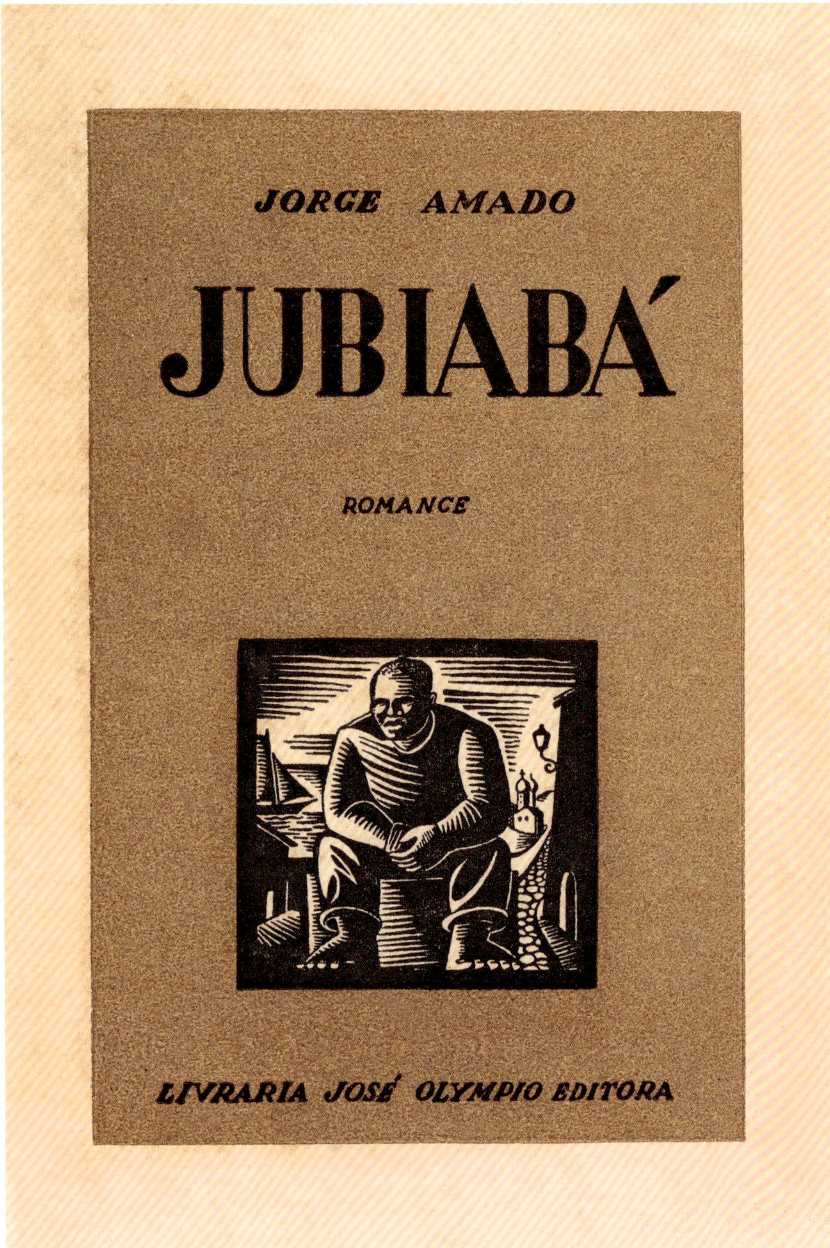


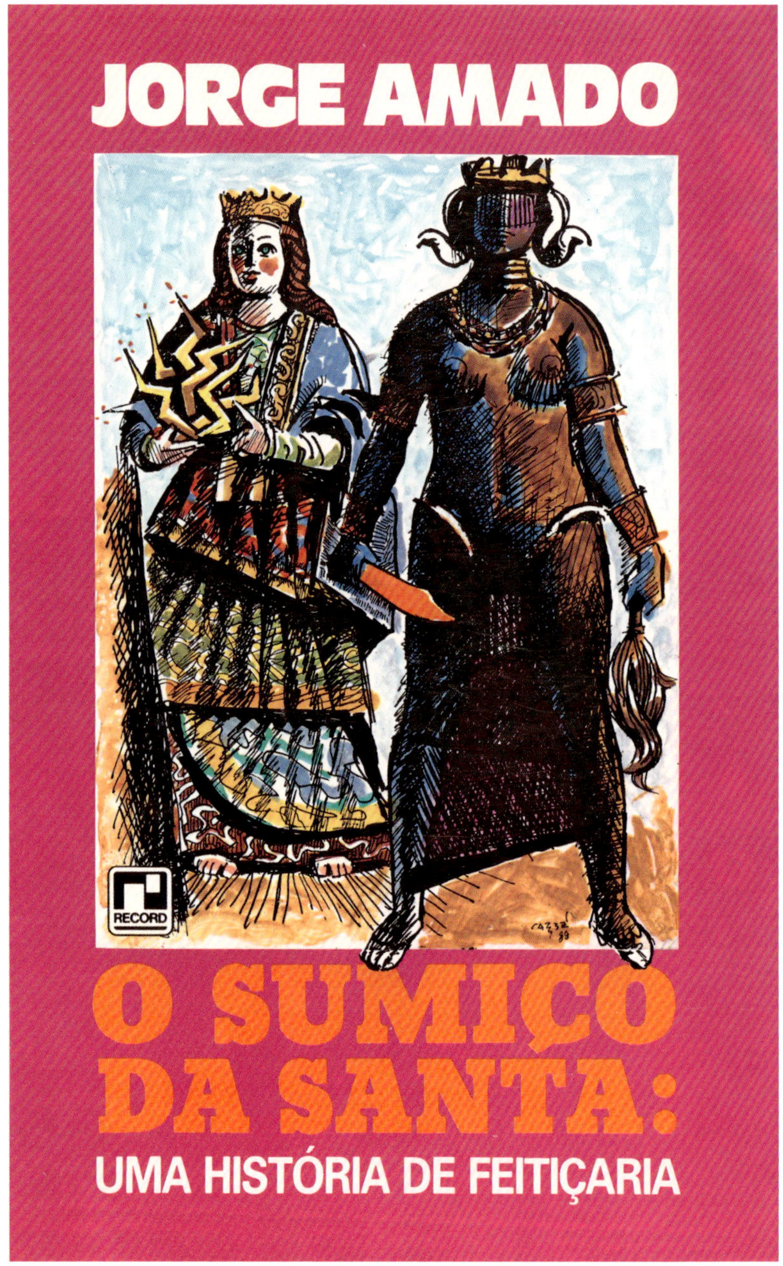


**7.8**
Jorge Amado (b, 1912, Itabuna, Bahia, Brazil; d. 2001)
*Jubiabá* (Rio de Janeiro: Livraria José Olympio Editora, 1935)
Ink on Paper
19 x 13 cm
PRIVATE COLLECTION

**7.9**
Jorge Amado (b, 1912, Itabuna, Bahia, Brazil; d. 2001)
*O sumiço da santa* (*The War of the Saints*; Rio de Janeiro: Editora Record, 1988)
Ink on Paper
20.5 x 13.5 cm
PRIVATE COLLECTION

It is well known that both Carybé and Verger became interested in visiting Bahia after reading *Jubiabá* (1935), and Carybé served as illustrator for several of Amado's books.[7] In many ways, one can say that Caymmi, Carybé, and Verger all reproduce, each in his own fashion, their own visions of the cultural universe that Amado describes in these and later works. In other words, what occurred was a convergence of distinct artistic practices, developed in different professional trajectories, around a common set of themes related to the people and cultures of Bahia.

Central to these themes is Candomblé. This is not surprising, since all four were Obás of Xangô at the Ilê Axé Opô Afonjá Candomblé house and were either active in one or more temples or engaged to different degrees in the defense of Afro-Brazilian religion and culture (fig. 7.9).[8] In this sense, their association with Candomblé goes far beyond artistic elaboration or documentation. Jorge Amado, for example, wrote the article of the 1946 constitution that guaranteed religious freedom in the country. Verger undertook extensive research into *orixás* and Candomblé on both sides of the Atlantic and became a *babalaô*, or diviner of Ifá prophecies, for which he earned the name "Fatumbi" (meaning "one who was reborn for Ifá"). He was involved in numerous Candomblé temples in Salvador, including Ilê Axé Opô Afonjá, the Terreiro do Gantois, and Ilê Axé Opô Aganju. At Opô Afonjá, Carybé served as an Obá, an Ogã,[9] and president of the house's civil society, the Sociedade Cruz Santa. He also "became something of the right arm of Mãe Stella from the administrative standpoint" (Fundação Pierre Verger 2012, 183).

Both Verger and Carybé documented multiple aspects of Candomblé, the former through his photography, which includes hundreds of photographs of Bahian Candomblé, among them iconic images of Mãe Senhora[10] and Iemanjá. Verger's publications on African and Afro-Brazilian religion are also extensive. Carybé worked in diverse media in his artistic representations of a broad range of Candomblé figures and activities. Most notable are perhaps the 27 wood panels of the *orixás* (1967) held by the Museu Afro-Brasileiro in Salvador (see figs. 10.7, 10.8) and the book *Iconografia dos deuses africanos no Candomblé da Bahia* (1980), which brings together 128 watercolors resulting from 40 years of research and observation (see Conduru, this volume, for a discussion of the work of Carybé).

As indicated above, Dorival Caymmi's "É doce morrer no mar" and other songs were inspired by—and its lyrics largely taken from—Amado's *Mar morto*. The song evokes the goddess of the sea, Iemanjá, in its final verses:[11]

| | |
|---|---|
| Saveiro partiu de noite foi | The sloop left at night |
| Madrugada não voltou | And did not return at dawn |
| O marinheiro bonito | The handsome sailor |
| Sereia do mar levou | A siren took away |
| É doce morrer... (bis) | It's sweet to die at sea (bis) |
| Nas ondas verdes do mar, meu bem | In the green waves of the sea, my love |
| Ele se foi afogar | He went away to drown |
| Fez sua cama de noivo | He made his wedding bed |
| No colo de Iemanjá | In the arms of Iemanjá |
| É doce morrer... (bis) | It's sweet to die at sea (bis) |

Caymmi refers to Iemanjá in numerous other songs: "Rainha do mar" (1939),[12] "Promessa de pescador" (1939), "O bem do mar" (1954), "Quem vem pra beira do mar" (1954), "Dois de Fevereiro" (1957), "Sargaço Mar" (1985), and "Caminhos do mar" (2001), among others. Close to both the Terreiro do Gantois and the Ilê Axé Opô Afonjá Candomblé houses, he also wrote songs in honor of their leaders, Mãe Menininha[13] ("Oração de Mãe Menininha," 1972) and Mãe Stella de Oxossi ("Mãe Stella," 1994),[14] as well as in honor of the *orixá* Xangô, "Canto de Obá" (with Jorge Amado, 1972).[15] As indicated above, it was Jorge Amado who inspired all three of these artists in different ways.

**Jorge Amado**

Jorge Amado is one of Brazil's most popular and widely translated novelists. With a career lasting almost seventy years, his novels have been translated into forty-nine languages in fifty-five countries. From the early 1930s until at least the late 1950s, he was affiliated with the Brazilian Communist Party. Because of his political activism, he was arrested several times (1936, 1937, 1942, 1945), had books burned in a public square in Salvador (1937), and lived in exile outside of Brazil on several occasions (1941–1945: Argentina and Uruguay; 1948–1950: Paris; 1951–1952: Prague). In 1945, during a brief period of party legality, he was elected federal deputy (from São Paulo) on the Communist Party slate. It was in this capacity, and as a participant of the 1946 Constituent Assembly, that he wrote the constitutional amendment that guaranteed religious freedom in the country, an amendment specifically designed to protect the Candomblé community (Amado 2001, 73–74). Recent reports indicate that he was monitored by both the CIA (starting in the 1940s) and the Brazilian government (1936–1985) because of his political activities (Sperb 2017). Despite his political inclinations, Amado once described himself as a "baiano romântico e sensual" (a romantic and sensual Bahian), and there is no doubt that the image he came to transmit of Bahia could, in many respects, be characterized in these terms as well.[16] The self-description was not entirely evident in his work until the late 1950s, when a shift in focus became apparent and when, shortly thereafter, he again established residence in Salvador after many years in Rio de Janeiro and elsewhere.

Born in 1912 on a farm near the southern Bahian city of Itabuna, Amado first went to Salvador in 1922 to study at a boarding school. Near the end of the decade, he formed part of a literary/intellectual group known as the "Academia dos rebeldes" (Academy of Rebels, 1928–1933), led by symbolist poet Pinheiro Viegas. In addition to Amado, the group was important in the intellectual development of such figures as poet Sosígenes Costa (1901–1968), poet and novelist Áydano Couto Ferraz (1914–1985), cultural critic and political militant Dias da Costa (1907–1979), film critic Walter da Silveira (1910–1970), novelist Clóvis Amorim (1912–1970), and ethnographer Édison Carneiro (1912–1972), who would play an important role in the legitimation of Afro-Bahian religion and culture in the 1930s and 1940s through his writings.[17] According to Amado, it was at that time—the late 1920s and early 1930s—that he began to be interested in Bahian popular culture, including Candomblé temples, where he witnessed the discrimination and violence the adherents suffered: "sacred places invaded and destroyed, *iyalorixás* and *babalorixás* arrested, beaten, humiliated.... Such misery and the greatness of the Bahian people are the raw material of my novels" (2001, 71–72). This early involvement led him to participate in the second Afro-Brazilian Congress, organized by Édison Carneiro in Salvador in 1937 (Amado 2001, 235).

A precocious writer, in 1931, at the age of nineteen, Amado published his first novel, *O país do Carnaval* (The Country of Carnaval), a fictional portrait of his intellectual generation, but his focus would shift drastically in his subsequent novels. In the early 1930s, Brazil's intellectual/artistic field was extremely polarized, and writers felt pressured to choose between extremes on the left or the right. Amado opted for the left, initiating an affiliation with the Brazilian Communist Party that would last at least until the 1950s.

Amado's political turn is evident in his literary production. In the preface to his second novel, *Cacau* (1933), which deals with workers on a cacao plantation in southern Bahia, Amado asks, "Could this be a proletarian novel?" His third novel, *Suor* (Sweat, 1934), offers a portrait of the sordid, degrading life in a tenement house in Salvador's historical district (Pelourinho). None of these early novels portends the image of Salvador that Amado would develop later in his career. As already noted, that image began to be developed in his next three novels, *Jubiabá*, *Mar morto*, and *Capitães da areia*. After a very brief discussion of the contribution of these works to the construction of a certain image of Bahia, I will focus on two later novels—*Tenda dos milagres* and *O sumiço da santa* (*The War of the Saints*, [1988] 1993)—that offer a somewhat different, but clearly related, view, one that continues to give centrality to Candomblé, but with a much stronger defense of racial and cultural miscegenation. This later view is also arguably more romantic, idealized, and humorous than that of his novels from the 1930s and 1940s.

The three novels in question have a number of things in common. First, they all deal with the lower classes. *Jubiabá* is the story of Antônio Balduíno (fig. 7.8), one of the first black heroes in Brazilian literature, and his trajectory from a boy living in a favela, the Morro do Capa Negro,[18] through numerous situations and occupations—street kid, boxer, worker on a Recôncavo tobacco plantation, stevedore—to becoming the leader of a dockworkers' strike in Salvador. In *Mar morto*, Amado turns to sailors and captains of small boats in the Bay of All Saints in a tale that is much more lyrical than political. *Capitães de areia*, in turn, focuses on a group of street children who live along the wharfs of Salvador in a kind of primitive communism, begging or stealing during the day, sharing what they obtained at night. In tune with Amado's political inclinations at the time, the group's leader, Pedro Bala, like Antônio Balduíno in *Jubiabá*, comes to lead a strike on the city's docks. All three of the novels reveal solidarity with the lower classes, who survive in the face of hardship, marginalization, and exploitation.

The second thing they have in common is that they all involve Candomblé. The title character of *Jubiabá* is a *pai de santo*, or Candomblé priest:

> Jubiabá always carried a bunch of herbs that rustled in the wind, and muttered words in the African Nagô dialect. He would come along the street talking to himself and blessing people....
>
> On certain nights, the sound of strange music would come from Jubiabá's house. Antônio Balduíno would toss and turn relentlessly on his straw mat. The music seemed to be calling him with rhythmic drumbeats, sounds of dancing, mysterious voices. (Amado [1935] 1984, 13)

Right from the beginning of the novel, Amado imbues the city of Salvador with air of mystery associated with Afro-Brazilian religion. Jubiabá is not the novel's main character, but as Antônio Dimas notes, "[He] is the moral conscience of those who live on Capa Negro Hill. Reserved and mysterious, which suits his function, Jubiabá only appears when called, because his availability is not that of common mortals... [he] has reached a higher level, the domicile of those who no longer need materiality to govern the living" (Dimas 2008, 329). *Jubiabá* is also the first novel in Brazil to represent, "without exoticism or bewilderment," a syncretic Candomblé ceremony (Dimas 2008, 328):

> The deity paid reverence to Jubiabá. Arms at sharp angles greeted Oxossi, the god of hunting. Lips were pursed, hands trembled, bodies shook in the hysteria of the sacred dance. Then suddenly, Oxalá, the greatest of all the gods, appeared, knocking down Maria dos Reis, a black girl of fifteen with a rounded, virgin's body. Oxalá divides himself in two: Oxadiã [Oxaguiã], who is young, and Oxolufã, who is old. This time he appeared as Oxolufã, old and bent, supported by a decorated staff. He came out of the dressing room attired in white to receive the reverence of the audience, who all bowed lower than ever.
>
> "Okê, Okê, Okê!"
>
> Only then did the high priestess sing, "Ê inun ójá la o lô, inun li a ô lo." She was advising, "Prepare yourselves, O people of the marketplace, for we are going to invade."
>
> And the audience chanted, "Erô ójá é pará món, ê inun ójá li a o lô."
>
> "Be careful, O crowds of people, we will enter the market place." Yes, they would enter the market place because they were with Oxalá, the greatest of all the spirits. (Amado [1935], 1984, 83-84)

Just as Jubiabá marks a presence, even when absent, Candomblé pervades Amado's novel, even when not explicitly mentioned.

The same occurs in *Mar morto*, which takes place largely on or around the Bay of All Saints in Salvador and the Recôncavo. The title of the book's initial section is "Iemanjá, Mistress of Seas and Sloops." Iemanjá, of course, is the goddess of the sea in Candomblé, and her presence permeates the novel.

> Iemanjá, who is mistress of the docks, of the sloops, of the lives of all of them, has five names, five sweet names that everyone knows. She is called Iemanjá, she has always been called that and it is her real name, as mistress of waters, lady of the oceans. Canoemen, however, like to call her Dona Janaína, and the blacks, who are her favorite children, who dance for her and fear her more than any others, call her Inaê, with devotion, or they make entreaties to the Princess of Aiocá, queen of those mysterious lands hidden behind the blue line that separates them from other places. The women of the docks, who are simple and valiant...call her Dona Maria, because Maria is a pretty name.... She is a siren, she is the mother-of-waters, the mistress of the sea, Iemanjá, Dona Janaína, Dona Maria, Inaê, Princess of Aiocá. (Amado [1936] 1984, 69)

José Benedito dos Santos has argued that in *Mar morto* Amado uses the myth of Iemanjá and her son Orungã, which explains the origins of the waters of the oceans, as a symbol of the construction of Brazilian identity based on its African heritage. In the novel Amado makes extensive use of oral traditions, as well as descriptions of Candomblé rituals, all in a romantic and lyrical setting (Santos 2013).

Although Candomblé doesn't have the same structural importance in *Capitães da areia* as in does in the two previous novels, it is nonetheless a factor. One of Amado's characters is Candomblé priestess Mãe Aninha, who founded and led the Ilê Axé Opô Afonjá house from 1910 until her death in 1938, and "who knows everything that Iá tells her" by consulting cowry shells on stormy nights" (Amado [1937] 1988, 21).[19] The novel's narrator explains that "all blacks and all poor people in Bahia are friends of the great *mãe-de-santo*" (Amado [1937] 1988, 80–81). Beyond that, Mãe Aninha represents a healing spirit for those in need and a central force of resistance to police violence against Candomblé houses.

These three novels, from Amado's earliest political phase, offer a vision of Bahia as socially and economically stratified, with the poor suffering from violence and marginalization, yet intriguing and romantic. As he writes near the beginning of *Capitães de areia*, "The city of Bahia, black and religious, is almost as mysterious as the green sea" (Amado [1937], 1988, 18).

Two later novels, *Tenda dos milagres* and *O sumiço da santa*, are imminently representative of a vision of Bahia that Amado would express starting in the late 1950s. The former, written during a period of repressive military rule, is explicitly anti-racist and anti-authoritarian. In a kind of foreword, the narrator posits an opposition between "a vast university" that encompasses the historical center of Salvador, "wherever there are men and women who work," creating "a fresh, original image of novel colors and sounds" (Amado [1968] 2003, 3), and the nearby School of Medicine, where students learn to care for the sick and "other things as well—bad rhetoric, and how to spout sonnets, and theories of dubious value" (Amado [1968] 2003, 9). The latter include the forms of scientific racism that prevailed in the nineteenth century and continued into the twentieth. The novel is much too complex to go into in any detail. Suffice to say that, like his earlier work, it denounces police violence against Candomblé temples, racism, authoritarianism, and the hypocrisy of dominant social institutions such as the press and the Catholic Church. It also involves an ardent defense of racial and cultural mixing. It does all of this with an infectious sense of humor and local color. Appropriately, the old building of the School of Medicine, where "theories of dubious values" were spouted, now houses the Museu Afro-Brasileiro (MAFRO), which is dedicated to the exhibition of the arts and cultures of Africa and the African diaspora in Brazil.

In *O sumiço da santa*, Amado again takes humorous, satirical aim at dominant social institutions in a story that illustrates the notion of religious syncretism that has long characterized discourses about Candomblé (fig. 7.9). In the novel, a statue of Saint Barbara of the Thunder is transported from Santo Amaro da Purificação, a town in the Recôncavo, to Salvador, where it is to be exhibited in the Museum of Sacred Art. Saint Barbara is traditionally syncretized with Iansã, the goddess of lightning, wind, and storms (thus the qualification "of the Thunder"). When the sloop carrying the statue arrives at the dock in Salvador, something miraculous happens:

> Before Master Manuel and Maria Clara had finished mooring the sloop and managed to lift out the saint, the saint herself got down from her litter, took a step forward, smoothed the folds of her cape, and walked off.
>
> With a sway of her hips, Saint Barbara of the Thunder slipped between Master Manuel and Maria Clara and gave them a smile of complicity and affection. The *êbômin* then held her hands open before her breasts in a ritual gesture and said: "*Eparrei, Oyá!*" When she passed the priest and the nun, she waved politely to the nun and winked at the priest....
>
> Before the lights came on in their lampposts Saint Barbara Yansan had disappeared into the midst of her people. (Amado [1988] 1993, 7)

Here, Amado's view of Bahia as a magical space comes into full view. *O sumiço da santa* is a novel that offers a defense of Candomblé and well as religious and cultural syncretism. It involves large doses of sensuality, a love for Brazilian culture, political and social satire, and a wonderful sense of humor. It also offers a summary of Amado's vision of Bahia.

# 8 Seeking the *Orixás* in Brazilian Popular Music

**Christopher Dunn**

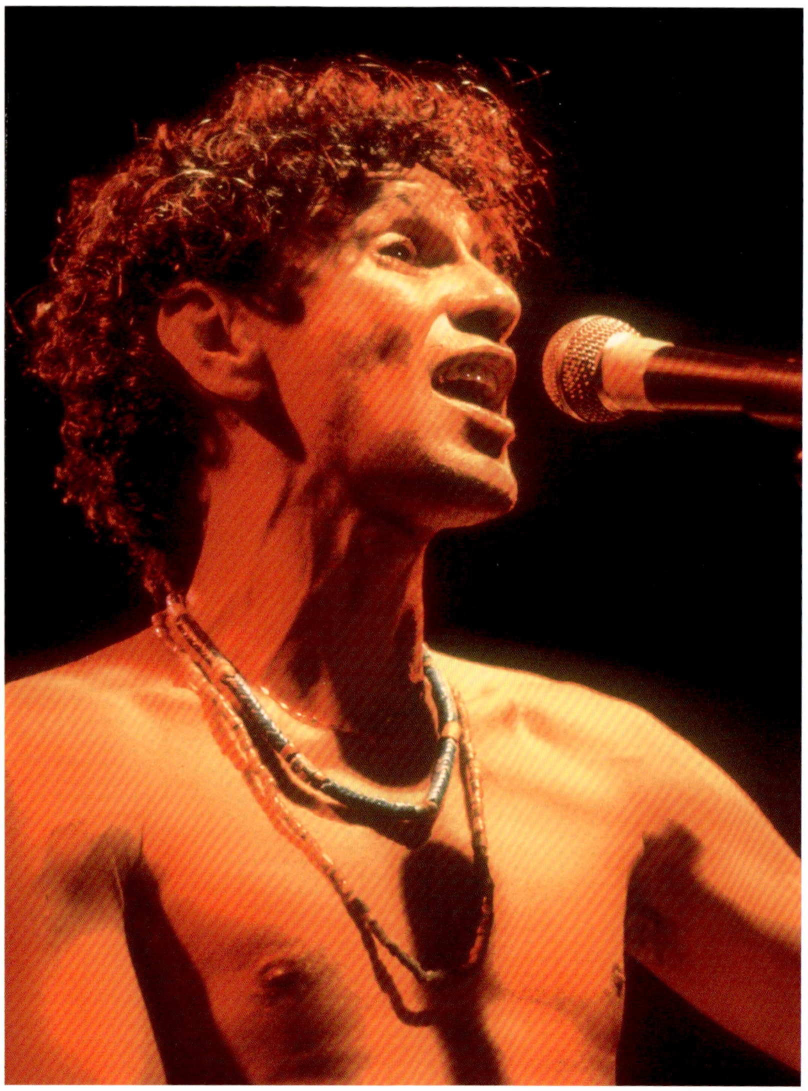

**8.1**
Caetano Veloso performs, 1989. PHOTOGRAPH BY H. JOHN MAIER JR./THE LIFE IMAGES COLLECTION GETTY IMAGES.

| | |
|---|---|
| Quem descobriu o Brasil<br>Foi o negro que viu<br>A crueldade bem de frente<br>E ainda produziu<br>milagres de fé no extremo Ocidente | Those who discovered Brazil<br>Were blacks who confronted<br>Cruelty head on<br>And still produced<br>Miracles of faith in the extreme Occident |
| Ojúobá ia lá e via<br>Ojúobá ia<br>Xangô manda chamar<br>Obatalá guia<br>Mamãe Oxum chora<br>Lágrima alegria<br>Pétala de Iemanjá<br>Yansã Oyá ria | Ojúobá went there and saw<br>Ojúobá went<br>Xangô calls out<br>Obatalá guides<br>Mama Oxum cries<br>Tears joy<br>Petals of Iemanjá<br>Yansã Oyá laughed |

—Caetano Veloso, "Milagres do povo"

CAETANO VELOSO'S "MILAGRES DO POVO" ("Miracles of the People"), cited in the epigraph,[1] calls our attention to a significant strand of Brazilian popular music that exalts Afro-Brazilian Candomblé with its pantheon of West African deities—the *orixás*—who animate the cosmology and mythology of this world religion (fig. 8.1). Veloso recorded the song in 1985 for a televised miniseries based on *Tenda dos milagres* (*Tent of Miracles*), Jorge Amado's famous novel of mysticism and social protest published in 1969 (see Johnson, this volume). The key protagonist of Amado's novel, Pedro Arcanjo, is an organic intellectual and divination priest known as Ojúobá, or "eyes of the king" in the Yoruba language. He leads a struggle against racial discrimination in Salvador da Bahia during the 1920s at a time when elite intellectuals firmly believed in the innate inferiority of black people. Despite this history of racialized oppression in Brazil, as Veloso's song asserts, black people produced "miracles of faith" that provided refuge in the "extreme Occident"—a vast country on the margins of "the West" that received more enslaved Africans than any other nation of the Americas. In his quest for truth and justice, Ojúobá beckons the *orixás*—Xangô, Obatalá, Oxum, Iemanjá, and Iansã—for their guidance and power.

Since the early twentieth century, the spirit world of the *orixás* and their interventions in the everyday lives of mortals have frequently appeared in the sambas of Rio and Bahia, but in recent decades they have also been evoked in romantic ballads, rock anthems, rap manifestos, as well as the most experimental precincts of the Brazilian pop avant-garde. As J. Lorand Matory observes, "Brazilian audiences of popular music all know a smattering of African-inspired gods," even without any direct experience with Afro-Brazilian religions.[2]

The lion's share of popular music that evokes the *orixás* is from, or at least about, Salvador da Bahia, a city that occupies a special space in the Brazilian cultural imaginary. As the first colonial capital during Portuguese rule (until 1763), it has foundational status as the place where "Brazil was born," a slogan that still appears in advertising for tourism to Bahia. Renowned for its magnificent colonial-era structures, from ornately gilded churches to imposing maritime forts, the city has long been associated with baroque opulence connected to the sugar economy of the seventeenth and eighteenth centuries. This very same economy relied on massive slave labor imported from Central and West Africa, which made Bahia the principal point of debarcation for African captives sent to Brazil. Starting in the eighteenth century, economic and political power shifted south to Rio and São Paulo, leaving Bahia and the rest of the northeast marginalized from national affairs.

With the abolition of slavery in 1888, many former slaves migrated to Rio de Janeiro where they settled in overcrowded slums (*cortiços*) and shantytowns (*favelas*) near the city center. By end of the century, Bahians, especially Bahian women, or Baianas, had gained iconic status in Brazilian culture, especially in Rio, long before the lusitanized terms from Candomblé, such as *orixá* and *axé* (life-giving force), circulated widely in popular culture. The figure of the Baiana was by then a stock character in *teatro ligeiro*, the light comedies staged for popular audiences, alongside other familiar social types such as the Portuguese immigrant, the policeman, the *malandro* (street hustler), and the *coronel* (local boss; [Santanna 2009, 120]). The Baiana typically appeared as a coquettish street vendor who charmed the guys with song and dance. Aluísio Azevedo's naturalist novel *O Cortiço* (*The Slum*, 1890) introduced readers to Rita Baiana, a brash and beguiling *mulata* who seduces Jerônimo, a sober Portuguese immigrant and family man, eventually leading him astray.

In contrast to the figure of the sly seductress, Baianas also entered the cultural imaginary as matronly figures of cultural preservation through religion, music, and cuisine. The early history of modern samba is closely associated with a Bahian woman known as Tia Ciata (Aunt Ciata), who had migrated from Salvador to Rio de Janeiro in 1876 and settled near the Praça Onze, which samba musician and painter Heitor dos Prazeres dubbed "little Africa" for its large Afro-Brazilian population. A Candomblé priestess renowned for her culinary skills and hospitality, Tia Ciata opened her house to the local community for religious ceremonies as well as for parties where people ate, drank, and danced samba. Pioneers of the genre, such as Pixinguinha, Donga, Sinhô, and João da Baiana (the son of another renowned Bahian "aunt," Tia Perciliana) were habitués of these events. The first recorded samba, "Pelo telefone" ("By Telephone," 1917) is credited to Donga, but was composed collectively at one of Tia Ciata's legendary house gatherings. When the *escolas de samba* (neighborhood-based samba clubs with elaborate floats, dancers, and percussionists), began competing during Carnaval of Rio de Janeiro in the 1930s, they were required to have an *ala das baianas* (a "wing" within the parade composed of women dressed in traditional Bahian garb) to honor Tia Ciata and the other "aunts" who played key roles in cultural preservation and transmission.

In Salvador, Baianas entered the popular imagination as Candomblé devotees and as vendors of *acarajé*, fried bean cakes with origins in West Africa that had become a popular street food. The most renowned religious leaders in Candomblé are female priestesses, especially those affiliated with the Nagô (also referred to as Ketu or Quêto) and Jeje traditions, or "nations," with respective origins among Yoruba and Aja-Fon people of present-day Nigeria and Benin. One priestess, Mãe Aninha (Eugênia Anna Santos, 1869–1938), who led one of Bahia's most venerated temples, Ilê Axé Opô Afonjá, famously described Salvador as *Roma negra* (Black Rome), the Afro-diasporic counterpart to the epicenter of Catholicism. Mãe Aninha and other Candomblé dignitaries of the time played a key role convincing local and foreign anthropologists of the African "purity" of the Nagô-Jeje tradition in contrast with other nations, such as Candomblé Angola, which adopted the pantheon of Yoruba deities, but retained a liturgical language based on the Kikongo and Kimbundu languages of present-day Angola and Congo (Matory 2005, 156). In an effort to defend their religion from persecution, they forged strategic alliances with artists, intellectuals, and local politicians who increasingly embraced Candomblé as a cultural symbol of regional identity, or Baianidade. The forging of Baianidade was part of a broader tendency among artists and intellectuals to acknowledge African contributions to Brazilian culture, one of the central literary themes and visual motifs of Brazilian *modernismo* in the 1920s. In his watershed study, *Casa grande e senzala* (*The Masters and the Slaves*, 1933), Gilberto Freyre placed black people at the center of a story about the creation of a unique Portuguese-speaking and mix-raced civilization in the tropics. Although he was from Recife, Freyre bestowed special praise on Salvador as "the most harmoniously *mestiço*" of all Brazilian cities (Freyre 1990, 29; and see Pinho 2010, 184–85).

The long rule of Gétulio Vargas (1930–1945), an authoritarian populist who sought to foster a sense of national identity in a vast and ethnically diverse country, gave institutional heft to these artistic and scholarly trends. Vargas promoted the expansion of radio stations and transmission networks throughout the country, which coincided with a golden age in Brazilian popular music, mostly recorded or broadcast live from studios in Rio de Janeiro (McCann 2004, 50–51). A relatively small but significant portion of popular music was dedicated to the allure and seduction of Bahia. The version of the young flirty Baiana, a staple of popular theater, figured in many of these songs from the 1930s. Ary Barroso, the most acclaimed composer of popular music of the time, created several hit songs about love found and lost in the streets of Salvador. A native of Minas Gerais who settled in Rio, Barroso composed these songs from the perspective of a male visitor to Bahia who falls in love with a brown-skinned woman, or *morena*. In Barroso's gorgeous lament, "Na Baixa do Sapateiro" ("In the Shoemaker's Alley," 1938), a desperate man longs to return to Bahia), where he failed to win the heart of the "most elegant *morena* of Bahia."

In one of his best known songs, "No tabuleiro da baiana" ("On the Baiana's Tray") Barroso stages a dialogue between a Baiana street vendor and a would-be suitor. The original 1936 recording featured Carmen Miranda, who sang the part of the Baiana, a role for which she would find fame and fortune in the following years. The first stanza introduces listeners to some of the culinary delicacies on the Baiana's tray such as vatapá, carurú, mungunzá, and angu.[3] The second stanza reveals her spiritual powers with reference to a *canjerê*—a gathering to worship African deities:

| | |
|---|---|
| No coração da baiana tem | In the heart of the Baiana there is |
| Sedução, canjerê, ilusão, Candomblé | seduction, *canjerê*, illusion, Candomblé. |

The song implies a strong connection between Candomblé and the Baiana's allure for this man, who claims to "have even gone to a *canjerê*" to win her over. Songs from this period associated Candomblé with seductive power, sometimes referred to as *feitiço*, from which the English word "fetish" is derived. Bereft of the overtly sexual connotations that the word accrued in English, *feitiço* is closer to "sorcery" or even "charm." "Na Bahia" ("At Bahia," 1938), another samba first recorded by Carmen Miranda, adopts the perspective of the Baiana who beckons the distant visitor to return:

| | |
|---|---|
| A Bahia da magia, dos feitiços e da fé. | The Bahia of magic, charm, and faith |
| Bahia que tem tanta igreja | Bahia with so many churches |
| que tem tanto candomblé. | And so much Candomblé |
| Vem, vem, vem | Come, come, come |
| Vem em busca da Bahia | Come in search of Bahia |
| Cidade da tentação | City of temptation |
| Onde o meu feitiço impera | Where my charm reigns |
| Vem | Come |
| Se me trazes o teu coração | Bring me your heart |
| Vem | Come |
| Que a Bahia te espera | For Bahia awaits you |

The Baiana's allure is conflated with the mystical powers of Candomblé as well as the enticing qualities of Bahia, described as the "city of temptation."

Around the time that Ary Barroso was scoring hits with his paeans to the sultry magic of Bahia, Dorival Caymmi, an aspiring singer-songwriter from Salvador migrated to Rio de Janeiro to make his way in the music business. A handsome young man of African and Italian descent, Caymmi had a penchant for writing Carnaval *marchas* and sambas, which had earned him some modest recognition in Salvador. He soon found work at the Rádio Tupí, which employed some of the most popular singers of the day to perform live broadcasts with a full orchestra. His talent as a songwriter came to the attention of Wallace Downey, an American film director and producer who worked in Brazil for much of the 1930s. At the time, Downey was producing the film *Banana da terra*, starring Carmen Miranda, and needed a song to replace "Na Baixa do Sapateiro," because Ary Barroso was seeking a small fortune for the rights to use it. Caymmi offered "O que é que a baiana tem?" ("What Is It That the Baiana Has?") and even helped Miranda with her stylized Baiana costume, for which she would become famous in the years to come.

"O que é que a baiana tem" uses a simple call and response pattern typical of the traditional sambas of Bahia to ask and answer a series of questions about the "typical" Baiana, her unique sartorial style, and her way of moving. Unlike Barroso's hit songs about Bahia, Caymmi's songs make no reference to male longing or appeals to supernatural forces for success in love. Caymmi's Baiana is not a coquettish street vendor, but rather a stately woman of elegance and prestige described in almost ethnographic detail:

| | |
|---|---|
| O que é que a baiana tem? | What does the Baiana have? |
| Tem torso de seda tem | She has a silk turban, yes |
| Tem brinco de ouro tem | She has golden earrings, yes |
| Corrente de ouro tem | A gold chain, yes |
| Tem pano da costa tem | She has a woven shawl, yes |
| Tem bata rendada tem | She has a lace blouse, yes |
| Pulseira de ouro tem | A gold bracelet, yes |
| E tem saia engomada tem | And she has a starched skirt, yes |
| Tem sandália enfeitada tem | She has adorned sandals yes, |
| E tem graça como ninguém! | And has the most grace of them all! |

Some listeners, especially in Bahia, would have recognized the lyrics as a description of a Candomblé priestess in her *pano da costa*, a distinctive woven shawl originally from the coast of West Africa, a white lace blouse, starched skirt, and ornate jewelry. The final stanza makes reference to a *balangandãs*, a silver assemblage strung with miniature amulets worn by Candomblé devotees to ward off evil spirits. An instant hit, the song would become Miranda's calling card as she embarked in 1939 on an extraordinarily successful career on Broadway and eventually in Hollywood, where she would make a string of musical comedies in which she reprised and further embellished her Baiana shtick. For Dorival Caymmi, "O que é que a baiana tem" was his big break into the upper echelons of Brazilian popular music.

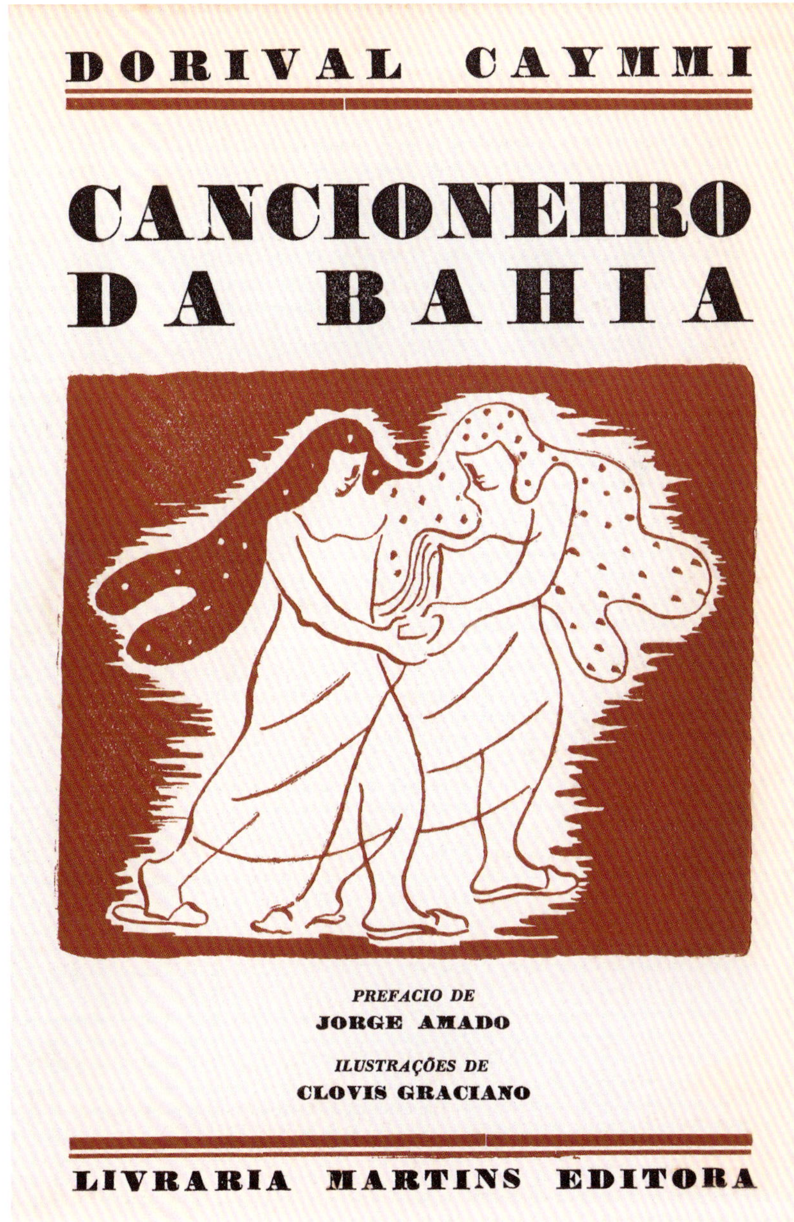


**8.2**
Dorival Caymmi (b. 1914, Salvador, Bahia, Brazil, d. 2008)
*Cancioneiro da Bahia* (Bahia Songbook; São Paulo: Livraria Martins Editora, 1947)
Ink on paper
24 x 13 cm
PRIVATE COLLECTION

In the following decades, Caymmi would consolidate his status as one of the greatest Brazilian singer-songwriters of the twentieth century, such that we may speak of a distinctly Caymmian tradition. He is best known for his songs about Bahia, which evoke images of an eternal city of matronly *baianas de acarajé*, beautiful *morenas*, and valiant capoeira fighters (fig. 8.2). Antonio Risério has noted that Caymmi's songs recall the bucolic Bahia of his youth at a time when metropolises of the south were undergoing rapid urbanization and industrialization. His utopian evocation of Bahia as a timeless idyll was central to the appeal of his songs among urban audiences exposed to social change and conflict (Risério 1993, 108). Some of his most famous songs are devoted to fishermen, the loved ones they leave behind when they set out to sail, their harrowing adventures, and their devotion to Iemanjá, the maternal *orixá* of the sea. Already in 1939, he recorded "Promessa de Pescador" ("Promise of a Fisherman") about an old fisherman who calls on Iemanjá to protect his son out on the high seas. Opening with the ritual invocation "a alodé Iemanjá odoiá," the fisherman promises her a gift in exchange:

| | |
|---|---|
| Quando chegar o seu dia | When his day arrives |
| Pescador velho promete | Old fisherman promises |
| Pescador vai lhe levar | Fisherman will bring to her |
| Um presente bem bonito | A very nice present |
| Para dona Iemanjá | For miss Iemanjá |
| Filho seu é quem carrega | His son will carry it |
| Desde terra até o mar | From land out to sea. |

Caymmi belonged to a generation of artists and intellectuals, including Bahian natives and transplants, who were devoted to documenting Afro-Bahian culture, including street festivals, religious processions, and Candomblé ceremonies, as well as scenes from everyday life on the streets, docks, and beaches of Salvador. The watercolors, oil paintings, and sculptures of Carybé, an Argentine who settled in Salvador in 1950, provide an obvious companion to Caymmi's oeuvre, as do the ethnographic images of Pierre Verger, the French photographer, historian, and ethnographer who also made the city his home. Caymmi's sambas and *toadas* (a kind of lament) also resonate with the novels of Jorge Amado (see Johnson, this volume), who achieved international fame with his vivid evocation of the sacred and profane in Bahia. Unlike Amado, however, Caymmi rarely made reference to social injustice or racial inequality in his songs. Amado's novels that are set in Salvador portray the hardscrabble streets and the fetid bayside docks of the lower city, populated by stevedores, street vendors, hustlers, prostitutes, and street urchins in revolt against a socially stratified society and a brutal police force assigned to maintain order. Caymmi's Bahia looks out over the Atlantic Ocean; his characters may struggle to eke out a living from the sea, but they don't understand themselves to be oppressed (Risério 1993, 51). Life is hard, but Iemanjá will protect and provide.

With his use of complex harmonies, understated vocals, and minimalist lyrics about love, beauty, and ludic pleasure in everyday life, Dorival Caymmi would have a profound impact on a new generation of musicians who proposed a new approach to samba, which they called bossa nova (Caymmi 2001, 374–75). With a series of recordings in the late 1950s, João Gilberto, a native of Juazeiro, Bahia, joined composer-pianist Antonio Carlos Jobim and poet Vinícius de Moraes in defining this new style. Like Caymmi's oeuvre, the first wave of bossa nova was, as Lorenzo Mammí has noted, a "utopian project" that held out the "promise of happiness" during a period of national optimism (Mammí 1992, 63). In 1958, when João Gilberto launched the movement, Brazil had a democratically elected government that had embarked on an ambitious plan for national development and modernization, epitomized by the construction of Brasília, the futuristic planned capital built in the hinterland.

By the early sixties, however, some of the musicians affiliated with bossa nova believed that artists should engage in social critique, especially in unevenly developed societies such as Brazil. In this context, singer-songwriters asserted the redemptive power of the *orixás* to right the wrongs here on earth. For example, the song "Maria Moita" (1963), composed by Carlos Lyra and Vinícius de Moraes, describes a poor Bahian woman who is under the thumb of her abusive husband, pointing to widespread social injustice in which lazy bosses lord over their downtrodden workers. While the motherly Iemanjá is the most referenced *orixá* in Caymmi's songs, this song speaks of visiting a Candomblé priest, or *babalorixá,* to make an appeal to Xangô, the male *orixá* of thunder and fire who is revered as a warrior for justice.

| | |
|---|---|
| Vou pedir ao meu babalorixá | I'm going to ask my *babalorixá* |
| Pra fazer uma oração pra Xangô | To make an oration to Xangô |
| Pra pôr pra trabalhar | To put to work |
| Gente que nunca trabalhou | People who have never worked |

In its treatment of the *orixás*, "Maria Moita" strayed from the Caymmian tradition. It exemplified a trend toward social critique as middle-class, university-educated artists and intellectuals put their faith in the political power of art. Inspired by the Cuban Revolution, an emergent generation of musicians, playwrights, visual artists, poets, and critics believed that they had a key role to play in leading their country toward a social revolution. These artists often took aim at the gross inequalities and injustices found in the rural northeast, the poorest region of the country and one that was still dominated by the *latifundio* system, which confined land ownership and political power to a few families. Other compositions by Vinícius de Moraes from this period were more aligned with the Caymmian tradition. In 1966 he collaborated with guitar virtuoso Baden Powell on *Os Afro-Sambas*, a pioneering effort to combine samba and bossa nova with percussive elements from Candomblé. Nearly all of the songs were dedicated to the mythology of the *orixás* and their unique attributes and personalities.

**8.3**
Lita Almeida Cerqueira (b. 1952, Salvador, Bahia, Brazil)
*Doces Bárbaros* (Sweet Barbarians), 1978
Photograph
COURTESY LITA ALMEIDA CERQUEIRA

From left to right are members of the group Doces Bárbaros (Sweet Barbarians): Gilberto Gil, Maria Bethânia, Gal Costa, and Caetano Veloso.

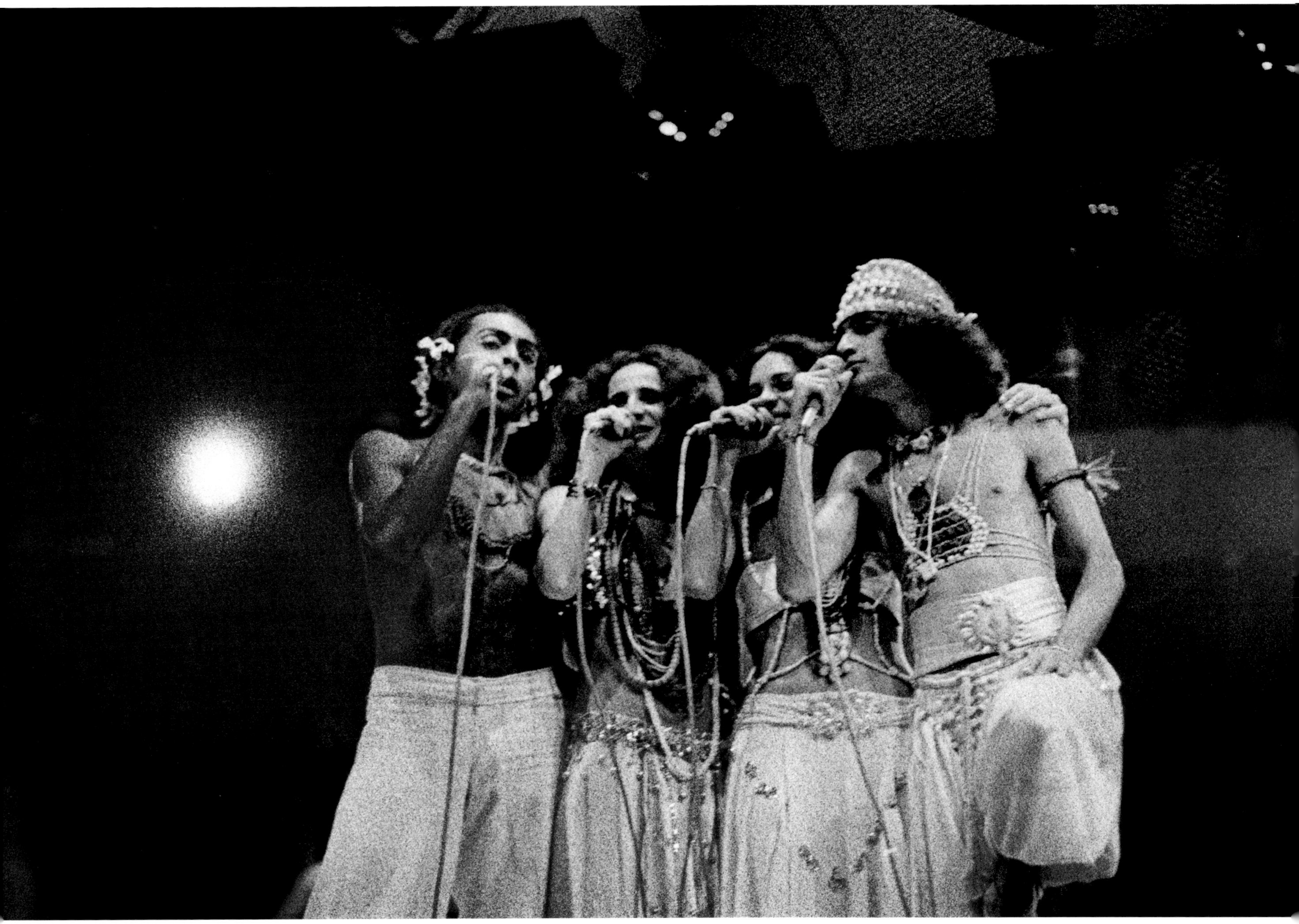

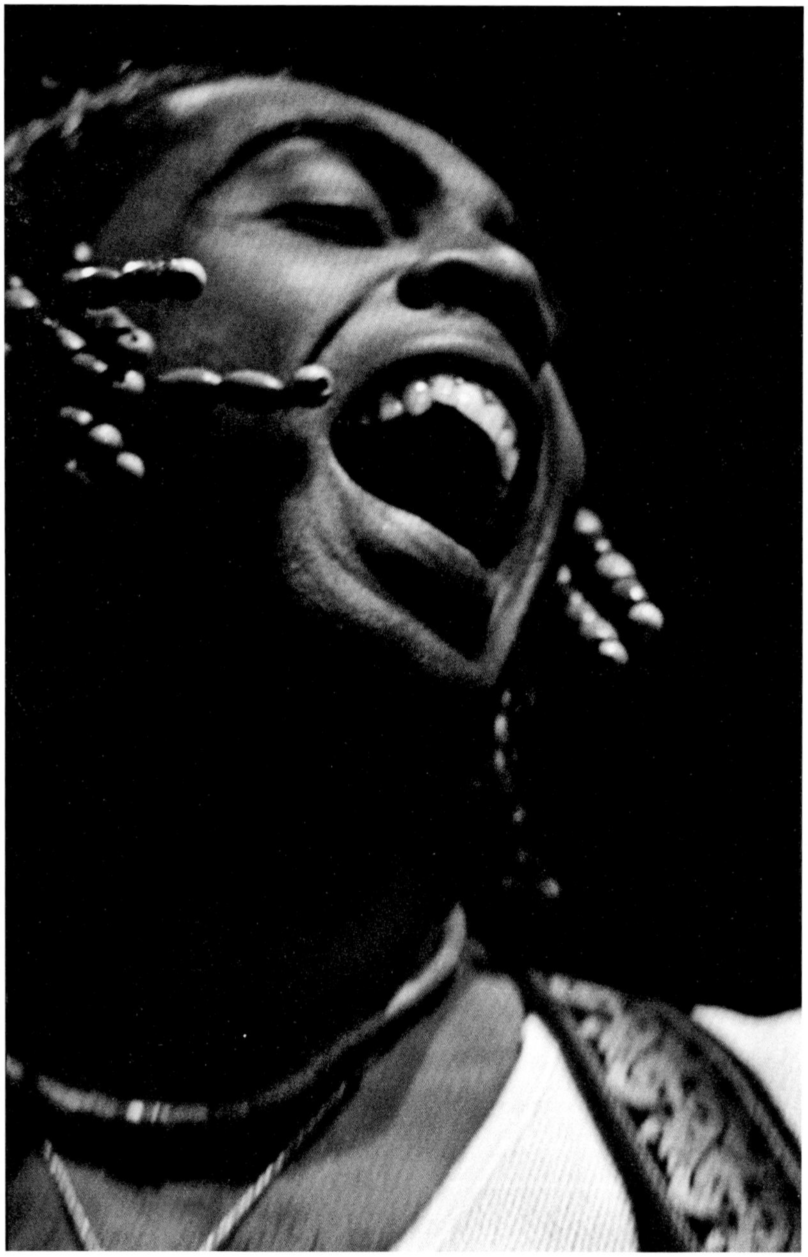

**8.4**
Lita Almeida Cerqueira (b. 1952, Salvador, Bahia, Brazil)
*Realce* (Highlight), 1980
Photograph
COURTESY LITA ALMEIDA CERQUEIRA

Gilberto Gil performs in Morro da Urca, Rio de Janeiro.

In 1964, a US-backed military coup ushered in twenty years of military rule, effectively curtailing left-wing political and social movements, but it also inspired a vibrant protest culture with manifestations in all artistic fields. An emerging cohort of Bahian musicians—Caetano Veloso, Gilberto Gil, Tom Zé, Gal Costa, and Maria Bethânia—came of age around the time of the military coup. Known as the *grupo baiano*, they were steeped in the cultural traditions of Bahia, but also deeply inspired by bossa nova, a sign of cosmopolitan modernity. They began their careers at time when there was considerable tension between homegrown rockers, who used electric instruments, and those who defended Brazilian popular music based on samba and a variety of "folk" genres, especially from the northeast. To varying degrees, they were invested in popular music as a vehicle for social protest and critique. One of Gil's earliest recordings, "Roda," for example, darkly warned a powerful landowner to heed his warning: "Hey mister, be careful/ with your exploitation/ or else I'll give you as a present/ a hole in the ground." At the same time, however, Gil composed "Eu vim da Bahia" ("I Came from Bahia"), a Caymmian tribute to Salvador, which acknowledges poverty, but affirms that the *orixás* will provide.

| | |
|---|---|
| Onde a gente não tem pra comer | Where we don't have enough to eat |
| Mas de fome não morre porque | But we don't die of hunger |
| Na Bahia tem Mãe Iemanjá | Because in Bahia there is Mother Iemanjá |
| De outro lado o Senhor do Bonfim | And our Lord of Bonfim on the other side |

Mother Iemanjá reigns over the Atlantic coast, while the Bay of All Saints is protected by the Lord of Bonfim (Jesus Christ in Ascension), who is identified with Oxalá, the father of all *orixás*. Like so many other Bahians who sought to pursue careers in popular music, the *grupo baiano* migrated south to Rio and São Paulo, where they found opportunities in musical theater, TV showcases, and a lively televised festival scene. Veloso and Gil reached a wide audience at the 1967 Festival of Brazilian Popular music, where they won over audiences with compositions based on traditional Brazilian genres but performed with electric instruments. As much as they loved the traditional musical culture of Bahia, as well as the new innovations of bossa nova, they also embraced post–British Invasion trends in international rock.

In 1968, they launched a movement, known as Tropicália, to revolutionize Brazilian popular music in dialogue with international pop. One of their objectives was to project a more urban and cosmopolitan view of Bahia. Whereas most popular music about Bahia since the 1930s represented black culture as timeless folklore, tropicalist songs tended to situate Afro-Bahian culture in contemporary urban life. For example, the song "Batmacumba" (a track written by Veloso and Gil for the concept album *Tropicália, ou panis et circencis* (*Tropicália, or Bread and circuses*, 1968) is structured as a verbal montage based on a simple phrase ("batmacumbaiêiê batmacumbaobá") containing discrete semantic fragments pertaining to popular culture (the comic hero Batman and *iê-iê-iê*, a popular term for sixties-era Brazilian rock inspired by the refrain of the Beatles' hit "She Loves You") and Afro-Brazilian religion (*macumba*, an antiquated designation for Afro-Brazilian religion in Rio de Janeiro, and Obá, a Yoruba honorific title as well as the name of a female *orixá*). "Batmacumba" also strayed from the Caymmian tradition, but not in the same way as "Maria Moita" with the latter's suggestion that the *orixás* intervened on behalf of social justice. Instead, "Batmacumba" represented Afro-Brazilian religion as a facet of contemporary culture in urban Brazil, not a premodern vestige of an African past (Dunn 2001, 105).

The tropicalists drew criticism from left-wing nationalists, who associated rock and electric guitars with US cultural imperialism, but also provoked suspicions among regime agents, who were troubled by their irreverent live performances and by their identification with the international youth counterculture. Gil and Veloso were arrested in late December 1968, weeks after hardline forces within the military government had assumed power, and were exiled to London. They returned in 1972 during the height of the Brazilian counterculture. Thousands of young Brazilians flocked to Salvador, where they camped on the beach, reveled in the local culture, and went searching for alternative spiritual experiences in Candomblé temples. As icons of the Brazilian counterculture, the tropicalists took a leading role in celebrating and decoding Candomblé for a national audience. They cultivated a relationship with the most famous Candomblé priestess of the twentieth century, Mãe Menininha (Maria Escolástica da Conceição Nazaré Assunção), who had led one of Bahia's most venerated temples since 1922. To celebrate her fifty years as priestess, Dorival Caymmi composed "Oração de Mãe Menininha," which was recorded by Gal Costa and Maria Bethânia. Caymmi's homage to "this daughter of Oxum" (that is, a devotee of Oxum, the *orixá* of fresh water) enhanced Menininha's fame, especially among Brazilian youth with no prior connection to the religion (Nóbrega and Echeverria 2006, 158). In interviews, they name dropped the *orixás* and proudly wore the colored bead necklaces associated with their personal deities. Bethânia is famously a daughter of Iansã, the goddess of lightning and tempests, while Gal is devoted to Omolú, the deity of disease and rebirth. Veloso is the son of Oxóssi, the hunter god, while Gil belongs to Logunedé, the child of Oxóssi and Oxum who possesses both masculine and feminie traits.

In 1976, the Bahian group (Maria Bethânia, Gal Costa, Gilberto Gil, and Caetano Veloso) reunited as the Doces Bárbaros (Sweet Barbarians) for a national tour (figs. 8.3, 8.4), which resulted in a double live album and a feature-length documentary by Jom Tob Azulay (Azulay 2007). The Doces Bárbaros project focused heavily on Candomblé and the mythology of the *orixás*. Each of the four performers wore a specially designed outfit with the colors and symbols of specific *orixás*. The concert featured several songs about the *orixás*, including "São João/Xangô Menino," a celebration of religious syncretism that casts Xangô, the deity of thunder and fire, as the divine eminence that presides over the annual winter festivals for Saint John the Baptist throughout Brazil's northeast, especially in the rural areas. "As Ayabás," a four-part song composed by Veloso in homage to female *orixás* (Iansã, Obá, Euá, and Oxum), made use of the 12/8 tempo polyrhythms used to call the *orixás*. All four performers took turns singing praise songs in Portuguese backed by only by the *atabaques* (drums) used in Candomblé festivals. During her performance Bethânia simulated the act of spirit possession, thrusting her shoulders to the rear and throwing her head back while shouting a salutation to Iansã.

The theme song of the show, "Os mais doces bárbaros" ("The Sweetest Barbarians"), likened their tour to an invasion of "sweet barbarians" who brought a message of joy, expressed in terms of both countercultural revelry and the spiritual power of Candomblé. They arrived "with love in their hearts," bearing "the sword of Ogum, the blessing of Olorum, and the lightening flash of Iansã." In a salvo of diverse references, the refrain combines hippie lingo with references to Afro-Bahian culture, space travel, nature, and Carnaval processions:

| | |
|---|---|
| alto astral, altas transas, lindas canções | good vibes, groovy plans, lovely songs |
| afoxés, astronaves, aves, cordões | *afoxés*, spaceships, birds, parades |

The Doces Bárbaros represented a confluence of symbols and discourses that associated Candomblé with Brazilian youth counterculture (Dunn 2016, 142–43). Around this time, Gilberto Gil helped to revitalize the Filhos de Gandhy, a traditional percussion-based group known as an *afoxé*, which had been founded in 1949 as an homage to Mahatma Gandhi.[4] Composed entirely of men, mostly practitioners of Candomblé, the Filhos de Gandhy sing praise songs to the *orixás* during Carnaval parades.

The Doces Bárbaros project coincided with an emergent movement in Bahia that sought to reaffirm cultural connections and political commitments to Africa and the African diaspora. Inspired by African American Black Power and national liberation movements in Africa, young blacks began to question the official discourse of the regime, which held that Brazil was a "racial democracy," a concept defended by Gilberto Freyre and other conservative intellectuals. In 1974, a group of friends from the predominantly black, working-class neighborhood of Liberdade founded a Carnaval group to promote black pride and denounce racism in Bahian society. Led by Antônio dos Santos, known as Vovô ("grandpa"), the group called itself Ilê Aiyê, a Yoruba term meaning "house of life" or "house of this world" (fig. 8.5). Ilê Aiyê would represent a secular counterpart to Candomblé temples, also known as *ilês*, which commune with the spirit world, or Orun. Vovô's mother, Mãe Hilda, was the head priestess of the Candomblé temple Ilê Axé Jitolú and provided orientation to the group as it developed an Afrocentric approach to cultural expression (Tosta 2010, 181). Ilê Aiyê was the first *bloco afro*, a term that distinguished the group from other Carnaval organizations, such as the *blocos de trio*, which paraded with large, amplified trucks, known as *trios elétricos*. Ilê Aiyê provided a space for young Afro-Bahians who were largely excluded from the middle-class *blocos de trio*. Its mission was to celebrate black history, praise famous black leaders, and disseminate information about Africa and the African diaspora through music and dance. The group's musical directors developed a unique fusion of *samba* and *ijexá* (a rhythm used in Candomblé festivals). Ilê Aiyê's signature song, "Que bloco é esse?," announced the groups intent:

| | |
|---|---|
| Que bloco é esse | What group is this? |
| Eu quero saber | I want to know |
| É o mundo negro | It's the black world |
| Que viemos mostrar para você | That we've come to show you |

In 1977, Gilberto Gil recorded a version of the song for *Refavela*, an album that marked his own turn toward African and diasporic concerns, following his participation in FESTAC '77, the Second World Black and African Festival of Arts and Culture, in Nigeria. Throughout the 1980s, Ilê Aiyê's directors would choose specific African countries to celebrate during Carnaval, such as Angola, Ghana, Nigeria, and Senegal, as well as nations that had little historic connection to Bahia, such as Zimbabwe and Rwanda. Starting in the early 1990s, the group took up themes connected to black history in Brazil such as Palmares (a community of fugitive slaves in the seventeenth century; see introduction, fig. 25), the Malê Slave Revolt of 1835, and the role of Candomblé in black resistance. In 1993, Ilê Aiyê celebrated the achievements and struggles of African Americans with references to Martin Luther King, Malcolm X, and Fannie Lou Hamer. The following year, Ilê Aiyê's theme was "Uma nação africana chamada Bahia" (An African Nation called Bahia), which proclaimed Bahia's diasporic nationhood reminiscent of the various transatlantic "nations" (Nagô, Jeje, Angola) of Candomblé.

Ilê Aiyê paved the way for new *blocos afro* that emerged in the late 1970s and early 1980s, such as Olodum, Muzenza, Malê Debalê, and Araketu, which developed specific identities within the movement. Based in the historic center Pelourinho, Olodum took its name from Olodumaré, the supreme deity of Candomblé, known as the "God of Gods." Its musical director, known as Neguinho do Samba, created a new rhythm, samba-reggae, which was soon adopted by other *blocos* and pop bands in the city in the 1980s (fig. 8.6). By that time, roots reggae from Jamaica had gained a mass audience, especially among the city's black youth, some of whom embraced the Rastafarian religion. Bob Marley visited Rio de Janeiro in 1980, the same year that Jimmy Cliff joined Gilberto Gil for a highly successful tour of Brazil. The *bloco afro* Muzenza brought together local rastas, known as the "warriors of Jamaica," who paraded during Carnaval waiving Jamaican flags and large photos of Bob Marley. Of all these groups, Araketu was most devoted to the iconography and mythology of Candomblé. Its logo is the *ofá* (a bow and arrow), which is the symbol of Oxóssi, the *orixá* of hunting. One of their most popular songs, "Elegibô," celebrated Ejigbo, a Yoruba town in Nigeria, as well as Ketu (Kétou), a Yoruba town in the Republic of Benin that provided the namesake for the group, which means "the people of Ketu."

| | |
|---|---|
| Cidade reluzente | Shining city |
| Cidade florescente | Flourishing city |
| Ejibô cidade encantada | Ejigbo enchanted city |
| Elegibô sua majestade real | Elejigbô its royal monarch |
| Araketu ritual do candomblé | Araketu Candomblé ritual |
| Exalta as cidades de Ketu e Sabé | Exalts the cities of Ketu and Sabé |

"Elegibô" is typical of *bloco afro* songs from the 1980s in connecting celebratory portrayals of African places and ethnicities to the cultural traditions of Bahia, especially Candomblé. These songs popularized the historical ethnographies dedicated to the affinities and continuities that linked coastal West Africa to Bahia.

In the mid-1980s, local singers and bands in Salvador began to appropriate the songs and rhythms of the *blocos afro* to make radio-friendly pop songs. While the *blocos afro* recorded and performed as percussion troupes, these bands featured a full complement of electric instruments in order to reach a wider audience. The singer Margareth Menezes scored a local hit with an electric version of Araketu's "Elegibô," which later brought her international attention when David Byrne, formerly of the Talking Heads, invited her to join his North American tour for the album *Rei Momo* (1989). Banda Reflexus achieved success with their version of Olodum's "Madagascar" as well as Ilê Aiyê's "Canto para o Senegal" ("Song for Senegal"), both of which were popular Carnaval theme songs. These recordings were early examples of what would come to be known as *Axé* Music, a term that combines the Yoruba term for life-giving force with the English noun, which suggested its insertion into the emergent US and European markets for "world music." *Axé* Music does not designate a specific genre or style, but rather the encounter between the *trios elétricos* and the *blocos afro* starting in the mid-1980s (Guerreiro 2000, 133).

In one of the great odes to Salvador, the singer-songwriter known as Gerônimo composed (with Vevê Calazans) the anthem "É d'Oxum" (1985), which proclaimed that the city belonged to the *orixá* deity of fresh water and love. Set to a lilting *ijexá* rhythm, Gerônimo's song portrayed Salvador as a socially integrated, racially harmonious city enveloped in the loving embrace of Oxum:

| | |
|---|---|
| Seja tenente ou filho de pescador | Whether you're a lieutenant or fisherman's son |
| Ou importante desembargador | Or an important judge |
| Se der presente é tudo uma coisa só | If you offer a gift it's all the same |
| A força que mora n'água | The force that lives in the water |
| Não faz distinção de cor | Makes no distinctions based on color |
| E toda a cidade é d'Oxum | And the whole city belongs to Oxum |

As a song in the Caymmian tradition, "É d'Oxum" evokes the *orixás* as a natural force of social harmony that unites people, despite differences of class and color. In other songs, however, Gerônimo confronted the racial and social tensions in the city, as in "Eu sou negão," ("I'm a Big Black Guy"), his homage to the *blocos afro*, which had to struggle for physical and sonic space during Carnaval. The song narrates a tense encounter between a flashy and loud *trio elétrico* that interrupts a *bloco afro* parade during Carnaval. When the lead singer of the *trio elétrico* tries to get the *bloco afro* to accompany his music, the director of the *bloco*, affirming his identity as a *negão*, tells him to move on and allow his group to continue with their own percussion-based sound (Guerreiro 2000, 22).

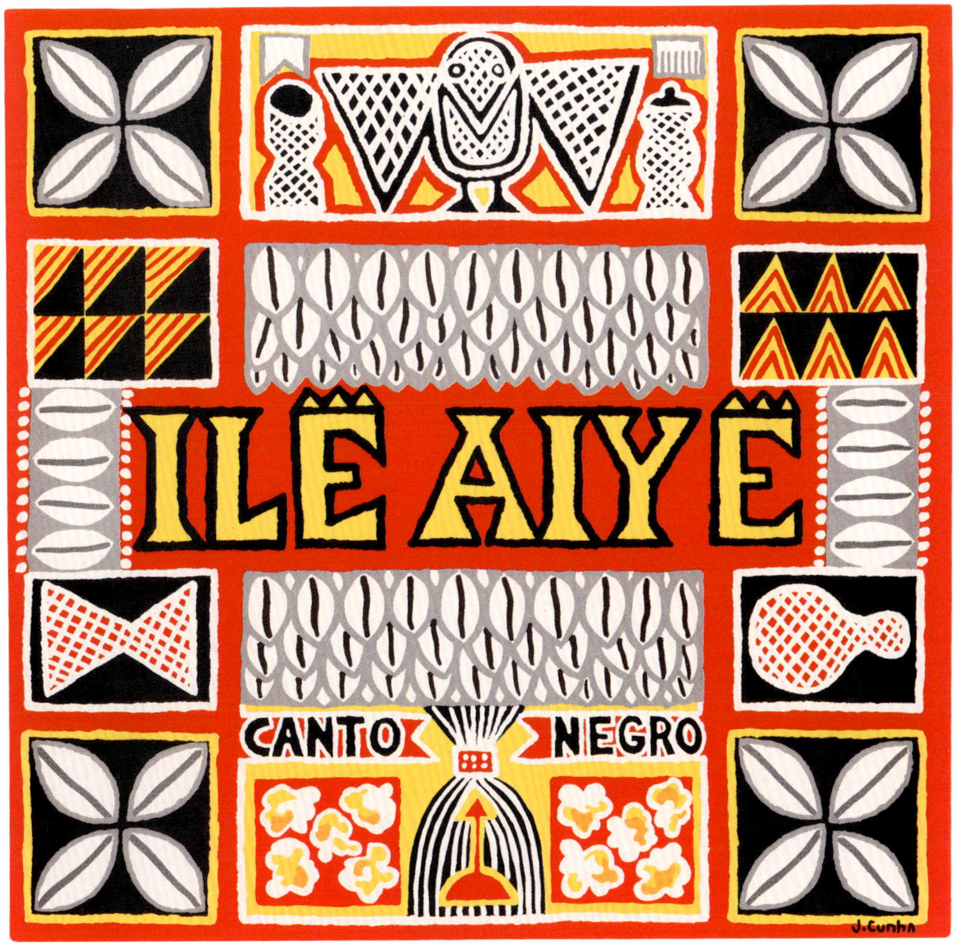


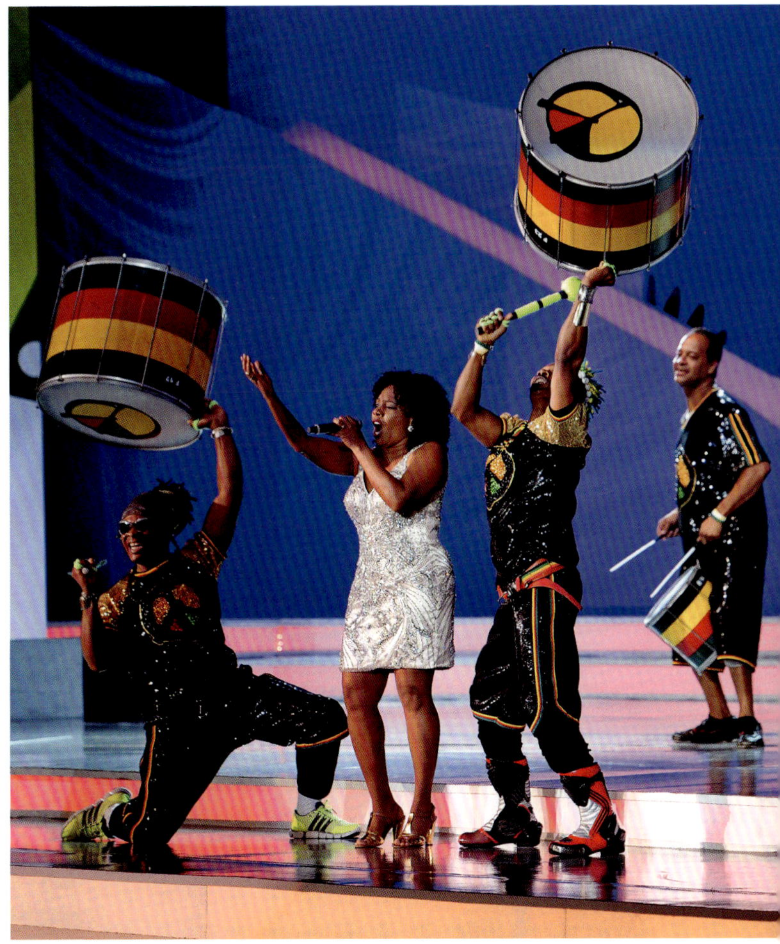

**8.5**
J. Cunha (José Antônio Cunha, b. 1948, Salvador, Bahia, Brazil)
Ilê Aiyê album cover, 1984
Ink on paper
COURTESY J. CUNHA
PHOTOGRAPH BY ANDREW KEMP

**8.6**
Margareth Menezes and Olodum perform at the Final Draw for the 2014 FIFA World Cup, Bahia, 2013. PHOTOGRAPH BY SHAUN GOTTERILL. GETTY IMAGES.

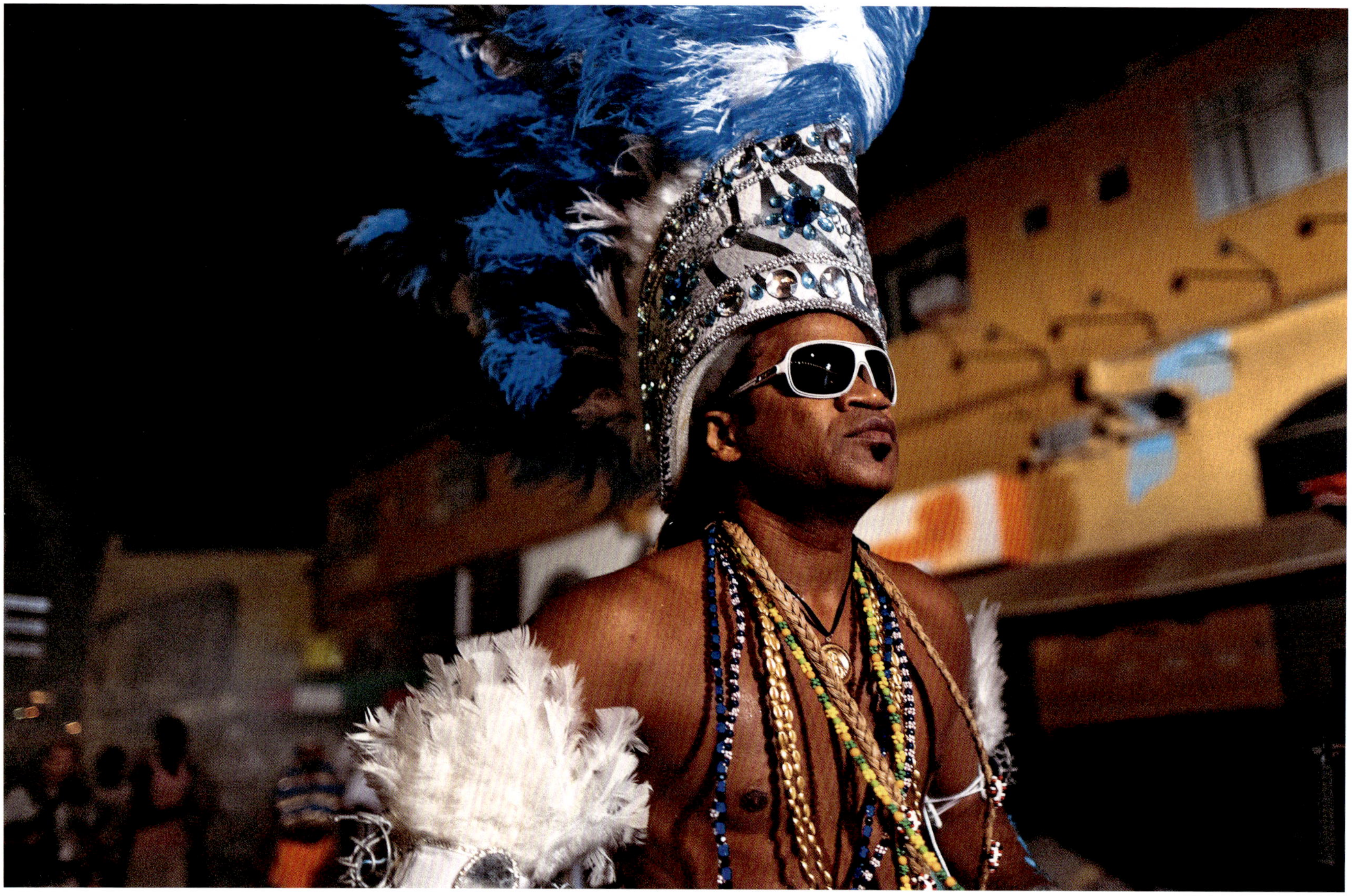

**8.7**
Carlinhos Brown dances at the Iemanjá festival, Bahia, 2012.
PHOTOGRAPH BY JAN SOCHOR. GETTY IMAGES.

By the early 1990s, the *blocos afro* had begun to attract local, national, and international media attention. Olodum's percussion troupe was featured on recordings by Paul Simon, Michael Jackson, Wayne Shorter, and the heavy metal band Sepultura. Ilê Aiyê collaborated with pop star Daniela Mercury on her chart-topping album *O Canto da Cidade*, which brought *Axé* Music into the mainstream of Brazilian pop. Araketu effectively ceased to be a *bloco afro*, drastically reduced its drum ensemble, and morphed into an *axé* band playing a wide range of styles with a full complement of electric instruments. While many of the early classics of *axé* used the samba-reggae rhythm associated with Olodum, Araketu also incorporated elements of northeastern genres such as *frevo*, *forró*, and *lambada*, Caribbean genres such as reggae and calypso, as well as Bahian pop samba known as *pagode*. *Axé* Music also benefitted from the development of a local recording industry, notably Wesley Rangel's WR Studios, which allowed local artists to pursue successful careers in Bahia. New percussion-based groups emerged, most notably among women whose role in *blocos afro* had been largely singing and dancing. In 1994, Neguinho do Samba founded the Banda Didá with proceeds from his collaboration with Paul Simon on the album *Rhythm of the Saints* (1990). The all-female Banda Didá opened the way for more young women to play percussion, a domain long dominated by men.

Carlinhos Brown is emblematic of the *axé* generation (fig. 8.7). He grew up in Candeal Pequeno, which he refers to as a "ghetto" to suggest commonalities with other marginalized urban communities. Brown achieved renown in the 1980s before founding Timbalada, a massively successful Carnaval group that uses light, high-pitched hand drums called *timbaus*. Brown embraced the musical aesthetics of Africa and the diaspora, but dispensed with the black politics of the *blocos afro*. Like the *blocos afro*, he parlayed financial and cultural capital into community projects, such as the Pracatum music school and the Candyall Ghetto Square, a state-of-the-art recording studio in the heart of Candeal Pequeno. A prolific composer, Brown's songs address a wide variety of themes, including quotidian life in Candeal. His song, "Dandalunda" pays homage to Mãe Maiamba, the priestess of the Terreiro de Mutuiçara, a Candomblé temple in Candeal Pequeno that cultivates both Ketu and Angola traditions (Santanna 2009, 323).

| | |
|---|---|
| Bem pertinho da entrada do gueto | Close to the ghetto where you enter |
| Um terreiro de Angola e Ketu | An Angola and Ketu temple |
| Mãe Maiamba que comanda o centro | Mãe Maiamba commands the center |
| Dona Oxum dançando Oxóssi no tempo | Miss Oxum dancing Oxóssi outside |

Mãe Maiamba is a daughter of Oxum in the Ketu tradition, which corresponds to Dandalunda in the Angola tradition. Brown adopted the refrain "Dandalunda maiambanda coquê," which the priestess and her community sing in praise of Oxum. Recorded and performed by Margareth Menezes, "Dandalunda" was the most popular song of the 2001 Carnaval season and the hit song of her album *Afropopbrasileiro*. Neither a Caymmian ode nor a song of social protest, "Dandalunda" celebrates cultural hybridity in which African gods of different traditions come together and where this moment may be commemorated in the mass euphoria of Carnaval.

In the last decade, a vibrant hip-hop scene has developed in Salvador, especially among predominantly black working-class youth. While the epicenter of Brazilian hip-hop is São Paulo, where rap, graffiti, and breakdance form part of community-based social movements, the genre has spread throughout the country. The Bahian hip-hop group, Opanijé, incorporates Candomblé rhythms, chants, and invocations in songs about the marginalized communities of Salvador's periphery. The group's name references the dance and rhythm associated with the *orixá* Omolú (also known as Obaluayê), a deity associated with sickness, death, and rebirth through the natural life cycle. The group frequently invokes the *orixás* as agents of resistance against dominant forces in society that have marginalized blacks and disparaged their cultural traditions. The affirmation of Candomblé as a cornerstone of Afro-Brazilian social organization has become more urgent in the last decade with the rise of verbal and physical attacks on practitioners of Candomblé by evangelical Protestants, who associate the religion with devil worship. Their song, "Encruzilhada" ("Crossroads"), references Exú, the messenger *orixá* who is responsible for communication, transformation, and protection. Exú, the lord of the crossroads, is present whenever a decision must be made.

| | |
|---|---|
| Quem tem fé no axé não dá ré, segue adiante | Those who have faith in *axé* go forward, not in reverse |
| Extrai o êxtase extremo, exuberante | Extracting extreme exuberant ecstasy |
| Exu nasceu no Jitolú, não teme nada | Exú was born in Jitolú, fears nothing[5] |
| Mora na comunidade, a encruzilhada é sua morada | He lives in our community, the cross-roads is his home |

In this song, Exú is invoked as a guide to "those who have faith in *axé*" so that they may move through life with "exuberant ecstasy" and as a guardian to the communities coping with poverty and violence. Opanijé's song reminds us that people identify with and derive strength from the *orixás*, who confront adversity with unique powers and personalities.

For nearly a century popular music has been the primary conduit through which aspects of Candomblé, notably its celebrated gods, the *orixás*, have been transmitted to the general public, reaching people who have little or no personal connection to the religion. These songs have also made Bahia, especially its capital, Salvador, arguably the most mythologized regional culture in the country. Early references to Bahia in popular music typically focused on the beauty and charm of the Baianas, imagined to derive their seductive power from sorcery, or *feitiço*. The most famous of these songs were composed by white, middle-class composers from the center-south, such as Ary Barroso. Bahian native Dorival Caymmi further innovated this tradition by introducing a measure of ethnographic detail in songs about the *orixás*, their unique domains and powers, and their interventions in the everyday lives of their devotees. Songs in the Caymmian tradition portayed Bahia as a timeless place of hardship, joy, and devotion, largely devoid of social conflict and change. Since the 1960s, the *orixás* have appeared in Brazilian popular music as avengers of social justice, avatars of modernity, and divine fixers who intervene on behalf of mortals. With the rise of the *blocos afro, Axé* Music, and local strains of hip-hop, Afro-Bahian artists have exalted the *orixás* as icons of black dignity, identity, and empowerment. In popular music, the *orixás* have been invoked in ongoing national and regional conversations about the blackness of Brazil and (to recall Ilê Aiyê's 1994 Carnaval theme) an "African nation called Bahia."

# 9 Afro-Revels Notes on the Black Presence in Salvador da Bahia's Carnaval

**Paulo Miguez**

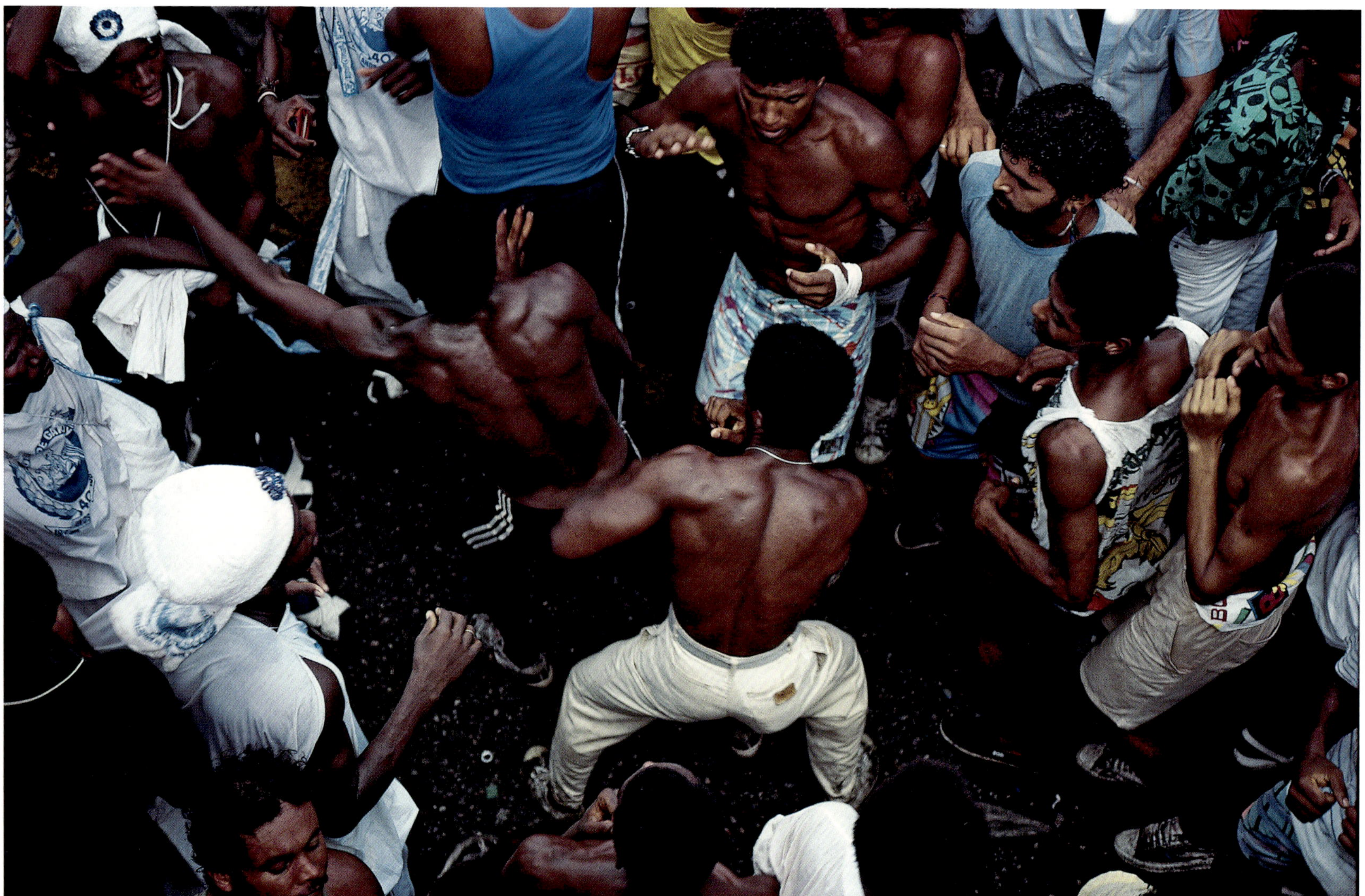

CARNAVAL FESTIVITIES IN THE AMERICAS are rooted in Baroque Iberian festive traditions. Introduced to Brazil in the form of the Portuguese Shrovetide festival known as Entrudo, they came to Hispanic America as Antruejo, the name given to the three days devoted to King Momo, a period referred to as Carnestolendas, in Spain. In both parts of the so-called New World, whether Portuguese or Spanish speaking, African cultures have played a highly significant role in the consolidation and development of Carnaval. In Brazil, they are key elements in the development of the important and famous Carnavals of Bahia, Rio de Janeiro, Recife, and Olinda, as well as the revels held in countless towns and smaller cities in that country. In Latin America and the Caribbean, the presence of African cultural roots in the shaping and development of Carnaval festivities is equally significant as can be seen in the Carnavals of Barranquilla and Pasto, in Colombia; Trinidad and Tobago; Santo Domingo in Cuba; Uruguay; and New Orleans in the United States.

In Bahia, the cultural repertoire is especially linked to Africa. This contributes decisively and definitively to ensuring the uniqueness of the event. The African presence has been visible since the times of the Entrudo, which entailed festive games of Portuguese origin during the forty-day period leading up to Lent. These games were recorded in Brazil as early as the seventeenth century. During the Entrudo, aristocratic colonial families amused themselves with a kind of "war" in which the contenders' "weapons" were "*limões*" or "*laranjinhas de cheiro*"—small wax "limes" or "little oranges" filled with scented water, and sometimes with other less-pleasant liquids, such as urine, often leading to violence. Members of the black population, both enslaved and free, ensured the festive atmosphere of the games, taking to the city streets with songs and dances typical of their cultures, generally in the later afternoon (fig. 9.2). By this time of day, the elite festivities typically became more domestic, marked by great feasts inside their townhouses.

In both the Entrudo and other festivals of the time, particularly the many religious festivities,[1] the presence of black and mixed-race peoples followed the line of socio-ethnic segregation that was a hallmark of daily life in colonial society. Distance was thus maintained, and the attitude of those in power toward cultural expressions of the black population ranged from tolerance to outright suppression. The strict hierarchy that governed relations between white masters and the black population in a slave-holding, patriarchal society, both in colonial Brazil and after independence, continued to reign supreme during the Entrudo festivities. The second half of the nineteenth century, however, saw the decline of the Entrudo, which the authorities had always opposed, not only because it disrupted public order—the festivities often became anarchic and violent—but also because the revels were an opportunity for public expressions of the customs of peoples of African origin (fig. 9.1).

**9.1**
Mário Cravo Neto (b. 1947, Salvador, Bahia, Brazil; d. 2009)
Carnaval Fight Club, circa 1990
Photograph
COURTESY OF THE ESTATE OF MÁRIO CRAVO NETO ©IMCN

The unrestrained energy of Carnaval occasionally results in altercations. Here the Filhos de Gandhy (in white turbans) uphold their traditional role as peacekeepers.

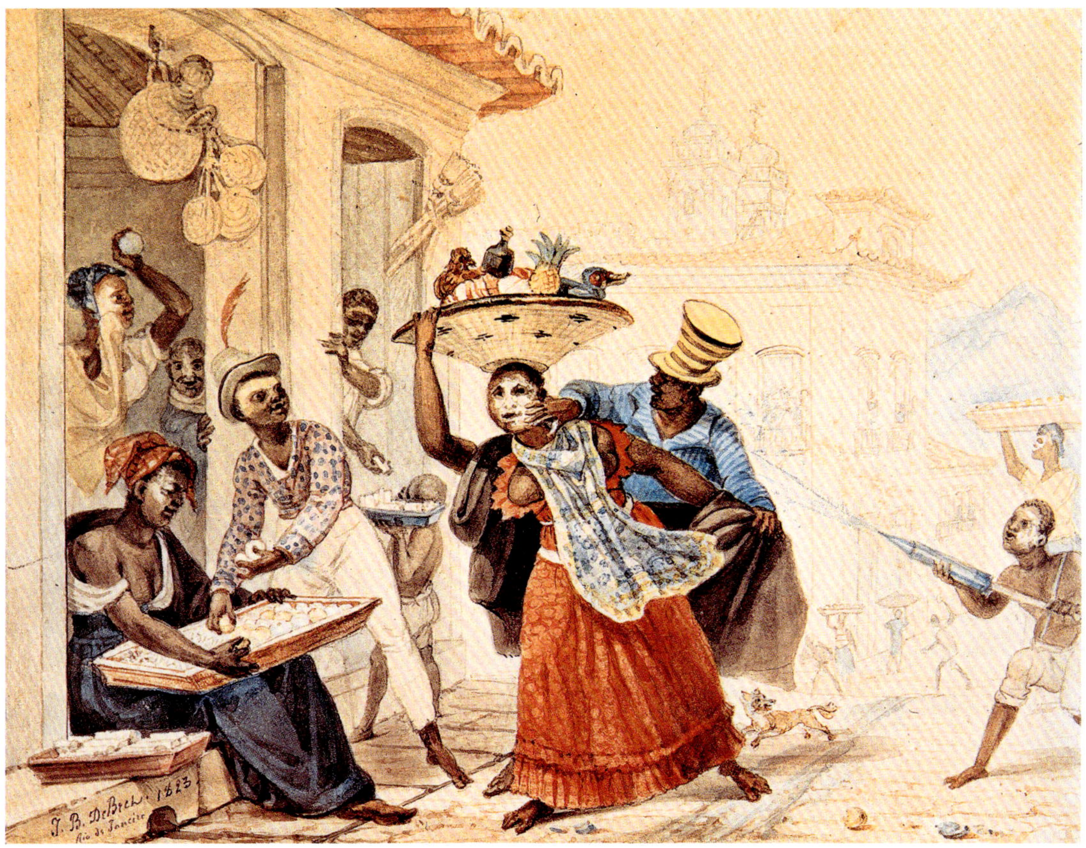


**9.2**
Jean-Baptiste Debret (b. 1768, Paris, France; d. 1848)
*Scéne de Carnaval* (Carnaval Scene), circa 1817–1829
Watercolor
8.1 x 13.9 cm
COURTESY CASTRO MAYA MUSEUM, RIO DE JANEIRO, BRAZIL

### The First Modern Carnavals

Although it is difficult to assign exact dates, we do know that Carnaval began to replace the Entrudo in the last two decades of the nineteenth century.[2] The transition points to the "Europeanization" of the festival, which was modeled on the Carnaval held in Nice, France. Indeed, it was this model that would be adopted by most modern-day Carnavals in the West, replacing the "barbarity" of the Entrudo and its revels, which were incompatible with the sophisticated aspirations of the Brazilian upper classes.

The emergence of Carnaval, however, did not prevent Africans and Afro-descendants from taking part in the festivities. To the contrary, the black populace—now organized in clubs such as the Embaixada Áfricana, Pândegas d'África, Chegada Áfricana, and Filhos de África—was encouraged to take part in the parades, the high point of "Carnaval à la Nice," and occupied a prominent place there despite the "Europeanizing" and "civilizing" ethos that had replaced the rough-and-tumble Entrudo. The new character of the event was well represented by the processions parading to the sound of military marches and opera music, themes linked to European history and culture, and the masked balls, enlivened by polkas and opera music, which were held in two bastions of the Bahian elite—the Polytheama and the São João Theater—places that were obviously off-limits to the black and enslaved population.

During the first twentieth-century Carnavals, however, the strong French influence made the presence of blacks something of an embarrassment to the elite and a bit too similar to the old Entrudo. The black "clubs" took part in the parades, legitimizing the rules of the "civilized" Carnaval through a "conformist" strategy, but black people also filled the city streets with their drumming, bands of masked revelers, and *afoxés* (traditional Carnaval groups formed by Afro-Brazilian communities and explicitly linked to Candomblé). That awkward black presence translated into systemic racial and cultural intolerance on the part of those in power, whether expressed through newspaper condemnations or police repression. In 1905, for example, after insistent journalistic demands, the chief of police issued an edict, which was reissued in the following years, expressly banning and harshly punishing the expression of African customs such as *batuques* (drumming) during Carnaval. Once again, this reaffirmed the socio-ethnic segmentation of spaces and the artistocratic and elitist character of society.

It is important to note that the intolerant and repressive attitudes of those in power toward the participation of black peoples in Carnaval was particularly focused on the *batuques*, *mascarados* (groups of masked revelers), and *afoxés*, which consisted entirely of poor people who, due to their clear ties to African traditions—particularly Candomblé—were seen as "primitive" and "barbarous." Their involvement was perceived as a form of resistance to "civilized society." The participation of blacks through organizations that took part in the procession was, however, tolerated, and even encouraged, precisely because it represented a form of social co-optation, therefore signaling the reverse of "resistance."

The presence of the white aristocracy in Bahia's street Carnaval was, however, short lived. They quickly retreated into Carnaval balls at the tennis club, the yacht club, and the Bahia Athletic Association, abandoning the open territory of the streets for the enclosed space of their social groups, an option that, strictly speaking, persisted until the 1960s and 1970s, fully corresponding to the tradition of patriarchal Brazilian families for whom the streets were the enemy of the elegant townhouse and a place devoid of social prestige.[3]

The streets have continued to be festively occupied by black and mixed-race populations. In addition to the *afoxés*, with their percussion orchestras playing the rhythms and accompanying the joyful songs typical of the Yoruba liturgy in the Candomblé *terreiros*, the groups that paraded through the city streets included the *batucadas*, or orchestras made up of drums, *cuícas*,[4] *reco-recos*,[5] and *agogôs*[6] that marched in single file; the *blocos*, clubs in which the number of participants was larger than that of the *batucadas*, and they wore identical costumes; as well as the *cordões*, so called because they used ropes to cordon off an area for their participants and had larger orchestras than the *batucadas* and *blocos*, even using floats in their parades.

From a territorial standpoint, the occupation of the streets during Carnaval involved clear segregation. *Préstitos*, *corsos*, and *pranchas*,[7] as well as some *blocos* and *cordões*, paraded through the fashionable part of the city center, Rua Chile. Families would set up chairs on the sidewalks so they could sit and watch the Carnaval parades of the elite white clubs—Fantoches da Euterpe, Cruz Vermelha, Inocentes em Progresso. *Afoxés* and any other group made up of black people were a rare and furtive presence. They occupied the low-income parts of the city, Piedade, Terreiro de Jesus, Baixa dos Sapateiros, and Largo de São Miguel, which formed the backdrops of public balls and parades of *batucadas*, *blocos*, *cordões*, and *mascarados*. Vibrant Carnavals held in several underprivileged districts such as Tororó, Garcia, Liberdade, Saúde, Cosme de Farias, Engenho Velho de Brotas, Itapagipe, and Ribeira were an obligatory stop for the Afro-Carnaval groups, who took part in the popular and spirited contests organized by associations and community groups.

### Bahia's Afro-Carnaval Festivities in the 1950s and 1960s

The 1950s and 1960s witnessed new and important actors in Salvador's Carnaval who further reinforced the public and primarily black and mixed-race nature of King Momo's festivities in the city streets. The first of these was the Afoxé Filhos de Gandhy, an Afro-Carnaval association founded in 1949 by black and mixed-race stevedores in the port of Salvador, almost all of whom had direct links to the Candomblé *terreiros*. Many years later, this group would become one of the chief symbols of Bahia's Carnaval. The association clearly set forth an anticolonial policy by paying tribute to Mahatma Gandhi and his struggle for India's independence at a time when dock workers in Salvador were refusing to unload the British ships anchored there (it is important to remember that some of the Afoxé's founders were trade union activists linked to the Brazilian Communist Party). The presence of elements of Candomblé, such as the songs, the musical instruments, and the ceremony that precedes participation in the festivities, can also be understood as a bold gesture of resistance and confrontation in a historically segregated festival from the social-ethnic standpoint. The founders of the group, however, did not confront the issue of race relations and ended up adopting an integrationist policy regarding white society's culture and values. Confrontation would be clearly expressed only by the *blocos afro* that emerged on the Carnaval scene a quarter of a century later at a clearly different time in terms of the presence of the issue of race relations on the Brazilian agenda.

The creation of the *trio elétrico* by two top-notch musicians Dodô and Osmar in 1950 was a revolution that radically changed the festival. With the *trio elétrico*, a kind of moving stage that drives through the city (see fig. 9.4), Carnaval conquered the streets, redefining them, and making them accessible to all without distinction. As a result, the people's Carnaval, mainly made up of the black and mixed-race population, invaded the central parts of the city, eliminating the hierarchy of the festival's social arena and introducing an absolutely egalitarian space where the "democracy of the ludic" began its joyous reign. Triumphing over the streets and attracting throngs of revelers with their music, the *trios elétricos* broke down the duality of stage and audience that had once predominated in the festivities and has made the essentially participatory nature of Bahia's Carnaval its most distinctive trait ever since.

The arrival of the *trio elétrico* also brought about other changes. On the aesthetic and musical level, the "trio-electrification" of Pernambuco's *frevo*[8] brought about by Dodô and Osmar—and later developed by major names in Brazil's music scene, like Caetano Veloso (see Dunn, this volume)—was so original that it ended up creating a new musical genre. It opened up a line of development that would lead to an unprecedented musical hybrid in Brazilian popular music, incorporating a varied range of styles such as rock, acid rock, reggae, and *ijexá*.[9] This resulted in the birth of what is now called "*Axé* Music" in the 1980s.

The highly visible *trio elétrico* also proved to be an excellent advertising medium and marked the first commercial interventions in Carnaval. This led to further mercantile involvement in the organization and production of the festival, which could no longer be sustained by the old system of spontaneous contributions and occasional donors. Although the market-driven side of the Carnaval festivities was initially limited to displaying brand names, by the end of the 1980s, the *trio elétrico*, linked with *blocos* and bands, came to dominate the Carnaval business, a characteristic feature of the revelries in modern-day Salvador.

The *trio elétrico* also brought about another important innovation. Over the course of the 1940s, Dodô and Osmar, the former an electrical technician and the latter a specialist in mechanical engineering, managed to overcome the problem of inadequate amplification by building an "electric rod" to use when they performed in shows and dances in the city. They can therefore be considered to have produced a precursor of the electric guitar, which, invented in the United States by Les Paul, was still unknown in Brazil. The *trio elétrico* also sparked a permanent process of technological transformation that extended to various areas such as sound and lighting engineering, and especially architecture and design, which met the challenges of transforming the mobile stage from a small automobile to trucks, and to the thirty-ton truck trailers that today house, in addition to a huge stage, comfortable dressing rooms and sophisticated live-recording studios.

Samba schools also erupted on Salvador's Afro-Carnaval scene during the period in question. They emerged in Bahia's revelries near the end of the 1950s, more precisely 1957, the year when the first samba school, Ritmistas do Samba, was founded. Its appearance in the Bahian frolics was clearly inspired by the Carnaval samba schools of Rio de Janeiro, which by then were well known and admired throughout the country thanks to newspapers and magazines, which gave tremendous visibility to exuberant samba parades, and to the radio, which played its catchy *sambas-enredo*.[10] Like their counterparts in Rio, Salvador's Carnaval samba schools were generally anchored in strong territorial identity, always associated with the low-income districts of the city where participants lived. In Rio de Janeiro, they originated in the *ranchos* of that city's first Carnavals. In Salvador, they emerged from the *batucadas* and *cordões* that made the people's Carnaval a lively event in that city.[11] There were more than fifty, and they made their presence felt in Salvador's Carnaval until the mid-1970s.[12] Then, they went into decline and disappeared, possibly because of the end of government funding for their organization, which involved high costs, or due to the changes those festivities underwent with the emergence of the *blocos afro*, a new type of association that mobilized vast swaths of the Afro-Carnaval community.

The *blocos de índio* (Amerindian groups) also impacted Salvador's Carnaval in the 1950s and 1960s. They were inspired by the Bloco Carnavalesco Cacique de Ramos, a Carnaval association founded in Rio in 1961 that was entirely devoted to samba and became a benchmark for that city's celebration.[13] In Salvador, they appeared during the last Carnavals of the 1960s and were organized by youths from the black and mixed-race community who took part in Carnaval by parading with the samba schools. The first *bloco de índio*, for example, was the Bloco Carnavalesco Caciques do Garcia, which was founded in 1966 and made up of participants of the Escola de Samba Juventude do Garcia, who decided to hit the streets with their *bloco de índio* on the day their samba school did not join the parades. The Apaches do Tororó, famous for its large number of participants, songs, and vast and boisterous drumming section, was founded in 1968 by members of the Escola de Samba Filhos do Tororó.

From the time they emerged on Bahia's Carnaval scene to the early 1980s, over twenty *blocos de índio* took part in the festivities and, in some cases, paraded with thousands of participants. Since then, however, they have lost ground, particularly to the new Carnaval associations organized by the black and mixed-race community that began to emerge—the *blocos afro*. Their presence in Carnaval is now limited to just two groups: Apaches do Tororó and Comanches do Pelô.

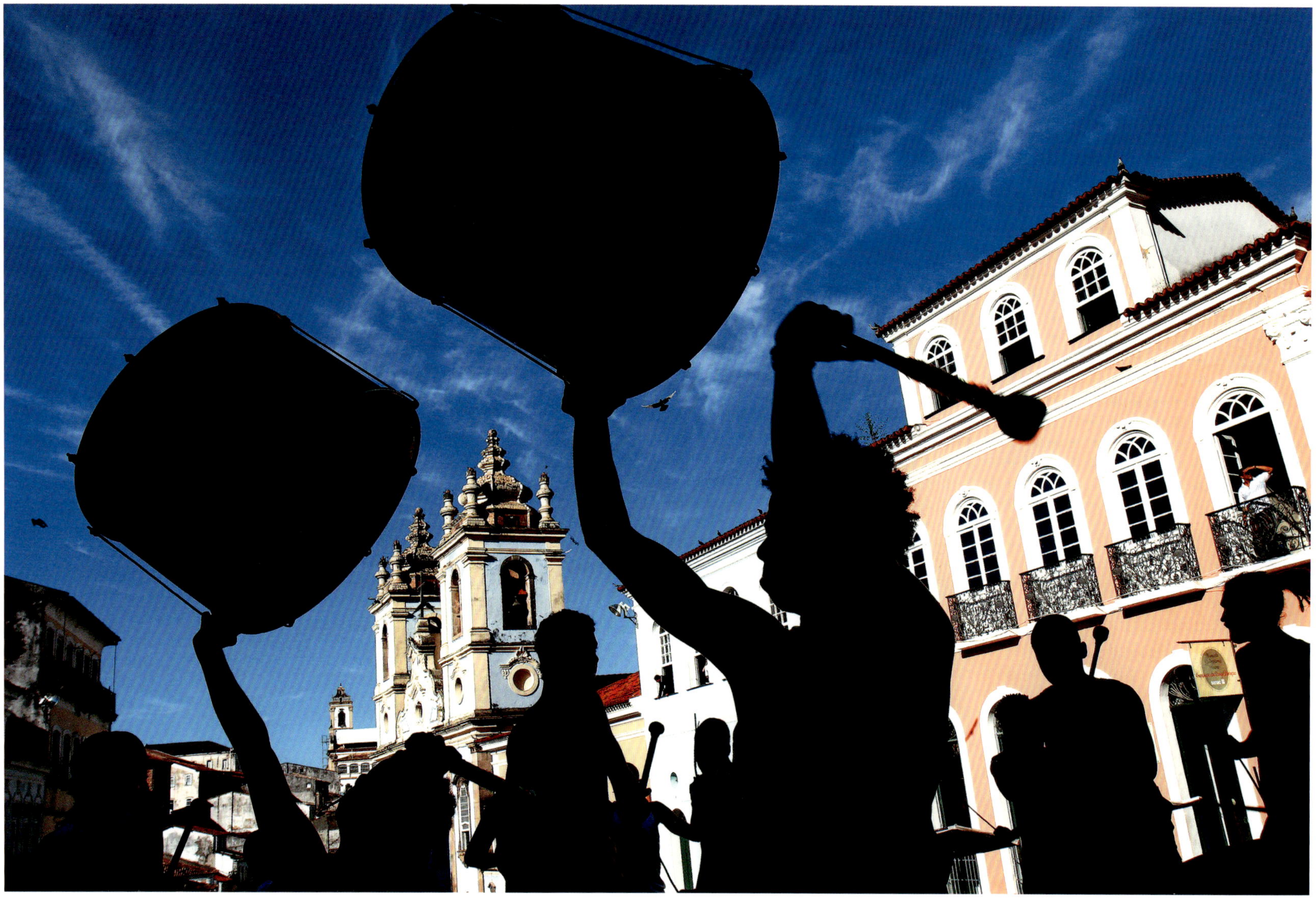

**9.3**
Roberto Faria (b. 1968, Salvador, Bahia, Brazil)
Olodum performs in Pelourinho during Carnaval, 2006
Photograph
COURTESY ROBERTO FARIA

### A Cultural Revolution: The Rise of the *Blocos Afro*

In the mid-1970s, Salvador's Carnaval underwent a significant change, the effects of which exceeded the festival itself and are strongly felt to this day. This consisted of the emergence of the *blocos afro* and their aesthetic-political repertoire with its deep Afro-Bahian roots. The first of these associations, Ilê Aiyê, came to life in Curuzu, part of a low-income district called Liberdade, and took to the streets in 1975.[14] Dozens of *blocos afro* were subsequently created around the city and joined the numerous *afoxés* that powerfully reemerged at this time.

These new Afro-Carnaval organizations clearly intended to affirm their ethnic character. Thus, the black and mixed-race youth of Salvador took charge of the festivities, and through *blocos afro* and *afoxés*, dances, songs, and costumes, they occupied the space of Carnaval and anchored it in Afro-Bahian cultural traditions. This was done with the unquestioned political aim of confronting racism, which had never before been attempted by Bahia's Afro-Carnaval associations.[15] The *blocos afro* arose during Brazil's "economic miracle"[16] and the economic changes it entailed. At that time the younger members of Salvador's black and mixed-race community were powerfully influenced by the African American aesthetic-political scene of the 1960s, especially the struggle for civil rights and the emergence of "soul music." They were inspired as well by the successful process of national liberation in Africa and the victorious struggle against Portuguese colonialism.

The *blocos afro* not only unleashed a process of renewal and innovation in Bahian Carnaval—dominating the festivities from the standpoint of aesthetics, music, and gesture—but also expanded their transformative activities to areas previously reserved for the white elite. This enabled them to demonstrate the black roots of Bahian culture in an unprecedented way. The black and mixed-race community's new organizations were able to produce greater levels of inclusion in society, encompassing the arts and culture, politics and business. Perhaps the best-known *bloco afro*, even internationally, is Olodum, which was created in 1979 (fig. 9.3).

Today, Bahia's Carnaval includes a large number of *blocos afro* with gorgeous percussion rhythms and thousands of revelers taking part in their parades. In addition to the pioneer, Ilê Aiyê, with its discourse and performance anchored in a more traditional perspective, and Olodum, with markedly "pop" characteristics, other groups worthy of note in the streets include Muzenza, inspired by the Afro-Jamaican world and strongly linked to the Rastafari and reggae aesthetic; Malê de Balê, from the famous Itapoã district, inspired by the black Muslims who led an important slave revolt in Bahia in 1835; and Cortejo Afro, the youngest *bloco afro*, founded in 1998, which parades with tremendous aesthetic finesse in its costumes, floats, and songs, fully justifying its adopted motto: the "elegantly sophisticated" *bloco*.

### Bahia's Carnaval Today: Commerce and Exclusion

The changes that the Carnaval festivities have undergone in Salvador since the mid-1980s have established the boundaries of its current configuration, the predominant feature of which is commercial (fig. 9.4). Today, the festival presents a diverse organizational ecology made up of over two hundred entities, such as *blocos* of various types and sizes and *trios elétricos*. The Afro-Carnaval presence is especially represented in that universe by numerous *afoxés*, *blocos afro*, and *blocos de samba*. The latter have gained strength in the last fifteen years, mobilizing vast portions of the city's black and mixed-race community and dominating the festivities during the first two days of Carnaval.

Central to the current organization of Carnaval is a commercial logic and dynamic dominated by the large *blocos de trio*. These emerged in the mid-1970s and experienced rapid growth. They became highly important when those whose membership came especially from the city's middle- and upper-class youth started organizing themselves as businesses. The *bloco de trio* got its name because, in the area cordoned off for the *bloco*, a *trio elétrico* replaces the *charangas*, the percussion and wind orchestras that characterized the traditional *blocos*. Privatizing the *trio elétrico* by imprisoning it within the ropes reintroduced the socio-spatial hierarchy of the festival—separating the revelers who pay to frolic within the cordon from those who frolic outside it. This in effect reestablished a type of festival that had been deconstructed following the appearance of the *trio elétrico* in the 1950s.[17]

At the top of the Carnaval business pyramid, these *blocos de trio* joined forces with the interests of the tourist industry and, even more important, established privileged relationships with the media, particularly television, creating the conditions for the emergence of the star system within the genre of Carnaval music known as *Axé*. This became the major asset of the festival's market, the essential basis for broadening its business potential, such as its massive presence in music and show business arenas, and for exporting that model of Carnaval to other cities in Brazil, as well as other countries. The result is a gigantic market that is highly concentrated in the hands of a few large *blocos de trio* with professional management structures and the economic and financial capital as well as the political clout to operate in Carnaval's numerous businesses.[18]

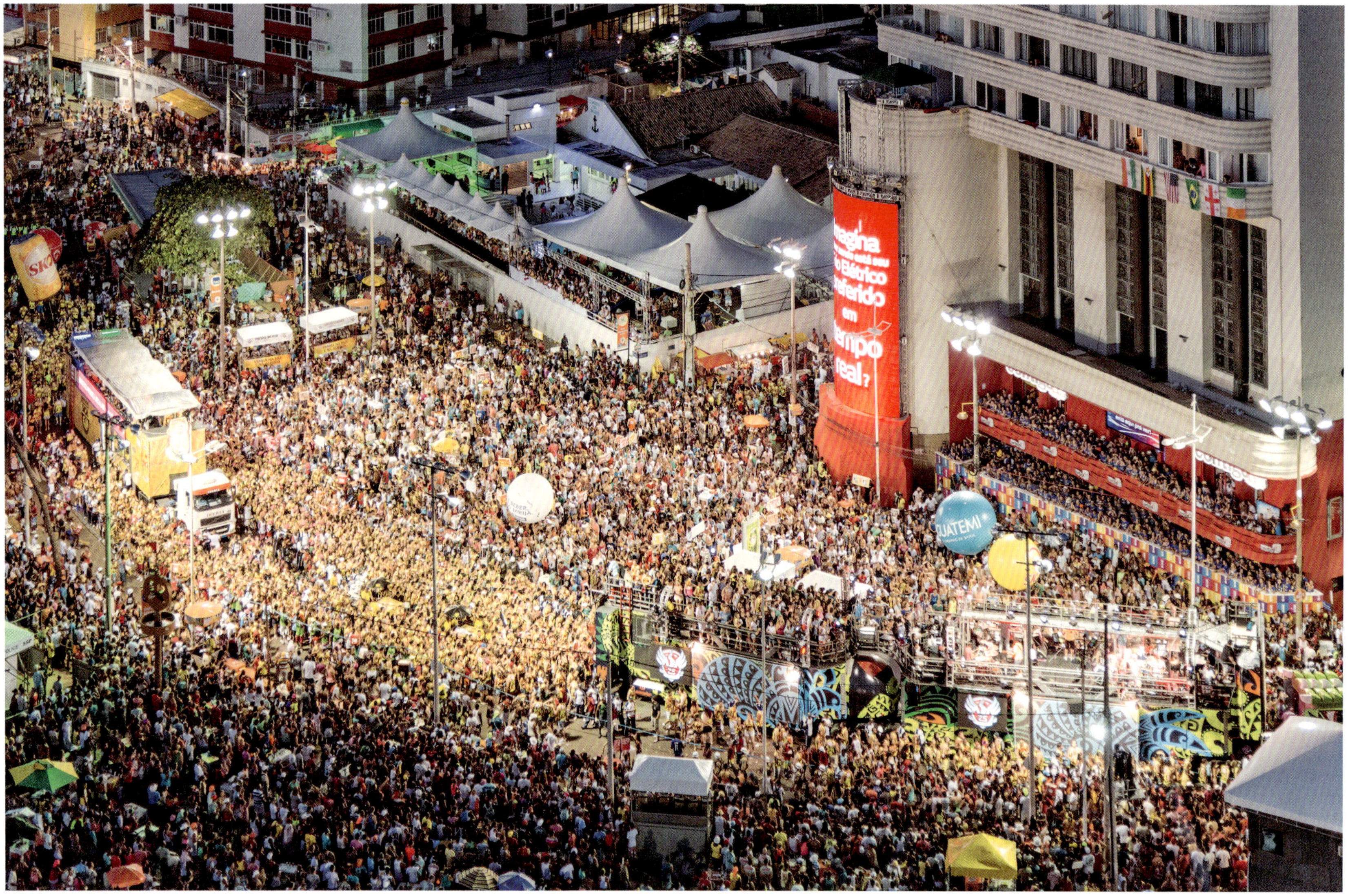


**9.4**
Nilton Souza (b. 1950, Varzedo, Bahia, Brazil)
Crowds fill the streets during Carnaval in Salvador, Bahia, 2013
Photograph
COURTESY NILTON SOUZA

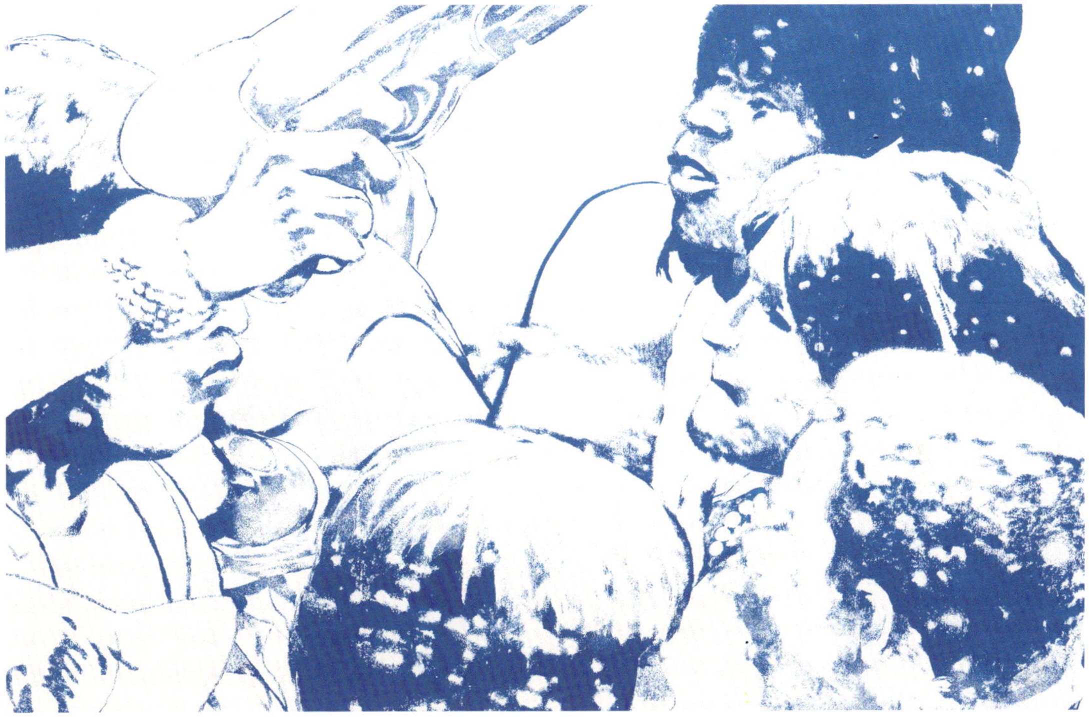

**9.5**
Pedro Marighella (b. 1979, Salvador, Bahia, Brazil)
Detail of an untitled work from the *Série mata* (Mata Series), 2014
Acrylic paint on wood
2.3 x 2.6 m
COURTESY GALLERY RV CULTURA E ARTE
PHOTOGRAPH BY ANDREW KEMP

For a photograph of the entire work, see figure 11.5. The use of squirt guns recalls the nineteenth-century watercolor by Debret (see fig. 9.2).

Other entities struggle at the bottom of the pyramid, vying with each other in tough competition for the commercial sponsorships essential for organizing Carnaval parades. Afro-Carnaval associations like *afoxés*, *blocos afro*, and other small *blocos* face an even tougher challenge in this contest. They are entities that maintain sociocultural ties with their communities, where they are intensely active in the fields of education, culture, and social services. The *afoxés* in particular are nonprofit entities managed on the basis of the traditional systems of Candomblé *terreiros*. They are not organized as businesses, and not even the large, traditional *blocos afro* like Ilê Ayiê, Olodum, Malê Debalê, Muzenza, and Os Negões have sufficiently mature organizational and management structures to compete for funding in the Carnaval market. Furthermore, they face racial prejudice on the part of many sponsors and end up depending on government subsidies[19] to finance their presence in the festival.[20]

### Challenges in Momo's Kingdom

Today, Salvador's Carnaval would be unthinkable without the vibrant contributions that the black populace has made over time, despite confrontations, disputes, and prejudices. Furthermore, from a business standpoint, the exploitation of these features represents valuable symbolic/cultural capital. The modern-day Bahian Carnaval—particularly as characterized within the arts industry—is organized on a scale that surely guarantees it the title of the largest street party in the world (fig. 9.5).[21] This requires an understanding of its implications regarding the Afro-Carnaval side of the story and, on a broader scale, the very nature of the participation of the populace, which has always set that festival apart. Here, the challenge is twofold and imposes inescapable responsibilities on the government to protect the cultural dimension of the Carnaval. Otherwise, its meaning and significance will be compromised and even make it impossible to achieve the more inclusive socioeconomic development that this great celebration represents.

Thus, specifically regarding the economic side of the festivities, it is imperative to radically renew the frameworks that regulate Carnaval-related businesses and now support a market characterized by oligopolistic practices, tending to broaden and deepen the unjust and precarious situation with which the most vulnerable actors in the revels must cope. Like dozens of Afro-Caribbean entities, it keeps them on the margins of a better share of the economic benefits generated by the business. On a broader scale, the most urgent and fundamental challenge is the effective recognition of Carnaval as part of Bahia's intangible cultural heritage and its meaning for the soul of the city and its people, an issue that requires the formulation and implementation of cultural policies that identify, recognize, and guarantee the visibility and coexistence of the diversity of Carnaval expressions with deep roots in ancient traditions and in the most contemporary repertoires of the revels— an indispensable element for the continuity of the participatory character that has made the Bahian Carnaval a major festival.

Interleaf **H**

# The Art of J. Cunha and His *Códice* (Codex)

*Jeri Bernadette Williams*

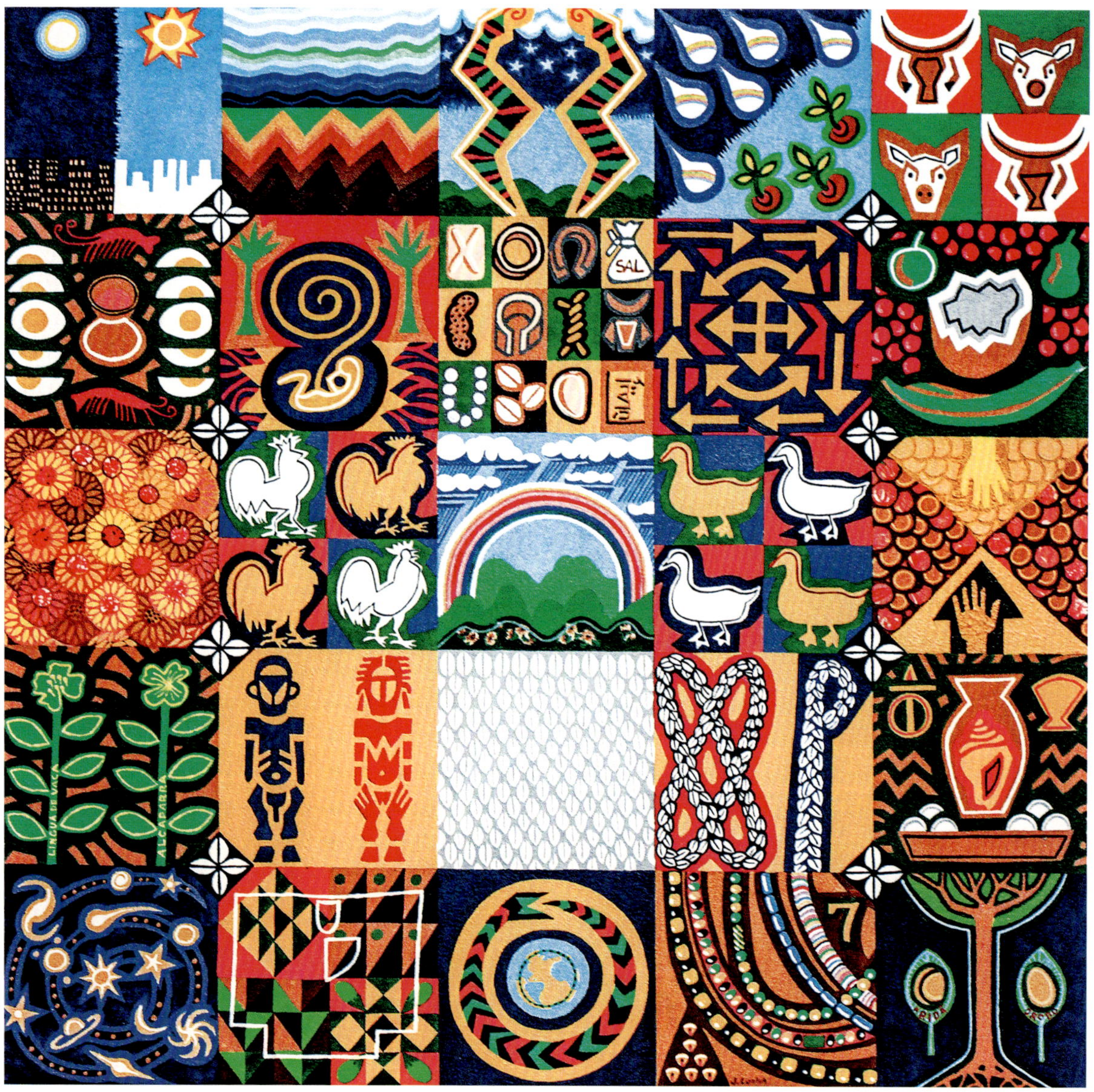

AN INTERNATIONALLY ACCLAIMED VISUAL ARTIST, José Antônio Cunha (J. Cunha) was born June 13, 1948, on the feast day of Santo Antônio (Saint Anthony of Padua), patron saint of Brazil. Raised in Ponta de Humaitá, Itapagipe, in the Monte Serrat district of Salvador, he credits his upbringing in the *cidade baixa* ("the lower city," i.e., the bayside section of Salvador) as the foundation of his artistic vision. Surrounded by fishermen and the culture of the sea, Cunha constantly sketched community events such as festivals and Candomblé ceremonies. After earning a reputation as a sign painter at an early age, he won a scholarship to attend the prestigious Escola de Belas Artes (School of Fine Arts) at the Federal University of Bahia in the *cidade alta* (upper city). There he was inspired by established Bahian artists such as Mário Cravo Neto, Edmídio Magalhães, and Juarez Paraíso.

Cunha extracts elements of his personal and cultural heritage to portray the essence of a *vida Baiana* (Bahian life), an artistic code that is a journey of discovery into what is means to be Afro-Bahian. He proudly incorporates his own multiethnic roots—indigenous Amerindian (Kiriri Tupi group) and African (Bantu from Angola) on his maternal side and European (Armenian Roma) on his paternal side. The activist social climate of the 1960s, an era of revolution and social awareness, further led him to consider the purpose of art and to explore its ability to address inequalities in urban and rural life, the impact of colonialism, racism, political corruption, and environmental dilemmas.

Early in his career he served as the set and costume designer for Emília Biancardi's famed Brazilian folkloric dance group Viva Bahia, and later he developed the graphic identity (logo, textiles, album covers, etc.) for Ilê Aiyê, one of the groundbreaking Afrocentic Carnaval troupes (*blocos afro*) in Bahia (see Miguez, this volume). As Ilê Aiyê's main designer for several decades, he utilized four basic hues to express the organization's political and social agenda: black representing African skin tone, red for sacrifice and bloodshed, yellow for wealth and prosperity, and white for peace (see Dunn, this volume).

Vibrant primary colors with emblematic or "archetypal" meanings clearly play a dominant role in Cunha's art. His bright palette is strongly influenced by the aesthetics of indigenous Amerindian and African cultures as well as by the tropical flora and fauna of northeastern Brazil. He considers his full body of work (*carteira*) to be a portfolio of the rich tones that the world possesses. Cunha also draws an analogy to musical composition, asserting "Color is to art as musical notes are to song."[1] Not surprisingly, music is a mandatory element of his creative process whether he is singing to himself or listening to recorded compositions.

Created from 2011 to 2014, Cunha's masterpiece *Códice* (Codex) offers an expansive chart of the iconography and central tenets of the historically related but theologically distinct religions Candomblé and Umbanda. Comprised of twenty-one panels, it has been described as a "holy book of color" (Moreira 2016, 17). Each segment is dedicated either to an *orixá* (divinity), a spiritual category such Egungun (ancestors), *erês* (child spirits), and *caboclos* (Native American entities), or a ritual such as Ifá divination. Furthermore, each panel or chapter contains twenty-five distinct visual cells depicting ceremonies, symbolic colors, sacred animals and plants, and liturgical objects as well as invoking relevant mythological narratives, cosmological themes, and historical events.

Fundamentally, *Códice* celebrates Afro-Brazilian spirituality in vivid detail. It is also challenges viewers, Brazilian or otherwise. Most, in all likelihood, would require a deeper degree of Bahian cultural-religious literacy to comprehend fully the intricate layers of meaning embedded in the work. Part narrative illustration and part meditative space, Cunha's complex rendering of religious symbolism invites exploration of Candomblé and Umbanda in terms of the past, present, and future of Brazil and the broader world.

Enlargement of figure H.1f

Enlargement of figure H.1k

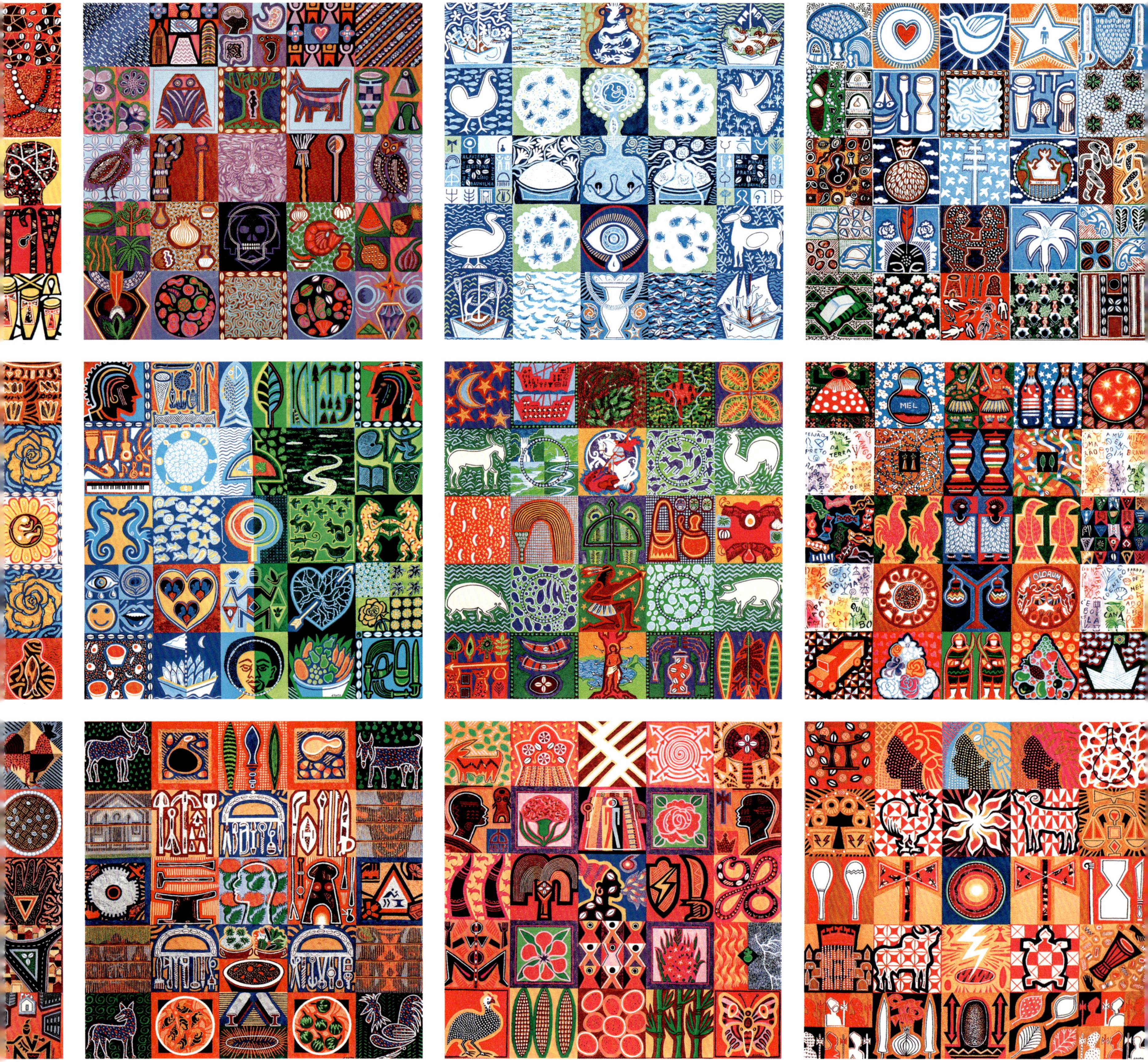
MEL

**H.1a-u**
J. Cunha (José Antônio Cunha, b.1948, Salvador, Bahia, Brazil)
*Códice* (Codex), 2010–2014
Acrylic paint on canvas
Each panel 100 x 100 cm
COLLECTION OF J. CUNHA, PHOTOGRAPHS BY SORA MAIA

According to the artist, the panels should preferably be read from left to right and from the bottom row to the top.

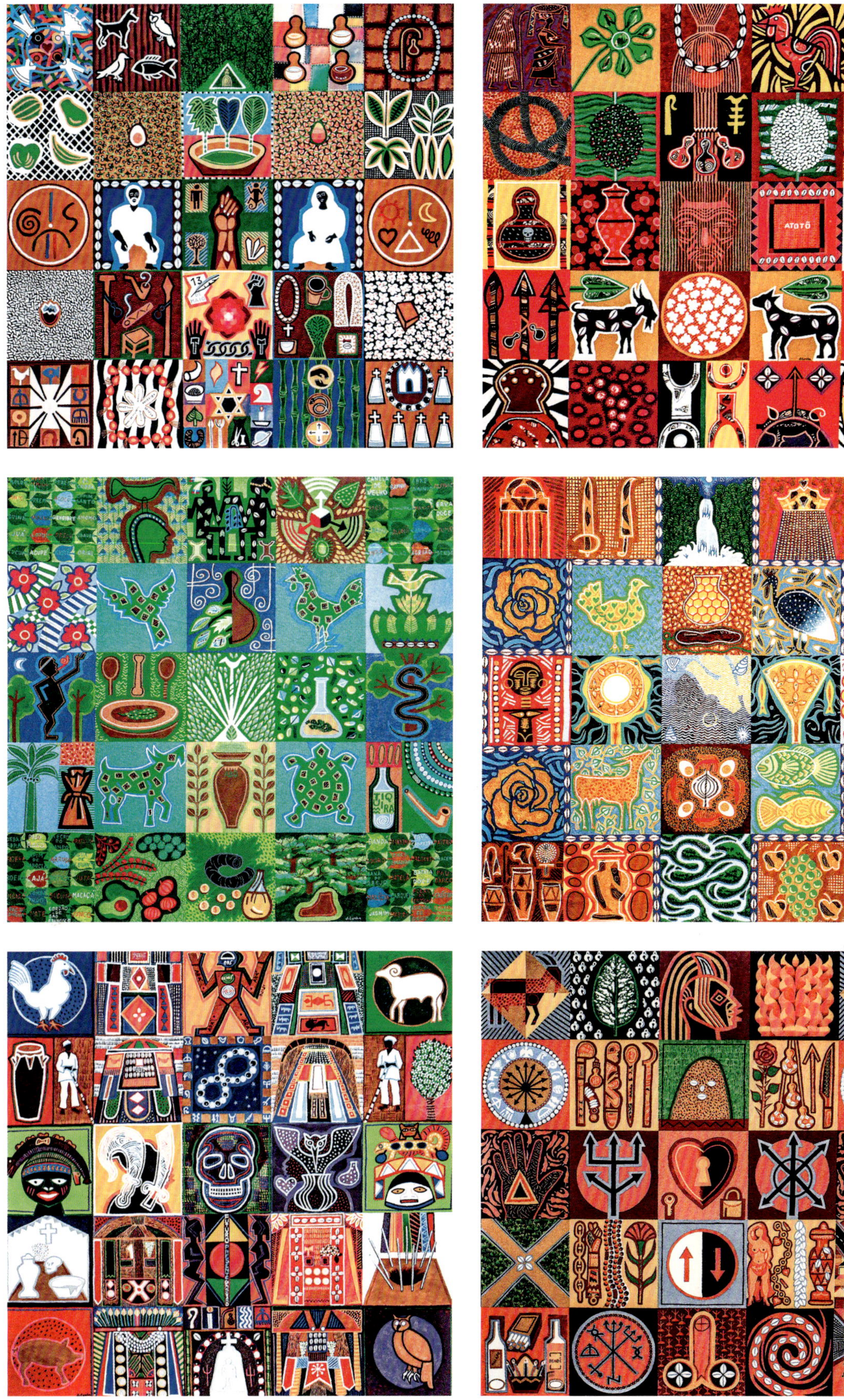

#### BOTTOM ROW

**a**
*Egungum* are ancestors who return during special Candomblé ceremonies held almost exclusively on the island of Itaparica. Notable here are references to carved Yoruba masks, shrines, and offerings.

**b**
*Exu* is the embodiment of phallic virility, master of the crossroads, and facilitator of communications between humans and the other *orixás*. His associated colors are red and black, and he favors fiery-hot substances.

**c**
*Ogum* is the *orixá* of war, iron, and technology. His dominant hues are blue and green, and his special emblems include weapons and tools, dogs, horned animals, and the blade-like leaves of the plant *Sansevieria trifasciata*.

**d**
*Iansã* is goddess of wind and storms. A fierce *orixá* who confronts the spirits of the dead, she prefers reddish tones, copper accoutrements, and offerings of Guinea fowl and female goat.

**e**
*Xangô*, the *orixá* of thunder and lightning, is husband to Iansã, Oxum, and Obá. His defining implement is the double-headed axe (*oxê*), and his dominant colors are red and white.

**f**
*Oxumaré* embodies the rainbow linking sky and earth and is associated with the growth that accompanies rainfall. Also symbolized with paired serpents, this *orixá* is thought to spend half the year in the form of a male and half in the shape of a woman.

**g**
*Rituais Afrobrasileiros* (Afro-Brazilian Rituals) presents crucial aspects of belief shared by the African-inspired religions of Candomblé and Umbanda. These include the *orixás*, divination using cowry shells, and many liturgical objects.

#### MIDDLE ROW

**h**
*Ossaim* is keeper of the knowledge of sacred plants and herbal medicine. Often represented as a one-legged tree-like figure covered with leaves, he is also symbolized with the *operé*, a seven-pointed metal sculpture surmounted by a bird.

**i**
*Oxum* is an *orixá* associated with fresh water, feminine beauty, and fertility. Her sacred colors are yellow and gold, and her icons include a mirror (*abebé*) and a crown (*adé*) with a beaded veil.

**j**
*Logunedé*, the child of Oxóssi and Oxum, inherited the characteristics of both parents. Viewed by some as androgynous, this *orixá* spends half the year hunting in the forest and the other half fishing in rivers.

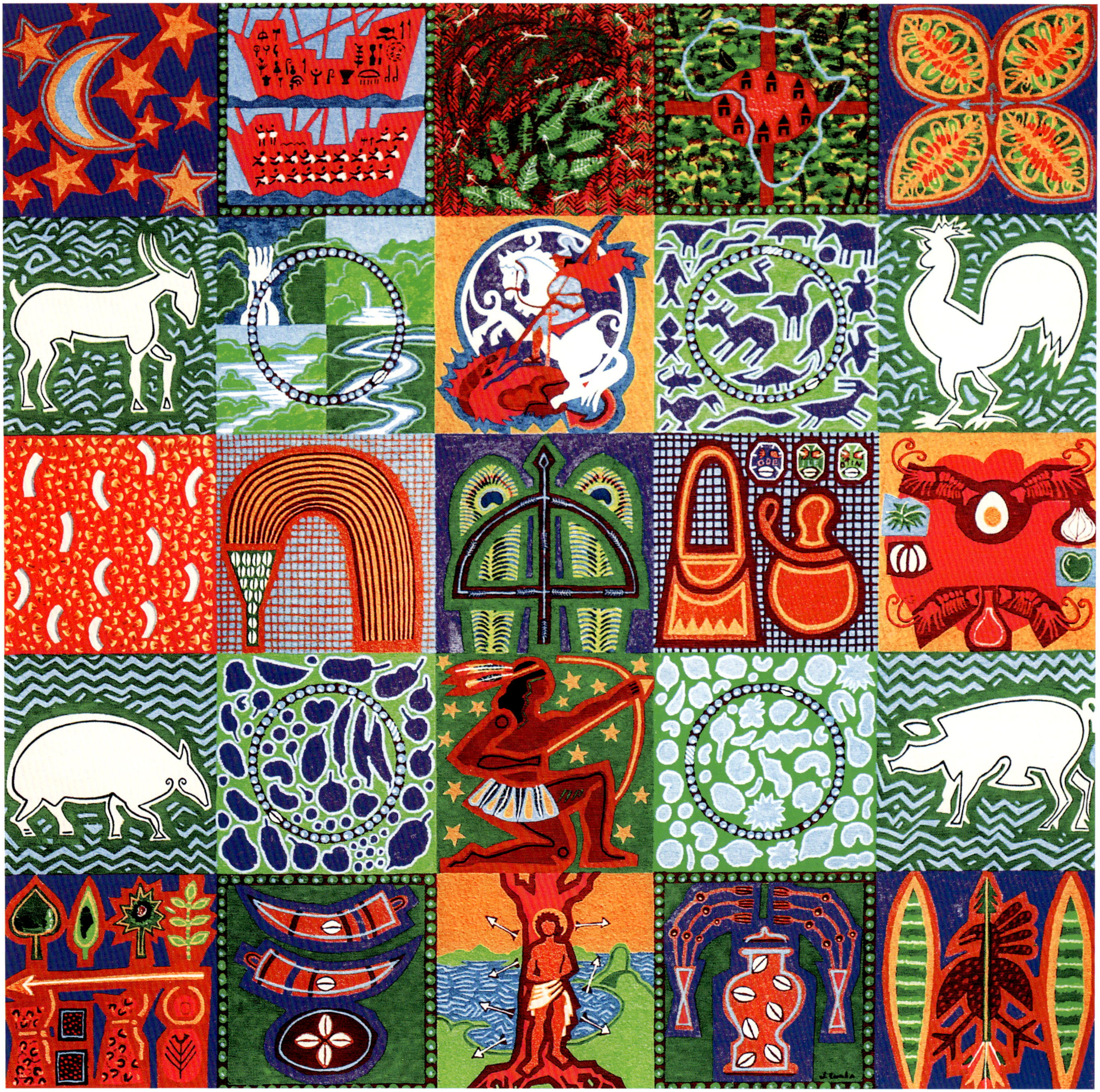

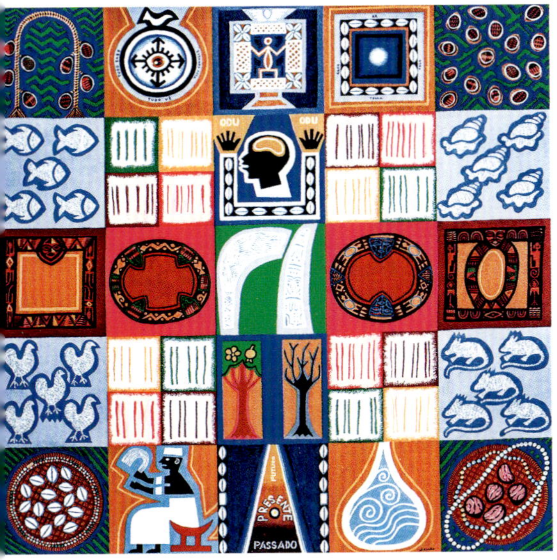

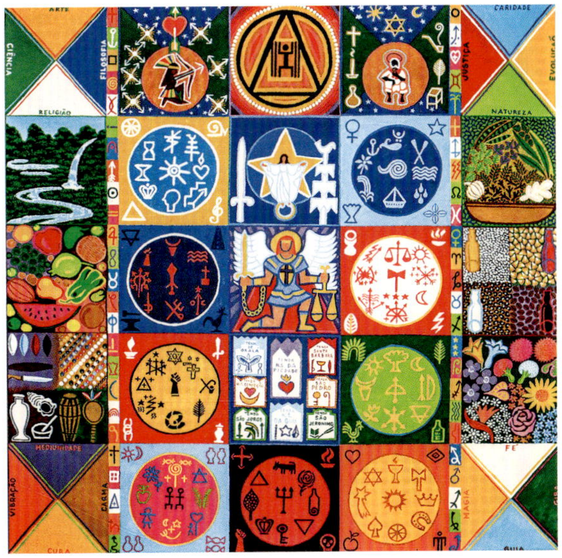

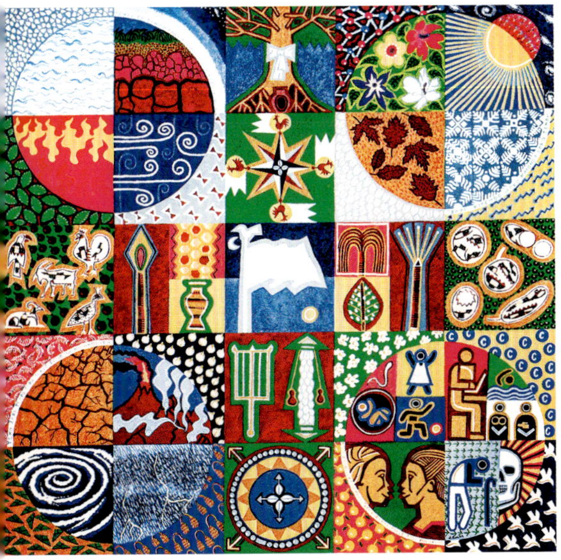

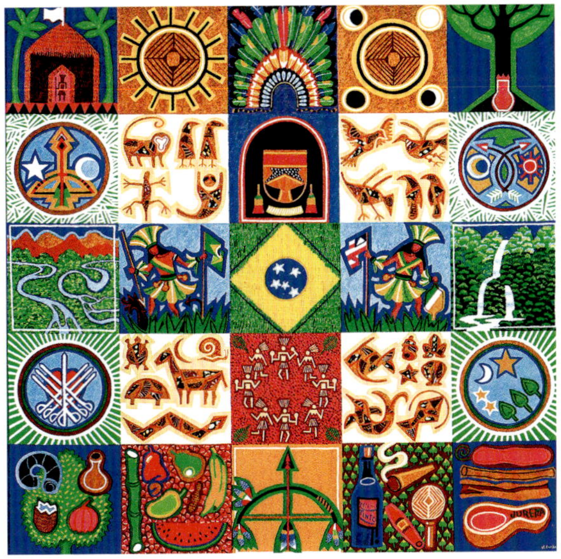

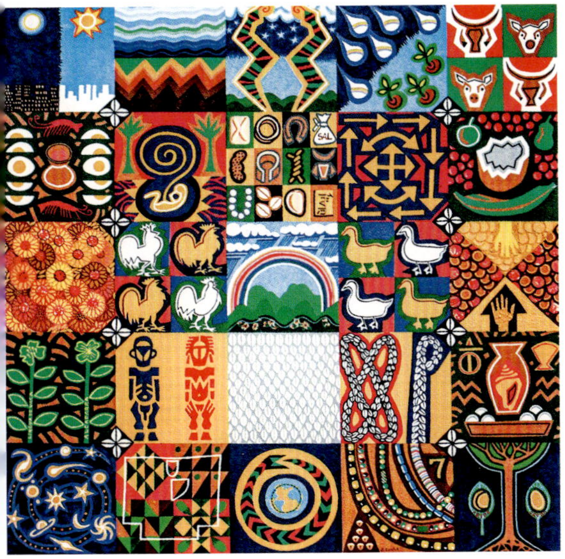

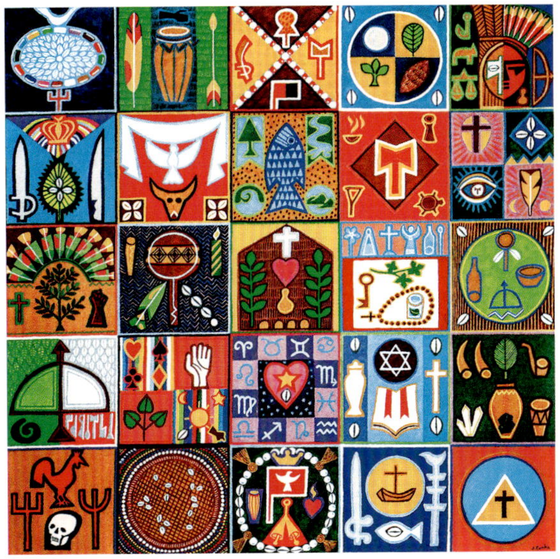

k
*Oxóssi* is brother to Ogum. An archetypal hunter, he is symbolized by the bow and arrow (*ofá*), the freedom of the wilderness, and the shades of the forest. He is associated with the Catholic Saint George and Saint Sebastian.

l
*Erês* are the youthful spirits that inhabit all people. Ceremonies held for them are much like children's parties with toys, candy, and other special foods. Some link them with the Ibeji (twin *orixás*).

m
*Tempo* is the personification of time and the cycle of seasons. An aged figure, he is closely associated with the earth's fundamental elements, environmental conditions, and the phases of human lives.

n
*Caboclo* references a category of indigenous spirits associated most closely with the practice of Umbanda. Romanticized figures, who are often linked to the colonization of Brazil and the foundation of Bahia, they embody Native American sacred knowledge.

**TOP ROW**

o
*Pretos Velhos* (Old Blacks) in Umbanda are the souls of elderly Africans who lived and died in Brazil prior to abolition (May 13, 1888). With wisdom gained from age and suffering, they serve as spirit guides for the living.

p
*Omolu* is *orixá* of infectious diseases. His face and upper body are obscured by strips of palm fiber (raffia), and he is represented with hues of red, black, and white. Canes, crutches, and popcorn—which evokes bursting sores—are his key symbols.

q
*Nanã*, one of the oldest female *orixás*, represents still waters, marshes, and the primordial mud from which life emerged.

r
*Iemanjá* is the *orixá* of the oceans. A nurturing mother figure often envisioned as a mermaid, her dominant colors are blue and white, and her primary symbols are fish, shells, and a boat laden with votive offerings.

s
*Oxalá* is the divinity of wisdom, purity, and peace. He is widely regarded as the father of the *orixás* and the creator of humankind. His color is white, and his key emblems are the dove-topped staff (*opaxorô*), the snail, and the red tail feather of the African gray parrot.

t
*Ifá* is a Yoruba-derived divination system that utilizes sacred narratives (Odu Ifá) to interpret human dilemmas and suggest appropriate courses of action. A primary method is the casting of sixteen palm nuts or cowry shells onto a round or square board (Opon-Ifá). Based on the patterns in which the objects land, vertical marks are traced in white powder (*iyerosun*) to determine the relevant tale.

u
*Umbanda*, which mixes Candomblé traditions with a wide variety of elements from other global faiths and mystical practices, has been described as the Brazilian religion par excellence. "I'm not a prophet by any means," Cunha relates, "but I believe that Umbanda is the Afro-religion of the future in Latin America" (Moreira 2016, 7).

# 10 Candomblé as Artistic Inspiration

## Syncretic Approaches

**Kimberly L. Cleveland**

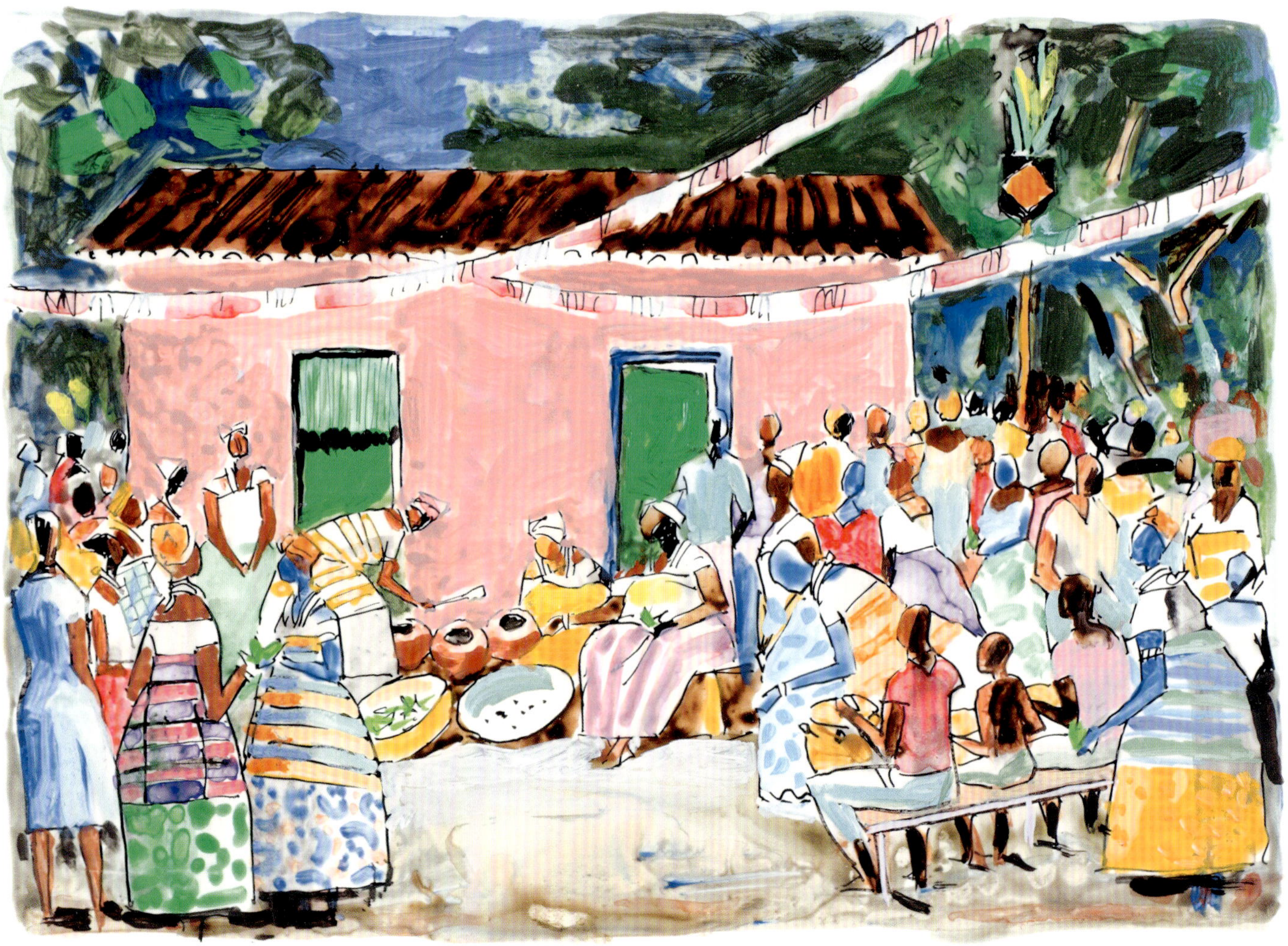

IN BRAZIL ENSLAVED WEST AFRICAN PEOPLES and their descendants combined elements of their own religions with aspects of Catholicism (see Matory and Sansi, this volume). This was done, at least in part, to safeguard indigenous traditions under the guise of adopting the belief system of Portuguese colonists. The Afro-Brazilian religion of Candomblé emerged from this syncretism (fig. 10.1), which has been given lengthy and serious consideration by scholars and religious adherents and continues to be a topic of discussion today.

Academics and spiritual communities seem to have overlooked another form of syncretism, however, which is apparent in the works of artists who combine sacred and secular elements in their Candomblé-related production. Beginning in the mid-twentieth century, several artists from Bahia took Candomblé as a source of inspiration. These individuals, some of whom were religious initiates, did not strictly adhere to the symbols, colors, and materials prescribed for liturgical pieces produced for use and viewing within sacred spaces. Rather, they combined religious subjects and forms with secular influences and elements in accordance with their own styles, preferences, and objectives. Agnaldo Manoel dos Santos, Carybé, Rubem Valentim, and Mestre Didi were among the first generation to create a bridge between the sacred and secular spheres of artistic production and to introduce Candomblé-influenced pieces to the broader Brazilian public. A brief examination of their work underscores how the members of this otherwise diverse group each took a syncretic approach toward creating art inspired by Candomblé.

**Agnaldo Manoel dos Santos, Carybé, Rubem Valentim, and Mestre Didi**

In the mid-twentieth century, a number of established artists began to produce Candomblé-inspired works for secular spaces and audiences. At that time, the majority of the public, as well as individuals in the mainstream art circles were unfamiliar with Afro-Brazilian religious subject matter. Through their exploration of Candomblé-influenced forms and themes, these artists played a pivotal role in exposing the wider Brazilian population to this Afro-Brazilian religion and its visual vocabulary.

Agnaldo Manoel dos Santos was born on the island of Itaparica in 1926. In 1946, he relocated to Salvador, where he supported himself by working as a warehouse loader and a laborer at a lime pit, among other jobs. Five years later, a chance encounter with one of Bahia's most beloved artists, the sculptor Mário Cravo Júnior, changed the course of his life. Agnaldo initially worked as a watchman for Cravo's studio and later as his assistant.

An adept carver, Agnaldo had acquired an understanding of woodworking over the years, and through his involvement with Cravo, he honed his artistic skills (fig. 10.2). He also learned about regional artistic forms and subject matter and gained insight into the workings of the professional art world. The association with Cravo made possible his introduction to a number of important artistic and cultural figures, including art dealer Terzo Lombardi, museum director José Valladares, and photographer and researcher Pierre Verger.

**10.1**
Carybé (Héctor Julio Páride Bernabó, b. 1911, Lanús, Buenos Aires Province, Argentina; d. 1997)
*Olubajé de Omolú: Engenho Velho* (Annual Festival for Omolú: Engenho Velho), undated
Ink and watercolor (gouache) on paper
83 x 63 cm
COURTESY INSTITUTO CARYBÉ / COPYRIGHTS CONSULTORIA LTDA.

**10.2**
Pierre Verger (b. 1902, Paris, France; d. 1996)
Agnaldo Manoel dos Santos (left) and Mário Cravo Júnior (right)
Photograph
PHOTO PIERRE VERGER ©FUNDAÇÃO PIERRE VERGER

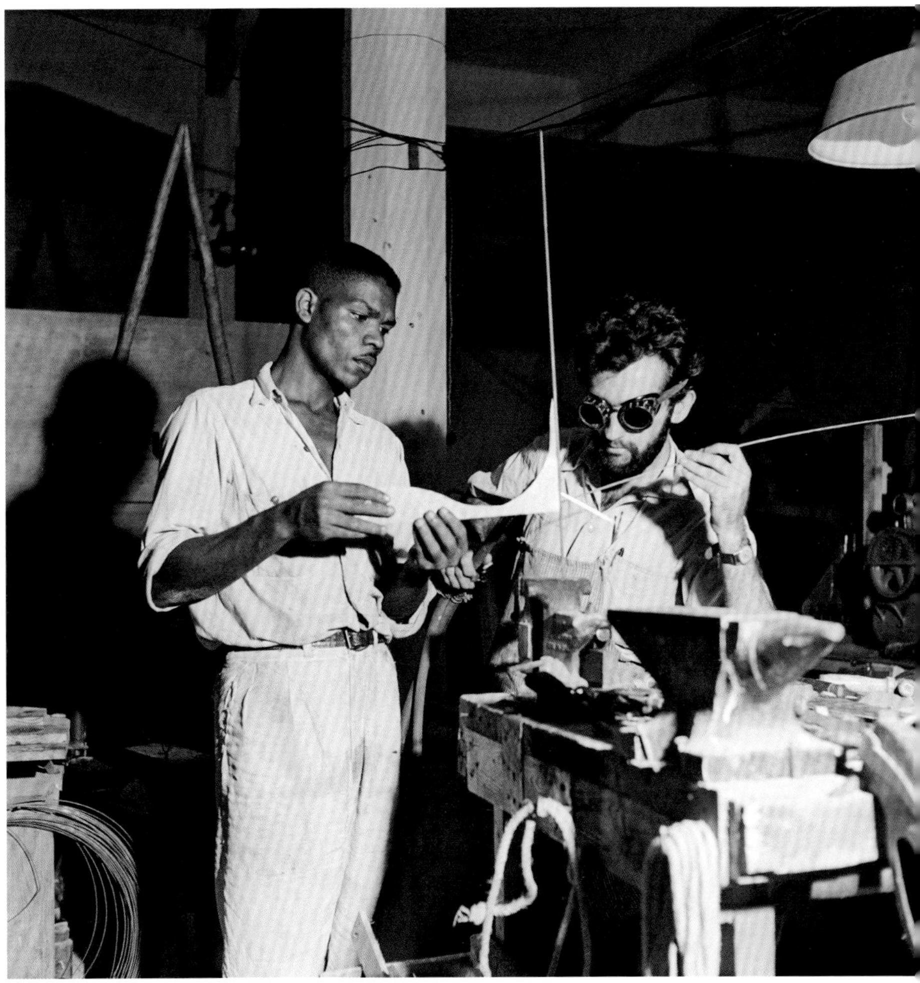

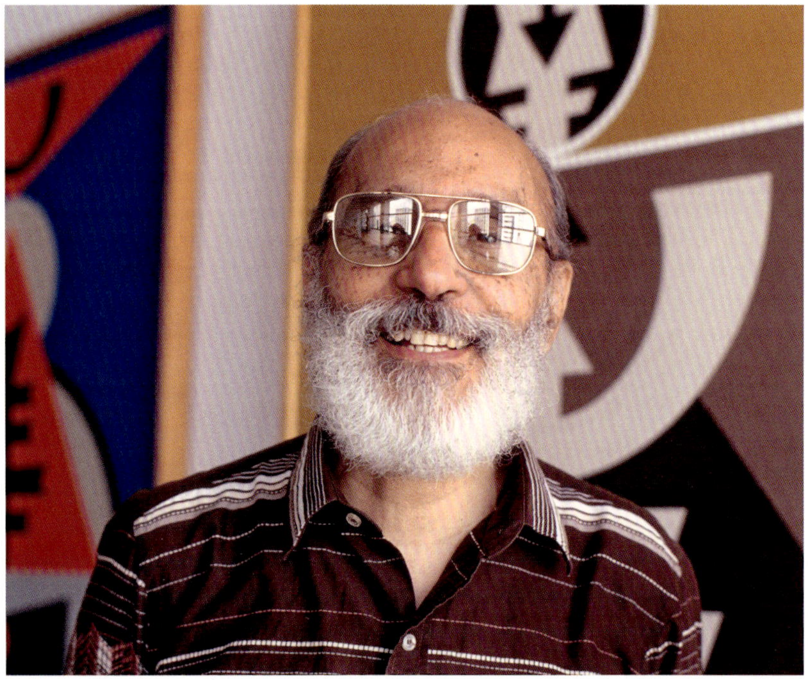

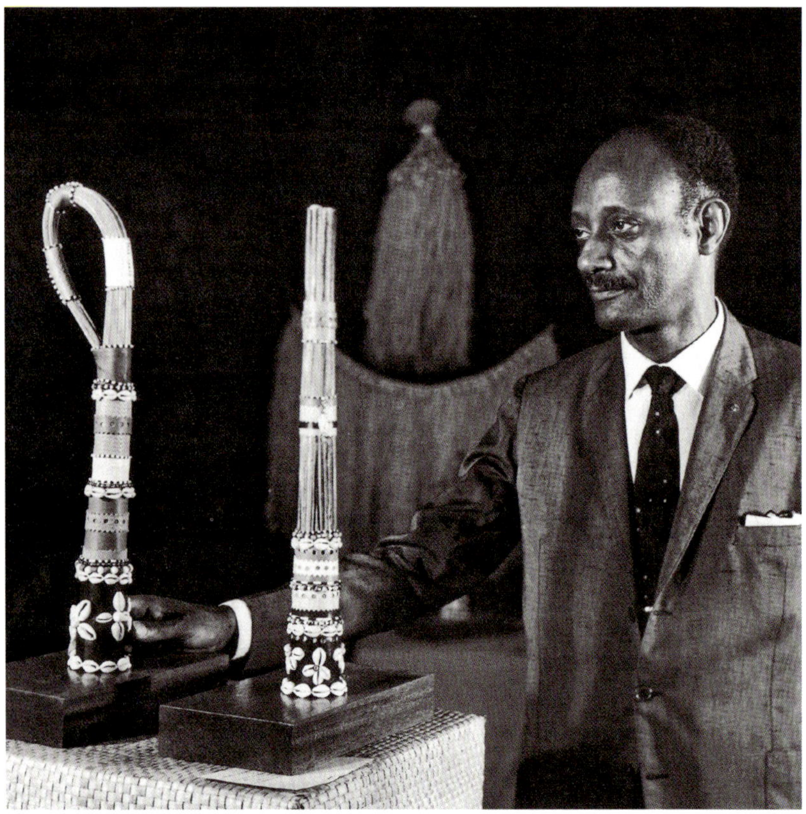

By 1957 Agnaldo had established himself as a professional sculptor and had left Cravo's studio, dedicating himself to his own work. Unfortunately, this lasted only five years, as he died prematurely in 1962 at the age of thirty-six. Although his professional artistic career was brief, he gained recognition during his lifetime. Before his death, his sculptures were shown in exhibitions in several cities, including at the 1957 São Paulo Biennial. Unlike the other artists discussed in this essay, however, he never publically addressed his personal involvement in Candomblé or his use of it as a source of artistic inspiration.[1] His comparatively small body of work also includes examples influenced by Catholic subjects, African sculpture, and quotidian themes.

Carybé was not originally from Bahia, but by the second half of the twentieth century, he had become virtually synonymous with its regional culture. Although he was born Héctor Julio Páride Bernabó in Lanús, a province of Argentina, in 1911, his most significant artistic, spiritual, and cultural development would take place in Brazil. During several short-term stays there, he managed to complete a two-year course of study at the Escola Nacional de Belas Artes in Rio de Janeiro in the late 1920s, learn the Afro-Brazilian martial art of capoeira, and frequent a number of Candomblé *terreiros*. Carybé was drawn to the strong African influences he found in Salvador and settled there permanently in 1950. He quickly integrated into the local artistic and religious communities.

It was almost immediately following the move to Salvador that Candomblé became a significant influence on Carybé. Within a decade, he was deeply involved in Ilê Axé Opô Afonjá, one of the region's most well-known and traditional houses of Candomblé. He strengthened his religious affiliation when he achieved his first spiritual title at Ilê Axé in 1957, the same year he became a naturalized citizen (Carybé 2009). Carybé was a prolific artist, who worked in diverse media. He represented themes and subjects from Candomblé in many of the pieces he produced until his death in 1997.

**10.3**
Silvestre Silva (b. 1945, Minas Gerais, Brazil)
Rubem Valentim in front of his paintings, 1984
Photograph
COURTESY SILVESTRE SILVA

**10.4**
Artist Unknown
Mestre Didi (Deoscóredes Maximiliano dos Santos) at an exhibition of his work at the University of Ibadan, Nigeria
Photograph
REPRODUCED WITH THE PERMISSION OF JUANA ELBEIN DOS SANTOS

**10.5**
Pierre Verger (b. 1902, Paris, France; d. 1996)
*Mãe Senhora, Candomblé Ilê Axé Opô Afonjá* (The High Priestess Senhora, Candomblé Temple Axé Opô Afonjá), Salvador, Brazil, 1948–1951
Photograph
PHOTO PIERRE VERGER ©FUNDAÇÃO PIERRE VERGER

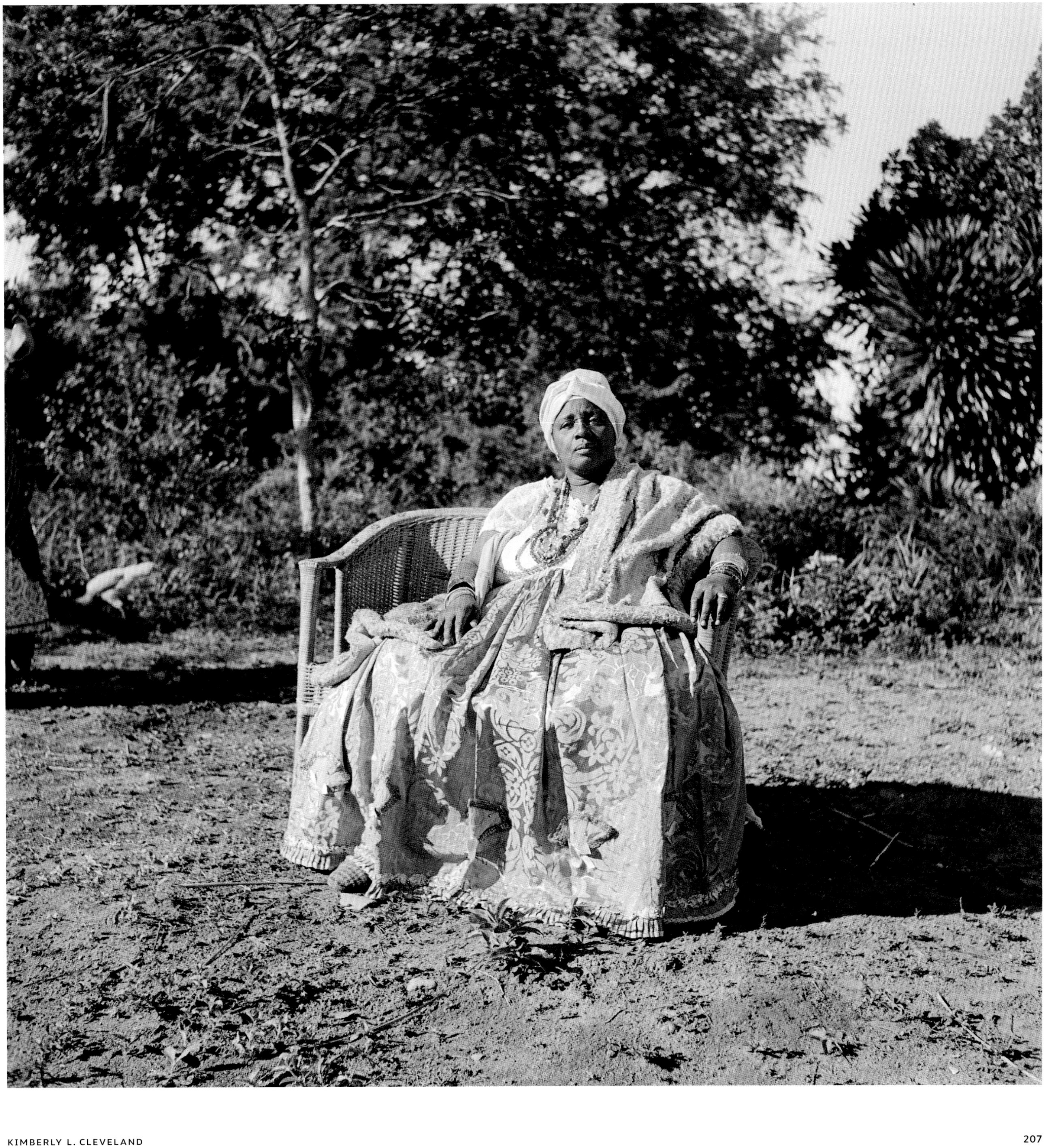

Another of the region's most important artists, Rubem Valentim would leave his birthplace of Salvador in the late 1950s (fig 10.3). Valentim, who was born in 1922, was self-taught and began to paint in 1946, the same year he obtained a degree in dentistry. Eventually, however, he abandoned the latter to dedicate himself completely to painting. He quickly became active in Bahia's artistic and literary circles, and ten of his works were featured in an exhibition of upcoming regional artists in 1950 (Coelho 1968, 10). At mid-decade, he began to produce increasingly abstract works, which he based on the forms and symbols of Candomblé. Unhappy with what he felt was a lack of acceptance of his work in Salvador, he relocated to Rio de Janeiro in 1957 (Valentim 2001, 196).

Although Valentim never again resided in his home region, his paintings and later prints and sculptures were forever linked to Bahia through the visual language of Candomblé. As a child, the artist had attended both Catholic Church services and several Candomblé houses with family members (Valentim 2001, 189, 193). In his 1976 "Manifesto ainda que tardio" ("Manifesto although Late"), he addressed the significant influence that Bahia, with its mixture of cultures, had on him:

> My plastic-visual-signographic language is linked to the deep mythical values of Afro-Brazilian culture (mestizo-animist-fetishist). With the weight of Bahia on me—the culture experienced; with black blood in my veins—the atavism; with eyes wide open toward what is going on in the world—contemporaneity; creating one's sign-symbols I seek to transform the enchanted, magic, probably mystic world into a plastic language that has flown continually within me. The substratum comes from the earth, as I am so closely linked with the complex culture of Bahia; a city that is the product of a great collective synthesis based in the fusion of ethnic and cultural elements of European, African, and Amerindian origins (Valentim 2001, 28).[2]

Taking his cue from the region's syncretic character, Valentim created his own plastic language based on Candomblé.

Although not to the extent he desired, Valentim's works had been featured in local exhibitions before he left Bahia. Somewhat ironically, his turn toward abstract representations of Candomblé subject matter occurred within a year of his departure. Soon after, Valentim became nationally known for his unique visual language with its regional roots. He was the only artist whose work was selected by the Brazilian government to represent the nation in the First (1966) and Second (1977) World Festivals of Black Art and Culture, held in Senegal and Nigeria, respectively. Today, permanent galleries dedicated to Valentim's work exist in both the Pinacoteca do Estado de São Paulo and the Museu de Arte Moderna da Bahia.

Mestre Didi was a native son of Bahia and spent his entire life in the region. Born Deoscóredes Maximiliano dos Santos in Salvador in 1917, he was linked from birth with Ilê Axé Opô Afonjá (fig. 10.4), and his mother, Mãe Senhora (fig. 10.5), ultimately headed the community from 1942 until her death in 1967. Because of the primary role that religion played in Didi's life, the sacred affected his artistic training and his choice of form and material. In recognizing the inextricability of his sacred affiliation from all other aspects of his life, Juana Elbein dos Santos described her late husband as a "priest-artist" (Santos 1997, 173).

Didi's artistic formation was in fact part of his religious instruction. As a child, he was inclined to make objects (Munanga and Gomes 2006, 215), and his creative training took place within the physical spaces of the Candomblé community with spiritual elders who taught him to "understand and manipulate forms, objects, and emblems that personify sacred entities" (Santos 1997, 173). At the same time that he honed his artistic skills, he attained higher religious positions. He became a priest at seventeen, and was made an *asogbá* (high priest) of Obaluaê (the deity of illness and also the masculine principle of Earth) before the age of twenty. As a priest, Didi was required to create and consecrate ritual emblems and scepters, thus drawing upon his artistic skills. As his creations were intended for use within the sacred realm, those who saw them were almost exclusively members of Ilê Axé Opô Afonjá. It was not until he was in his fifties that Didi began to exhibit his work outside of the religious space, expanding his audience.

Didi studied African influences in Bahia and was active in preserving the region's Afro-Brazilian heritage. In 1946 he authored a Yoruba-Portuguese dictionary. In the 1960s he collaborated with other key cultural figures—including author Jorge Amado, artists Carybé and Pierre Verger, and scholar Roger Bastide—on publications about Candomblé and African influences in Salvador. He also collaborated with his wife, an anthropologist and fellow initiate, on studies of Afro-Bahian culture and exhibitions of his own Afro-Brazilian art related to Candomblé as well as that of other artists. As soon as he began to present his work outside Ilê Axé Opô Afonjá, there was immediate interest in his production. Galleries in Salvador, Rio de Janeiro, and São Paulo held solo exhibitions of his sculptures, and in 1967 he was awarded the Bahia State prize at the National Biennial. He continued to produce exclusively Candomblé-influenced pieces and exhibit his art nationally and internationally until his death in 2013.

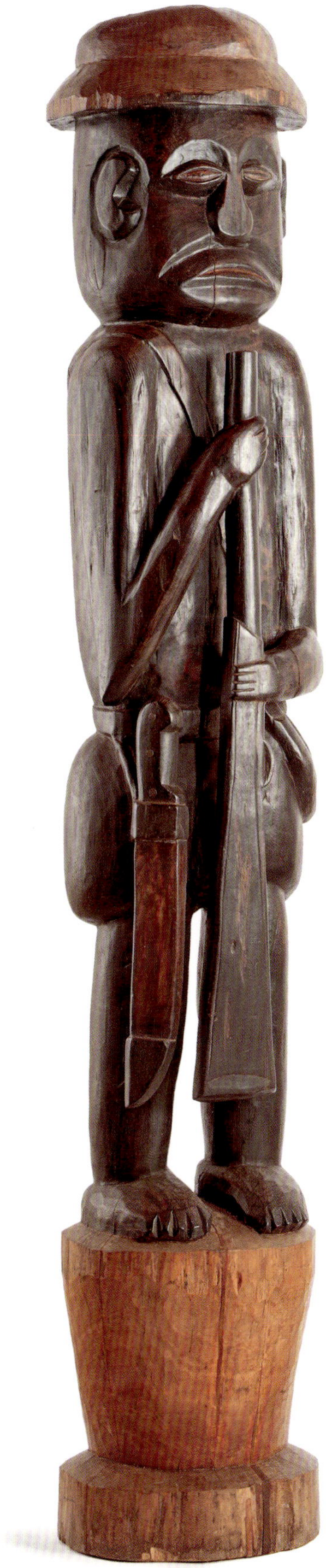

### The Artworks

Candomblé uses a number of artistic forms and materials in its practices, as did the four artists discussed here. Both Agnaldo and Mestre Didi were sculptors, although Agnaldo worked exclusively in wood and Didi with a variety of materials traditionally used to create liturgical instruments. Carybé created paintings, sculptures, and drawings in diverse media. Valentim was a painter, sculptor, and printmaker, who also worked with a range of materials.

An undated sculpture by Agnaldo features the *orixá* Oxóssi, the hunter god who lives in the forest (fig. 10.6). The instruments traditionally associated with this deity are the bow and arrow. Agnaldo, however, has syncretized the immortal *orixá* with a human hunter who wears a hat and holds a shotgun to his chest. At his waist is a machete and across his chest the strap of a bag he carries. In his representation of this deity, Agnaldo has also taken inspiration from the northeastern figure of the *cangaceiro* made famous in the early twentieth century. *Cangaço* was a form of banditry that was especially prevalent in northeastern Brazil in the 1920s. Rather than incorporate the god's traditional bow and arrow, Agnaldo bestows upon him some of the elaborate attire and weapons for which these bandits were known (Mello 2001, 54–71). Agnaldo created several representations of Oxóssi in which he syncretized the powerful deity with the infamous *cangaceiro*. Because he was producing with a secular audience in mind, the sculptor did not follow the religious conventions in his representations. For many local viewers, however, both the sacred and secular elements had relevance.

Carybé's carved panel of *Oxum* represents another Candomblé *orixá*. Oxum is the goddess associated with grace, love, and vanity (see figs. 10.7o). In the artist's wood carving, she wears her elegant crown (*adé*) and waist chain (*penca*), and holds her fan (*abebé*) in an elevated position, as if she were admiring her reflection in a mirror. She is adorned with earrings, beaded necklaces, and bracelets, all of warm, glowing gold. Carybé also skillfully intimates Oxum's seductive dance, suggesting that the goddess moves on tiptoe while holding up her skirts. This goddess rules the sacred river named for her in Oshogbo, Nigeria, and her swaying form follows the undulating waves of the water. Below her image on the panel is a nanny goat, one of her preferred sacrifices.

**10.6**
Agnaldo Manoel dos Santos (b. 1926, Ilha de Itaparica, Bahia, Brazil; d. 1962)
*Oxóssi caçador* (Oxóssi the Hunter), undated
Wood
H: 197 cm
COLLECTION OF MUSEU DE ARTE MODERNA DA BAHIA (MAM, BAHIA)
PHOTOGRAPH BY ANDREW KEMP

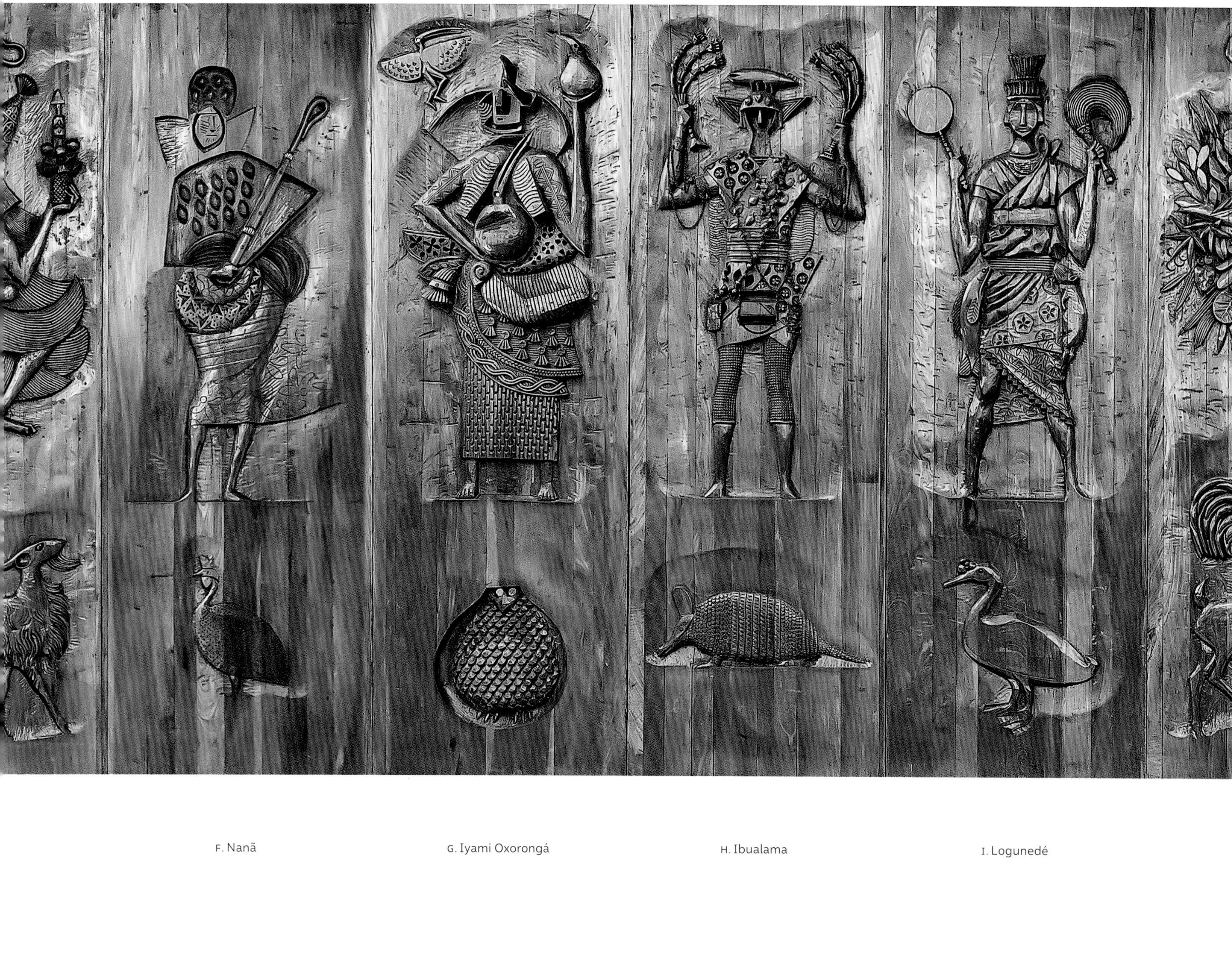

F. Nanã

G. Iyami Oxorongá

H. Ibualama

I. Logunedé

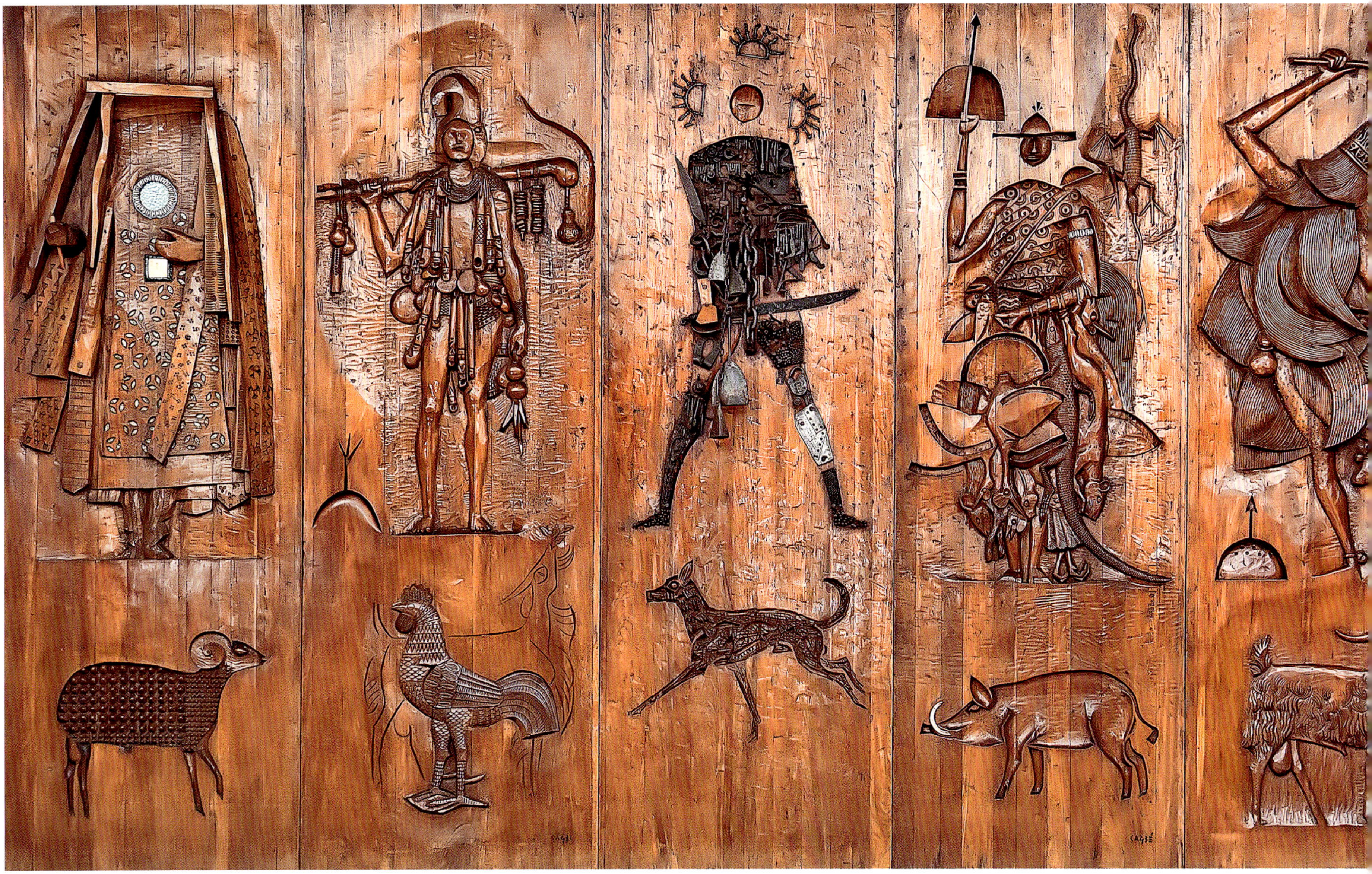

A. Babá Abaolá B. Exú C. Ogum D. Oxóssi E. Omolú

Ogum's intimidating and bellicose appearance counterbalances Oxum's charming and seductive presence. Ogum, the god of war, rules over all metal, including iron. Above his head Carybé has placed representations of the deity's unique crown (*akoro*). His armor is composed of pieces of scrap metal, which give shape to his form. His weapon of choice, a sword, cuts across his body in a bold horizontal line. Metal chains and links emanate from this god, spilling forth like an iron waterfall. At Ogum's feet is a dog, one of the animals he eats (Amado 1979, 24).

These two carvings are part of a series of twenty-seven wood panels depicting the *orixás* that Carybé created in 1968 (figs. 10.7a-s, 10.8a-h). They were collectively titled, *Grande Mural dos Orixás* and originally commissioned by the Banco da Bahia in Salvador. The majority of the pieces are uniform in size, three meters tall and one meter wide, making each deity appear larger than life. The artist imparted a sense of rhythm and motion through his careful use of line and also appealed to the sense of touch through a textural combination of materials. Today, Carybé's *Mural dos Orixás* stands in a dedicated gallery of the Museu Afro-Brasileiro in Salvador.

Valentim used the symbolic forms and symbols associated with the various *orixás* in his own signature style. In his *Objeto emblemático 11* (Emblematic Object 11) from 1969, the artist featured the double-headed axe of Xangô, the Candomblé deity of thunder and lightning. According to curator Paulo Herkenhoff, "Xangô's double-edged machete able to slash on both sides was [Valentim's] most significant symbol as well as an artistic metaphor which encompassed western tradition as well as a genuine approach to the African roots which integrate Brazilian culture" (Herkenhoff 1996, 418). The artist also employed other sacred forms in *Objeto emblemático 11*. During religious rites, Candomblé initiates may use *pontos riscados*, or marked points, which are graphic symbols drawn on the floor with chalk, to call the deities from the otherworldly sphere to communicate with select individuals in the world of the living. In this sculpture, Valentim uses several variations of the marked point for Exú, god of the crossroads that exist between the mortal and immortal spheres. The arrows pointing up and down, as well as the "pitchfork-style" symbols allude to this Candomblé deity, who guards the intersection of different realms. The color red, which dominates the work, is associated with both Xangô and Exú.

**10.7a–s**
Carybé (Héctor Julio Páride Bernabó, b. 1911, Lanús, Buenos Aires Province, Argentina; d. 1997)
Larger panels from the Grande mural dos *orixás*, 1968
Cedar with metal inlay
Each panel 3 x 1 m
MUSEU AFRO-BRASILEIRO, SALVADOR

A. Babá Abaolá
B. Exú
C. Ogum
D. Oxóssi
E. Omolú
F. Nanã
G. Iyami Oxorongá
H. Ibualama
I. Logunedé
J. Ossanyin (Ossaim)
K. Irôko
L. Xangô
M. Bayani
N. Oxumaré
O. Oxum
P. Iansã
Q. Ewá
R. Iemanjá
S. Oxalufã

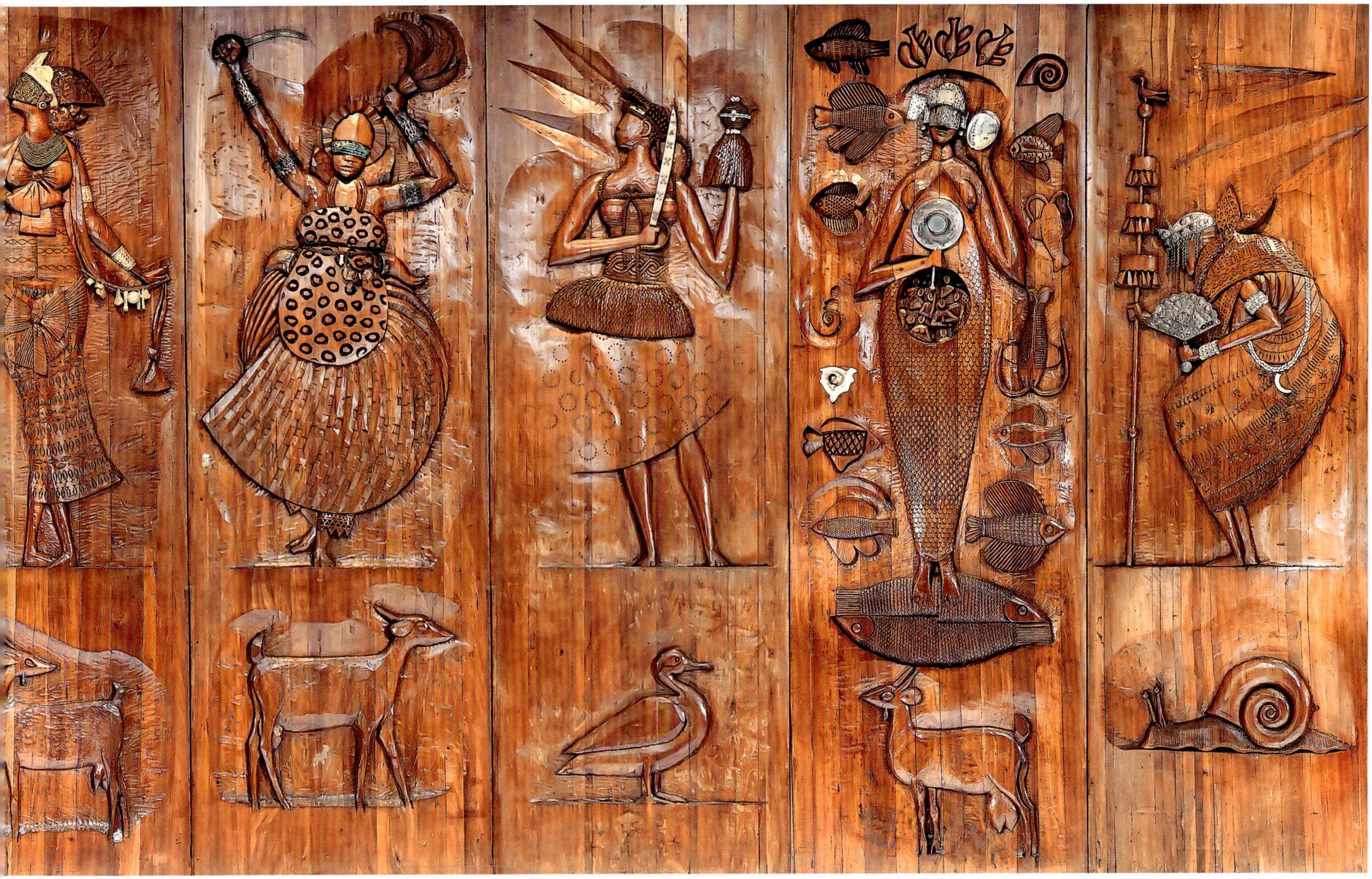

O. Oxum P. Iansã Q. Ewá R. Iemanjá S. Oxalufã

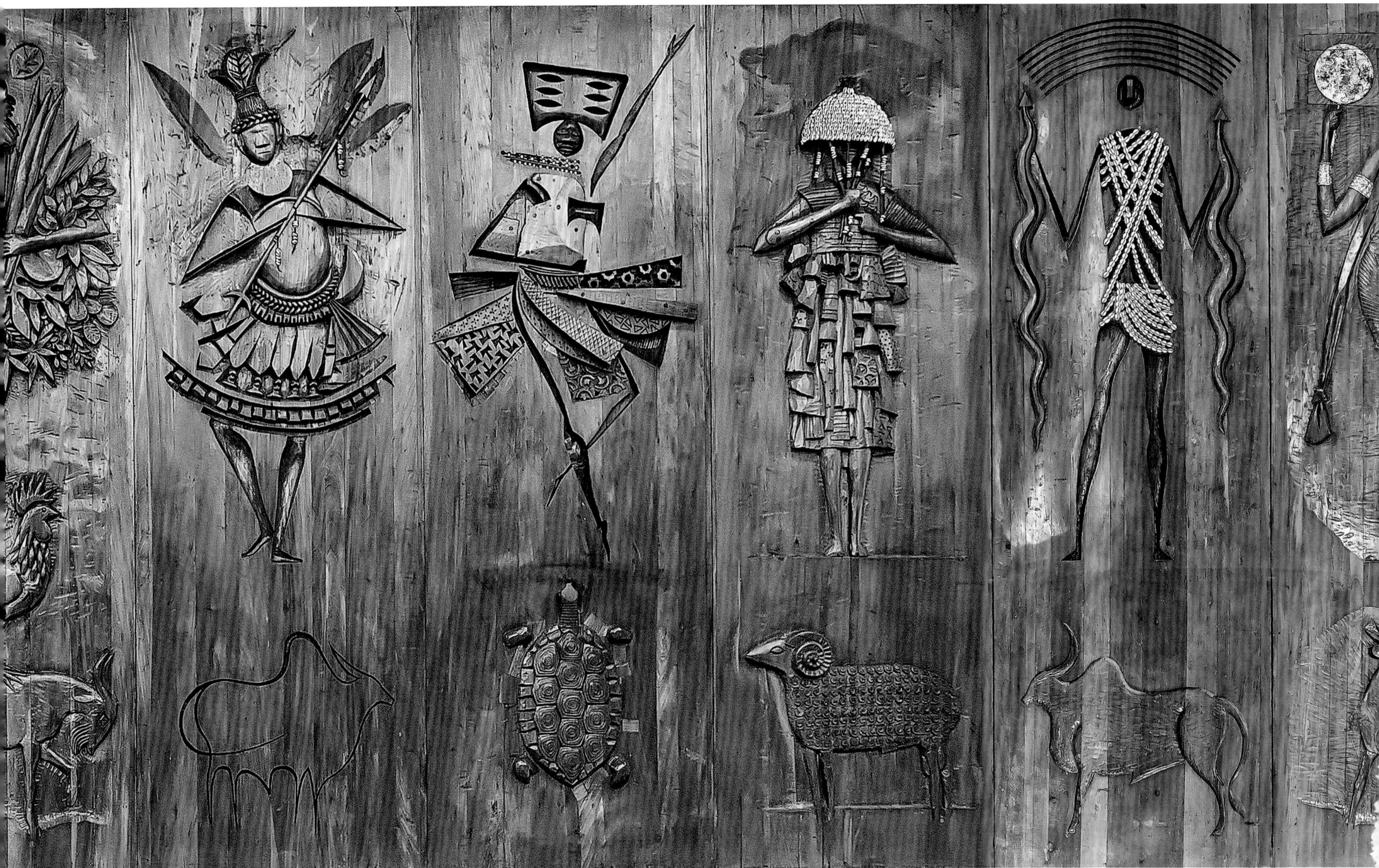

J. Ossayin (Ossaim)

K. Irôko

L. Xangô

M. Bayani

N. Oxumaré

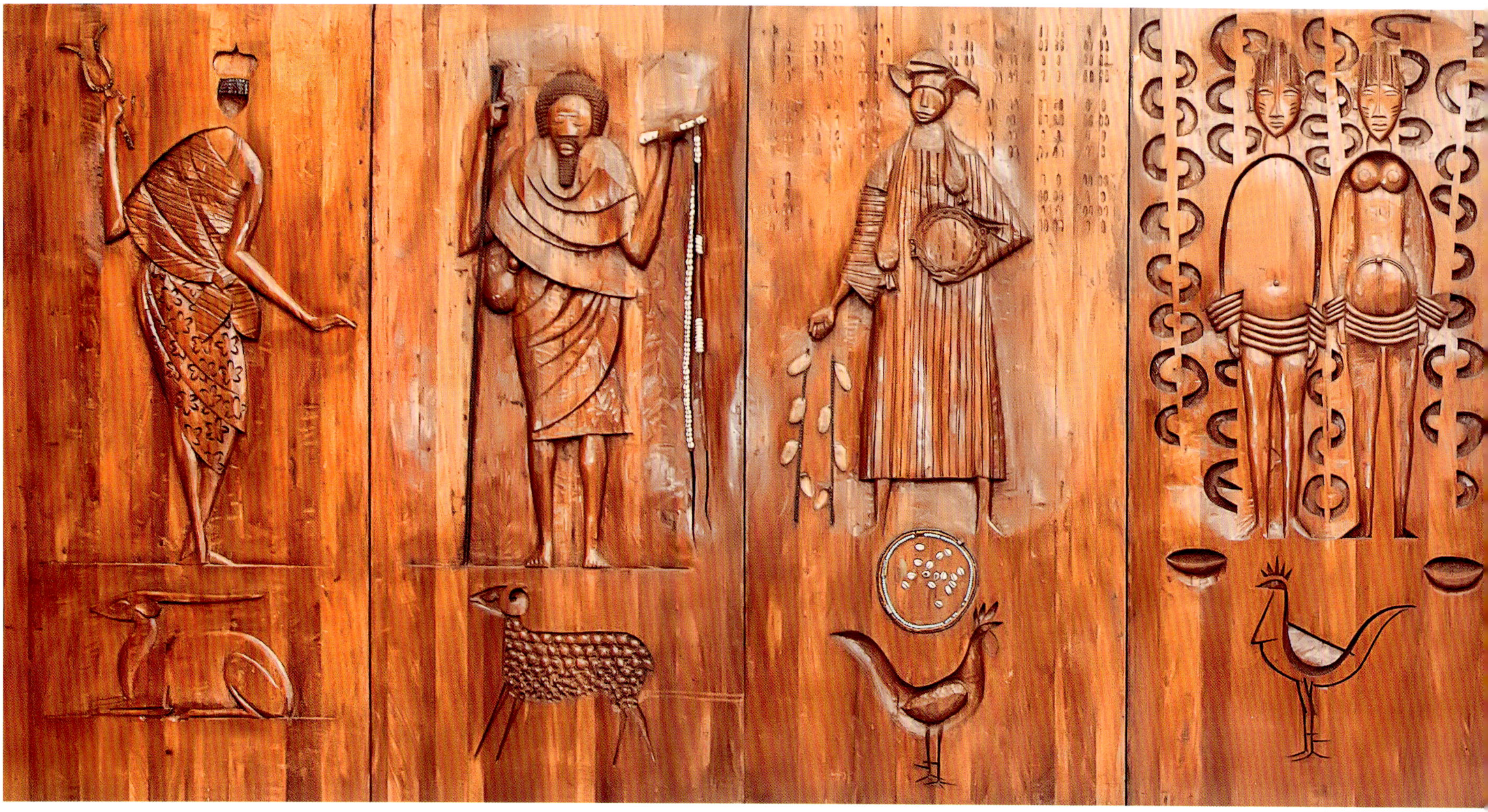

A. Axabó

B. Orixá Okô

C. Ifá

D. Ibeji

**10.8a–h**
Carybé (Héctor Julio Páride Bernabó, b. 1911, Lanús, Buenos Aires Province, Argentina; d. 1997)
Smaller panels from the Grande mural dos *orixás*, 1968
Cedar with metal inlay
Each panel 2 x 1 m
MUSEU AFRO-BRASILEIRO, SALVADOR
PHOTOGRAPHS BY DARÍO GUIMARÃES NETO

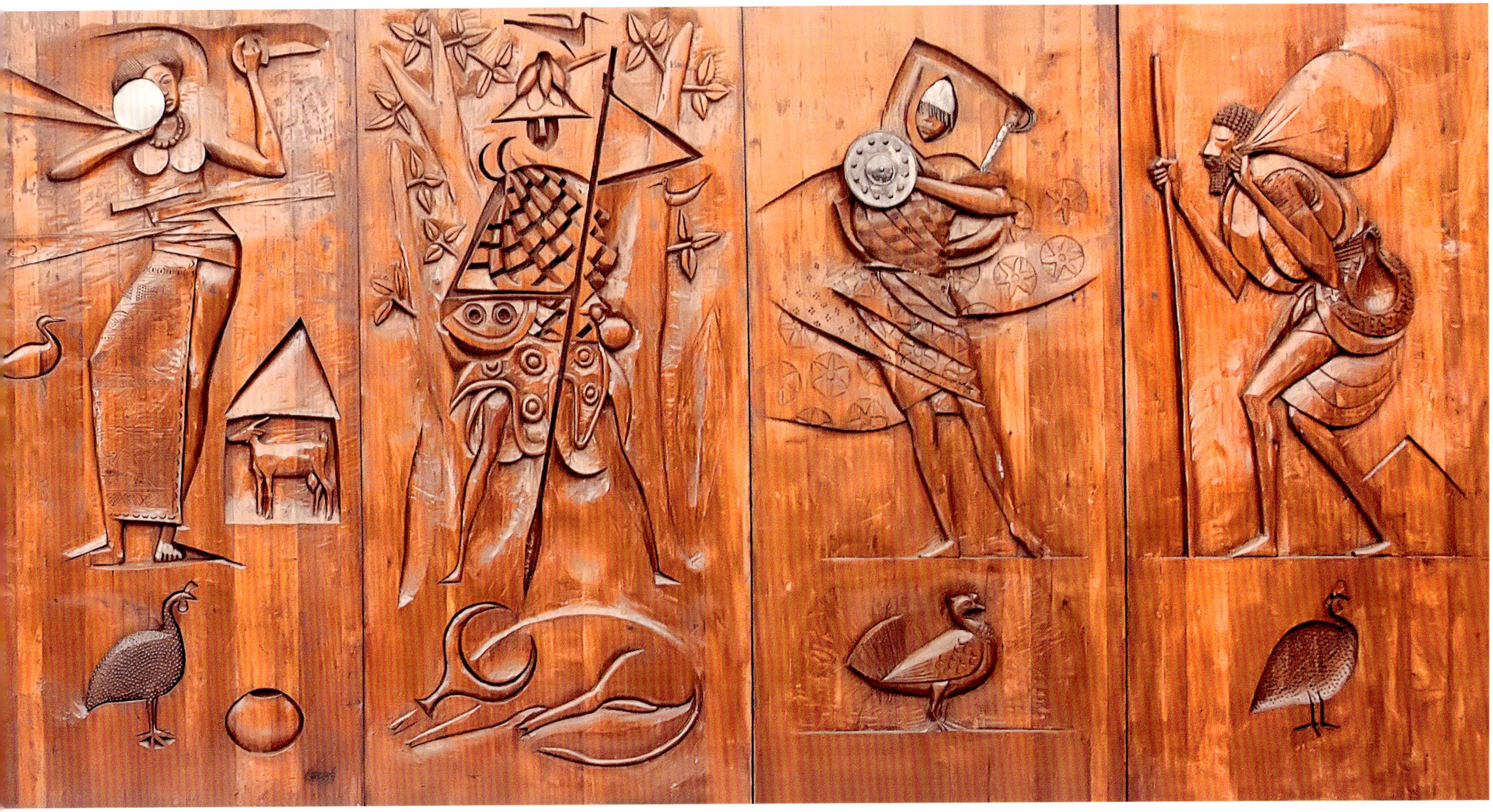

E. Obá

F. Otin

G. Oxaguiã

H. Onilé

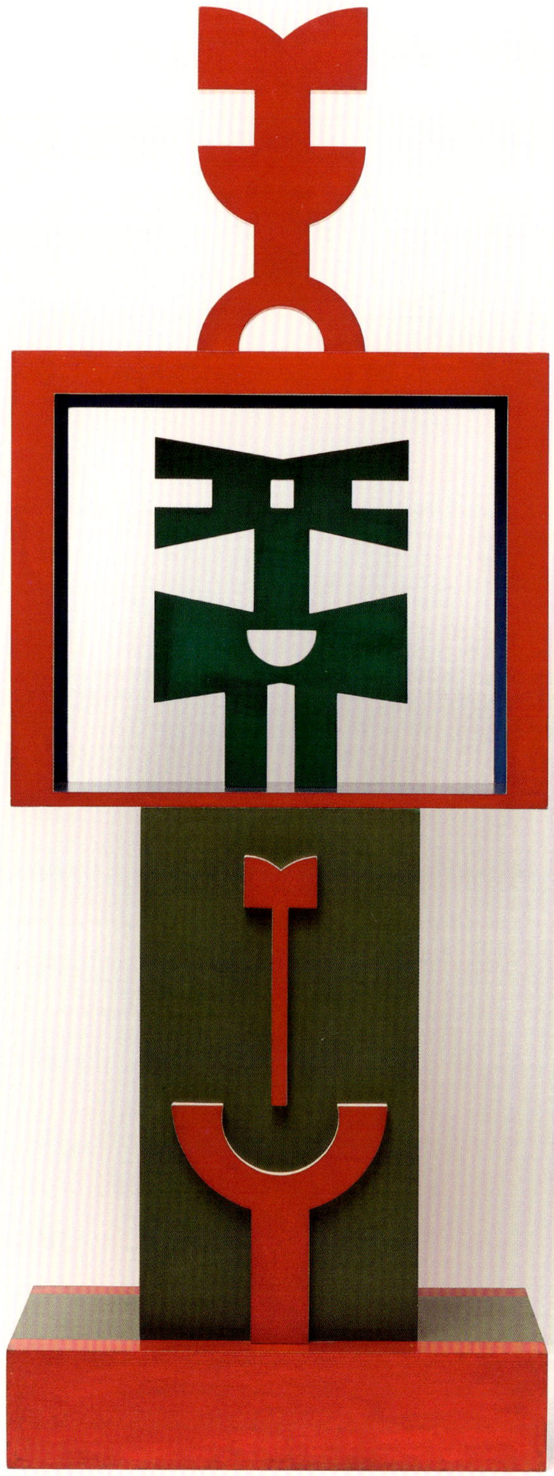

**10.9**
Rubem Valentim (b. 1922, Salvador, Bahia, Brazil; d. 1991)
*Objeto emblemático 4* (Emblematic Object 4), 1969
Acrylic paint on wood
H: 206 cm
COLLECTION OF THE PINACOTECA DO ESTADO DE SÃO PAULO, BRAZIL; DONATION OF LIA BICCA DE ALENCASTRO AND BALTHAZAR BICCA DE ALENCASTRO
PHOTOGRAPH BY ISABELLA MATHEUS

*Objeto emblemático 4* is one of a number of emblematic objects, which Valentim began creating in 1969 (fig. 10.9). He had already transitioned from two-dimensional paintings to three-dimensional forms, primarily emblematic reliefs, two years earlier (figs. 10.10, 10.11). From reliefs he moved onto freestanding sculptures. Despite this switch of medium from the paintings that defined the first few decades of his production, the artist maintained his focus on Candomblé and his emphasis on symmetry. His exploration of freestanding three-dimensional sculpture was a reference to religious altars, or *pejis*. Unlike the names, symbols, and colors of the various *orixás*, which were more frequently used in public celebrations and references to Candomblé, the altars were seen only by certain ranking initiates inside the sacred grounds of the religious communities. Valentim based *Objeto emblemático 4*, as well as his other emblematic objects, on the altars, which, he noted, had a "composite, almost geometric organization" (Valentim 1994, 78).

Mestre Didi's *Idilê Aiyê* (Scepter Combining the Symbols of the Earth Pantheon) celebrates the trio of deities constituting the pantheon of the Earth (Santos 1997, 173). The artist represents Nanã and her two sons, Obaluaê and Oxumaré, through their respective liturgical objects or forms (fig. 10.12). Obaluaê's thick hand-held broom (*xaxará*) made of bound palm leaf ribs forms the base of the sculpture (figs. 10.13, 10.14). The curved lines on each side, together with the *xaxará* base, morph into two staffs (*ibirís*) for Nanã. A priestess of this *orixá* would normally carry a staff of this type, made of palm leaf ribs, in her hand. Weaving in, out, and around these forms are the double *ejó* (snakes) that represent Oxumaré. The artist has embellished the traditional materials used for the liturgical instruments with leather, beads, and cowry shells in this sculpture.

Whereas for the uninitiated, Didi's sculpture is visually captivating, for the Candomblé initiate, each form and line within the work is symbolic. Nanã is the great Earth Mother, an elder female deity who is linked with the cycle of life. Her son, Obaluaê, is the male principle of the Earth. Nanã shares his *xaxará* toward the base, but ultimately branches off to form her own *ibirí* on either side. Nanã's other son, Oxumaré, is associated with the "mythical pythons who rose out of the depths of the Earth, touched the sky and returned to penetrate the Earth.... As a winding, multicolored serpent, Oxumare represents the cyclical relation of this world and beyond" (Santos 1998, 12). The snakes spiral in and out of the curves of the *ibirí* and twist around the *xaxará* to create a harmonious family unit.

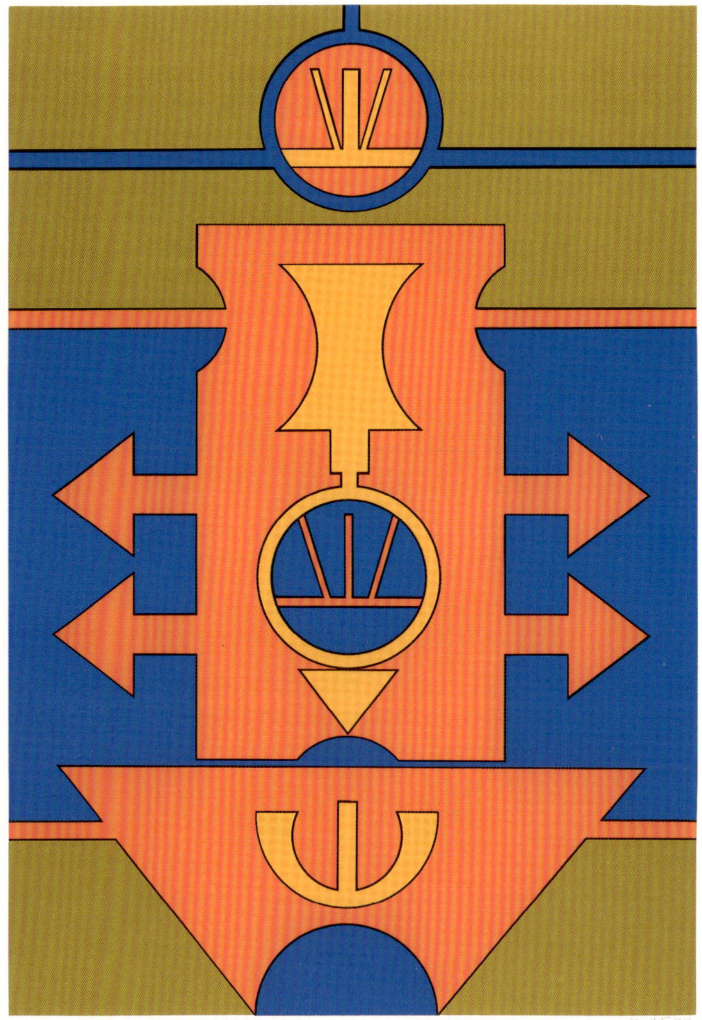

**10.10**
Rubem Valentim (b. 1922, Salvador, Bahia, Brazil; d. 1991)
*Sem título* (Untitled), 1989
Colored silk-screen print on paper
100 x 70.5 cm
COLLECTION OF THE PINACOTECA DO ESTADO DE SÃO PAULO, BRAZIL;
DONATED BY ASSOCIAÇÃO DOS AMIGOS DA PINACOTECA DO ESTADO, 2003
PHOTOGRAPH BY ISABELLA MATHEUS

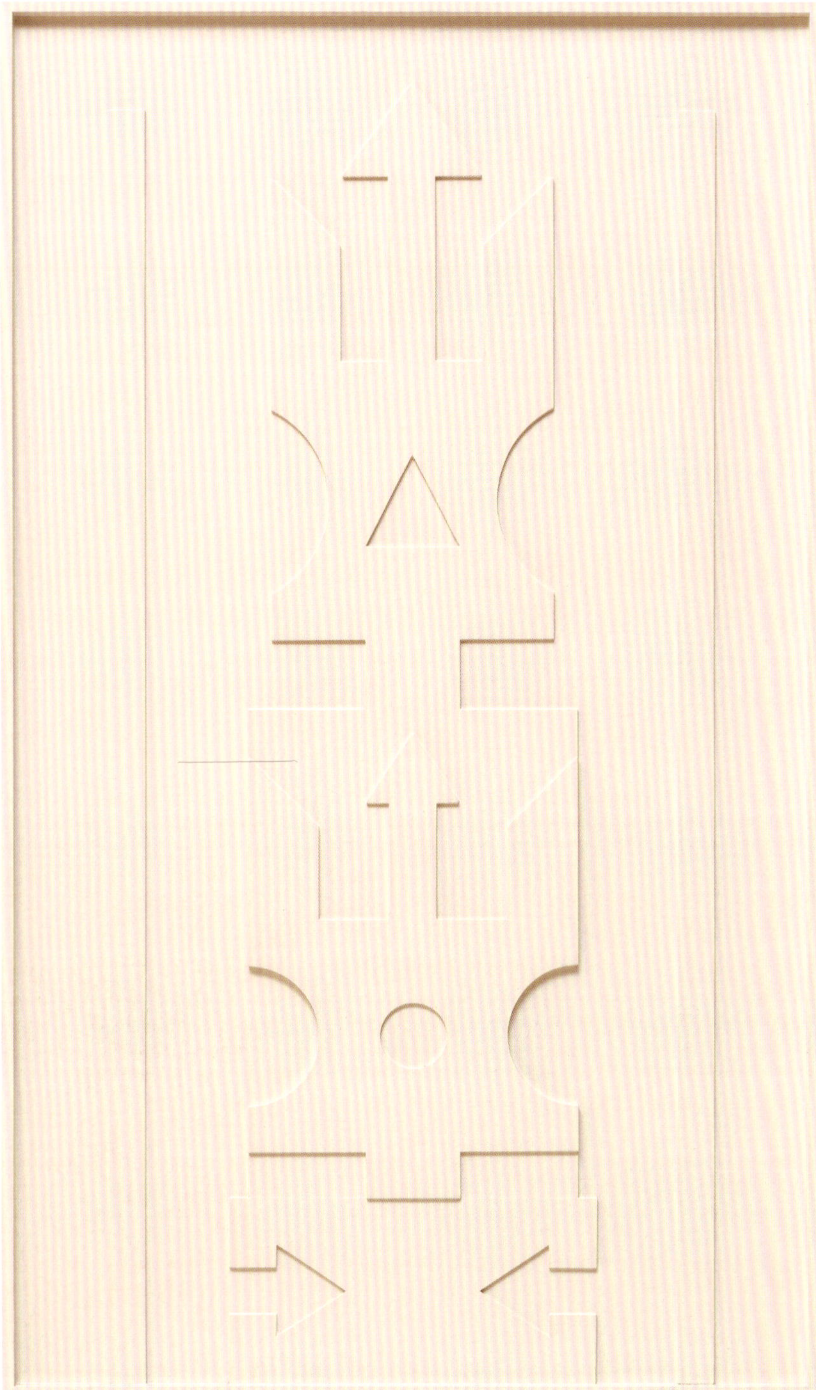

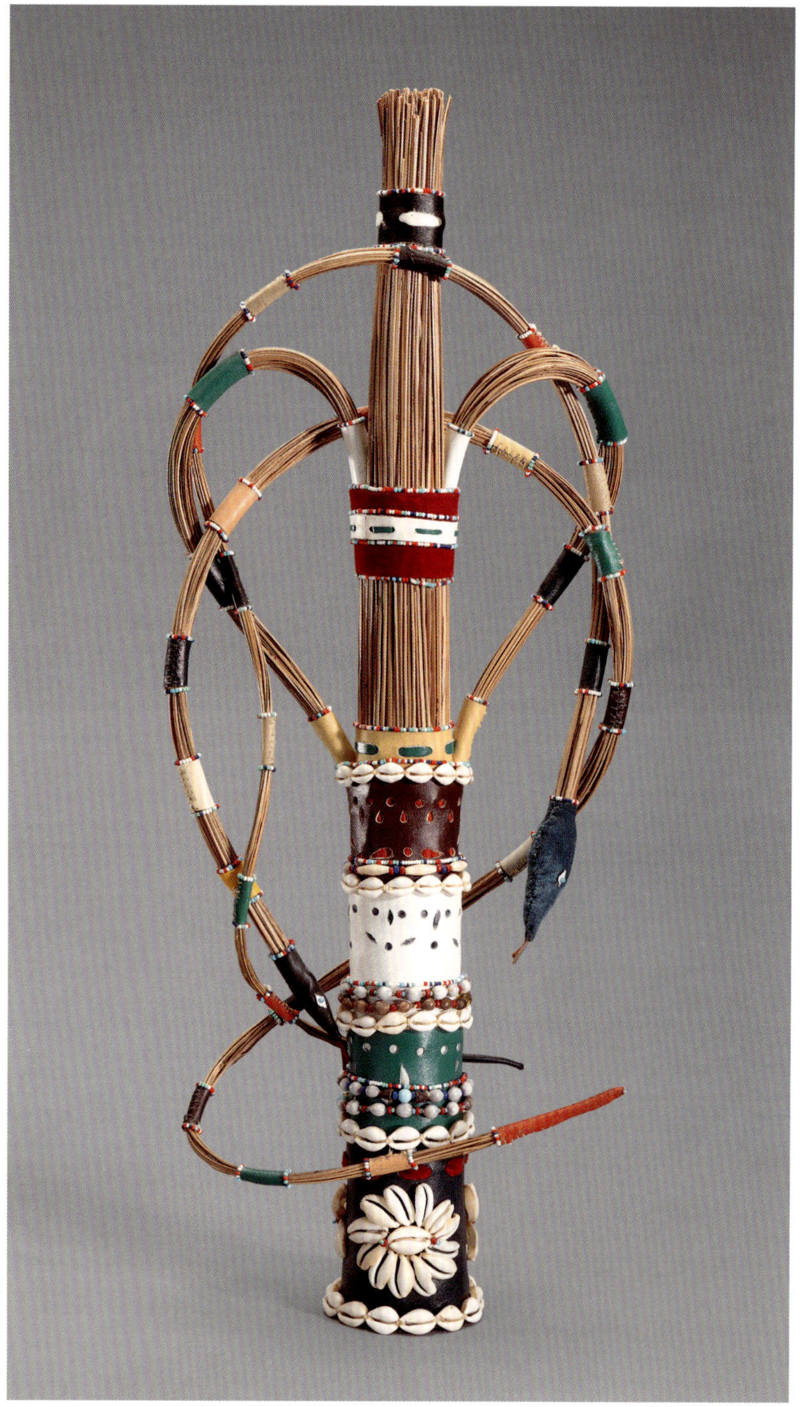

**10.11**
Rubem Valentim (b. 1922, Salvador, Bahia, Brazil, b. 1991)
*Relevo emblema 78* (Relief Emblem 78), 1978
Acrylic paint on wood
119.6 x 69.6 cm
COLLECTION OF THE PINACOTECA DO ESTADO DE SÃO PAULO, BRAZIL; PURCHASED BY GOVERNO DO ESTADO DE SÃO PAULO, 2013
PHOTOGRAPH BY ISABELLA MATHEUS

**10.12**
Mestre Didi (Deoscóredes Maximiliano dos Santos, b. 1917, Salvador, Bahia, Brazil; d. 2013)
*Idilê Aiyê: Sasará [xaxará] ejo ati ibirí* (Scepter Combining the Symbols of the Earth Pantheon), 1995
H: 71 cm
Vegetal fiber, leather cowries
COLLECTION OF THE BASS MUSEUM OF ART

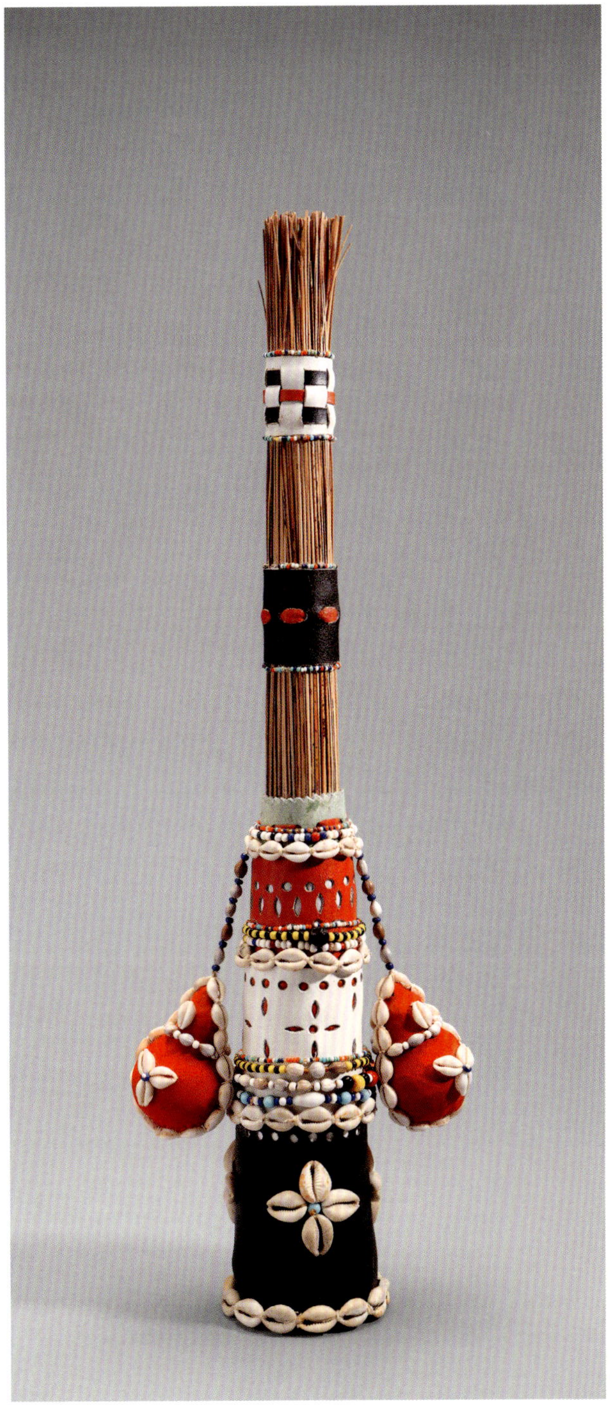

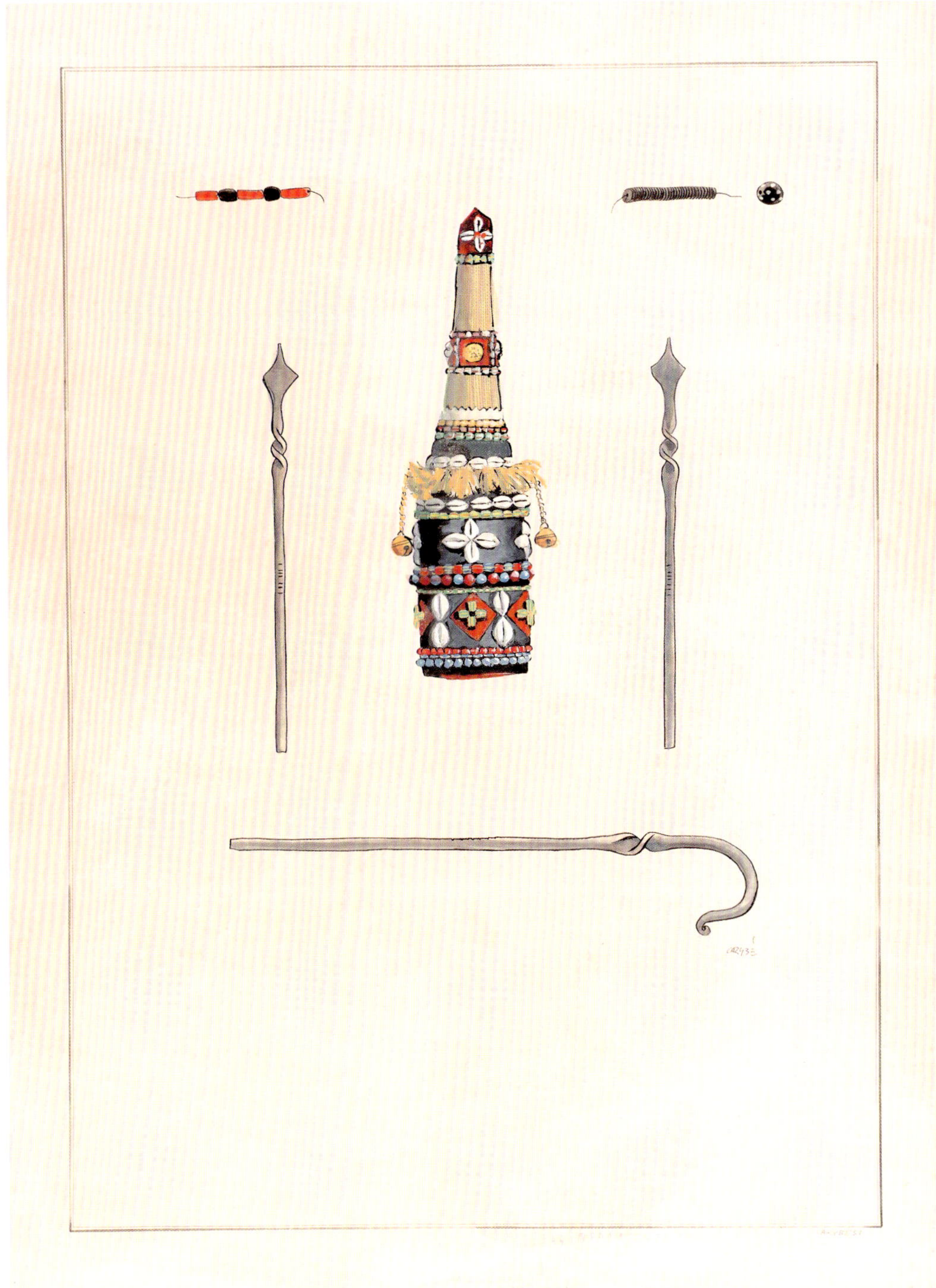

**10.13**
Mestre Didi (Deoscóredes Maximiliano dos Santos;
b. 1917, Salvador, Bahia, Brazil; d. 2013)
*Xaxará ati adô meji* (Scepter with Two Heads), 1989
Vegetal fiber, leather, cowries
H: 60 cm
COLLECTION OF MARK STEVEN GREENFIELD AND VALERIE ZAVALA

**10.14**
Carybé (Héctor Julio Páride Bernabó, b. 1911,
Lanús, Buenos Aires Province, Argentina; d. 1997)
*Ferramentas de Omolú, o orixá da varíola, das pestes e das doenças em geral: Xaxará, lanças curtas e gancho. Filho de Nanã Buruku e, como Oxumaré, originário da Nação Mabi* (Implements of Omolú, the *Orixá* of Smallpox, Plague, and Diseases in General: *Xaxará*, Short Spears, and Hook. Son of Nanã Burukú and, Like Oxumaré, Originally of the Mabí Nation), 1951
Ink and watercolor (gouache) on paper
83 x 63 cm
COURTESY INSTITUTO CARYBÉ / COPYRIGHTS CONSULTORIA LTDA.

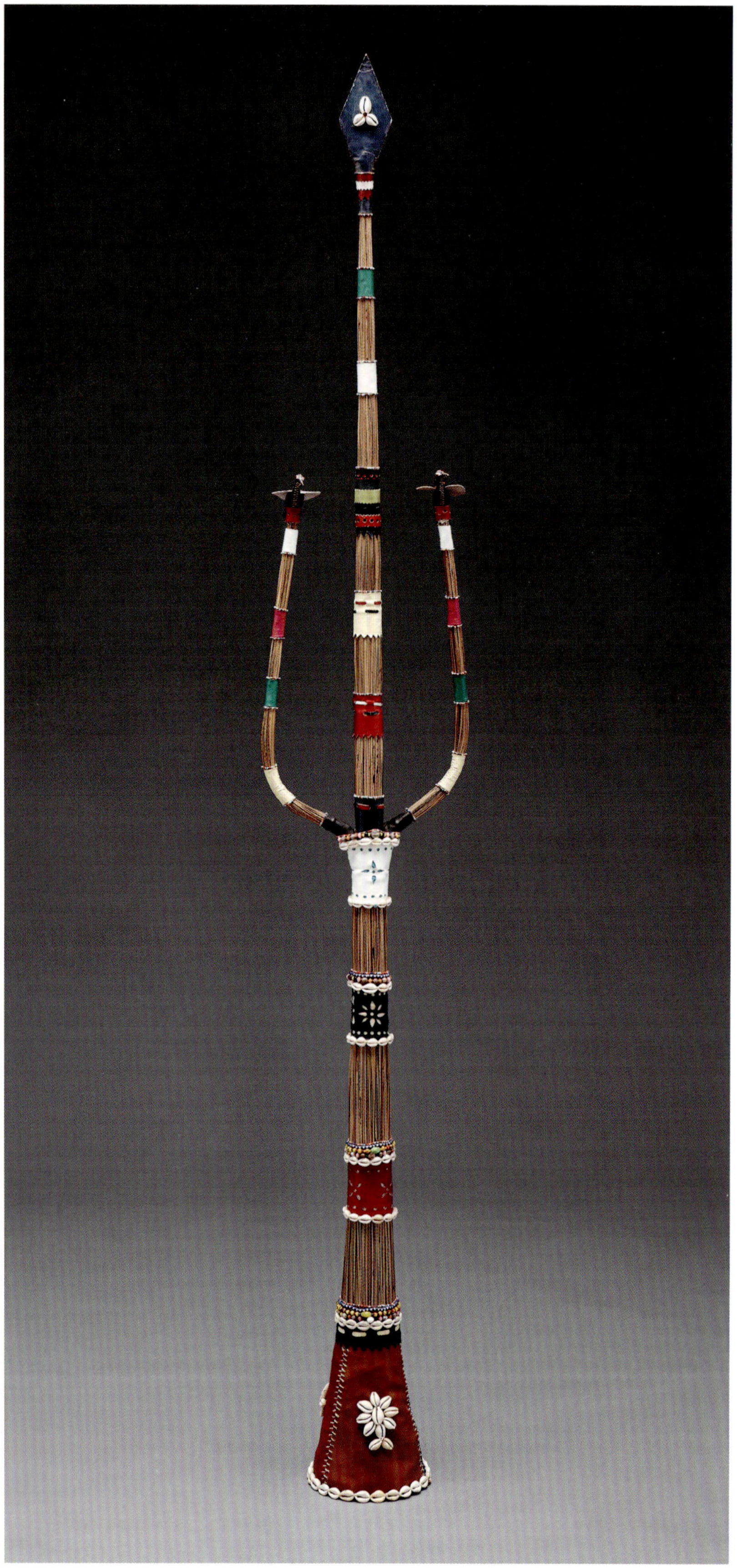

## Syncretic Approaches Embodied in Candomblé-Inspired Artworks

In his sculpture of *Oxóssi caçador*, Agnaldo combined aspects of a Candomblé deity with those of the *cangaceiro*, a secular figure, in his exploration of regional subjects that would speak to a local audience. He privileged this objective above adherence to the prescribed religious iconography, even in instances when it was financially disadvantageous to do so. This point is emphasized in an anecdote that appears in Jorge Amado's *Tent of Miracles*, in which the author tells of a Candomblé priest who commissioned an Oxóssi sculpture from the artist:

> As [Agnaldo] carved the trunk with ineffable delight, he gave Oxóssi a rifle to hold instead of a bow and arrow. It was a different kind of Oxóssi: still...the lord of the forest, of course, but with a strong resemblance to Lucas de Feira, the bandit from the backlands, or a rough-and-ready *cangaceiro*.... That's how Agnaldo saw Oxóssi and that's the way he carved him, with a fish knife and a rifle.... But the [priest] refused to accept the profane image. (Amado 1971, 6)

Although Agnaldo's deviation from established representations of Oxóssi made his sculpture undesirable to religious traditionalists, his amalgamation of the god with the god-like figure of the *cangaceiro* was a celebration of several aspects of regional culture. He underscored Candomblé's resonances and applicability beyond the physical boundaries of the religious space by making Oxóssi and the outlaw one. In contrast to the tendency of scholars and collectors to emphasize an "atavistic" approach in their discussions of the artist, analysis of Agnaldo's representations of Oxóssi reveals a clearly syncretic approach (Bevilacqua 2015, 108–16).

In the second half of the twentieth century, Carybé helped to define a regional aesthetic through numerous exhibitions of his works, many of which were based on Candomblé subjects. In the 1960s, through commissioned murals and panels that decorated banks and companies in Salvador and other parts of Brazil, he spread awareness of the religion even further. In acknowledging the impact that such large-scale installations could have, Carybé remarked, "murals are public, [whereas] paintings and drawings disappear in private homes" (Hein 1992, 27). In the case of his *Mural dos Orixás*, the carvings are a visual dictionary or guide, containing information about the numerous deities, their liturgical vestments, associated objects, movements, and animals. Carybé's firsthand experiences and his access to sacred spaces and information informed his detailed representations of

**10.15**
Mestre Didi (Deoscóredes Maximiliano dos Santos; b. 1917, Salvador, Bahia, Brazil; d. 2013)
*Opá exin ati eye meji* (Large Spear-Scepter with Two Birds), circa late 1990s
Leather, cowry shells, and palm leaf ribs
H: 243.8 cm
DALLAS MUSEUM OF ART; GIFT OF DEEDIE AND RUSTY ROSE

the religion in the built environment. He exercised a syncretic approach in merging the private and public worlds of Candomblé.

As one of a number of, mostly white, members of the intelligentsia, who took regional culture as their main source of inspiration, Carybé was able to introduce what was then still a largely marginalized religion into the mainstream regional culture prior to the "re-Africanization" movement of the 1970s. Artists, authors, poets, and other creative figures featured Candomblé and other aspects of Bahian culture in their production, although crafting what has often been labeled a romanticized or "folkloric" picture of regional life. These individuals, many of whom were Candomblé initiates, were not subject to the same social marginalization and racial discrimination that the majority of Afro-Brazilian practitioners faced. Key religious leaders embraced these cultural ambassadors, who in turn, introduced Afro-Brazilian religious subject matter into regional cultural representations, making Candomblé part of the public face of Bahia.

While Carybé looked "outward," Valentim looked inward, translating the sacred signs and symbols of Candomblé into his own abstract plastic language. Although highly personal, because of its reductive, semiotic character, Valentim's form of expression visually resembled the avant-garde style of Concrete Art popular in Brazil at that time. In the 1970s, several national and international curators and art critics praised Valentim's non-figural style of representation, which distinguished his production from what they considered the "folkloric," provincial representations of some of Bahia's other artists (Valentim 1970; 1978). Whereas Carybé introduced Candomblé's forms into mainstream spaces, Valentim inserted Afro-Brazilian religious symbols into the mainstream arts scene through his plastic language.

Although rooted in historical influences, Valentim's symbolic form of expression was about the future; and although his visual language was regional in its inspiration, it aimed for universal appeal. Importantly, Valentim relocated to Brasília in 1967, just seven years after it became the new national capital. Architect and urban planner Lúcio Costa designed the city around the shape of an airplane to represent the dynamism and boldness associated with this new center of government (Barnitz 2001, 184–88). The city's urban landscape and "metaphysical" religious atmosphere offered the perfect backdrop to Valentim's own graphic language and his leap from two-dimensional abstract paintings to three-dimensional emblematic reliefs and objects (Valentim 1994, 75). Valentim translated a regional visual language based in the mystery and culture of the country's less-economically developed northeast into a more accessible plastic language rooted in rationalism and symmetry in line with Brazil's financial and cultural centers in the south, as well as with dominant European artistic and cultural trends. Art critics lauded the creation of what Valentim called his "poetic, contemporary, universal language" (Valentim 2001, 28). The artist syncretized Candomblé symbols and ideas with avant-garde artistic concerns and styles of expression to create a unique plastic language.

For individuals in Bahia's art circles who were eager to see someone translate the esoteric and unfamiliar concepts of Candomblé into aesthetically pleasing pieces, Mestre Didi was an obvious match. Even before he became known as an artist, many Bahians knew of his familial connection to Ilê Axé Opô Afonjá. Furthermore, his religious and artistic instruction took place within the space of the Candomblé community. Of the artists who were producing Candomblé-inspired artworks in the mid-twentieth century, including those discussed earlier in this essay, Didi's sculptures were the truest in form and material to the liturgical instruments used within the religious communities. All of these factors created an unparalleled aura of knowledge and authenticity surrounding Didi's works once he began to create for audiences outside Ilê Axé Opô Afonjá.

Analysis of Didi's sculptures underscores that even a high-ranking priest has individual affiliations and predilections. The artist's widow confirms that with regard to the pieces "not actually intended for ritual use," Didi "used his own elaborations and his experience as an initiate to abstract symbolic meanings and transform them" (Santos 1997, 174). Although in many ways Didi, the artist, could not be separated from Didi, the priest, his production underscores the place of the individual within the religion as a whole. In Didi's works for the secular audience he syncretized aspects of Candomblé with aspects of *his* Candomblé (Cleveland 2015, 102–4).

Candomblé is complex, as is the historic and current role of syncretism in this religion. The foregoing examination of the religious-influenced artworks demonstrates that a combinatory approach applies to aspects of Candomblé beyond the often-discussed association of Yoruba deities with Catholic saints. Although Agnaldo Manoel dos Santos, Carybé, Rubem Valentim, and Mestre Didi appear more frequently in studies of Afro-Brazilian art history than Afro-Brazilian religion, they were among the first generation to introduce Candomblé-influenced works to the broader Brazilian public. Employing approaches based in the sacred and secular, public and private, regional and universal, and general and individual, these artists bridged different spheres of artistic production. Motivated by their own styles, preferences, and objectives, their work is evidence of the diverse fruits that the artistic tree of Candomblé bears.

*Interleaf* **I**

# Caetano Dias

**Roberto Conduru**

**I.1**
Caetano Dias (b. 1959, Feira de Santana, Bahia, Brazil)
*1978—Cidade sumersa* (1978—Submerged City), 2010
Video, 14:41
PHOTOGRAPH BY WALLACE NOGUEIRA, TATIANA DE LIMA
COURTESY PAULO DARZÉ GALERIA DE ARTE

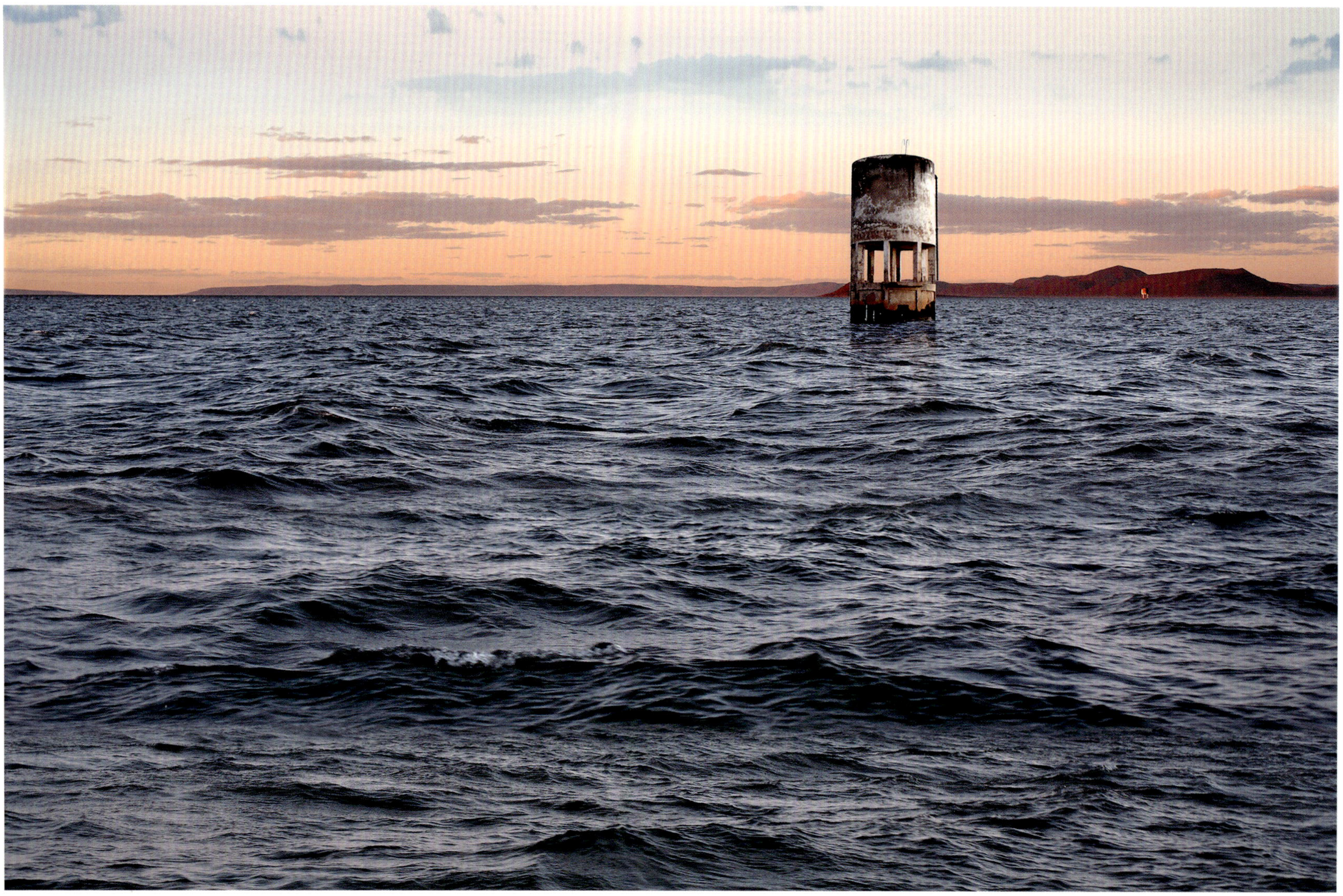

BORN IN FEIRA DE SANTANA, Bahia, in 1959, Caetano Dias moved to the state capital of Salvador in 1976. He began exhibiting ten years later and continues to live and work in the city. His oeuvre, however, does not in any way suggest fixity, uniformity, or monotony. Moving freely among the media currently available to artists, he has explored in particular the production of objects, installations, photography, and videos. Among other art historical issues, he has considered: the work of art as an intersubjective opening, based on Neoconcretism (a movement that flourished in Rio de Janeiro between 1959 and 1961); meanings added to materials, pursuing the path of German artist Joseph Beuys, who has other followers in Bahia (for example, Ayrson Heráclito and Tiago Sant'Ana); and the luminous chromatism with which Mário Cravo Neto photographically revealed Bahia. The hinterland and the coastal areas of Bahia are poles that also nourish Dias's thought and work, but they alone are not sufficient to encapsulate the arc of his interests.

There are some themes that recur; the first being his attraction to the unusual. Sometimes, he produces it himself. This is the case with *Mar de dentro* (Inner Sea, 2005), the artifact he made from wood and cement scraps with the help of people from a low-income community on the outskirts of Salvador (fig. I.2). On other occasions, he appropriates odd scenes and objects. Among his many photographs and video captures, highlights are the paradoxical images of the inoperative water tanks of Remanso, a rural town in Bahia that was submerged in the 1970s to build an artificial lake for the Sobradinho Dam (fig. I.1).

**I.2**
Caetano Dias (b. 1959, Feira de Santana, Bahia, Brazil)
*Mar de dentro* (Inner Sea), 2005
Wood, concrete, iron nails, wire mesh
W: 1.45 m
PHOTOGRAPH BY CAETANO DIAS
COURTESY PAULO DARZÉ GALERIA DE ARTE

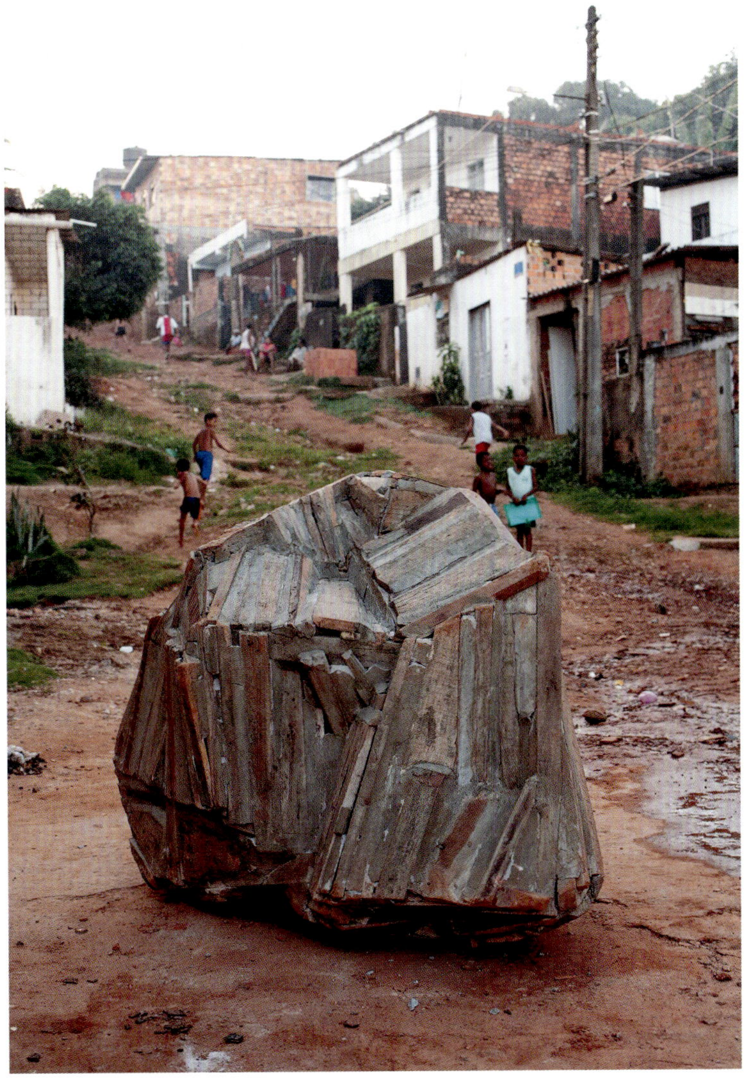

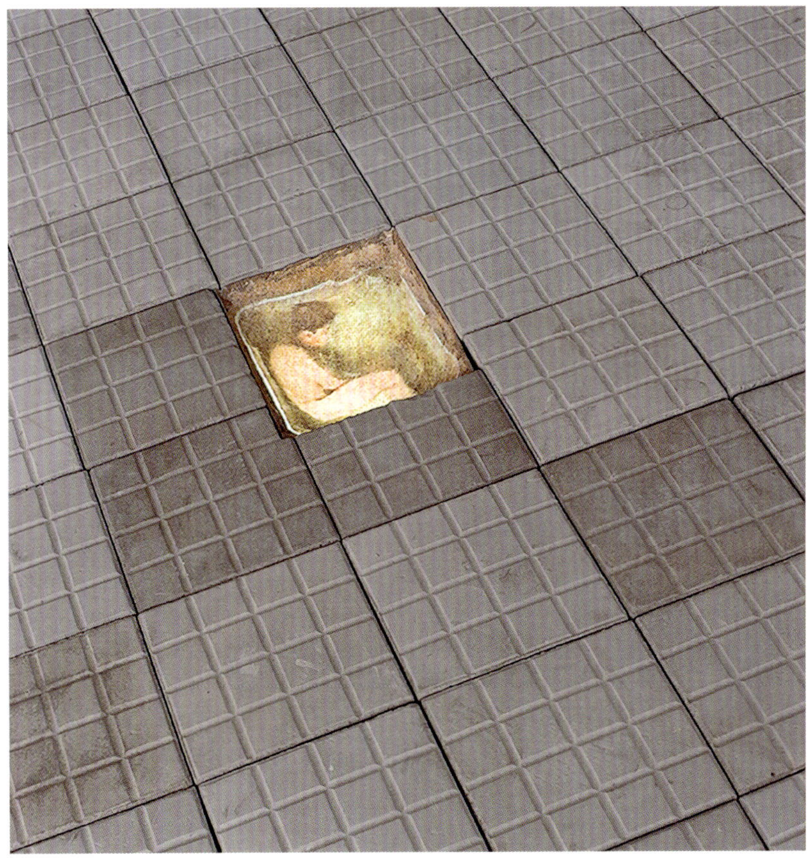

**I.3**
Caetano Dias (b. 1959, Feira de Santana, Bahia, Brazil)
*Passeio Neoconcreto* (Neoconcrete Passage), 2010
Fifth of a series of five installations
Video projection, concrete slabs, fiberglass shell, steel rod
Dimensions variable
Video, 15:00; Video directed by Caetano Dias
PHOTOGRAPH BY ANDREW KEMP
COURTESY PAULO DARZÉ GALERIA DE ARTE

Along with other materials, Dias has frequently employed sugar in his work. The production of this crop began in Bahia in the sixteenth century under Portuguese colonial rule and relied upon the forced labor of enslaved Africans and Afro-descendants. It became an essential factor in shaping the Bahian landscape and sociocultural relations. Using this substance, Dias has made children's toys, a pile and pillar of bricks, a maze, numerous heads cast from real-life subjects, a homeless man, and even an image of Jesus Christ. These objects and bodies, constructions and spaces use sugar to access the history of Bahia, indicating the persistence of its potential and its stigmas (see fig. 1.1).

Violence is also a key, and not infrequent, theme. Through the work of Dias, we can see how it pervades the process of history and shapes the Brazilian environment as it manifests in: Portuguese colonization; the enslavement of Africans and Afro-descendants between the sixteenth and nineteenth centuries; the extermination of Canudos, a quasi-religious rural commune in Bahia that was destroyed in 1897 and later flooded by the Cocorobó Dam; engineering works carried out during the military and civilian dictatorship that dominated Brazil between 1964 and 1985; the favela, or ghetto, as a place of social segregation; and ruined buildings, people, and landscapes. Despite these preoccupations, however, Dias manages to find beauty in the degraded, activating it poetically to instigate reflection.

Thus, his works open up meanings that go beyond the interplay between local and global. Both in the body of Jesus Christ and in that of a homeless

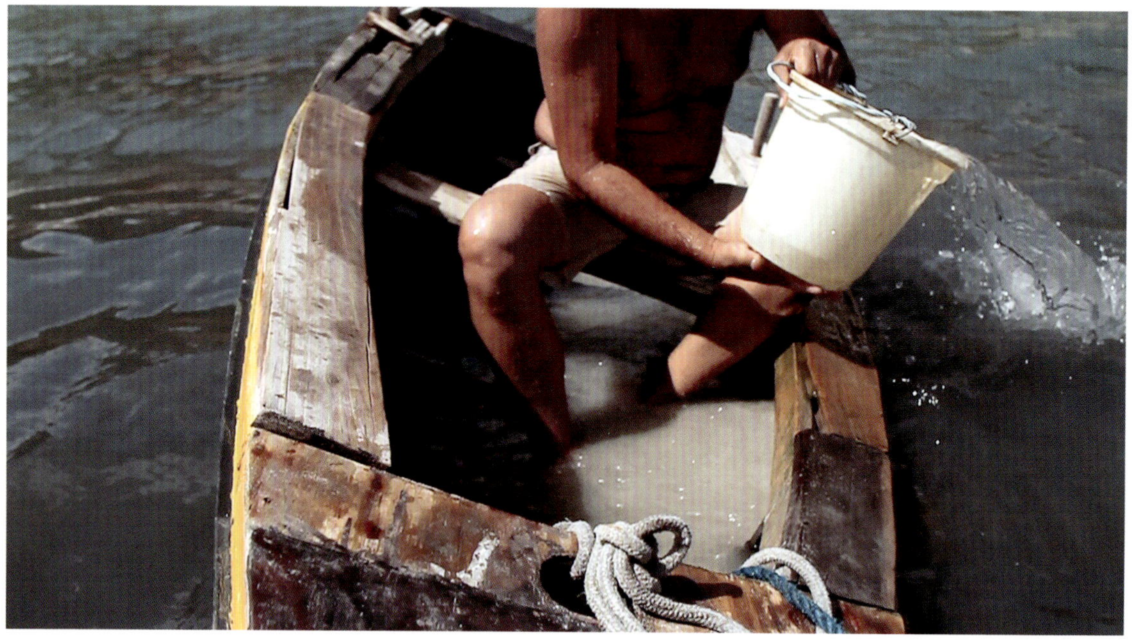

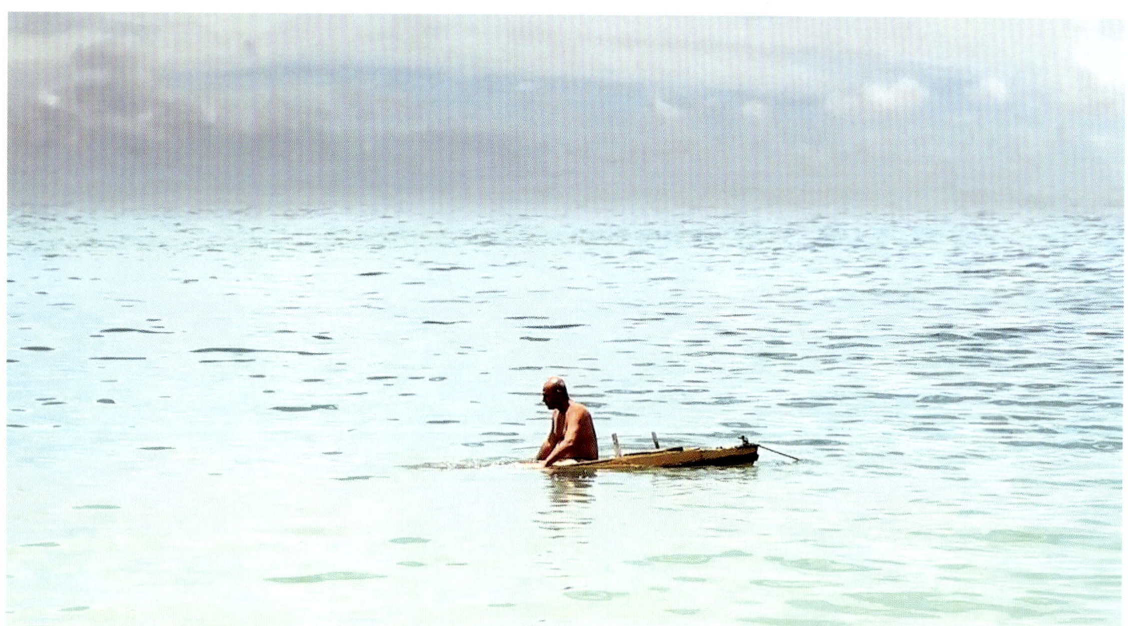

**I.4a-d**
Caetano Dias (b. 1959, Feira de Santana, Bahia, Brazil)
*Águas* (Waters), 2010
Video, 3:11
PHOTOGRAPH BY CAETANO DIAS
COURTESY PAULO DARZÉ GALERIA DE ARTE

man made of sugar echoes are to be found of marginalized peoples from the most varied latitudes and dates. In the video installation *O mundo de Janiele* (Janiele's World, 2007), we can understand the girl's continuous hoola-hooping as a ludic way of resisting physical, sociocultural, and existential limitations that are present as much for her in the Don Avelar neighborhood in Salvador as they are for Afro-descendants in the diaspora, or any person in his or her context (see fig. 11.9).

There is also broad resonance in the experience of *Mar de dentro* (fig. I.2), in which the unusual wood and cement object is repeatedly pushed uphill, only to be set loose and roll down again, running the risk of being destroyed and playing with the myth of Sisyphus. If the installation *Passeio Neoconcreto* (Neoconcrete Passage) holds an unfulfilled promise of happily overcoming tensions by harking back to the experience in the maternal womb and the imminence of birth (fig. I.3), it also indicates much less optimistic meanings about the infinite aquatic cloister associated with the sociocultural processes of restriction and even the limits naturally imposed on the human body. This pessimism only grows in *Águas* (Waters, 2010), a film that shows a man in a boat, bailing water into the vessel as he and it gradually sink before vanishing altogether (fig. I.4). This can be interpreted both as a parable about the process of the destruction of the environment by human beings today and a metaphor for human existence. This fatalism is not exempt from enchantment: Dias's placid images recall Dorival Caymmi when he combines sugar and saltwater in his song "É doce morrer no mar" ("It Is Sweet to Die in the Sea").

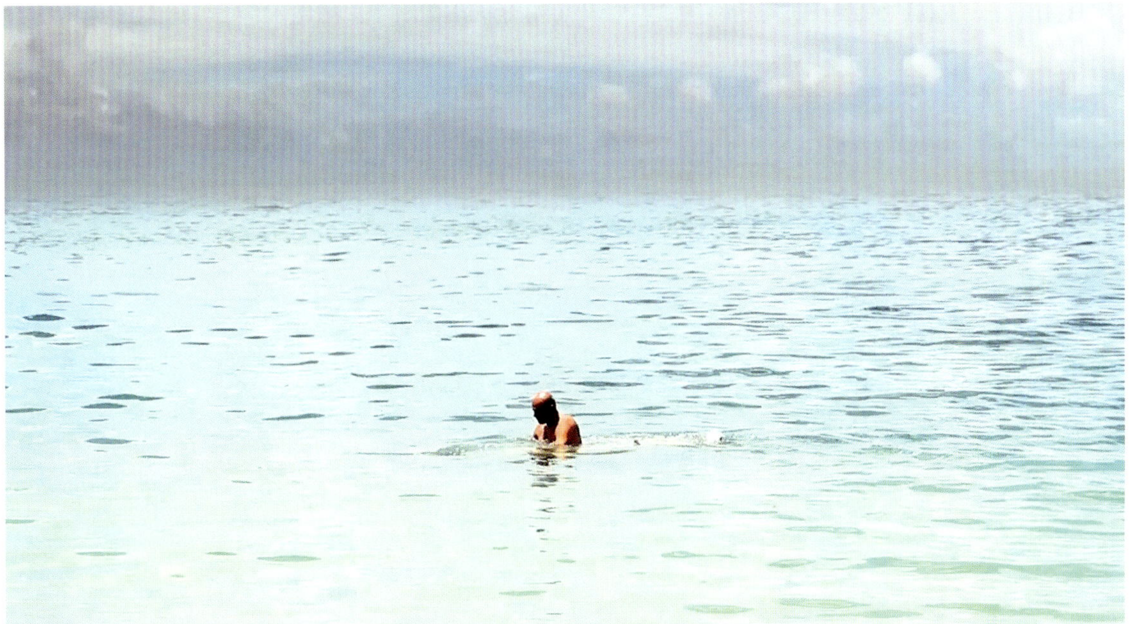

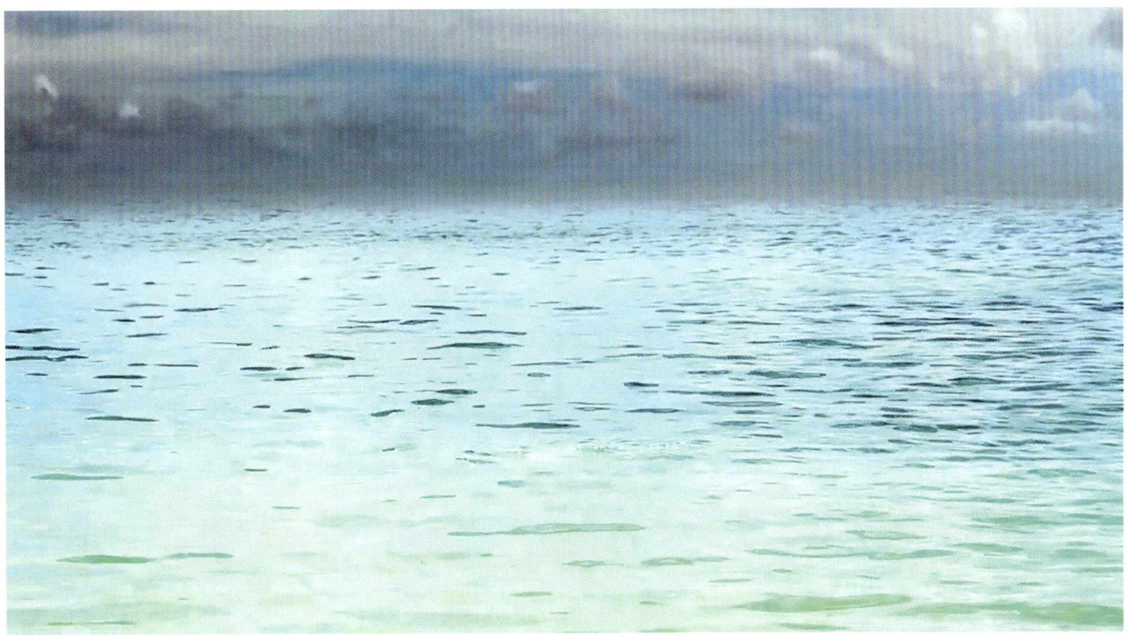

*Interleaf* **J**

# Mário Cravo Neto's Literal and Metaphorical Bahia

***Sabrina Gledhill and Roberto Conduru***

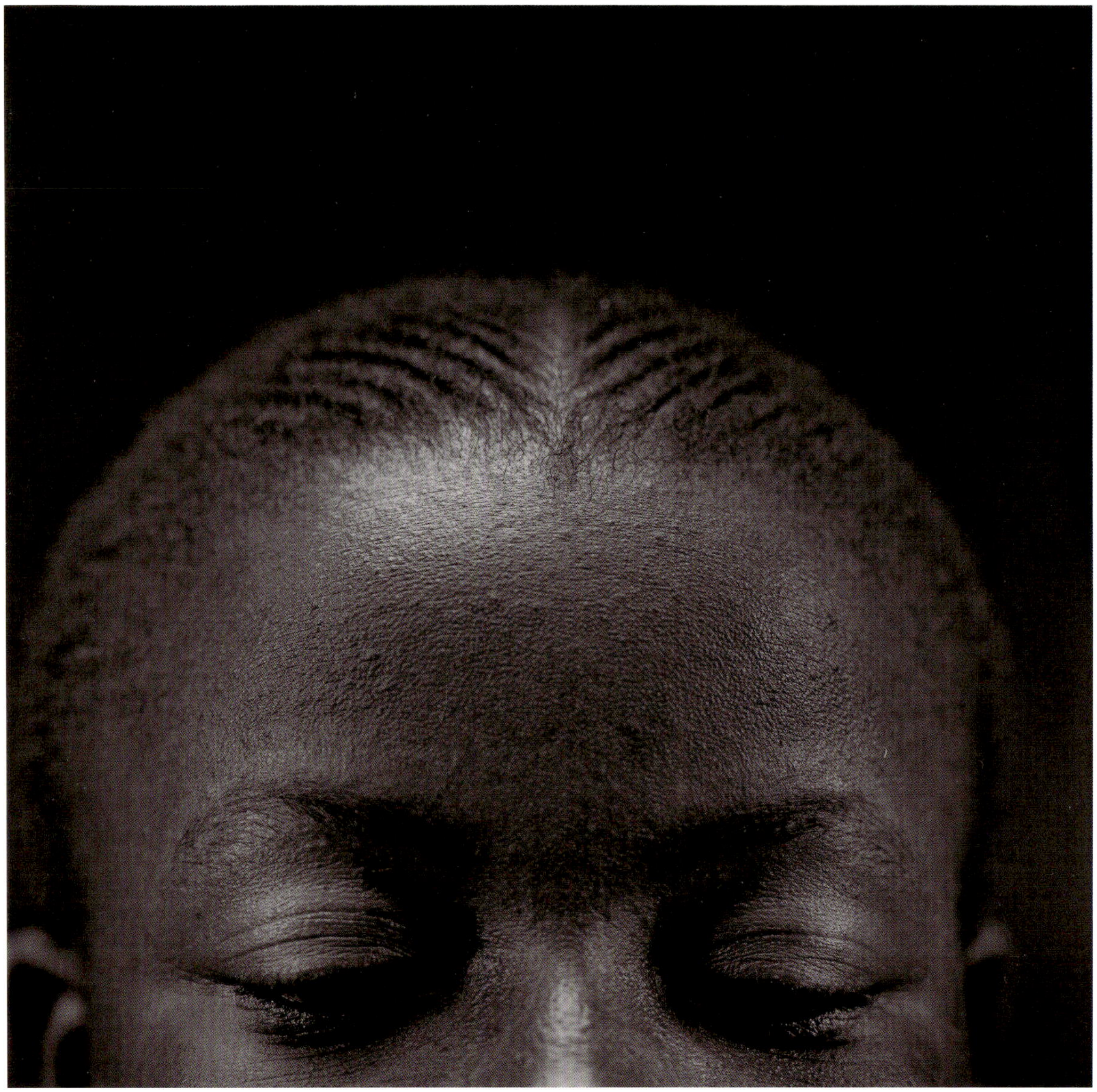

**J.1**
Mário Cravo Neto (b. 1947, Salvador, Bahia, Brazil; d. 2009)
*África I* (Africa I), 1992
Photograph
COURTESY OF THE ESTATE OF MÁRIO CRAVO NETO ©IMCN

**J.2**
Mário Cravo Neto (b. 1947, Salvador, Bahia, Brazil; d. 2009)
Sem título da série A flecha em repouso (Untitled from the series An Arrow at Rest), circa 2000
Photograph
COURTESY OF THE ESTATE OF MÁRIO CRAVO NETO ©IMCN

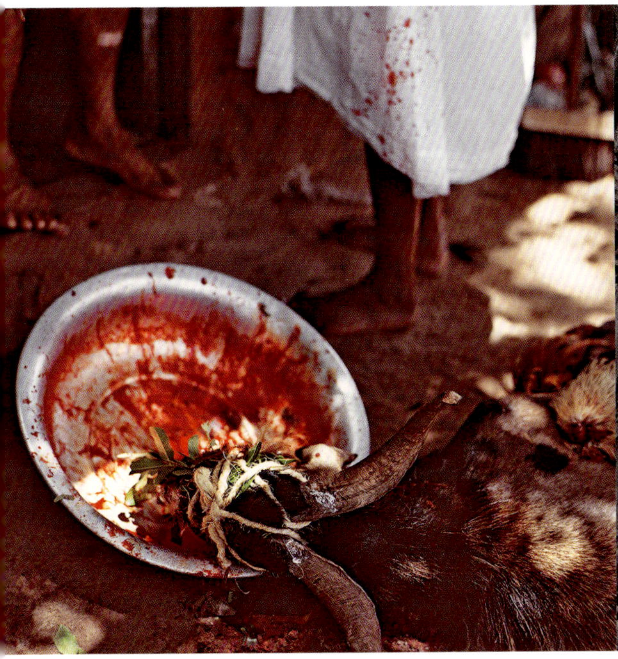

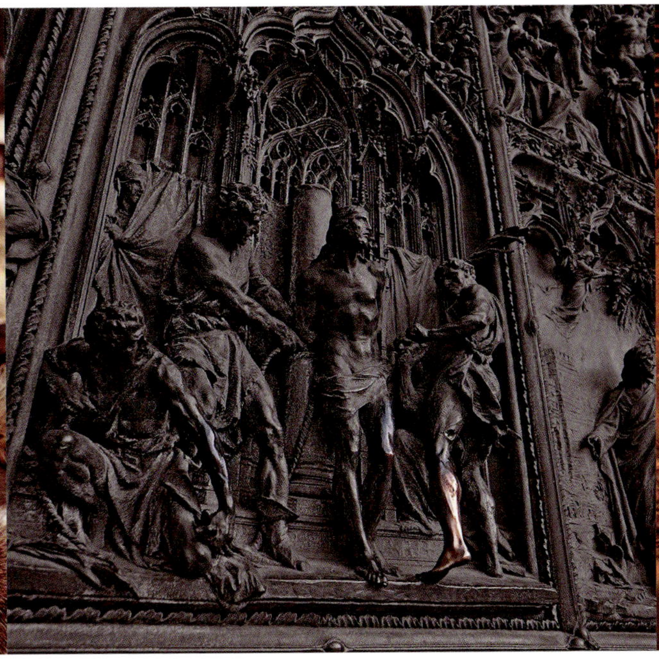

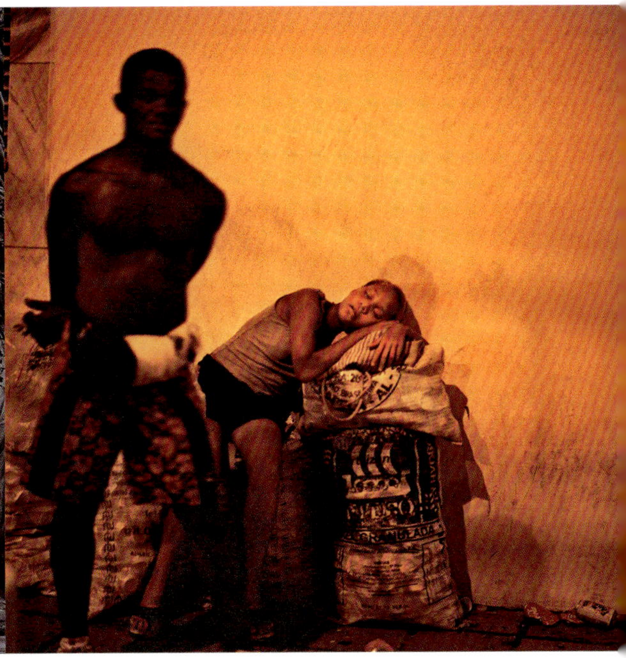

WHETHER RE-MAKING BAHIA IN HIS STUDIO or venturing out to create a veritable atelier of its inhabitants, streets, Catholic churches, and Candomblé temples, Mário Cravo Neto (1947–2009) produced vivid images in color and black-and-white (figs. J.1, J.2). Abstract and iconic, sculptural and painterly, they present his unique vision of Bahian aesthetics, daily life, festivals, spirituality, and culture. His main focus, however, was the city's people—particularly its majority, Afro-descendant population. One of Brazil's leading photographers, his work has been exhibited in the country's major cities, as well as in Germany, the United States, France, Colombia, and the United Kingdom. His influence has inspired generations of photographers, among them his sons Christian and Akira.

The scion of a family of artists that now extends through three generations, Cravo Neto was clearly aware of his rock-star status in Bahia's art world, not only due to his famous surname but as a result of the international recognition his work received. He knew how to make an entrance—fashionably late with an entourage—at his own exhibitions and those of others, but he could also be seen emerging among the flower baskets, camera in hand, in the early morning at the Iemanjá Festival in Rio Vermelho (see interleaf B, this volume). He often spent hours crouched in the urine-drenched alleys near Castro Alves Square to get the best angles on Carnaval revelers and parades.

Cravo Neto's grandfather Mário Cravo (*neto* means "grandson" in Portuguese) was a coffee mogul and local kingmaker whose wealth helped send Cravo Neto's father, Mário Cravo Júnior, to study sculpture abroad. Once there, he dropped the "junior" from his name and, as Mário Cravo, became famous for monumental works, many of which can be seen in the city of Salvador, where he still lives and works. Mário Cravo's close circle of friends included Carybé and Pierre Verger, and Cravo Neto thus grew up immersed in the world of the arts and Afro-Brazilian culture.

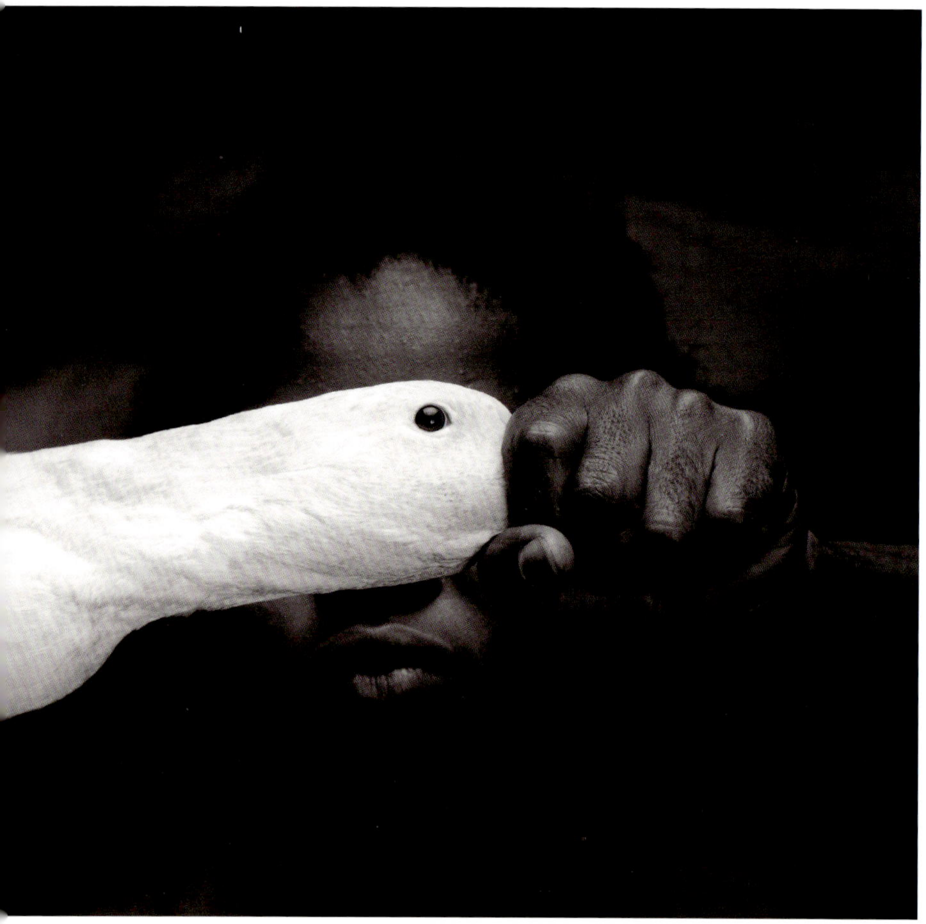

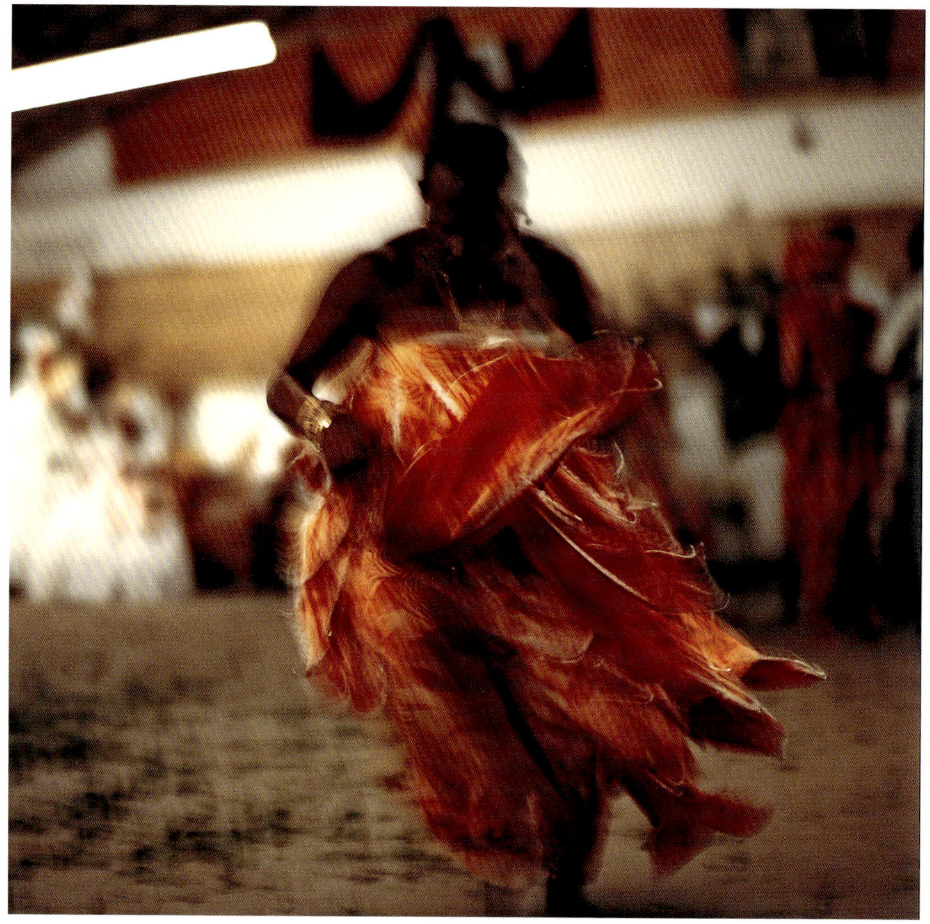

**J.3**
Mário Cravo Neto (b. 1947, Salvador, Bahia, Brazil; d. 2009)
*Odé*, 1998
Photograph
COURTESY OF THE ESTATE OF MÁRIO CRAVO NETO ©IMCN

**J.4**
Mário Cravo Neto (b. 1947, Salvador, Bahia, Brazil; d. 2009)
*Xangô*, circa 2000
Photograph
COURTESY OF THE ESTATE OF MÁRIO CRAVO NETO ©IMCN

Cravo Neto started out as a sculptor, like his father. In 1968 he went to New York City, where he spent two years studying sculpture and photography at the Art Students League, producing a series of photos titled "On the Subway." He became a studio photographer while convalescing from a serious car accident in 1975. Particularly influenced by Robert Mapplethorpe, his work abounds with muscular black bodies and sexual overtones, especially the book *Laróyè*, his homage to the Afro-Brazilian divinity Exú, whose symbols include a phallus. Cravo Neto also employed objects and animals such as tortoises, birds, and stones that could be associated with Afro-Brazilian religious rites but may also evoke double entendres. The black hand wrapped around the beak of a white fowl in figure J. 3, for example, could be a reference to animal sacrifice, but it also suggests an idiomatic expression for intercourse, "*afogar o ganso*" (literally, "drown the goose"). The dreamy beauty of *Luciana* could be a reference to the "trance" of possession, the threads spiralling around her face instead of hanging down to cover her eyes, as they would in a traditional *orixá* crown (see fig. 11.8).

Although his outdoor photos may seem spontaneous, Cravo Neto crafted many of them as carefully as he did his studio work. Some of the "anonymous" people he portrayed in the streets were actually friends. This allows us to see continuities and breaks between the series produced inside and outside the atelier, between black-and-white representations of static subjects under artificial, controlled light and color photos of bodies in motion under natural light. Through arrangements of people, animals, and objects in space, he composed images that are at the same time iconic, symbolic, and indicial, speaking literally and metaphorically about Bahian culture,

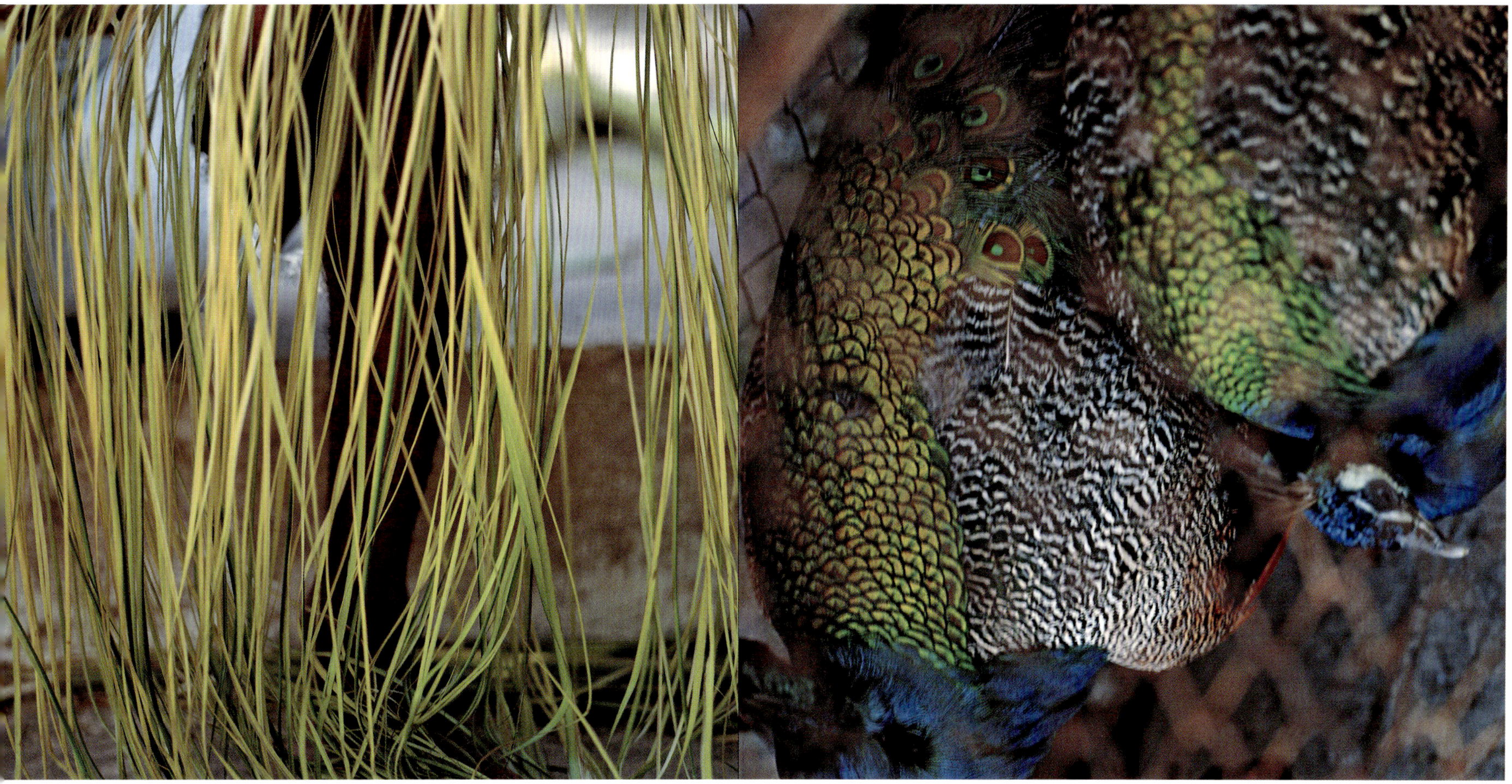

its stereotypes and contingencies, in addition to discussing slavery and ethno-racialism, gender and intergenerational relations, European and Afro-Brazilian religions, sexuality and (post)colonialism.

A culmination of his intertwining experience of Afro-Brazilian culture and art was his initiation by one of Bahia's leading high priests, Pai Balbino (Balbino Daniel de Paula), a descendant of a line of Alapinis (high priests of temples that worship Egunguns, or ancestral spirits), who founded his *terreiro*, Ilê Axé Opô Aganjú, with the help of Pierre Verger. Although some assume that Cravo Neto was only initiated to gain more access to rites and ceremonies, he appeared to believe in Candomblé, the Afro-Brazilian religion into which he was initiated for Omolú, the fearsome *orixá* of plague and smallpox, also known as Obaluaê, the "King of the Earth."

When photographing religious ceremonies, mainly at Ilê Axé Opô Aganjú, he took care to portray the embodied divinities as a blur, as in his portrait of Pai Balbino while Xangô danced in his body (fig. J.4). Cravo Neto did so out of respect for the ban most *terreiros* place on photography, particularly of embodied *orixás*. Another way of portraying divinities without actually photographing them was to seek out their symbols, such as the *ofá* (stylized bow and arrow) of Oxóssi, the leaves of Ossaim, peacocks sacred to Oxum, and the palm fringes that protect windows and adorn the body of Ogum (fig. J.5).

Cravo Neto is a key figure in the process of renewing photography in Bahia by minimizing the ethnographic gaze that dominated the works of Voltaire Fraga and Pierre Verger, and by emphasizing artistic experimentation, opening (with Miguel Rio Branco) the path for Ayrson Heráclito, Caetano Dias, and other younger artists.

**J.5**
Mário Cravo Neto (b. 1947, Salvador, Bahia, Brazil; d. 2009)
Sem título da série Territórios em transe (Untitled from the series Trance Territories), circa 2000
Photograph
COURTESY OF THE ESTATE OF MÁRIO CRAVO NETO ©IMCN

*Interleaf* **K**

# Ayrson Heráclito

***Roberto Conduru***

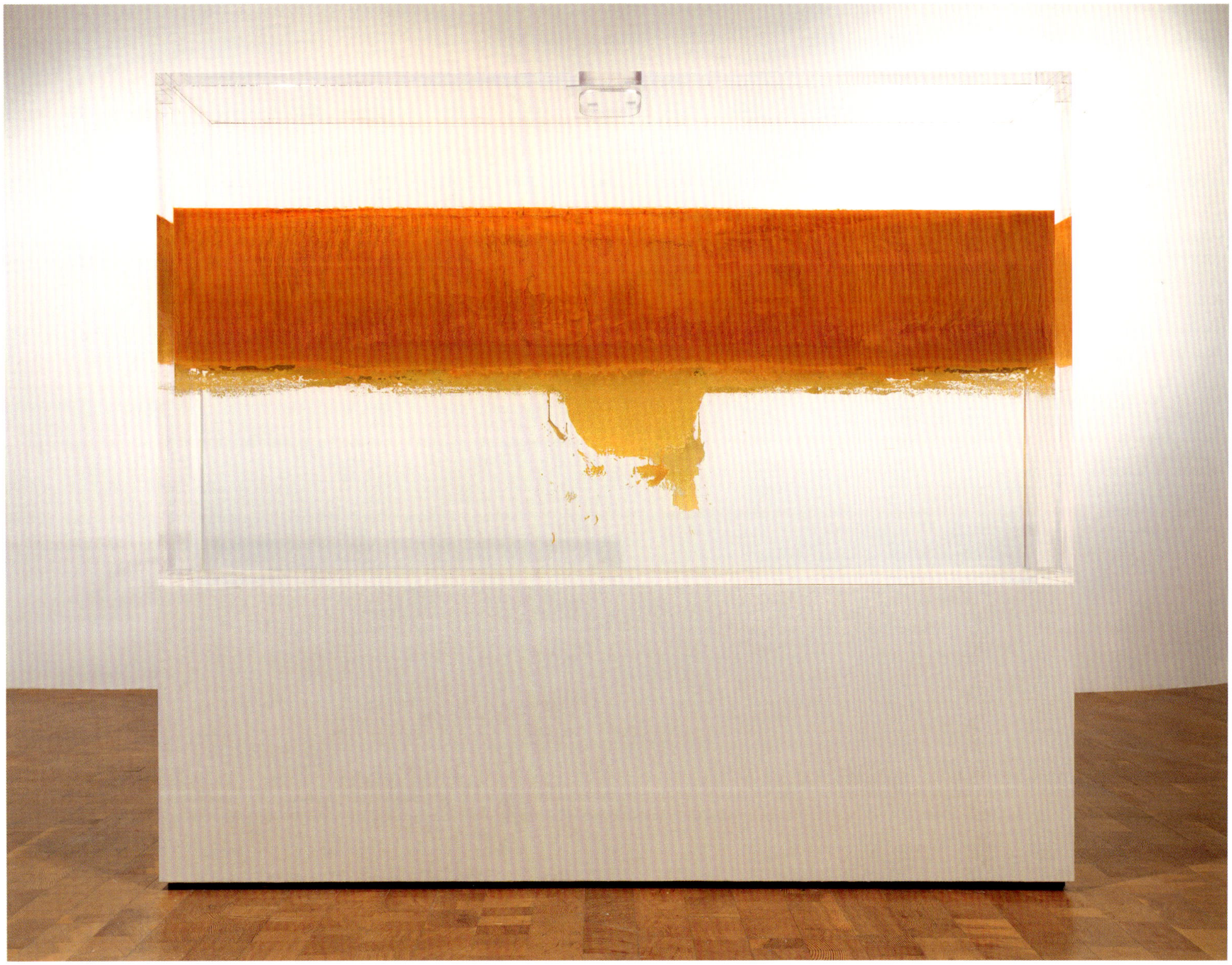

**K.1a,b**
Ayrson Heráclito (Ayrson Heráclito Novato Ferreira;
b. 1968, Macaúbas, Bahia, Brazil)
*Divisor* (Divider), 2017
Red palm oil (*dênde*), salt, water, acrylic
H: 300 cm

WITH *DIVISOR* (DIVIDER; fig. K.1), the first version of which was shown in 2000, Ayrson Heráclito achieved a simple, elegant formulation of the research he has conducted since the mid-1990s: an exploration of the historical significance and ethno-cultural resonances of organic materials such as sugar, meat, and red palm oil (*dendê*). These elements, which figure prominently in both the coastal and inland culture of Bahia, connect the Americas with Africa. In using them, Heráclito rethinks Afro-Bahian culture, closely examining colonialism and slavery and their contemporary reverberations. This is revealed in *Segredos internos* (Inner Secrets, 1994; fig. K.2), where he takes a dramatic look at the effects of the transatlantic slave trade and the Portuguese colonial system established on the basis of the sugar economy.

In addition to experimentation with unusual media, the artist draws inspiration from public religious ceremonies and centuries-old hallmarks of quotidian experience in Bahia. As a result, his processes of production and diffusion have drawn considerable attention. In 2000, for example, he used nearly 800 kilograms of salted beef, once a dietary staple of poor Brazilians, to create a collection of clothing that was then displayed in fashion shows—both on Salvador's catwalks and downtown streets—becoming part of the performance called *Transmutação da carne* (Transmutation of the Flesh; fig. K.3). These robes were then branded with a hot iron, dramatizing the torture endured by enslaved Africans in Brazil. Subsequently, the artist donated the meat to feed the poor.

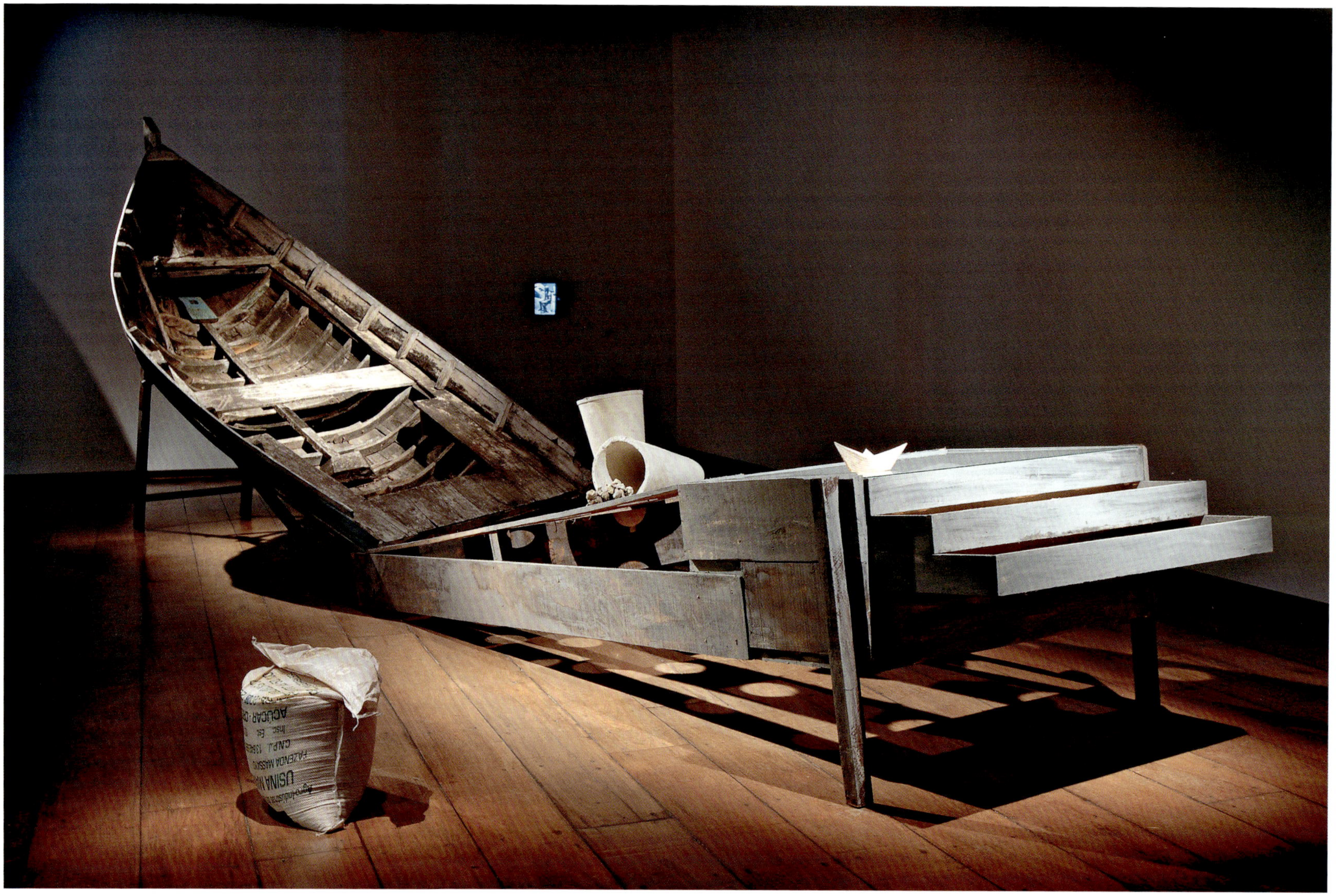

Palm oil, which is regularly employed in local cuisine, also has symbolic reverberations within the Afro-Brazilian religion of Candomblé, and the substance has been significant in Heráclito's work since the beginning of his career in the 1980s. It is perhaps worth noting here that there are some precedents for such usage, as the material culture of Afro-Brazilian religions has overflowed into the art world at least since the mid-1960s. Rubem Valentim used the structure of *pejis* (altars) to compose his works, and Deoscóredes Maximiliano dos Santos, or Mestre Didi, made the ceremonial insignia of the *orixás* transcend the boundaries of the Candomblé *terreiro* to become objects of aesthetic appreciation as well (see Cleveland, this volume).

In this borderland between artistic and religious realms, Heráclito has expanded the link between local and global languages and cultures. He not only makes use of everyday materials and objects used in the *terreiros*, he also incorporates rituals that engage in dialogue with the performing arts. He does not seek merely to attest to the contemporary validity of Candomblé through art or to use religion to re-enchant art. Exploring the fusion of their magical dimensions, he aims to re-empower both realms by making them capable of healing individual and collective, artistic and social ills.

In *Bori* (Feeding the Head, 2008; see figs. 3.11a-l), Heráclito's starting point is one of the most complex and important rituals of Candomblé, in which the heads of initiates and others are nourished with food, song, prayer, and dance to achieve mental and physical regeneration. As an artist, he performs some of the acts usually undertaken by a *babalorixá* (caretaker of the divinities), cooking roots, vegetables, and grains to prepare religious delicacies and using them to crown the heads of people lying on straw mats, each representing an *orixá* from the Afro-Brazilian pantheon. If in *Bori*, people witness the rite involving the artist and his collaborators, in *Buruburu* (Popcorn, 2010), they are invited to take part in the ritual by receiving a purifying shower of popcorn from the hands of the artist (fig. K.4).

Afro-Brazilian religious rituals and sociopolitical concerns are intertwined in the artist's paired performance interventions that appear in the video *Sacudimentos* of 2015. Heráclito carried these out in two sixteenth-century buildings on two continents—the ruins of the Garcia d'Ávila House, built in Mata de São João, north of Salvador, Bahia, which was once the largest slave-owning estate in Brazil (fig. K.5a), and the Maison des Esclaves (House of the Slaves) on Gorée Island, near Dakar, Senegal, originally built by the Portuguese and now a memorial to the transatlantic slave trade (fig. K.5b). The *sacudimento* is a spiritual cleansing ritual practiced in Candomblé for both individuals and environments. By reenacting this process the artist unites the two Atlantic shores to banish the negative spirits and meanings ingrained in those sites over the course of history and to help heal the effects of colonialism.

These performance interventions are not entirely religious. They are also political. Far removed from the idea of purity, they blur the boundaries between those realms and their rites. The photographs and videos derived from them empower the self-image of Africans, people of African descent, and followers of Afro-Brazilian religions. Running the risk of aestheticizing at a time when art is commercially showcased and these religions are suffering hypertrophy, the propagation of images of symbolic actions has been a key strategy for Heráclito's simultaneously sacred and activist art.

**K.2**
Ayrson Heráclito (Ayrson Heráclito Novato Ferreira; b. 1968, Macaúbas, Bahia, Brazil)
*Segredos internos* (Inner Secrets), 1994
Wood, glass, sugar, brown sugar
W: 10 m
COURTESY AYRSON HERÁCLITO
PHOTOGRAPH BY MARCIO LIMA

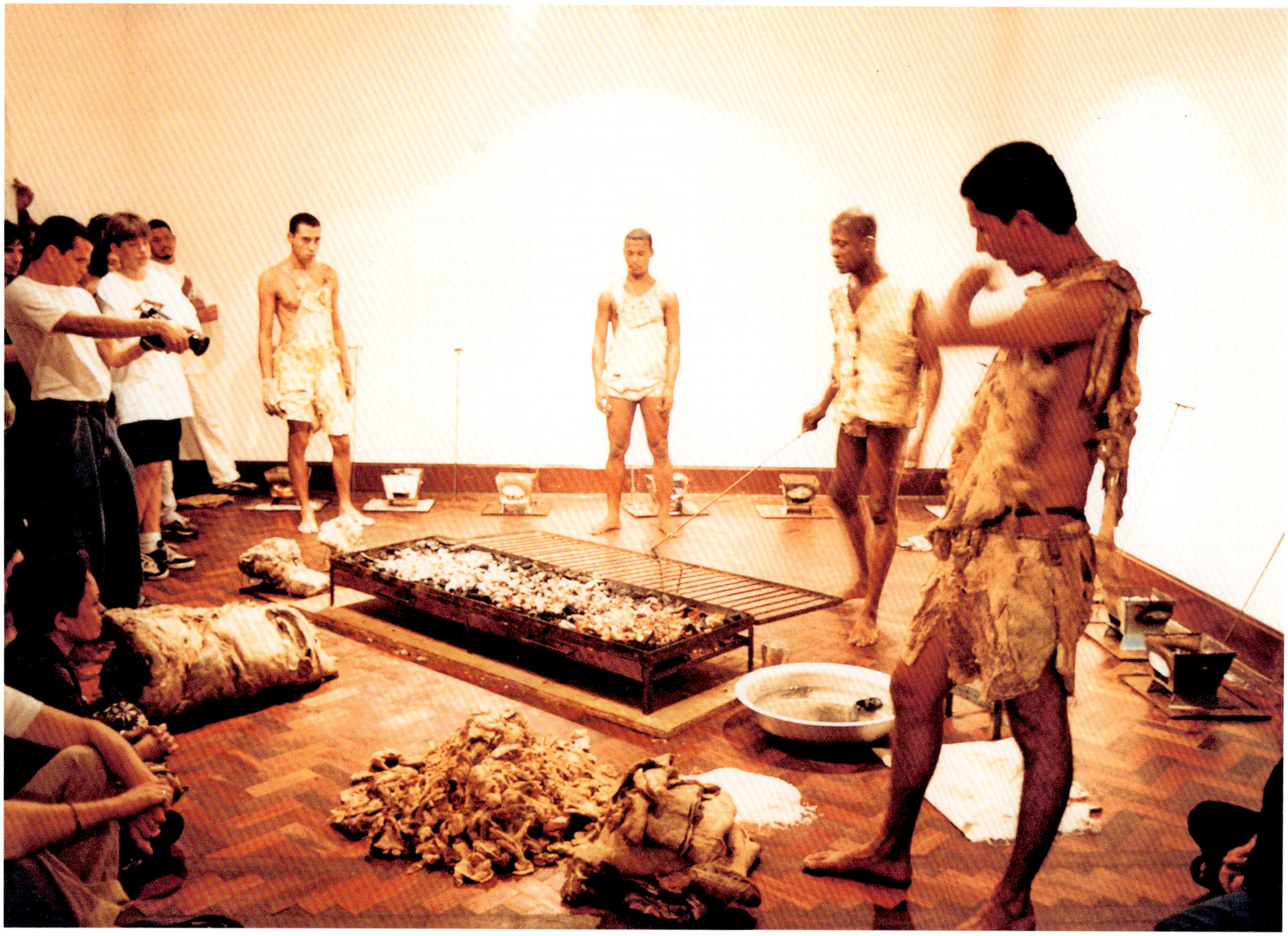

**K.3**
Ayrson Heráclito (Ayrson Heráclito Novato Ferreira;
b. 1968, Macaúbas, Bahia, Brazil)
*Transmutação da carne* (Transmutation of the Flesh), 2000
Performance
COURTESY AYRSON HERÁCLITO
PHOTOGRAPH BY EDGARD OLIVA

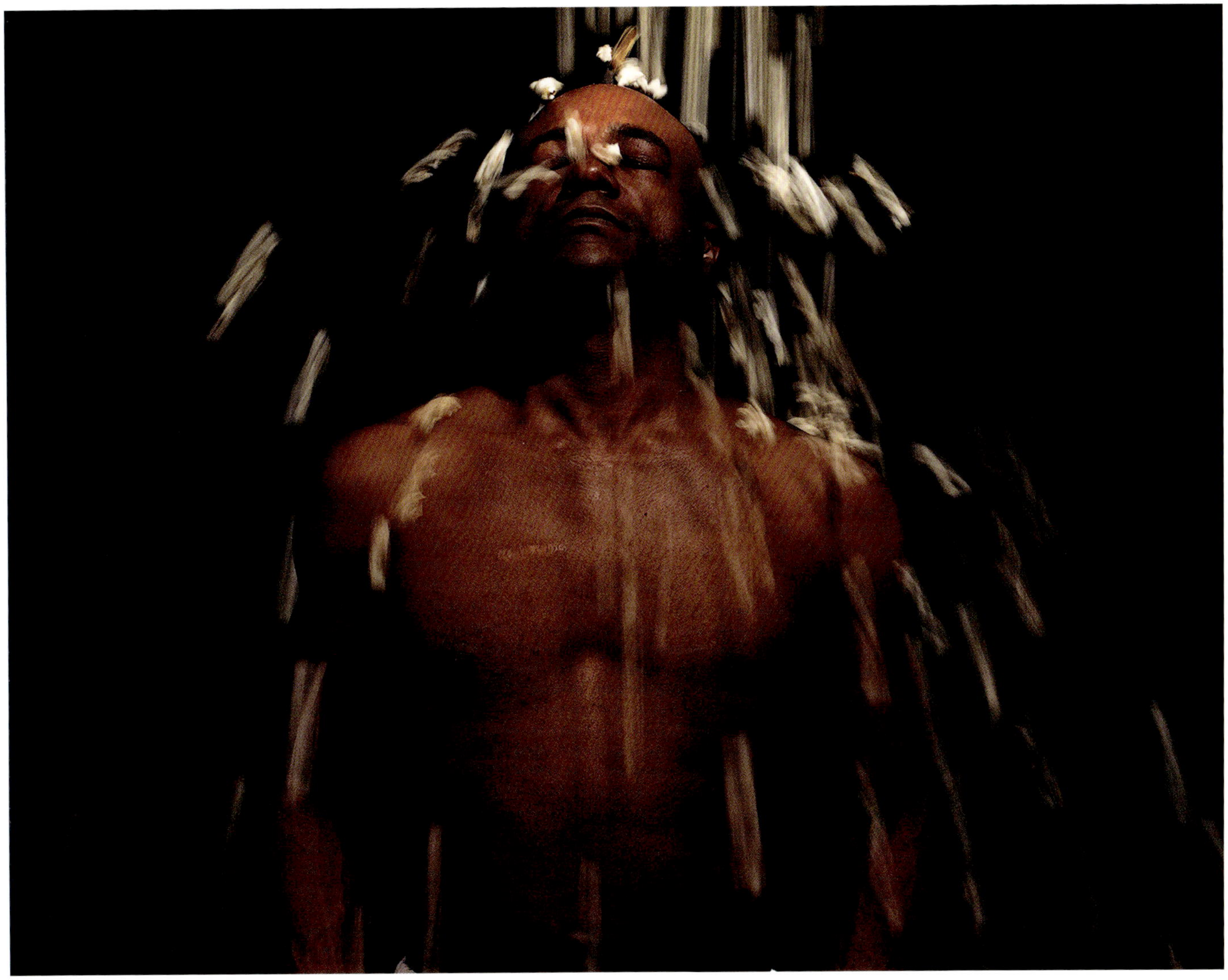

**K.4**
Ayrson Heráclito (Ayrson Heráclito Novato Ferreira; b. 1968, Macaúbas, Bahia, Brazil)
*Buruburu* (Popcorn), 2013
Video, color, sound, 2:25
COURTESY AYRSON HERÁCLITO

**K.5a** (OVERLEAF)
Ayrson Heráclito (Ayrson Heráclito Novato Ferreira; b. 1968, Macaúbas, Bahia, Brazil)
*O sacudimento da Casa da Torre na Bahia: Diptico I* (The Cleansing of the Tower House in Bahia: Diptych I), 2015
Photograph
COURTESY AYRSON HERÁCLITO

**K.5b** (OVERLEAF)
Ayrson Heráclito (Ayrson Heráclito Novato Ferreira; b. 1968, Macaúbas, Bahia, Brazil)
*O sacudimento da Maison des Esclaves em Gorée: Diptico I* (The Cleansing of the House of Slaves in Gorée: Diptych I), 2015
Photograph
COURTESY AYRSON HERÁCLITO

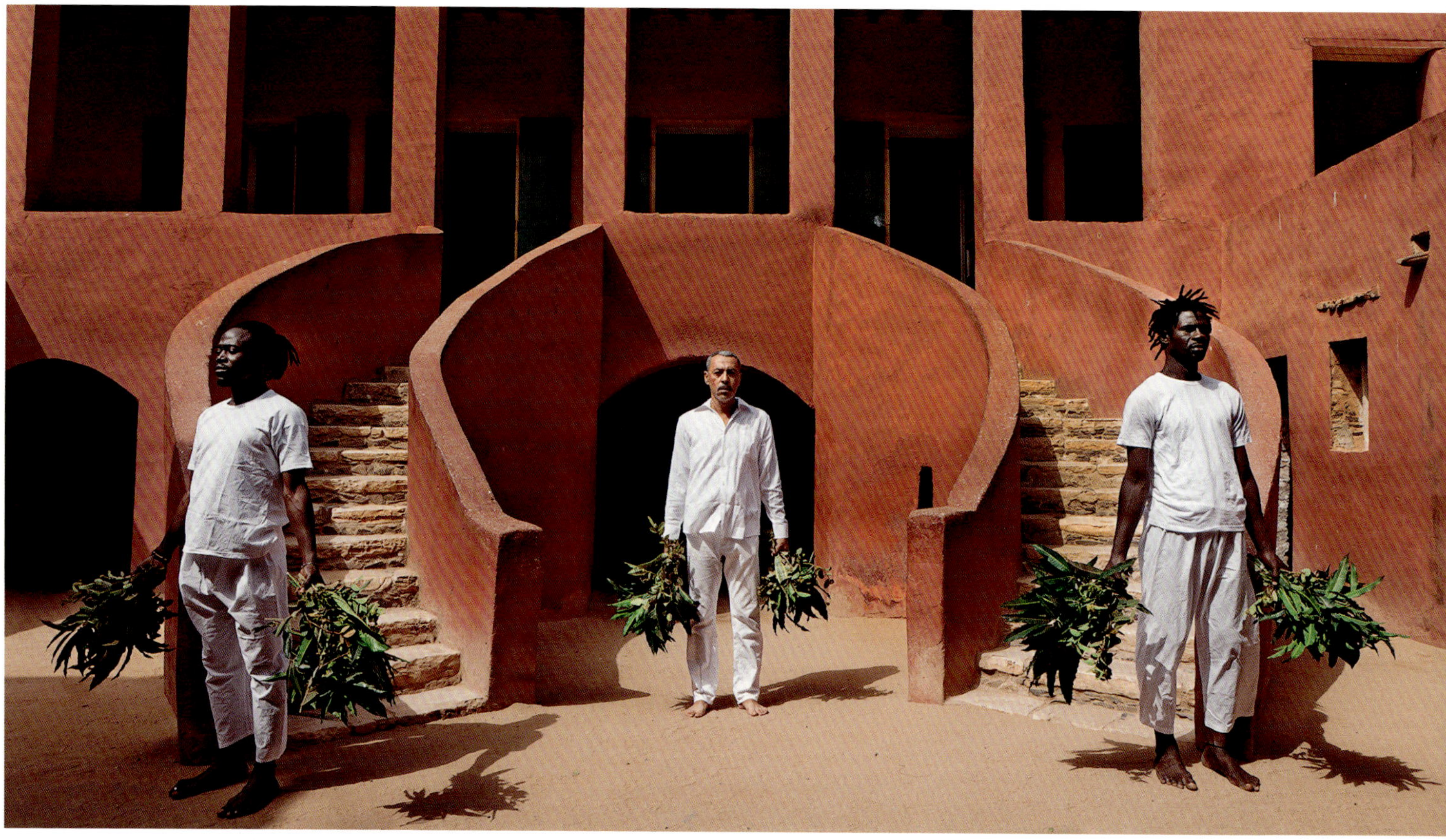

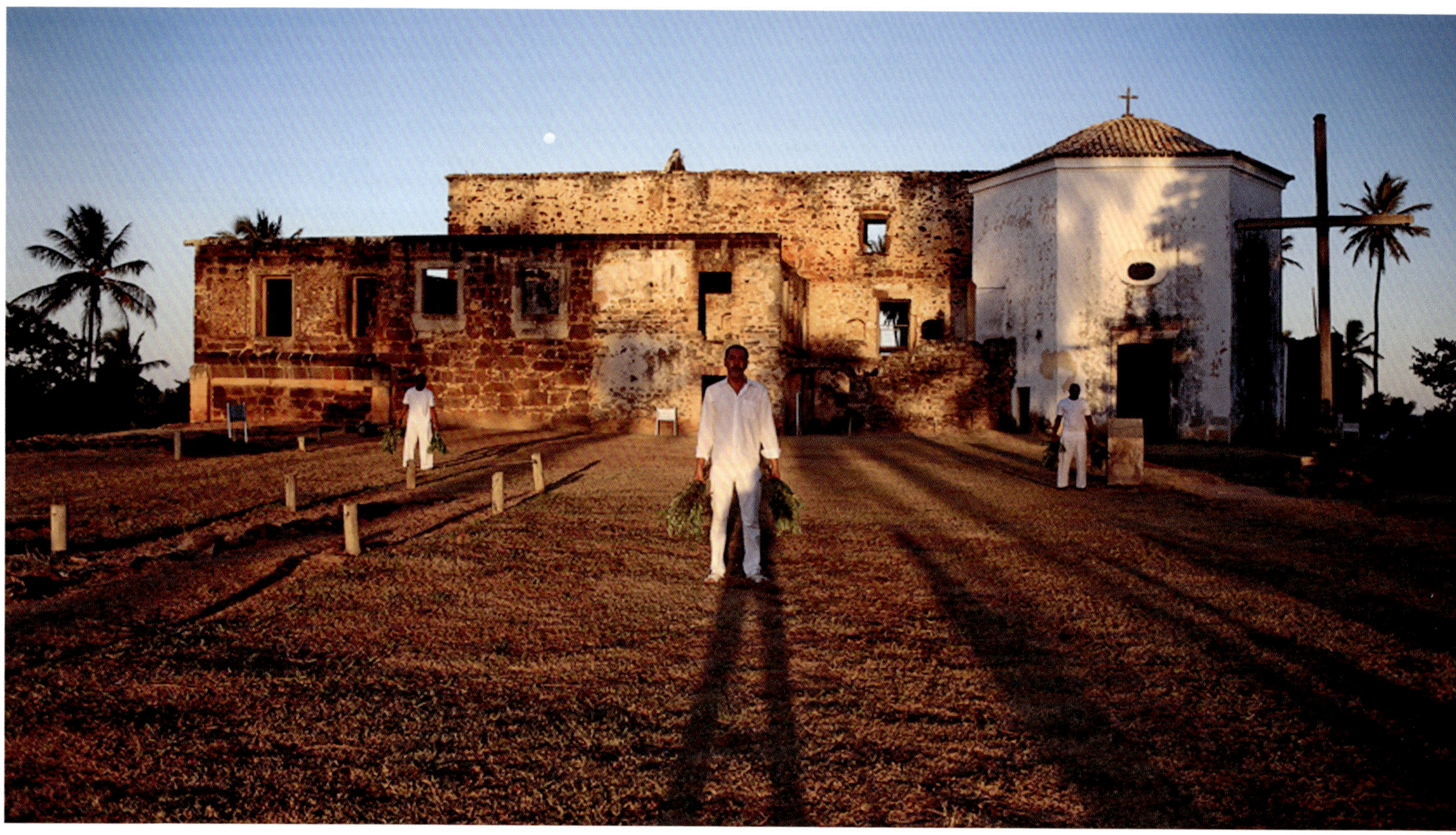

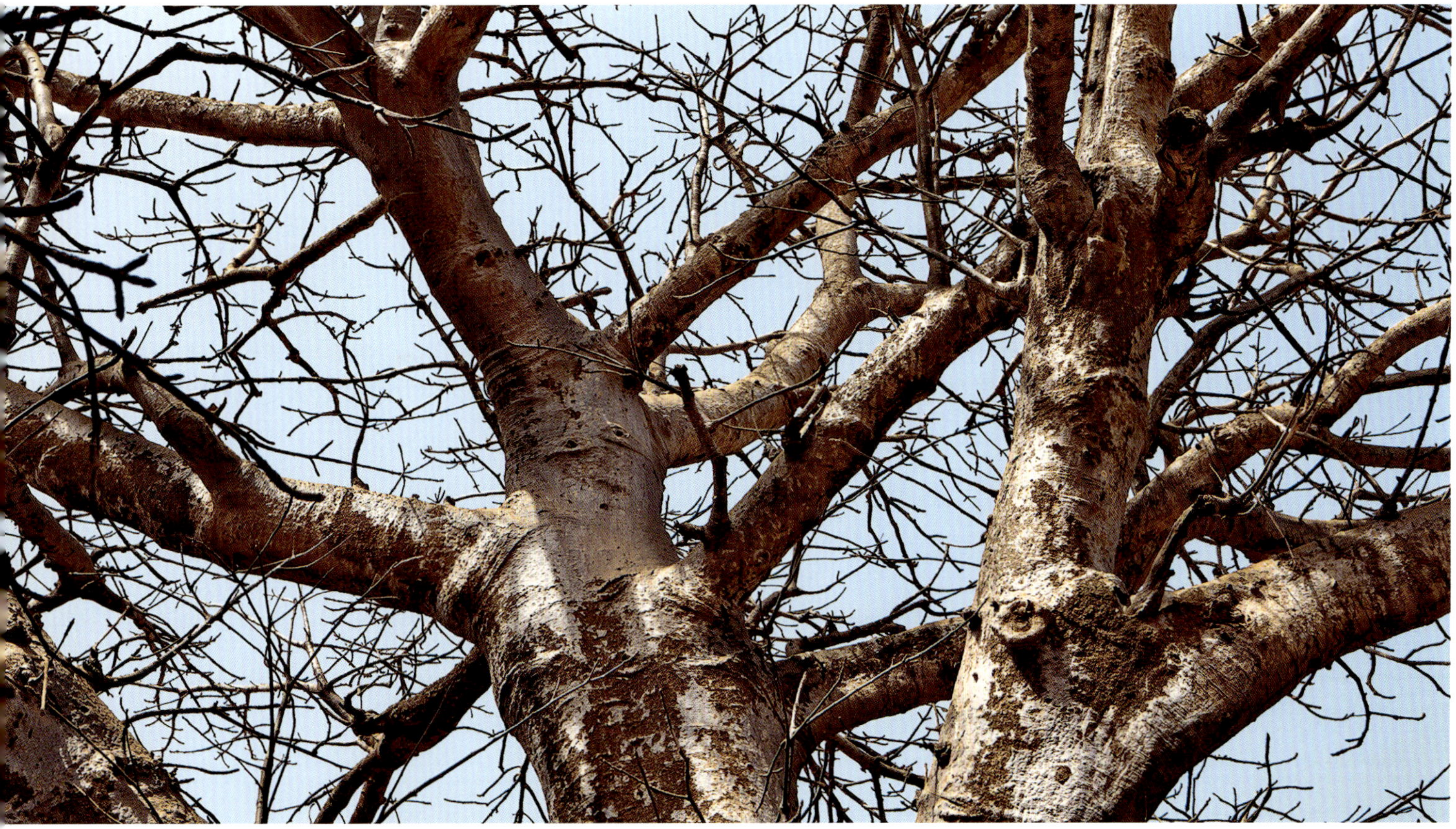

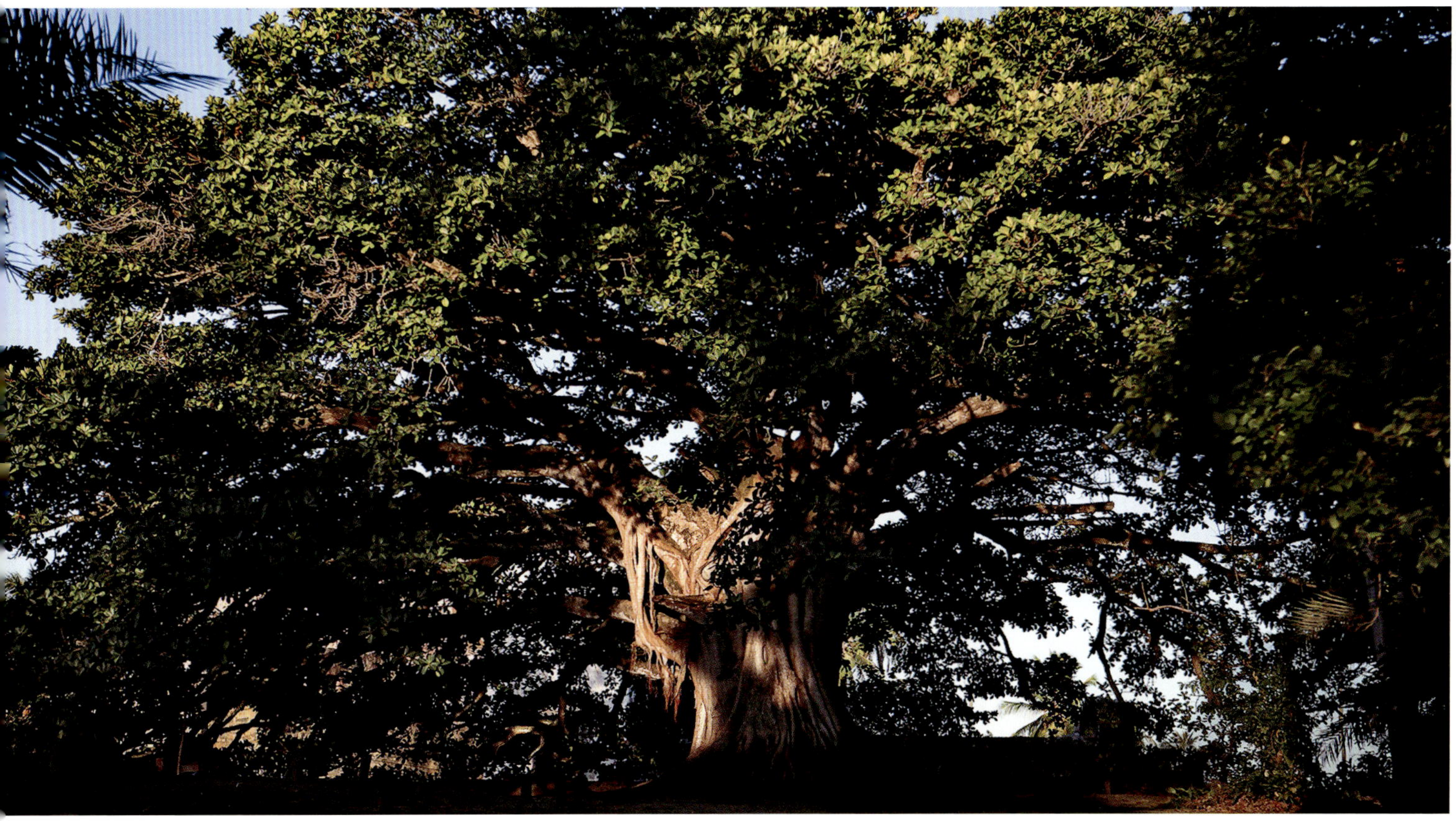

# 11 Confronting the World with Art, Beauty, and *Axé*

Roberto Conduru

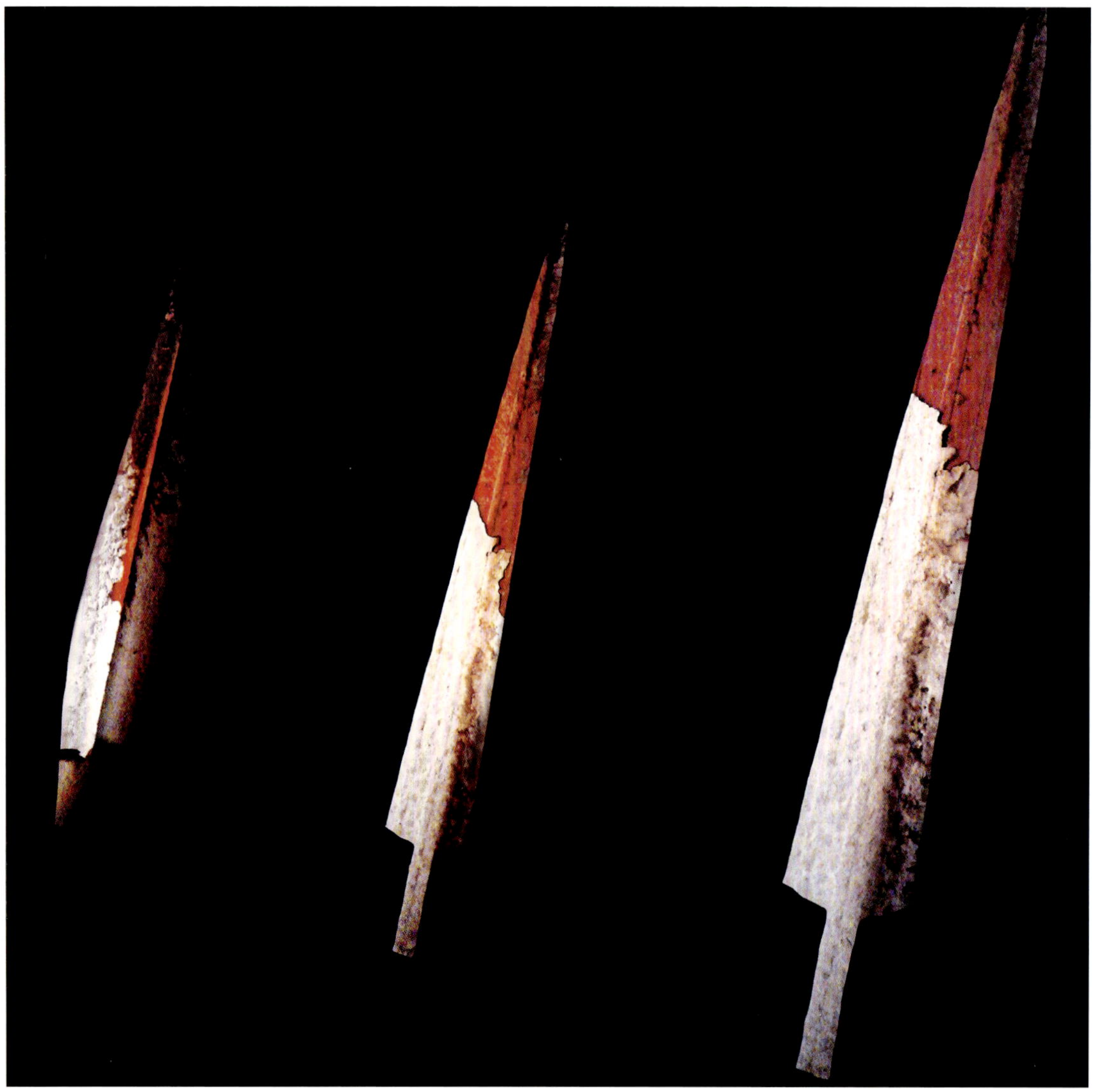

Bahia, *minha preta…*

Persist with what is beautiful
And the world will see
You return laughing to the place that is yours on the blue globe
Queen of the South Atlantic

*E ô!* Bahia, mythical font, enchanted
*E ô!* Expand your *axé*, don't hide a thing
Your cry of joy echoes far, [in] time and space
Queen of the Atlantic.[1]

THE VERSES ABOVE are from "Bahia, minha preta," a song written by Caetano Veloso in 1993 for fellow Bahian singer Gal Costa (Costa 1993). "*Minha preta*," a term of endearment that can be somewhat patronizing, literally means "my black woman." In this context, however, it emphasizes that Bahia is black. Although Bahia has a multiethnic and mixed-race population, like all Brazilian states, and can therefore be understood in its multiplicity and presented as multicolored, it has often been simply identified as black. This is not necessarily because it has the largest population of Afro-descendants in Brazil and is the city with the largest black population outside of Africa. It is a mistake to restrict Brazil's blackness to Bahia, but unquestionably, it is in Bahia that blackness is cultivated in a singular fashion and has achieved prominence in the cultural imaginary. In this regard, Bahia is unique within Brazil. This symbolic status, however, rarely leads to substantial changes in the social situation of peoples of African descent and is often profitable for those who exploit it through tourism and entertainments, including Carnaval, music and dance performances, and gastronomic events.

Not all works of art produced in Bahia in recent years, however, are based on blackness,[2] and artists in other parts of Brazil have tackled sociocultural issues surrounding race.[3] In Bahia, nonetheless, a chain of at least five generations of artists has focused on experiencing, examining, and showcasing black cultures—peoples, their locales, and their daily lives. From Carybé's drawings and paintings and Pierre Verger's photographs of the 1940s to the recent performances by Tiago Sant'Ana, interventions by Àlex Ìgbó, murals by Pedro Marighella, and photographs by Tacun Lecy, artists have reiterated some topics, set others aside, moved in new directions, reviewed approaches, and broadened the field of representations. The dialogues about black culture that Bahian artists have initiated for over seven decades have, however, consciously formed a tradition. Composed of a few different strands, it is an important feature in Brazil's cultural field, and it may have emerged as a result of the discontinuity and weak institutionalization of Brazil's fine arts or as a form of resistance to the strategy of disparaging and marginalizing peoples and cultures of African descent—not to mention the genocide of these peoples in the past.

Given the significance Bahia has attained in issues of blackness, it must be acknowledged that some decisive agents in the formulation of this tradition, among them Carybé, Verger, and Mário Cravo Neto, are not people of African descent. This is an important factor in the consolidation of the idea of Afro-Brazilian art based not only on the theme of the work but also on the artist's ethnic and racial origins (Conduru 2015, 77–90). The demand that African descent be a priority, if not a determining factor, for being active in that realm, which is currently being propagated in other Brazilian contexts, especially São Paulo, is less evident in Bahia.

Also unique to the work of Bahian artists is the appreciation and maintenance of ties with Africa. This is seen to a much lesser extent in the rest of the country.[4] Although capoeira, Carnaval, and Afro-Brazilian religions are not cultural expressions that originated from or are exclusive to Bahia, due to the intensity and quality of their local inflections and the way they are connected to Africa, they have become the pillars of a culture that is not infrequently called Afro-Bahian. It is no coincidence that Bahia is considered the African capital of Brazil by peoples on both sides of the Atlantic.

Many artists active in Bahia have visited Africa at some point their careers.[5] This travel has stimulated or resulted in works that played a role in the lengthy process of cultural (re)Africanization of Bahia in the second half of the twentieth century[6]: the sacred sculptural works of Deoscóredes Maximiliano dos Santos, better known as Mestre Didi, the photographs and writings of Verger,[7] the woodcut series Suíte Afríquia by Emanoel Araújo, the textile prints José Antônio Cunha designed for Ilê Aiyê, and the pair of performance works titled O *sacudimento de Casa da Torre na Bahia* (The Cleansing of the Tower House in Bahia) and O *sacudimento da Maison des Esclaves em Gorée* (The Cleansing of the House of Slaves in Gorée) by Ayrson Heráclito. Both the cultivation of ties with Africa and this range of artistic achievements have helped Bahia garner a special place in the cultural geo-history of the African diaspora. Like Havana and Harlem, New Orleans and Port-au-Prince, Salvador is one of the brightest stars in the constellation of metropolises that cultivate Afro-American art in the Americas.

**11.1a**
Detail of figure 11.1c.

**11.1b**
Detail of figure 11.1c.

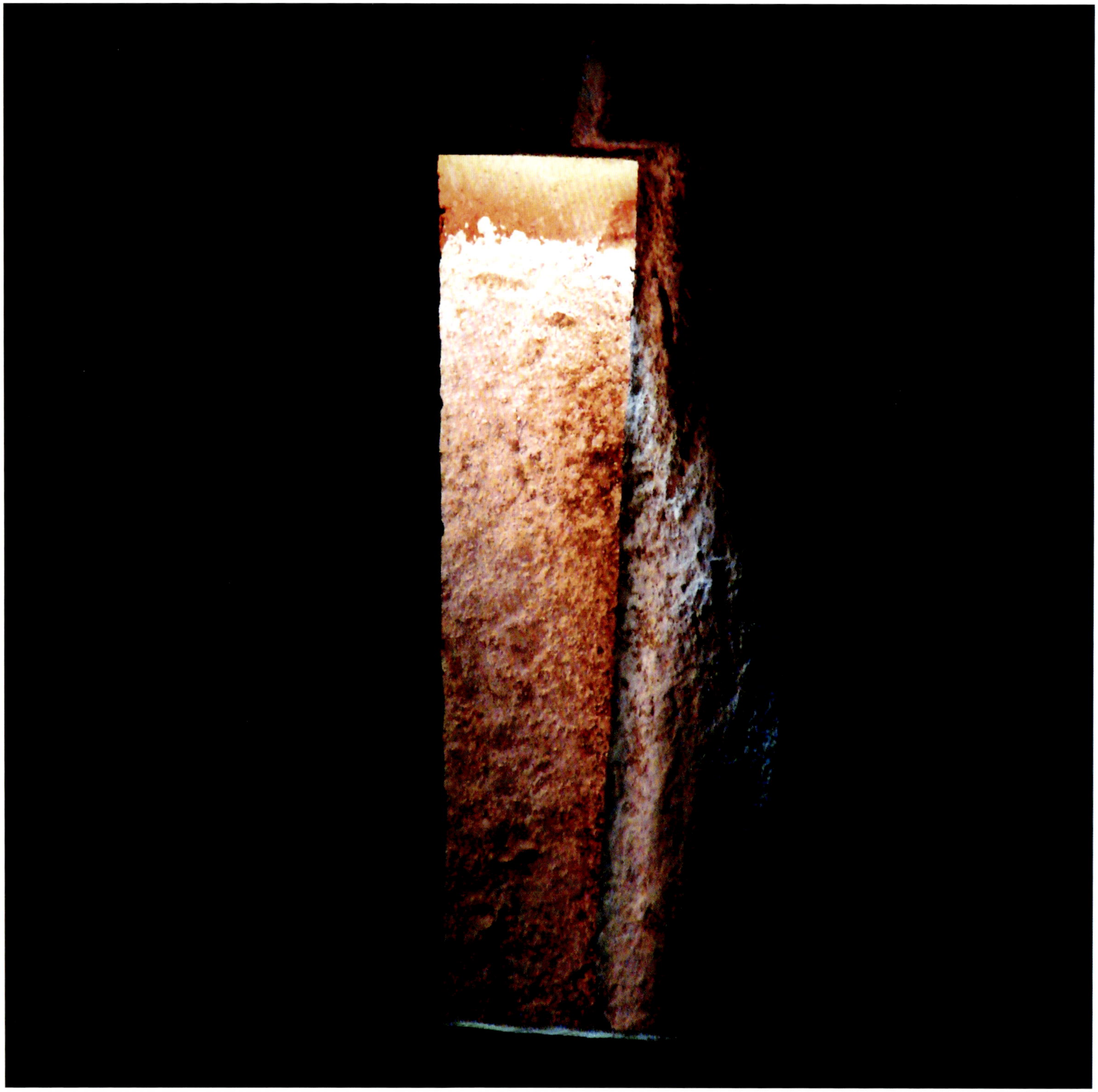

## The Art of *Axé*

In the song that opens this essay, Caetano Veloso turns to religion, reiterating that Bahia is a "mythical font, enchanted," and in the context of the persecution of Afro-Brazilian religions, particularly by followers of Neo-Pentecostal sects, he exhorts, "Expand your *axé*." Like Caetano, many others, before and after him, have been seduced by the power of the *orixás*, *voduns*, *inquices*, and *encantados* and have devoted themselves to the artistic celebration of those divinities. This explains the omnipresence of Afro-Brazilian religions in the arts related to blackness, which is not unique to Bahia.[8]

In the late nineteenth century, in writings that were certainly not devoid of racial prejudice, the physician and amateur ethnologist Raimundo Nina Rodrigues qualified some artifacts used by followers of Candomblé as "black art" (Rodrigues [1896] 2006) and even "fine art"[9] (see Romo, this volume). This, however, did not mean that they were accepted within the elite system of art in Brazil. On the contrary, such ceremonial objects were still randomly seized by the police in their efforts to suppress those religious practices, since the penal code enacted in Brazil in 1890 criminalized "the practice of Spiritism, magic and its spells."[10] That process led to the formation of collections that are currently housed in a varied range of institutions but still lack attention, visibility, and public access (see Sansi, this volume).[11] Despite critical and curatorial efforts to rethink objects made and used in *terreiros*,[12] it was only in 1964 that this type of artifact began to migrate from religious spheres to arts institutions.

That year, Mestre Didi began exhibiting the *xaxarás* and *ibirís* (ceremonial scepters) that he made for the worship of Obaluaê and Nanã, respectively, in galleries and cultural centers in Brazil and abroad. The inclusion of his work in the *Magiciens de la Terre* (Magicians of the Earth) exhibition, held at the Centre Georges Pompidou in 1989, and in other exhibitions in Brazil and abroad, can be viewed as an important stage in the artistic valorization of such works. The positioning of his works in exhibitions as a counterpoint to the other works of art and the presentation of their creator as a "priest-artist" (Santos 2000), however, made Mestre Didi's work the exception that confirmed the rule of the exclusion of the arts of Candomblé from erudite and vanguard art circles in Brazil. Produced for the use of religious communities that appreciate them for their symbolic and aesthetic value, portrayals of divinities, like the dolls created by Valdete Ribeiro da Silva, known as Detinha de Xangô (see interleaf F, this volume), and the iron sculptures forged by José Adário dos Santos, known as Zé Diabo (see interleaf E, this volume), still confront resistance from art critics, curators, and historians who often make judgments based on the prejudices of their fields and their own sociocultural status.

Less problematic was the acceptance of figurations of deities and Afro-Brazilian religious practices that, having previously appeared sporadically in Rio de Janeiro,[13] became more and more common as an artistic theme in Brazil, especially in Bahia from the 1940s onward.[14] The negative public responses to Candomblé initiation rites in Bahia, photographed by Henri-Georges Clouzot and by José Medeiros and published in the magazines *Paris Match* and *O Cruzeiro*, respectively, in 1951 (Tacca 2009), however, traumatized the Afro-Brazilian religious milieu. As a result the photographing of rites and ceremonies remains controversial and non-consensual to this day. This has not prevented photographers—including Verger, Cravo Neto, Adenor Gondim, and Lecy, among others—from finding ways of getting around restrictions. Religious communities are less strict about controlling portrayals that are not as committed to realism.

The problem is in fact nearly the opposite: the excess and banalization in the iconic portrayal of the world of Candomblé, particularly the *orixás*, even though the proliferation of this imagery can be seen as a political response to persecution of Afro-Brazilian faiths. It is also undeniable, however, that noteworthy innovations arise from time to time, such as the still lifes Hélio de Oliveira composed from objects used in the *terreiros* or more sculptural or pictorial portrayals in the images Mário Cravo Neto produced inside and outside the studio. It is nonetheless hard to avoid the abundant and uncreative elaborations on the imaginary shaped by Carybé, Verger, and others in works of art, decorative objects, tourist souvenirs, graffiti murals, and other media. These precedents are, however, sometimes taken up in intelligent dialogues that revere and expand on strands of the local artistic tradition. Lecy and Sant'Ana, for example, have openly expressed their affiliations with the works of Verger and Heráclito, respectively.

There is, therefore, no lack of major artistic achievement focused on Candomblé: Verger's monumental dedication, on both sides of the Atlantic; the ethnographic detail of Carybé's graphic-sculptural *orixás*; the artistic updating of myths in the work of Mestre Didi; Rubem Valentim and his constructive translation of the Afro-Brazilian religious-artistic aesthetic; *Laroyé*, the explicit and metaphorical, critical and reverent book by Mário Cravo Neto; *Códices*, the mural in which Cunha pictorially reconciles hagiographic and historical meanings; the enlightening and memorial series Opô, by Oscar Dourado; the pair of *Sacudimentos* in which Ayrson Heráclito connects architecture and performance, history and religion, Brazil and Africa in a decolonial key.

In his Opô series, Dourado embodies the emotional states experienced during initiation through color photographs of filtered patterns of light coming through worn ceramic tiles (fig. 11.1a-c). He explores the possibilities of peering inside without disrespecting the limits established in the religious sphere on the reproducing of rituals. Cravo Neto challenges the ban in flickering portrayals of embodied *orixás*, as well as in other images. He follows the path opened by Verger in showing public ceremonies as well as environments and artifacts configured in ritual. Although the work of Dourado and Cravo Neto is different (see interleaf J, this volume), both artists keep their distance from ethnography, which has and continues to dominate the photography of Afro-Brazilian religions. They also share the linking of artistic and religious experience, another peculiarity of Bahia. Just as it has been perceptible in the past, in the trajectories and works of Carybé, Cravo Neto, Detinha de Xangô, Mestre Didi, Valentim, and Verger, so it is now, with Marco Aurélio Damaceno, Heráclito, Lecy, Sant'Ana, and Zé Diabo, among others. Running the risk of slipping into the sensationalizing of Candomblé, which has contributed to the hypertrophy of Afro-Brazilian religions, these artists have publicly disseminated aesthetic values experienced in the daily life of the *terreiros*, relying on *axé*, the power of the *orixás*, as a means of reactivating the artistic sphere. Whether they are images, materials, objects, or performances, artistic representations can be seen as indications of the slow process of unrestricted inclusion of Candomblé in Brazil's sociocultural dynamics.

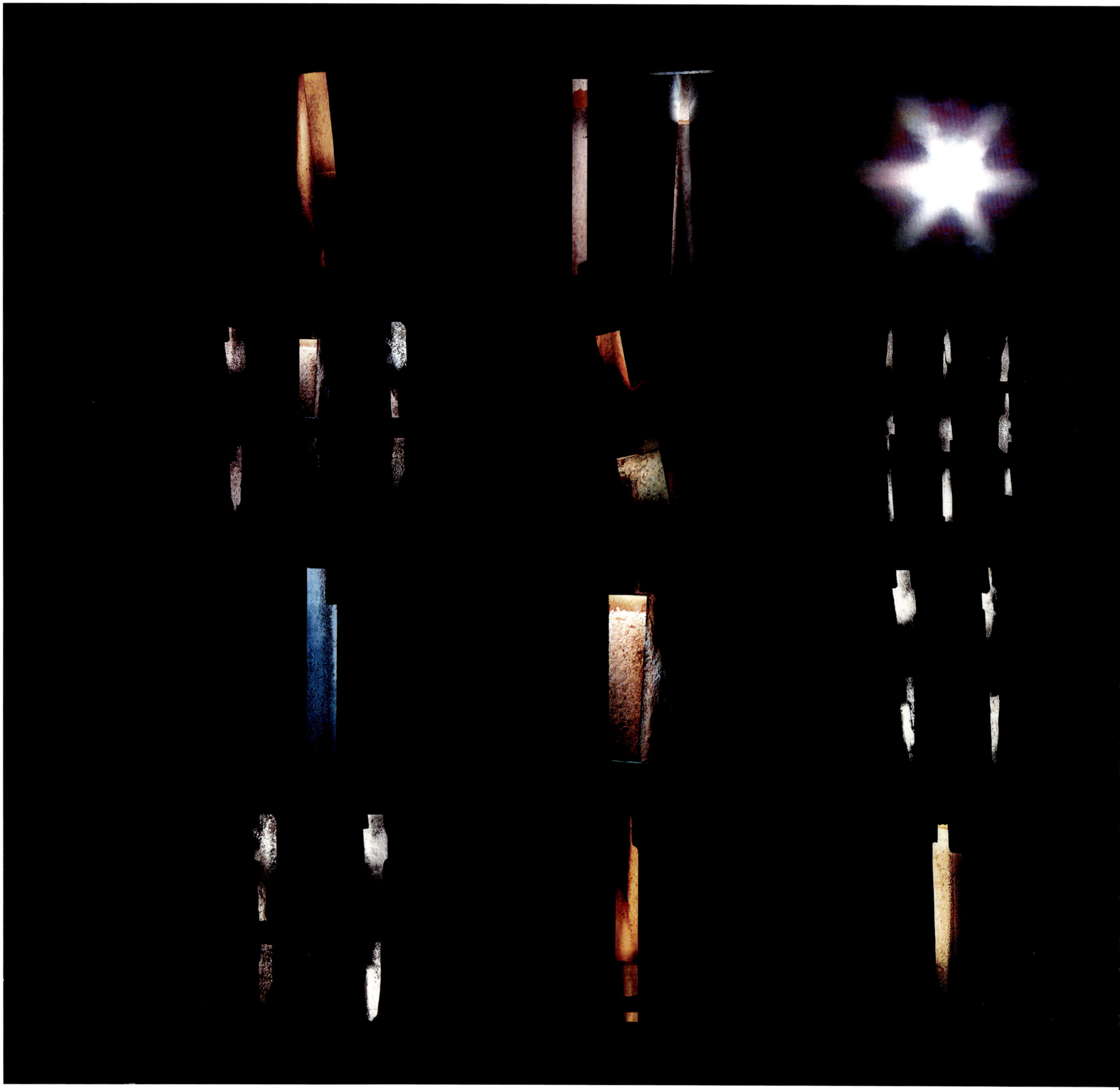

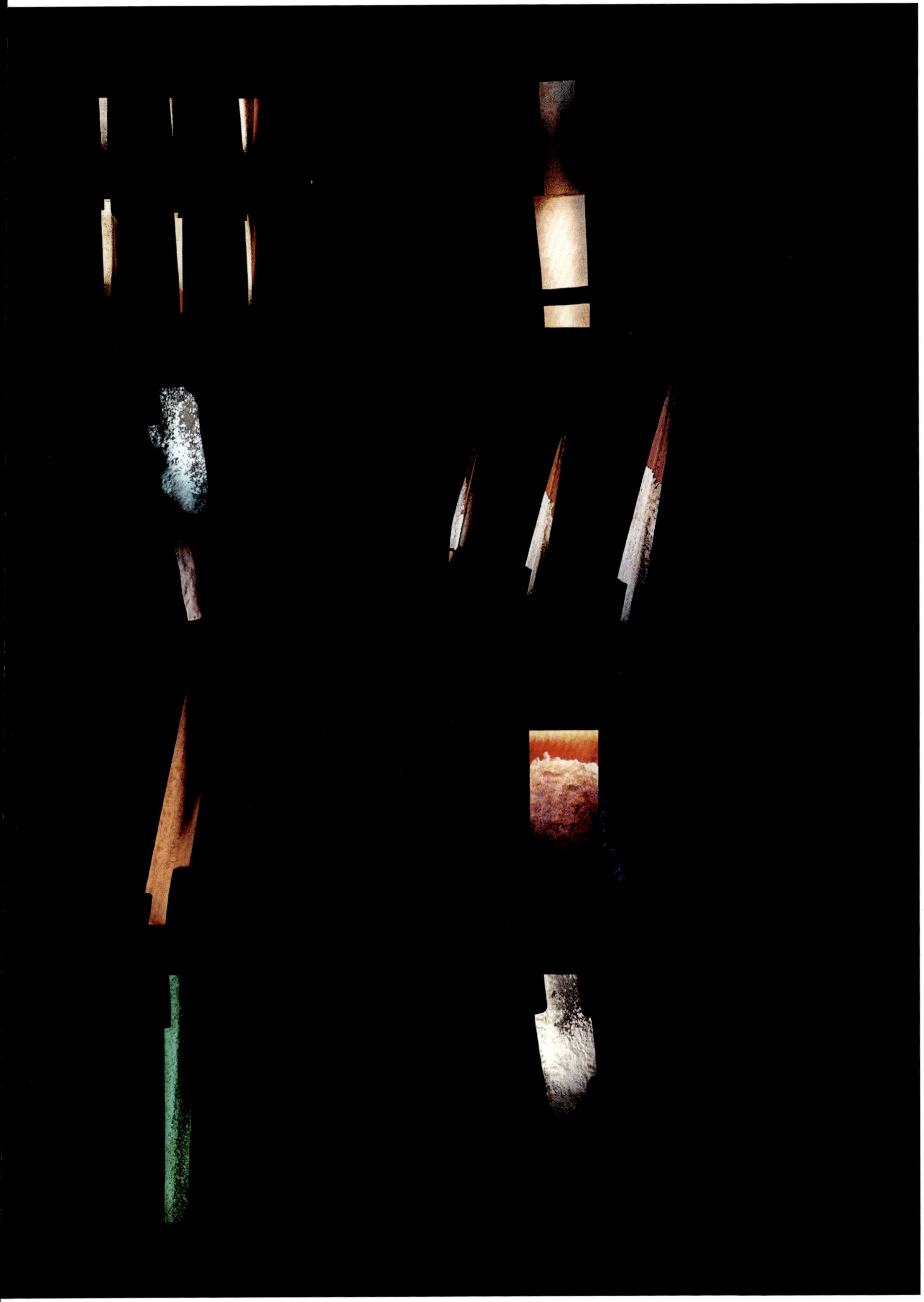

**11.1c**
Oscar Dourado (b. 1954, Salvador, Bahia, Brazil)
*Opô elo imemorial* (Opô, Immemorial Chain), 2017
Digital color photographs printed on Duratrans
COURTESY OSCAR DOURADO

According to Dourado this series consists of twenty photographs and speaks of the experience of initiatory seclusion within Candomblé. As with initiation where sacred knowledge is revealed over time, these images are the result of a slow process of observation during which Dourado lay on floor of a tiny, windowless room in an old house where the only illumination came from the passage of sunlight through the slits between the roof tiles.

The individual titles of the photographs are given below (right to left, top to bottom):

1. *Opô Onipin* (*Opô* of the Supreme Being, Oludumaré, Who Has Dominion over Everything but Shares Power with the *Orixás*)
2. *Opô ododo lailai* (*Opô* of the Ancestral Flowers)
3. *Opô Egungun I* (*Opô* of the Ancestral Spirits I)
4. *Opô Egungun II* (*Opô* of the Ancestral Spirits II)
5. *Opô Onirê* (*Opô* of the *Orixá* Ogum, the Ruler of Irê [a city in ancient Nigeria])

6. *Opô Wari* (*Opô* of Ogum of the Waters)
7. *Opô Alafia* (*Opô* of the Energy That Brings Peace, Well-Being, and Harmony)
8. *Opô abi Ilú* (*Opô* of the Birth of the Drums)
9. *Opô ohun-oná obé I* (*Opô* of the Old Knives or Ritual Implements [*ferramentas*] I)
10. *Opô Padá I* (*Opô* of the *Orixá* Oyá Who Lights the Path of Returning Spirits of the Dead [Egungun] I)

11. *Opô etá aranlê* (*Opô* of the Three Relatives in the House)
12. *Opô etá alaikú* (*Opô* of the Three Immortal Beings)
13. *Opô Ilú* (*Opô* of the Drums)
14. *Opô ohun-oná obé II* (*Opô* of the Old Knives or Ritual Implements [*ferramentas*] II)
15. *Opô ekodidê* (*Opô* of the Red Tail Feather of the African Gray Parrot That Is Worn by the *Orixá* Oxalá)

16. *Opô Orôminan* (*Opô* of the *Orixá* Ogum Who Uses Fire)
17. *Opô Ajagun* (*Opô* of the Warrior Oxaguiá, the Youthful Incarnation of Oxalá)
18. *Opô agadá* (*Opô* of the Scimitar Used by the *Orixás* Ogum and Oyá )
19. *Opô obé* (*Opô* of the Knife, the Main Tool Used by Ogum, Placed in Its Sheath)
20. *Opô Ohun-oná Exin* (*Opô* of the Old Spears or Ritual Implements [*ferramentas*])

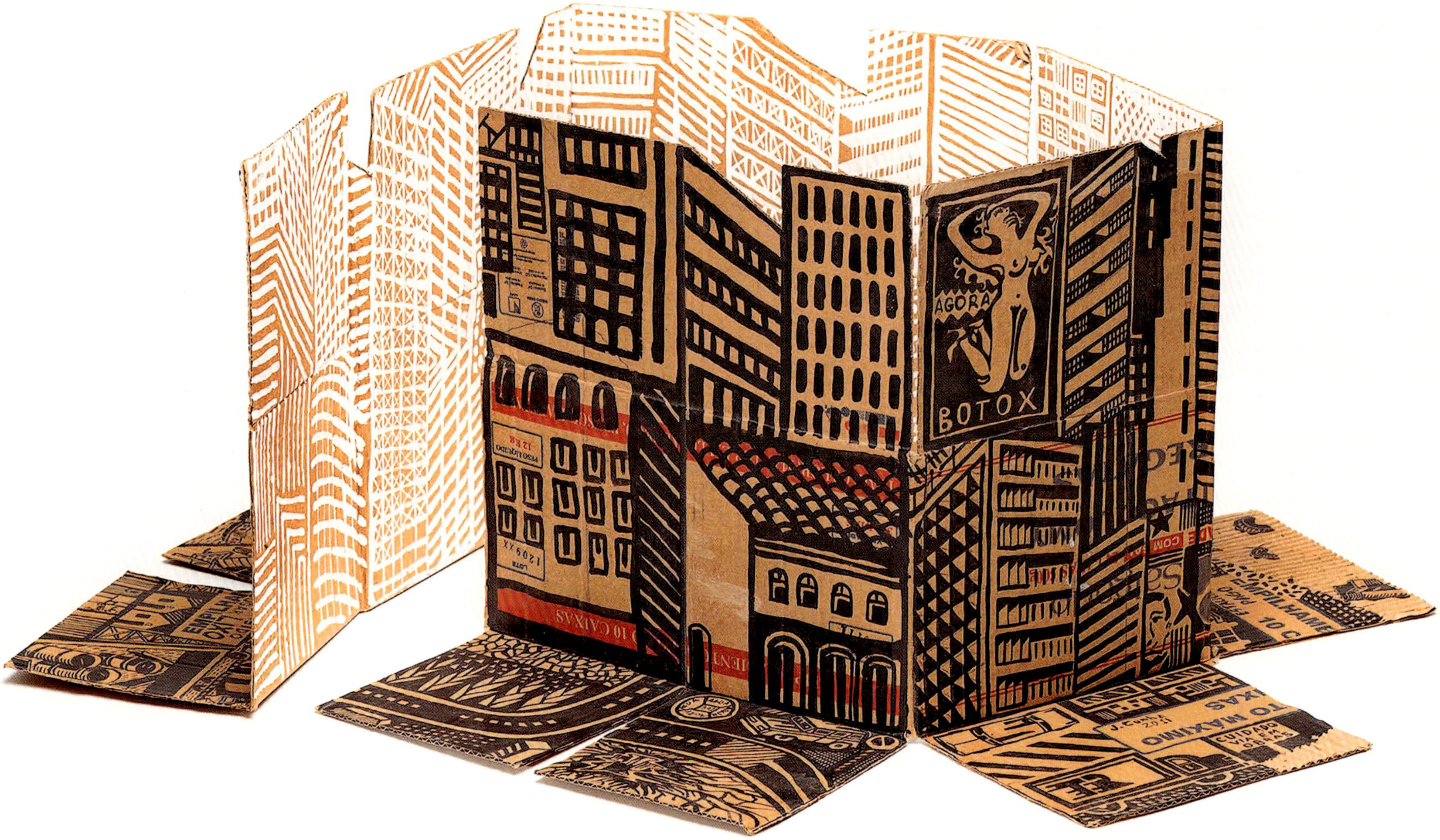


**11.2**
J. Cunha (José Antônio Cunha, b. 1948, Salvador, Bahia, Brazil)
*Cidade tropical* (Tropical City), 2016
Acrylic paint on cardboard
L: 1.45 m
COLLECTION OF J. CUNHA
PHOTOGRAPH BY ANDREW KEMP

### Street Art

Life experience is an issue that goes beyond each artist's individual religious affiliation. Insufficiencies and discontinuities in the local art scene (Almandrade 2001, 9–10) result in lack of recognition of the breadth of the visual arts in Bahia, their dissemination throughout the city, and the variety of media employed. If dialogue and collaborations with other fields such as literature, music, architecture, the dramatic arts, and cinema are common—following modern forms of artistic integration, as well as the more compromising dependency on the governmental and economic spheres—other connections and exchanges also stand out. These involve institutions from other social spheres, such as religious communities and popular festivals like Carnaval.

The diversity that characterizes this volume corresponds to the fluidity with which the black imaginary pervades a variety of social sectors, including a wide range of subjects, institutions, and spaces in the city. These range from tattoos to clothing and other forms of corporal reinvention, from art galleries and museums to temples and shops, from decorative objects and buildings to street furniture and monuments, from graffiti to souvenirs, from social activism to public- and private-sector marketing campaigns. From the artistic institutionalization of Afro-Bahian culture to the reverberation of cultural and artistic repertoires in commercial artifacts, an intense and little-studied[15] exchange has arisen among the arts, material culture, corporeity, and imaginary in Bahia, constituting a unique public role for the arts without parallel in other Brazilian contexts.

The special dialogue between agents of the arts and other fields in Bahia goes beyond the reverberation of daily life in the art world. It is not restricted to breaking through traditional barriers and taking it to the streets to make art accessible to a broader swath of people. It could reside in modernist strategies of popularization, such as book illustrations, print series, murals, and sculptures erected in public places, in which Carybé explored his talent like no other. It may lurk in the contemporary domestication of what first emerged as transgression—the movement in which Eder Muniz uses graffiti art to express a notion of Bahia shaped more in the association of nature with the black self-image than by history and culture (see Polk, this volume). It could also exist in the reverberation of a repertoire already institutionalized in social programs, such as the use of paintings by Gil Abelha in posters for public health campaigns (see fig. 3.13). On a smaller scale, this art would correlate with "the music of Bahia's Carnaval, particularly the most commercial, which has become known as *Axé* Music,"[16] which Caetano defends directly in the song with which this essay begins.

Artistic portrayals of characters and cultural practices that have shaped the predominant Bahian cultural identity, such as Baianas, capoeira, and Candomblé have contributed to another sociocultural valuation of historically excluded social groups, institutions, and cultural expressions. We should not, however, ignore the presence of portrayals of Afro-Bahian culture in public settings in a society that systematically marginalizes and makes the black population and cultures socially invisible. It does present the risk of reinforcing stereotypes conducive to various kinds of exploitation.

In this regard, one of the factors that distinguishes the visual arts in Bahia is their integration with street practices that link hedonism, reflection, and activism. Aurelino dos Santos's colorful cityscapes are a case in point (figs. 11.3, 11.4). Other instances include the ceremonies that overflow from the *terreiros* into street festivals and culminate in Carnaval. This is a domain in which the performance of Cunha as artistic director of the Carnaval group Ilê Aiyê is particularly noteworthy (see interleaf H, this volume, and fig. 11.2). Between 1979 and 2005, he created prints for fabrics, costumes, and the stage sets for that group, conceiving a visual identity in keeping with the struggle for the preservation of cultural values and the promotion of social equality for Afro-descendants (see fig. 24). In this case, lived experience implies an exceptional moment, a celebration in which people, objects, and the senses merge into playful and combative ecstasy. Furthermore, after the celebrations are done, the fabrics are adapted to a range of uses as everything from curtains to blouses and are incorporated into all walks of life in the city.

This is a phenomenon that the concept of fine art cannot circumscribe, whether due to the fact that Cunha is almost completely self-taught,[17] or to the way multiple artistic and cultural references are combined with the Carnaval group as their origin and driving force (see Miguez, this volume). Since Carnaval has become one of the dynamos of Bahia's cultural and economic life, the scale and scope of production is not surprising. Furthermore, the power of religious celebrations and Carnaval festivities greatly surpasses the dynamics of the art galleries and museums in Salvador. A revised and broader view of the art world is required in this context.

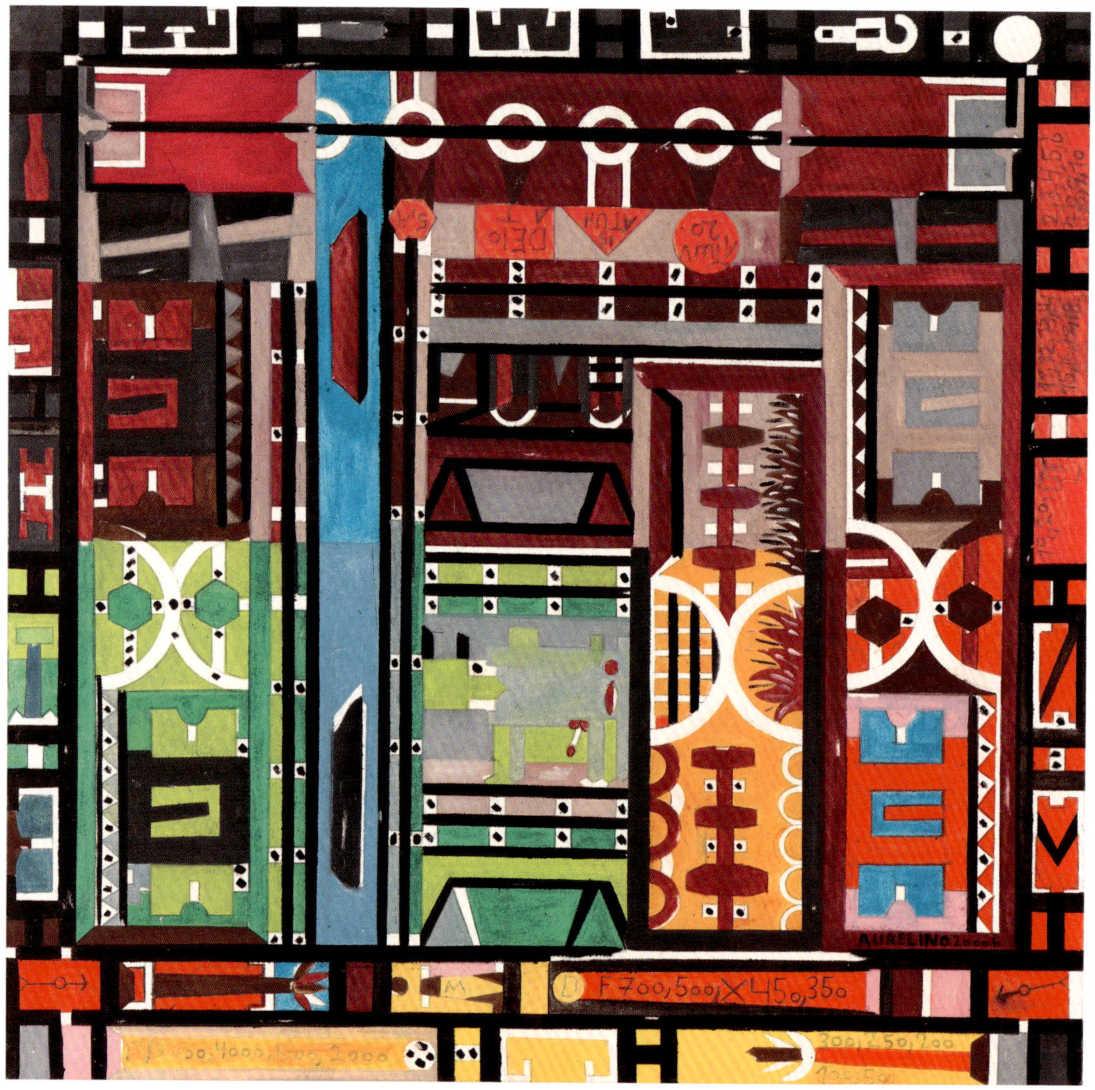

**11.3**
Aurelino dos Santos (b. 1942, Salvador, Bahia, Brazil)
*Sem titulo* (Untitled), 2006
Oil on canvas
80 x 80 cm
COLLECTION OF ROBERTO ALBAN GALERIA
PHOTOGRAPH BY ANDREW KEMP

A self-taught visionary artist, Aurelino appears to translate his experience of the urban design of Salvador—or perhaps some other metropolis of the mind—into brightly colored and wildly geometric cityscapes. Highlighted with letters and numbers of uncertain meaning and the occasional bit of discarded paper, they have the effect of providing both aerial and street-level views.

**11.4**
Aurelino dos Santos (b. 1942, Slavador, Bahia, Brazil)
*Sem titulo* (Untitled), 2012
Oil and collage on canvas
100 x 100 cm
COLLECTION OF ROBERTO ALBAN GALERIA
PHOTOGRAPH BY ANDREW KEMP

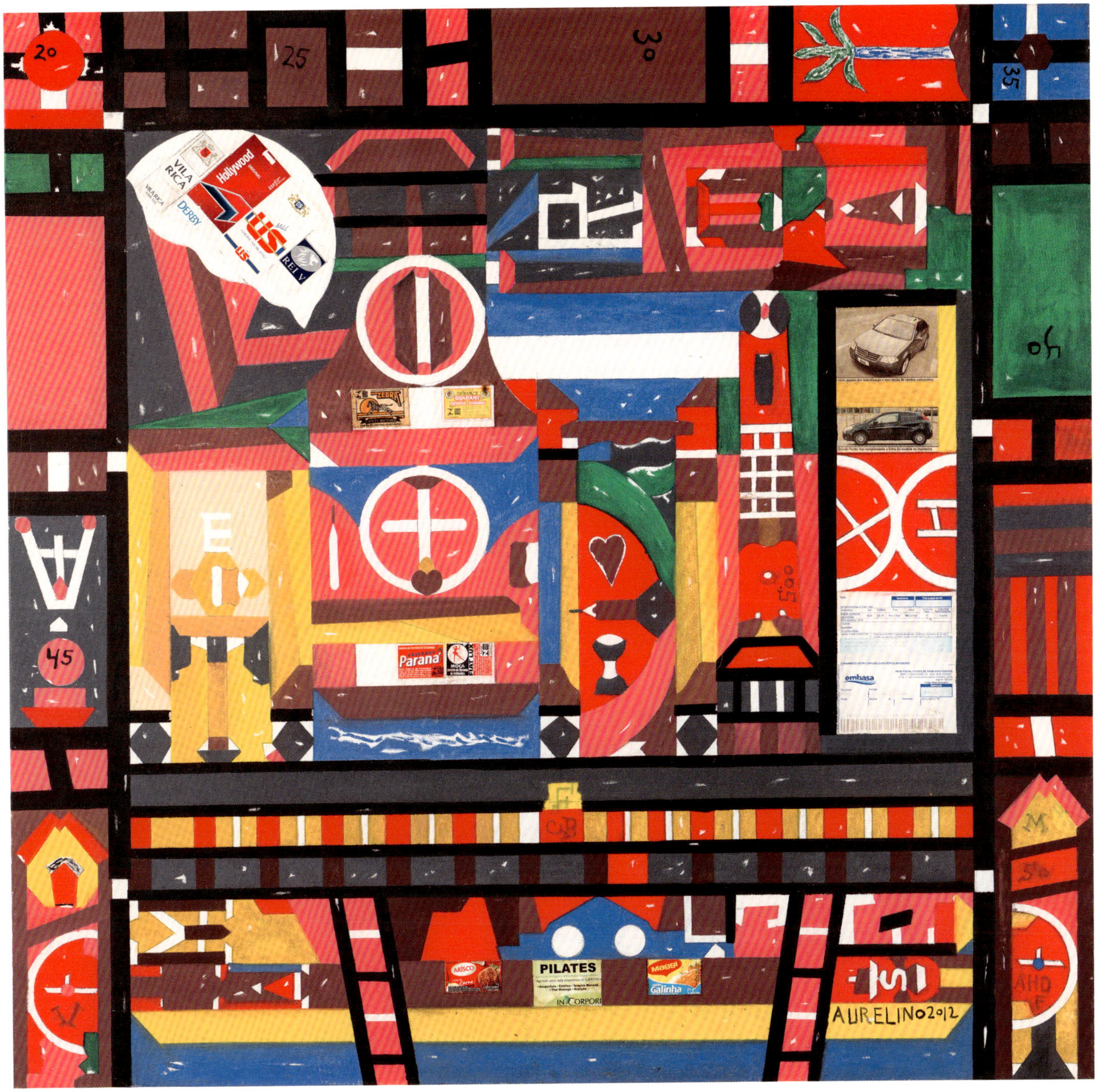
20
25
30
35
40
45
VILA RICA
Hollywood
DERBY
US
REI V
Parana
PILATES
INCORPORE
ARISCO
Maggi
Galinha
embasa
AURELINO 2012

**11.5**
Pedro Marighella (b. 1979, Salvador, Bahia, Brazil)
*Sem titulo* (Untitled), 2014
Acrylic paint on wood
2.3 x 2.6 m
COURTESY GALLERY RV CULTURA E ARTE
PHOTOGRAPH BY ANDREW KEMP

This painting is a part of Marighella's *Série mata* (Mata Series). It features a boisterous Carnaval crowd—some members armed with squirt guns—as it reaches critical mass. The word *mata* can mean both "jungle forest" and "kill" in Portuguese, reflecting the often ambiguous energy of the celebration.

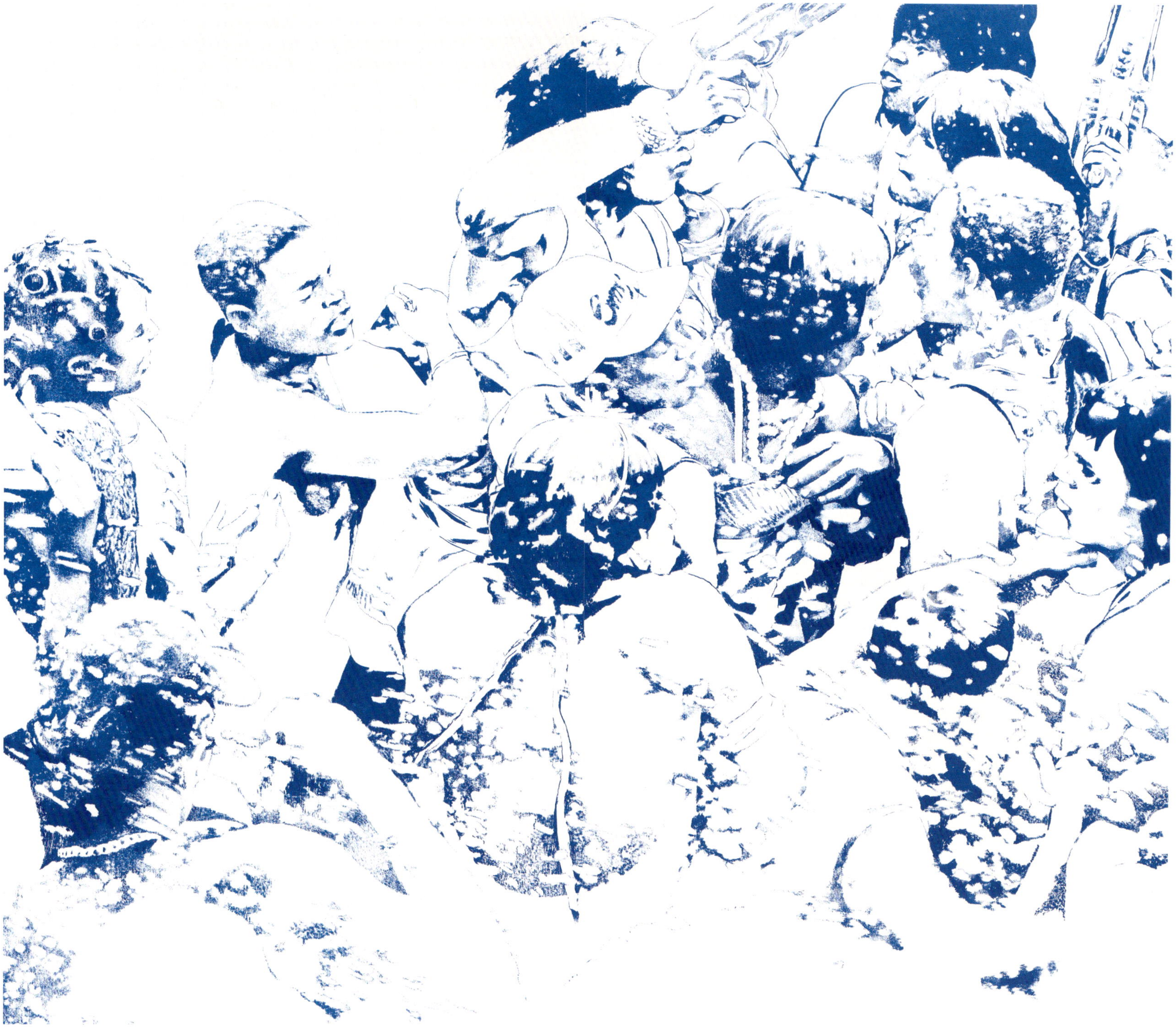

In the intervention *De lama lâmina* (From Mud, A Blade), Matthew Barney evoked the primordial *orixá* Nanã Buruku with a float featuring an enormous logging truck carrying at its front an entire uprooted tree. It was followed by Arto Lindsay's band performing on an attached logging trailer, flanked by drummers and dancers of the Cortejo Afro group. This took place during Carnaval in Bahia of 2004. Barney interwove complex themes of Afro-Brazilian religion, sexuality, and ecology in this rare attempt to respond artistically to the festivities in Salvador, with their multiplicity of languages and scale.

It is not difficult, however, to find reflections of the unique ways in which Bahian Carnaval activates the senses in recent artistic production. Heráclito has confronted the question of scale in *O condor do Atlântico: Moqueca* (The Atlantic Condor: Stew), held at the Museu de Arte Moderna da Bahia in 2002. Visitors and the nearby community of Gamboa were invited to cook and eat a stew called *moqueca*, a popular local dish, made with an enormous stingray, a cheap and popular fish in Bahia, which was figuratively linked with the great Andean condor to characterize the ritual as a metaphor for the liberation of the Americas. Marepe (Marcos Reis Peixoto) also performed a symbolic public act when he poured thirteen thousand freshwater pearls into the Tietê River in São Paulo in 2006, both as an offering to Oxum[18] and a protest against pollution and environmental degradation, stressing the environmental aspects of Candomblé. Damaceno went out into the streets and returned with Encruzilhada: Troca de passagem (Crossroads: The Passage), a video-performance in which, opposed to the acrobatic showmanship typical of capoeira, he engages without an opponent within the self-imposed boundaries of a manhole cover inscribed with a Kongo cosmogram (see figs. 5.11a,b). This suggests how this martial art evokes myths and tales of the diasporic streams that connect Africa, Rio de Janeiro, Bahia, and beyond. Pedro Marighella focuses on masses of people in his murals and paintings (fig. 11.5). Using somewhat abstract and decorative patterns generated from photographs, he portrays groups at play and sometimes in conflict to graphically condense the energy that the crowd can produce in festive events and other settings.

### The Art of Struggle

For a long time, the political dimension of Bahian arts linked to Africanness resided primarily in the visual presentation of that which was socially marginalized. Increased appreciation of these arts aided the struggle for inclusion of Afro-descendants and their cultural practices. While this artistic visibility led to some integration, it was not immune from exploitation, nor did it guarantee equality. The preference for pandering to the taste for cultural exoticism to the detriment of explicitly presenting people's real living conditions often won out. This, in addition to poor critical response, bolstered representations of Afro-Bahian culture as visual expressions of the myth of the harmonious racial mixture alleged to constitute Brazilian society.

We must carefully sift through Carybé's output to find any scathing social content.[19] The nature of photography makes Verger's images more realistic, but it does not transform them into involuntary denunciations of social malaise. One exception is Hansen Bahia, in whose work social issues carry a different weight, as in the series of prints that illustrate Castro Alves's poem *O navio negreiro* (The Slave Ship) with dramatic scenes of men and women enduring the Middle Passage (see interleaf A, this volume). Another exception is the photography of Cravo Neto, whose images are both indicative and allegorical, addressing topics such as colonialism, slavery, and racism.[20]

As usual in Bahia, religion is fertile ground for politics. In *Divisor* (Divider), Heráclito explores the symbolism of red palm oil (*dênde*) in Afro-Brazilian religions to speak of the blood spilled during the transatlantic slave trade (see fig. K.1). If in this work the materials recall that sacrifice and expose its present-day ramifications, in Heráclito's *Sacudimentos*, carried out in two important sites of the slave trade, enslavement, and colonialism, located in Brazil and Africa, the duo of performance and religious ritual aims to free those places from persistent aftereffects (see figs. K.5a,b). While Heráclito uses religious procedures to heal historical wounds, Àlex Ìgbó turns to the tactics of present-day urban culture to intervene in the religious war underway in Salvador and throughout Brazil. With his rough-hewn graffiti and *lambe-lambe* posters, he provocatively connects the Christian and Yoruba messengers Jesus and Exú in *Jexus* (see. figs. 3.3, 3.4).

The artistic production of the last three decades has confronted tensions from the past and present, whether latent or explicit in the social arena, with various degrees of engagement and mediation. It would be a mistake to include in the plots of the constructive tradition, harking back to the works of Valentim and Araújo, the installation *A fragilidade dos negócios humanos pode ser um limite espacial incontestável* (The Fragility of Human Affairs Can Be an Incontestable Spatial Boundary) by Rommulo Vieira Conceição, whose work critically avoids the exaltation of Afro-Bahian culture (figs. 11.6a,b). Although one can accept a reading associated with constructivism, as well as an interpretation regarding intersubjectivity, this work brings together in a lively and incisive manner the more recent failures of modern architecture in the long-standing tradition of segregating slaves and the poor, particularly black people, in Salvador, as in other Brazilian cities.

Another emphatic message comes from Caetano Dias in *Delírios de Catarina* (The Ravings of Catherine; see fig. 1.1), in which he juxtaposes a table made from bull's blood in the King Manuel style of the late fifteenth to early sixteenth century, a work bench, a vise, and a pile of heads made of brown sugar to confront us with the oppressive legacy of Bahia's former primary economy. Clearly, however, it also addresses the perverse contemporary impacts of colonialism and slavery. Focused on the present, while also looking to the past with a less allegorical tone, is *Apagamento #1—Cabula* (Elimination #1—Cabula), a video-performance that Sant'Ana has composed with photos of his head, on which the word *cabula* is written, referring to the district in Salvador of the same name where twelve young black men were killed by military police officers on February 6, 2015. In images that somewhat parody mug shots, the word disappears as his hair grows back to the sound of drums (figs. 11.7a-c), both as a condemnation of how killings of young men, especially black men, are forgotten in Brazil and subsumed in statistics, and as a call to reflection on violence and racism.

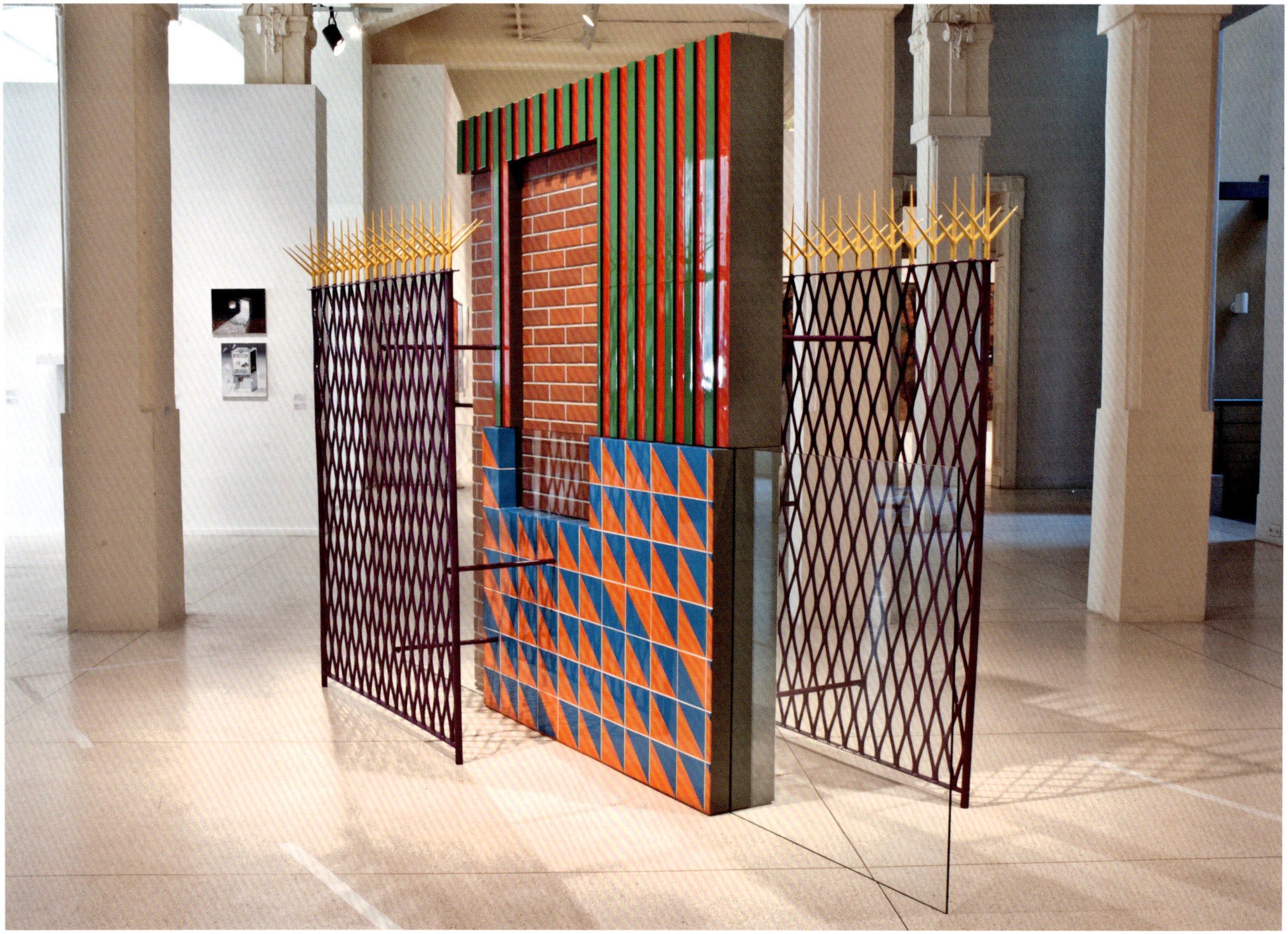

**11.6a,b**
Rommulo Vieira Conceição (b. 1968, Salvador, Bahia, Brazil)
*A fragilidade dos negócios humanos pode ser um limite especial incontestável* (The Fragility of Human Affairs Can Be an Incontestable Spatial Boundary), 2015
Wood, metal, glass, automotive paint
W: 3.8 m
COLLECTION OF THE ARTIST

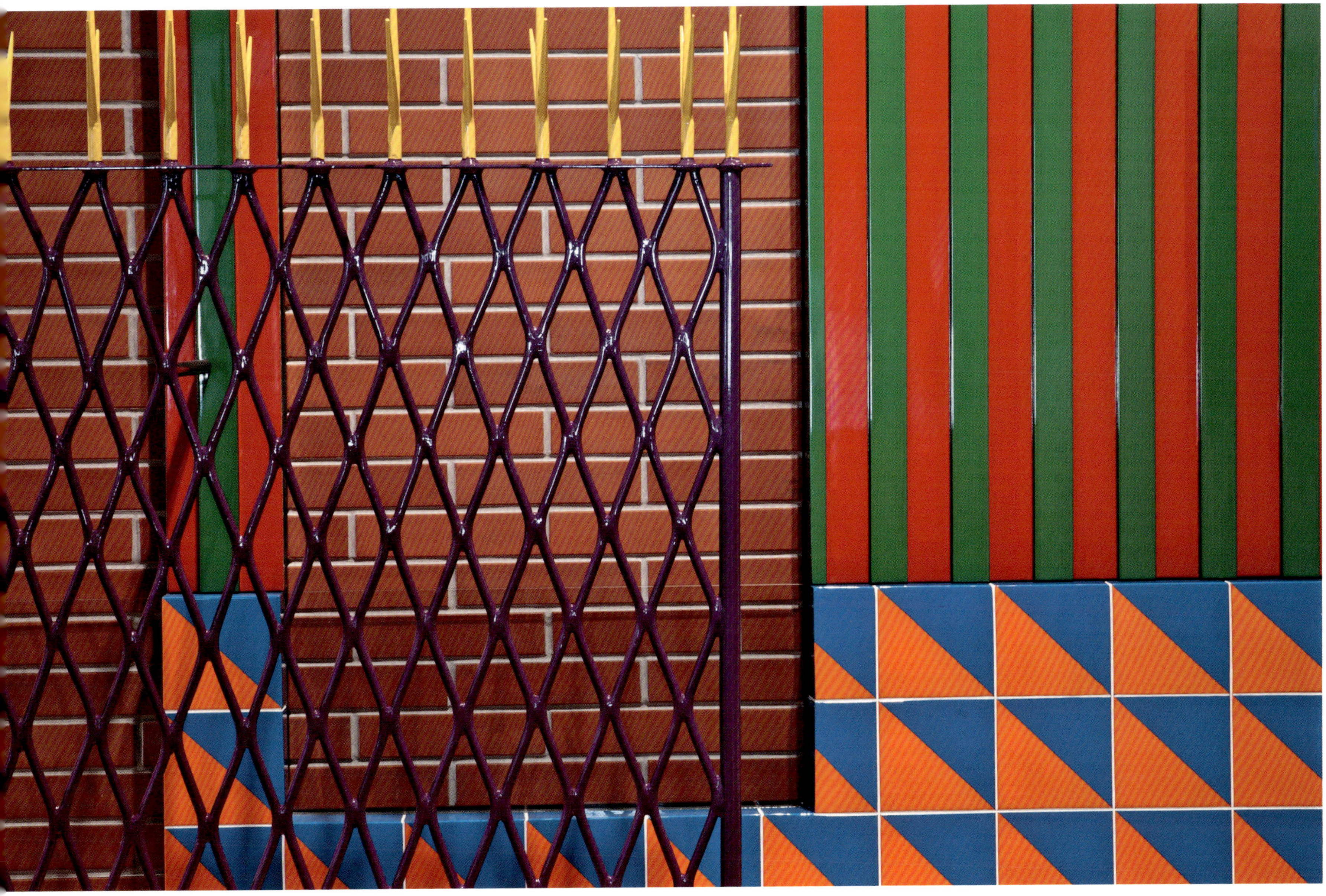

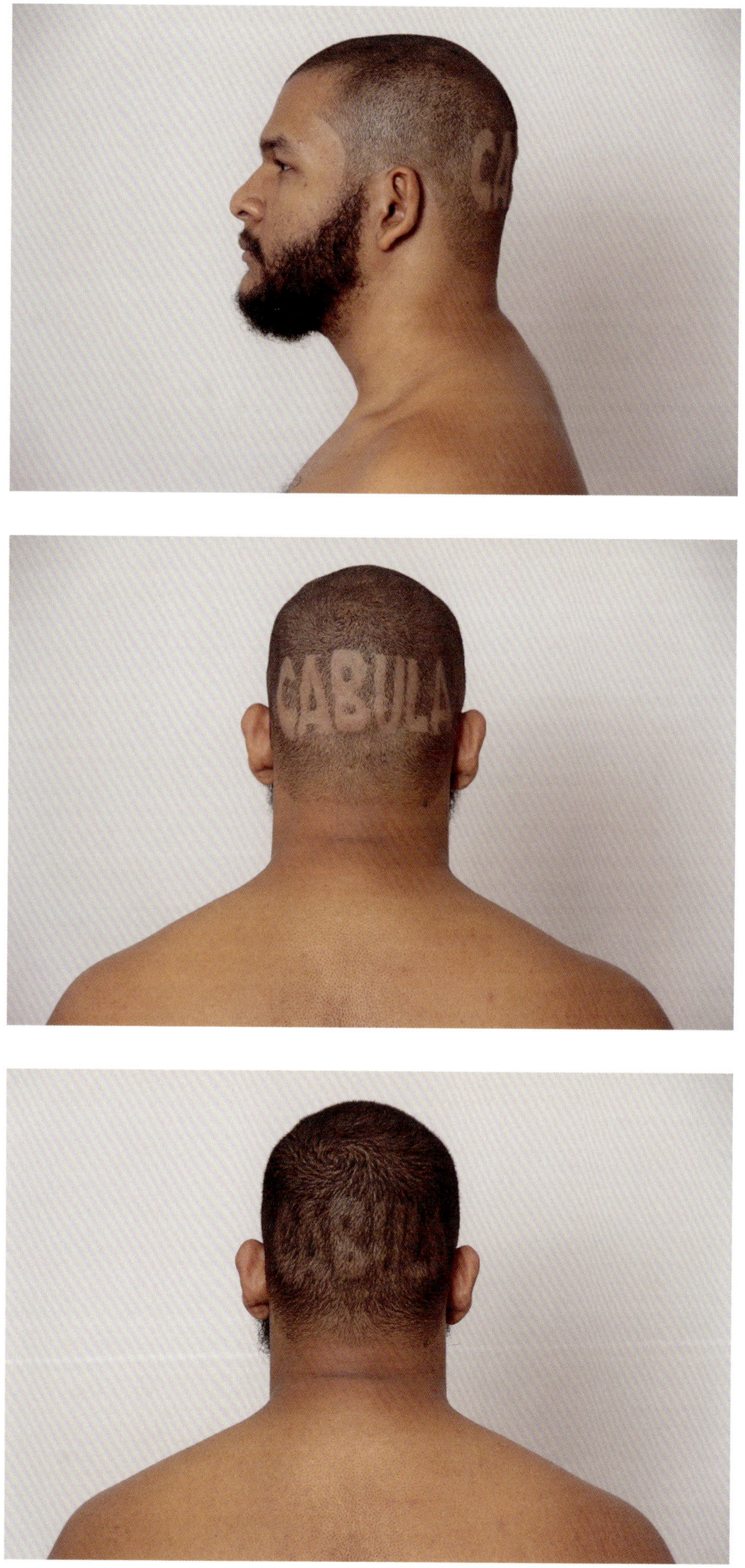


**11.7a-c**
Tiago Sant'Ana (b. 1990, Salvador, Bahia, Brazil)
*Apagamento #1—Cabula* (Elimination #1—Cabula), 2017
Video, 48 seconds
COURTESY TIAGO SANT'ANA

Sant'Ana writes that in low-income areas of Salvador, some young people style their hair with designs made using razors. Words and globally recognized logos reveal their sense of identity—a way of representing and writing about themselves. *Apagamento #1—Cabula* immerses itself in this double context. The artist had the word *Cabula* shaved into his hair and then photographed it, day after day, until the name disappeared completely. This work is a means of highlighting the cruel process of strategically silencing young blacks and even exterminating them and their presence in the contexts of the metropolis where they were born.

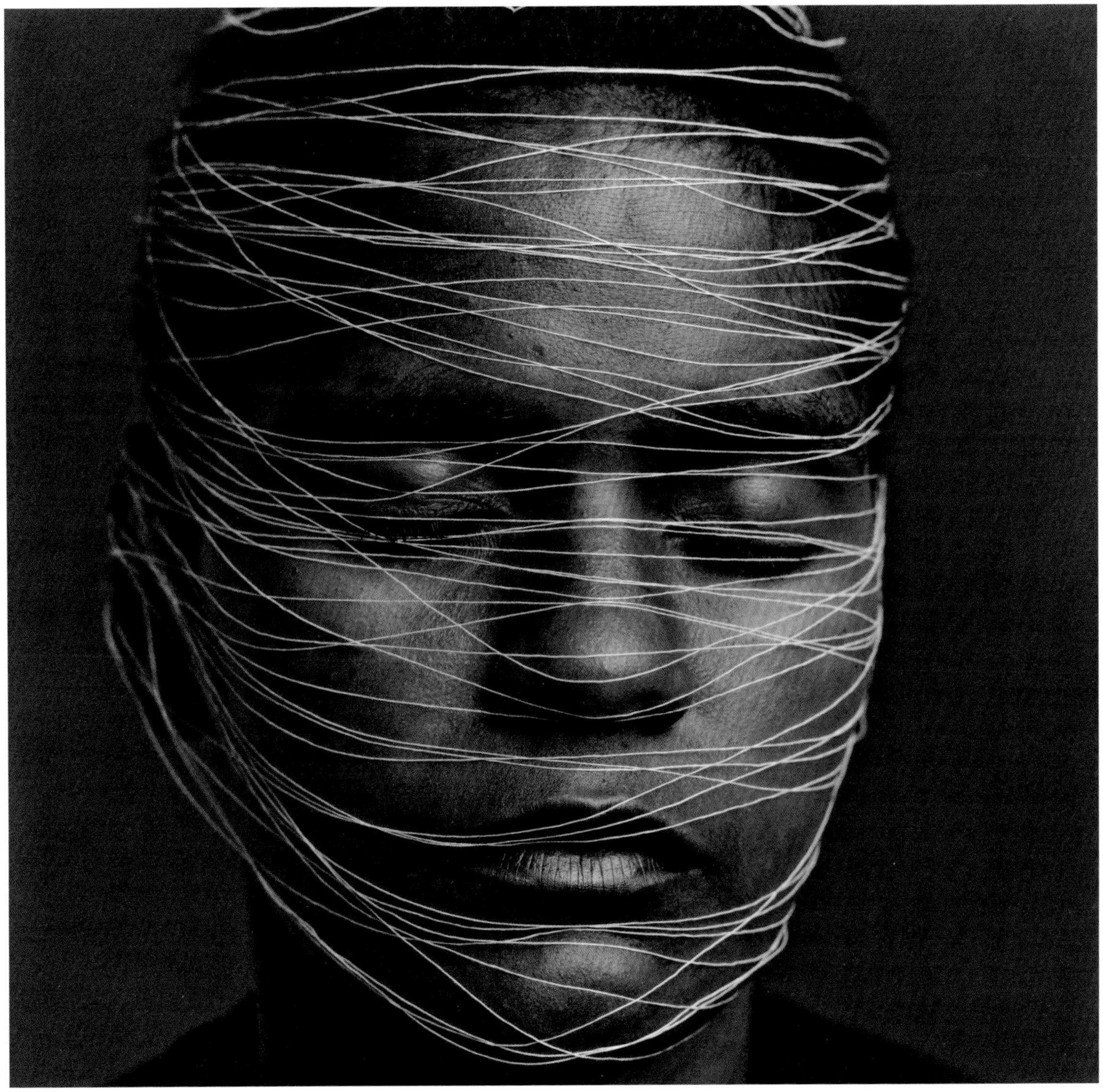

**11.8**
Mário Cravo Neto (b. 1947, Salvador, Bahia, Brazil; d. 2009)
*Luciana*, 1994
Photograph


**The Arts (of Suffering and) of Beauty**
In addition to history and culture, religion and art, there is a political vein in the prints created by Goya Lopes, both for everyday clothing and for installations such as *Sentidos afros-baianos* (Afro-Bahian Senses). This is clear in the unusual patterns she has created on the basis of the schematic cross-section of a slave ship (see fig. T.1, p. 50) and the icon of "Escrava Anastácia," or Anastácia the Slave (see interleaf L, this volume, and see fig. T.3, p. 52). If it is easy to understand the desire to pay tribute to a figure who is popular in the folk religion of Brazil, it is harder to understand who would want to wear a symbol of human barbarity, even if the slave ship is somewhat imperceptible in the curvilinear pattern created by the linkage of its design with the figures of *ibejis* and other graphic elements.[21] Along with Cunha's creations for Ilê Aiyê and other interventions in Carnaval *abadás* (costumes), Goya's fabrics showcase prints that are engaged with the processes of emancipating the black community. In Bahia, cultural expression and the struggle for civil rights are taking place in Carnaval and daily life, mixing religion and politics with beauty, sweetness, sensitivity, and sensuality.

It is also with considerable delicacy that Cravo Neto alludes to the imprisonment of women, blackness, beauty, and light in his photograph titled *Luciana* (fig. 11.8). This image acts as a metaphor for the condition of the Baiana, or Bahian woman. On the basis of songs, we are informed that, with charms "like no other,"[22] the Baiana comes from "Bahia, land of happiness."[23] This praise of grace and happiness nourishes the widespread assumption about the sunny lifestyle and culture of Bahia, which is believed to overcome, or at least attenuate, its social insufficiencies (see Shirey, this volume). As Cravo Neto's image subtly and charmingly helps its viewers realize, however, not everything is beauty and joy for Luciana, the Baiana, or for other people of African descent in Bahia.

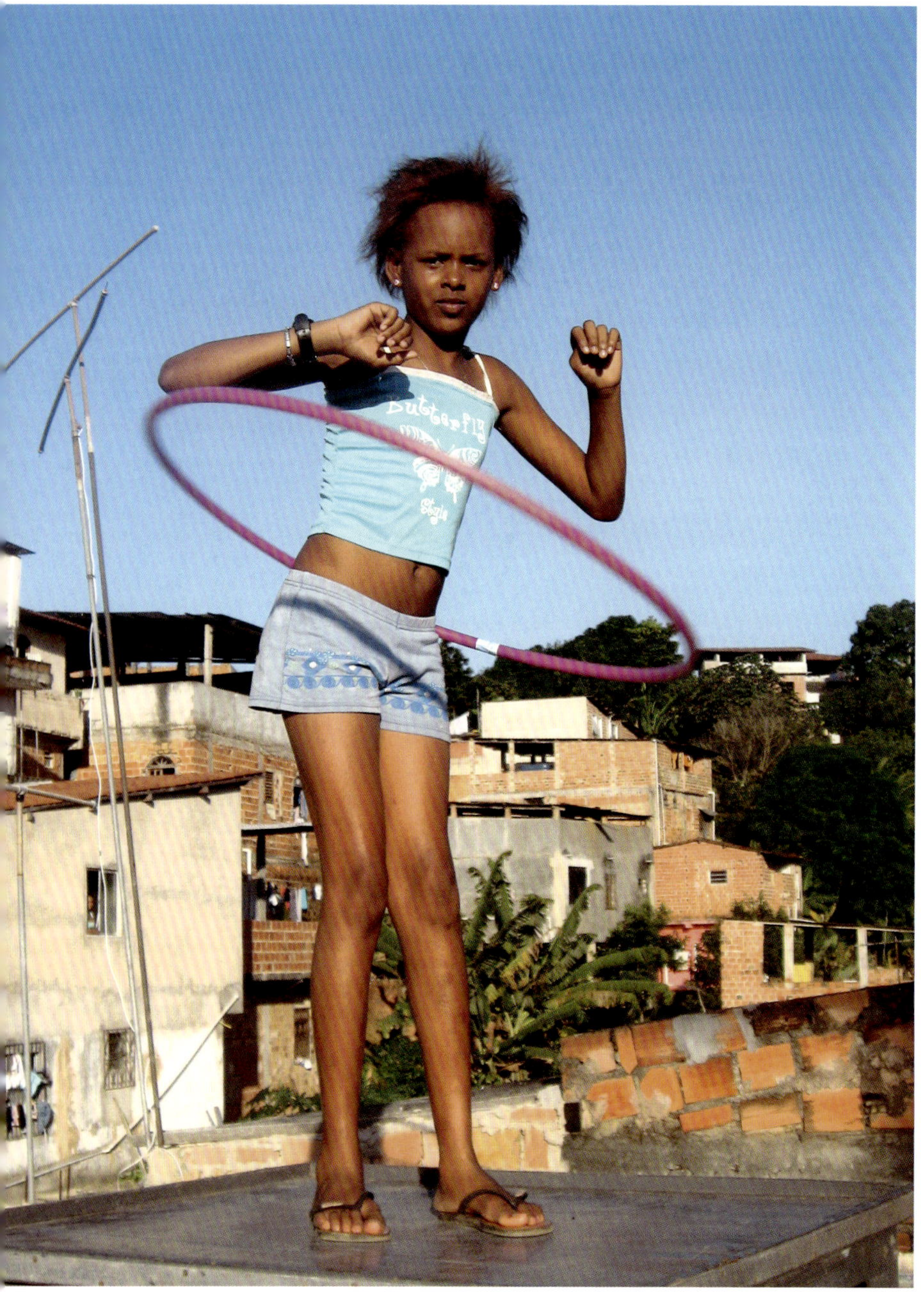


**11.9**
Caetano Dias (b. 1959, Feira de Santana, Bahia, Brazil)
*O mundo de Janiele* (Janiele's World), 2007
Video, 3:58 mins.
COURTESY CAETANO DIAS

Despite past and present hardships, many artists have insisted on preserving harmonious views, even when dealing with degrading themes. Recently, however, that artistic equation has been balanced and in rare cases inverted. This is in response to criticisms regarding previous alienation, the commitment of artistic modernism to the exaltation of Bahian culture, and the demand for greater engagement from artists in sociopolitical causes. Furthermore, there is a strong belief in Afro-Bahian *axé*. It is not just a matter of celebrating the beautiful power of life. Although Bahian culture emerged from barbaric processes, its charm can be seen as a special weapon to overcome adversity. If pain can generate beauty, art can participate in individual and collective emancipation. Suffering and beauty are balanced in *O mundo de Janiele* (Janiele's World) by Caetano Dias (fig. 11.9). To the repetitive and banal sound of a music box, a young girl sways, dances, and bobs while hoola-hooping—rising proudly and gracefully above the favela and the social ills that surround her. Like Janiele, Bahia uses the power of beauty, art, and culture to confront the world.

**Central Margin**

Following in the steps of the vast musical soundtrack extolling Bahia, Veloso also refers to grace and happiness in the lyrics that guide this essay. He bases Bahia's resumption of her place in the globalized world on the insistence of what is beautiful. A reconquest based on felicity, because the cry that he says should echo "far, [in] time and space" is one of joy. He also sees the city of São Salvador da Bahia de Todos os Santos[24] regaining the geopolitical status it enjoyed in the past, particularly between 1549 and 1763, when it was the capital of Brazil and held a privileged position in the exchanges established across the Atlantic Ocean, inside and outside of the Portuguese Empire.

Jorge Amado, Dorival Caymmi, João Gilberto, and Glauber Rocha—like Veloso and Costa—are some of the art-world figures who have garnered a prominent position in the Brazilian imaginary for themselves and their home state. Not just a theme for artists born or based there, Bahia has been configured as a special place in a country that, since the 1910s, has been organized into regions with physical, economic, and sociocultural characteristics that give rise to contrasting and complementary identities.[25] Seen as an idyllic place whose delights stem from an amalgam of the tropics and deep-rooted cultural traditions, Bahia is believed to be one of the necessary counterpoints[26] to the configuration of São Paulo and Rio de Janeiro as cosmopolitan cities and capitals of modernity in Brazil.

Unlike in literature and music, and later on filmmaking, however, Bahia occupied second place in the fine arts. Its peripheral status as a center of artistic production and debate derived from the persistence of academicism, backwardness, and the slow modernization of Salvador compared to the primacy and dynamism of São Paulo and Rio de Janeiro.[27] Beginning in 1944, according to Walter Zanini, modernism in Bahia was "extremely attached to the stimuli of the physical and human world" (Zanini 1983, 638). The unique, opulent, and vivacious imaginary propagated by the novels of Amado and the songs of Caymmi since the 1930s would only begin to expand visually in the middle of the following decade through the varied artistic output of Carybé, and the photographs of Verger (see Johnson, this volume). The unique artistic research of Valentim, who combined abstract-geometric principles and shapes with Afro-Brazilian religious symbolism, grew with increased density when he migrated from Salvador to Rio de Janeiro in 1957. Although he was warmly received in Bahia's art world, the predominant portrayal of scenes, people, and local customs was scorned by Brazilian art critics as a regionalist and somewhat conservative expression, in contrast with the abstract, constructive, and informal trends that had spread in that country as vanguard movements after World War II.

Undeniably, São Paulo and Rio de Janeiro played a central role in Brazilian modernism. It is no coincidence that migrating permanently or temporarily to the southeast of the country has been a factor in the careers of many Bahian artists, musicians, and writers in the twentieth century. The peripheries are not necessarily pale shadows of the centers, however, nor are they identical. Moreover, they can have exclusive traits, unique delights.

The permanent or temporary establishment of artists from other parts of Brazil and abroad in Bahia[28] indicates its status as an alternative place in which they saw the possibility of combining a way of life with artistic experimentation. For many, Salvador's somewhat archaistic character was attractive and could serve as a liberating option, given the provincialism that could often be detected in ostensibly cosmopolitan intellectual and artistic circles in Rio de Janeiro and São Paulo. From the late 1950s until the eruption of the military-civilian dictatorship a decade later, it became one of the most dynamic vanguard locales in the country.

If we recall that relations between centers and peripheries are complementary, conflicting, complex, and changeable (Ginzburg 1991, 5–7), we can argue that the centrality of those cities is relative. In addition to depending on the periphery to affirm their central status, they can be viewed as marginal, backward centers with less-intense dynamics when compared with other hubs of artistic modernization in Europe and the Americas. This was accentuated over time. Although Rio and São Paulo continue to function as artistic centers in the country and on the continent, other cities—Salvador among them—have recently attained greater power and vitality, particularly for foreign audiences. Following the restructuring of artistic networks and hierarchies in the process of globalization, the mediating function of Brazilian centers has become virtually meaningless. Real and virtual flows of people, objects, and ideas enable direct contact with places, agents, institutions, and processes that were once nearly inaccessible.[29]

Salvador offers enormous attractions in this globalized setting. Its history as the capital of the largest Portuguese colony and as a key port on the economic and cultural routes of the first modern era are significant. These factors made the city a locus where the ideas, techniques, instruments, and forms of artistic systems that were being brought together by the activities of the Portuguese—including influences from Africa, the Americas, and Asia—converged, have been re-elaborated and disseminated (Freyre 2003). This suggests that the artworks produced in the past and present should be reviewed, questioning the hierarchies established by interpretative matrices imbued with colonial and nationalist forms of logic without naively relying on the relativism propagated by globalization or overlooking the idiosyncrasies of Bahia's cultural world.

It is important to stress the factors that have tinged obdurate provincial conservatism, instilling cosmopolitanism in the arts of Bahia: the comings and goings of the Bahians who migrated, the foreign training of some artists in different contexts,[30] and more extensive or merely occasional stimuli from outsiders who sought creative alternatives and challenges there.[31] These are precedents that help us understand the increasingly free transit of Bahia's artists in the international art world, who, to paraphrase Caetano Veloso, purchased "the equipment and know how to use it, selling talent, and know how to cash in, profit."[32]

Two cases are exemplary here. The first is that of Emanoel Araújo, whose student activism in the 1960s led to interventions in museums beginning in the 1980s in Bahia and São Paulo. These culminated in the establishment of the Museu Afro Brasil, created in 2004, which he conceived and directs to this day. It is based on the outstanding collection of artworks and other objects related to Afro-Brazilian and African cultures that Araújo has assembled over his lifetime. In that institution, Bahia, its culture, and arts occupy a central, predominant place. The other example is Heráclito's work as one of the curators of the Third Bahia Biennial in 2014, which sought to reaffirm the ex-centric, alternative, and anti-hegemonic view of Bahia based on its location in the Brazilian northeast.

It is also important to rethink the backwardness of modernism in Bahia in the light of the current situation of the arts. Paradoxically, its slow development and position in the rear-guard would have helped some of its artists become current with contemporary artistic flows. The persistence of past and local values, which meant being out of step with the dynamics in the artistic centers, their vogues and rhythms, has taken on a less-negative aspect in the face of recent disenchantment with the prospects and universalist aims of modernism. Previously scorned, the compromise solutions that reconciled new and old, international and regional elements, began to serve as valuable precedents when taking on the solution that now recommends, when it does not require, linking the global to the local. The prominence of the theme, of cultural specificity and even of exoticism, which was previously paternalistic, has also gained a different kind of power through increasingly blurred boundaries between art and culture, history and anthropology.

In this sense, artistic production in the last decades has minimized Salvador's peripheral status, not because artists have broken with previously dominant choices, but precisely because they insist on some of them, unfolding them reflexively; because they maintain the attachment criticized by Zanini, although less to the stimuli of the physical environment and more to those of the human environment, to social types and customs, to the culture that, for some time, has been commonly identified as Bahian. Whether artists have heeded Caetano Veloso's recommendation or whether he has voiced what so many have expressed in many languages, it is a fact that recently artists have kept to the trail blazed by Amado and Caymmi, corroborated by Carybé and Verger, and reiterated by Valentim, Araújo, and Cravo Neto: extolling Bahia and particularly its blackness, its Africanness. The prominent position in artistic relations with Africa and other diasporic contexts is a good example of how Bahia not only unfolds artistic propositions generated elsewhere but also spreads ideals and ideas of its own, regionally, nationally, and internationally. When it comes to being black and wanting to be black in Brazil, a country where racism is entrenched in institutions and daily life, Bahia is indeed the center, not the periphery—the Afro-Brazilian metropolis.

*Interleaf* **L**

# Goya Lopes

## *Sentidos Afro-Baianos*

**Sabrina Gledhill**

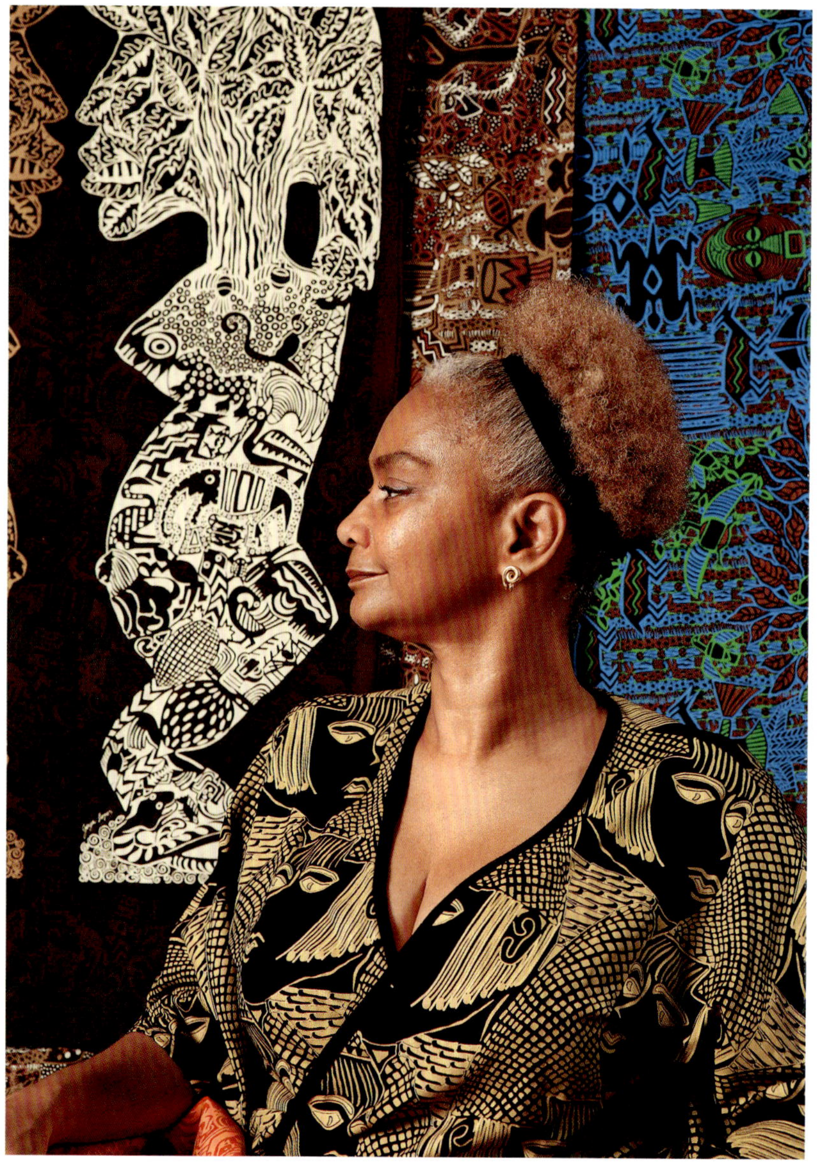

**L.1**
Portrait of Goya Lopes
COURTESY GOYA LOPES
PHOTOGRAPH BY ARTUR VIANA

**L.2a**
Detail of figure L.2c. PHOTOGRAPH BY ANDREW KEMP.

**L.2b**
Detail of figure L.2c. PHOTOGRAPH BY ANDREW KEMP.

BEST KNOWN AS GOYA LOPES, or simply Goya, which has become her artist's name, Maria Auxiliadora dos Santos Goya Lopes (b. 1954) is a designer, businesswoman, lecturer, and black activist who lives and works in Bahia (fig. L.1). Her artistic abilities were first noted in childhood, and in the course of private lessons, her instructor suggested that she observe Bahian folk culture as a source of inspiration. Goya eventually graduated from the School of Fine Art at the Universidade Federal da Bahia (UFBA) and went on to obtain a scholarship to study in Italy. There, she spent three years at the Universitá Internazionale dell'Arte di Firenze and decided to pursue design, which she viewed as the "profession of the future."

Goya's work has been included in solo and group exhibitions in the United States, Italy, and Brazil with *Goya Lopes: African Diaspora in Brazil* opening at Columbia College in Chicago in 2008. Her palette is typically tropical, and her unique designs combine elements drawn from African, Amerindian, European, and Asian cultures with the result that a mandala can deliberately resemble an *abebé*, a fan/mirror associated with the Afro-Brazilian divinity Oxum. This reflects the mixing that produced Bahia's own unique culture.

For the *Axé Bahia* exhibition at the Fowler Museum, Goya created an installation based on the senses to elicit the Afro-Brazilian experience. Called *Sentidos afro-baianos* (Afro-Bahian Senses),[1] it is composed of five different cloth panels printed on both sides. The back of each panel shows enlarged details of some motifs appearing on the front as well as other relevant images. As visitors walk past scenes designed to awaken their senses, the artist intends them to experience something of the journey of the African diaspora and the myriad ways it has become part of the fabric of life in Bahia. The first of these panels, *Visão ancestral* (Ancestral Vision), portrays various facets of West African life, spirituality, and art (figs. L.2a-d). The artist observes, "When visitors use their eyes, this segment of the installation awakens feelings and enables them to discover the meanings, beauty, and contribution of African culture" (pers. comm.). The principal images on this panel are mothers and children, masks, and spirits. The aesthetics of different cultural groups are represented by women with a variety of African hairstyles and jewelry. All of these elements eventually had a profound influence on Brazilian culture. In the top six registers of the front of this panel, the artist directly references motifs found in carved Yoruba doors. Below this section, in a row of masks, are examples inspired by a Yoruba Gẹlẹdẹ mask, a hip mask from Benin, a Luba Kifwebe mask, and a Baule Goli mask. Figures with fin-like appendages recall mudfish, which appear in the mythologies of the Yoruba and other West African peoples as symbols of wealth and divine power. Near the bottom are hair combs from Ghana and possibly East Africa as well.

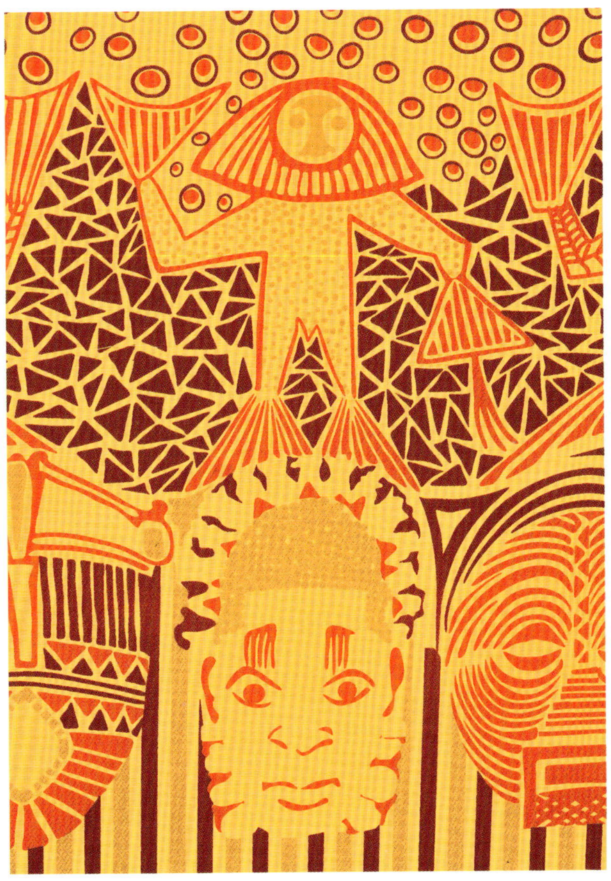

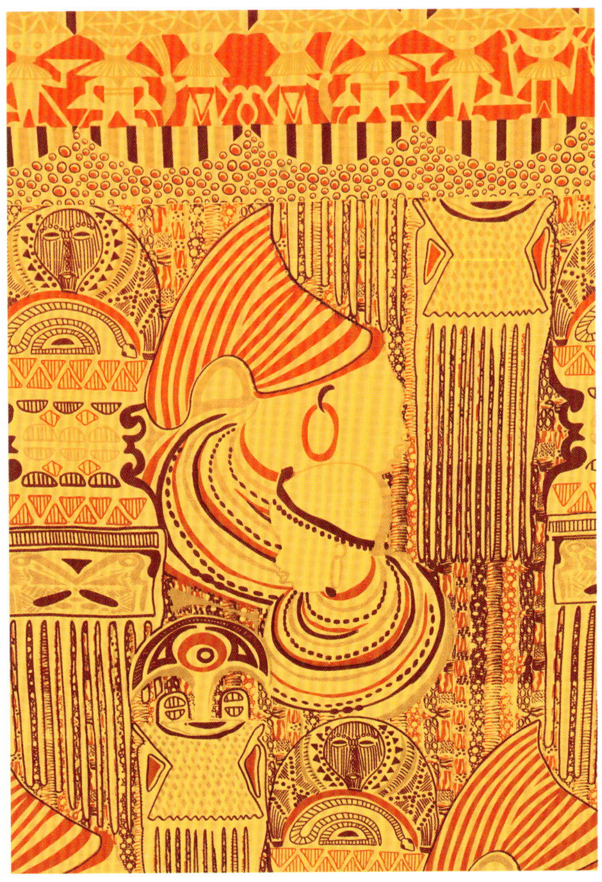

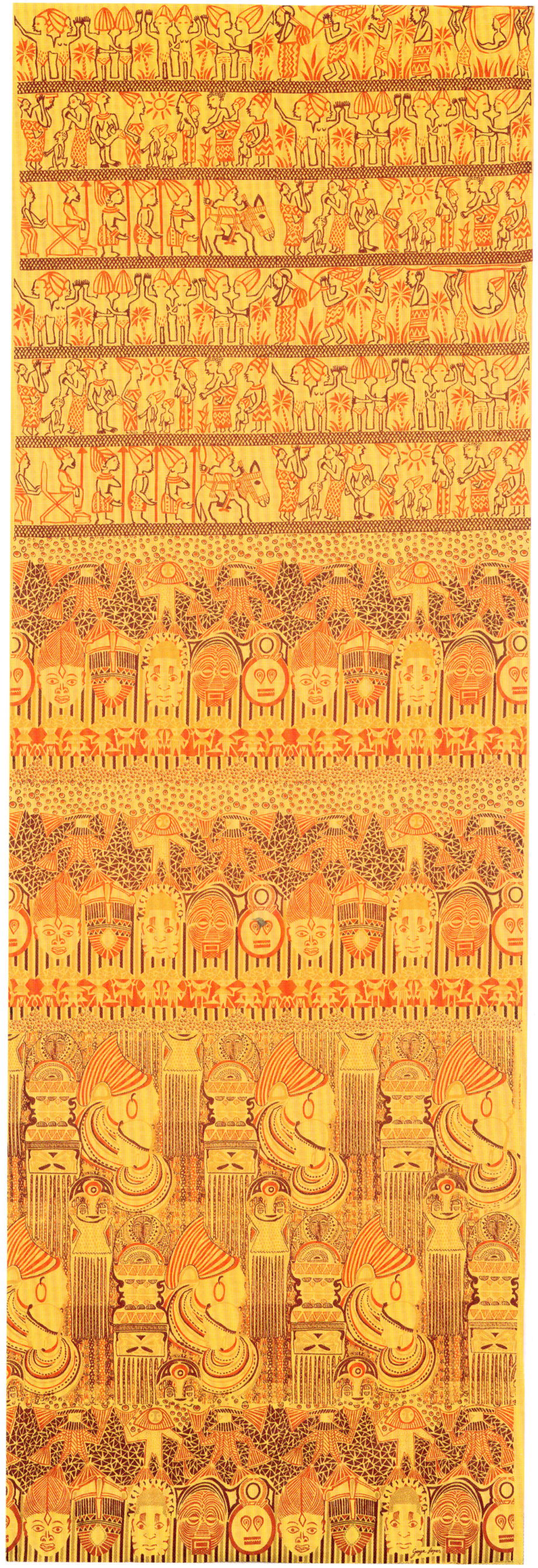

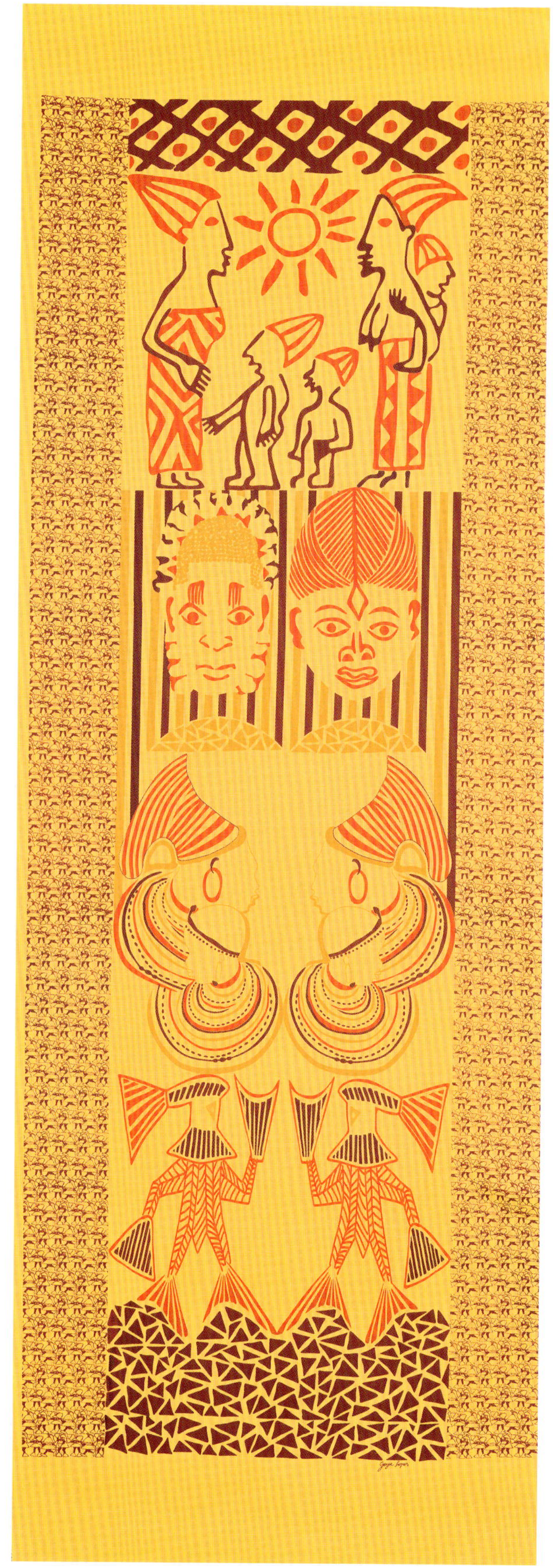

**L.2c**
Goya Lopes (b. 1954, Salvador, Bahia, Brazil)
*Visão ancestral* (Ancestral Vision), 2016
Silk screen on cotton
3 x 1 m
COURTESY GOYA LOPES
PHOTOGRAPH BY ANDREW KEMP

**L.2d**
Reverse of figure L.2
PHOTOGRAPH BY ANDREW KEMP

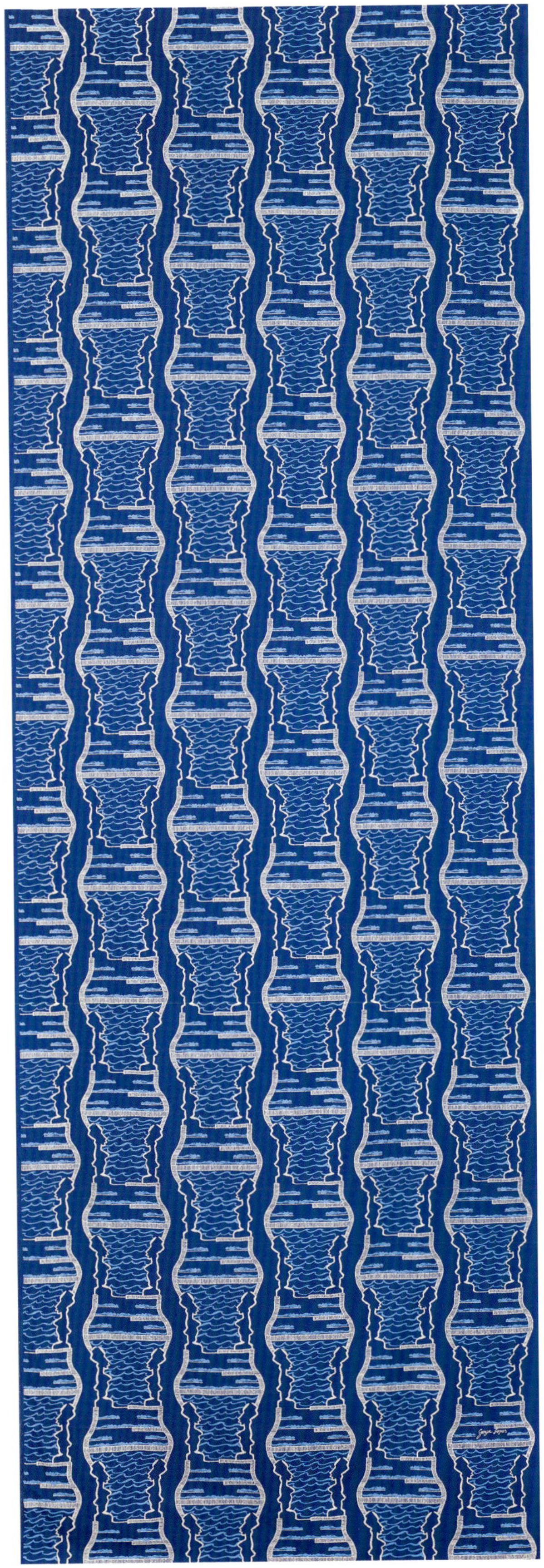

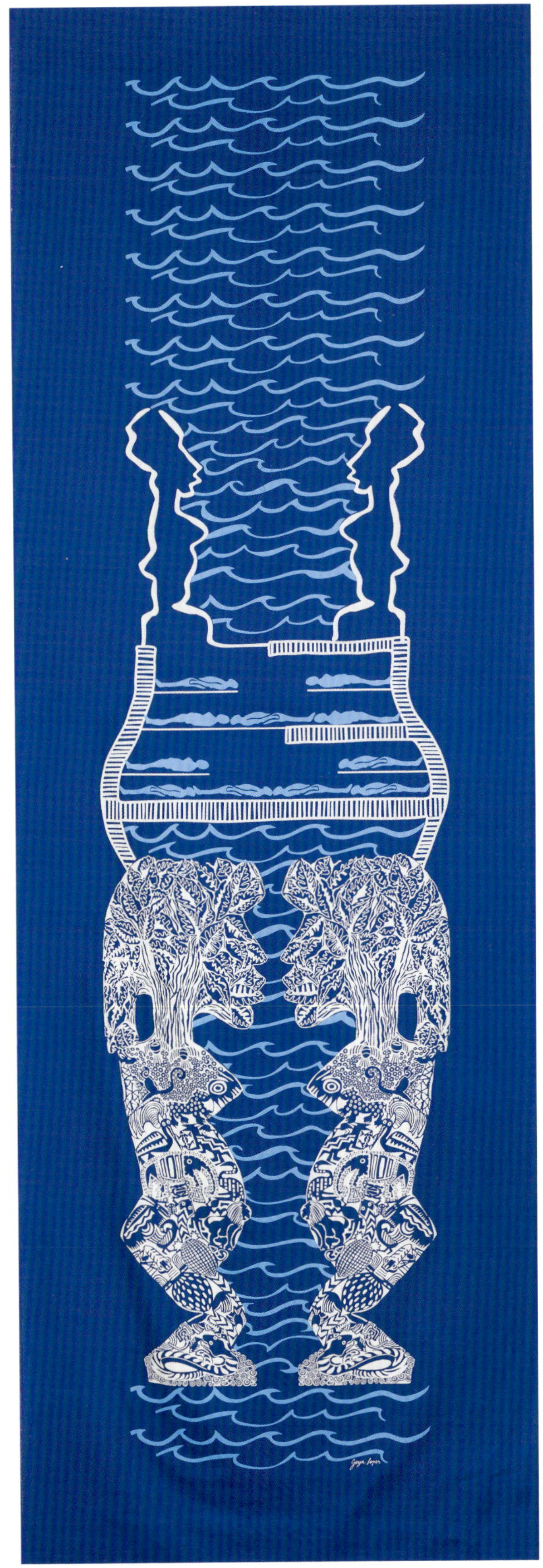

**L.3a**
Goya Lopes (b. 1954), Salvador, Bahia, Brazil
*Olfato memória* (Olfactory Memory), 2016
Silk screen on cotton
3 x 1 m
COURTESY GOYA LOPES
PHOTOGRAPH BY ANDREW KEMP

**L.3b**
Reverse of figure L.3a
PHOTOGRAPH BY ANDREW KEMP

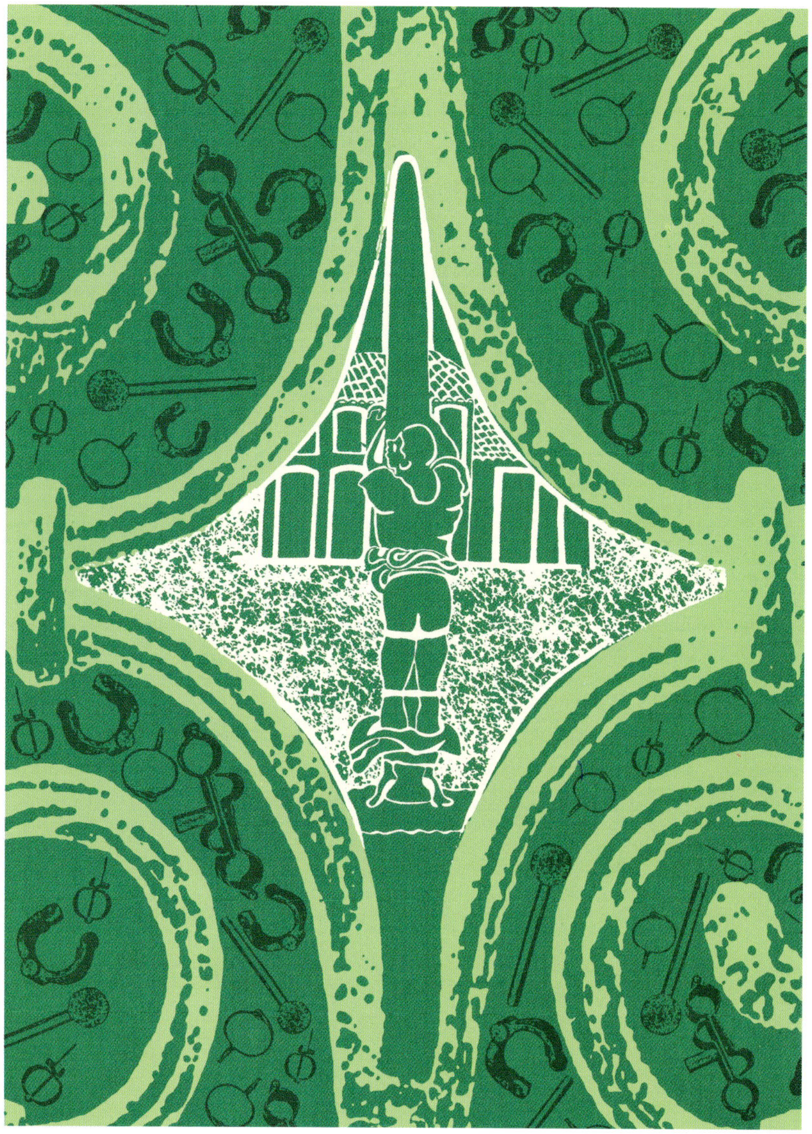

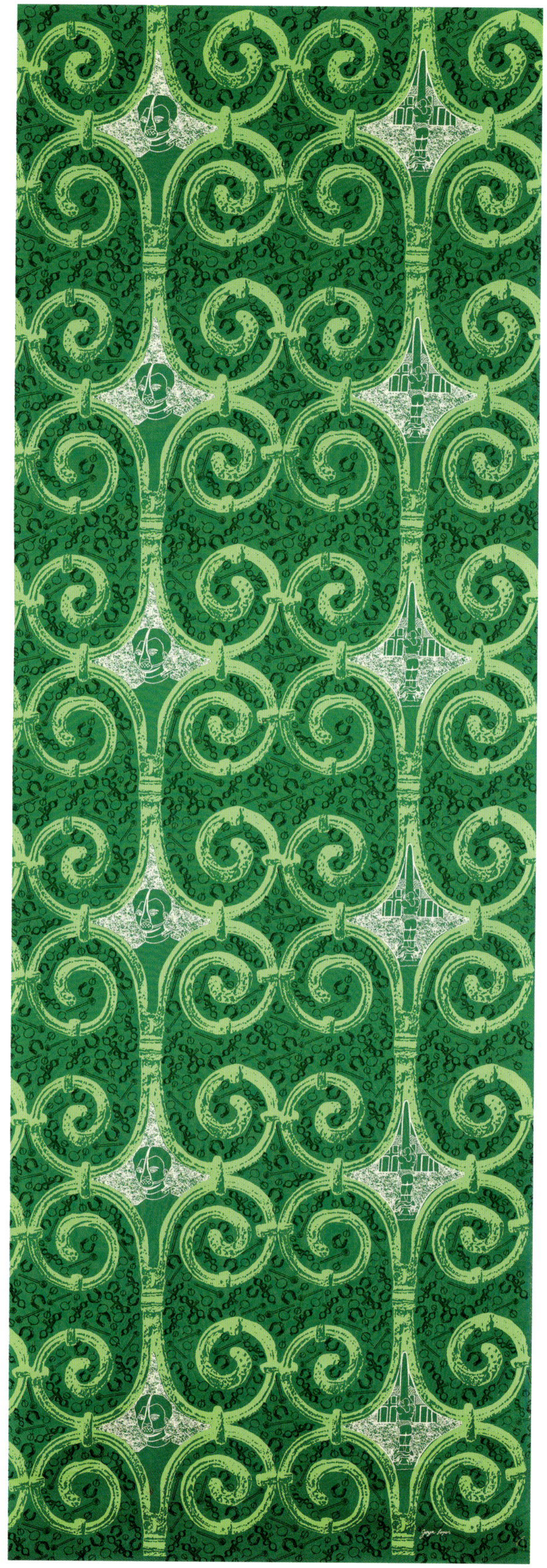

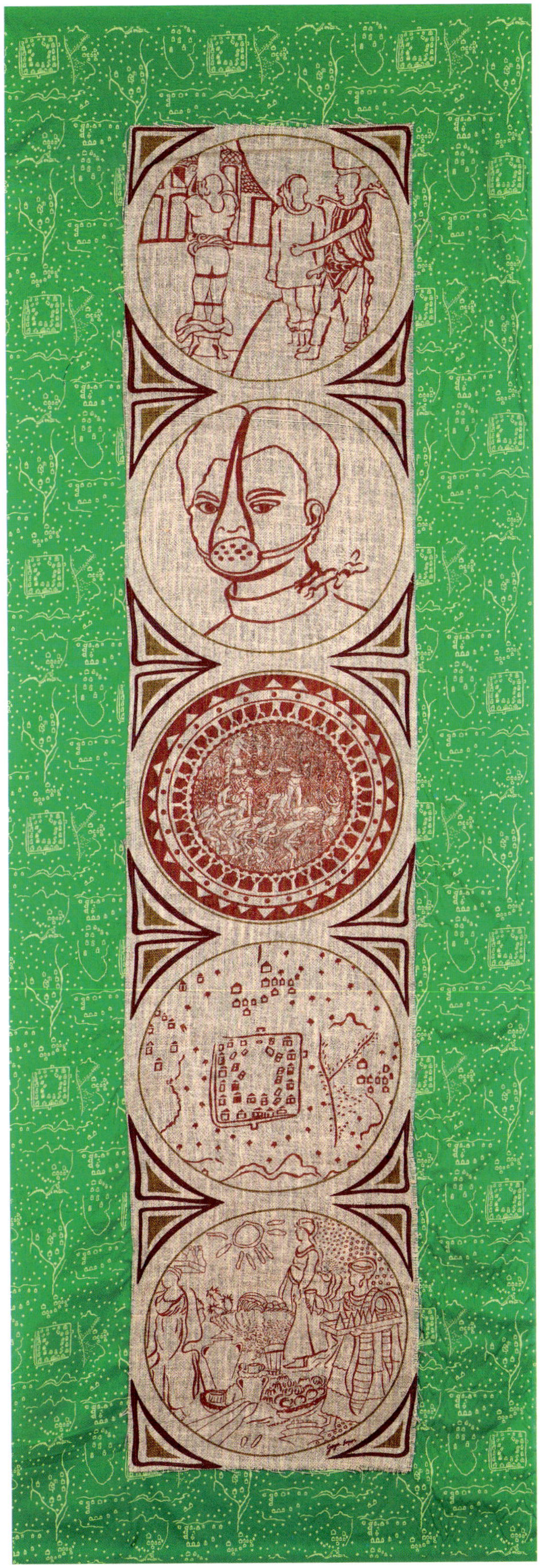

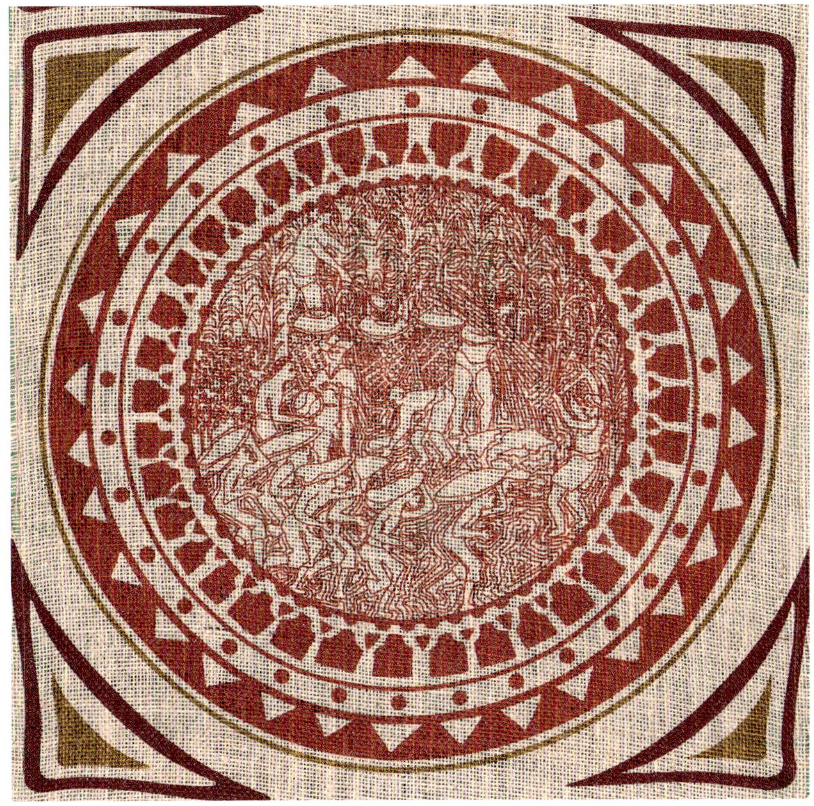

**L.4a**
Detail of figure L.4b
PHOTOGRAPH BY ANDREW KEMP

**L.4b**
Goya Lopes (b. 1954, Salvador, Bahia, Brazil)
*Tato essencial* (Essential Touch), 2016
Silk screen on cotton
3 x 1 m
COURTESY GOYA LOPES
PHOTOGRAPH BY ANDREW KEMP

**L.4c**
Reverse of figure L.4b
PHOTOGRAPH BY ANDREW KEMP

**L.4d**
Detail of figure L.4c
PHOTOGRAPH BY ANDREW KEMP

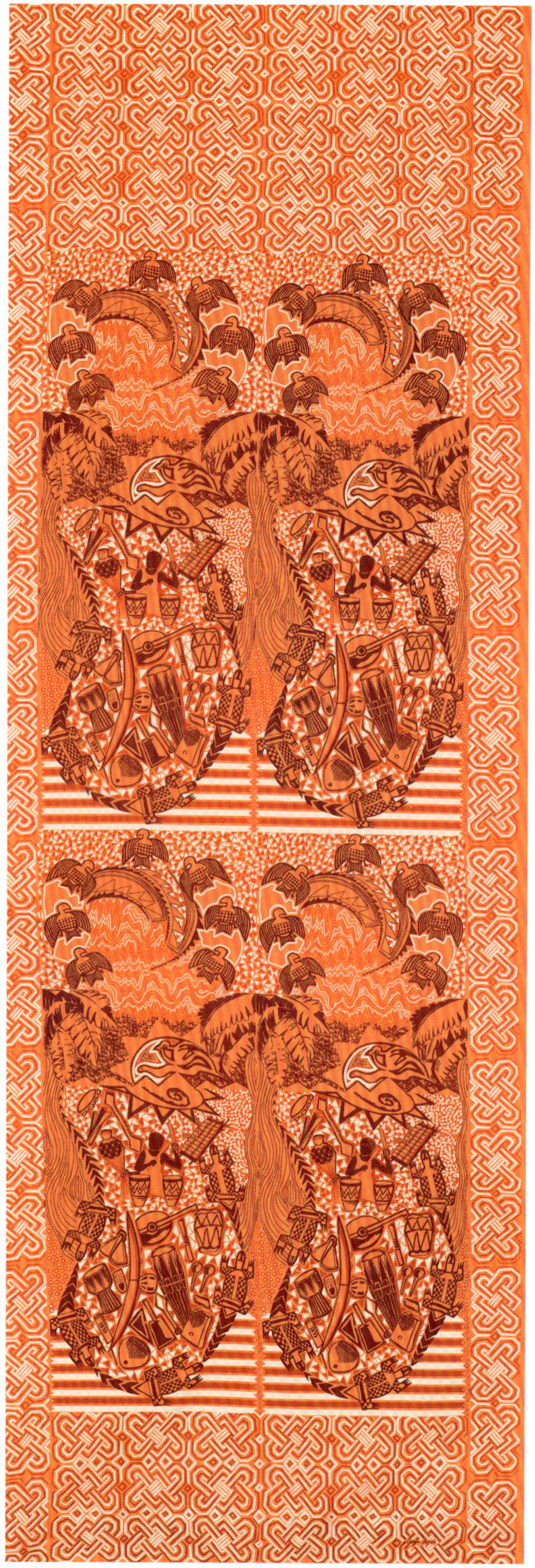

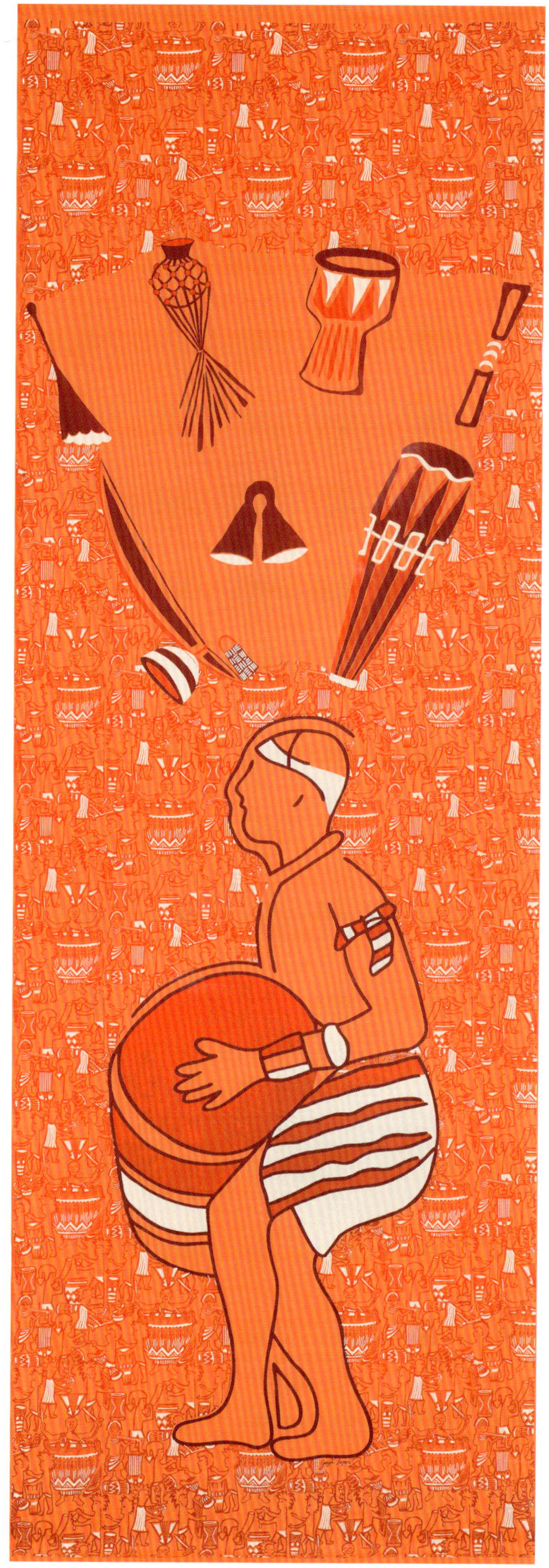

**L.5a**
Goya Lopes (b. 1954, Salvador, Bahia, Brazil)
*Audição e musicalidade baiana*
(Bahian Hearing and Musicality), 2016
Silk screen on cotton
3 x 1 m
COURTESY GOYA LOPES
PHOTOGRAPH BY ANDREW KEMP

**L.5b**
Reverse of figure L.5a
PHOTOGRAPH BY ANDREW KEMP

**L.5c**
Detail of figure L.5a
PHOTOGRAPH BY ANDREW KEMP

**L.5d**
Detail of figure L.5b
PHOTOGRAPH BY ANDREW KEMP

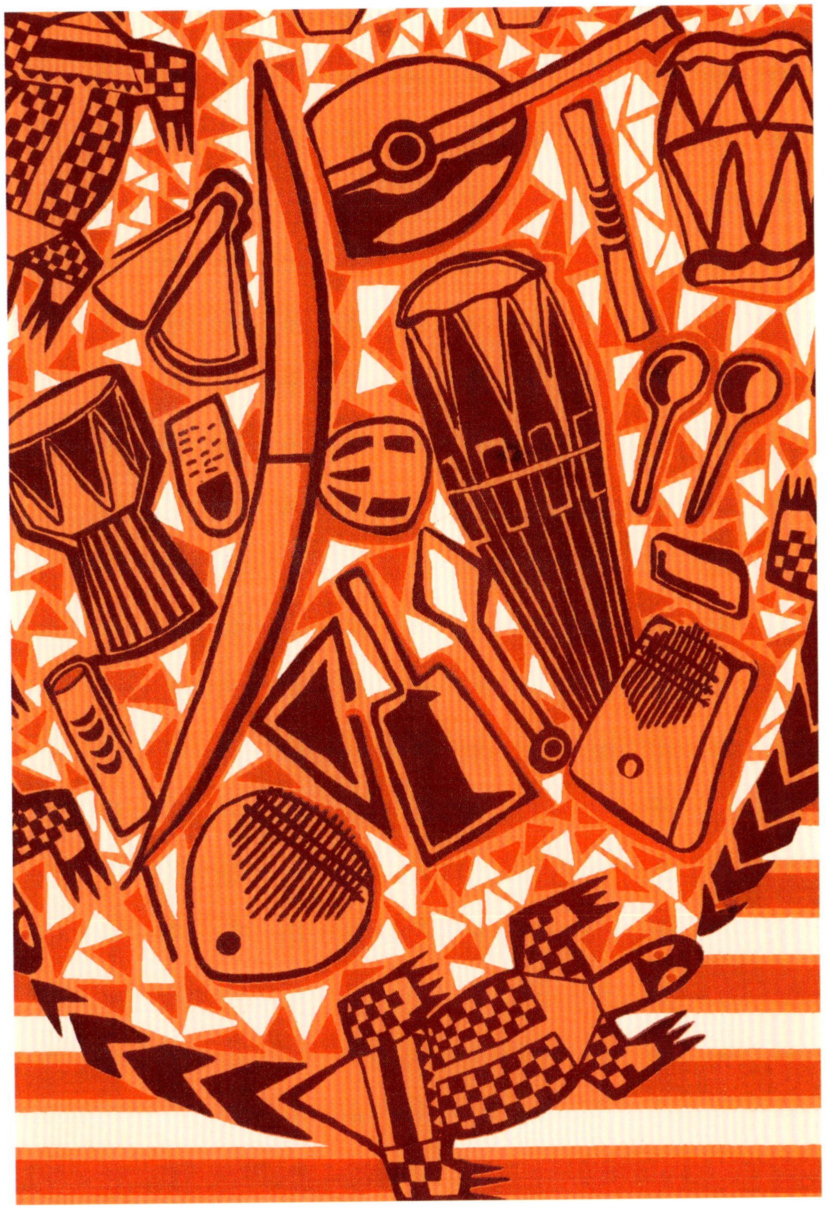

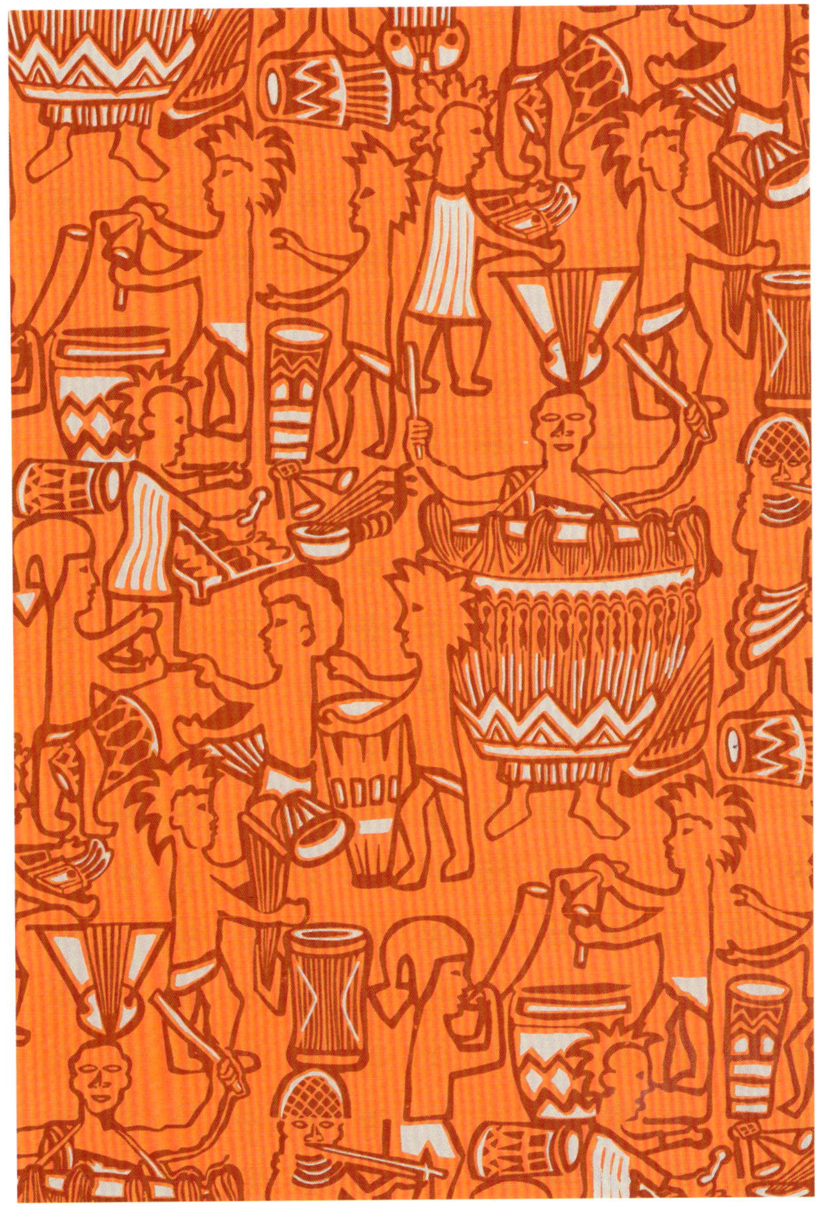

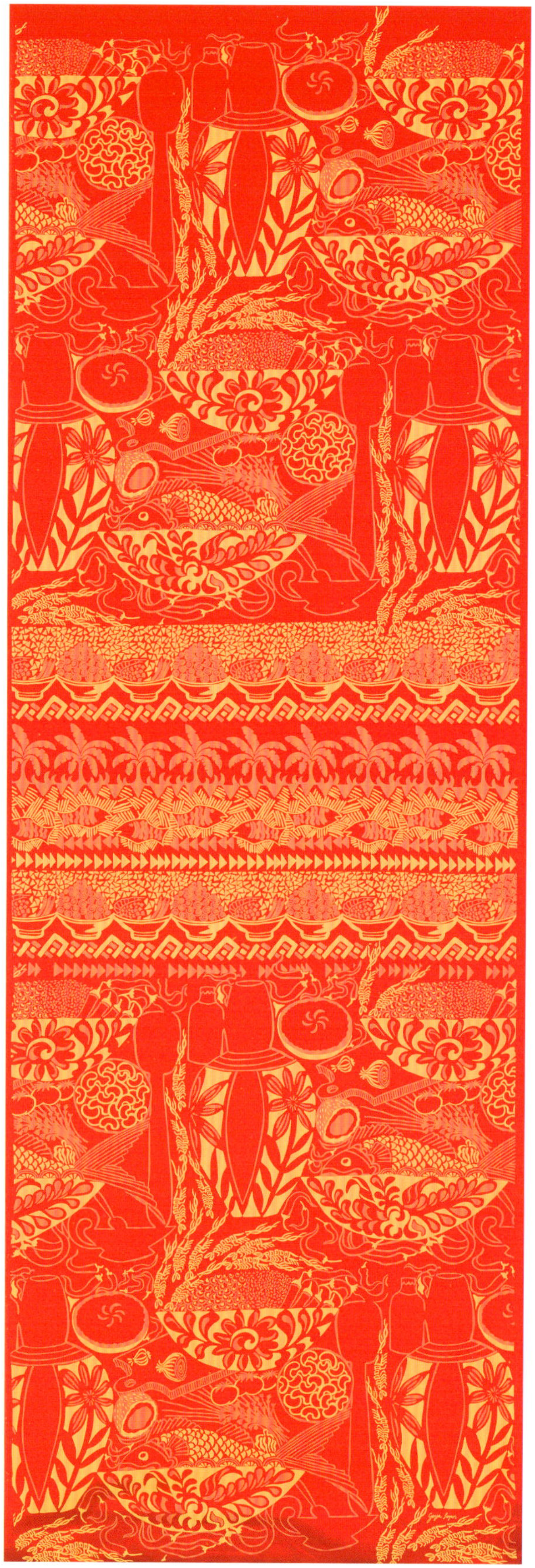

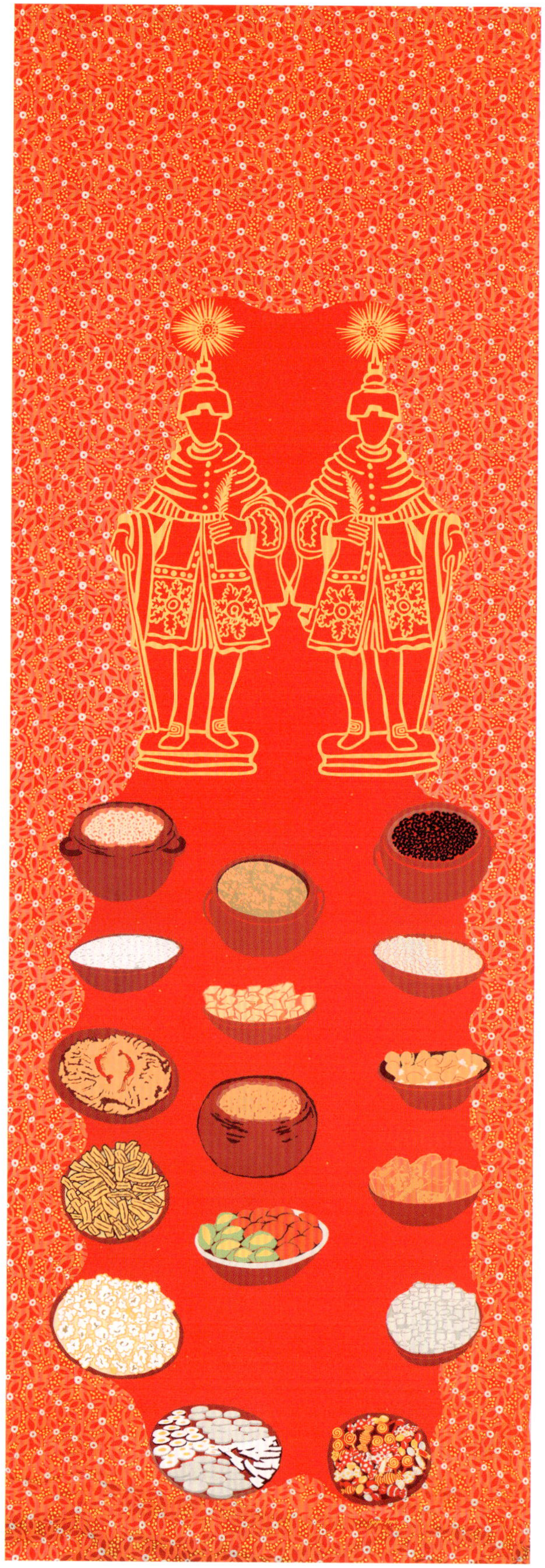

**L.6a**
Goya Lopes (b. 1954, Salvador, Bahia, Brazil)
*Paladar afro-baiano* (Afro-Bahian Palate), 2016
Silk screen on cotton
3 x 1 m
COURTESY GOYA LOPES
PHOTOGRAPH BY ANDREW KEMP

**L.6b**
Reverse of figure L.6a
PHOTOGRAPH BY ANDREW KEMP

*Olfato memória* (Olfactory Memory), the next panel (figs. L.3a,b), "takes our thoughts much farther by conjuring up odors that represent the crossing of over five million Africans from several ethnic groups who were torn from their Mother Africa" (pers. comm.). It reminds us of the horrors endured by enslaved Africans on the high seas. The Middle Passage is represented by waves that are flanked by African sculptures of women seen in profile. These figures resemble the caryatids that support Luba royal stools from the Democratic Republic of the Congo. Immediately below them is a cross-section of a slave ship that is based on an image of the *Brookes* (circa 1788), which would become a famous abolitionist symbol (see timeline, p. 50). The diagram shows how captive Africans were crammed into the hold. Slave ships were called *tumbeiros*, or "floating tombs," in Brazil, a reflection of the high mortality rate among their human cargo. On the reverse of the panel, in the register below the slave ship, the profiles of the African statues are shown again, but this time they are pregnant with memories of the homeland—a giant tree with broad leaves appears atop their heads and hair, the trunks become their throats, and their bodies are filled with stylized images of African wildlife.

Goya explains that the third panel, *Tato essencial* (Essential Touch; figs. L.4a-d), portrays "survival,...it was through those hands, with hard work, pain and suffering, that a new history, a new feeling in a new world was built." The images here point to the terrible punishments meted out to enslaved peoples, the resistance of *quilombos* (maroon communities), as well as the arts, religious rituals, and cultural heritage of the diaspora. Physical pain and suffering are made vivid by shackles and instruments of torture. Among the latter is the metal mask worn by Escrava Anastácia (Anastácia the Slave), an image inspired by a portrait of a black woman wearing such a mask by Jacques Arago (see timeline, p. 52). Anastácia is a folk saint widely revered in several parts of Brazil because of the miracles attributed to her. According to legend, she was forced to wear the mask because her mistress was jealous of her beauty and because she openly condemned slavery. An image of a black man tied to a post, stripped naked for whipping (see fig. L.4d), is derived from Jean-Baptiste Debret's early nineteenth-century work *Espèce de châtiment qui s'exécute dans le diverses grandes places de villes* (The Type of Punishment Carried out in Various Public Squares of the Cities; see timeline, p. 53). Both portraits are well-known in Brazil and abroad—an image of Escrava Anastácia is displayed in the Museum of Slavery in Liverpool—as symbols of suffering and resistance. Other details portray work on the plantations and the jobs done by hired-out slaves as well as a schematic map of a *quilombo*, which symbolizes the captives who dared to escape and form their own communities, some of which later became districts of cities like Salvador.

*Audição e musicalidade baiana* (Bahian Hearing and Musicality) highlights Afro-Brazilian instruments (fig. L.5a-d). Sounds that originated in Africa intermingled with the musical traditions of other Brazilian ethnic groups to create new rhythms and melodies. From samba to samba-reggae, Afro-Brazilian music is part of Bahia's way of life and being. The *berimbau* (a musical bow strung with heavy wire, using a calabash for a sounding board), the *atabaque* (conga drum), *reco-reco* (scraper), and *agogô* bells are essential instruments for bouts of *capoeira angola*, the traditional form of the Afro-Brazilian martial art. Three *atabaques*, called, *rum*, *rumpi*, and *le*, *agogôs* and *shekeres* (calabashes covered with bead netting), also called *afoxés*, produce the rhythms that are vital to Candomblé ceremonies, praising and calling on the *orixás* to dance and bless their children and followers.

*Paladar afro-baiano* (Afro-Bahian Palate; fig. L.6a,b) features different kinds of food and offerings for the *orixás*, including the famous *caruru*, a feast for children honoring both the Ibeji (Yoruba twin deities) and Saints Cosmas and Damian. The details show the Catholic saints, who are associated with the Yoruba divinities that protect young children, as well as the traditional dishes served at the feast—including the okra stew that gives it its name, coconut, popcorn, and black beans, as well as candy and sweet foods, including sugar cane. Held in September, these feasts are an important part of Bahian culture. Today, however, their ritual form is threatened by Neo-Pentecostal rejection of the tradition, and it is becoming harder and harder to find seven children to open the feast by sitting around a large clay bowl filled with portions of all the dishes and eating them with their hands.

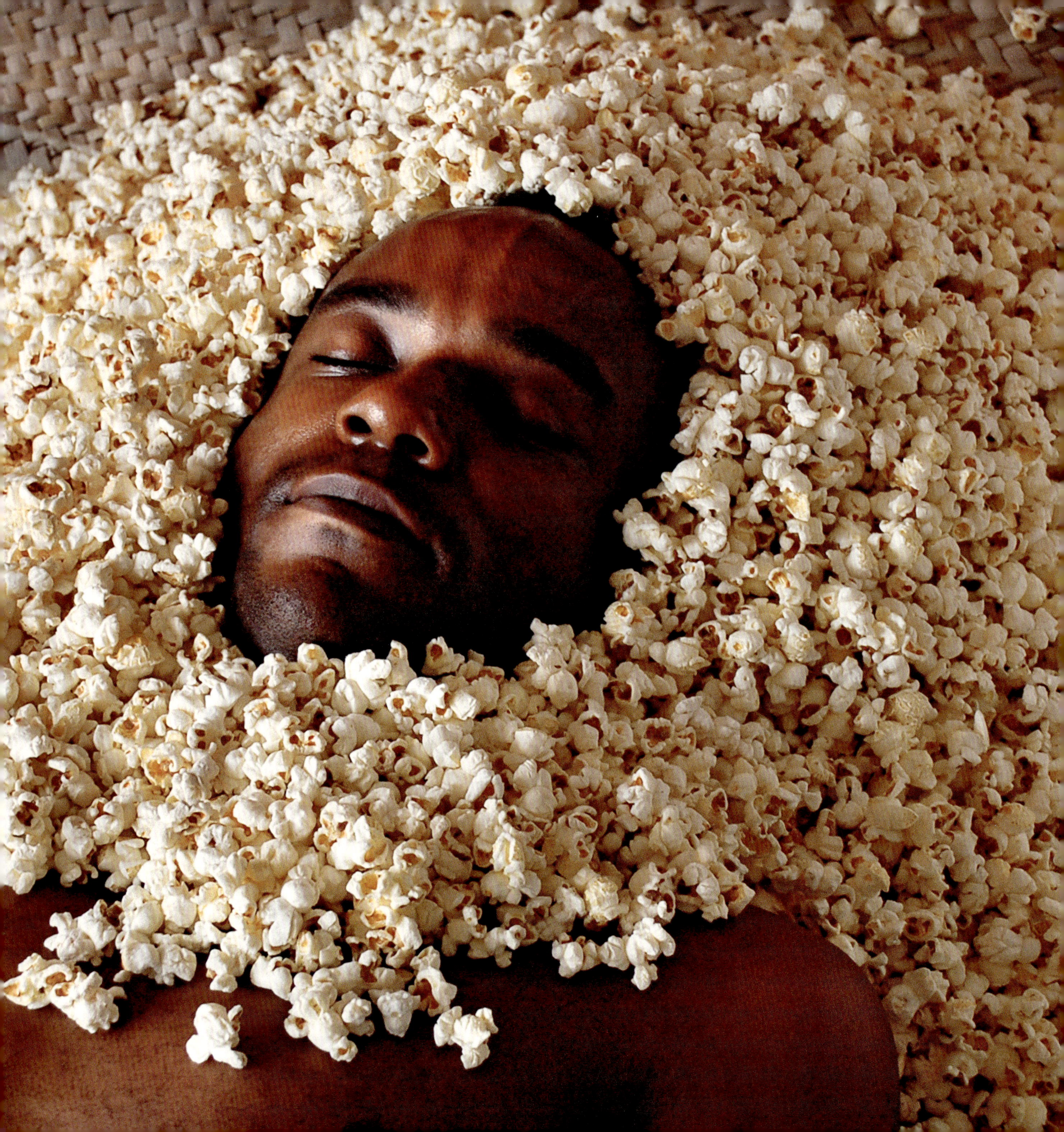

# List of Objects in the Exhibition

Christian Cravo, (b. 1974, Salvador, Bahia, Brazil)
*Afternoon with Bonfim Church in the Background*, 2003
Photograph
L2017.2.1; COURTESY CHRISTIAN CRAVO

Goya Lopes (b. 1954, Salvador, Bahia, Brazil)
*Sentidos afro-baianos* (Afro-Bahian Senses), 2016
Silk screen on cotton
L2017.1.1-5; COLLECTION OF GOYA LOPES

Ayrson Heráclito (Ayrson Heráclito Novato Ferreira, b. 1968, Macaúbas, Bahia, Brazil)
*Divisor* (Divider), 2017
Red palm oil (*dênde*), salt water, glass
L2017.6.1; COURTESY AYRSON HERÁCLITO

*The Atlantic Slave Trade in Two Minutes*: 315 years. 20,528 voyages. Millions of Lives, by Jamelle Bouie and Andrew Kahn, 2015
L2017.2.1; COURTESY OF SLATE MAGAZINE

Hansen Bahia (Karl Heinz Hansen; b. 1915, Hamburg, Germany; d. 1978)
*Caminho de lágrimas* (Trail of Tears), 1958
Ink stamp on woven plant fiber
L2017.4.2; PRIVATE COLLECTION

Hansen Bahia (Karl Heinz Hansen; b. 1915, Hamburg, Germany; d. 1978)
*Caminho de lágrimas* (Trail of Tears), 1958
Woodcut print on paper
L2017.4.4; PRIVATE COLLECTION

Hansen Bahia (Karl Heinz Hansen; b. 1915, Hamburg, Germany; d. 1978)
*Caminho de lágrimas* (Trail of Tears), 1958
Woodcut print on paper
L2017.4.5 PRIVATE COLLECTION

Hansen Bahia (Karl Heinz Hansen) (b. 1915, Hamburg, Germany; d. 1978)
*Caminho de lágrimas* (Trail of Tears), 1958
Woodcut print on paper
L2017.4.6; PRIVATE COLLECTION

Caetano Dias (b. 1959, Feira de Santana, Bahia, Brazil)
*Delírios de Catarina* (The Ravings of Catherine), 2017
Wood, metal, sugar, ox blood, resin
L2017.5.1; COURTESY CAETANO DIAS

Ayrson Heráclito (Ayrson Heráclito Novato Ferreira, b. 1968, Macaúbas, Bahia, Brazil)
*O sacudimento da Maison des Esclaves em Gorée: Diptico I* (The Cleansing of the House of Slaves in Gorée: Diptych I), 2015
Video Diptych. 8:37 mins.
L2017.6.2; COURTESY AYRSON HERÁCLITO

Ayrson Heráclito (Ayrson Heráclito Novato Ferreira, b. 1968, Macaúbas, Bahia, Brazil)
*O sacudimento da Casa da Torre: Diptico I* (The Cleansing of the Tower House: Diptych I), 2015
Video Diptych. 8:37 mins.
L2017.6.3; COURTESY AYRSON HERÁCLITO

Artist Unknown
Egungun masquerade ensemble representing an Egun (ancestral spirit) called Babá Xangô, Itaparica, Bahia, Brazil, early 20th century
Cloth, beads, cowries, mirrors
GIFT OF MRS. THOMAS DAVIS, X82.1359; FOWLER MUSEUM AT UCLA

Artist Unknown
*Correntão de crioula* (Creole necklace), 18th century
Gold-plated silver
L2017.10.1; PRIVATE COLLECTION

Artist Unknown
*Correntão de crioula* (Creole necklace), 18th century
Gold-plated silver
L2017.10.2; PRIVATE COLLECTION

Artist Unknown
*Correntão de crioula* (Creole necklace), 18th century
Gold alloy
L2017.10.3; PRIVATE COLLECTION

Artist Unknown
*Correntão de crioula* (Creole necklace), 18th century
Silver, coral
L2017.10.4; PRIVATE COLLECTION

Artist Unknown
*Pulseira de crioula* (Creole bracelet), 19th century
Gold, coral
L2017.10.5; PRIVATE COLLECTION

Artist Unknown
*Pulseira de crioula* (Creole Bracelet), 18th century
Silver, coral
L2017.10.6; PRIVATE COLLECTION

Artist Unknown
*Penca de balangandãs* (Charm brooch), circa 19th century
Silver
L2017.10.7; PRIVATE COLLECTION

Artist Unknown
*Penca de balangandãs* (Charm brooch), ca. 19th century
Gold, metal alloys, coral, bone
L2017.10.8; PRIVATE COLLECTION

Nadia Taquary (b. 1967, Salvador, Bahia, Brazil)
*Béérè—A primeira filha* (Béérè—The First Daughter), 2009
Tinted coconut, wood, chiseled brass, silver-plated alloy
L2017.11.1; PRIVATE COLLECTION

Helen Salomão (b. 1994, Salvador, Bahia, Brazil)
*Gorda flor* (Full Bloom), 2016
Photograph
L2017.51.2; COURTESY HELEN SALOMÃO

Helen Salomão (b. 1994, Salvador, Bahia, Brazil)
*Igbagbo* (*Fé*) (Faith), 2015
Photograph
L2017.51.1; COURTESY HELEN SALOMÃO

Adenor Gondim (b. 1950, Rui Barbosa, Bahia, Brazil)
*Velha guarda da Irmandade de Nossa Senhora da Boa Morte* (Old Guard of the Sisterhood of Our Lady of the Good Death), August 6, 1994
Photograph
L2017.9.1; COURTESY ADENOR GONDIM

Voltaire Fraga (b. 1911, Salvador, Bahia, Brazil; d. 2006.)
*Baiana de acarajé, vatapá na Barra* (Seller of Acarajé, Vatapá in Barra), 1940
Photograph
L2017.8.1; COURTESY AROLDO DE OLIVEIRA PEIXOTO

*Banana da Terra* (Plantain), 1939
Video. 2:18 mins.
L2017.13.1; COURTESY MARIA BYINGTON

*Turbante-se* (Turban Yourself), project by Thaís Muniz (b. 1987, Feira de Santana, Bahia, Brazil) and photographs by Shai Andrade (b. 1992, Salvador, Bahia, Brazil), 2012–2016
L2017.14.1-10; COURTESY THAÍS TUNIZ

1. *Turbante-se Tutorial by Thaís Muniz*, Salvador, Bahia
2. *Turbante-se in the Street 1*, Rio de Contas, Bahia
3. *On Her Ori—Crowning Ceremony by Thaís Muniz*, Rio de Contas, Bahia
4. *Queens: Mother and Daughter*, Rio de Contas, Bahia
5. *Turbante-se in the Street 2*, Rio de Contas, Bahia
6. *Turbante-se in the Street 3*, Rio de Contas, Bahia
7. *Turbante-se in the Street 4*, Rio de Contas, Bahia
8. *Other Narratives: Turbante-se against Cancer 1*, Aristides Maltez Hospital, Salvador, Bahia
9. *Other Narratives: Turbante-se against Cancer 2*, Aristides Maltez Hospital, Salvador, Bahia
10. *Smiles for Reconnections*, Aristides Maltez Hospital, Salvador, Bahia

Mário Cravo Neto (b. 1947, Salvador, Bahia, Brazil; d. 2009)
*Luciana*, 1994
Photograph
L2017.12.1; COURTESY OF THE ESTATE OF MÁRIO CRAVO NETO ©IMCN

Tacun Lecy (b. 1977, Salvador, Bahia, Brazil)
*Candomblés Nagô: Ilê Axé Ogunjá* (Nagô Candomblés: Axé Ogunjá Temple), January 18, 2014
Photograph
L2017.23.1; COURTESY TACUN LECY

Carybé (Héctor Julio Páride Bernabó; b. 1911, Lanús, Buenos Aires Province, Argentina; d. 1997)
*Iaôs de Oxumaré, Ogum, Oxossi, Oxum* (Initiates of Oxumaré, Ogum, Oxóssi, Oxum), undated
Ink and watercolor (gouache) on paper
L2017.24.1; COURTESY INSTITUTO CARYBÉ

Carybé (Héctor Julio Páride Bernabó; b. 1911, Lanús, Buenos Aires Province, Argentina; d. 1997)
*Olubajé de Omolú: Opô Afonjá* (Annual Festival for Omolú: Opô Afonjá Temple), undated
Ink and watercolor (gouache) on paper
L2017.24.2; COURTESY INSTITUTO CARYBÉ

Tacun Lecy (b. 1977, Salvador, Bahia, Brazil)
*Candomblés Nagô: Ilê Axé Ogunjá* (Nagô Candomblés: Axé Ogunjá Temple), May 17, 2015
Photograph
L2017.23.2; COURTESY TACUN LECY

Zé Diabo, aka Zé Bahia (José Adário dos Santos; b. 1947, Cachoeira, Bahia, Brazil)
*Ogum Ajá*, 2015
Metal
MUSEUM PURCHASE, X2015.17.1; FOWLER MUSEUM AT UCLA

Mário Cravo Júnior (b. 1923, Salvador, Bahia, Brazil)
*Exú*, mid-20th century
Metal
L2017.25.2; COLEÇÃO ESTÁCIO DE LIMA—MUSEU AFRO-BRASILEIRO DA UFBA

Artist Unknown
*Boneca* (doll), early 20th century
Cloth, beads, metal
L2017.25.2; COLEÇÃO ESTÁCIO DE LIMA—MUSEU AFRO-BRASILEIRO DA UFBA

Detinha de Xangô (Valdete Ribeiro da Silva); b. 1928, Salvador, Bahia, Brazil; d. 2014)
*Xangô*, ca. 1990s
Cloth, metal, beads
GIFT OF DR. JULIO CASOY, X2015.4.7; FOWLER MUSEUM AT UCLA

Detinha de Xangô (Valdete Ribeiro da Silva; b. 1928, Salvador, Bahia, Brazil; d. 2014)
*Oxum*, ca. 1990s
Cloth, metal, beads
GIFT OF DR. JULIO CASOY, X2015.4.3; FOWLER MUSEUM AT UCLA

Gil Abelha (Gildásio Feliciano Costa; b. 1955, Salvador, Bahia, Brazil; d. 2006)
Omolú, ca. 1990s
Acrylic paint on wood
GIFT OF DR. JULIO CASOY, X2015.4.101; FOWLER MUSEUM AT UCLA

Artist Unknown
Centro Baiano Anti-AIDS (Bahian Anti-AIDS Center)
*Candomblé—Saúde—Axé* (Candomblé—Health—Life Force), ca. 1980s
Ink on paper
L2017.40.1; SAM L. SLICK COLLECTION OF LATIN AMERICAN AND IBERIAN POSTERS, CENTER FOR SOUTHWEST RESEARCH, UNIVERSITY LIBRARIES, UNIVERSITY OF NEW MEXICO

Tauan Carmo (b. 1993, Salvador, Bahia, Brazil)
*Orixás*, 2016
Digital photographs enhanced with Microsoft Paint
COURTESY TAUAN CARMO

1. *Oxum—A Rainha das águas doces* (Oxum—The Queen of Fresh Waters)
L2017.29.1; DRAWING BY TAUAN CARMO, PHOTOGRAPH BY TIAGO TROCCOLI

2. *Iansã—A Rainha dos raios* (Iansã—The Queen of Lightning)
L2017.29.2; DRAWING BY TAUAN CARMO, PHOTOGRAPH BY EDGAR AZEVEDO

3. *Ossain—O Senhor das folhas* (Ossaim—The Lord of Leaves)
L2017.29.3; DRAWING BY TAUAN CARMO, PHOTOGRAPH BY MARCO MENEZES

4. *Iemanjá—A Rainha do mar* (Iemanjá—The Queen of the Sea)
L2017.29.4; DRAWING BY TAUAN CARMO, PHOTOGRAPH BY HELEMOÃO

5. *Ogum—O Senhor do ferro* (Ogum—The Lord of Iron)
L2017.29.5; DRAWING BY TAUAN CARMO, PHOTOGRAPH BY JOÃO LIMA

Artist Unknown
*Adé* (crown) for Iemanjá, ca. early 1980s
Tin, glass beads
MUSEUM PURCHASE, X83.536A; FOWLER MUSEUM AT UCLA

Artist Unknown
*Abébé* (fan) for Iemanjá, ca. early 1980s
Tin
ANONYMOUS GIFT, X83.536B; FOWLER MUSEUM AT UCLA

Artist Unknown
*Espada* (sword) for Iemanjá, ca. early 1980s
Tin
ANONYMOUS GIFT, X83.524; FOWLER MUSEUM AT UCLA

Artist Unknown
*Penca* (belt-like charm) for Iemanjá, ca. early 1980s
Tin
MUSEUM PURCHASE, X83.536C; FOWLER MUSEUM AT UCLAA

Artist Unknown
*Fios de contas* (Beaded necklaces for Iemanjá), late 20th century/early 21st century
Glass beads, monofilament
L2017.4.21A-B; PRIVATE COLLECTION

Pierre Verger (b. 1902, Paris, France; d. 1996)
*Candomblé Joãozinho da Goméia* (Candomblé Temple of Joãozinho da Goméia), 1946
Photograph
L2017.17.5; PHOTO PIERRE VERGER ©FUNDAÇÃO PIERRE VERGER

Adenor Gondim (b. 1950, Rui Barbosa, Bahia, Brazil)
*Terreiro de Mãe Filhinha* (Temple of the High Priestess Filhinha), February 2, 1990
Photograph
L2017.26.1; COURTESY ADENOR GONDIM

Adenor Gondim (b. 1950, Rui Barbosa, Bahia, Brazil)
*Presente para Iemanjá* (Present for Iemanjá), February 2, 2005
Photograph
L2017.17.6; COURTESY ADENOR GONDIM

Tacun Lecy (b. 1977, Salvador, Bahia, Brazil)
*Festa de Yemonjá* (The Iemanjá Festival), February 2, 2014
Photograph
L2017.23.3; COURTESY TACUN LECY

Oscar Dourado (b. 1954, Salvador, Bahia, Brazil)
*Opô, elo imemorial* (Opô, Immemorial Chain), 2017
Digital color photographs printed on Duratrans
L2017.6.1-20; COURTESY OSCAR DOURADO

1. *Opô Onipin* (*Opô* of the Supreme Being, Oludumaré, Who Has Dominion over Everything but Shares Power with the *Orixás*)
2. *Opô ododo lailai* (*Opô* of the Ancestral Flowers)
3. *Opô Egungun I* (*Opô* of the Ancestral Spirits I)
4. *Opô Egungun II* (*Opô* of the Ancestral Spirits II)
5. *Opô Onirê* (*Opô* of the *Orixá* Ogum, the Ruler of Irê [a city in ancient Nigeria])
6. *Opô Wari* (*Opô* of Ogum of the Waters)
7. *Opô Alafia* (*Opô* of the Energy That Brings Peace, Well-Being, and Harmony)
8. *Opô abi Ilú* (*Opô* of the Birth of the Drums)
9. *Opô ohun-oná obé I* (*Opô* of the Old Knives or Ritual Implements [*ferramentas*] I)
10. *Opô Padá I* (*Opô* of the *Orixá* Oyá Who Lights the Path of Returning Spirits of the Dead [Egungun] I)
11. *Opô etá aranlê* (*Opô* of the Three Relatives in the House)
12. *Opô etá alaikú* (*Opô* of the Three Immortal Beings)
13. *Opô Ilú* (*Opô* of the Drums)
14. *Opô ohun-oná obé II* (*Opô* of the Old Knives or Ritual Implements [*ferramentas*] II)
15. *Opô ekodidê* (*Opô* of the Red Tail Feather of the African Gray Parrot That Is Worn by the *Orixá* Oxalá)
16. *Opô Orôminan* (*Opô* of the *Orixá* Ogum Who Uses Fire)
17. *Opô Ajagun* (*Opô* of the Warrior Oxaguiá, the Youthful Incarnation of Oxalá)
18. *Opô agadá* (*Opô* of the Scimitar Used by the *Orixás* Ogum and Oyá )
19. *Opô obé* (*Opô* of the Knife, the Main Tool Used by Ogum, Placed in Its Sheath)
20. *Opô Ohun-oná Exin* (*Opô* of the Old Spears or Ritual Implements [*ferramentas*])

Mário Cravo Neto (b. 1947, Salvador, Bahia, Brazil; d. 2009)
*Xangô*, ca. 2000
Photograph
L2017.12.2; COURTESY OF THE ESTATE OF MÁRIO CRAVO NETO ©IMCN

Mário Cravo Neto (b. 1947, Salvador, Bahia, Brazil; d. 2009)
Untitled, from the series Transe territoires (Trance Territories), ca. 2000
Photograph
L2017.12.3; COURTESY OF THE ESTATE OF MÁRIO CRAVO NETO ©IMCN

Ayrson Heráclito (b. 1968, Macaúbas, Bahia, Brazil)
*Bori* (Feeding the Head), 2008–2011
Photographs
L2017.6.4-15; COURTESY AYRSON HERÁCLITO

1. Ogum
2. Oxóssi
3. Omolú
4. Xangô
5. Ossaim
6. Oxumaré
7. Tempo
8. Oxum

Bauer Sá (b. 1950, Salvador, Bahia, Brazil)
*Olhos de* Xangô (Xangô's Eyes), 2007–2009
Photograph
L2017.28.1; COURTESY BAUER SÁ

Mestre Didi (Deoscóredes Maximiliano dos Santos; b. 1917, Salvador, Bahia, Brazil; d. 2013)
*Xaxará ati adô meji* (Scepter with Two Heads), 1989
Vegetal fiber, leather, cowries
L2017.30.1; COLLECTION OF MARK STEVEN GREENFIELD AND VALERIE ZAVALA

Mestre Didi (Deoscóredes Maximiliano dos Santos)
(b. 1917, Salvador, Bahia, Brazil; d. 2013)
*Idilê Aiyê: Sasará [xaxará] ejo ati Ibirí* (Scepter Combining the Symbols of the Earth Pantheon), 1995
Vegetal fiber, leather, cowries
L2017.32.1; COLLECTION OF THE BASS MUSEUM OF ART

Mestre Didi (Deoscóredes Maximiliano dos Santos)
(b. 1917, Salvador, Bahia, Brazil; d. 2013)
*Opá exin ati eye meji* (Large Spear-Scepter with Two Birds), ca. late 1990s
Leather, cowries, and palm leaf ribs
L2017.31.1; DALLAS MUSEUM OF ART, GIFT OF DEEDIE AND RUSTY ROSE

Agnaldo Manoel dos Santos (b. 1926, Ilha de Itaparica, Bahia, Brazil; d. 1962)
*Oxóssi caçador* (Oxóssi the Hunter), undated
Wood
L2017.33.1; COLLECTION OF MUSEU DE ARTE MODERNA DA BAHIA (MAM BAHIA)

Rubem Valentim (b. 1922, Salvador, Bahia, Brazil; d. 1991)
*Objeto emblemático 4* (Emblematic Object 4), 1969
Acrylic paint on wood
L2017.34.1; COLLECTION OF THE PINACOTECA DO ESTADO DE SÃO PAULO, BRAZIL. DONATION OF LIA BICCA DE ALENCASTRO AND BALTHAZAR BICCA DE ALENCASTRO

Rubem Valentim (b. 1922, Salvador, Bahia, Brazil; d. 1991)
*Relevo emblema 78* (Relief Emblem 78), 1978
Acrylic paint on wood
L2017.34.2; COLLECTION OF THE PINACOTECA DO ESTADO DE SÃO PAULO, BRAZIL. PURCHASED BY GOVERNO DO ESTADO DE SÃO PAULO, 2013

Rubem Valentim (b. 1922, Salvador, Bahia, Brazil; d. 1991)
*Sem Titulo* (Untitled), 1989
Colored silk-screen print on paper
L2017.34.3; COLLECTION OF THE PINACOTECA DO ESTADO DE SÃO PAULO, BRAZIL. DONATED BY ASSOCIAÇÃO DOS AMIGOS DA PINACOTECA DO ESTADO, 2003

J. Cunha (José Antônio Cunha; b. 1948, Salvador, Bahia, Brazil)
*Códice* (Codex), 2010–2015
Acrylic paint on canvas
L2017.27.1A-U; COLLECTION OF J. CUNHA

1. Egungum
2. Exu
3. Ogum
4. Iansã
5. Xangô
6. Oxumaré
7. *Rituais afrobrasileiros*
8. Ossaim
9. Oxum
10. Logunedé
11. Oxóssi
12. Erês
13. Tempo
14. Caboclo
15. Pretos Velhos
16. Omolu
17. Nanã
18. Iemanjá
19. Oxalá
20. Ifá
21. Umbanda

Alexandre Robatto Filho (b. 1908, Salvador, Bahia, Brazil; d. 1981) with drawings and set design by Carybé (Héctor Julio Páride Bernabó) (b. 1911, Lanús, Buenos Aires province, Argentina; d. 1997)
*Vadiação* (Vagrancy), 1954
Video. 8:14 mins.
L2017.15.1; COURTESY YÊDA ROBATTO STASI

Marco Aurélio Damaceno (b. 1965, Aracajú, Sergipe, Brazil)
*Encruzilhada: A Passagem* (Crossroads: The Passage), 2017
Video. 5:21 mins.
L2017.16.1; COURTESY CARCO AURÉLIO DAMACENO

Pierre Verger (b. 1902, Paris, France; d. 1996)
*Capoeira*, Salvador, Brazil, ca. 1946–1947
Photograph
L2017.17.1; PHOTO PIERRE VERGER ©FUNDAÇÃO PIERRE VERGER

Arlete Soares (b. 1940, Valença, Bahia, Brazil)
*Capoeira*, 1973
Photograph
L2017.19.1; COURTESY ARLETE SOARES

Lita Almeida Cerqueira (b. 1952, Salvador, Bahia, Brazil)
*Dança da capoeira II* (The Dance of Capoeira II), 1976
Photograph
L2017.18.1; COURTESY LITA ALMEIDA CERQUEIRA

Jorge Amado (b. 1912, Itabuna, Bahia, Brazil; d. 2001)
*Jubiabá*, 1935
Livraria José Olympio Editora
L2017.4.7; PRIVATE COLLECTION

Carybé (Héctor Julio Páride Bernabó, b. 1911, Lanús, Buenos Aires Province, Argentina; d. 1997)
*Alexandrina e sua cidade* (Alexandrina and Her City), 1944
Oil on canvas
L2017.20.1; COLLECTION OF ADRIANA VAREJÃO, RIO DE JANEIRO, BRAZIL

Pierre Verger (b. 1902, Paris, France; d. 1996)
*Carybé*, Salvador, Brazil, ca. 1948–1951
Photograph
L2017.17.3; PHOTO PIERRE VERGER ©FUNDAÇÃO PIERRE VERGER

Carybé (Héctor Julio Páride Bernabó; b. 1911, Lanús, Buenos Aires Province, Argentina; d. 1997)
*Obrigação do Ojá Obalá: Opô Afonjá* (Ritual for Ojá Obalá: Opô Afonjá), undated
In *Os deuses africanos no Candomblé da Bahia* (*African Gods in the Candomblé of Bahia*), 1993
Editora Bigraf
L2017.11.2; PRIVATE COLLECTION

Pierre Verger (b. 1902, Paris, France; d. 1996)
*Mãe Senhora, Candomblé Ilê Axé Opô Afonjá, Salvador, Brazil* (The High Priestess Senhora, Candomblé Temple Axé Opô Afonjá), ca. 1948 – 1950
Photograph
L2017.17.4; PHOTO PIERRE VERGER ©FUNDAÇÃO PIERRE VERGER

Carybé (Héctor Julio Páride Bernabó; b. 1911, Lanús, Buenos Aires Province, Argentina; d. 1997)
*As sete portas da Bahia* (The Seven Gates of Bahia), 1962
Livraria Martins Editora, São Paulo
L2017.4.10; PRIVATE COLLECTION

Pierre Verger (b. 1902, Paris, France; d. 1996)
*Dorival Caymmi*, Salvador, Brazil, 1946
Photograph
L2017.17.2; PHOTO PIERRE VERGER ©FUNDAÇÃO PIERRE VERGER

Dorival Caymmi, (b. 1914, Salvador, Bahia, Brazil, d. 2008)
*Cancioneiro da Bahia* (Bahia Songbook), 1947
Livraria Martins Editora, São Paulo
L2017.4.8; PRIVATE COLLECTION

Dorival Caymmi (b. 1914, Salvador, Bahia, Brazil, d. 2008) and Jorge Amado (b. 1912, Itabuna, Bahia, Brazil; d. 2001)
*Canto de amor a Bahia e quatro acalantos de "Gabriela, Cravo e Canela"* (Love Song for Bahia and Four Lullabies from "Gabriela, Clove and Cinnamon"), 1958
Festa Discos with cover photograph by Pierre Verger (b. 1902, Paris, France; d. 1996)
L2017.4.12; PRIVATE COLLECTION

Artist Unknown
*Bahia: Salvador City of Churches*, ca. 1938
Tourist brochure distributed at the 1939 New York World's Fair
L2017.4.14; PRIVATE COLLECTION

Ada Peacock (b. United States; dates unknown)
Menu cover, early 1940s
S. S. Argentina, Moore and McCormack Lines; Bridgetown, Barbados to Bahia, Tuesday, July 7, 1953
L2017.4.15; PRIVATE COLLECTION

Artist Unknown
*Bahia: Land of Happiness*, late 1980s
Bahiatursa tourism campaign poster
L2017.4.19; PRIVATE COLLECTION

Adenor Gondim (b. 1950, Rui Barbosa, Bahia, Brazil)
*Barraca de festa de largo de Salvador* (Vendor's Stall at a Bahian Street Festival), January 11, 1985
Photograph
L2017.37.1; COURTESY ADENOR GONDIM

J. Cunha (José Antônio Cunha; b. 1948, Salvador, Bahia, Brazil)
*Cidade tropical* (*Tropical City*), 2016
Acrylic paint on cardboard
L2017.38.1; COLLECTION OF J. CUNHA

Aurelino dos Santos (b. 1942, Salvador, Bahia, Brazil)
*Sem titulo* (Untitled), 2012
Oil and collage on canvas
L2017.39.2; COLLECTION OF ROBERTO ALBAN GALERIA

Aurelino dos Santos (b. 1942, Salvador, Bahia, Brazil)
*Sem titulo* (Untitled), 2006
Oil on canvas
L2017.39.1; COLLECTION OF ROBERTO ALBAN GALERIA

Àlex Ìgbó (b. 1986, Salvador, Bahia, Brazil): *Jexus* Series, 2014–2017
*Jexus*, Bairro do Canela, 2014
Collage
L2017.41.1-2; COURTESY ÀLEX ÌGBÓ

Àlex Ìgbó (b. 1986, Salvador, Bahia, Brazil): *Jexus* Series, 2014–2017
*Jexus*, Bairro Gamboa, 2015
Stencil, paint
L2017.41.1-2; COURTESY ÀLEX ÌGBÓ

Tiago Sant'Ana (b. 1990, Salvador, Bahia, Brazil)
Apagamento #1 – Cabula (Elimination #1 – Cabula), 2017
Video. 48 seconds
L2017.42.1; COURTESY TIAGO SANT'ANA

Rommulo Vieira Conceição (b. 1968, Salvador, Bahia, Brazil)
*A fragilidade dos negócios humanos pode ser um limite espacial incontestável* (The Fragility of Human Affairs Can Be an Incontestable Spatial Boundary), 2015
Wood, metal, glass, automotive paint
L2017.43.1; COLLECTION OF THE ARTIST

Caetano Dias (b. 1959, Feira de Santana, Bahia, Brazil)
*O mundo de Janiele* (Janiele's World), 2007
Video. 3:58 mins.
L2017.5.2; COURTESY CAETANO DIAS

J. Cunha (José Antônio Cunha; b. 1948, Salvador, Bahia, Brazil)
*Organizações de resistencia negra—Ilê Aiyê* (Black Resistance Organizaions—Ilê Aiyê), 1995
Block printed cotton textile
L2017.44.1; HELEN LOUISE ALLEN TEXTILE COLLECTION, UNIVERSITY OF WISCONSIN-MADISON

Eder Muniz (b. 1982, Salvador, Bahia, Brazil)
*A força que habita em mim* (The Force That Resides within Me), 2017
Aerosol paint, varnish, wood
TR2017.52.1A-B; COURTESY EDER MUNIZ

Pedro Marighella (b. 1979, Salvador, Bahia, Brazil)
*Sem titulo* (Untitled) from the *Serie mata* (Mata Series), 2014
Acrylic paint on wood
L2017.45.1; GALERIA RV CULTURA E ARTE

# Notes to the Text

### Introduction (Polk)

1. These verses are from the song "*Alienação*" ("Alienation") by the *bloco afro* Ilê Aiyê. It was composed by Mario Pam and Sandro Teles.
2. Throughout the Americas, the recognition of national centers of black or African diasporic culture is common. Similar descriptions have been applied to Harlem, New York, and New Orleans, Louisiana, in the United States, the city of Mantanzas in Cuba, and the Costa Chica region of Mexico.
3. They are titled with many misspellings as follows: "Candoblé da Nação de Keto"; "A Famosa Puxada de Rede na Pesca do Xareu"; "Bahianas na Lavagem do Bomfim"; "Samba de Roda, Fôrça Viva de Platicidade Corporal"; "Bahianas na Lavagem do Bomfim"; "Coco da Bahia"; "Bahiana con Tabuleiro de Acarajé"; and Capoeira, Luta ou Jogo em Forma de Dança." The Candomblé, samba, and capoeira images feature uncredited performers from Emília Biancardi's Viva Bahia folklore troupe.
4. Greatly influenced by European colonialism and global tourism, these themes can be seen as variants of broader traditions of representation. Nearly identical fishing scenes, for example, have been routinely featured in twentieth-century postcards and tourist advertisements related to other maritime cultures.
5. The series uses the archaic spelling *typica* rather than the more standard *típica*.
6. See Brenken (1993, 88–91). The sprig of leaves in Alexandrina's hand appears to be rosemary for remembrance of the dead, but also for blessing.
7. Argentine illustrator Manuel Kantor (1912–1990), for example, should have expected negative reviews when he included drawings directly copied from Verger photographs in his book; see Kantor (1955). See also Paesani and Branco (1955, 4–5).
8. The song was co-written by the Bahian journalist César Rasec.
9. The Brazilian República, like Portugal's national symbol of the same name, was essentially modeled after the "Marianne" of the French Republic. All, ultimately, derive from ancient European sources.
10. Robert W. Slenes has discussed anti-slavery symbolism employed by Rugendas in representing Afro-Brazilians (2002, 147–68).
11. In 2014 the proposal of congressional candidate and evangelical pastor Elionai Muralha to remove the *orixá* sculptures from public space was widely reported in the Brazilian press.
12. Visual creativity within the context of African diasporic religion is well described by Leiris (1953, 201–11) and Cosentino (2005, 231–46).
13. In Brazil, the *orixá* Iemanjá is also associated with Nossa Senhora dos Navegantes (Our Lady of Seafarers), Nossa Senhora das Candeias (Our Lady of the Candles), and Nossa Senhora da Piedade (Our Lady of Piety) among other incarnations of the Virgin Mary.
14. The song "*Lá no céu abriu uma porta*" ("There in Heaven, a Door Opened)" is popular with practitioners of the African-inspired religion Umbanda.
15. Although "Gandhi" is often used to describe the association, the official spelling used by the organization is "Gandhy."
16. Each star on the banner represents a specific Brazilian state (plus the capital district). Their positioning is said to reflect the night sky over Rio de Janeiro on November 15, 1889, when the Brazilian Republic was established.

### Chapter 1 (Fromont)

1. See http://slavevoyages.org/. The project's team of experts estimate "that the total number of voyages that set out to obtain captives was 43,600"; see http://www.slavevoyages.org/voyage/understanding-db/methodology-2. The official slave trade to Bahia was abolished in 1850.
2. http://www.slavevoyages.org/voyages/tfZjA6Ut.
3. About *minkisi*, see MacGaffey (1986).
4. Gilroy (1993, 6, 15–16). About the Black Atlantic, see also Thompson (1983).
5. Joseph Roach also uses the term "vortex" to speak of what he terms the "circum-Atlantic world." See Roach (1996, 4).
6. Dana Rush (1999, 64–65). Chacha VIII passed away in 2014.
7. "Elevasam, e Fasada, que mostra em prospeto pela marinha a Cidade de Salvador Bahia de Todos of Santos na America Meridional aos 13 graos de latitude, e 345 graos, e 33 minutosde longitude com as plantas e prospetos embaixo em ponto maior de toda a fortificação que defende a ditta cidade.

   Este prospeto foi tirado por Carlos Julião Cap. M de Mineiros de Reg.to de Artt.a da corte, na ocasião que foi na Nao Nossa Senhora Madre De Deus em Maio de 1779." In Gabinete de Estudos Arqueológicos de Engenharia Militar/Direcção de Infra-Estruturas do Exército (Reg. 8756, cota 4756-3-38-52) 53x86 cm.
8. "Modo de trajar das mulatas da cidade da Bahia"; "Preto que vende leite na Bahia"; "Carruagem, ou cadeirinha em que andaõ as senhoras na cidade do Salvador Bahia de Todos os Santos"; "Mossa dançando o landú de bunda a cinta"; "Traje das pretas minas da Bahia quitandeiras"
9. "Illuminated Drawings of Figures of Whites and Blacks about the Mores of Rio de Janeiro and the Serro Frio." See Carlos Julião (1960).
10. Note that it is unclear who titled and labeled the Rio de Janeiro images, likely not Julião himself.
11. In the Biblioteca Nacional of Lisbon, Manuela Tenreiro uncovered a volume of Julião's *Dicionário de árvores e arbustos* (Dictionary of Trees and Bushes), printed in 1801. See Tenreiro (2008, 79).
12. See Lundu or Landú in Cascudo (1962). See also Fryer (2000, 116–26).
13. About the *bolsas de mandinga*, see Sweet (2003), Mott (1988), Buono, (2015, 23–26).

### Interleaf A (Gledhill)

1. All translations are mine.
2. The "one-drop rule" indicates that even a single drop of African blood would determine whether a person was black. This was obviously not enforced in Brazil where there was high degree of racial mixing.

### Interleaf B (Gledhill)

1. Also known as the Fort of Itapagipe Passage, Fort São Bartolomeu was built in the early seventeenth century and demolished in 1900. It was located at the mouth of the Pirajá River, north of Salvador. See http://fortalezas.org/?ct=fortaleza&id_fortaleza=78&muda_idioma=PT. Accessed April 18, 2017.
2. http://g1.globo.com/bahia/noticia/2017/02com-fe-e-oferendas-fieis-lotam-rio-vermelho-para-reverenciar-iemanja.html. Accessed April 10, 2017.
3. http://noticiasdapauliceia.blogspot.co.uk/2013/02/odo-iya-yemanja-ataramagba-ajeje-lodo.html. Accessed April 18, 2017.

### Chapter 2 (Matory)

1. "Yarriba" had originally been the term that the West African Hausa people used to refer specifically to the subjects of the Ọyọ Kingdom. In the mid-nineteenth century, however, the Reverend Samuel Ajayi Crowther—a British-rescued Ọyọ captive educated in Freetown and serving as a missionary for the Anglican Church—cobbled together a hybrid language largely understandable to all of these populations (in Freetown and in the hinterland of Lagos) for the sake of efficient proselytization, and he called that language "Yoruba." The Bibeli Mimọ, or the Holy Bible, was the first book published in this language. In the 1880s and 1890s, as improvements in Western tropical medicine allowed larger numbers of white Britons to settle in Lagos, and, as both racism and an economic downturn marginalized the loyalist black bourgeoisie of colonial Lagos, the Yoruba language, a British-style documentation of the Yoruba royal past, and a re-dignification of this new people's pre-Christian past became banners of a cultural nationalism with circum-Atlantic reverberations.

### Interleaf D (Alves Barton)

I am indebted to Adenor Gondim for sharing his thoughts and essays with me. See Gondim (2005). All translations are mine.

1. Jeje refers to a Dahomean-descended ethnic group related to Vodun. See Castillo and Pares (2010, 1–27); Castro (2006).
2. The relation between the Irmãs da Boa Morte and Gẹlẹdẹ was confirmed in several interviews with local priestesses, local and foreign anthropologists, religious scholars and cultural historians. See Silveira (2010, 437, 450); Clarke (2004, 29); Ferreira (2005); Gondim (2005).
3. The sisters have a tradition of jewelry making that dates from the colonial era and mobilizes both West African and Portuguese aesthetics and techniques (see interleaf G). Today few examples exist in the hands of the Irmandade. As one now-deceased sister explained to me, "When you need new teeth your jewels have no other value than the price of the teeth."
4. "A partir desse dia, passei a perceber que a fotografia era muito mais que uma atitude mecânica de pressionar um botão ou fazer um clique—não gosto dessa palavra. Comecei a percorrer a periferia de Itabuna, pegava minha bicicleta e saía fotografando tudo o que achava triste e alegre, feio e bonito, no universo da pobreza e natureza. É interessante como a maioria dos

fotógrafos, no início de carreira, mergulha seus olhares na miséria humana! Tive sérios aborrecimentos com meu pai quando voltava dessas aventuras. 'Gastando filmes, papéis, químicos e perdendo tempo com essas bobagens. Jogando dinheiro fora!'" Gondim (2005, 99).

5. "Em 1982, mergulhei no universo encantado do imaginário do Catolicismo Popular, a Romaria do Bom Jesus da Lapa. Em 1990, como fotógrafo e voluntário, me apaixonei pela Irmandade de Nossa Senhora da Boa Morte de Cachoeira. Num mergulhei, no outro me apaixonei. Uma estória sem fim, beco sem saída." Adenor Gondim, "Um pouquinho de estória," in Gondim (2005, 100).

6. Estes ritos ficavam os meios para articular práticas culturais que são um aspecto fundamental da identidade baiana. Para mim a possibilidade de documentar o festival como um exemplar da autodeterminação e da cultura crioula teve o potencial de anunciar uma reforma cultural através da circulação de imagens de práticas patrimoniais que, à minha chegada [no festival], estavam em ruínas. (Adenor Gondim, personal communication with the author February 12, 2017).

7. "Não sou fotógrafo da natureza, da violência, da miséria humana, da dor... Sou fotógrafo da dignidade de um povo que desdenha da fome e do abandono com a alegria da festa. Meu trabalho pessoal é totalmente focado na cultura popular da Bahia que passa por dois troncos que interagem com a maior naturalidade: 1. Catolicismo Popular: procissões, romarias, Paixão de Cristo, festas do Divino, Reis, Cosme e Damião... 2. Candomblé: das diversas nações, Angola, Ijexá, Ketu, Jeje—Presentes de Iemanjá, Mandus, festas em homenagem a todos os orixás. 3. Sincretismo: festa da Irmandade de Nossa Senhora da Boa Morte, em Cachoeira, Cosme e Damião, São Lázaro e São Roque...Não fotografo pensando nas galerias. Fotografo pelo simples prazer de fotografar, buscando no outro ou no meio um fragmento que falta em mim. Há momentos em que a emoção me faz deixar de lado o ato de fotografar para vivê-los. Gosto de fotografar essencialmente em preto-e-branco, mas reconheço a importância da cor e sei quando é a melhor opção. Sou interétnico. Nas minhas veias, correm sangue índio, negro, português e seus derivados. Sou um ecumênico. Passei pelo limbo da Igreja Batista, Espiritismo, Catolicismo e do Candomblé. Aprendi e incorporei um pouco da bondade de cada uma. O bem ou o mal está no Homem. Sou contra a intolerância religiosa. Sou contra a globalização cultural. Sou contra qualquer tipo de preconceito. Sou Baiano, Brasileiro, Sul-americano. Sou cidadão do Mundo.O meu mundo é a Bahia. A Bahia me basta.

   Em conclusão, eu acredito que às vezes é melhor parar de tirar fotos e viver no momento que acontece na frente dos meus olhos. Recebi permissão para o fotógrafo designado, permitindo-me estar lá naquele momento. No entanto, eu prefiro atrasar o meu processo, parar tudo, e experimentar o momento até que eu não estou mais superado com emoção." Gondim, "Um pouquinho de estória" in Gondim (2005, 100).

### Chapter 3 (Sansi)

1. http://oglobo.globo.com/sociedade/mpf-recorre-de-decisao-da-justica-que-nao-reconhece-umbanda-candomble-como-religioes-12507234. Accessed March 27, 2017.

### Chapter 4 (Shirey)

1. The Black Issue is an annual issue of *Vogue Brasil* that features models of African descent. Women of color remain dramatically underrepresented in fashion in Brazil, both on the runway and in print. In fact, the advertisements in the January 2011 Black Issue, dedicated to black models, primarily featured white models. See Correa and Santos (2012, 15–16).
2. Lody (2015, 22–23). See also Graham (1992, 50–52). Graham discusses *quintadeiras* in Rio de Janeiro.
3. See Lody (2015, 25). See also Godoy (2006, 18). Godoy notes the important fact that slaveholders at times provided opulent jewels to the enslaved women in their households as a way of flaunting their own wealth.
4. Trinidade (2006, 63–74). See page 64 for a particularly detailed description of *balangandãs*. Godoy (2006) traces the origins of *balangandãs* in northern Portugal and West Africa and also highlights similarities to objects from Martinique.
5. Butler (1998a, 168) discusses the Baiana in the context of resistance to the dominant culture.
6. Lody (2015, 30) discusses the history of *richelieu*, named after the Cardinal and Duke of Richelieu, Armand Jean du Plessis.
7. Gage (2005, 410). Godoy (2006, 21) discusses the use of jewelry as a security account, to save up to buy one's own freedom or that of others. Conduru (2013b, 33).
8. Nívea Alves dos Santos (2013, 54) notes that for early twentieth-century initiates in Candomblé, vending traditional foods in the street was an obligation to be fulfilled as a sign of devotion.
9. In 1993 the Central Bank of Brazil introduced the *cruzeiro real*, a short-lived currency. It was replaced by the *real* in 1994 with the implementation of a new economic plan. The *cruzeiro real* was released in denominations of 1,000, 5,000, and 50,000. The Baiana appeared on the 50,000 *cruzeiro real* banknote, which had an extremely short period of circulation (March-September 1994).
10. *Museu de Valores do Banco Central*. http://www.bcb.gov.br/htms/museu-espacos/cedulas/CRR.asp?idpai=CEDBC#CRreal5000000. Accessed October 11, 2016. See also Lody (2015 41–42) and Lody (2001, 34–36), for a detailed discussion of auxiliary items added to strings of beads and *balangandãs*.
11. Whether this was produced in Ferrez's studio in Rio de Janeiro or in another space in Salvador da Bahia remains to be determined. Ferrez was known to have made a trip to Bahia between 1875 and 1876, sponsored by the Imperial Geological Commission. During this time, he is thought to have searched for photographic models, and he may have used other photographers' studios. See Isis Freitas dos Santos (2014). Freitas dos Santos reproduces an image by Marc Ferrez shot in Salvador's Praça Castro Alves from the Arquivo Instituto Moreira Salles that is dated 1885, but notes that the photograph was more likely taken during an earlier trip (see pp. 44, 45, n. 85). As a result, it is not possible to make a definitive determination as to whether this photograph was produced in Salvador or in Rio de Janeiro, but certainly images like this were part of the visual culture in both places.
12. See Ferrez (1984; 1990). On the similar use of photographic types in Rio de la Plata; see Cuarterolo (2015).
13. See for example, *Vendedoras da rua*, reproduced in Freitas dos Santos (2014, image 9, 47).
14. The Estado Novo refers to the era of authoritarian rule under populist leader Getúlio Vargas, who promoted corporatism and the centralization of government, and with this an emerging national identity. Vargas was also instrumental in shifting foreign policy to develop stronger relationships with the United States. The Good Neighbor policy, which emerged during this period, involved the promotion of a new image of Brazil in the United States.
15. See Harris (2003, 83–124). The full skirt and head wrap of the traditional Baiana allow for some comparisons with the stereotype of the Mammy in the United States, who as Michael Harris has noted, was desexualized. In emphasizing sexuality, however, Carmen Miranda's performance of the Baiana departs significantly from the stereotype of the Mammy.
16. See Ickes (2013a, 116–18) for additional details on the significance of the washing of Bonfim during the Estado Novo. This is, as Patricia de Santana Pinho notes, a significant event at which Bahian identity is constructed, especially in relation to the political sphere. See Pinho (2010, 195). See also Butler (1998b, 164–65).
17. This was particularly true with the *balangandãs*, which Romo has noted was an antiquated reference rather than a popular accessory by the time Caymmi wrote about it in his samba. See Romo ( 2010, 98).
18. "Praias de Vicente de Carvalho," with text by Arlindo Silva and photographs by Roberto Maia.
19. Nancy de Souza e Silva, known as Dona Cici, who worked closely with Pierre Verger, identified the subject of this photograph as Dona Angorence in a conversation in May 2015.
20. Paula Bastos identifies the models as Lailane Dórea, Tania Neres, and Dandana França. See Bastos (2016).

### Chapter 5 (Höfling)

1. My English translation is from Sergio Milliet's Portuguese translation (1954). Johann Moritz Rugendas, *Viagem pitoresca através do Brasil*, 5th ed., Biblioteca histórica brasileira (São Paulo: Livraria Martins Editôra, 1954). Unless otherwise noted, all translations are mine.
2. *Vadiação* (lit., "vagrancy") is related to the verb *vadiar*, Portuguese for "loitering" or "being idle."
3. Summarized from an interview by Roberto Freire published in the magazine *Realidade* in 1967. Reprinted in Abreu and Castro (2009, 25).
4. "Somos registrados, temos uma sede, temos carteiras, documentos legalisado, e assinado pelo parlamentares do pais que é nosso Presidente." Pastinha (c. 1955–1960, 34–35).
5. For a full discussion of both Afro-Brazilian congresses, see Romo (2010).
6. His family name and birthdate are my approximations based on the available literature. In the first edition of *Bahia de Todos os Santos* (1945), Jorge Amado describes Samuel Querido de Deus as a Bahian fisherman in his

mid-sixties (which would place his birthdate around 1880). By the eighth edition of this same book (published in 1960), we know that Querido de Deus was no longer alive because Amado includes a note to say that his portrait of Querido de Deus was written while he was still living, placing his death between 1946 and 1960. Newspaper records from the 1936 pugilistic season in Salvador suggest that his family name might have been de Souza. See Abreu (1999, 65).

7. My translation of the original text. Robatto Filho (1954).

8. For a full discussion of Mestre Canjiquinha's stage work, see Höfling (forthcoming).

9. *Canto orfeônico* (orpheonic song) was the cornerstone of a nationalist musical education project formulated by conductor and composer Heitor Villa-Lobos during the Getúlio Vargas regime. See Flávio Oliveira (2011, 44–63); Goldenberg (1995, 6, no. 3: 103–9).

10. For a detailed analysis of the trajectory of Viva Bahia, see my article "Staging Capoeira, Samba, Maculelê, and Candomblé: Viva Bahia's Choreographies of Afro-Brazilian Folklore for the Global Stage" (2015).

### Chapter 6 (Romo)

1. I trace this evolution in *Brazil's Living Museum: Race, Reform, and Tradition in Bahia* (2010). Scott Ickes (2013a) examines changes in Bahian identity from the 1930s through the 1950s. See also Risério ( 1988, 143–66). For explorations of Bahian identity in the latter half of the century, see especially Pinho (2010) and Jocélio Teles dos Santos (2005). The changing views and status of Salvador's Afro-Bahian population are addressed in Alberto (2011) and Butler (1998a).

2. Skidmore (1993, 67). It should be noted that this is based on the census figures for 1890, which were generally regarded at the time as incomplete.

3. The 1890 census did not report race or color for individual states, thus I've consulted the earlier 1872 census. Amazons and Piauí were lower, but just barely. I have compiled these state-level statistics myself based on the data from the 1872 census; see below for tables and sources.

4. Color and race categories are of course notoriously unstable and subject to different interpretations over time. They are accurate, however, in reflecting the understanding of the time. Source: 1872 Census Microfilm, unnumbered page, "Quadro geral da população escrava considerada em relação aos sexos, estados civis, raças, religião, nacionalidades, e grão de instrucção;" and "Quadro geral da população livre considerada em relação aos sexos, estados civis, raças, religião, nacionalidades, e grão de instrucção, com indicação dos numeros de casas e fogos."

5. These ideas are too complicated to fully develop here, but see chapter 1 of Romo (2010).

6. See Matory (2005). Matory's argument here does not preclude a domestic scene with its own dynamic, something that Capone and Pares treat with great insight. See Capone (2010) and Parés (2013).

7. Hermano Vianna highlights the constructed nature of this association between samba and authenticity in *The Mystery of Samba: Popular Music and National Identity in Brazil* (1999).

8. Other corporations such as the Moore and McCormack steamship lines seized on the policy for their own commercial purposes, naming three ships to South America the "Good Neighbor Fleet." Figure 6.6 shows how a menu for this cruise line promoted Bahia as part of this project.

9. As would become a common trope in later advertising for tourism, the scene centered around a male visitor overwhelmed by the charms of Bahian women. For exploration of the gendering of images of Bahia, see Pinho (2010).

10. I develop more in-depth treatment in my forthcoming book, *Race and the Art of Tourist Promotion in Bahia, Brazil: Crafting an Urban Landscape, 1900–1964* and in my forthcoming article, "Writing Bahian Identity: Crafting New Narratives of Blackness in Salvador, Brazil, 1940s–50s," *The Journal of Latin American Studies* (2018).

11. See Scaldaferri (1998, 660). Scaldaferri would perhaps date the first exhibition to 1932, with the show of José Guimarães, but this date has not generally been taken up by critics. Amado (1977, 50–51) indicates that some of the pieces displayed came from his own collection as well as the private holdings of Tavares. The artists displayed included Di Cavalcanti and Lasar Segall. As Roger Sansi notes (2007, 127), this was probably one of the first direct exposures for Bahian artists to the modernism of the South.

12. "A cidade negra por excelência" in the original Portuguese. See Amado (1945, 26).

13. Collected in Carybé, "Coleção rencôncavo: Desenhos de Carybé" (1955).

14. See Carybé (1962). For a retrospective of his work, see Emanoel Araújo, ed. (2006).

### Chapter 7 (Johnson)

1. The title of an article in *The New York Times* once said in reference to Bahia, "If It's 'Black Brazil,' Why Is the Elite So White?"

2. Eugênia Anna Santos (1869–1938), or Mãe Aninha,founded the Ilê Axé Opô Afonjá Candomblé house in Salvador in 1910 and led it until her death almost three decades later.

3. "Na Baixa do Sapateiro" is known in this U.S. as "Bahia," but it should not be confused with Barroso's 1931 composition of the same name.

4. See, for example, studies by Anadelia Romo, Patricia Santana de Pinho, Scott Ickes, Roger Sansi, and Jocélio Telles dos Santos, among others.

5. In 2016, the state and federal governments signed an agreement to turn a building next to the Amado Foundation into a cultural center dedicated to Zélia Gattai: see "Zélia Gattai" (2016).

6. For information on Verger, see the Web site of the Pierre Verger Foundation: http://www.pierreverger.org/en/.

7. Carybé illustrated *Jubiabá* (1961), *O compadre de Ogum* (1964), *O gato malhado e a andorinha sinhá* (1976), *A morte e a morte de Qunicas Berro d'Água* (1978), and *O sumiço da santa* (1992).

8. In the 1930s, the Opô Afonjá Candomblé temple established the institution of the Obás of Xangô, which were honorary positions generally held by intellectual elites to enhance the house's "value and fame," to use the words of Roger Sansi (2007, 68–69).

9. An Ogã is a Candomblé official who does not incorporate the *orixá* and does not go into a trance.

10. Maria Bibiana do Espírito Santo (1890–1967), or Mãe Senhora, led the Ilê Axé Opô Afonjá Candomblé house from 1942 until her death.

11. The excessively literal translation is my own.

12. The date of the song's initial recording. See Caymmi (2001, 579–604), for a complete discography.

13. Maria Escolástica da Conceição Nazaré (1894–1986), or Mãe Menininha do Gantois, headed the Gantois Candomblé house from 1922 until her death.

14. Maria Stella de Azevedo Santos, or Mãe Stella (b.1925), became the head of the Ilê Axê Opô Afonjá Candomblé house in 1976

15 According to Stella Caymmi, "Canto de Obá" was written for a theatrical staging of Amado's novel, *Terras do sem-fim* (1943; *The Violent Land*, 1988).

16. The same can be said of Caymmi and Carybé, but probably not Verger, at least not in the same sense.

17. Romo and Ickes both discuss Carneiro at some length in their respective studies of Bahia.

18. In her translation, Margaret A. Neves chooses to leave "Capa Negro" in Portuguese, in all probability because of its violence and offensiveness. The term literally means "castrate blacks." Amado certainly used the term to invoke historical and contemporary violence against enslaved Africans and black Brazilians.

19. Gregory Rabassa erroneously translated *búzio* as a "game of seeds." Amado's reference is to the *jogo de búzios*, an art of divination using cowry shells that is very common in Candomblé.

### Chapter 8 (Dunn)

1. All translations of song lyrics are by the author, who wishes to thank Roberto Conduru, Sabrina Gledhill, Lynne Kostman, J. Lorand Matory, and Patrick A. Polk for their comments and suggestions.

2. Matory (2005, 15). Reginaldo Prandi has assembled a useful database of Brazilian songs from the twentieth century that reference Afro-Brazilian religions: http://www.fflch.usbr/sociologia/prandi/mpb-down.htm.

3. Bishop-Sanchez (2016, 26–28). *Vatapá* is a savory dish made from bread, palm oil, coconut milk, dried shrimp, and peanuts mashed into a paste that typically accompanies *acarajé*, a fried bean cake that is a popular snack food in Bahia. *Carurú* is an okra dish seasoned with palm oil, dried shrimp, and ground peanuts. *Munguzá* is a sweet porridge made with white maize kernels cooked in milk, sugar, and cinnamon. *Angú* is a savory maize porridge that accompanies meat and vegetable dishes.

4. Risério (1981, 53). The first *afoxés* emerged in the late nineteenth century following the abolition of slavery, led by a group called the Embaixada Africana (African Embassy). See Butler (1998a, 176–78).

5. Ilê Axé Jitolú is the Candomblé temple founded by Mãe Hilda, the spiritual guide of the *bloco afro* Ilê Aiyê. An early formation of Opanijé went by the name of Erê Jitolú.

**Chapter 9 (Miguez)**

1. Until the mid-nineteenth century, when the Catholic Church gradually withdrew from the festival scene, *batuques* (drum corps) played a major role in Brazil's religious processions and festivities. In many instances, their participation was advocated by the colonial power, which saw such expressions as a way of encouraging religion among the masses. By promoting the regrouping of slaves on the basis of ethnicity, drumming also exacerbated existing rivalries and acted as a deterrent to any concerted rebellion against slavery.

2. Reputedly, the first Carnaval was held in Bahia in 1884.

3. In today's Carnaval, the difference between those two spaces—"home" and "street"—is especially apparent in the form of *camarotes* (grandstands), facilities developed by the Carnaval business that are installed along the circuits in which Salvador's Carnaval *blocos trios elétricos* parade.

4. The *cuíca* is a musical instrument that originated in Africa, particularly among Bantu peoples. Similar to a drum, it consists of a wooden rod attached to the center of a leather membrane, from the inner side. The sound is obtained by rubbing the rod with a piece of moistened cloth and pressing the outside of the *cuíca* with a finger, producing its characteristic snoring sound. The closer the musician's finger is to the center of the *cuíca*, the higher-pitched the sound will be. The *cuíca* occupies a prominent place in Brazilian percussion, particularly in samba, but it is also used in many Latin rhythms, such as salsa.

5. The *reco-reco* is a percussion instrument of African origin, originally used in Candomblé ceremonies. In its most common form, it consists of a piece of bamboo or a small slat of wood that is cut crosswise and scraped with a stick to produce a rasping and intermittent sound. In the samba schools, the *reco-reco* takes on another form. Instead of being made of wood, it consists of a metal box with a stretched spring.

6. The *agogô* is a musical instrument that originated among Yoruba-speaking peoples of West Africa. It is made of iron with a loop connecting two or more cones of different sizes that are struck with a metal rod. The *agogô* is both used in Candomblé ceremonies and secular cultural expressions like Carnaval and capoeira. It is an instrument with a prominent presence in Brazilian samba and many other Latin Americna and Caribbean musical genres.

7. In addition to the masked balls, the *préstitos*, *corsos*, and *pranchas* were typical manifestations of the presence of the aristocratic elites in the Carnavals of the first half of the twentieth century. The *préstitos* were the sumptuous parades of the Carnaval clubs, in the manner of the Carnaval parades of Nice. The *corso* was a parade of decorated private cars that drove along the central boulevards, their occupants wearing costumes. The *pranchas* were trucks, richly ornamented and filled with costumed revelers, which traveled alongside the *corsos*.

8. The *frevo*—which comes from *ferver* (to boil) and from the bastardization "frever" to designate the effervescence, agitation, and buzz typical of Carnaval celebrations—is a Carnaval musical rhythm that emerged in Pernambuco between the end of the nineteenth century and the beginning of the twentieth century, as a result of the fusion of other musical genres like *marcha*, *maxixe*, *dobrado*, and polka. Originally played by military bands and without lyrics, *frevo* is also a dance with complicated steps that require tremendous technique. The dancers, called *passistas do frevo*, use a colorful parasol during the performance and execute their footsteps mixing twirls, sways, and improvised jugglery. In 1950 Dodô and Osmar attended a presentation by a famous *frevo* group from Recife, the Clube Carnavalesco Misto Vassourinhas, which was passing through Salvador on its way to Rio de Janeiro. This gave them the idea of taking it into the streets, atop of the body of an old Ford Bigode (Model T), while they performed *frevos* with their electric guitars. Thus the tradition of the electric trio and *frevo trieletrizado* was ushered in. *Frevo* has been registered as a form of Brazilian Intangible Cultural Heritage since 2007, and in 2012 it was recognized by UNESCO as an Intangible Cultural Heritage of Humanity.

9. *Ijexá* is a rhythm of African origin played in Candomblé *terreiros* in Bahia. During Carnaval, it is played by *afoxés* with their orchestras of *atabaques* (conga drums), *agogôs*, *xequerês*, etc.

10. The nationwide success attained by the samba schools of Rio's Carnaval in the 1950s eventually influenced Carnaval festivities throughout Brazil. Thus, for many Brazilian cities the parades of local samba schools are the high point of the festivities. In some cases, like São Paulo, the samba school parades display the same sophistication as their counterparts in Rio de Janeiro.

11. The first, Ritmistas do Samba, for example, was an offshoot of the Nega Maluca Batucada from Ladeira da Preguiça. Many imprinted their territorial identity in their very names, such as the famous Diplomatas de Amaralina, Filhos da Liberdade, Juventude do Garcia, and Filhos do Tororó. The latter two were founded in districts with strong Carnaval traditions. Juventude do Garcia was an offshoot of the former Filhos do Garcia *cordão*, established in 1959, and Filhos do Tororó issued from the equally famous Cordão Carnavalesco Filhos do Tororó, in 1963.

12. For an overview (in Portuguese) of the samba schools, *cordões*, and *batucadas* that took part in Salvador's Carnaval from the 1950s to 1975, see the Web site of the "Memórias do Reinado de Momo: Cordões, batucadas e escolas de samba no carnaval de Salvador—1950–1975" project: http://memoriasdemomo.com.br/.

13. The association of Afro-descendants and Amerindians on the Carnaval scene is not uncommon. This is the case, for example of the "black Indians" of New Orleans's Mardi Gras. In Bahia's Carnaval, although *blocos de índio* were officially inspired by the Cacique de Ramos group from Rio de Janeiro's Carnaval. There is no question that their appearance somehow pays homage to the divinities of what is called Candomblé de Caboclo, a variation of the African religion that is strongly present in Bahian life.

14. On Carnaval Saturday, the departure of Ilê Aiyê from its headquarters, Senzala do Barro Preto, in the neighborhood of the Liberdade district known as Curuzu, is marked by a beautiful ceremony attended by thousands of people. After the presentation and placement of the head wrap on the Ebony Goddess, a title given to the group's queen, who is chosen annually through a big and festive contest, a ceremony of a religious character takes place with requests for the *orixás'* blessing, showers of popcorn, and the release of white doves. Ilê Aiyê has strong ties with a Candomblé *terreiro*, Ilê Axé Jitolú, whose recently deceased *iyalorixá*, Mãe Hilda, was the mother of Vovô, one of the group's founders.

15. It is interesting to note that the names of many *blocos de índio*, such as the Apaxes, Comanches, and Sioux, among others, were inspired by "Indians" from westerns, a film genre that was very popular among low-income audiences in Salvador's movie theaters. That inspiration, which arose from their identification with the Native Americans who were usually defeated in the films, was a way of dramatizing the socio-racial position of black people in the city of Salvador. Unlike the *blocos afro*, the *blocos de índio* did not use cultural expressions of African origin, with the exception of the musical repertoires of *blocos* like the Apaxes do Tororó.

16. The expression "Brazilian economic miracle" refers to the period of major economic growth in Brazil between 1968 and 1973 during the civilian-military dictatorship (1964–1985). Although it was characterized by a substantial increase in Brazils GDP growth, that period was also marked by extreme concentration of income and increased social inequality in an atmosphere of strong political repression.

17. Until the end of 1999, when the Salvador City Council established a Parliamentary Inquiry Commission to investigate charges of racism in Carnaval, *blocos de trio* used discriminatory practices to select their revelers, obliging them to submit a photo and proof of residence when purchasing costumes, a mechanism that guaranteed the exclusion of blacks and residents of low-income districts from their parades.

18. Today, Salvador's Carnaval economy involves resources totaling roughly a billion *reais*. Studies and research involving statistics and indicators on the festival and its economy can be found in numbers 1, 3, 4, and 6 of *Infocultura*, a publication of the State Department of Culture (Secult-Ba) and available on its Web site: http://www.cultura.ba.gov.br/modules/conteudo/conteudo.php?conteudo=89.

19. Afro-Carnaval organizations (*blocos afro*, *blocos de samba*, *afoxés*, *blocos de reggae*, etc.) now receive government funding, although much less than they need to finance their presence in the festivities. The state government's Ouro Negro (Black Gold) Program is particularly noteworthy.

20. The highly concentrated Carnaval market imposes similar difficulties on the independent *trios elétricos* in attracting the resources from sponsors that are necessary to meet the high costs of their presence in the festivities as well as the large army of tens of thousands of informal workers, to a large extent drawn from the black/mixed-race population of the city, who try to make a scanty living as street vendors and *cordeiros*—the name given to the men whose job is to hold the ropes of the blocos during the parades.

21. The festivities last over seven days, take up most of the city center, mobilize a massive effort from city and state agencies to organize the infrastructure and logistics (safety, health, sanitation, transport, etc.), and bring over a million people per day into the streets.

### Interleaf H (Williams)

1. See *A Vida Estampada de J. Cunha*, Fundo do Quintal Cinema e Video. TVE Educativa da Bahia (HD) (#84045 3759345676; February 15, 2015). Length: 25:42. https://www.facebook.com/tvebahia/videos/840453759345676/ http://www.tve.ba.gov.br/tveonline.

### Chapter 10 (Cleveland)

1. Antonio Vieira da Silva states that Agnaldo was a ranking initiate of Candomblé, although this assertion has never been substantiated elsewhere (1983, 14, 181).
2. "Minha linguagem plástico-visual-signográfica está ligada aos valores míticos profundos de uma cultura afro-brasileira (mestiça-animista-fetichista). Com o peso da Bahia sobre mim—a cultura vivenciada; com o sangue negro nas veias—o atavismo; com os olhos abertos para o que se faz no mundo—a contemporaneidade; criando seus signos-símbolos procure transformer uma linguagem visual o mundo encantado, mágico, provavelmente místico que flui continuamente dentro de mim. O substrato vem da terra, sendo eu tão ligado ao complexo cultural da Bahia; cidade produto de uma grande síntese coletiva que se traduz na fusão de elementos étnicos e culturais de origem européia, africana e ameríndia." Translation mine.

### Chapter 11 (Conduru)

1. Bahia, minha preta
   Insiste no que é lindo
   E o mundo verá
   Tu voltares rindo ao lugar que é teu no globo azul
   Rainha do Atlântico Sul

   E ô! Bahia, fonte mítica, encantada
   E ô! Expande teu axé, não esconde nada
   Teu grito de alegria ecoa longe, tempo e espaço
   Rainha do Atlântico.

   Translator's Note: In Bahia, "*minha preta*," can be used as an endearment for a woman of any color. Here, however, Caetano Veloso's intention is clearly to show affection for Bahia while pointing out the predominant color of its people. Caetano Veloso (2003, 4).
2. See artists from different generations, such as Almandrade and Virginia de Medeiros. Regarding Almandrade, see http://barogaleria.com/artist/almandrade/ and http://www.antoniomiranda.com.br/poesia_visual/almandrade.html. Regarding Medeiros, see http://virginiademedeiros.com.br.
3. See, for example, such dissimilar artists as Heitor dos Prazeres, Abdias Nascimento, Eustáquio Neves, and Rosana Paulino, among many others.
4. In other parts of Brazil, the links with Africa in artistic production are more recent, because they have mainly focused on the history and cultures of Africans and people of African descent in Brazil.
5. This is the case with Pierre Verger, Carybé, Mestre Didi, Rubem Valentim, Emanoel Araújo, José Antônio Cunha, and Ayrson Heráclito.
6. Regarding the process of (re)Africanizing Bahia, see Capone (2004); Pinho (2004).
7. Among other titles, Verger's works include: *Orixás: Deuses iorubás na África e no novo mundo* (1981); *Fluxo e refluxo do tráfico de escravos entre o golfo de Benin e a Bahia de Todos os Santos dos séculos XVII a XIX* (1987); *Notas sobre o culto aos orixás e voduns na Bahia de Todos os Santos, no Brasil, e na antiga costa dos escravos, na África* (1999). For a full list of his works, see http://www.pierreverger.org/br/pierre-fatumbi-verger/sua-obra/bibliografia-detalhada/livros-e-artigos.html. Accessed June 10, 2016.
8. Those who have devoted themselves to reflecting artistically on Afro-Brazilian religions include Modesto Brocos, Heitor dos Prazeres, Wilsom Tibério, and Abdias Nascimento, among others.
9. See Raimundo Nina Rodrigues ([1904] 2002, 158–63).
10. Decree No. 847of October 11, 1890. In http://legis.senado.gov.br/legislacao/ListaPublicacoes.action?id=66049. Accessed April 5, 2016.
11. The existing collections in Brazil have different conceptual frameworks, based on the institutions that house them: Instituto Histórico e Geográfico de Alagoas, Maceió; Museu Afro-Brasileiro da Universidade Federal da Bahia, Salvador; Museu da Polícia Civil do Estado do Rio de Janeiro, Rio de Janeiro; Museu do Estado de Pernambuco, Recife; Museu Nacional da Universidade Federal do Rio de Janeiro. Regarding these police seizures and the collections formed through them, see: Sansi (2007); Rafael and Maggie (2013, 276–342); Buono (2015, 9–34).
12. See Ramos (1937); Querino (1955a); Mário Barata (1957, 51–56). Also of note, the exhibition *Bahia no Ibirapuera*, curated by Lina Bo Bardi and Eros Martim Gonçalves and presented at the time of the Fifth International Biennial of São Paulo in 1959.
13. The following can be mentioned: the painting *A Mandinga*, produced by Modesto Brocos between the late nineteenth and early twentieth centuries; the series of drawings on Macumba produced by Cecília Meireles between 1926 and 1934; the series of drawings of Afro-Brazilian religious rituals by Oswaldo Goeldi, probably dating from the 1930s.
14. It should be noted that this increased visibility is linked to the Brazilian constitutions of 1937 and 1946, which guaranteed freedom of worship.
15. One exception is Roger Sansi (2007, 143–63).
16. See Veloso (2003, 26).
17. J. Cunha took the open course at the Universidade Federal da Bahia School of Fine Arts in Salvador from 1968 to 1969. Danillo Barata (2016, 154).
18. A divinity of the Afro-Bahian pantheon who is strongly linked with freshwater.
19. This is the case with the mural *Navio negreiro* (1955), located in the Castro Alves Building in Salvador. Emanoel Araújo, ed. (2006, 111).
20. Regarding the emergence of issues related to the slave trade and slavery in the work of Cravo Neto, see Heeren (2015). Available on http://cral.in2p3.fr/artelogie/spip.php?article351.
21. In this regard, it is worth noting the controversial reactions to a print showing scenes of black slavery that was used in the *Pindorama* series of the Maria Filó fashion label in Rio de Janeiro in 2016. "Marcas de roupas cria estampa com desenho racista e revolta consumidores." *Folha de S. Paulo*, October 14, 2016. http://f5.folha.uol.com.br/voceviu/2016/10/marca-de-roupas-cria-estampa-com-desenho-racista-e-revolta-consumidores.shtml. Accessed October 14, 2016.
22. Carmen Miranda began dressing as a Baiana to sing *O que é que a baiana tem?* a song written by Caymmi, in the film *Banana da Terra*, 1939. Among the many answers to the question, "What Is It That the *Baiana* Has?" one verse informs us that she "charms like no other."
23. Caymmi wrote the song "*O que é que a baiana tem?*" to replace "*Na Baixa do Sapateiro*," written in 1938 by Ary Barroso, who failed to close a deal with the film's producers, and sums up in one of his verses: "Bahia, land of happiness."
24. Bahia, the archaic Portuguese spelling of "bay" (which is now spelled *baía*), can designate: (1) the city whose full name is São Salvador da Bahia de Todos os Santos, but is usually called Salvador, and was founded by the Portuguese in 1549 overlooking a bay in northeastern South America as the capital of its largest colony at the time, Brazil; (2) the state of Bahia, whose capital is Salvador.
25. Wagner de Cerqueira e Francisco "Divisão Regional Brasileira." In *Brasil Escola*. http://brasilescola.uol.com.br/brasil/divisao-regional-brasileira.htm. Accessed April 14, 2016).
26. Others would say Minas Gerais, the Amazon, the Sertão (Backlands), and the northeast, but Bahia plays a special role in the latter, as a place where the balance between nature and culture was manifested longer and with greater intensity.
27. In this regard, see Denisson de Oliveira, "A arte da bahia e seu mercado de arte no século XX" in Oliveira, ed. (2001, 14–15); Scaldaferri (1998); Zanini (1983, 637–38); and Zanini (1991, 76–77).
28. In addition to the above-mentioned Carybé, Verger, and Hansen Bahia, we can include José Pancetti, Oswaldo Goeldi, Henrique Oswald, Lina Bo Bardi, and Arthur Scovino, among others.
29. In addition to the individual experiences of many artists, it is worth noting the Sacatar Institute's residency for artists. For more information, see http://www.sacatar.com.br/site/index.asp. Accessed April 15, 2016).
30. This is the case with artists from other parts, whether Brazilian or foreign, who were based in Bahia, including Carybé, Pierre Verger, Hansen Bahia, and Aristides Alves, as well as Bahians such as Mário Cravo Júnior, Mário Cravo Neto, Goya Lopes, and Ayrson Heráclito.
31. This is the case with artists based in Brazil, such as José Pancetti, Henrique Oswald, Lina Bo Bardi, and Miguel Rio Branco, as well as foreigners like the Spaniard Isabel Muñoz, the Portuguese Cristina Lamas, the Italian Antonello Veneri, the Frenchman Pierre David, and the Americans Matthew Barney, Gerald Cyrus, and Fran Siegel, among others.
32. "Comprar o equipamento / E saber usar / Vender o talento e saber cobrar, lucrar." Caetano Veloso (2003).

### Interleaf L (Gledhill)

1. In addition to "senses," *sentidos* also means directions and meanings.

# References Cited


Abreu, Frederico José de
1999 *Bimba é bamba: A capoeira no ringue*. Bahia: Insituto Jair Moura.

Abreu, Frederico José de, and Maurício Barros Castro
2009 *Capoeira*. Rio de Janeiro: Beco do Azougue Editorial.

Alberto, Paulina L
2011 *Terms of Inclusion: Black Intellectuals in Twentieth-Century Brazil*. Chapel Hill: University of North Carolina.

Almandrade
2001 "A vanguarda e o contemporâneo: O circuito de arte na Bahia: A arte da Bahia e seu mercado de arte no século XX." In *+100 Artistas plásticos da Bahia*, edited by Denisson de Oliveira. Salvador: Prova do Artista.

Alves, Antônio Frederico de Castro
1958 *Navio negreiro*. Salvador: Universidade da Bahia.

Amado, Jorge
[1935] 1984 *Jubiabá*. Translated by Margaret A. Neves. New York: Bard/Avon.
[1936] 1988 *Captains of the Sands*. Translated by Gregory Rabassa. New York: Bantam.
[1937] 1993 *The War of the Saints*. Translated by Gregory Rabassa. New York: Bantam.
1945 *Bahia de Todos os Santos: Guia das ruas e dos mistérios da cidade do Salvador*. São Paulo: Livraria Martins Editora.
1964 *Bahia de Todos os Santos: Guia das ruas e dos mistérios da cidade do Salvador*. 10th ed. São Paulo: Livraria Martins Editora.
[1968] 2003 *Tent of Miracles*. Translated by Barbara Shelby. Madison: University of Wisconsin Press.
1971 *Tent of Miracles*. Translated by Barbara Shelby. New York: Alfred A. Knopf.
1977 *Bahia de Todos os Santos: Guia das ruas e dos mistérios da cidade do Salvador*. 27th ed. Rio de Janeiro: Editora Record.
1979 *Mural dos orixás*. Salvador: Banco da Bahia Investimentos.
1984 "Jorge Amado." *Américas* 36, no. 3 (May/June): 16–19.
[1988] 1993 *The War of the Saints*. Translated by Gregory Rabassa. New York: Bantam.
2001 *Navegação de cabotagem: Apontamentos para um livro de memórias que jamais escreverei*. Rio de Janeiro: Editora Record.

Andrews, George Reid
1991 *Blacks and Whites in São Paulo, Brazil, 1888–1988*. Madison: University of Wisconsin Press.

Angelou, Maya
1978 "Still I Rise." In *Still I Rise: A Book of Poems*. New York: Random House.

Aquino, Patricia de
2002 "No Freeze-Frame on Gods." In *Iconoclash: Beyond the Image Wars in Science, Religion, and Art*, edited by Bruno Latour and Peter Weibel. Karlsruhe: 2km/Center for Art and Media; Cambridge, MA: The MIT Press.

Araújo, Emanoel
2000 *Negro de corpo e alma*. . São Paulo: Associacão Brasil 500 Anos Artes Visuals: Fundacão Bienal de São Paulo.
[2010] *A mão afro-brasileira: Significado da contribuição artística e histórica*. São Paulo: Museu Afro Brasil.
2014 *A nova mão afro-brasileira*. São Paulo: Museu Afro Brasil.

Araújo, Emanoel, ed.
2006 *O universo mítico de Hector Julio Paride Bernabó, o baiano Carybé*. São Paulo: Museu Afro Brasil.

Araújo, Vânia Maria Mourão, and Luiz Felipe Ferreira
2012 "Tradição e modernidade no traje da baiana de escolar de samba." *Visualidades* 10, no. 1: 301–15.

Associacão Brasil 500 Anos Artes Visuals
2000 *Arte afro-brasileira*: Mostra do redescobrimento. São Paulo: Associacão Brasil 500 Anos Artes Visuals.

Assunção, Matthias Röhrig
2015 "Angola in Brazil: The Formation of *Angoleiro* Identity in Bahia." In *African Heritage and Memories of Slavery in Brazil and the South Atlantic World*, edited by Ana Lúcia Araújo, 109–48. Amherst, MA: Cambria Press.

Azulay, Jom Tob
2007 *Doces Bárbaros*. DVD. Rio de Janeiro: Biscoito Fino.

Barata, Danillo, ed.
2016 *O universo de J. Cunha*. Salvador: Corrupio.

Barata, Mário
1957 "A escultura de origem negra no Brasil." *Arquitetura contemporânea*, no. 9.

Barbosa, Juciara Maria Nogueira
2007 "Imagens de Salvador, por Pierre Verger, na revista *O Cruzeiro*." *Cadernos do PPGAV: Programa de Pós-Graduação em Artes Visuais—EFA/UFBA*: 29–42.

Barnitz, Jaqueline
2001 *Twentieth-Century Art of Latin America*. Austin: University of Texas Press.

Bastide, Roger
1971 *African Civilizations in the New World*. New York: Harper and Row.

Bastos, Paula
2016 "Editorial: Gorda Flor, entre curvas e cores." *Comportamento* (April 7). http://grandesmulheres.com.br/2016/04/07/editorial-gorda-flor-entre-curvas-e-cores/.

Bevilacqua, Juliana Ribeiro da Silva
2015 "Beyond the Revealed Unconscious: Agnaldo Manoel dos Santos as the Protagonist of His Own Art." *Critical Interventions Journal of African Art History and Visual Culture* 9, no. 2: 108–16.

Bimba, Mestre
Circa 1960 *Curso de capoeira regional*. Sound disc (analog, 33 1/3 rpm) with booklet. Salvador: JS Discos.

Bishop-Sanchez, Kathryn
2016 *Creating Carmen Miranda: Race, Camp, and Transnational Stardom*. Nashville, TN: Vanderbilt University Press.

Brenken, Anna
1993 "Imagens da miscigenação cultural brasileira: O artista Carybé em Salvador da Bahia." *Humboldt* (Bonn), no. 67: 88–91.

Brooke, James
1991 "Bahia Journal: If It's 'Black Brazil,' Why Is the Elite So White?" *The New York Times* (September 24).

Buono, Amy
2015 "Historicity, Achronicity, and the Materiality of Cultures in Colonial Brazil." *Getty Research Journal*, no. 7: 9–34.

Burdick, John
1998 *Blessed Anastacia: Women, Race, and Popular Christianity in Brazil*. New York: Routledge.

Butler, Kim D
1998a *Freedoms Given, Freedoms Won: Afro-Brazilians in Post-Abolition São Paulo and Salvador*. New Brunswick, NJ: Rutgers University Press.
1998b "Ginga Baiana—The Politics of Race, Class, Culture, and Power in Salvador, Bahia." In *Afro-Brazilian Culture and Politics: Bahia, 1790s to 1990s*, edited by Hendrik Kraay. New Brunswick, NJ: M.E. Sharpe.

Capone, Stefania
2004 *A busca da África no Candomblé: Tradição e poder no Brasil*. Rio de Janeiro: Contra Capa Livraria.
2010 *Searching for Africa in Brazil: Power and Tradition in Candomblé*. Durham, NC: Duke University Press.

Carneiro, Édison
1937 *Negros bantus: Notas de ethnographia religiosa e folk-lore*. Rio de Janeiro: Civilização Brasileira.

Carneiro, Édison, and Aydano do Couto Ferraz
1940 "Congresso Afro-Brasileiro da Bahia." In *O Negro no Brasil*, 7–11. Rio de Janeiro: Civilização Brasileira.

Carybé [Héctor Julio Páride Bernabó]
1951–55 *Coleção Rencôncavo: Desenhos de Carybé*, edited by Bahia Museu do Estado. Salvador: Livraria Progresso Editora.
1962 *As sete portas da Bahia*. São Paulo: Martins.
2009 *Carybé*. Salvador: Museu de Arte Moderna da Bahia.

Cascudo, Luis da Camara
1962 *Dicionário do folclore brasileiro*. Rio de Janeiro: Instituto Nacional do Livro, Ministério da Educação e Cultura.

Castillo, Lisa Earl

2008 *Entre a oralidade e a escrita: A etnografia nos Candomblés da Bahia*. Salvador: EDUFBA.

Castillo, Lisa Earl, and Luis Nicolau Pares

2010 "Marcelina da Silva: A Nineteenth-Century Candomblé Priestess in Bahia." *Slavery and Abolition* 31, no. 1: 1–27.

Castro, Armando Alexandre Costa de

2006 *Irmãs de fé: Tradição e turismo no Recôncavo baiano*. Rio de Janeiro: E-papers. http://books.google.com/books?id=H1VZAAAAMAAJ.

Caymmi, Stella

2001 *Dorival Caymmi: O mar e o tempo*. São Paulo: Editora 34.

Clarke, Peter Bernard

2004 *New Trends and Developments in African Religions*. Westport, CT: Greenwood.

Cleveland, Kimberly L.

2012 "Afro-Brazilian Art as a Prism: A Socio-Political History of Brazil's Artistic, Diplomatic, and Economic Confluences in the Twentieth Century." *Luso-Brazilian Review* 49, no. 2: 103–13.

2015 "Sacred/Secular Nexus: Afro-Brazilian Religion in the Afro-Brazilian Art of Mestre Didi and Ronaldo Rego." *Critical Interventions Journal of African Art History and Visual Culture*, no. 2: 102–4

Coelho, Antônio Alves

1968 *Contribuição ao estudo das artes brasileiras; quatro artistas baianos: Agnaldo Manoel dos Santos, Genaro de Carvalho, Mário Cravo Júnior, Rubem Valentim*. Salvador: Centro de Estudos Baianos.

Coelho, Brenda

2012 "Fundação reúne acervo da vida e obra de Jorge Amado no Pelourinho." *G1— Bahia* (August 9). http://g1.globo.com/bahia/noticia/2012/08/fundacao-reune-acervo-da-vida-e-obra-de-jorge-amado-no-pelourinho.html. Accessed January 12, 2017.

Coelho, José Ligiéro

1998 *"Carmen Miranda: An Afro-Brazilian Paradox."* PhD diss., New York University.

Collins, John F.

2015 *Revolt of the Saints: Memory and Redemption in the Twilight of Brazilian Racial Democracy*. Durham, NC: Duke University Press.

Conduru, Roberto

2013a *Pérolas negras—primeiro fios: Experiências artísticas e culturais nos fluxos entre África e Brasil*. Rio de Janeiro: Editora da Universidade do Estado do Rio de Janeiro.

2013b "Pérolas da liberdade: Joalheria afro-brasileira." *Textos escolhidos de cultura e artes populares*10, no. 1 (May): 33.

2015 "Jorge dos Anjos and the Colorful Blackness of the Art That Connects Africa and Brazil." *Critical Interventions* 9, no. 2: 77–90.

Correa, Suzamar, and Robson de Souza dos Santos

2012 "Modelo negra e nomunicacão de noda no Brasil: Análise de conteúdo dos anúnicios publicados no revista *Vogue Brasil*." *Iniciacom* 4, no. 2: 15–16.

Cosentino, Donald J.

2005 "Vodou in the Age of Mechanical Reproduction," *RES: Anthropology and Aesthetics*, no. 47 (Spring): 231–46.

Costa, Gal

1993 *O sorriso do gato de Alice*. CD. Rio de Janeiro: RCA.

Coutinho, Daniel

1993 *O ABC da capoeira de angola: Os manuscritos do Mestre Noronha*. Brasília: CIDOCA.

Cuarterolo, Andrea

2015 "Social Construction of the Photographic Portrait in Nineteenth-Century Rio de la Plata." *Oxford Research Encyclopedia of Latin American History*. http://latinamericanhistory.oxfordre.com/view/10.1093/acrefore/9780199366439.001.0001/acrefore-9780199366439-e-105.

Cunha, Laura

2011 *Joias de Crioula: Jewelry of the Brazilian Crioula*. Translated by Ive Brunelli. São Paulo: Editora Terceiro Nome.

Dantas, Beatriz Góis

1988 *Vovó nagô e papai branco: Usos e abusos de África no Brasil*. Rio de Janeiro: Graal.

Deleuze, Gilles, and Félix Guattari

1980 *Mille plateaux*. Paris: Minuit.

Dimas, Antônio

2008 "Da praça ao palanque." In Jorge Amado, *Jubiabá*. São Paulo: Companhia das Letras, 325–41.

Drewal, Henry J., ed.

2008 *Mami Wata: Arts for Water Spirits in Africa and Its Diasporas*. Los Angeles: Fowler Museum at UCLA.

Drewal, Henry J., and David C. Driskell

1989 *Introspectives: Contemporary Art by Americans and Brazilians of African Descent*. Los Angeles: California Afro-American Museum.

Duccini, Luciana

2016 *Diplomas e decás: Identificação religiosa de membros de classe média no Candomblé*. Salvador: EDUFBA.

Dunn, Christopher

2001 *Brutality Garden: Tropicália and the Emergence of a Brazilian Counterculture*. Chapel Hill: University of North Carolina Press.

2007 "Black Rome and the Chocolate City: The Race of Place." *Callaloo* 30, no. 3 (Summer): 847–61.

2016 *Contracultura: Alternative Arts and Social Transformation in Authoritarian Brazil*. Chapel Hill: University of North Carolina Press.

Durão, José de Santa Rita

1781 *Caramurú: Poema epico do descubrimento da Bahia*, canto X. Lisbon: Regia Officina Typografica.

Ewbanks, Thomas

1856 *Life in Brazil*. New York: Harper and Brothers.

Falcon, Gustavo, and Goya Lopes

2010 *Imagens da diaspora*. Salvador: Solisluna Design.

Farelli, Maria

1981 *Balangandãs e figas da Bahia: O poder mágico dos amuletos*. Rio de Janeiro: A. C. Fernandes.

Ferreira, Luzia Gomes

2005 "O Samba de Roda nas festividades de N. Sª da Boa Morte em Cachoeira Bahia." www.cult.ufba.br/enecul2005/LuziaGomesFerreira.pdf.

Ferreira, Roquinaldo Amaral

2012 *Cross-Cultural Exchange in the Atlantic World: Angola and Brazil during the Era of the Slave Trade*. African Studies Series. New York: Cambridge University Press.

Ferrez, Gilberto

1984 *O Rio antigo do fotógrafo Marc Ferrez: Paisagens e tipos humanos do Rio de Janeiro, 1865–1918*. Rio de Janeiro: Editora Ex Libris.

1990 *Photography in Brazil, 1840–1900*. Translated by Stella de Sá Rego. Albuquerque: University of New Mexico Press.

Freyre, Gilberto

1990 *Bahia e Bahianos*. Salvador: Empresa Gráfica da Bahia.

2003 "Arte e civilização moderna nos trópicos: A contribuição portuguesa e a responsabilidade brasileira." In Gilberto Freyre, *China tropical*, edited by Edson Nery da Fonseca. Brasília: Editora da UnB; São Paulo: Imprensa Oficial do Estado.

Fryer, Peter

2000 *Rhythms of Resistance: African Musical Heritage in Brazil*. Hanover, NH: University Press of New England.

Fundação Pierre Verger

2012 *Carybé, Verger & Jorge: Obás da Bahia*. Lauro de Freitas: Solisluna Editora; Salvador: Fundação Pierre Verger. English translation: Sabrina Gledhill, 170–91.

Gage, Kelly M.
2005 "Nineteenth-Century Afro-Brazilian Women's Dress." In *Berg Encyclopedia of World Dress and Fashion: Latin America and the Caribbean*, edited by Margot Blum Schevill. Oxford: Bloomsbury Academic.

Garcia, Antonia dos Santos
2009 *Desigualdades raciais e segregação urbana em antigas capitais: Salvador, cidade d'Oxum, e Rio de Janeiro, cidade de Ogum*. Rio de Janeiro: Garamond.

Gilroy, Paul
1993 *The Black Atlantic: Modernity and Double Consciousness*. Cambridge, MA: Harvard University Press.

Ginzburg, Carlo
1991 "História da arte italiana." In Carlo Ginzburg, *A micro-história e outros ensaios*. Lisbon: Difel.

Giumbelli, Emerson
2007 "Um projecto de cristianismo hegemônico." In *Intolerância religiosa: Impactos do neopente costalismo no campo religioso afro-brasileiro*, edited by V. Gonçalves da Silva. São Paulo: EDUSP.

Gledhill, Helen Sabrina
2014 "Travessias racialistas no Atlântico Negro: Reflexões sobre Booker T. Washington e Manuel R. Querino." PhD diss., Federal University of Bahia.

Godoy, Solange de Sampaio
2006 *Círculo das contas: Jóias de crioulas baianas*. Salvador: Museum Carlos Costa Pinto.

Goldenberg, Ricardo.
1995 "Educação musical: A experiência do canto orfeônico no Brasil." *Pró-posições* 6, no. 3: 103–9.

Gomes, Tiago de Melo
2003 "Para Além da Casa de Tia Ciata: Outras experiências no universo cultural carioca, 1830–1930." *Afro-Ásia* (UFBA), nos. 29–30: 175–88.

Gondim, Adenor
2005 *Itaylê Ogun: Adenor Gondim fotografias*. São Paulo: Pinacoteca do Estado.

Graham, Sandra L.
1992 *House and Street: The Domestic World of Servants and Masters in Nineteenth-Century Rio de Janeiro*. Austin: University of Texas Press.

Guerreiro, Goli
2000 *A trama dos tambores: A música afro-pop de Salvador*. São Paulo: Editora 34.

Guran, Milton
1999 *Agudás: Os "brasileiros" do Benim*. Rio de Janeiro: Editora Nova Fronteira and Editora Gama Filho.

Haberly, David T.
1983 *Three Sad Races: Racial Identity and National Consciousness in Brazilian Literature*. Cambridge: Cambridge University Press.

Hall, Stuart
1990 "Cultural Identity and Diaspora." In *Identity: Community, Culture, Difference*, edited by Jonathan. Rutherford. London: Lawrence and Wishart.

Harding, Rachel E.
2000 *A Refuge in Thunder: Candomblé and Alternative Spaces of Blackness*. Bloomington: Indiana University Press.

Harris, Michael D.
2003 *Colored Pictures: Race and Visual Representation*. Chapel Hill: The University of North Carolina Press.

Heeren, Alice
2015 "Specters of Brazilian History in the Early Photographic Work of Mário Cravo Neto." *Artelogie*, no. 7.

Hein, Martin
1992 "The Miracle of Bahia." In *Carybé*, edited by Bruno Furrer. St. Gallen: Edition Diá.

Herkenhoff, Paulo
1996 "Rubem Valentim's Lightening Stone: Obá-Painter of the Casa de Mãe Senhora." In *Salas especiais = Special Exhibitions: 23. Bienal internacional São Paulo*, edited by Nelson Aguilar and Agnaldo Farias. São Paulo: Fundação Bienal de São Paulo.

Hertzman, Marc A.
2013 *Making Samba: A New History of Race and Music in Brazil*. Durham, NC: Duke University Press.

Höfling, Ana Paula
2015 "Staging Capoeira, Samba, Maculelê, and Candomblé: Viva Bahia's Choreographies of Afro-Brazilian Folklore for the Global Stage." In *Performing Brazil: Essays on Culture, Identity, and the Performing Arts*, edited by Severino João Medeiros Albuquerque and Kathryn Bishop-Sanchez, 98–125. Madison: University of Wisconsin Press.
Forthcoming *Staging Capoeira: Choreographies of Brazil*. Middletown, CT: Wesleyan University Press.

Ickes, Scott
2013a *African-Brazilian Culture and Regional Identity in Bahia, Brazil*. Gainesville: University Press of Florida.
2013b "Salvador's Modernizador Cultural: Odorico Tavares and the Aesthetics of Baianidade, 1945–1955." *The Americas* 69, no. 4: 437–66.

Johnson, Paul Christopher
2002 *Secrets, Gossip, and Gods: The Transformation of Brazilian Candomblé*. New York: Oxford University Press.

Johnson, Paul Christopher, ed.
2014 *Spirited Things: The Work of "Possession" in Afro-Atlantic Religions*. Chicago: University of Chicago Press.

Julião, Carlos, and Lygia da Fonseca Fernandes da Cunha
1960 *Riscos illuminados de figurinhos de brancos e negros dos uzos do Rio de Janeiro e Serro do Frio*. Rio de Janeiro: Biblioteca Nacional.

Kantor, Manuel
1955 *Bahia*. São Paulo: Edigões Melhoramentos.

Landes, Ruth
1940 "A Cult Matriarchate and Male Homosexuality." *Journal of Abnormal and Social Psychology* 35: 386–97.
1947 *The City of Women*. New York: Macmillan.

Lara, Sílvia Hunold
2000 "Sedas, panos e balangandãs: O traje de senhoras e escravas nas cidades do Rio de Janeiro e de Salvador (século XVIII)." In *Brasil colonização e escravidão*, edited by Maria Beatriz Nizza da Silva. Rio de Janeiro: Nova Fronteira.

Law, Robin, and Kristin Mann
1999 "West Africa in the Atlantic Community: The Case of the Slave Coast." *The William and Mary Quarterly* 56, no. 2: 307–34.

Leal, Maria das Graças de Andrade
2009 *Manuel Querino entre letras e lutas: Bahia, 1851–1923*. São Paulo: Annablume.

Leiris, Michel
1953 *"Notes sur l'usage* de chromolithographies catholiques par les vodouisants d'Haiti." In *Les Afro-Américains*, 27, 201–11. Dakar: IFAN.

Lody, Raul
2001 *Joias de axé: Fios-de-contas e outros adornos do corpo a joalheria afro-brasileira*. Rio de Janeiro: Bertrand Brasil.
2015 *Moda e história: As indumentárias das mulheres de fé*. São Paulo: Editora SENAC.

Lopes, Goya
2016 "Goya Lopes—Trajetória de uma Criadora." *Moda palavra* 9, no. 18 (July-Dec.).

Lühning, Angela
1995–1996 "Acabe com este santo, Pedrito vem aí: Mito e realidade da perseguição ao candomblé entre 1920 e 1941." *Revista USP* 28 (Dec.-Feb.): 194–220.

MacGaffey, Wyatt
1986 *Religion and Society in Central Africa: The BaKongo of Lower Zaire*. Chicago: University of Chicago Press.

Maggie, Yvonne

1992 *Medo do feitiço: Relações entre magia e poder no Brasil*. Rio de Janeiro: Arquivo Nacional.

Mammí, Lorenzo

1992 "João Gilberto e o projeto utópico da bossa nova." *Novos Estudos Cebrap* 34 (November).

Mann, Kristin, and Edna G. Bay

2001 *Rethinking the African Diaspora: The Making of a Black Atlantic World in the Bight of Benin and Brazil*. Studies in Slave and Post-Slave societies and Cultures. London: F. Cass.

Martins, José de Barros, ed.

1961 *Jorge Amado: 30 anos de literatura*. São Paulo: Martins.

Matory, J. Lorand

[1994] 2005 *Sex and the Empire That Is No More: Gender and the Politics of Metaphor in Oyo Yoruba Religion*. New York: Berghahn.

1999 "Afro-Atlantic Culture: On the Live Dialogue between Africa and the Americas." In *Africana: The Encyclopedia of the African and African American Experience*, edited by Henry Louis Gates Jr. and K. Anthony Appiah, 36–44. New York: Basic/Civitas.

2003 "Gendered Agendas: the Secrets Scholars Keep about Yoruba-Atlantic Religion." *Gender and History* 15: 408–38.

2005 *Black Atlantic Religion: Tradition, Transnationalism and Matriarchy in the Afro-Brazilian Candomblé*. Princeton: Princeton University Press.

McCann, Bryan

2004 *Hello, Hello Brazil: Popular Music in the Making of Modern Brazil*. Durham, NC: Duke University Press.

Meireles, Cecília

2003 *Batuque, samba e macumba: Estudos de gesto e de ritmo 1926–1934*. São Paulo: Martins Fontes.

Mello, Frederico Pernambuco de

2001 "The Aesthetics of the *Cangaço* as an Expression of Brazilian Libertarianism." In *Heroes and Artists: Popular Art and the Brazilian Imagination*, edited by Tania Costa Tribe, 54–71. Cambridge: BrasilConnects and the Fitzwilliam Museum.

Moreira, Marcello

2016 *O Universo de J. Cunha*. Edited by Danillo Barata. Bahia: Editora Corrupio.

Mott, Luiz

1988 "A vida mistica e erotica do escravo Jose Francisco Pereira." *Tempo Brasileiro* 153, no. 1: 85–104.

Moura, Roberto

1983 *Tia Ciata e a pequena África no Rio de Janeiro*. Rio de Janeiro: FUNART.

Munanga, Kabengele, and Nilma Lino Gomes

2006 *O negro no Brasil de hoje*. São Paulo, Brazil: Global Editora.

Nóbrega, Cida, and Regina Echeverria

2006 *Mãe Menininha do Gantois*. Salvador: Corrupio.

Nussbaum, Barbara

2003 "Ubuntu: Reflections of a South African on Our Common Humanity." *Reflections* 4, no. 4: 22. http://www.barbaranussbaum.com/downloads/reflections.pdf.

Oliveira, Denisson de

2001 "A arte da bahia e seu mercado de arte no século XX." In *+100 artistas plásticos da Bahia*, edited by Denisson de Oliveira. Salvador: Prova do Artista.

Oliveira, Denisson de, ed.

2001 *+100 artistas plásticos da Bahia*. Salvador: Prova do Artista.

Oliveira, Flávio

2011 "Orpheonic Chant and the Construction of Childhood in Brazilian Elementary Education." In *Brazilian Popular Music and Citizenship*, edited by Idelber Avelar and Christopher Dunn, 44–63. Durham, NC: Duke University Press.

Omari, Mikelle Smith

1984 *From the Inside to the Outside: The Art and Ritual of Bahian Candomblé*. Monograph Series of the Museum of Cultural History, 24. Los Angeles: Museum of Cultural History, UCLA.

Omari-Tunkara, Mikelle Smith

2005 *Manipulating the Sacred: Yorùbá Art, Ritual, and Resistance in Brazilian Candomblé*. Detroit, MI: Wayne State University Press.

Paesani, Alfredo, and Bernardo Castelo Branco

1955 "Bahia feita em casa." *Acropole* (São Paulo) 18, no. 205: 4–5.

Parés, Luis Nicolau

2013 *The Formation of Candomblé: Vodun History and Ritual in Brazil*. Chapel Hill: The University of North Carolina Press.

Pastinha, Vicente Ferreira

c. 1952–1957 "Quando as pernas fazem miserêr." In *Manuscritos do Mestre Pastinha*. Private collection of Raimundo César Alves de Almeida, Salvador.

c. 1955–1960 "Pensamentos." In *Manuscritos do Mestre Pastinha*. Private collection of Raimundo César Alves de Almeida, Salvador.

Pato, Ana

2015 " Arte contemporânea e arquivo: reflexões sobre a 3a Biennal da Bahia." *Revista CPC* (São Paulo), no. 20: 122–36.

Patterson, Orlando

1982 *Slavery and Social Death: A Comparative Study*. Cambridge, MA: Harvard University Press.

Pinho, Osmundo S. de Araujo

1998 "A Bahia no fundamental: Notas para uma interpretação do discurso ideológico da baianidade." *Revista brasileira de ciências sociais* 13, no. 36: 109–20.

Pinho, Patrícia de Santana

2004 *Reinvenções da África na Bahia*. São Paulo: Annablume.

2010 *Mama Africa: Reinventing Blackness in Bahia*. Durham, NC: Duke University Press.

Pitombo, João Pedro

2014 "Casa de Jorge Amado e Zélia Gattai é aberta como museu em Salvador." *Folha Ilustrada* (November 30). http://www1.folha.uol.com.br/ilustrada/2014/11/1554192-casa-de-jorge-amado-e-zelia-gattai-e-aberta-como-museu-em-salvador.shtml. Accessed December 20, 2016.

Puff, Jefferson

2016 "Por que as religiões de matriz africana são o principal alvo de intolerância no Brasil?" http://www.bbc.com/portuguese/noticias/2016/01/160120_intolerancia_religioes_africanas_jp_rm. Accessed March 3, 2017.

Pullen, Kirsten

2014 *Like a Natural Woman: Spectacular Female Performance in Classical Hollywood*. New Brunswick, NJ: Rutgers University Press.

Querino, Manuel

1955a *A raça africana e os seus costumes na Bahia*. Salvador: Livraria Progresso.

1955b *A Bahia de outrora*. 3rd ed. Salvador: Livraria Progresso Editora. http://noticiasdapauliceia.blogspot.co.uk/2013/02/odo-iya-yemanja-atara magba-ajeje-lodo.html.

Rafael, Ulisses N., and Yvonne Maggie

2013 "Sorcery Objects under Institutional Tutelage." *Vibrant—Virtual Brazilian Anthropology* (Brasília) 10, no. 1 (Jan.-June): 276–342.

Raillard, Alice

1990 *Conversando com Jorge Amado*. Rio de Janeiro: Record.

Ramos, Arthur

1937 *As culturas negras no novo mundo*. Rio de Janeiro: Civilização Brasileira.

Rego, Waldeloir

1968 *Capoeira angola: Ensaio sócio-etnográfico*, Coleção Baiana. Rio de Janeiro: Gráf. Lux.

Reis, João José

1993 *Slave Rebellion in Brazil: The Muslim Uprising of 1835 in Bahia*. Baltimore: Johns Hopkins University Press.

Reis, Letícia Vidor de Sousa

2000 *O mundo de pernas para o ar: A capoeira no Brasil*. 2nd ed. São Paulo: Brasil.

Ribeyrolles, Charles

[1859] 1980 *Brasil pittoresco: História, descripções, viagens, colonização, instituições, colonisação*. Coleção reconquista do Brasil. Belo Horizonte e São Paulo: Editora Itatiaia; Editora da Universidade de São Paulo.

Riggs, Miriam Elizabeth

2008 "'There's Room for Everyone': Tourism and Tradition in Salvador's Historic District, 1930 to the Present." PhD diss., University of California at San Diego.

Risério, Antonio

1981 *Carnaval Ijexá*. Salvador: Corrupio.

1988 "Bahia com 'H'—Uma leitura de cultura baiana." In *Escravidão e invenção da liberdade: Estudos sobre o negro no Brasil*, edited by João José Reis, 143–66. São Paulo: Editora Brasiliense.

1993 *Caymmi: Uma utopia de lugar*. São Paulo: Perspectiva.

Roach, Joseph R.

1996 *Cities of the Dead: Circum-Atlantic Performance*. New York: Columbia University Press.

Robatto Filho, Alexandre

1954 *Vadiação*. Film.

Rodrigues, Raimundo Nina

[1896] 2006 *O animismo fetichista dos negros baianos*. Rio de Janeiro: Fundação Biblioteca Nacional; Editora UFRJ.

[1904] 2002 "As bellas-artes nos colonos pretos do Brazil—A esculptura." In *Para nunca esquecer: Negras memórias/memórias de negros*, edited by Emanoel Araújo 158–63. Rio de Janeiro: Museu Histórico Nacional.

Romo, Anadelia

2007 "Rethinking Race and Culture in Brazil's First Afro-Brazilian Congress of 1934." *Journal of Latin American Studies* 39, no. 1: 31–54.

2009 "O que é que a Bahia representa? O Museu do Estado da Bahia e as disputas em torno da definição da cultura baiana (O que é que a Bahia representa? Bahia's State Museum and the Struggles to Define Bahian Culture)." *Afro-Ásia* 39: 115–52.

2010 *Brazil's Living Museum: Race, Reform, and Tradition in Bahia*. Chapel Hill: University of North Carolina Press.

Forthcoming "For Brazilian Eyes: Race and the Emergence of Native Tourist Guides in Post-War Salvador, Brazil." *The Journal of Latin American Studies*.

Forthcoming *Race and the Art of Tourist Promotion in Bahia, Brazil: Crafting an Urban Landscape, 1900–1964*.

Rugendas, Johann Moritz

1835 *Voyage pittoresque dans le Brésil*. Paris: Engelmann & Cie.

1835 *Malerische Reise in Brasilien*. Paris: Engelmann & Cie.

1954 *Viagem pitoresca através do Brasil*. Translated by Sergio Milliet. 5th ed. Biblioteca histórica brasileira. São Paulo: Livraria Martins Editora.

Rush, Dana

1999 "Eternal Potential: Chromolithographs in Vodunland." *African Arts* 32, no. 4: 61–75, 94.

"Salvador ganha"

2016 "Salvador ganha espaços Carybé das artes e Pierre Verger de fotografia." *Jornal Grande Bahia* (May 14). http://www.jornalgrandebahia.com.br/2016/05/salvador-ganha-espacos-carybe-das-artes-e-pierre-verger-de-fotografia/. Accessed January 2, 2017.

Sansi, Roger

2005 "The Hidden Life of Stones: Historicity, Materiality, and the Value of Candomblé Objects in Bahia." *Journal of Material Culture* 10, no. 2: 139–56.

2007 *Fetishes and Monuments: Afro-Brazilian Art and Culture in the 20th Century*. New York: Berghan.

Santanna, Marilda

2009 *As donas do canto: O sucesso das estrelas-intérpretes no Carnaval de Salvador*. Salvador: Edufba.

Santos, Deoscredes Maximiliano dos (Mestre Didi)

1967 "West African Sacred Art and Ritual in Brazil: A Comparative Study." Manuscript. Ibadan, Nigeria.

Santos, Isis Freitas dos

2014 "'Gosta dessa Baiana?' Crioulas e outras baianas nos cartões postais de Lindemann (1880–1920)." MA thesis, Universidade Federal da Bahia.

Santos, Jocélio Teles dos

2005 *O poder da cultura e a cultura no poder: A disputa simbólica da herança cultural negra no Brasil*. Salvador: EDUFBA.

Santos, José Benedito dos

2013 "A recriação do mito de Iemanjá e Orungã: Uma leitura do romance *Mar morto*, de Jorge Amado." *Revista decifrar* (Manaus) 1, no. 1 (Jan.-June): 42–60.

Santos, Juana Elbein dos

1997 "Mestre Didi." In *Brazilian Sculpture: An Identity in Profile*, edited by Emanoel Araújo et al. São Paulo, Brazil: Associação dos Amigos da Pinateca.

1998 "Mestre Didi Is a Priest Artist." In *Mestre Didi: Sacred Afro-Brazilian Sculpture*, edited by Deoscoredes Maximiliano dos Santos, Diane W. Camber, and Juana Elbein dos Santos. Miami Beach, FL: Bass Museum of Art.

2000 "Tradição e contemporaneidade: Poesia mítica." In *Mestre Didi*. São Paulo: Galeria São Paulo.

Santos, Maria Stella de Azevedo

2010 *Meu tempo é agora*. 2nd ed. Salvador: Assembléia Legislativa do Estado da Bahia.

Santos, Nívea Alves dos

2013 "Entre ventos e tempestades: Os caminhos de Uma Gaiaku de Oiá." PhD diss., Federal University of Bahia.

Scaldaferri, Sante

1998 *Os primórdios da arte moderna na Bahia*. Salvador: Fundação Casa de Jorge Amado.

Selka, Stephen

2014 "Demons and Money: Possessions in Brazilian Pentecostalism. In *Spirited Things: The Work of "Possession."* In *Afro-Atlantic* Religions, edited by Paul Christopher Johnson, 155–76. Chicago: University of Chicago Press.

Silva, Antonio Vieira da

1983 "Reflexos da cultura Iorubá na arte e nos artistas brasileiros." *Afro Ásia* 14: 181.

Silva, Paulo Santos

1952 "Estatuto do Centro Esportivo de Capoeira Angola." Salvador: Centro Esportivo de Capoeira Angola.

2000 *Âncoras de tradição: Luta política, intelectuais e construção do discurso histórico na Bahia, 1930–1949*. Salvador: EDUFBA.

Silva, Vagner Gonçalves da

2007 *Intolerância religiosa: Impactos do neopentecostalismo no campo religioso afro-brasileiro*. São Paulo: EDUSP.

Silveira, Renato da

2010 *O candomblé da Barroquinha: Processo de constituição do primeiro terreiro baiano de keto*. Salvador: Edições Maianga.

Skidmore, Thomas E.

1993 *Black into White: Race and Nationality in Brazilian Thought*. 2nd ed. Durham, NC: Duke University Press.

Slenes, Robert W.

2002 "African Abrahams, Lucretias, and Men of Sorrows: Allegory and Allusion in the Brazilian Anti-slavery Lithographs (1827–1835) of Johann Moritz Rugendas." *Slavery & Abolition* 23, no. 2: 147–68.

Soares, Cecília Moreira

1996 "As ganhadeiras: Mulher e resistência negra em Salvador no século XIX." *Afro-Ásia* 17: 57–72.

Sperb, Paula

2017 "Documentos da CIA revelam investigacões sobre Jorge Amado." *Folha de São Paulo, Ilustrada* (February 11). http://www1.folha.uol.com.br/ilustrada/2017/02/ 1857598-documentos-da-cia-revelam-investigacoes-sobre-jorge-amado.shtml. Accessed February 11, 2017.

Sullivan, Edward J., Michael M. Hall, and Roberto DaMatta

2001 *Brazil: Body and Soul*. New York: Guggenheim Museum Publications.

Sweet, James H.

2003 *Recreating Africa: Culture, Kinship, and Religion in the African-Portuguese World, 1441–1770*. Chapel Hill: University of North Carolina Press.

Tacca, Fernando de

2009 *Imagens do sagrado—entre* Paris Match *e* O Cruzeiro. Campinas: Editora da Unicamp; Imprensa Oficial do Estado de São Paulo.

Tavares, Odorico

1951 *Bahia, imagens da terra e do povo*. 2nd ed. Rio de Janeiro: Olympio.

Telles, Edward E.

2004 *Race in Another America: The Significance of Skin Color in Brazil*. Princeton, NJ: Princeton University Press.

Tenreiro, Maria Manuela

2008 "Military Encounters in the Eighteenth Century: Racial Representations in the Work of Carlos Julião and Colonial Discourse in the Portuguese Empire." PhD diss., SOAS.

Thompson, Robert Farris

1983 *Flash of the Spirit: African and Afro-American Art and Philosophy*. 1st ed. New York: Random House.

Tosta, Luciano

2010 "Resistance and Citizenship in the Songs of Ilê Aiyê and Olodum." *Afro-Hispanic Review* 29, no. 2 (Fall): 181.

Trinidade, Simone

2006 "Penca de balangandãs." *Cadernos do PPGAV/EBA/UFBA* 3.

Valentim, Rubem

1970 *31 objetos emblemáticos e relevos emblemas de Rubem Valentim*. Rio de Janeiro: Museu de Arte Moderna.

1976 "Manifesto ainda que tardio." Manuscript.

1978 *Mito e magia na arte de Rubem Valentim: Emblemática: 20 pinturas, 10 relevos, 10 esculturas*. Rio de Janeiro: Galeria Bonino.

1994 *Rubem Valentim: Construção e símbolo*. Rio de Janeiro: Centro Cultural Banco do Brasil.

2001 "Rubem Valentim: Statements Made to Bené Fonteles, Sao Paulo 1989–1990." In *Rubem Valentim: Artista da luz*. São Paulo: Edições Pinacoteca.

Valladares, José

[1951] 2012 *Bêabá da Bahia: Guia turístico*. 2nd ed. Salvador: EDUFBA.

Van de Port, Mattijs

2011 *Ecstatic Encounters: Bahian Candomblé and the Quest for the Really Real*. Amsterdam: Amsterdam U.P.

Vargas, Getulio

1938–1941 "A instrução profissional e a educação." Speech given in Bahia, August 18, 1933. Reprinted in volume 2 of *A nova politica do Brasil*. Rio de Janeiro: Jose Olympio, 1938–1941.

Vassallo, Simone Pondé

2003 "Capoeiras e intelectuais: A construção coletiva da capoeira 'autêntica.'" *Estudos históricos* 32 (2003): 106-24.

Veblen, Thorstein

1947 *What Veblen Taught*. Edited by Wesley C. Mitchell. New York: Viking.

Veloso, Caetano

2003 "Bahia, minha preta" In *Letra só/Sobre as letras*, edited by Eucanaã Ferraz. São Paulo: Companhia das Letras

Veloso, Monica Pimenta

1990 "As tias baianas tomam conta do pedaço: Espaço e identidade cultural no Rio de Janeiro." *Estudos históricos* (Rio de Janeiro) 3, no. 6: 207–28.

Verger, Pierre

1968 *Flux et reflux de la traite des nègres entre le Golfe de Bénin et Bahia de Todos os Santos, du XVIIe au XIXe siècle*. Le Monde d'outre-mer, passé et présent, 1 sér. Paris: Mouton.

1981 *Orixás: Deuses iorubás na África e no novo mundo*. Salvador: Editora Corrupio Comércio; São Paulo: Círculo do Livro S.A.

1987 *Fluxo e refluxo do tráfico de escravos entre o Golfo de Benin e a Bahia de Todos os Santos dos séculos XVII a XIX*. São Paulo: Corrupio; Brasília: Ministério da Cultura.

1999 *Notas sobre o culto aos orixás e voduns na Bahia de Todos os Santos, no Brasil, e na antiga costa dos escravos, na África*. Salvador: Corrupio.

Verger, Pierre Fatumbi, and Carybé

1997 *Lendas africanas dos Orixás*. Translated by Maria Aparecida da Nóbrega. 4th ed. Salvador: Corrupio.

Verger, Pierre, and Angela Lühning

2003 *Pierre Verger, repórter fotográfico*. Rio de Janeiro: Bertrand Brasil.

Vianna, Hermano

1999 *The Mystery of Samba: Popular Music and National Identity in Brazil*. Translated by John Charles Chasteen. Chapel Hill: University of North Carolina Press.

Weinstein, Barbara

2015 *The Color of Modernity: Sao Paulo and the Making of Race and Nation in Brazil*. Durham, NC: Duke University Press.

Wood, Marcus

2013 *Black Milk: Imagining Slavery in the Visual Cultures of Brazil and America*. Oxford: Oxford University Press.

Yunes, Daniela Daflon

2011 *Eu fiz tudo pra você gostar de mim: A construção da legenda de Carmen Miranda (1929–1939)*. MA thesis, Pontifícia Universidade Católica do Rio de Janeiro.

Zanini, Walter

1983 "Arte Contemporânea." In *História geral da arte no Brasil*, edited by Walter Zanini. São Paulo: Instituto Walther Moreira Salles; Fundação Djalma Guimarães.

1991 *A arte no Brasil nas décadas de 1930–40: O Grupo Santa Helena*. São Paulo: EDUSP.

Zélia Gattai

2016 "Zélia Gattai será homenageada com espaço cultural no Pelourinho." *G1—Bahia* (May 7). http://g1.globo.com/bahia/noticia/2016/05/zelia-gattai-sera-homenageada-com-espaco-cultural-no-pelourinho.html. Accessed December 20, 2016.

# Index

# Contributors

*Scott Alves Barton* is Assistant Adjunct Professor in the Nutrition and Food Studies Department at New York University, New York, and is also a filmmaker.

*Sarah K. Chenault* was Curatorial Assistant for the *Axé Bahia* project and is based in Los Angeles, California.

*Kimberly L. Cleveland* is Associate Professor of Art History at The Ernest G. Welch School of Art & Design, Georgia State University, Atlanta.

*Roberto Conduru* is the Endowed Distinguished Professor of Art History in the Meadows School of the Arts at Southern Methodist University, Dallas, Texas.

*Christopher Dunn* is Professor of Brazilian Literary and Cultural Studies with a joint appointment in Africana Studies at Tulane University, New Orleans, Louisiana.

*Cécile Fromont* is Associate Professor in the Department of Art History at the University of Chicago, Illinois.

*Sabrina Gledhill* is an independent scholar and translator based in Birmingham, England.

*Ana Paula Höfling* is Assistant Professor in the School of Dance at the University of North Carolina, Greensboro.

*Randal Johnson* is Distinguished Professor in the Department of Spanish and Portuguese at UCLA.

*Vanda Machado* is Associate Professor at the Universidade Federal do Recôncavo da Bahia, Brazil.

*Lucas Marques* is a PhD student in Social Anthropology at the Museu Nacional/Universidade Federal do Rio de Janeiro, Brazil.

*J. Lorand Matory* is the Lawrence Richardson Professor of Cultural Anthropology and Director of the Sacred Arts of the Black Atlantic Project at Duke University, Durham, North Carolina.

*Paulo Miguez* is the Vice-Chancellor of the Universidade Federal da Bahia, Brazil.

*Patrick A. Polk* is Curator of Latin American and Caribbean Popular Arts at the Fowler Museum at UCLA.

*Anadelia Romo* is Associate Professor in the Department of History at Texas State University, San Marcos.

*Roger Sansi* is Professor of Social Anthropology at the Universitat de Barcelona, Spain.

*Heather Shirey* is Associate Professor and Director of Graduate Studies in the Art History Department at University of Saint Thomas, Saint Paul, Minnesota.

*Jeri Bernadette Williams* is an independent scholar based in Los Angeles, California.

# Fowler Museum at UCLA

The Fowler Museum is part of UCLA's School of the Arts and Architecture

Lynne Kostman, *Managing Editor*
Gassia Armenian, *Editorial Assistant*
Danny Brauer, *Designer and Production Manager*
Don Cole, *Principal Photographer*
Derek Dubler, *Title Design*


Fowler Museum at UCLA
Box 951549
Los Angeles, California 90095-1549



Printed and bound in Hong Kong by Great Wall Printing Company Limited

Library of Congress Cataloging-in-Publication Data

Names: Polk, Patrick Arthur, editor. | Conduru, Roberto, editor. | Gledhill, Sabrina, editor. | Johnson, Randal, 1948- editor. | Fowler Museum at UCLA, organizer, host institution.
Title: Axé Bahia : the power of art in an Afro-Brazilian metropolis / Patrick A. Polk, Roberto Conduru, Sabrina Gledhill, and Randal Johnson, editors ; with essays by Scott Alves Barton, Sarah K. Chenault, Kimberly L. Cleveland, Roberto Conduru, Christopher Dunn, Cécile Fromont, Sabrina Gledhill, Ana Paula Höfling, Randal Johnson, Vanda Machado, Lucas Marques, J. Lorand Matory, Paulo Miguez, Patrick A. Polk, Anadelia Romo, Roger Sansi, Heather Shirey, Jeri Bernadette Williams.
Description: Los Angeles : Fowler Museum at UCLA, 2018. | Includes bibliographical references.
Identifiers: LCCN 2017039441 | ISBN 9780990762652 (hbk.)
Subjects: LCSH: Art, Brazilian—Brazil—Salvador—Exhibitions. | Art, Brazilian—African influences—Exhibitions. | Ethnicity in art—Exhibitions. | Salvador (Brazil)—Civilization—African influences—Exhibitions.
Classification: LCC N6657.S25 A94 2017 | DDC 709.81—dc23
LC record available at https://lccn.loc.gov/2017039441